KT-364-184

J. Christopher Holloway & Claire Humphreys

THE BUSINESS OF TOURISM

11th EDITION

Los Angeles | London | New Delhi
Singapore | Washington DC | Melbourne

Los Angeles | London | New Delhi
Singapore | Washington DC | Melbourne

SAGE Publications Ltd
1 Oliver's Yard
55 City Road
London EC1Y 1SP

SAGE Publications Inc.
2455 Teller Road
Thousand Oaks, California 91320

SAGE Publications India Pvt Ltd
B 1/I 1 Mohan Cooperative Industrial Area
Mathura Road
New Delhi 110 044

SAGE Publications Asia-Pacific Pte Ltd
3 Church Street
#10-04 Samsung Hub
Singapore 049483

© J. Christopher Holloway and Claire Humphreys 2020

This eleventh edition first published 2020

Apart from any fair dealing for the purposes of research or private study, or criticism or review, as permitted under the Copyright, Designs and Patents Act, 1988, this publication may be reproduced, stored or transmitted in any form, or by any means, only with the prior permission in writing of the publishers, or in the case of reprographic reproduction, in accordance with the terms of licences issued by the Copyright Licensing Agency. Enquiries concerning reproduction outside those terms should be sent to the publishers.

Editor: Matthew Waters
Editorial assistant: Jasleen Kaur
Assistant editor, digital: Sunita Patel
Production editor: Sarah Cooke
Copyeditor: Sharon Cawood
Proofreader: Leigh Smithson
Marketing manager: Lucia Sweet
Cover design: Francis Kenney
Typeset by: C&M Digitals (P) Ltd, Chennai, India
Printed in the UK by Bell and Bain Ltd, Glasgow

Library of Congress Control Number: 2019943757

British Library Cataloguing in Publication data

A catalogue record for this book is available from the British Library

ISBN 978-1-52645-944-2
ISBN 978-1-52645-945-9 (pbk)

At SAGE we take sustainability seriously. Most of our products are printed in the UK using responsibly sourced papers and boards. When we print overseas we ensure sustainable papers are used as measured by the PREPS grading system. We undertake an annual audit to monitor our sustainability.

THE BUSINESS OF TOURISM

BATH SPA UNIVERSITY
DISCARD
LIBRARY

Sara Miller McCune founded SAGE Publishing in 1965 to support the dissemination of usable knowledge and educate a global community. SAGE publishes more than 1000 journals and over 800 new books each year, spanning a wide range of subject areas. Our growing selection of library products includes archives, data, case studies and video. SAGE remains majority owned by our founder and after her lifetime will become owned by a charitable trust that secures the company's continued independence.

Los Angeles | London | New Delhi | Singapore | Washington DC | Melbourne

BRIEF CONTENTS

CONTENTS

PREFACE TO THE ELEVENTH EDITION

The first edition of this text appeared in 1983. Since that time, tourism and its industry have changed out of all recognition. That edition was a scant 246 pages long; its cover bore a picture (black and white) of a group of tourists boarding a Dan-Air propeller aircraft (plus ça change: the current edition was completed as news was received of FlyBMI's collapse). The text focused predominantly on traditional elements of the business: tour operations and retailing. There was no dedicated chapter dealing with business tourism, nothing on managing tourism and little recognition of the importance of tourist destinations, attractions or events as motivating factors in travel. The role of the public sector was downplayed, while environmental and sociocultural impacts were restricted to just three pages each.

Perhaps the most interesting issue raised appeared in the closing section, in which the author forecast, with a leap into the future:

> Advances in computer reservations systems … will permit the holidaymaker to select his holiday, book it and pay for it by direct debit to his account … will this make the tasks of both tour operator and travel agent obsolete by the year 2000?

While both these sectors have survived, their numbers and roles have seen significant change – and today the authors would certainly not make reference exclusively to male holidaymakers!

It would have stretched imagination to have believed in 1983 that the text would enter its eleventh edition well into the twenty-first century, and be considering issues like global pollution and climate change, terrorism and tariffs, and the consequences of political events such as Brexit. That first edition, however, did recognise even then the fast-changing nature of the tourism business, its preface pointing out 'the danger of content becoming outdated before it went to print'. Consequently, while the original structure of this text has changed little over the years, each edition has seen significant changes to content and emphasis.

Another issue inherent in frequent editions is that the inclusion of new material without cuts to the earlier work can result in the textbook becoming both cumbersome and expensive. We have addressed this in this new edition by tightening the text and excluding some material that has become less pertinent over the years. We hope and trust that this new edition remains relevant to, and valued by, students of tourism as a comprehensive introduction to this fascinating subject.

Chris Holloway and Claire Humphreys

LIST OF ABBREVIATIONS

AA	(1) American Airlines (2) Automobile Association
AAA	American Automobile Association
ABTA	Association of British Travel Agents
ABTAC	Association of British Travel Agents' Certificate
ABTOT	Association of Bonded Travel Organizers Trust
ACE	(1) Association of Conference Executives (2) Association of Cruise Experts
ACORN	A Classification of Residential Neighbourhoods
ACTE	Association of Corporate Travel Executives
ADS	approved destination status
AENA	Aeropuertos Españoles y Navegación Aérea
AFTA	Australian Federation of Travel Agents
AFI	Airline Failure Insurance
AI	all-inclusive
AIC	Airbus Integrated Company
AIDA	Awareness, Interest, Desire, Action
AIEST	International Association of Scientific Experts in Tourism
AIT	Air inclusive tour
AITO	Association of Independent Tour Operators
ALM	additive layer manufacturing
ALVA	Association of Leading Visitor Attractions
AONB	area of outstanding natural beauty
APD	Air Passenger Duty
APEC	Asia-Pacific Economic Cooperation
APEX	Advance purchase excursion fare
APM	air passenger miles
ARDA	American Resort Development Association
ARTAC	Association of Retail Travel Agents' Consortia
ASEAN	Association of South East Asian Nations
ASM	available seat mile
ASTA	American Society of Travel Agents
ATC	air traffic control
ATOC	Association of Train Operating Companies
ATOL	Air Travel Organizer's Licence
ATP	Accredited Travel Professional
ATIF	Air Travel Trust Fund
AUC	Air Transport Users' Council
AVE	Alta Velocidad Española (Spanish high-speed train)
B2B	business to business
B2C	business to consumer
BA	British Airways
BAA	British Airports Authority (organisation that operates airports, now privatised, formerly publicly owned)
BABA	book a bed ahead
B&B	bed-and-breakfast accommodation
BCG	Boston Consulting Group
BEA	British European Airways (later merged with BOAC to form British Airways)
BHA	British Hospitality Association
BH&HPA	British Holiday and Home Parks Association
BIS	Department for Business, Innovation and Skills
BITOA	British Incoming Tour Operators' Association (now renamed UKinbound)
BITS	Bureau International de Tourisme Sociale
BOAC	British Overseas Airways Corporation, later merged with BEA to form British Airways
BRADA	British Resorts and Destinations Association
BRIC	Brazil, Russia, India and China
BSR	Business for Social Responsibility
BTA	(1) British Tourist Authority (now VisitBritain) (2) British Travel Association
BVEP	Business Visits and Events Partnership
CAA	Civil Aviation Authority

CAB	Civil Aeronautics Board (USA)
CBI	Confederation of British Industry
CECTA	Central European Countries Travel Association
CI	Conservation International
CILT	Chartered Institute of Logistics and Transport
CIM	Chartered Institute of Marketing
CIMTIG	Chartered Institute of Marketing Travel Industry Group
CITES	Convention on International Trade in Endangered Species
CLIA	Cruise Lines International Association
CPD	continuous professional development
CPT	Confederation of Passenger Transport
CRC	Cooperative Research Centre
CRN	Countryside Recreation Network
CRS	computer reservations system
CSR	corporate social responsibility
CTAC	Creative Tourist Agents' Conference
CTC	(1) Certified Travel Counsellor (2) Cyclists' Touring Club
DCLG	Department for Communities and Local Government
DCMS	Department for Culture, Media and Sport
DDA	Disability Discrimination Act
DEFRA	Department for Environment, Food and Rural Affairs
DfF	Department for Transport
DMO	(1) Destination Management Organisation (2) Destination Marketing Organisation
DTCM	Department of Tourism and Commerce Marketing (responsible for planning and marketing tourism in Dubai)
DTI	Department of Trade and Industry
DVT	deep vein thrombosis
EADS	European Aeronautic Defence and Space Company
EC	European Commission
ECPAT	End Child Prostitution, Pornography and Trafficking
EIA	environmental impact assessment
ELFAA	European Low Fares Airlines Association
EPA	Environmental Protection Agency
ERDF	European Regional Development Fund
ETB	English Tourist Board (later, the English Tourism Council)
ETC	(1) English Tourism Council (now integrated with VisitBritain) (2) European Travel Commission
ETS	emissions trading scheme
EU	European Union
FFP	frequent flyer programme
FHA	Family Holiday Association
FIT	(1) free independent travellers (when referring to markets) (2) fully inclusive tour (when referring to ticketing) (3) foreign inclusive tours (when referring to ticketing of international packages)
FOC	flag of convenience
PTO	Federation of Tour Operators
FTTSA	Fair Trade in Tourism South Africa
GBTA	Guild of Business Travel Agents
GDP	gross domestic product
GDS	global distribution system
GIP	Global Infrastructure Partners
GIT	group inclusive tour-basing fare
GNP	gross national product
GRT	gross registered tonnage
GWR	Great Western Railway
HAA	Historic Houses Association
HCIMA	Hotel and Catering International Management Association (now Institute of Hospitality)
HSS	high-speed sea service
IAAPA	International Association of Amusement Parks and Attractions
IAE	International Aero Engines
IAG	International Airlines Group
IATA	International Air Transport Association
IBTA	International Business Travel Association
ICAO	International Civil Aviation Organization
ICE	intercity express

IGT	Information and communications technology
IEFT	International Education Fairs of Turkey
IHEI	International Hotel Environment Initiative
IHG	Intercontinental Hotels Group
II	Interval International
IIT	independent indusive tour
ILG	International Leisure Group
IMO	International Maritime Organization
IPS	International Passenger Survey
IRTS	International Recommendations for Tourism Statistics
ISIC	International Standard Industrial Classification
ISP	Internet service provider (a company providing Internet access for commercial payment)
ISTO	International Social Tourism Organization
IT	(1) inclusive tour
	(2) information technology
ITG	Institute of Tourist Guiding
ITM	Institute of Travel and Meetings (formerly Institute of Travel Management)
ITT	Institute of Travel and Tourism
ITX	inclusive tour-basing excursion fare
IUCN	International Union for the Conservation of Nature
IWM	Imperial War Museum
IYE	International Year of Ecotourism
LAC	Limits of Acceptable Change
LCCs	Low-cost Carriers
LCLF	low-cost low-fare
LDC	lesser-developed countries
LEP	Local Enterprise Partnership
LGBT	lesbian, gay, bisexual and transgender
LMS	London, Midland and Scottish Railway
LNER	London and North Eastern Railway
LOCOG	London Organising Committee of the Olympic and Paralympic Games
MIA	Meetings Industry Association
MICE	meetings, incentives, conferences and events
MMC	Monopolies and Mergers Commission (now Competition Commission)
MOMA	Museum of Modem Art, New York
MTOW	maximum take-off weight
NAITA	National Association of Independent Travel Agents (later Advantage, now part of Triton)
NBC	National Bus Company
NEAP	Nature and Ecotourism Accreditation Programme
NFC	Near-field Communication
NGO	non-governmental organisation
NHS	National Health Service
NITS	Northern Ireland Tourist Board
NQAS	National Quality Assurance Schemes
NRS	National Readership Survey
NTB	(1) National Tourist Board
	(2) former National Training Board of ABTA
NTO	National Tourist Organization
NVQ	National Vocational Qualifications
ODA	Olympic Delivery Authority
OECD	Organisation for Economic Co-operation and Development
OITS	International Organisation of Social Tourism
ONS	Office for National Statistics
OTE	Organization for Timeshare in Europe
PATA	Pacific Area Travel Association
P&O	Peninsular and Oriental Steam Navigation Company
PCO	Professional Conference Organiser
PNR	passenger name record
PPP	public-private partnership
PSA	Passenger Shipping Association
PSO	Public Service Obligation
PSR	passenger-space ratio
PTA	Polytechnic Touring Association
QAA	Quality Assurance Agency
QC	quota count
RAC	Royal Automobile Club
RCI	Royal Caribbean International
RDAs	Regional Development Agencies

RFF	Reseau Ferré de France (French equivalent of Britain's Network Rail, responsible for operating the national rail track)
RFID	radio frequency identification
RPK	revenue passenger kilometres
RTB	Regional Tourist Board
RV	recreational vehicle
SARS	severe acute respiratory syndrome
SAS	Scandinavian Airlines System
SATH	Society for Accessible Travel and Hospitality
SOR	Special Drawing Rights
SME	small- to medium-sized enterprise
SMERF	social, military, educational, religious and fraternal
SNCF	Societé Nationale des Chemins de Fer
SOLAS	Safety of Life at Sea, International Convention for the
SPR	size to passenger ratio
SR	Southern Railway
SSSI	Site of Special Scientific Interest
STB	Scottish Tourist Board (now VisitScotland)
STOL	short take-off and landing
SUV	sports utility vehicle
TAC	Travel Agents' Council
TALC	Tourist Area Life Cycle
TCF	Travel Compensation Fund
TCN	Tourism Society Consultants' Network
TDAP	Tourism Development Action Plan
TEFL	Teaching English as a Foreign Language
TEN-T	Trans-European Network for Transport
TGV	Train à Grande Vitesse
TIC	Tourist Information Centre
TIER	Tourism Industry Emergency Response Group
TIES	The International Ecotourism Society
TIM	Tourism Income Multiplier
TIP	tourist information point
TMC	travel management companies
TOC	Tour Operators' Council
TOP	Thomson Open-line Programme (Thomson Holidays' computer reservations system)
TOSG	Tour Operators' Study Group (now Federation of Tour Operators, FTO)
TSA	Tourism Satellite Account
TTA	Travel Trust Association
TUI	Touristik Union International
UAIT	Universal Air Travel Plan (the airline-owned payment network)
UGC	user-generated content
UKTS	United Kingdom Tourism Survey
UN	United Nations
UNEP	United Nations Environment Programme
UNESCO	United Nations Educational, Scientific and Cultural Organization
UNWTO	United Nations World Tourism Organization
VAQAS	Visitor Attraction Quality Assurance Schemes
VAT	value added tax
VFR	visiting friends and relatives
VLJ	very light jet
VTOL	vertical take-off and landing
WAM-V	Wave Adaptive Modular Vessel
WCS	Wildlife Conservation Society
WHO	World Health Organization
WHS	World Heritage Sites
WIG	wing-in-ground
WISE	wing-in-surface effect
WPC	wave-piercing catamaran
WTB	Wales Tourist Board
WTO	World Tourism Organization (now UNWTO)
WTTC	World Travel and Tourism Council
WWF	World Wide Fund for Nature
WWW	World Wide Web
YHA	Youth Hostels Association

ONLINE RESOURCES

The Business of Tourism is supported by a wealth of online resources for both students and lecturers to help support learning and teaching. These resources are available at: https://study.sagepub.com/bot

FOR LECTURERS

- **Shape your course** using the handy **introduction** on how to make best use of the book and online resources in your teaching.
- **Save time** and support your teaching each week by using the author-prepared **PowerPoint slides** for each chapter.
- **Structure** your teaching around the **learning outcomes** provided by the authors.
- **Consolidate** your understanding of the chapters by reviewing the **summary of the key areas** covered in the chapter.
- **Encourage discussion** with the **in-class questions** for two examples within each chapter and **their suggested answers**.
- **Help students apply their knowledge** by using the **suggested answers to the in-text tasks** to guide your seminars.
- **Discover** more information with additional **website links** curated by the author.

FOR STUDENTS

- **Expand** on what you learn in the textbook by watching the **videos** provided to support each chapter and **reflect** on what you've watched by answering the **questions** provided.
- **Review** everything you've learnt by comparing the **answers to the three questions** at the end of each chapter.

PART 1

DEFINING AND ANALYSING TOURISM AND ITS IMPACTS

1

AN INTRODUCTION TO TOURISM

CONTENTS

LEARNING OUTCOMES

After studying this chapter, you should be able to:

- recognise why tourism is an important area of study
- define what is meant by tourism – both conceptually and technically – and distinguish it from travel, leisure and recreation
- identify the composition and major characteristics of tourism products
- outline the various forms of tourist destination and their appeal
- explain why destinations are subject to changing fortunes.

> Over the decades, tourism has experienced continued growth and deepening diversification to become one of the fastest growing economic sectors in the world. Modern tourism is closely linked to development and encompasses a growing number of new destinations. These dynamics have turned tourism into a key driver for socio-economic progress. (UNWTO, 2018)

WHY STUDY TOURISM?

As the UNWTO highlights in the quote above, tourism is a global industry, with more than a billion international trips taken annually, and it is forecast that this will expand to 1.8 billion by 2030 (UNWTO, 2017). This book introduces you to this vast and fascinating industry. Through its various chapters, you will first learn about the factors that have led up to making this the world's fastest-growing business, and then examine what that business entails. You will look at the nature of tourism, its appeal, its phenomenal growth over the past half century, the resulting impact on both developed and developing societies and, above all, its steady process of **institutionalisation** – that is to say, the manner in which tourism has become commercialised and organised since its inception. It will also be about travel, but only those forms of travel specifically undertaken within the framework of a defined tourism journey.

The tourism business deals with the organisation of journeys away from home and the way in which tourists are welcomed and catered for in destination countries. Those who plan to work in this industry will be responsible for ensuring that the outcome of such journeys, whether domestic or international in scope, maximises satisfaction with the tourist experience.

Formal study of tourism was introduced, in part, to address a perceived lack of professionalism in the industry. Indeed, in many destination countries it remains the case that much of the industry is in the hands of amateurs – sometimes inspired amateurs, whose warmth and enthusiasm are enough to ensure that their visitors are adequately satisfied, but amateurs nonetheless. However, a warm climate, friendly natives and a few iconic attractions are no longer enough in themselves to guarantee a successful tourism industry, least of all within the principal destination countries of the developed world, which now find themselves in an increasingly competitive environment in the battle to attract global tourists.

It was the expansion of tourism in the 1960s and 1970s that finally led to a recognition that the study of tourism was something to be taken seriously. Up to that point, the educational focus had been on training for what were perceived to be low-level craft skills that could be learned principally by working alongside experienced employees, to watch how they did the job and emulate them. This would be typical of the way in which hotel and catering workers, travel agents, tour operator resort representatives, visitor attraction employees and airline ground handling staff would be expected to learn their jobs. Not surprisingly, in many cases this merely helped to perpetuate outdated modes of work, not to say errors in practice. In due course, those who performed best in these skills would be promoted to management roles – once again with no formal training – and expected to pick up their management skills as they went along. Gradually, it became recognised that this was not the ideal way to amass knowledge and skills, and that a more formal process of learning, based on a theoretical body of knowledge and its practical application, would lead to improved professionalism in the industry. From basic-level craft skills, academic courses emerged in the 1970s, 1980s and 1990s at diploma, degree and, ultimately, postgraduate levels to educate the workers and managers of the future, as well as equip them with the necessary knowledge and skills to cope at all levels with the rapid changes that were to occur in the tourism industry in the closing years of the last century.

Recognition of the need for formal training is one thing. Determining the body of knowledge that should be appropriate for someone planning to spend a lifetime career in the industry is something else. Tourism is a complex, multidisciplinary subject, requiring knowledge of not only business and management but also of such diverse disciplines as law, town and country planning, geography, sociology and anthropology. One difficulty the tourism industry faces is that trainers will deliver only the knowledge required by their specific tourism sector, while a career in that industry today is likely to involve frequent transfers between the different sectors – and thus an understanding of how each of these operates. Any formal programme of tourism education must take these needs into account and prepare students for a life in the industry as a whole. Due to the multidisciplinary nature of tourism, however, courses offered in this subject in colleges and universities around the world differ substantially in content, with some choosing to deliver what is essentially a business and management programme tuned to the specific needs of the industry, and others focusing on issues such as sustainable tourism or public-sector planning for tourism. Still others may choose to deliver courses where the focus is on understanding tourists, drawing on the disciplines of psychology, sociology and anthropology. A well-rounded student of tourism is going to require some knowledge of all of these disciplines.

EXAMPLE

UK Quality Assurance Agency: Benchmark for tourism programmes

The QAA introduced benchmark statements to clarify academic expectations and standards related to degree qualifications. Initially developed in 2000, the tourism benchmark statements were last reviewed and updated in 2016 to reflect developments in the industry. As part of this review, the QAA acknowledges that degrees in tourism often involve the study of:

- the concept and characteristics of tourism – this is often considered in the context of business management but may also be appreciated for its sociological perspective
- the behaviour and characteristics of tourists
- the structure of the tourism industry, including operations and the interactions between sectors
- the management and governance of tourism destinations – this may include the policy and strategies influencing destination development and protection
- the economic impacts of tourism and its contributions to the economy
- tourism's influence on society, its cultures and communities
- the environmental impact of tourism and the ethical and sustainable management of resources used by tourism
- crisis management along with security, safety, risk and resilience issues relevant to the tourism industry
- the role of technology, digital media and data in the production and consumption of tourism.

Source: QAA, 2016

DEFINING TOURISM

A good starting point for any textbook that sets out to examine the tourism business is to try to define what is meant by the terms 'tourist' and 'tourism' before going on to look at the many different forms that tourism can take. While an understanding of the term's meaning is essential, in fact the task of defining it is very difficult. It is relatively easy to agree on technical definitions of particular categories of 'tourism' or 'tourist', but the wider concept is ill defined.

We can say that, self-evidently, the tourist is one who engages in tourism. Tourism involves the movement of a person or persons away from their normal place of residence: a process that usually incurs some expenditure, although this is not *necessarily* the case. Someone cycling or hiking in the countryside on a camping weekend during which they carry their own food may make no economic contribution to the area in which they travel, but can nonetheless be counted as a tourist. Many other examples could be cited in which expenditure by the tourist is minimal. We can say, then, that tourism usually, but not invariably, incurs some expenditure of income and that, further, money spent has been earned within the area of normal residency, rather than at the destination.

The term 'tourism' is further refined as the movement of people away from their *normal* place of residence. Here we find our first problem: Should shoppers travelling short distances of several kilometres be considered tourists? Is it the *purpose* or the *distance* that is the determining factor? Just how far must people travel before they can be counted as tourists for the purpose of official records? What about that growing band of people travelling regularly between their first and second homes, sometimes spending equal time at each?

Clearly, any definition must be specific. In the USA, in 1973, the National Resources Review Commission established that a domestic tourist would be 'one who travels at least 50 miles (one way)'. That was confirmed by the US Census Bureau, which defined tourism 11 years later as a round trip of at least 100 miles. However, at that time the Canadian government defined it as a journey of at least 80 kilometres from home, while the English Tourism Council proposed a measure of not less than 20 miles and three hours' journey time away from home for a visit to constitute a leisure trip, thus showing no consensus towards consistency.

EARLY ATTEMPTS AT DEFINING TOURISM

One of the first attempts at defining tourism was that of Professors Hunziker and Krapf of Berne University in 1942. They held that tourism should be defined as 'the sum of the phenomena and relationships arising from the travel and stay of non-residents, in so far as they do not lead to permanent residence and are not connected to any earning activity'. This definition helps to distinguish tourism from migration, but it makes the assumption that both *travel* and *stay* are necessary for tourism, thus precluding day tours. It would also appear to exclude business travel, which is connected with 'earning activity', even if that income is not earned in the destination region. Moreover, distinguishing between business and leisure tourism is, in many cases, extremely difficult as most business trips will combine elements of leisure activity.

Earlier still, in 1937, the League of Nations had recommended adopting the definition of a 'tourist' as one who travels for a period of at least 24 hours in a country other than that in which he or she usually resides. This was held to include persons travelling for pleasure, domestic reasons or health, those travelling to meetings or otherwise on business and those visiting a country on a cruise vessel (even if for less than 24 hours). The principal weakness in this definition is that it ignores the movements of domestic tourists.

Later, the United Nations' Conference on International Travel and Tourism, held in 1963, considered recommendations put forward by the International Union of Official Travel Organizations (later the United Nations World Tourism Organization (WTO)) and agreed to use the term 'visitor' to describe any person visiting a country other than that in which they have their usual place of residence, for any reason other than following an occupation remunerated from within the country visited.

This definition was to cover two classes of visitor:

1. Tourists, who were classified as temporary visitors staying at least 24 hours, whose purpose could be categorised as leisure (whether for recreation, health, sport, holiday, study or religion) or business, family, mission or meeting.
2. Excursionists, who were classed as temporary visitors staying less than 24 hours, including cruise travellers but excluding travellers in transit.

TOWARDS AN AGREED DEFINITION

Once again, these definitions fail to take into account the domestic tourist. The inclusion of the word 'study' above is an interesting one as it is often excluded in later definitions. A working party for the proposed Institute of Tourism in the UK (which later became the Tourism Society) attempted to clarify the issue and reported, in 1976:

> Tourism is the temporary short-term movement of people to destinations outside the places where they normally live and work, and activities during their stay at these destinations; it includes movement for all purposes, as well as day visits or excursions.

This broader definition was reformulated slightly, without losing any of its simplicity, at the International Conference on Leisure-Recreation-Tourism, organised by the International Association of Scientific Experts in Tourism (AIEST) and the Tourism Society in Cardiff, Wales, in 1981:

> Tourism may be defined in terms of particular activities selected by choice and undertaken outside the home environment. Tourism may or may not involve overnight stay away from home.

Efforts to standardise data gathering for tourism led the UNWTO to review and revise definitions. In 1993, their definition was endorsed by the UN's Statistical Commission following an international government conference held in Ottawa, Canada, in 1991:

> Tourism comprises the activities of persons travelling to and staying in places outside their usual environment for not more than one consecutive year for leisure, business or other purposes.

More recently, the 2008 International Recommendations for Tourism Statistics further revised these definitions, declaring:

> A visitor is a traveler taking a trip to a main destination outside his/her usual environment, for less than a year, for any main purpose (business, leisure or other personal purpose) other than to be employed by a resident entity in the country or place visited.

Finally, the UNWTO glossary of terms clarifies that a visitor (domestic, inbound or outbound) is classified as a tourist if his/her trip includes an overnight stay.

These definitions have been quoted here at length because they reveal how broadly the concept of tourism must be defined in order to embrace all forms of the phenomenon and how exceptions can be found for even the most narrowly focused definitions. Indeed, with the growth of timeshare and second-home owners, who in some cases spend considerable periods of time away from their main homes, it could be argued that a tourist is no longer necessarily 'outside the home environment'. Furthermore, it is increasingly recognised that defining tourists in terms of the distances they have travelled from their homes is unhelpful, as locals can be viewed as 'tourists' within their own territory if they are engaged in tourist-type activities, and certainly their economic contribution to the tourism industry in the area is as important as that of the more traditionally defined tourist.

CLASSIFYING TRAVELLERS

Figure 1.1 illustrates the guidelines produced by the United Nations World Tourism Organization (UNWTO) (then, the WTO) to classify travellers for statistical purposes. Some loopholes in the definitions remain, however. Even attempts to classify tourists as those travelling for purposes unconnected with employment can be misleading if one looks at the social consequences of tourism. Ruth Pape (1964) drew attention to the case of nurses in the USA who, after qualifying, gravitated to California for their first jobs, as employment was easy to find and they would thus enjoy the benefits of the sunshine and leisure pursuits for which the state is famous. They might spend a year or more in this job before moving on, but the point is that they were motivated to come to that area not because of the work itself, but because of the area's tourist attractions. Frequently, too, students of tourism, after completing their course, return to work in the areas in which they undertook work placements during their studies, having found the location (and often the job) sufficiently attractive to merit spending more time there. People increasingly buy homes in areas where they can enjoy walking, skiing or other leisure activities, so that tourism is literally on their doorsteps, yet this growing group of 'resident tourists' is not taken into consideration for statistical purposes. Indeed, the division between work and leisure is further blurred today by the development of e-mail and Wi-Fi, which offer immediate access from wherever a worker happens to be spending time. This has led many to buy second homes, where work may be engaged in between bouts of leisure and relaxation. Cafés with Internet access, mobile computing and smartphones allow workers to keep in touch with their business while away from home, further blurring the distinction between travel for work and travel for leisure.

Finally, we must consider the case of pensioners who choose to retire abroad in order to benefit from the lower costs of living in other countries. Many Northern Europeans move to Mediterranean countries after retirement, while Americans similarly seeking warmth gravitate to Mexico; they may still retain homes in their country of origin, but spend a large part of the year abroad. Canadians, and Americans living in northern states, are known as 'snowbirds' because of their migrant behaviour, coming down in their mobile homes and caravans to the sunshine states of the US south-west during the winter months to escape the harsh winters of the north. Once again, the motivation for all of these people is not simply to lower their costs of living but also to enjoy an improved climate and the facilities that attract tourists to the same destinations.

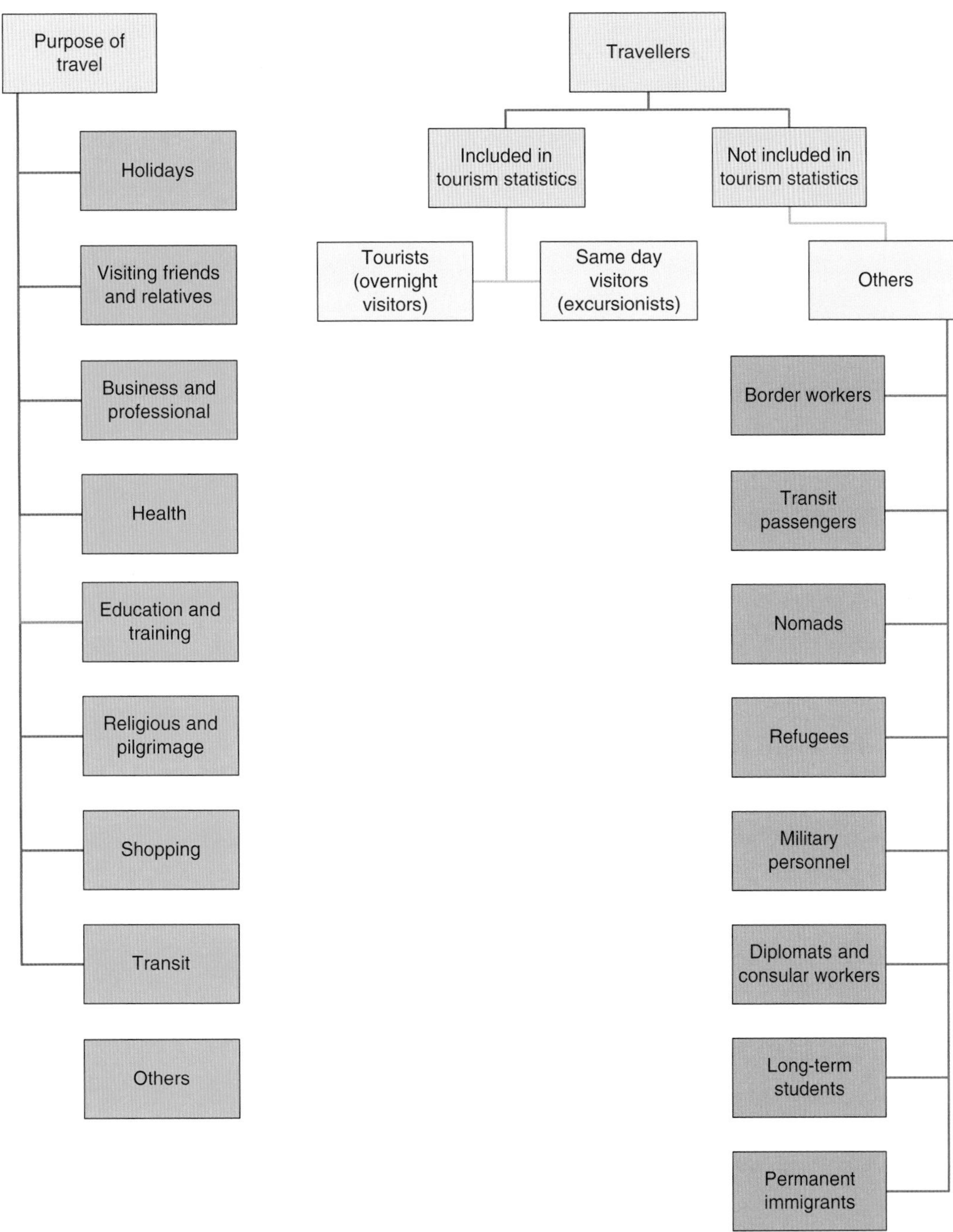

FIGURE 1.1 Classifying travellers

Source: Adapted from UNWTO, 2007

EXAMPLE

Classifying tourists

The UNWTO classifies three basic forms of tourism based on border crossing:

- domestic tourism, involving residents of the given country travelling only within this country
- inbound tourism, involving non-residents travelling in the given country
- outbound tourism, involving residents travelling in another country

For example, if the country being considered is Australia, then visitors arriving in Australia for a holiday would be counted as inbound tourists, while Australian residents travelling out of the country on vacation would be counted as outbound tourists. Australians visiting any other part of this vast country would be measured as domestic tourists, regardless of distance travelled.

It is important to consider the country of reference (in the example above, Australia) because an outbound traveller for one country will be an inbound tourist for another. Thus, any Australian travelling to Singapore would be counted as an outbound tourist for Australia, but an inbound tourist from Singapore's perspective.

Source: Adapted from UNWTO (2007)

Up to this point, definitions and classifications have been discussed in terms of their academic importance and for the purposes of statistical measurement. We need to recognise that the terms are used much more loosely within the industry itself, with a distinction being made between travel and tourism. If we think of **tourism as a system** (Leiper, 1979) (see Figure 1.2) embracing a generating region (where the market for tourism develops), a destination region or regions (places and areas visited by the tourist) and a transit zone (where some form of transport is used to move the tourist from, and back to, the generating region and between any destinations visited), it is becoming common practice among practitioners to refer to the second of these as comprising the *tourism industry*, with the other two referred to as the *travel industry*.

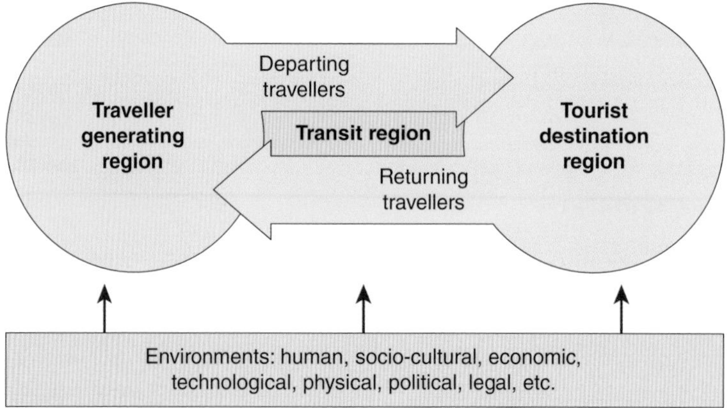

FIGURE 1.2 The tourism system

Source: Adapted from Leiper, 1979

Conceptually, defining tourism precisely is a near-impossible task. To produce a technical definition for statistical purposes is less problematic. As long as it is clear what the data comprise, and one compares like with like, whether inter-regionally or internationally, we can leave the conceptual discussion to the academics.

THE TOURIST PRODUCT

Having made an attempt to define the concept of the 'tourist' and 'tourism', we can now look at the tourist product itself.

INTANGIBILITY

The first characteristic to note is that this is a **service** rather than a tangible good. This intangibility poses particular difficulties for those whose job it is to market tourism. A tourist product cannot, for example, be inspected by prospective purchasers before they buy, as can a washing machine, laptop computer or other consumer durable. The purchase of a package tour is a speculative investment, involving a high degree of trust on the part of the purchaser, the more so as a holiday is often the most expensive purchase made each year (although, with increasing affluence, many consumers are now able to purchase two or more such holidays annually). The necessary element of trust is heightened by the development of sales via the Internet and the introduction of electronic ticketing for much air travel.

It has often been said that 'selling holidays is like selling dreams'. When tourists buy a package tour abroad, they are buying more than a simple collection of services, such as an airline seat, a hotel room and the opportunity to sit on a sunny beach; they are also buying the temporary use of a strange environment, incorporating what may be, for them, novel geographical features – old-world towns, tropical landscapes – plus the culture and heritage of the region and other intangible benefits, such as service, atmosphere and hospitality. The planning and anticipation of the holiday may be as much a part of its enjoyment as is the trip itself. Then, recalling the experience later and reviewing videos or photos are further extensions of the experience. These are all part of the product, which is therefore a psychological as well as a physical experience.

HETEROGENEITY

The challenge for the marketer of tourism is to match the dream to the reality. The difficulty of achieving this is that tourism is not a homogeneous but a **heterogeneous** product; that is, it tends to vary in standard and quality over time and under different circumstances, unlike, say, a television. A package tour or even a flight on an aircraft cannot be consistently uniform: a bumpy flight, or a long technical flight delay, can change an enjoyable experience into a nightmare, while a holiday at the seaside can be ruined by a prolonged rainy spell.

Because a tour comprises a compendium of different products, an added difficulty in maintaining standards is that each element of the product should be broadly similar in quality. A good room and fine service at a hotel may be spoilt by poor food, or delays to a flight may mar an otherwise enjoyable hotel stay. Thus, an element of chance is always present in the purchase of any service, including tourism.

The introduction of **dynamic packaging**, which is rapidly changing the traditional package tour, is beginning to complicate this. Dynamic packaging (discussed in Chapter 19) is the process by which travel agents, or other retailers of travel, themselves put together flights, accommodation and other elements of travel and sell the resulting package of components to consumers. Of course, today tourists can put their own packages together through Internet suppliers, but if they choose to do so, uncertainty about the uniformity of the product is heightened. Even when packages are tailor-made by the travel agent or other retailer in a similar manner, the lack of a single tour operator or supplier to oversee the final package threatens to undermine the concept of a 'standard quality' product.

INSEPARABILITY

One of the factors influencing the heterogeneity of the product is that often people are involved in the delivery of the service, and this human involvement may not be consistent in behaviour or demeanour. The interaction between the service provider – a waiter in a restaurant, for instance, or the holiday representative at a resort – and the customer can be influenced by the moods and emotions of each. But this highlights another characteristic of tourism, in that it cannot be brought to the consumer. Rather, the consumer must be brought to the product and be present for the delivery of the service. This **inseparability** also means that the tourism product cannot be 'manufactured' at a place and time convenient to the supplier. For example, if the holidaymaker has been sold a guided tour then both the tour guide and the tourist need to be present at an agreed time and place for the transaction to take place.

PERISHABILITY

A fourth characteristic of tourism is its inability to be stockpiled for future use. If the hotel room is not sold for a particular night then that 'product' is lost forever; no one would buy a hotel room for use last month! Similarly, the unsold aircraft seat cannot be stored for later sale, as is the case with tangible products, but is lost forever once the plane is airborne; hence the great efforts that must be made by those in the industry to fill empty seats. This has implications for the industry and, as we will discuss in Chapter 18, tour operators work hard to ensure they maximise sales, perhaps offering last-minute discounted deals, to ensure that they earn money from these products before they are lost.

In the short term, at least, the supply of this product is fixed; the number of hotel bedrooms available at a particular destination cannot be varied to meet the changing demands of holidaymakers during the season. If market demand changes, as it does frequently in the business of tourism, the supply will take time to adapt. A hotel is built to last for many years, and must remain profitable throughout that period. These are all problems unique to tourism and call for considerable marketing and management ingenuity on the part of those in the business.

THE NATURE OF TOURISM

It is useful to examine the characteristics of a tour in terms of the following five broad categories: motivation for the trip, the characteristics of the trip, the mode of organisation, the composition of the tour and the characteristics of the tourist.

THE MOTIVATION FOR A TRIP

Motivation identifies, first, the purpose of a visit. As we saw in Figure 1.1, there are many purposes for travel. We can group these into three distinct categories:

- holidays (including visits to friends and relatives, known as VFR travel)
- business (including meetings, conferences, etc.)
- other (including study, religious pilgrimages, sport, health, etc.).

It is important to be aware of the underlying purpose behind the tourist's travels, because each of these categories will reveal a different set of characteristics. Let us consider, for example, how business travel differs from leisure travel. The business traveller will have little discretion in choice of destination or the timing of the trip. In general, destinations will bear little similarity to the destinations of the leisure traveller, as enjoyment of the attractions and facilities does not form part of the purpose of the trip (even if those that exist may be enjoyed as an adjunct to it). Business trips frequently have to be arranged at short notice and for specific and brief periods of time, often only a day, even where substantial journey time is involved. For these reasons, business travellers need the convenience of frequent, regular transport, efficient service and good facilities (in terms of accommodation and catering) at the destination. Because their company will usually be paying for all the travel arrangements, business travellers will be less concerned about the cost of travel than they would be if they were paying for it themselves. Higher prices are not likely to deter travel, nor will lower prices encourage more frequent travel. We can say, therefore, that business travel is relatively **price inelastic**. Holiday travel, however, is highly price elastic; lower prices for holidays to a particular destination will tend to lead to an increase in the total number of travellers, as tourists find the holiday more affordable, while others may be encouraged by the lower prices to switch their planned destination. Leisure travellers will be prepared to delay their travel or will book well in advance of their travel dates if this means that they can substantially reduce their costs.

While these generalities continue to hold, we must also recognise the fact that growing disposable income among the populations of the developed world is having the effect of reducing price elasticity for many holidaymakers as upmarket winter sports holidays, cruises, special interest and long-haul travel attract a greater percentage of mass-market travellers (especially the growing numbers taking second and third holidays every year). For these travellers, service is becoming more important than price. At the same time, narrowing profits in the business world, and restrictions placed on corporate travel budgets, are driving up price elasticity among business travellers. In the latter case, the growth in low-cost air carriers has made discounted air travel so attractive by comparison with fares on the established carriers (particularly first and business class) that low-cost airlines now claim that a large proportion of their passengers are people travelling on business.

Beyond price, we must also identify other reasons for a specific type of holiday or resort being chosen. Different people will look for different qualities in the same destination. A particular ski resort, for example, may be selected because of its excellent slopes and sporting facilities, its healthy mountain air or the social life it offers to skiers and non-skiers alike. The variety of motivations influencing demand for holidays is extensive, and these are discussed in more detail in Chapter 3.

THE CHARACTERISTICS OF A TRIP

These define what kind of visit is made and to where. First, one can differentiate between **domestic** tourism and **international** tourism. The former refers to travel taken exclusively within the national boundaries of the traveller's home country. The decision to take one's holidays within the borders of one's own country is an important one economically as it will reduce the outflow of money from that country and have an impact on the balance of payments. Many governments therefore encourage residents to holiday in their own countries in order to aid the economy. Recession in the early part of the twenty-first century saw the growth of 'staycations', a new term describing the growing number of holidays taken in areas local to home.

EXAMPLE

Why take a staycation?

The growth in 'staycations' – holidaying in your home town – has been given greater press attention since the term emerged during the global recession which started towards the end of the last decade.

The idea of a staycation is to make use of local resources – those often attractive to tourists visiting the area – to provide opportunities to relax, unwind and break with routine. For example, staycation activities may include visiting a local museum or attraction, taking a guided walking tour or sampling a restaurant in another part of town. However, the term is being increasingly misused to refer to taking a domestic holiday rather than international travel.

Staycations can offer some advantages. For example, the cost of travel can be lower, leaving more in the budget for other activities. Exploring the local area can eliminate stresses caused by transport issues, such as flight delays and long queues at passport control. Furthermore, exploring local tourist attractions can also provide a new appreciation for one's home town.

Next, what kind of destination is being chosen? Will travel be to a seaside resort, mountain resort, country town, health spa or major city? Is it to be a single-centre visit, a multi-centre one (involving a stopover at two or more places) or a longitudinal tour that will involve extensive travel with brief overnight stays along the route? If a cruise is to be taken, statisticians have to decide whether or not to count this as international travel if the vessel visits foreign ports and, if so, whether to count each country visited as a separate visit to a foreign country. Does a one-night stopover in Miami before boarding a cruise vessel bound for the Caribbean count as a separate visit to the USA for the European or Asian visitor?

Next, what length of time is being spent on the trip? A visit that does not involve an overnight stay is known, as we saw earlier, as an excursion, frequently referred to as a 'day trip'. The expenditure of day trippers is generally less than that of overnight visitors and statistical data on these forms of tourism are often collected separately. A visitor who spends at least one night at a destination is termed a 'tourist', but can, of course, make day trips to other destinations which could even involve an international trip. For instance, a visitor staying on the Greek island of Rhodes may take a trip for the day by boat to the Turkish mainland; another in Corfu can go on an excursion to the nearby coastal resorts of Albania. For the purposes of Turkey's and Albania's records, that visitor will be recorded as an excursionist. Domestic American tourists travelling through New England often make a brief visit to the Canadian side of the Niagara Falls, hence are excursionists as far as the Canadian tourism authorities are concerned.

Finally, in order to maintain accurate records, some maximum length of time must be established beyond which the visitor can no longer be looked on as a tourist. There are different approaches here, with some using a low figure of three months, others six months and, in some cases, a full year is viewed as the maximum period.

MODES OF TOUR ORGANISATION

This further refines the form that the travel takes. A tour may be **independent** or **packaged**. A package tour, for which the official term is 'inclusive tour' (IT), is an arrangement in which transport and accommodation are purchased by the tourist at an all-inclusive price. The price of individual elements of the tour cannot normally be determined by the purchaser. The tour operator putting together the package will buy transport and accommodation in advance, generally at a lower price because each of the products is being bought in bulk, and the tours are then sold individually to holidaymakers, either directly or through travel agents. Agents and operators can also package independent inclusive tours by taking advantage of special net fares and building the package around the specific needs of the client. This is explained more fully in Chapter 18.

As explained earlier in this chapter, **dynamic package** is the term used to describe holidays that are put together as tailor-made programmes, whether by the operator, the retailer or even by the holidaymakers themselves. This form of holiday package is rapidly changing the standard inclusive tour, although it is not thought that this will lead to the demise of the traditional package. Rather, operators are adjusting their products to make them more flexible by means of tailor-made alterations to duration and other arrangements.

THE COMPOSITION OF THE TOUR

This consists of the elements comprising the visit. All tourism involves travel away from one's usual place of residence and in the case of 'tourists' – as opposed to 'excursionists' – it will include accommodation. So, we must identify the form of travel – air, sea, road or rail – that is to be used. If air transport is involved, will this be by charter aircraft or scheduled flight? If there is to be an overnight stay, will this be in a hotel, a guest house, a campsite or self-catering accommodation? How will the passenger travel between airport and hotel – by coach, taxi or private limousine? A package tour will normally comprise transport and accommodation, often with transfers to and from the accommodation included, but in some cases additional services will be provided in the programme, such as car hire at the destination, excursions by coach or theatre entertainment.

THE CHARACTERISTICS OF THE TOURIST

Analysis of tourism must include analysis of the tourist. We have already distinguished between the holidaymaker and the business traveller. We can also identify the tourist in terms of nationality, social class, sex, age and lifestyle. What life stage are they in? What type of personality do they have? This is discussed in more detail in Chapter 3.

Such information is valuable not only for the purpose of record-keeping; it will also help to shed light on the reasons why people travel, why they select certain destinations and how patterns of travel differ between different groups of people. Research is now focusing much more intently on personality and lifestyle as characteristics that determine the choice of holidays, rather than looking simply at social class and occupation. The more that is known about such details, the more effectively those in the industry can produce the products that will meet the needs of their customers, and develop the appropriate strategies to promote such products.

THE TOURIST DESTINATION

We can now examine the tourist destination itself. The nature of destinations will be explored in Chapter 8, but at this point in the book an initial understanding of what attracts tourists to different destinations will be helpful. A **destination** can be a particular resort or town, a region within a country, the whole of a country or even a larger area of the globe. For example, a package tour may embrace visits to three separate countries in Latin America that have quite distinct attractions – say, an initial visit to Peru to see the cultural life of the Peruvian Indians and the ruins at Machu Picchu, followed by a flight to Buenos Aires, Argentina, for a typical capital city experience of shopping and nightlife, returning home via Cancún, Mexico, where a few days of recuperation are enjoyed at a beach resort.

This 'pick and mix' approach to the varieties of destination and their relative attractions is becoming increasingly common, with the earlier concept of being expected to choose between a beach holiday, a cultural holiday, a short-break city tour and some other uniform package arrangement no longer holding true. Cruise companies have come to recognise this and now commonly market fortnight combination holidays, consisting of several days of cruising, preceded or followed by a few days at a beach resort close to the port of embarkation.

In the case of cruises, for many tourists the 'destination' is the ship itself, and its actual ports of call may be secondary to the experience of life on board. Indeed, it is by no means unusual for regular cruise passengers to fail to disembark at ports of call, preferring to enjoy the company of the cruise staff and entertainment on board while the ship is in port.

In other examples, the destination and accommodation are inseparable, as in the case of a resort hotel that provides a range of leisure facilities on site. In such cases, it may be the tourist's objective to visit the hotel purely and simply because of the facilities that hotel provides and the entire stay will be enjoyed without venturing beyond the precincts of the hotel grounds. An example would be the Sandals all-inclusive resorts in the Caribbean and Club Med resorts across the world.

EXAMPLE

A resort destination

Club Med operates premium all-inclusive resorts around the globe, providing an extensive range of facilities to keep holidaymakers entertained. To take one example – and this is representative of many of their resorts – we can look at the Cargèse resort on the French island of Corsica. Located on the west coast, it is immediately adjacent to a beach suited to swimming and other watersports. To encourage holidaymakers onto the water, the resort offers a sailing academy and provides catamarans, windsurfing and kayaking facilities.

For tourists preferring dry land, the tennis academy may be more suited to their desires. Alternatively, a chance to try archery, badminton, basketball, volleyball or to participate in fitness classes may be preferred. The less active holidaymaker may choose to relax by the pool, or enjoy the concerts and shows. For those who wish to venture outside of the resort, full- and half-day excursions are offered. These might include visits to local World Heritage Sites.

Although it has been operating for more than half a century, Club Med launched its current approach to holiday resorts in 2004, reinvigorating its appeal to markets demanding upmarket, all-inclusive resorts. This has proved popular, and the company provided holidays for 1.34 million tourists in 2017.

All destinations share certain characteristics. Their success in attracting tourists will depend on the quality of three essential benefits that are offered: **attractions, amenities** (or facilities) and **accessibility** (or ease with which they can travel to the destination). At this point, we will do no more than outline the variety of destinations attractive to tourists, before considering their attractions, amenities and accessibility.

VARIETIES OF DESTINATIONS

Destinations are of two kinds – either 'natural' or 'constructed'. Most are 'managed' to some extent, whether they are natural or constructed. National parks, for example, are left in their natural state of beauty as far as possible, but nevertheless have to be managed, in terms of the provision of access, parking facilities, accommodation (such as caravans and campsites), litter bins and so on.

Broadly, we can categorise destinations by delineating them according to geographical features, under the following three headings:

- urban tourism – this will include visits to cities and towns
- coastal tourism – this will include seaside resorts, natural beaches, boating holidays along coasts, coastal footpaths and so on
- rural tourism – this will include the most common category of lakes and mountains, but also countryside touring, 'agritourism' such as farm holidays, visits to vineyards, gardens, visits and stays at villages or rural retreats, river and canal holidays, wildlife parks and national parks.

Health resorts, including spas (which are important to the tourist industries of many countries), may be based in rural, seaside or urban areas. Adventure holidays and active holidays, such as winter sports, are commonly associated with rural sites, but if one thinks of the appeal of towns such as St Moritz in Switzerland, Aspen in Colorado or Jackson Hole, Wyoming, in the USA, which developed primarily to attract winter sports enthusiasts, it must be recognised that pigeonholing all forms of tourism as being one or other of only these three types of destination is inappropriate.

All destinations can suffer from overuse and, for the most popular, this is a growing problem. The difficulties created by too great a demand and the need for careful management of city centres, beaches and natural countryside are subjects that are discussed in Chapters 5 and 6.

ATTRACTIONS, AMENITIES AND ACCESSIBILITY

All destinations require adequate attractions, amenities and accessibility if they are to appeal to large numbers of tourists. In this section, we will look at these issues.

The more attractions a destination can offer, the easier it becomes to market that destination to the tourist. Listing and analysing attractions is no easy matter, especially when one recognises that what appeals to one tourist may actually deter another.

Many of the attractions of a destination depend on its physical features: the beauty of mountains, the fresh air of a seaside resort and the qualities of a particular beach, the historical architecture, shopping and entertainment opportunities and the 'atmosphere' of a great city. These can be added to the numerous purpose-built attractions that increase the pulling power of the destination. Key cities and capitals build new museums, art galleries or exhibition centres, while former stately homes or castles are transformed by development into focal points for visits by tourists and day trippers alike.

Sometimes, the constructed attraction becomes a destination in its own right, as is the case with theme parks such as the Disney complexes in Anaheim (California), Orlando (Florida), Paris, France, Hong Kong and Shanghai. Similarly, the success of many spa towns on the Continent rests on their ability to combine constructed attractions such as casinos with the assumed medical benefits of the natural springs, while the popular ski resorts must provide adequate ski runs, ski lifts and après-ski entertainment to complement their combination of suitable weather and mountain slopes. The operation of managed visitor attractions is dealt with in Chapters 9 and 16. At this point, therefore, it is sufficient to highlight certain distinctions between attractions.

First, attractions may be either *site* or *event* attractions (Figure 1.3). Site attractions are permanent by nature, while event attractions (discussed in Chapter 10) are temporary and may be mounted in order to increase the number of tourists to a particular destination. Some events have a short timescale, such as an air display; others

	Site-based attractions	Event-based attractions
i. Natural	1. Grand Canyon, Arizona	2. Aurora Borealis (Northern Lights)
ii. Man-made	3. Eiffel Tower, Paris	4. Olympic Games

FIGURE 1.3 Classifying attractions

Source: Adapted from Leiper 1979

may last for many days (the Edinburgh Festival, for example) or even months (for instance, the Floriade Garden Festival in the Netherlands). Some events occur at regular intervals – yearly, biennially, four-yearly (the Olympic Games) or even less frequently (the Oberammergau Passion Play in Germany and the Floriade Festival mentioned above occur only once every ten years), while other festivals are organised on an ad hoc basis and may, indeed, be one-off events. A destination that may otherwise have little to commend it to the tourist can, in this way, succeed in drawing tourists by mounting a unique exhibition, while a site destination can extend its season by mounting an off-season event, such as a festival of arts.

Second, destinations and their attractions can be either *nodal* or *linear* in character. A nodal destination is one in which the attractions of the area are closely grouped geographically. Seaside resorts and cities are examples of typical nodal attractions, making them ideal for packaging by tour operators. This has led to the concept of 'honey pot' tourism development, in which planners concentrate the development of tourism in a specific locality. Whistler in Canada is an example of a purpose-built nodal tourism resort, built largely to satisfy the growing needs of winter sports enthusiasts (Figure 1.4). With its extensive range of accommodation, attractions and amenities, it now draws high-spend tourists throughout the year from all over the world. Linear tourism, however, defines an

FIGURE 1.4 Whistler, Canada, has purpose-built facilities catering to snow-sport enthusiasts in winter and hikers and golfers in summer.

Photo: Claire Humphreys

attraction spread over a wide geographical area, without any specific focus. Examples include the Shenandoah Valley region in the USA, the Highlands of Scotland or the so-called 'romantische Strasse' (romantic trail) through central Germany – all ideal for touring holidays, rather than just 'stay put' holidays. Motels or bed-and-breakfast accommodation spring up in such areas to serve the needs of the transient tourist, who may spend only one or two nights at a particular destination. Cruising is another form of linear tourism, currently enjoying growing popularity as it enables tourists to see a multitude of different sites conveniently and with minimal disruption.

It is important to remember that much of the attraction of a destination is intangible and greatly depends on its image, as perceived by the potential tourist. India may be seen by one group of travellers as exotic and appealing, while others will reject it as a destination because of its poverty or its unfamiliar culture. Images of a destination, whether favourable or unfavourable, tend to be built up over a long period of time and, once established, are difficult to change. Overcoming such stereotyping is an important task for a country's national tourist board.

Amenities are those essential services that cater to the needs of the tourist. These include accommodation and food, evening entertainment such as theatres, nightclubs and bars, local transport, and the necessary infrastructure to support tourism: roads, public utility services and parking facilities. Naturally, such amenities will vary according to the nature of the destination itself: it would clearly be inappropriate to provide extensive infrastructure in an area of great scenic beauty, such as a national park, and those planning to visit such a destination will recognise that the availability of hotels and restaurants must inevitably be limited. Such sites are likely to attract the camper and those seeking only limited amenities – indeed, this will be part of the attraction for them.

It should also be recognised that, on occasion, the amenity itself may be the attraction, as was discussed earlier in the case of a resort hotel offering a comprehensive range of *in situ* attractions. Similarly, a destination such as France, which is famed for its regional foods, will encourage tourists whose motive in visiting may be largely to enjoy their meals. In this case, the amenity is itself an attraction.

Finally, a destination must be accessible if it is to facilitate visits from tourists. While more intrepid travellers may be willing to put themselves to great inconvenience in order to see some of the more exotic places in the world, most tourists will not be attracted to a destination unless it is relatively easy to reach. This means, in the case of international travel, having a good airport nearby, regular and convenient air transport to the region at an affordable price and good local connections to the destination itself (or, at the very least, good car hire facilities). Cruise ships will be attracted by well-presented deep water ports with moorings available at reasonable cost to the shipping line and situated within easy reach of the attractions in the area. Cities such as Helsinki, Stockholm and Tallinn have the great advantage of providing deep water moorings close to the very heart of the capital, allowing passengers to disembark and walk into the centre of the city. Warnemünde is a popular port for cruise visitors wanting to visit Germany, as Berlin is a comfortable day's excursion by fast motorway from the coast. Access is also important in getting around the locality at a destination. This may be achieved through local public transport, or providing facilities targeting visitors.

However, if access becomes too easy, this may result in too great a demand and resultant congestion, making the destination less attractive to the tourist. The building of motorways in the UK opened up the Lake District and the West Country to millions of motorists, many of whom now find themselves within a two-hour drive of their destination. This has led to severe congestion due to the large numbers of weekend day trippers and summer holidaymakers during the peak tourist months.

It should be noted that the *perception* of accessibility on the part of the traveller is often as important as a destination's *actual* accessibility. In particular, the introduction of low-cost airlines to less familiar destinations has led many holidaymakers to perceive some destinations as being conveniently accessible in terms of both cost and travelling time. Such perceptions will undoubtedly affect decision-making when tourists are formulating their travel plans.

SUMMARY

This chapter has highlighted the problem of defining tourism, but much of this difficulty can be appreciated in recognising that this industry has many subsectors. This provides the student planning their career in tourism with many opportunities, whether they wish to work in travel operations, retail travel, the numerous transport sectors, the accommodation sector, marketing destinations or the many other areas we have not listed here. It is also important that the impacts of tourism are recognised, and, for tourism to remain sustainable, planning and management are vital activities.

QUESTIONS AND DISCUSSION POINTS

1. Why is it difficult to define tourism?
2. In this chapter, we note that tourism is influenced by characteristics such as intangibility, inseparability, heterogeneity and perishability. What are the implications of each of these characteristics for tourism managers?
3. How does the perception of the available amenities and attractions influence a tourist's choice of destination?

TASKS

1. You are considering a staycation. Investigate your local area and produce a short report that offers a critical view of the attractions and amenities available.
2. Each month, the UNTWO produces a newsletter (published online at http://media.unwto.org/newsletters). Review a sample of recent editions to identify some key issues facing the tourism industry today. Produce a poster that displays your findings.

REFERENCES

Hunziker, W. and Krapf, K. (1942) *Grundriss der Allgemeinen Fremdenverkehrslehre*. Zurich: Polygraphischer Verlag.

Leiper, N. (1979) The framework of tourism: Towards a definition of tourism, tourist, and the tourist industry. *Annals of Tourism Research*, 6 (2), 390–407.

Pape, R. (1964) Touristry: A type of occupational mobility. *Social Problems*, 11 (4), 327–36.

QAA (2016) *Subject Benchmark Statement: Events, hospitality, leisure, sport and tourism*. Gloucester: The Quality Assurance Agency for Higher Education.

United Nations World Tourism Organization (UNWTO) (2007) *2008 Draft International Recommendations for Tourism Statistics*. Madrid: UNWTO. Available online at: http://unstats.un.org/unsd/statcom/doc08/bg-tourismstats.pdf [Accessed October 2018].

UNWTO (2017) *Tourism Highlights*. Madrid: UNWTO.

UNWTO (2018) *Why Tourism*? Available online at: www2.unwto.org/content/why-tourism [Accessed October 2018].

2

TOURISM IN ITS HISTORICAL CONTEXT

CONTENTS

LEARNING OUTCOMES

After studying this chapter, you should be able to:

- explain the historical changes that have affected the growth and development of the tourism industry from its earliest days
- understand the relationship between technological innovation and tourism development
- explain why particular forms of travel and destinations were chosen by early tourists
- be aware of the part played by travel writers and guides in encouraging tourism
- identify the factors giving rise to mass tourism
- describe the origins and changing characteristics of package holidays
- understand the influence of political, social and economic factors as they have affected tourism over time.

> Ancient and modern conceptions of the meaning of travel are very different, as are their emphases on the transformations effected by a journey. The ancients valued travel as an explication of human fate and necessity, for moderns it is an expression of freedom and an escape from necessity and purpose. (Leed, 2007: 5)

INTRODUCTION: THE ORIGINS OF TRAVEL

Some knowledge of the history of travel and tourism is an essential ingredient in any serious study of the subject, not purely as a matter of academic interest, but because it underpins our understanding of the business of tourism today. We learn from history that this mass movement of people, from its earliest days some 3000 years ago, shares many of the characteristics of the business as we know it today. Many of the facilities and amenities demanded by modern tourists had to be provided – albeit in a more basic form – for early travellers: not just accommodation and transport, but also catering services, guides and souvenir shops. Only the sophistication with which these facilities are provided today marks out the difference between early travel and the temporary mass movement of people around the world.

The earliest forms of travel can be traced at least as far back as the Babylonian and Egyptian empires, some three millennia BC, but these originated for business purposes rather than leisure. People travelled largely out of obligation, for reasons of government administration, trade or military purposes. However, there is also evidence of significant movements of religious tourists to the sites of sacred festivals. Leisure travel took a little longer to develop, though this, too, is traceable as far back as c.1500 BC. At that time, Egyptians began to visit their pyramids, partly for reasons of religion but largely out of curiosity or for pleasure (Casson, 1974). It would be true to say, however, that such travel entailed very little pleasure and was viewed as a stressful necessity by travellers. Indeed, the origin of the word 'travel' is to be found in its earlier form of *travail* – literally, a painful and laborious effort.

While some limited travel along the coasts and rivers of those ancient empires must have occurred even earlier, travel was greatly facilitated when shipwrights first designed vessels capable of travelling safely and relatively comfortably over open water, sometime after 3000 BC (Casson, 1994). Primarily used to carry freight, they would have also carried a few passengers. Ashore, transport was limited to donkey riding pending, around 3000 BC, the introduction – probably by the Sumerians – of solid-wheeled wagons drawn by oxen or onagers (a type of wild ass).

By the first millennium BC the world had changed, as new empires grew, fought and died. Most forms of transport around this time (such as the chariot) were first developed for military purposes, but this soon led to the use of horse-drawn wagons to convey goods and people. Horse riding also appeared, at first in military guise, as warriors from Asia swept down from the Steppes. From about 500 BC, however, it was adopted by the Western nations, first in the form of cavalry, but later as a more peaceful form of transport.

Cultural tourism had developed by at least the sixth century BC, with Babylon's museum of 'historic antiquities' one notable example. The Egyptians held many religious festivals, attracting the devout, while others came to see famous buildings and works of art in the cities. To provide for these throngs during the festivals, services sprang up: street vendors of food and drink, guides, hawkers of souvenirs, touts and, inevitably, prostitutes. Some early tourists took to vandalising buildings with graffiti to record their visit – with examples in Egypt dating back to 2000 BC.

From about the same date, and notably from the third century BC, Greek tourists travelled to visit the sites of healing gods. Because the independent city states of ancient Greece had no central authority to order the construction of roads, most of these tourists travelled by water, and as most freight also travelled in this fashion, the seaports prospered. The Greeks, too, enjoyed their religious festivals, which, in time, became increasingly orientated towards the pursuit of pleasure and, in particular, sport. Athens had become an important destination for travellers visiting major sights like the Parthenon, and so inns – often adjuncts of the temples – were established in major towns and seaports to provide for travellers' needs. Innkeepers of this period were known to be difficult and unfriendly, and the facilities they provided were very basic: a pallet to sleep on, but no heating, no windows and no toilet facilities.

EXAMPLE

The first travel writers were critics

Around 500 BC, some travellers took to recording their observations. Aristides, for example, made reference to the appalling conditions of the highways in Asia Minor in his Sacred Discourses, while Herodotus (c.484–424 BC), a noted historian and early travel writer, recorded extensively, and with some cynicism, the tall stories recounted by guides. The quality and accuracy of information these provided varied greatly, whether their task was to shepherd the tourists around the sites (the periegetai) or to provide information (the exegetai) (Casson, 1974). Some would recount that the great pyramids at Giza extended downwards into the Earth to the same extent as their height; others that the white marble used in the greatest statues was so dazzling that viewers should avert their gaze to avoid eyesight damage. The philosopher Plutarch wrote to complain that guides insisted on talking too much about the inscriptions and epitaphs found at the sites, ignoring visitors' entreaties to cut this short.

Guidebooks appeared as early as the fourth century BC, covering destinations such as Athens, Sparta and Troy. Pausanias, a Greek travel writer, produced a noted 'Description of Greece' between AD 160 and 180 that, in its critical evaluation of facilities and destinations, acted as a model for later writers. Advertisements, in the form of signs directing visitors to wayside inns, also date from this period, and both Greeks and Romans produced geographical and travel texts.

The Roman Empire boosted international travel markedly. With no foreign borders between England and Syria, and with the seas safe from piracy owing to Roman military patrols, conditions favouring travel had at last arrived. Roman coinage was acceptable everywhere, and Latin was the common language of the day. Romans travelled to Sicily, Greece, Rhodes, Troy, Egypt and, from the third century AD, the Holy Land. Guidebooks (*itineraria*) similar to present-day Michelin Guides listed hostels with symbols to indicate quality.

Growth in travel bureaucracy also intensified. Reference to passport-type documents can be traced to at least as far back as 1500 BC and there are biblical references to 'letters', allowing passage for travellers, relating to the period around 450 BC (Lloyd, 2003). Later, exit permits were required in order to leave by many seaports and a charge was made for this service. The Roman *tractorium* is an early example of a passport-type document, issued during the reign of Augustus Caesar. Souvenirs acquired abroad were subject to an import duty and a customs declaration had to be completed.

The Roman Empire suffered its share of 'cowboy operators', both at home and abroad. Among the souvenirs offered to Roman travellers were forgeries of Greek statues, especially works bearing the signature of Greece's most famous sculptor, Praxiteles. Popular souvenirs of the day included engraved glass vials, while professional stonecutters offered their services to inscribe graffiti on tourist sites. Roman writers of the day complained that Athens was becoming a 'city of shysters', bent on swindling the foreign tourist.

EXAMPLE

Early market segmentation of tourism

Domestic tourism flourished within the Roman Empire's heartland. Second homes were built by the wealthy within easy travelling distance of Rome – for use particularly during the springtime social season.

The most fashionable resorts were to be found around the Bay of Naples, and there is evidence of early market segmentation for these destinations. Naples itself attracted the retired and intellectuals, Cumae became a high-fashion resort, while Puteoli attracted the more staid tourist and Baiae, which was both a spa town and a seaside resort, attracted the downmarket tourist, becoming noted for its rowdiness, drunkenness and all-night singing. As the Roman philosopher Seneca put it, 'Why must I look at drunks staggering along the shore, or noisy boating parties?' (Casson, 1974: 32).

The distribution of Roman administrators and military led to journeys abroad to visit friends and relatives, a precedent for today's VFR movements. Better communications resulting from conquest aided the growth of travel: first-class roads, coupled with staging inns (precursors of the modern motels), led to comparatively safe, fast and convenient travel unsurpassed until modern times.

THE DEVELOPMENT OF TRAVEL IN THE MIDDLE AGES

Following the collapse of the Roman Empire and the onset of the so-called Dark Ages (fifth to eleventh centuries AD), travel became more dangerous, difficult and considerably less attractive. Most pleasure travel was undertaken closer to home, but adventurers still sought fame and fortune, while merchants sought new trade opportunities abroad, and strolling players and minstrels made their living by performing as they travelled (the most famous of these must be Blondel, a native of Picardy and friend of King Richard I, the Lionheart, whom he is reputed to have accompanied during the latter's crusade to the Holy Land). However, all these forms of travel would be identified either as business travel or travel from a sense of obligation or duty. In order for people to travel for pleasure, the conditions that favour travel must be in place.

Holidays played an important role in the life of the public. The word 'holiday' has its origin in the old English *haligdaeg*, or 'holy day', and from earliest times, religion provided the framework within which leisure time was spent. For most people, this implied a break from work rather than movement from one place to another. The village 'wakes' of the Middle Ages, held on the eve of patronal festivals, provide an example of such 'religious relaxation'. Such public holidays were, in fact, quite numerous – up until as recently as 1830, there were as many as 33 saints' days in the UK holiday calendar, which dispels the myth of peasants being engaged almost constantly in hard manual labour. Pilgrimages would be undertaken to places of worship, notably including Canterbury, York, Durham and, by the thirteenth century, Walsingham Priory in Norfolk. Chaucer's tales of one pilgrimage to Canterbury provide evidence that there was a pleasurable side to this travel, too.

Once political stability was achieved on the Continent and in England following the Norman invasion in 1066, pilgrimages to important sacred sites abroad became increasingly commonplace. Among the most notable were Santiago de Compostela (where the ever-increasing flow of pilgrim tourists led to the creation of relatively sophisticated travel facilities along the pilgrim route by the fifteenth century), Rome and the Holy Land itself. Visits to the latter countries were generally routed via Venice, which itself became a wealthy and important stopover point and a trading centre for the pilgrims.

In the Middle East, religious travel meant visits to Mecca, the birthplace of Mohammed, the founder of Islam, following his death in 632, while Arab explorers included the Moroccan Ibn Battuta (1165–1240) (Dunn, 1986). A spiritual philosopher, he undertook journeys comparable to those of Marco Polo, travelling over 70,000 miles in 25 years, visiting Russia, India, Manchuria and China, as well as nearer countries in North Africa and the Middle East. His travelogue, the *Ribla* examined the social and cultural history of Islam as well as politics, immigration and gender relations within the countries he visited.

THE DEVELOPMENT OF ROAD TRANSPORT

Before the sixteenth century, those who sought to travel had three modes of doing so. The poor walked, regardless of distance involved; others travelled on horseback or were carried, either on a litter (borne by servants – an option restricted largely to the aristocracy) or on a carrier's wagon. This horse-drawn vehicle without springs was slow and appallingly uncomfortable: roads were poorly surfaced, potholed and, in winter, deeply rutted by wagon wheels, making any journey an endurance test.

Road tolls appeared as early as 1267, and tollgates on turnpike roads became common from around 1663, adding to travel cost. Journeys were unsafe; highwaymen abounded on the major routes, posing an ever-present threat to wayfarers. Apart from royalty and the court circle, who were always well guarded, only a handful of wealthy citizens, such as those with 'country seats' (second homes in the country), travelled for pleasure, until well into the eighteenth century.

The development of the sprung coach was a huge advance for those obliged to travel. Initially, the body of the coach was 'sprung' by being suspended from primitive leather straps, offering some small measure of comfort. The later introduction of metal, leaf-spring suspension greatly improved comfort.

By the mid-1600s coaches were operating regularly in Britain, with daily services between London and Oxford. Stagecoaches appeared in Britain in the seventeenth century, using teams of horses changed at regular points along the route, greatly aiding mobility, and by the eighteenth century, turnpike roads, with improved surfaces, enabled stagecoaches carrying between eight and 14 passengers to cover upwards of 40 miles a day during the summer. However, this still meant that a journey from London to Bath would take some three days, while the 400 miles to Edinburgh took fully ten days.

Across the Atlantic, stagecoaches helped develop the North American colonies, with services between Boston and New York introduced in 1772, and other routes serving Providence (Rhode Island), Philadelphia and Baltimore.

Travel of some distance requires accommodation. Inns sprang up to serve the needs of overnight guests and provide fresh horses, while lodgings or 'chambers' were available for rent to visitors when they arrived at their destinations. However, facilities were fairly basic.

Around 1815, the introduction of tarmacadam revolutionised the road systems of Europe and North America. For the first time, a hard surface less subject to pitting and ruts enabled rapid increases to be made in the average speed of coach services. Charabancs (public coaches drawn by teams of horses, with rows of transverse seats facing forwards) appeared as early as 1832 (the name was later applied to the first motor coaches used for leisure travel in the early twentieth century), and the horse-drawn omnibus became a common sight in London and Paris. Mail coaches covered the distance between London and Bath in 12 and a half hours, and the London to Brighton run was reduced to a little over five hours.

THE GRAND TOUR

From the early seventeenth century, the Renaissance heralded a new form of tourism encouraging the quest for learning. Young men seeking positions at court were encouraged to travel to the Continent to complete their education. It eventually became customary for the education of a gentleman to be completed by a 'Grand Tour' (a term in use as early as 1670) of major European cultural centres, accompanied by a tutor and often lasting three years or more. A special licence had to be obtained from the Crown in order to travel abroad, but universities were privileged to grant licences themselves for purposes of scholarship. The publication in 1749 of a guidebook by Dr Thomas Nugent entitled *The Grand Tour* provided a further boost. While ostensibly educational, as with the spas, the appeal soon became social, with pleasure-seeking young men of leisure travelling predominantly to France and Italy to enjoy the cultures and social life of Paris, Venice and Florence. Other Northern Europeans, too, travelled south, visiting Italian cities to develop their cultural knowledge of antiquity, architecture, music and arts. These travels also provided opportunities to develop useful political and social contacts.

European towns and cities opened up to tourism (it was not until the close of the eighteenth century that the countryside, lakes and mountains began to appeal), with Aix-en-Provence, Montpellier and Avignon becoming notable bases, especially for those using the Provence region as a staging post for travel to Italy. When pleasure travel followed in the nineteenth century, eventually to displace educational tours as the motive for continental visits, the Riviera developed as the principal destination for British tourists, aided by the introduction of regular steamboat services across the Channel from 1821 onwards. While growth was interrupted for some 30 years by the Napoleonic wars, this interval led the British to take greater interest in touring their own country.

AUTHORISATION TO TRAVEL

Travel outside the boundaries of one's country, and sometimes between regions of the same country, had long been subject to restrictions, since the days of the Roman Empire and in some cases even earlier. In the eighteenth century, France required internal passports to travel between towns, and colonial America demanded similar documentation for interstate travel.

The earliest use of the term 'passport' in Britain is thought to have occurred in 1548 (Lloyd, 2003). These documents were similar to medieval *testimoniale* – a letter from an ecclesiastical superior given to a pilgrim to avoid the latter's possible arrest on charges of vagrancy. Later, formal state approval to travel, particularly during periods of warfare with neighbouring European countries, became the norm.

Monarchs were suspicious of alliances with foreign states and, throughout the sixteenth and seventeenth centuries, had the prerogative to control movements of their subjects abroad. Applications had to be made for a 'licence to pass beyond the seas'. Such 'licences' became more frequent in the eighteenth and nineteenth centuries, but were prohibitively expensive for all but the wealthy. However, demand for licences grew rapidly, to a point where it became impossible to issue passports in the traditional way. In Britain, the Foreign

Secretary issued all licences based on personal knowledge of the applicant, but this was clearly becoming impractical.

The Alien Bill 1792 – introduced in Britain at a time when the government was becoming concerned about who was coming to Britain (in the lead-up to war with France) – required foreigners entering Britain to be in possession of passports from 1793 onwards and to register on arrival – the first modern form of immigration control. This restriction was not lifted until 1826. Curiously, however, around this period, countries such as France and Belgium appeared willing to issue passports to non-citizens, including Britons. Lloyd (2003) recounts the story of the poet Robert Browning eloping with Elizabeth Barrett Browning in 1846, travelling on a French passport.

By the mid-nineteenth century, apart from times of war, issuance of passports became increasingly relaxed both in Europe and in North America. Regulations were introduced in 1846 in the UK for the movement of merchants and diplomats, but those travelling purely for leisure were no longer obliged to carry formal documentation (although immigration controls were reintroduced in Britain by the Aliens Act of 1905).

World War I was to change all this. New passports, accompanied by a photograph of the bearer, were widely introduced, the League of Nations standardising their design in 1921. In Britain, passports for foreign travel have been compulsory since 1916.

OTHER POLITICAL HINDRANCES TO TRAVEL

Another political factor affecting the movement of tourists between countries is the relationship between generating and destination countries. Throughout history, European nations have been at war with one another, limiting the desire to travel in the territories of a recent or former enemy, while enhancing a willingness to visit allied countries. Border controls will inhibit travel and some nationalities may be excluded, while, at the very least, visas or other documentary requirements may be imposed on less friendly nations. Countries may refuse entry to visitors who have travelled to or through a nation with which the destination country is in conflict or which it does not recognise (today, a number of countries refuse entry to visitors with an Israeli stamp in their passport, for example).

The use of common currencies in different countries facilitates travel, as we saw under the Roman Empire, and see again today with the adoption of the euro within 19 European Union countries. This has undoubtedly motivated inter-European tourism, but also has its downside, as we shall see later.

Similarly, taxation has affected travel from the very earliest periods of tourism history. The opportunity to enhance a nation's coffers at the expense of the foreign tourist was widely recognised during the Middle Ages. However, history has shown that travellers react to high taxation, switching to other destinations where costs are lower, so measures to tax tourists are always subject to economic sensitivity.

THE DEVELOPMENT OF THE SPAS

Spas have always played a significant role in the travel industry. Already well established during the time of the Roman Empire, their popularity, based on the supposed medical benefits of the waters, lapsed in subsequent centuries, but were never entirely out of favour, with the sick continuing to visit spas throughout the Middle Ages. However, interest in the therapeutic qualities of mineral waters re-arose with the influence of the Renaissance in Britain and other European centres.

In 1562, Dr William Turner published a book drawing attention to the curative powers of the waters at Bath and on the Continent. Bath itself, along with the spa at Buxton, had been showing a return to popularity among those 'seeking the cure' and the effect of Dr Turner's book was to establish the credibility of the resorts' claims. In 1626, Elizabeth

Farrow drew attention to the qualities of the chalybeate mineral spring in Scarborough and, in the same year, Dr Edmund Deane wrote his *Spadacrene Anglica*, which praised what he claimed were 'the strongest sulphur springs in Great Britain' at Harrogate. Thereafter, at one time or another, some 175 different spas opened in England, with three of these – at Bath, Buxton and Hotwells in Bristol – incorporating thermal springs in their cures.

EXAMPLE

Bath Spa

Bath in particular became a major centre for social life for high society during the eighteenth and early nineteenth centuries, aided by visits from the monarchs of the day. Under the guidance of Beau Nash at the beginning of the eighteenth century, it soon became a centre of high fashion, deliberately setting out to create a select and exclusive image. The commercial possibilities opened up by the concentration of these wealthy visitors were not overlooked and facilities to entertain or otherwise cater for these visitors proliferated, changing the spas into what we would today term holiday resorts rather than watering places. The building of the Pump Rooms as a focal point within Bath was a key development, leading to the town's success as a resort, while Harrogate, similarly, benefited from the construction of its own Pump Room in 1841–42.

By 1815, seven of the spas had purpose-built theatres to provide entertainment. 'Taking the cure' rapidly developed social status and the resorts changed in character. By the early nineteenth century, the common tendency of resorts to go 'downmarket' in the course of their life cycle (see The Tourist Area Life Cycle, Chapter 3) led to a changing clientele, with the landed gentry being replaced by wealthy merchants and the professional class. By the end of the eighteenth century, the heyday of the English spas was over.

However, they were to have a far longer life cycle on the Continent. There, the popularity of the spas lay in the popular belief in their efficacy, supported by members of the medical profession. Public funding was, and still is in some cases, provided by the state for those needing treatment. The town of Spa in Belgium (Figure 2.1) is said to have given its name to the concept of a centre for the treatment of illness through taking, or bathing in, the mineral waters (or later, by the application to the body of mud or other substances with perceived healing qualities). Spas rapidly became, and to a large extent remain, popular in Germany, Italy and middle European countries like Hungary and The Czech Republic. (Their role as attractions today is discussed further in Chapter 9.)

THE RISE OF THE SEASIDE RESORT

Until the Renaissance, bathing in the sea found little favour in Britain. Although not entirely unknown before then, such bathing as did occur was undertaken unclothed, and this behaviour conflicted with the values and customs of the day. Only when the sea became associated with certain health benefits did bathing gain popularity.

The association of sea water with health did not find acceptance until the early years of the eighteenth century and, initially, the objective was to drink it rather than bathe in it. It is perhaps to be expected that health theorists would eventually recognise that some of the minerals found in spa waters were also present in sea water.

FIGURE 2.1 The continental spa: the casino at Spa, Belgium

Photo: Chris Holloway

EXAMPLE

A justification for visiting the coast

By the early eighteenth century, small fishing resorts around the English coast were beginning to attract visitors seeking 'the cure', both by drinking and by immersing themselves in the sea water. It was Dr Richard Russell's noted medical paper 'A dissertation on the use of sea water in the diseases of the glands, particularly the scurvy, jaundice, king's evil, leprosy, and the glandular consumption', published in 1752, that is credited with popularising the custom of sea bathing more widely.

Moral doubts about exposing one's body in the sea were overcome by the invention of the bathing machine, and the seaside resorts prospered.

Undoubtedly, the demand for seaside cures could have been even greater in the early years if fast, cheap transport had been developed to cater for this need. In the mid-eighteenth century, however, it still took two days to travel from London to Brighton and the cost was well beyond the reach of the average worker, the equivalent of six weeks' pay. Accommodation provision, too, grew only slowly, outpaced by demand, but all this was to change in the early nineteenth century.

First, the introduction of steamboat services reduced the cost and time of travel from London to the resorts near the Thames Estuary. In 1815, a service began operating between

London and Gravesend and, five years later, to Margate. The popularity of these services was such that other pleasure boat services were quickly introduced to more distant resorts, with services between Scotland and Ireland established in 1819. This development required the construction of piers to provide landing stages for the vessels. The functional purpose of the seaside pier was soon overtaken by its attraction as a social meeting point and a place to take the sea air.

The introduction of steamboat services linking the UK and continental Europe posed the first threat to Britain's seaside resorts. Brighton established a ferry link with Dieppe as early as 1761 and later this was followed by links between Dieppe and the towns of Shoreham and Newhaven. It has been estimated that by the 1820s some 150,000 visitors a year were travelling from the UK to mainland Europe, many for the purpose of visiting coastal resorts.

At first, from about 1780 onwards, travel was concentrated along the Riviera, between the mouth of the Var and the Gulf of Spezia. The Italian resorts benefited from direct steamer services from London and Liverpool to Genoa. Before the advent of the railways, stagecoaches or hired carriages took three weeks to travel from London to Rome, but direct steamboats to Italy were to reduce this by half. Soon, French resorts were attracting UK visitors along the north coast between Boulogne and Cherbourg. The UK visitors insisted on facilities that met their particular needs, including churches of their favourite denominations and British shops, chemists, physicians and newspapers. The more successful French resorts quickly provided these. From 1880 onwards, the Train Bleu offered wealthy UK visitors elegant sleeping accommodation from Paris to the Riviera, popularising not only summer but also winter holidays to escape the cold of the British climate.

Seaside resorts were also finding favour with the nobility and wealthy of other countries by this time. Aristocratic Russians travelled to the Crimea, the Baltic and the South of France for their holidays, while wealthy Americans on the Eastern seaboard frequented the first resorts developed along the New Jersey, New York and New England coastlines, the most wealthy building second homes along the Rhode Island shores.

CONDITIONS FAVOURING THE EXPANSION OF TRAVEL IN THE NINETEENTH CENTURY

This brief history of travel, from earliest times to the nineteenth century, shows that a number of factors were at work encouraging travel. We can divide these into two categories: factors that make travel possible (**enabling factors**) and those that persuade people to travel (**motivating factors**).

HISTORICAL PERSPECTIVE OF ENABLING FACTORS

In order for travel to be possible at all, people must have adequate time and money to undertake it. Throughout most of history, however, and until very recently, both of these have been the prerogative of the elite in society. Leisure time for the masses was very limited. Workers laboured from morning to night, six days a week, and were encouraged to treat Sundays (and the not infrequent Saints' days) as days of rest and worship. Pay was barely adequate to sustain a family and buy the basic necessities of life. The idea of paid holidays was not even considered until the twentieth century.

No less importantly, the development of pleasure travel depends on the provision of suitable travel facilities. The growth of travel and transport are interdependent: travellers require transport that is priced within their budget and is fast, safe, comfortable and convenient. As we have seen, none of these criteria were being met until the latter half of the eighteenth century, but, from the early nineteenth century onwards, rapid improvements in technology led to transport that was both fast and moderately priced.

This development will be examined in greater detail shortly. Suffice it to say here that good transport must be complemented by adequate accommodation at the traveller's destination. The traditional places to stay for travellers in the Middle Ages were the monasteries, but these were dissolved in Britain during the reign of Henry VIII, and the resulting hiatus acted as a further deterrent to travel for everyone apart from those planning to stay with friends or relatives. The gradual improvement in lodgings that accompanied the introduction of the mail coaches and stagecoaches went some way to correcting this shortage. The general inadequacy of facilities away from the major centres of population, though, meant that towns such as London, Exeter and York, with their abundant social life and entertainment as a magnet, were to become the first centres to attract large numbers of visitors for leisure purposes.

Other constraints awaited those prepared to ignore these drawbacks to travel. In cities, public health standards were low, so travellers risked disease – a risk compounded in the case of international travel. Currency exchange facilities for international travel were unreliable, rates of exchange were inconsistent and travellers risked being cheated. They tended to carry large sums of money with them, attracting highwaymen. Foreign currencies were, in any event, chaotic. Political suspicion compounded the difficulty of arranging travel documents, sometimes leading to long delays in obtaining permission to travel. Removing these constraints encourages growth in travel.

HISTORICAL PERSPECTIVE OF MOTIVATING FACTORS

The real motivation for travel must be intrinsic – the desire to travel for its own sake, to get away from one's everyday surroundings and become acquainted with other places, cultures and people. This is explained in more detail in Chapter 3.

It was the rapid urbanisation of the population in the UK that provided the impetus for travel in the nineteenth century. The industrial revolution had led to massive migration of the population away from the villages and countryside and into the industrial cities, where work was plentiful and better paid. This migration was to have two important side-effects for the workers themselves. First, workers in dark and polluted cities became conscious of the beauty and attraction of their former rural surroundings for the first time. Now, they longed to escape from the cities in what little free time they had – a characteristic still evident among twenty-first-century city dwellers. Second, the type of work available in the cities was both physically and psychologically stressful. The comparatively leisurely pace of life in the countryside was replaced by monotonous factory work, so any escape from its routine and pace was welcome.

The expansion of the UK economy due to increased productivity created by the industrial revolution, led to a growth in real purchasing power for every worker, while worldwide demand for British goods created a huge business travel market. Increased wealth stimulated rapid growth in the population at this time, too. In short, the UK at the beginning of the nineteenth century stood poised on the threshold of a considerable escalation in the demand for travel. The introduction of modern transport systems at this point in history was to translate this demand into reality.

THE AGE OF STEAM: RAIL AND SEA TRANSPORT

Two technological developments in the early part of the nineteenth century were to have a profound effect on transport and the growth in travel generally. Driven by the arrival of steam power, the first of these was the advent of the railway, the second the development of steamships.

The first passenger railway was built in England, between Stockton and Darlington, in 1825. It was to herald a major programme of railway construction throughout the world and a dramatic increase in the ability to travel. Road transport had been dangerous and uncomfortable, with travel by canal possible since 1760 but at 3 mph too slow to attract travellers. Railways made travel at 13 mph possible – at least 3 mph faster than the quickest mail coaches.

EXAMPLE

Early rail travel

Invicta, the first steam-driven train, made the first passenger journey between Whitstable Bay and Canterbury on 3 May 1830, carrying day trippers. In the decade that followed the construction of a rail link between Liverpool and Manchester in the same year, trunk routes sprang up between the major centres of population and industry in the UK, on mainland Europe and throughout the world.

In the USA, for example, East Coast services were operative from the 1820s, and by 1869 a transcontinental link was in place. One of the last great rail routes – the Trans-Siberian – opened in 1903, connecting Moscow with Vladivostok and Port Arthur (now Lüshun, China).

In the UK, new routes emerged, linking cities and large towns (as the major centres of population) to popular coastal resorts. Rail companies were initially slow to recognise the opportunities this provided for pleasure travel, preferring to focus on the business traveller, a strategy which, in the 1840s, proved highly remunerative. Competition between railway companies was initially based on service rather than price, although a new market developed quickly for day trips. Before long, however, entrepreneurs, including Thomas Cook, were approaching the railways to organise excursions at special fares, at first on regular services, then later on whole train charters, setting a precedent for the air charter services which became such a feature a century later.

These enterprises led to substantial movements of pleasure-bound travellers to the seaside. With sympathetic support from public authorities like the Board of Trade, railway companies began actively promoting excursions by the 1850s, while at the same time introducing a range of discounted fares for day trips, weekend trips and longer journeys. By 1855, Thomas Cook had extended his field of operations to mainland Europe, organising the first 'inclusive tours' to the Paris Exhibition of that year. This followed the success of his excursions to the Great Exhibition in London in 1851, which in all had welcomed a total of 3 million visitors.

EXAMPLE

Thomas Cook

Born in 1808 in Derbyshire, Cook was a man of vision in the world of travel. The success of his operations was due to the care he took in organising his programmes to minimise problems. He had close contacts with hotels, shipping companies and railways throughout the world, ensuring that he obtained the best possible service as well as cheap prices for the services he provided. By escorting his clients throughout their journeys abroad, he took the worry out of travel for the first-time traveller. He also made the administration of travel easier by introducing the hotel voucher in 1867, which allowed tourists to prepay their hotel accommodation and produce evidence to the hotels that this had been done. In 1874, he also introduced the 'circular note', the precursor to today's traveller's cheque – a promissory note that could be exchanged abroad for local currency. This greatly helped to overcome the problems arising from the many different coinages in use in Europe. The latter was not a totally new concept – a certain Robert Herries set up the London Banking Exchange Company in 1772 in order to issue similar documents – but it was Cook (and, later, in North America, American Express, which introduced the first traveller's cheque in 1891) who popularised these ideas, making travel far more tolerable for the Victorian traveller.

The coincidental invention of photography in the mid-nineteenth century further stimulated overseas travel for reasons of prestige. For the first time, visitors abroad could be photographed against a background of the great historical sites of Europe, to the envy of their friends (a precursor to the 'selfie' craze in the twenty-first century).

The expansion of the railways led to a decline in stagecoach operations. Some survived by providing feeder services to the nearest railway stations, but overall road traffic shrank and, with it, the demand for the staging inns. These offered very different services from those expected of a hotel and, while the concept of the 'modern hotel' can be traced back as far as 1764, it was the railways, from around 1840 onwards, that were to drive the development of hotels as we know them today. A period of hotel construction began, in which the railway companies themselves were leaders, establishing the great railway terminus hotels that came to play such a significant role in the hotel industry over the next 100 years. The high capital investment called for by this development led to the formation of the first hotel chains and corporations.

Social change in the Victorian era further encouraged travel. Victorian society placed great emphasis on the role of the family as a social unit, leading to the type of family holidays for which the seaside was so well suited. The foundations of traditional seaside entertainment were soon laid – military bands, Punch and Judy shows, barrel organs, donkey rides, music hall and variety shows, and the seaside pier – and became essential components (BBC, 2011).

Resorts began to develop different social images, partly as a result of their geographical location: those near major centres of population developed a substantial market of day trippers, while others deliberately aimed for a more exclusive clientele. These latter generally tended to be situated further afield, but, in some cases, their exclusivity arose from the desire of prominent residents to resist the encroachment of the railways for as long as possible (Bournemouth, for example, held out against the extension of the railway from Poole until 1870). Some areas of early promise as holiday resorts were quickly destroyed by the growth of industry – in Swansea, Hartlepool and Southampton, for example, beaches gave way to dockland development.

Health continued to play a role in the choice of holiday destinations, but the emphasis gradually switched from the benefits of sea bathing to those of sea air. Climate became a feature of the resorts' promotion. Sunshine hours were emphasised, or the bracing qualities of the Scarborough air, while the pines at Bournemouth were reputed to help those suffering from lung complaints. Seaside resorts on the Continent also gained in popularity and began to develop their own social images – Scheveningen near The Hague, Ostend, Biarritz and Deauville offering the same magic for UK holidaymakers as the Mediterranean resorts were to provide a century later. Some overseas resorts flourished as a result of a reaction to middle-class morality in Victorian England – Monte Carlo, with its notorious gambling casino, being a case in point.

The desire to escape from one's everyday environment was as symptomatic of nineteenth-century life as it was to become in the middle of the twentieth century. Of course, destinations on the Continent were to attract only those who were relatively well off and the railways produced services to cater for these high-spend tourists. The Train Bleu, which entered service between Paris and the Côte d'Azur and Rome in 1883, and the Orient Express of the same year, operating from Paris to the Black Sea, provided unsurpassed levels of luxury for rail travellers on the Continent.

EXAMPLE

Development of European railways

Much of the development of railways in the UK was undertaken by private enterprise. In continental Europe, state involvement in development was more common. In Belgium, the rail network was developed and tightly controlled by the state, while France used a public–private partnership approach (Mitchell, 2006) with limited consideration given initially to the creation of a coherent network. Germany took an approach similar to that of the UK, raising capital for construction from private investors, which allowed extensive local networks to be quickly developed but which had limited national connectivity. The Association of German Railway Administrations was introduced in 1847 to standardise and coordinate the private and state networks.

Standardising railways, particularly the gauge – the distance between rails – helped improve network operations. Early railways in the Netherlands, parts of Germany and Norway initially used different gauges from that which has since become the European standard (and which was said to originate from mining tramways in use in Northern England (Puffert, 2009)).

Long-distance rail services became possible with the provision of sleeping cars, introduced in the USA by George Pullman and Ben Field in 1865, and in Europe by the French Wagons-Lits company in 1869. These luxury carriages first arrived in the UK on the London to Glasgow route in 1873 and were operating between London and Brighton by 1881. The first restaurant car arrived in 1879, on the London to Leeds route.

Other forms of holidaymaking – opened up by the advent of the railways on the Continent – arose from the impact of the Romantic Movement of mid-Victorian England. Rail charters were introduced for travel to Germany, Italy, the French Riviera and Spain. The Rhine and the French Riviera in particular benefited from their new-found romantic appeal, while the invigorating mountain air of Switzerland, combining the promise of better health with opportunities for strenuous outdoor activities, was already drawing tourists from the UK by the 1840s.

Mountaineering became a popular pastime for the British by the 1860s, later boosted by the introduction of skiing. Originating in Norway, by the beginning of the 1890s skiing had become firmly established in Switzerland and Austria. Sir Henry Lunn, the British travel entrepreneur, is credited with the commercialisation of winter ski holidays in Switzerland, having organised packages to Chamonix before the end of the nineteenth century. The railways made their own contributions to these developments, but, above all, they encouraged the desire to travel by removing the hazards of foreign travel that had formerly existed for travellers journeying by road.

The influence of rail travel on early tourism in North America

Tourism in North America paralleled that in Europe throughout the nineteenth century. Initially, a few seaside resorts grew up to cater for tourists from the major North American conurbations within the original 13 states. Fashionable resorts developed at Newport, Rhode Island, Cape May and Atlantic City in New Jersey and along the Massachusetts coast, while more popular resorts closer to New York City, such as those on the coast of New Jersey and Long Island, catered largely for day trippers. Spa resorts were also developing at this time, with Saratoga Springs in upstate New York becoming particularly popular. Others, in resorts such as French Lick, Indiana, White Sulphur Springs in West Virginia (popular with early US presidents), Hot Springs Arkansas and Glenwood Springs Colorado, prospered and they still owe some economic dependence to their attraction as tourist resorts today.

The Americans were quick to adopt the newly invented steam railways, with the Baltimore and Ohio Railroad formed as early as 1830. The Pacific Railroad Act (1862) gave the green light to a cross-continental rail service, completed in 1869, that served both business and leisure needs. Interest in rugged landscapes, especially mountain tourism, ran parallel with this development in Europe, with travellers visiting the mountainous regions of eastern USA by the 1820s.

Niagara Falls became the travellers' target, popularised by improved accessibility, with the development of paved roads and railways. Canadian tourism, meanwhile, was developing to cater to the needs of expanding populations in and around Toronto and Montreal, with visits to the St Lawrence Seaway, Niagara Falls and the Maine coast soon becoming popular. The absence of any border formalities between Canada and the USA, and the common language (at least for a large part of Canada), facilitated the movement of tourists between the countries, giving holidaymakers a comforting sense of reassurance with the familiar while 'travelling abroad' – a characteristic that continues to enhance travel in North America to this day.

THE EXPANSION OF STEAM-POWERED TRAVEL

As with the railways, so steam was harnessed at sea, driving new generations of ships. British railway companies were quick to recognise the importance of links to cross-Channel ferry ports and, by 1862, had gained the right to own and operate steamships themselves. Their control of the ferry services led to rapid cross-Channel expansion.

Deep sea services were introduced on routes to North America and the Far East, the paddle-wheel steamer *Savannah* being the first to operate across the Atlantic, sailing between Savannah and Liverpool in 1819 and using steam as an auxiliary to sails. The Peninsular and Oriental Steam Navigation Company (later P&O) is credited with the first regular long-distance steamship service, beginning operations to India and the Far East in 1838. This company was soon followed by the Cunard Steamship Company, which, with a lucrative mail contract, began regular services to the North American continent in 1840.

The UK, by being the first to establish regular deep sea services of this kind, came to dominate the world's shipping in the second half of the nineteenth century, although it was soon to be challenged by other leading industrial nations on the popular North American route. This prestigious and highly profitable route prospered both from mail contracts and from rising demand from passengers and freight as trade with the North American continent expanded. Later, the passenger trade would be boosted by the flow of emigrants from Europe (especially Ireland) and a smaller but significant number of American visitors to Europe. Thomas Cook played his part in stimulating the package tour market to North America, taking the first group of tourists in 1866. In 1872, he went on to organise the first round-the-world tour, taking 12 clients for 220 days at a cost of some £200 – more than the average annual salary at the time.

The Suez Canal, opened in 1869, stimulated demand for P&O's services to India and beyond, as Britain's Empire looked eastwards. The global growth of shipping led, in the latter part of the century, to the formation of shipping conferences, which developed cartel-like agreements on fares and conditions applicable to the carriage of traffic. The aim of these agreements was to ensure year-round profitability in an unstable and seasonal market, but the result was to stifle competition on the basis of price, eventually leading to excess profits for the shipping companies, until the advent of airline competition in the mid-twentieth century.

While long voyages by sea were popular, the concept of cruising caught on only slowly. Among early examples of ship voyages treated essentially as a cruise, the Matson Line services between the US West Coast and Hawaii were to open up those islands to tourism.

OTHER LATE NINETEENTH-CENTURY DEVELOPMENTS

As the Victorian era drew to a close, other social changes came into play. Continued enthusiasm for the healthy outdoor life coincided with the invention of the first modern bicycle in 1866. A London Bicycle Club was established in 1875 and, three years later, the formation of a national Cyclists' Touring Club did much to promote the enjoyment of cycling holidays. This movement paved the way for interest in outdoor activities on holiday, and may well have stimulated the appeal of the suntan as a status symbol of health and wealth, in marked contrast to the earlier emphasis on the fair complexion as being symbolic of gentility and breeding. The bicycle offered, for the first time, opportunity for mobile rather than centred holidays.

Political stability in the final years of the nineteenth century and opening years of the twentieth also allowed for further expansion of travel. Significantly, no conflicts occurred on the European continent between 1871 and 1914 – one of the longest stretches of peacetime in history – and a Europe at peace was becoming an attractive place to visit, both for Europeans and others from further afield.

As tourism grew in the later years of the century, so the organisers of travel became established institutions. Thomas Cook and Sir Henry Lunn are two of the best-known names from the period, but many other UK companies became established brands in this era. In the USA, American Express (founded by, among others, Henry Wells and William Fargo of Wells Fargo fame) initiated money orders and travellers' cheques, later going on to promote holidays.

As the century drew to a close, the vogue for photography was accompanied by the cult of the guidebook. No UK tourist venturing abroad would neglect to take a guidebook, and a huge variety of these soon became available on the market. Many were superficial and inaccurate, but the most popular and enduring published were those of John Murray, whose 'Handbooks' appeared from 1837 onwards, and Karl Baedeker, who introduced his first guidebook (to the Rhine) in 1839. By the end of the century, Baedeker had become firmly established as the leading publisher of guidebooks in Europe.

THE TWENTIETH CENTURY AND THE ORIGINS OF MASS TOURISM

In the opening years of the twentieth century, travel continued to expand, encouraged by the gradually increasing wealth, curiosity (inspired, to some extent, by the introduction in the UK of compulsory education following the Education Act 1870) and outgoing attitudes of the post-Victorian population and the steady improvement in transport. Travellers were much safer from disease and physical attack, mainland Europe was relatively stable politically and documentation for UK travellers uncomplicated. Wealthy UK tourists increasingly over-wintered in the French Riviera in the period immediately before World War I (1914–1918).

Disastrous though that war was, it proved to be only a brief hiatus in the expansion of travel, although it led to the widespread introduction of passports for nationals of many countries. The prosperity that soon returned to Europe in the 1920s, coupled with large-scale migration, meant unsurpassed demand for travel across the Atlantic, as well as within Europe. The first-hand experience of foreign countries by combatants during the war aroused, for the first time, a sense of curiosity about foreign travel generally among the less well-off sectors of the community. These sectors were also influenced by the new forms of mass communication that developed after the war – the cinema, radio and, ultimately, television, all of which educated the population and encouraged an interest in seeing more of the world.

Forms of travel changed radically after the war. Railways declined, while motorised public road transport and improved roads led to the era of the charabanc – at first, adapted from army surplus lorries and equipped with benches to provide a rudimentary form of coach. These vehicles achieved immense popularity in the 1920s for outings to the seaside, but their poor safety record soon resulted in licensing regulations being brought in to govern road transport. For those who could afford superior public transportation, more luxurious coaches also made an appearance.

EXAMPLE

Luxury coach travel

The coach company Motorways offered Pullman coaches, generally accommodating 15 people in comfortable armchairs with tables, buffet bars and toilets. These coaches operated in many parts of Europe and North Africa, were used on safaris in East and Central Africa and even provided a twice-weekly service between London and Nice, taking a relaxing five to six days to make the trip.

However, it was the freedom of independent travel offered by the private motor car that contributed most to the decline of the railways' monopoly on holiday transport. The extensive use of the motor car for holidaying has its origins in the USA, where, in 1908, Henry Ford introduced his popular Model T at a price that brought the motor car within reach of the masses. By the 1920s, private motoring was a popular pastime for the middle classes in the USA and, soon, camping and caravanning followed. Caravans (or trailers in American terminology) had arrived by the 1930s, with 100,000 trailers on the road by 1937 (Löfgren, 1999).

By the 1930s, private motoring had arrived on a large scale in the UK to threaten domestic rail services, although rail services to the Continent survived and prospered until challenged by the coming of the airlines. In an effort to stem the decline, domestic rail services in the UK were first rationalised in 1923 into four major companies and later, following World War II, nationalised, remaining under public control until again privatised in the mid-1990s.

EXAMPLE

The first all-inclusive hotel?

The Royal Hawaiian Hotel – built to accommodate visitors in the 1920s to those then exotic islands – was one of the first to offer what we today know as 'all-inclusive' holidays, although hotels along the French Riviera and in Switzerland were to follow suit. Hawaii was to remain an upmarket destination until mass package tours arrived with air services in the 1950s.

THE ERA OF THE GREAT DEPRESSION

The 1930s are generally thought of as a period when the economic collapse in the Western world was similarly accompanied by the collapse of the international tourist market. While it is true that travel was severely curtailed, the Depression hit Europe rather later than the USA and, in the early 1930s, there remained a substantial market for those with sufficient wealth to travel. In the UK, however, government-imposed limits on foreign exchange for travel abroad proved a severe constraint.

The ever-resilient travel industry reacted with typical enterprise. The formation of the Creative Tourist Agents' Conference (CTAC) in the early 1930s brought together the leading travel agents (who were by this time also tour operators), including Thomas Cook, Dean and Dawson, Hickie Borman Grant, Frames, Sir Henry Lunn, Pickfords, Wayfarers' Touring Agency, the Workers' Travel Association and the Polytechnic Touring Association (PTA). These formed what amounted to a cartel to hold down and fix prices for foreign excursions. The PTA was instrumental in persuading the continental railways to discount their fares for bulk purchases – a move the railways had always resisted in the past. Soon, special rail charters were being organised to Germany, Italy, the Riviera and Spain and, by 1938, the PTA was operating its own regular train charters to Switzerland, then one of the most popular destinations on the Continent. This operator also packaged one of the first air charters, approaching Imperial Airways (which was in financial difficulties) in the opening years of the decade to charter a plane to carry 24 passengers from Croydon airport to Paris and to Basel in Switzerland (Studd, 1950). By 1932, the company was carrying nearly 1000 passengers by air to the Continent, mainly then as a means of avoiding foreign currency payments to rail and bus companies abroad, and the following year it organised a 14-day air cruise to seven European capitals. Doubtless these air charters would have continued, but the partial recovery of Imperial Airways' financial situation led the carrier to withdraw charter privileges, ending these first entrepreneurial modern package tours and making the point that tour operators of the future would have to avoid dependence on suppliers over whom they had no control – a lesson the first large-scale operators were quick to learn.

THE GROWTH OF THE AIRLINE INDUSTRY

The arrival of the airline industry signalled the beginning of the end for long-distance rail services and, more decisively, for the great steamship companies. UK shipping lines had been under increasing threat from foreign competition throughout the 1920s, with French, German and US liners challenging UK supremacy on the North Atlantic routes particularly.

The first commercial air routes were initiated – by Air Transport & Travel, the forerunner of British Airways (BA) – as early as 1919, from Hounslow airport, London, to Paris. In the same year, a regular service was introduced in Germany between Berlin, Leipzig and

Weimar. The infant air services were expensive (nearly £16 for the London–Paris service, equivalent to several weeks' average earnings) and uncertain (passengers were warned that forced landings and delays could occur). Consequently, initial growth in air services was limited to short-haul flights, over land. It was to be many years before air services achieved the reliability and low price that would make them competitive with world shipping routes.

In America, Pan American Airways was formed in 1927, introducing a transatlantic air service in the 1930s. Initially, the line employed flying boats. These flights were expensive and proved unreliable and uncomfortable by today's standards, necessitating frequent stopovers on long-distance journeys.

In the early years, commercial aviation was more important for its mail-carrying potential than for the carriage of passengers. Only with the technological breakthroughs in aircraft design achieved during and after World War II did air services prove a viable alternative to shipping for intercontinental travel. As for air package holidays, the holiday market would have to wait until the 1950s before this form of transport came into its own. The important sector of air travel is discussed in detail in Chapter 13.

THE ARRIVAL OF THE HOLIDAY CAMP

Among the major tourism developments of the 1930s, the creation of the holiday camp deserves a special mention. Aimed at the growing low-income market for holidays, the camps set new standards of comfort, offering 24-hour entertainment at an all-inclusive price. They were efficiently operated, with the added benefit of childminding services – a huge bonus for young couples on holiday with their children. This was in marked contrast to the lack of planned activities and the often surly service offered by the traditional seaside boarding houses of the day.

The origin of these camps goes back to early experiments by organisations in the UK such as the Co-operative Holidays Association, Workers' Travel Association and Holiday Fellowship. In the USA, summer camps for children were already a strong institution by the early twentieth century. The popularity and widespread acceptance of holiday camps by the adult public, however, has commonly been ascribed to the efforts and promotional flair of Billy Butlin. Supposedly, Butlin, who built his first camp at Skegness in 1936, met a group of disconsolate holidaymakers huddled in a bus shelter to avoid the rain on a wet summer afternoon. Butlin determined to build a camp with all-weather facilities, for an all-in price. The instant success of the concept led to a spate of similar camps being built by Butlin (see Figure 2.2) and other entrepreneurs such as Harry Warner and Fred Pontin in the pre-war and early post-war years. On the Continent, pre-war Germany had introduced the concept of the highly organised and often militaristic health and recreation camp that enabled many to enjoy holidays, who would otherwise have been unable to afford them.

In France, the 'villages de vacance' arose from similar political and social influences. The success of this concept of all-in entertainment was later to be copied by hotels. We noted earlier that the all-inclusive hotel with its own leisure complex had originated in the USA even earlier – for example, Grossingers resort hotel in the Catskills flourished as a popular all-inclusive destination in its own right, targeting principally the New York Jewish market.

Interest in outdoor holidays and healthy recreation was also stimulated by the Youth Hostels Association (YHA) in 1929 (the French equivalent opened in the same year), which provided budget accommodation for young people away from home.

THE POPULAR MOVEMENT TO THE SEASIDE

In spite of the rising appeal of holidays abroad for those who could afford them, mass tourism between the wars and in the early post-World War II era remained largely domestic. This period saw the seaside holiday become firmly established as the

FIGURE 2.2 **The holiday camp era – Butlin's camp at Skegness**

© Barry Lewis/Alamy

traditional annual holiday destination for the mass of the UK public. Suntans were, for the first time, seen as a status symbol, allied to health and time for leisure. In the UK, Blackpool, Scarborough, Southend and Brighton consolidated their positions as leading resorts, while numerous newer resorts – Bournemouth, Broadstairs, Clacton, Skegness, Colwyn Bay – grew rapidly in terms of both visitors and residential population. Until the Great Depression of the 1930s, hotels and guest houses proliferated in these resorts. The tradition of the family holiday, taken annually over two weeks in the summer, became firmly established in the UK.

The threat of competition from the European mainland started to became apparent from the 1920s onwards. The Mediterranean Riviera had begun to attract a summer, as well as a winter, market from the UK, while the resorts of northern France were seen as cheaper and began to offer competition for the popular south coast resorts of Brighton, Hove, Folkestone and Eastbourne. These nearby French resorts, however, were seen primarily as places for short summer holidays rather than the longer winter stays that had been popular with a wealthy UK clientele in the nineteenth century.

THE GROWTH OF PUBLIC-SECTOR INVOLVEMENT

It was in this period that the UK experienced the first stirrings of government interest in the tourism business. The UK was well behind other European countries in this respect. The government of Switzerland, for example, had long recognised the importance of its inbound tourism and was actively involved in both promoting tourism overseas and gathering statistics on its visitors.

The British Travel and Holidays Association was established by the government in 1929, but, with the theme 'travel for peace', its role was seen as essentially promotional and its impact on the industry was relatively light, until a change in status some 40 years later. By the outbreak of World War II in 1939, the UK government had at least recognised the potential contribution tourism could make to the country's balance of payments. Equally, it had recognised the importance of holidays to the health and efficiency of the nation's workforce. The French government had already introduced holidays with pay in 1936 and the publication of the Amulree Report in 1938 led to the first Holidays with Pay Act for the UK in the same year. This encouraged voluntary agreements on paid holidays and generated the idea of a two-week paid holiday for all workers. Although this ambition was not fulfilled until several years after the end of World War II, by the outbreak of war some 11 million of the 19 million workforce were entitled to paid holidays – a key factor in generating mass travel.

POST-WORLD WAR II TOURISM EXPANSION

In the aftermath of World War II, Europeans deprived of the opportunity to travel for six long years yearned to holiday abroad again. However, the ability to do so was limited, restricted by both political barriers and financial controls (including strict limits on access to foreign currency that created a huge barrier to cross-border travel). Although curiosity about battle sites never approached that which followed World War I, a slow but growing demand developed to visit sites like the 1944 landing beaches in Normandy, while North Americans and Japanese alike felt similarly drawn to sites of conflict in the Pacific, such as Pearl Harbour, Iwo Jima and Guadalcanal. Interest was also limited to the sites on the Western Front in Europe – the horrors of warfare on the Eastern Front were such that neither side showed much inclination to visit the former battlefields, many of which were, in any case, banned to visitors until after the fall of the Soviet government. The extensive theatre of war had introduced the many combatants not only to new countries but also to new continents, generating new friendships and an interest in diverse cultures.

Another outcome of the war, which was to radically change the travel business, was the advance in aircraft technology that was soon to lead to a viable commercial aviation industry for the first time. The first commercial transatlantic flights were soon introduced, initially between New York and Bournemouth, but operating a Douglas DC4 required stopovers at Boston, Gander and Shannon. The cost and duration of the journey ensured that long-haul flights in the age of piston-engined aircraft initially attracted only the rich in both time and money.

However, the surplus of aircraft in the immediate post-war years, a benevolent political attitude towards the growth of private-sector airlines and the appearance on the scene of air travel entrepreneurs like Harold Bamberg (of Eagle Airways) and Freddie Laker (of Laker Airways) soon led to a rapid expansion of air travel. Aircraft became more comfortable, safer, faster and steadily cheaper by comparison with other forms of transport. Military airports were soon adapted for civilian use, proving particularly valuable in opening up islands in the Mediterranean that were formerly inaccessible or time-consuming to reach by sea.

Commercial jet services began with the ill-fated de Havilland Comet aircraft in the early 1950s, but early post-war advances even in piston-engine technology helped to reduce the cost of air tickets. The breakthrough with jet aircraft arrived in 1958, when Boeing introduced the hugely successful model 707. Thereafter, rapid falls in the cost of air travel began to undermine demand for sea travel. Although liner services across the Atlantic continued for a further decade, their increasingly uncompetitive costs, high fares and lengthy journey time resulted in declining load factors (the ratio of numbers carried relative to full capacity).

EXAMPLE

The importance of speed

The new jets, with average speeds of 800–1000 kph, compared with older, propeller-driven aircraft travelling at a mere 400 kph, meant that air travellers could reach more distant destinations within a given time than had been possible before (for example, the key New York to London route fell from 18 hours in 1949 to just seven hours in 1969). This was particularly valuable for business journeys where time was crucial.

The early 1970s saw the arrival of the first supersonic passenger aircraft, the Anglo-French Concorde. Never truly a commercial success (the governments wrote off the huge development costs), it nevertheless proved popular with business travellers and the wealthy. Travelling from London or Paris to New York in three and a half hours, it allowed businesspeople for the first time to complete their business on the other side of the Atlantic and return home without incurring a hotel stopover. The limited range and carrying capacity (just over 100 passengers) of the aircraft, and restrictions regarding sonic booms over land, acted as severe constraints on operable routes. The fatal crash near Paris of a chartered Concorde in 2000 sealed the aircraft's fate, and low load factors led finally to withdrawal from service in 2003.

THE GROWTH OF THE PACKAGE TOUR

Inclusive tours by coach soon regained their former appeal after the war. The Italian Riviera was popular at first – French resorts proving too expensive – and resorts such as Rimini became affordable for the North European middle market. The inclusive tour by air – or 'package tour' as it became known – was soon to follow.

Cheap packages by air depend on the ability of tour operators to charter aircraft for their clientele and buy hotel beds in bulk, driving down costs and cutting prices. Initially, the UK government's transport policy restricted air charters to troop movements, but as official policy became more lenient, the private operators sought to develop new forms of charter traffic. Package holidays were the outcome, as the smaller air carriers and entrepreneurs learned to cooperate.

In the late 1950s, large airlines began purchasing the new jets, allowing smaller companies to buy second-hand propeller-driven aircraft, which were then put into service for charter operations. For the first time, holiday tourists could be transported to Mediterranean destinations faster than, and almost as cheaply as, trains and coaches. These new services proved highly profitable. Meanwhile, across the Atlantic, the first stirrings of an air package holiday industry emerged as regional operators began chartering aircraft from so-called 'supplemental' carriers on routes between major cities in the USA and Canada and the Caribbean Islands.

EXAMPLE

The introduction of the mass package tour

Vladimir Raitz is generally credited with founding the mass inclusive tour business, using air charters. In 1950, under the Horizon Holidays banner, he organised an experimental package holiday trip using a charter flight to Corsica. By chartering the aircraft and filling every seat instead of committing himself to a block of seats on scheduled air services, he was able to reduce the unit cost of his air transport and, hence, the overall price to his customers. He carried only 300 passengers in the first year, but repeated the experiment the following year and was soon operating profitably.

Other budding European tour operators like Club Méditerranée were soon copying his ideas, and by the early 1960s, the package holiday to the Mediterranean had become an established feature in the mass holiday market.

The Spanish coastline and the Balearic Islands were the first to benefit from the new influx of mass tourism from the UK, Germany and the Scandinavian countries, often transported by the Douglas DC-3 aircraft. First the Costa del Sol, then other coasts along the eastern seaboard, the islands of Majorca, Ibiza and, finally by the 1970s, the Canaries became, in turn, the destinations of choice for millions. By 1960, Spain, Italy, Greece and other Mediterranean coastal regions had all benefited from the 'rush to the sun'. Greece in particular, although slower to develop than Spain, provided a cheaper alternative as prices in the latter country rose.

The Nordic countries were also soon setting up their own package holiday arrangements to the Mediterranean and began to compete with the UK and their southern counterparts for accommodation along the Mediterranean coast. In Denmark, Tjaereborg dominated the Scandinavian market, first in low-cost package tours sold direct, and then with the formation of Sterling Airways, which became Western Europe's largest privately owned charter airline of the period.

The influence of currency restrictions

In post-war UK, tight controls were exercised over foreign exchange, with a total ban operating in 1947–8 followed by severe restrictions until the late 1960s, at which point a £50 per person allowance for leisure travel was in place (for business travellers, additional funds were available). There was, however, a silver lining to this particular cloud: it encouraged people to take package holidays rather than travel independently. As air transport costs were payable in sterling and as only the foreign currency element of the tour – the *net* costs of accommodation and transfers – had to be paid out of the allowance, the benefits of dealing with an operator became clear. The limits were relaxed from 1970 onwards and, with further liberalisation of air transport regulations and longer paid holidays, which encouraged a growing number of tourists to take a second holiday abroad each year, a new winter holiday market emerged in the 1970s. With a more even spread of package holidays throughout the year, operators found that they were able to reduce their unit costs still further, so package holiday prices continued to fall, boosting off-season demand.

Transport development and package tours

A further technological breakthrough in air transport occurred in 1970, when the first wide-bodied jets (Boeing 747s), capable of carrying over 400 passengers, appeared in service. Unit cost per seat fell sharply, resulting in more seats at potentially cheaper fares. This innovation meant that, once again, the aviation industry had to unload cheaply a number of obsolescent, although completely airworthy, smaller aircraft and these were quickly snapped up by charter operators.

North American visitors were increasingly demanding basic tours of the UK and the Continent, hitting as many 'high spots' as possible in a 10- to 14-day visit. This gave rise to the concept of the 'milk run' – a popular route that would embrace the top attractions in one or more countries in a limited timeframe for the first-time visitor (see Figure 2.3). Cheaper air transport enabled visitors to take short 'taster' tours around Western European cities, providing an introduction to long-haul travel for millions of Americans.

FIGURE 2.3 The linear tour – an example of the 'milk run' around Britain

By the 1960s, it was clear that the future of mass-market leisure travel was to be a North–South movement, from the cool and variable climates of North America and Northern Europe, where the mass of relatively well-off people lived, to the sunshine and warmth of the temperate to tropical lands in the southern part of the Northern Hemisphere (see Figure 2.4). These southern countries, being economically poorer, guaranteed low costs for tour operators. Major hotel chains, too, were quick to seize the opportunities for growth in these countries; Sheraton and Hyatt in the USA quickly expanded into Mexico and the Caribbean, as well as into Florida and Hawaii – the states offering the most attractive climates for tourism development. Hawaii, in particular, proved popular as an 'overseas' destination, following its incorporation into the USA.

In Europe, UK and German tour operators developed inclusive tours to the Mediterranean and North Africa in bulk, with the increased volumes making feasible

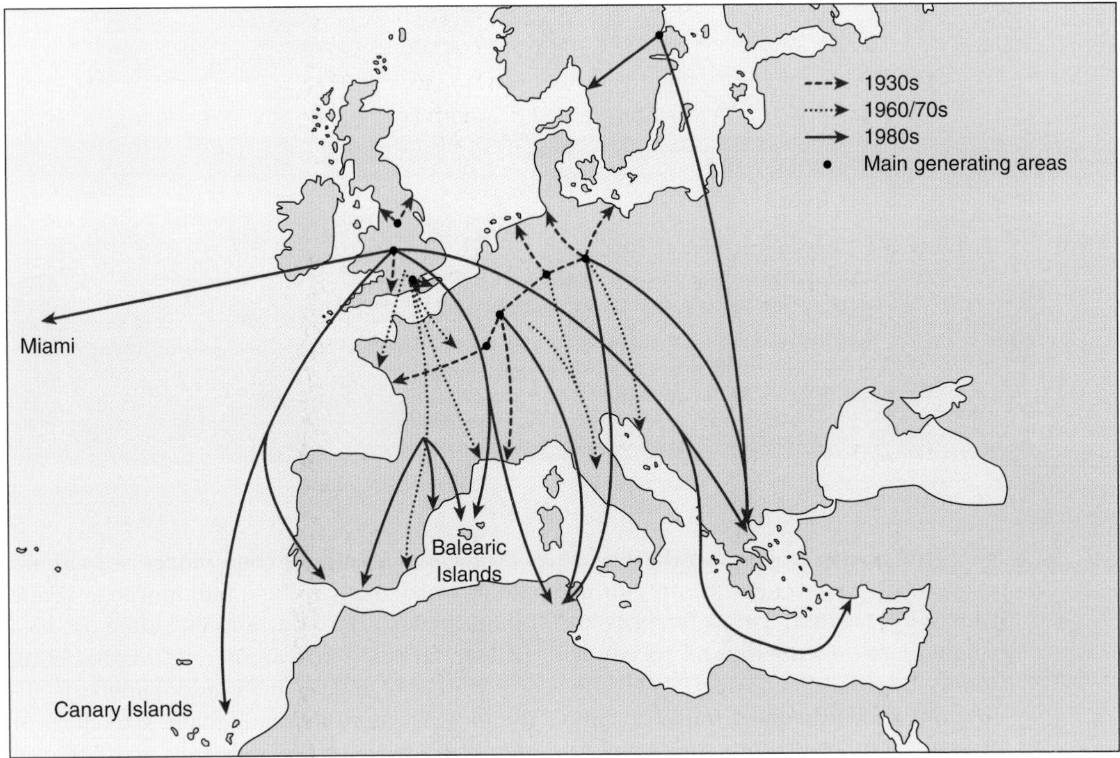

FIGURE 2.4 Changes in destination trends for mass-market holidays, 1930s to 1980s

the charter of jumbo jets for the first time, lowering prices further. Florida – boosted particularly by the attractions of the Walt Disney World Resort and Miami Beach – became almost as popular a destination for Europeans as the major Mediterranean resorts.

By the end of the twentieth century, expert packaging of these tours had been extended to include many other types of destination. Initially, tours to cultural and heritage sites, city breaks to major cities like London, Paris, Rome, Brussels and Amsterdam and river cruises on the Rhine or Danube were being efficiently packaged and sold to the Northern European market. Between the late 1960s and early 1980s, package holidays abroad enjoyed by British residents rose from 2.5 million per annum to over 11 million, and over 70% of the population had been abroad on holiday at least once in their lives.

IDENTIKIT DESTINATIONS

One important result of the growth of the mass tourism market was that those responsible for marketing tourist destinations recognised that they had to satisfy tourists sharing broadly similar aspirations, regardless of their country of origin. The destinations accepted that, apart from geographical location, there was little to differentiate one resort from another, and consumers' needs focused on good climate and beaches, reasonable standards of food and accommodation, enjoyable entertainment and cheap shopping. Often, consumers themselves cared little which country they were in, as long as these criteria were fulfilled.

EXAMPLE

The identikit destination

The larger the mass market, the less distinctive destinations are likely to be, especially if they are small and have only recently been developed. One can find newly built 'marina'-type resorts with yachting basins, hotel/apartment/villa accommodation, similar restaurants, cafés and shops, as well as golf, tennis, water sports, folk singers and barbecue nights in any one of a dozen countries around the Mediterranean, Caribbean, North Africa and the South Pacific.

Vernacular architecture gives way to standard monobloc development typical of beach resorts from Miami Beach to Australia's Gold Coast, by way of Benidorm and the faceless resorts of Romania and Bulgaria (including the optimistically named 'Golden Sands' and 'Sunny Beach').

This is also true even where business travellers attending conferences abroad are concerned. A convention centre, for example, is today likely to be a multipurpose venue containing facilities for conferences and committee/lecture rooms and including modern single or twin-bedded hotel rooms with private facilities, restaurants with banqueting rooms, bars, exhibition space, a leisure centre with pool, indoor and outdoor sports facilities and good scheduled transport links. The location may be Birmingham, Barcelona or Brisbane, but, once inside their hotel or conference centre 'cocoon', delegates may not even notice where they are. Indeed, one can find ubiquitous furniture of identical design (such as faux Regency chairs spray-painted in gold) in conference centres and hotels throughout the world.

We will employ the term **identikit destination** to define and identify this form of resort. They may be contrasted with the piecemeal development of resorts two or three generations previously, the attractions at which may have been developed with very different aims and markets in mind. This is not to say that all identikit destinations are chasing identical markets. Many may be 'downmarket' in their attractiveness – that is, they may offer cheap tourism to a large number of people with the image of great popularity – while others may offer a more upmarket, but nonetheless uniform image, offering the perception of higher quality and, thus, more expensive services to fewer visitors. In the former category, we may think of Benidorm, Magaluf and Benitses in the Mediterranean, Miami Beach in Florida or Seefeld in Austria, while in the latter category we may think of Tahiti, Fiji, Malindi in Kenya or Barbados.

Many identikit destinations have been developed through the activities of multinational tour companies, such as the all-inclusive resorts run by Sandals in the Caribbean and France's Club Méditerranée. Within their establishments, the mass tourist will find a comforting degree of uniformity. Mass tourism has therefore demanded, and been supplied with, products designed specifically for its needs, as revealed through the process of market research. Such products are *user-orientated* as opposed to *resource-orientated* (based on the resources available at a destination).

Many of these identikit destinations, however, have found themselves at a disadvantage as the world tourism market becomes more sophisticated. Research by the former English Tourism Council revealed that one of the weaknesses of many English seaside resorts has been their failure to project a unique image. Those that have succeeded – notably Blackpool and a handful of other major or minor resorts – have done so through a combination of significant investment and differentiation from other, often similar, resorts. Those resorts unable to make the investment needed to change their image are faced with the prospect of decline or have to appeal to newer, generally lower-spend markets. The later years of the last century found several of the formerly popular Mediterranean resorts attracting new tourists from the central European countries to replace the gradual decline in numbers of Western European visitors. One saving grace for those identikit destinations that developed around the core of an established town has been the ability to retain and improve the original 'old town', which is now promoted as a tourist attraction in its own right.

PRIVATE MOTORING AND HOLIDAYS

With improved standards of living throughout the Western nations, many people could contemplate buying their first car, even if second-hand. For the first time, the holiday masses had the freedom to take to the roads with their families in their own private cars and, in the UK, the popular routes between London and resorts on the south coast were, in those pre-motorway days, soon clogged with weekend traffic. The flexibility that the car offered could not be matched by public transport services, and both bus and rail lost the holiday traveller.

Camping and caravan holidays also rose sharply in line with car ownership. This form of tourism has been a cause for concern, however, as the benefits to a region of private camping and caravan tourism are considerably less than most other forms of tourism (owners can bring most of their own food with them and accommodation spend is limited only to park fees). Also, caravans tend to clog the holiday routes in summer, while both mobile and static caravans on site are perceived as something of an eyesore.

EXAMPLE

The resurgence of the camping holiday

The 1950s saw increased interest in camping holidays as they provided an affordable option for many holidaymakers. However, by the 1980s the availability of cheap hotel and self-catering accommodation through package holidays had reduced interest in this form of travel. Significantly, though, the market that had grown used to the freedoms of camping was ideally served with the introduction of packaged camping holidays, which arranged sea crossings where necessary, as well as providing tent, beds, stoves and kitchenware and, in some cases, private toilet facilities. The camping product further developed through the introduction of mobile homes (static caravans), chalets and lodges at holiday parks.

Companies like Canvas Holidays and Vacansoleil, both established in the 1960s, survived by updating their products to meet the changing demands of the customer. This meant greater levels of luxury and additional facilities within the accommodation. The diversity of accommodation within this sector can be seen in the example of Haven Holidays who, alongside their accommodation offerings of static caravans, chalets and apartments, provide four options for those holidaymakers wishing to sleep under canvas: safari tents, yurts, supertents and geodomes (Haven, 2014).

Campsites have also improved, with child-friendly sites offering play areas, family bathrooms and more varied entertainment. By 2010, camping was outstripping trips using bed-and-breakfast accommodation in the UK (Buscombe and Wallop, 2010).

The switch to private transport led to new forms of accommodation that catered for this form of travel. The UK saw the development of its first motels, modelled on the American pattern and a contemporary version of the staging inn for coach passengers. Furthermore, the construction of a new network of motorways and other road improvements made the journeys to more distant resorts manageable for those in centres of population and, in some cases, changed both the nature of the market served and the image of the resort itself.

The ever resourceful tour operators met the private car threat to package holidays by devising more flexible packages, such as fly-drive holidays, with the provision of a hire car at the airport on arrival. Hotels, too, spurred on by the need to fill their rooms off-peak, devised their own programmes of short-stay holidays, tailored to the needs of the private motorist. The demand for car rental abroad rose sharply as the overseas holidaymaker was emboldened to move further from their hotel.

THE DECLINE IN PASSENGER SHIPPING

By contrast with other elements of the travel business, passenger shipping companies, hit by rising costs and competition from the airlines, struggled to survive. Forced to abandon their traditional liner routes by the 1960s, some attempted to adapt their vessels for cruising. In this, they were far from successful as vessels purpose-built for long-distance, fast, deep-sea voyages are not ideally suited to cruising, either economically or from the standpoint of customer demand. Many were incapable of anchoring alongside docks in the shallower waters of popular cruise destinations such as the Caribbean islands.

Companies failing to embark on a programme of new construction, due to lack of either resources or foresight, soon ceased trading. Others, notably Cunard Line, were initially taken over by conglomerates outside the travel or transport industries. American cruise lines, beset by high labour costs and strong unions, virtually ceased to exist. New purpose-built cruise liners of Greek, Norwegian and, later, Russian registry soon appeared on the market to fill the gaps left by the declining maritime powers. These vessels, despite their registry, were based primarily in Caribbean or Mediterranean waters.

UK shipping was not entirely devoid of innovations at this time. Cunard, for instance, initiated the fly-cruise concept in the 1960s: vessels were based initially at Gibraltar and Naples, with passengers flying to join the cruise in chartered aircraft, avoiding rough sea crossings in the Bay of Biscay.

The rapid escalation of fuel and other costs during the 1970s threatened the whole future of deep-sea shipping, but, although declared dead by the pundits, this sector refused to lie down. A gradual stabilisation of oil prices and control of labour costs (largely by recruiting from developing countries) enabled the cruise business to stage a comeback in the 1980s and 1990s, led by entrepreneurial shipping lines like Carnival Cruise Line, the American operator that set out to put the fun back into cruising. More informality, to appeal to more youthful family markets, helped to turn the business round, so that, by the end of the twentieth century, cruising had again become a major growth sector. Carnival absorbed many of the traditional carriers, including UK companies Cunard and P&O, and had the financial backing necessary to make substantial investment in new vessels. This is discussed in greater detail in Chapter 14.

By contrast with the cruise business, ferry services achieved exceptional levels of growth between the 1950s and the end of the century, largely resulting from increased demand from private motorists taking their cars abroad, notably on routes between the Scandinavian countries and Germany, and between the UK and continental Europe. This growth in demand was also better spread across the seasons, enabling vessels to remain in service throughout the year with respectable load factors, with freight demand supporting weak passenger revenue in the winter period. Regular and frequent sailings, with fast turnarounds in port, encouraged bookings, and costs were kept down by offering much more restricted levels of service than would be expected on long-distance routes. Reliable, fast ferry services were further enhanced with the advent of the catamarans in the 1990s (Figure 2.5). This is discussed further in Chapter 14.

FIGURE 2.5 Ferries and catamarans provide passenger and car transport to the Isle of Wight

Photo: Shutterstock

THE GROWING IMPORTANCE OF BUSINESS TRAVEL

The growth in world trade in these decades saw a steady expansion in business travel, individually and in the conference and incentive travel fields, although recession in the latter part of the twentieth century affected both business and leisure travel. As economic power shifted between countries, emerging nations provided new patterns of tourism generation. In the 1970s, Japan and the oil-rich nations of the Middle East led the growth, while in the 1980s, countries like South Korea and Malaysia expanded both inbound and outbound business tourism dramatically. The acceptance of eight Eastern European nations (together with Malta and Cyprus) into the EU in 2004 led to new growth areas of tourism during the first decade of the new century, and the rise of a new, free-spending elite within the Russian community and adjacent countries resulted in those nationalities being among the fastest-growing sectors in international tourism, albeit from a low base. However, business uncertainty in the Western world, as demonstrated by the fall and slow recovery of the stock market in 2001 and the global economic recession which arrived in 2008, was reflected in wavering demand for business and leisure travel well into the twenty-first century.

Nevertheless, business travel of all kinds remains of immense importance to the industry, not least because the per capita revenue from the business traveller greatly exceeds that of the leisure traveller. We discuss motivational factors affecting business travel in the next chapter, and the nature of business travel is explored more fully in Chapter 11, but it should be stressed here that business travel often complements leisure travel, spreading the effects of tourism more evenly in the economy. Critically, business travellers are generally not travelling to areas favoured by leisure travellers (other than in the very particular case of the incentive travel market). Occasionally, spouses will travel to accompany the business traveller, so their leisure needs will have to be taken into consideration, too. In some cases, the business traveller will elect to stay at the destination after business has been concluded – such tourists are termed *extenders*. It is often not easy to distinguish between business and leisure tourism.

EXAMPLE

The value of extenders

Encouraging business travellers to stay longer in order to appreciate the tourist resources at a destination can add significantly to the value of tourism. The Business Tourism Partnership (an alliance of UK trade associations and government agencies interested in the sector) reported that 17% of conference delegates in the UK are accompanied by a guest who is not a delegate. While this is positive, it could be considered a paltry level when compared to Sydney where 42% of delegates are accompanied by a guest.

In Europe, conference visitors to France spend, on average, one day longer at the destination than delegates visiting the UK, while one-fifth of foreign conference visitors to Germany combine the visit with a holiday. It has been estimated that if just 10% of UK business visitors extended their trip by one day for leisure purposes, this would result in some £50 million more being spent on accommodation, food, entertainment and shopping (Business Tourism Partnership, n.d.).

CONFERENCES AND EXHIBITIONS

Conferences and formal meetings have become very important to the tourism industry, both nationally and internationally, with continued growth from the 1960s into the new century. In terms of the revenue for venues (Figure 2.6) and the wider economic benefits for host destinations, the UK conference and meetings market alone has been valued at £19.2 billion (BVEP, 2017). The conference market is often split into two sectors: corporate meetings and conferences, which mostly serve fewer than 200 delegates, and association conferences which often last two to four days, with 1000+ delegates.

Exhibitions have been important for business travel since at least the Great Exhibition at Crystal Palace, London, in 1851, and world fairs have become common events in major cities around the globe as a means of attracting visitors and publicising a nation's culture and products. Many national events are now organised on an annual basis, some requiring little more than a field and marquees or other temporary structures – the Royal Bath & West agricultural show being one example of a major outdoor attraction, held annually in the UK's West Country. The UK hosts thousands of exhibitions and trade shows annually, creating an economic benefit in excess of £11 billion (BVEP, 2017). As events have grown and become more professionally organised, they have become an important element in the business of tourism. A fuller discussion of event tourism is provided in Chapter 10.

THE ALL-INCLUSIVE HOLIDAY

The all-inclusive holiday is one that includes everything – food, drinks (including alcohol), water sports and entertainment at the hotel. The attractions of this form of tourism are obvious – it is often seen by tourists as offering better value, as they pay up front for the

FIGURE 2.6 The Excel Centre, London

Photo: Claire Humphreys

holiday, knowing what their budget will be well in advance, and unaffected by changes in the value of foreign currency.

In its modern form, all-inclusive tourism originated in the Caribbean, and upmarket tour operators like Sandals have promoted these programmes very successfully to the US and European markets. The concept later moved downmarket, however, and became popular in the more traditional European resorts, such as those of the Balearic Islands. Further expansion is seen as a direct threat to the livelihoods of many in the traditional coastal resorts.

EXAMPLE

All-inclusive holidays

Pressure to provide all-inclusive packages is coming from major international tour operators – First Choice now only offers all-inclusive holidays, while its parent company, TUI AG, also offers a wide range of all-inclusive holidays.

Research by the Travel Foundation (looking at both Cyprus and Tenerife) found that while all-inclusive holidaymakers spent less on food and drink, they were not the lowest spenders on excursions and shopping. Their conclusions were that hotel ratings, location and customer demographics were important influencers of likely spend outside of the resort.

Sources: Farmaki, 2013; Travel Foundation, 2013

MASS-MARKET TOURISM IN ITS MATURITY

By the 1980s, mass-market tourism to Southern European resorts had achieved maturity. Although still showing steady growth, expansion was not on the scale found between the 1950s and 1970s. Short-haul travel was changing geographically, while tourists sought new resorts and experiences. Portugal, having an Atlantic rather than a Mediterranean coast, wisely kept an upmarket image for its developments in the Algarve, while the Canaries, crucially within four hours' flying time from Northern European airports, were the closest destinations to offer guaranteed warm winter sunshine, and thus prospered from year-round appeal. Other, rather more exotic destinations attracted the upmarket winter holidaymaker. Tunisia, Morocco, Egypt and Israel pitched for the medium-haul beach markets, but following the upheaval in Middle East politics in the early part of the twenty-first century, many of the destinations in this region struggled to attract tourists. Tourism to Egypt was decimated, and in Tunisia it vanished almost entirely between 2015 and 2018 after a terrorist attack specifically aimed at foreign tourists.

As prices rose in the traditional resorts, tourists moved on to cheaper, and less developed, destinations still close at hand. Turkey – seen as cheap and mildly exotic – boomed, proving an attractive alternative to Greece. Balkan coastal resorts with attractive architecture and culture offered new appeal, despite lacking sandy beaches. Malta continued to appeal to the more conservative British tourist, while Crete and Cyprus began to attract larger numbers. Spain woke up to the despoliation of its resorts and made efforts to upgrade them, especially on the island of Majorca and in popular coastal towns like Torremolinos.

By the beginning of the new century, it had become clear that seaside tourism was moving in a new direction. Visitors were no longer willing to simply lie on a beach; they sought activities and adventure. For the young, this meant action, from sports to bungee jumping and dance clubs. Taking over popular resorts on Ibiza and in Greece, they encouraged the family holiday market to move on. For the older tourist, it meant more excursions inland to cultural sites and attractive villages.

The long-haul market was changing, too. Attempts to sell some long-haul destinations as if they were merely extensions of Mediterranean sunshine holidays failed to take into account the misunderstandings that could occur between hosts and guests, and destinations like The Gambia and the Dominican Republic suffered. Cruising, dormant for so long, suddenly found a new lease of life. Long-haul beach holidays in Kenya and Thailand, marketed at costs competitive with those in Europe, also attracted Western tourists.

The American and Northern European markets were joined by a rising flow of tourists from other parts of the world. The Asian market became a leading source of business for the travel industry – in the West as well as throughout Australasia. The flow of Japanese tourists to Australia was particularly noteworthy but this has been surpassed in recent years by the Chinese market, which now makes up about 15% of inbound tourism to the country (Tourism Australia, 2018). Travel times to Australia are shorter than those to Europe and, equally importantly, because the travel is largely within the same longitude, there is no time change or jet lag to face. South Africa similarly benefited from European visitors travelling longitudinally, although uncertainty over the country's crime and politics continues to cause concern.

Pacific destinations also began to attract Europeans in significant numbers, just as they have long attracted the Japanese and Australian markets. A large proportion of these visitors, however, were using the Pacific islands as stopover points for a night or two rather than as a holiday base. The impact of technology can be seen when, for the first time, aircraft became capable of flying direct between the west coast of the USA and Australia with the introduction of the Boeing 747-400SP aircraft. Tahiti, slightly off the direct route between these continents and long established as an attractive stopover point but expensive for longer holidays, immediately suffered a sharp decline in visitors as the airlines concentrated their promotion efforts on direct, non-stop services between Los Angeles and Sydney or Auckland.

THE INFLUENCE OF INFORMATION TECHNOLOGY

Perhaps the greatest change affecting the industry was occasioned by technological development. Reservation systems became computerised, first by the transport companies (airlines and shipping), then within tour operators and travel agencies. The introduction and rapid growth of the Internet allowed business-to-customer (B2C) and business-to-business (B2B) systems to develop, alongside the growth of personal computers. These issues will be examined in later chapters.

The affordability of computers, the penetration of the Internet and the availability of broadband access enabled customers to search for information about holiday destinations, compare travel companies (and user reviews) and reserve travel products online. The convenience of online bookings, coupled with budget airlines' offers of cheaper fares using this system, boosted travel; online travel agencies prospered, but the more traditional high street agencies suffered.

SUMMARY AND LESSONS FOR THE FUTURE

In this chapter, we have seen how social change led to a shift in the desire and motivation for holidays, influencing the growth of both domestic and international travel. We took account of technological change, especially within the transport sector, which enabled travel first to take place and then to expand over time. Finally, we discussed how tourist destinations and attractions first grew, then changed in response to changing demand, a process that has accelerated in more recent times. This ability to respond quickly as circumstances change and new forms of competition arise is the clearest lesson we can take away from our study of history.

QUESTIONS AND DISCUSSION POINTS

1. Explain how transport technology influenced demand for travel over time.
2. Discuss the appeal of traditional guidebooks vis-à-vis more recent means of acquiring travel information.
3. Identify key enabling factors that encouraged the growth of mass tourism in the twentieth century.

TASKS

1. There are many towns today that are popular as spa resorts. Investigate one resort of your choice and create a poster that addresses the following questions:
   - What motivates tourists to visit the town?
   - What spa resources are available for tourists today? Are these recent additions?
2. Write a brief that summarises how political hindrances influenced where people travelled pre-twentieth century. Do these influences impact on travel behaviour today?

FURTHER READING

Adams, C. and Laurence, R. (eds) (2011) *Travel and Geography in the Roman Empire*. London: Routledge.

Andrews, H. (2011) *The British on Holiday*. Bristol: Channel View Publications.

Barton, S. (2005) *Working-class Organisations and Popular Tourism: 1840–1970*. Manchester: Manchester University Press.

Boissevain, J. (1996) *Coping with Tourists: European reactions to mass tourism*. Oxford: Berghahn Books.

Bray, R. and Raitz, V. (2001) *Flight to the Sun: The story of the holiday revolution*. London: Continuum.

Butler, R. W. and Russell, R. (2010) *Giants of Tourism*. Wallingford: CABI.

Farr, M. and Guégan, X. (eds) (2013) *The British Abroad Since the Eighteenth Century, Vol. 1: Travellers and tourists* (Britain and the world). Basingstoke: Palgrave Macmillan.

Inglis, F. (2000) *The Delicious History of the Holiday*. London: Routledge.

Korte, B. (2000) *English Travel Writing: From pilgrimages to postcolonial explorations*. Basingstoke: Palgrave Macmillan.

Segreto, L., Manera, C. and Pohl, M. (2009) *Europe at the Seaside: The economic history of mass tourism in the Mediterranean*. New York: Berghahn Books.

Swinglehurst, E. (1982) *Cook's Tours: The story of popular travel*. London: Blandford Press.

Walton, J. K. (2000) *The British Seaside: Holidays and resorts in the twentieth century*. Manchester: Manchester University Press.

Ward, C. and Hardy, D. (2010) *Goodnight Campers! The history of the British holiday camp*. Nottingham: Five Leaves Publications.

REFERENCES

BBC (2011) *The Victorian Seaside*. Available online at: www.bbc.co.uk/history/british/victorians/seaside_01.shtml [Accessed July 2014].

Buscombe, C. and Wallop, H. (2010) More people camping than staying in B&Bs. *The Telegraph*, 31 July.

Business Tourism Partnership (n.d.) *Making the Most of our Business Visitors*. Available online at: www.tourisminsights.info/ONLINEPUB/BUSINESS/BUSINESS%20PDFS/BUSINESS%20TOURISM%20PARTNERSHIP%20(2004),%20Making%20the%20Most%20of%20our%20Business%20Visitors,%20BTP,%20London.pdf [Accessed January 2019].

Business Visits and Events Partnership (BVEP) (2017) *Opportunities for Global Growth in Britain's Events Sector*. Available online at: www.businessvisitsandeventspartnership.com/research-and-publications/research/category/4-bvep-research?download=285:opportunities-for-global-growth-in-britain-s-events-sector [Accessed January 2019].

Casson, L. (1974) *Travel in the Ancient World*. London: George Allen and Unwin; (1994) Baltimore, MD: Johns Hopkins University Press.

Dunn, R. E. (1986) *The Adventures of Ibn Battuta, a Muslim Traveler of the 14th Century*. Berkeley, CA: University of California Press.

Farmaki, A. (2013) Dealing with the growing issue of all-inclusive holiday packages. *Cyprus Mail*, 31 December.

Haven (2014) *Accommodation at Haven*. Available online at: www.haven.com/accommodation/index.aspx [Accessed July 2014].

Leed, E. (2007) The ancient and the moderns: From suffering to freedom. In S. L. Roberson (ed.), *Defining Travel: Diverse visions*. Jackson, MS: University Press of Mississippi.

Lloyd, M. (2003) *The Passport: The history of man's most travelled document*. Stroud: Sutton Publishing.

Löfgren, O. (1999) *On Holiday: A history of vacationing*. Berkeley, CA: University of California Press.

Mitchell, A. (2006) *The Great Train Race: Railways and the Franco-German rivalry, 1815–1914*. New York: Berghahn Books.

Nugent, T. (1749) *The Grand Tour: A journey through the Netherlands, Germany, Italy and France*. London: S. Birt.

Puffert, D. J. (2009) *Tracks across Continents, Paths through History: The economic dynamics of standardization in railway gauge*. Chicago, IL: University of Chicago Press.

Studd, R. G. (1950) *The Holiday Story*. London: Percival Marshall.

Tourism Australia (2018) *International Visitor Arrivals*. Available online at: www.tourism.australia.com/en/markets-and-stats/tourism-statistics/international-visitor-arrivals.html [Accessed January 2018].

Travel Foundation (2013) All-inclusive board basis one of many factors affecting customer spend on holiday. Available online at: www.thetravelfoundation.org.uk/images/media/Press_Release_-_new_all_inclusive_research.pdf [Accessed July 2014].

3

THE DEMAND FOR TOURISM

CONTENTS

LEARNING OUTCOMES

After studying this chapter, you should be able to:

- distinguish between motivating and enabling factors
- understand the nature of the psychological and sociological demands for tourism
- recognise how the product influences consumer demand
- be aware of some common theories of consumer behaviour, such as decision-making and risk avoidance
- appreciate the factors influencing demand and how demand is changing in the twenty-first century.

> Over the past six decades, tourism has experienced continued expansion and diversification to become one of the largest and fastest-growing economic sectors in the world. Many new destinations have emerged in addition to the traditional favourites of Europe and North America. (UNWTO, 2017: 2)

INTRODUCTION

The emergence of new destinations alongside long-established ones provides choice for those selecting their holiday. An understanding of why people buy the holidays or business trips they do, how they go about selecting their holidays, why one company is given preference over another and why tourists choose to travel when they do is vital to those who work in the tourism industry.

Motivation and purpose are closely related, and in Chapter 1 the principal purposes for which tourists travel were identified. These were classified into three broad categories: business travel, leisure travel and miscellaneous travel, which would include, *inter alia*, travel for one's health and religious travel. However, simply labelling tourists in this way only helps us to understand their *general* motivation for travelling; it tells us little about their specific motivation, or the needs and wants that underpin it, or how those needs and wants are met and satisfied. It is the purpose of this chapter to explain the terms and the complex interrelationship between factors that go to shape the choices of trips made by tourists of all kinds.

THE TOURIST'S NEEDS AND WANTS

If we ask prospective tourists why they want to travel to a particular destination, they will offer a variety of reasons, such as 'It's somewhere that I've always wanted to visit' or 'Some friends recommended it' or 'It's always good weather at that time of the year and the beaches are wonderful. We've been going there regularly for the past few years'. Interesting as these views may be, they actually throw very little light on the real motivations of the tourists concerned because they have not helped to identify their *needs* and *wants*.

People often talk about 'needing' a holiday, just as they might say they need a new carpet, a new dress or a better lawnmower. Are they, in fact, expressing a need or a want? 'Need' suggests that the products we are asking for are necessities for our daily life, but this is clearly seldom the case with these products. We are merely expressing a desire for more goods and services, a symptom of the consumer-orientated society in which we live.

Occasionally, a holiday (or at least a break from routine) can become a genuine need, as is the case with those in highly stressful occupations where a breakdown can occur if there is no relief from that stress. Families and individuals suffering from severe deprivation may also need a holiday, as is shown by the work of charitable organisations such as the Family Holiday Association (discussed in Chapter 17).

Let us start by examining what it is we mean by a need. People have certain physiological needs, and satisfying these is essential to survival: they need to eat, drink, sleep, keep warm and reproduce – all needs that are also essential to the survival of the human race. Beyond those needs, we also have psychological needs that are important for our wellbeing, such as the need to love and be loved, to enjoy friendship, to value ourselves as human beings and have others value and respect us. Many people believe that we also have inherently within us the need to master our environment and understand the nature of the society in which we live. Abraham Maslow conveniently grouped these needs into a hierarchy (see Figure 3.1), suggesting that the more fundamental needs have to be satisfied before we seek to satisfy the higher-level ones.

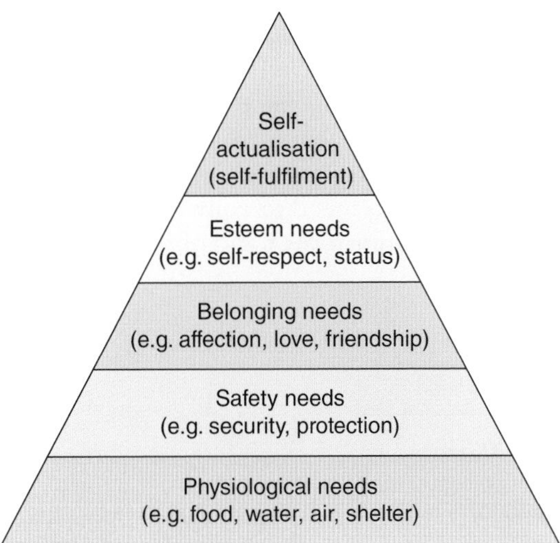

FIGURE 3.1 Maslow's hierarchy of needs

Source: Maslow, A. (1987) *Motivation and Personality*. Reprinted with permission.

The difficulty with exploring these needs is that many people may actually be quite unaware of their needs or how to go about satisfying them. Others will be reluctant to reveal their real needs. For example, few people would be willing openly to admit that they travel to a particular destination to impress their neighbours, although their desire for status within the neighbourhood may well be a factor in their choice of holiday and destination.

Some of our needs are **innate** – that is, they are based on factors inherited by us at birth. These include biological and instinctive needs such as eating and drinking. We also inherit genetic traits from our parents that are reflected in certain needs and wants. Other needs and wants arise out of the environment in which we are raised and are therefore **learned** or socially engineered. The early death of parents or their lack of overt affection towards us may cause us to have stronger needs for bonding and friendship with others, for example. As we come to know more about genomes, following the mapping of the human genetic code, DNA, early in the twenty-first century, so we are coming to appreciate that our genetic differences are, in fact, very slight, indicating that most of our needs and wants are conditioned by our environment.

Travel may be one of several means of satisfying a need and, although we feel needs, we do not necessarily express them and we may not overtly recognise how travel actually satisfies our particular needs. If we re-examine the answers given earlier to questions asking why we travel, it may be that, in the case where respondents are confirming the desire to return to the same destination year after year, they are actually expressing the desire to satisfy a need for safety and security, by returning to the 'tried and tested'. The means by which this is achieved, namely a holiday in a resort well known to them, reflects the respondents' 'want' rather than their need.

The process of translating a need into the motivation to visit a specific destination or undertake a specific activity is quite complex and can best be demonstrated by means of a diagram (see Figure 3.2).

Potential consumers must not only recognise that they have a need, but also understand how a particular product will satisfy it. Every consumer is different, and what one consumer sees as the ideal solution to the need, another will reject. A holiday in Benidorm that Mr A thinks will be something akin to paradise would be for Mr B an endurance test; he might prefer a walk in the Pennines for a week, which Mr A would find a torturous experience. It is important that we all recognise that each person's *perception* of a holiday, like any other product, is affected by experiences and attitudes. Only if the perception of the need and the attraction match will a consumer be motivated to buy the product. The job of the skilled travel agent is to subtly question clients in order to learn about their individual interests and desires and find the products to match them. Those selling more expensive holidays may need to convince their clients that the experience on offer is worth paying the difference over and above what they had expected for an ordinary holiday.

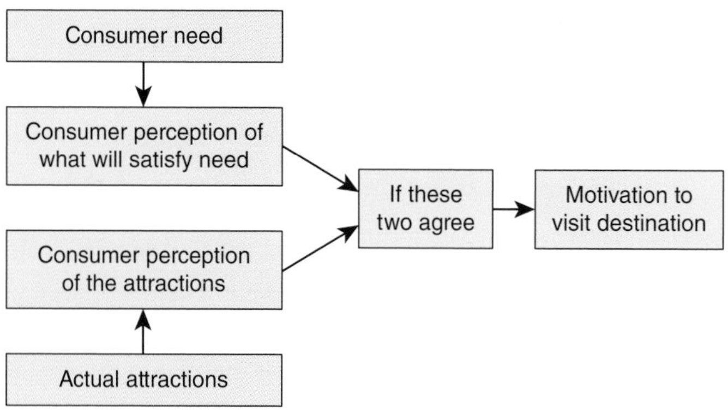

FIGURE 3.2 The motivation process

TRAVEL MOTIVATION

We have established that motivation arises out of the felt wants or needs of the individual. For some people, the motivation to travel is aimed at achieving a broad objective, such as getting away from the routine and stress of the workplace in order to enjoy different surroundings and a healthy environment. Alternatively, the tourist may decide to take a holiday in the Swiss Alps, for the opportunity to take walks in fresh mountain air and enjoy varied scenery, good food and total relaxation. Marketing professionals sometimes refer to these two forms of motivation as **'push' factors** and **'pull' factors** – that is, the tourist is being pushed into a holiday by the need to get away from their everyday environment, but other factors may be at work to pull, or encourage, them to travel to a specific destination. For this reason, marketing staff realise that they will have to undertake their promotion at two distinct levels, persuading the consumer of the need to take a holiday and also showing those consumers that the particular holiday or destination the organisation is promoting will best satisfy that need.

PUSH FACTORS

Among early academics who wrote about push and pull factors in relation to tourism, Graham Dann (1977), in his work relating to Barbados, revealed that greater interest had been shown in research into pull factors, while push factors were given minimal attention, despite the assertion that choice of destination is 'consequent on [a tourist's] prior need to travel' (p. 186). He suggested that push factors predispose the tourist to want to travel (for reasons such as escape and nostalgia). Ryan (1991) also explored the push factors that encouraged travel, categorising these into 11 themes:

- the motivation to escape from perceived mundane environments
- relaxation and recuperation
- the opportunity to play, providing adults with an opportunity to regress into the carefree state of childhood
- strengthening of family bonds and the opportunity to spend time with other family members
- gaining status and prestige among one's peers (both at home and while on holiday)
- social integration with hosts and other guests
- romance and sexual opportunity
- the opportunity for educational development and broadening of the mind
- self-fulfilment and self-discovery, which may potentially be life-changing
- wish fulfilment and the achievement of long-desired goals
- shopping.

While shopping may seem a somewhat banal reason, it is a popular and commonly expressed reason for travel and has led to increases in tourism numbers to destinations like New York and Dubai, as well as several border towns such as Calais in France. Importantly, these motivations, independently or in combination, stimulate individuals to travel. It is then down to the pull factors to determine which destination or resort is chosen to meet their desires.

EXAMPLE

Tactical holidays

One push factor noted in Ryan's list is that of escape. Sometimes this motivation might specifically relate to the need to escape stressful situations at home. A small survey by a UK travel company asked holidaymakers what determined the dates they chose for their holiday. More than two-thirds responded that it was to be out of the country to miss a stressful family or work commitment.

Other reasons for the choice of date included:

- wanting the weather to be good at the chosen destination (71%)
- the only time possible to be away from work (53%)
- wanting to celebrate a special event abroad (27%)
- wanting to get the best deal/price (21%).

While being out of the country might seem a good tactic for avoiding a family wedding or work problem, the survey revealed that one-fifth of those holidaymakers who had booked a tactical holiday felt that it had caused them more stress in the long run.

Sources: Anderson, 2014; Driver, 2014

PULL FACTORS

We have recognised that tourists may have many different motives for wanting to take a holiday. These motives may be fulfilled by a variety of destinations; therefore, distinguishing between one location and an alternative may be achieved by considering the pull factors for each. Richardson and Fluker suggest that these 'pull consumers towards a particular destination' (2004: 67). Pull factors may include:

- the range of attractions, including the natural environment, cultural resources and a welcoming host population
- the availability and quality of amenities
- special events
- infrastructure and accessibility
- suitable weather conditions
- a positive image as a safe, entertaining, interesting place to visit.

Pull factors can help the tourist choose the destination that best meets their motivations. However, it may be that some pull factors may stimulate motivation to travel; for example, the hosting of the 2012 Olympics in London stimulated some domestic tourists to visit the capital in order to witness this sporting occasion, whereas without the event a visit to London may never have been considered.

While on the subject of the Olympics as a pull factor, research also reveals that hosting this mega-event may actually deter tourists from visiting, perhaps concerned that costs and congestion would spoil the holiday experience (Preuss, 2005). The tourism industry hinted that this might have been the case for London 2012, and data supported this, with the number of international visitors during this period down on previous years. The UK government's post-games evaluation concluded that 'there was substantial displacement of regular visitors who were deterred by the potential for overcrowding, disruption and price rises because of the Games' (DCMS, 2013: 18).

CATEGORIES OF TOURIST MOTIVATION

If we look at the varied forms of leisure tourism that have become a part of our lives in the past few years, we will quickly see that certain types of holiday have become popular because they best meet common, and basic, needs. The 'sun, sea and sand' holiday that caters to the mass market is essentially a passive form of leisure, entailing nothing more stressful than a relaxing time on the beach, enjoyment of the perceived healthy benefits of sunshine and saltwater bathing, good food and reasonably priced alcohol (another relaxant). The tendency among certain groups of tourists abroad to drink too much and misbehave generally is, again, a reflection of need, even if the result is one that we have come to deplore because of its impact on others. Such tourists seek to escape from the constraints of their usual environment and enjoy an opportunity to 'let their hair down', perhaps in a more tolerant environment than they would find in their own home country.

Those travelling on their own might also seek opportunities to meet other people or even find romance (thus meeting the need to belong and other social needs). In the case of families, parents can simultaneously satisfy their own needs while also providing a healthy and enjoyable time for their children on the beach. Parents may also be given the chance to get away and be on their own while their children are being cared for by skilled childminders.

McIntosh et al. (1995) summarised these different tourism motivations into four categories: physical, cultural, interpersonal and status and prestige (Table 3.1). Fulfilling these motivations can be achieved through a range of activities; for example, tourists who choose to visit Machu Picchu in Peru may feel that the experience fulfils some of their cultural – and possibly status and prestige – motivations (see Figure 3.3).

TABLE 3.1 Tourism motivators

Physical motivators	Cultural motivators
• Refreshing the body • Reducing mental stress • Improve physical health • Exercising • Having fun and enjoyment	• Curiosity about foreign lands and people • Developing historical or cultural interests • Attending cultural events • Exploring local music, folklore, lifestyles, art, etc.
Interpersonal motivators	**Status and prestige motivators**
• Maintaining and enhancing relationships with friends and family • Making new friends • Escaping one's own routine environment (including escape from one's own family)	• Gaining status and recognition from others • Pursuing one's own hobbies • Continuing education and self-development

Source: McIntosh et al., 1995

FIGURE 3.3 Tourists visiting Machu Picchu in Peru may feel this experience fulfils some of their cultural or educational motivations

Photo: Claire Humphreys

What is provided, therefore, is a 'bundle of benefits', and the more a particular package holiday, or a particular destination, can be shown to provide the range of benefits sought, the more attractive that holiday will appear to the tourist compared with other holidays on offer. The bundle will be made up of benefits that are designed to cater to both general and specific needs and wants.

Today, there is a growing demand for holidays that offer more strenuous activities than are to be found in the traditional 'three S' (sun, sea and sand) holidays, such as trekking, mountaineering or yachting. These appeal to those whose basic needs for relaxation have already been satisfied (they may have desk-bound jobs that involve mental, rather than physical, strain) and they are now seeking something more challenging. Strenuous activities provide opportunities for people to test their physical abilities and, while this may involve no more than a search for health by other means, there may also be a search for competence, another need identified by Maslow (1954: 31). Because such holidays are purchased by like-minded people, often in small groups, they can also help to meet other ego and social needs.

The growing confidence and physical fitness of many tourists (and not just the young!) have put 'extreme sports' on the agenda of many holiday companies. Formerly limited to winter sports such as skiing and snowboarding and summer white water rafting, adventure holidays now embrace mountain climbing, windsurfing, BMX biking, paragliding, heliskiing, kitesurfing, landboarding, polar treks and base jumping (leaping off tall buildings with parachutes – seldom available as a legal activity!), with the range of activities increasing each year.

EXAMPLE

Bootcamp holidays

The desire to get fit has led to the growth of many holiday 'bootcamps'. These vacations provide health food regimes with organised physical activities and, in the case of many luxury bootcamps, massages and treatments to ease the aches and pains. While this may not seem like a holiday, demand has been increasing in recent years.

To serve more specialist markets, there are also training holidays for cyclists, triathletes and marathon runners. One such company is Embrace Sports, who regularly organise triathlon training holidays. A typical week-long holiday would include:

- a daily run (5–10 miles), swim (1–3 miles) or cycle ride (40–70 miles)
- an open water swimming technique session
- a strengthening and conditioning exercise class
- aquathon time trials
- running track sessions.

While such an intense exercise schedule would not suit everybody, part of the appeal for those who do take part is the opportunity to meet other people with a shared interest in triathlons.

It must also be recognised that many tourists are constantly seeking novelty and different experiences. However satisfied they might be with one holiday, they will be unlikely to return to the same destination. Instead, they will be forever seeking something more challenging, more exciting, more remote. This is, in part, an explanation for the growing demand for long-haul holidays. For other people, such increasingly exotic tourist trips satisfy the search for status.

The need for self-actualisation can be met in a number of ways. At its simplest, the desire to 'commune with nature' is common to many tourists and can be achieved through scenic trips by coach, fly-drive packages in which routes are identified and stopping-off points recommended for their scenic beauty, cycling tours or hiking holidays. Each of these forms of holiday will find its own market in terms of the degree of rural authenticity sought, but all, to some extent, meet the needs of the market as a whole.

Alternatively, the quest for knowledge can be met by tours such as those offered to cultural centres in Europe, often guided by experts in a particular field. Self-actualisation can be aided through packages offering painting or other artistic 'do-it-yourself' holidays. Some tourists seek more meaningful experiences through contact with foreign residents, where they can come to understand the local culture. This process can be facilitated through careful packaging of programmes arranged by organisers, who build up suitable contacts among local residents at the destination. Local guides, too, can act as 'culture brokers', overcoming language barriers or helping to explain local culture to inquisitive tourists, while at the same time reassuring more nervous travellers.

As people come to travel more and as they become more sophisticated or better educated, so their higher-level needs will predominate in their motivation to go on a particular holiday. Companies in the business of tourism must always recognise this and take it into account when planning new programmes or new attractions for tourists.

THE MOTIVATIONS OF BUSINESS TRAVELLERS

Those travelling on business often have different criteria that need to be considered. They are, in general, less price-sensitive. They are motivated principally by the need to complete their travel and business dealings as efficiently and effectively as possible within a given time frame; this reflects their companies' motivation for the trip. They will, however, also have personal agendas to take into account. Through the eyes of their companies, then, they will be giving consideration to issues such as speed of transport and how convenient it is for getting them to their destinations, the punctuality and reliability of the carriers and the frequency of flights so that they can leave at a time to suit their appointments and return as soon as their business has been completed. Decisions about their travel are often made at very short notice, so arrangements may have to be made at any time. They need the flexibility to change their reservations at minimal notice and are prepared to pay a premium for this privilege. The arrival of the low-cost airlines, however, has persuaded many to stick with a booking, as large savings can be achieved in this way, even for a flight within Europe. More recently, some low-cost carriers have been offering, at a slightly higher price, flexible tickets to attract business tourists.

Travel needs to be arranged on weekdays rather than weekends because most businesspeople like to spend their weekends with their families. Above all, businesspeople will require that those they deal with – agents, carriers, travel managers – have substantial, in-depth knowledge of travel products.

Personal motivation enters the scene when the business traveller is taking a spouse or partner with them and when leisure activities are to be included as an adjunct to the business trip. A businessperson may also be interested in travelling with a specific carrier in order to take advantage of frequent flyer schemes that provide seat upgrades or allow them to take a leisure trip with the airline when they have accumulated sufficient points. This may entail travelling on what is neither the cheapest nor the most direct route. Factors such as these can cause friction between travellers and their companies as the decision regarding whether or not to travel, how and when, may not rest with the travellers themselves, but rather with senior members of their companies, who may be more concerned with ensuring that the company receives value for money than the comfort or status of the traveller.

It was believed that when videoconferencing facilities were introduced a few years ago, this would herald the decline of business travel. In fact, this has had little impact; traditional meetings endure, while conferences and trade shows are continuing to expand.

TRAVEL FACILITATORS

Up to now, we have dealt with the factors that motivate tourists to take holidays. However, in order to take a holiday, the tourist requires both time and money. These factors make it possible for prospective tourists to indulge in their desires, and are therefore known as **facilitators**.

Facilitators play a major role in relation to the specific objectives of the tourist. Cost is a major factor in facilitating the purchase of travel, but equally, an increase in disposable income offers the tourist the opportunity to enjoy a wider choice of destinations. Better accessibility of the destination, or more favourable exchange rates against the local currency, easier entry without political barriers and friendly locals speaking the language of the tourist all act as facilitators, as well as motivating the choice of a particular destination over others.

A growing characteristic within wealthier countries is the presence of 'cash rich, time poor' consumers who are prepared to sacrifice money to save time. The implications of this phenomenon are significant for the industry. Those who can offer the easiest and fastest communication opportunities, prices and booking facilities, coupled with reliability and good service, can gain access to a wealthy, rapidly expanding market. Whether this race will be won by the direct selling organisations using websites and call centres or retailers using new sales techniques (such as experienced travel counsellors prepared to call on customers at times convenient to them and in their own homes, including evenings and weekends) remains to be seen.

SEGMENTING THE TOURISM MARKET

So far in this chapter, we have looked at the individual factors that give rise to our various needs and wants. In the tourism industry, those responsible for marketing destinations or holidays will be concerned with both individual and aggregate, or total, demand for a holiday or destination. For this purpose, it is convenient to categorise and segment demand according to four distinct sets of variables – namely, geographic, demographic, psychographic and behavioural.

GEOGRAPHIC VARIABLES

These are determined according to the areas in which consumers live. They can be broadly defined by continent (North America, South America, Asia, Africa, for example), country (such as the UK, France, Japan, Australia) or according to region, either broadly (for instance, Nordic, Mediterranean, Baltic states, US Midwestern states) or more narrowly (say, the Finger Lakes region of upstate New York, the Austrian Tyrol, Alsace-Lorraine, North Rhine-Westphalia, the UK Lake District). It is appropriate to divide areas in this way only where it is clear that the resident populations' buying or behaviour patterns reflect commonalities and differ from those of other areas in ways that are significant to the industry.

The most obvious point to make here is that chosen travel destinations will be the outcome of factors such as distance, convenience and how much it costs to reach the destination. For example, Europeans will find it more convenient, and probably cheaper, to holiday in the Mediterranean, North Americans in the Caribbean, and Australians in Pacific islands like Fiji and Bali. Differing climates in the generating countries will also result in other variations in travel demand.

DEMOGRAPHIC VARIABLES

Segmentation is frequently based on characteristics such as age, gender, family composition, stage in life cycle, income, occupation, education and ethnic origin. The type of holiday chosen is likely to differ greatly between 20–30-year-olds and 50–60-year-olds, to take one example. Changing patterns will also interest marketers – declining family size, increasing numbers of elderly consumers, greater numbers of individuals living alone and taking holidays alone, or increases in disposable income among some age groups – all these factors will affect the ways in which holidays are designed and marketed.

A significant factor influencing demand in the UK market in recent years has been the rise in wealth among older sectors of the public, after their parents (the first generation to have become property owners on a major scale) died, leaving significant inheritances to their offspring. This, and the general rise in living standards, fuelled demand for second homes both in the UK and abroad, changing leisure patterns and encouraging the growth of low-cost airlines to service the market's needs.

Demographic distinctions are among the most easily researched variables and, consequently, provide readily available data. Market differentiation by occupation is one of the commonest ways in which consumers are categorised, not least because it offers the prospect of a ready indication of relative disposable incomes. Occupation also remains a principal criterion for identifying social class.

The best-known socio-economic segmentation in the UK was introduced after World War II and is still widely used in market research exercises, including those conducted under the aegis of the National Readership Surveys (NRS). Using this tool, the consumer market is broken down into six categories on the basis of the occupation of the head of household (see Table 3.2).

TABLE 3.2 Social grade classification system based on occupation

Classes	Designation
A	Higher managerial, administrative and professional
B	Intermediate managerial, administrative and professional
C1	Supervisory, clerical and junior managerial, administrative and professional
C2	Skilled manual
D	Semi-skilled and unskilled manual
E	State pensioners, casual and lowest-grade workers, unemployed with state benefits only

The ABC1 grouping has been of key interest to the travel industry, which has identified this segment as major travellers, having both leisure time and the funds to purchase high-end holidays. However, this attempt to distinguish between market segments on the grounds of social class arising from occupation is open to criticism; indeed, patterns of purchasing or behaviour are now less clearly determined by social class. The belief that touristic motivations can be ascribed largely to occupation, given the changes taking place in twenty-first-century society, can be misleading. Furthermore, while the proportion of those travelling on holiday each year is, as one would expect, far higher among the higher-income brackets than among the lower, in an era where plumbers and electricians may earn up to twice as much as university lecturers, segmentation by occupation clearly has flaws.

Various attempts have been made in recent years to overcome this stigmatic characterisation by occupation. A new system of social classification was introduced in the UK in 2001 which then informed efforts to progress a European socio-economic classification system (see Table 3.3).

TABLE 3.3 European socio-economic classification system

Classes	Designation
1	Large employers, higher-grade professional, administrative and managerial occupations
2	Lower-grade professional, administrative and managerial occupations and higher-grade technician and supervisory occupations
3	Intermediate occupations
4	Small employer and self-employed occupations (excluding agriculture, etc.)
5	Self-employed occupations (agriculture, etc.)
6	Lower supervisory and lower technician occupations
7	Lower services, sales and clerical occupations
8	Lower technical occupations
9	Routine occupations
10	Never worked and long-term unemployed

Source: Adapted from Harrison and Rose, 2006

Despite concerns regarding the use of occupation as a segmentation method, categorising demand for a company's products by social class can be of some value in helping to determine advertising spend and the media to be employed. Similarly, breaking down demand by age group is also helpful, even vital if the aim is, say, to develop holidays that particularly appeal to young people.

Market research in recent years has been transformed by the efforts of researchers to bring together both geography and demography, through a process of pinpoint **geodemographic** analysis. This is based on combining census data and postcodes to reveal that fine-tuning by region can produce a picture of spend and behaviour that will be common to a large proportion of the population of that region. Among the best known of such systems is ACORN (A Classification of Residential Neighbourhoods), operated by CACI Limited, which takes into account such factors as age, income, lifestyle and family structure. However, even with the sophistication and refinement of this approach, it will not be sufficient to explain all of the variations in choice between different tourist products, and for this we must look to consumer psychographics for further enlightenment.

PSYCHOGRAPHIC VARIABLES

This approach to segmenting the market focuses on characteristics related to lifestyle, attitudes and personality (Reid and Bojanic, 2010). Beyond simple demographic distinctions, as buyers we are heavily influenced by those immediately surrounding us (our so-called **peer groups**), as well as those we most admire and wish to emulate (our **reference groups**). In the former case, while we may develop choices favoured by our parents and teachers in early life, as we become more independent, we prefer to emulate the behaviour of our immediate friends, fellow students, colleagues at work or others with whom we come into regular close contact. In the latter case, the influence of celebrities is becoming paramount, as the holiday choices and behaviour of pop idols, cinema and TV 'personalities' and those in the media and modelling worlds come increasingly to influence buying patterns, particularly those of younger consumers. Thus, the ways in which significant others live and spend their leisure hours exert a strong influence on holiday consumerism among all classes of client.

EXAMPLE

Elite segmentation

Some niche cruise companies have marketed themselves for many years on the basis that their passengers will mingle with celebrities and public figures, and the Caribbean island of Mustique successfully promoted itself as an exclusive hideaway for the rich, largely because Princess Margaret (the sister of Queen Elizabeth II) had been a frequent visitor. The choice of a private island in the Seychelles as the honeymoon destination of Prince William and his bride Kate Middleton in 2011 will undoubtedly have exerted an influence on travel demand to that destination in recent years.

Furthermore, numerous online lists exist that identify popular celebrity holiday destinations. These lists often include details of restaurants and hotels popular with the rich and famous in order to enhance the possibility of 'celebrity spotting', thus attracting a certain type of visitor to the destination.

As members of society, we tend to follow the norms and values reflected in that society. We all like to feel that we are making our own decisions about products, but do not always realise how other people's tastes influence our own and what pressures there are on us to conform. When we claim that we are buying to 'please ourselves', what exactly is this 'self' that we are pleasing? We are, in fact, composed of many 'selves'. There is the self that we see ourselves as, often highly subjectively; the ideal self, how we would like to be; the self as we believe others see us; and the self as we are actually seen by others. Yet none of these can be construed as our real self if, indeed, a real self can be said to exist outside of the way we interact with others. Readers will be aware that they put on different 'fronts' and act out different roles according to the company in which they find themselves, whether family, best friend, lover or employer. Do any of these relationships truly reflect our real self?

The importance attached to this theory of self, from the perspective of this text, is the way in which it affects those things that we buy and with which we surround ourselves. This means that, in the case of holidays, we will not always buy the kind of holiday we think we would most enjoy or even the one we feel we could best afford, but, instead, we might buy the holiday we feel will give us status with our friends and neighbours, or reflect the kind of holiday we feel that 'persons in our position' should take. Advertisers will frequently use this knowledge to promote a destination as being suited to a particular kind of tourist and will perhaps go further, using as a model in their advertisements some well-known TV personality or film star who reflects the 'typical tourist at the destination', with whom we can then mentally associate ourselves.

In the same way, status becomes an important feature of business travel as such travellers are aware that they are representing their companies to business associates and must therefore create a favourable impression. As their companies usually accept this view and pay their bills, this is one of the reasons business travel generates more income per capita than does leisure travel.

BEHAVIOURAL VARIABLES

This allows us to segment markets according to their usage of the products. This is a much simpler concept, and facts about consumer purchasing can be ascertained quite readily through market research. The frequency with which we purchase a product, the quantities we buy, where we choose to buy (from a travel agent or direct, using company websites, for example) and the sources from which we obtain information about products are of great interest to marketers, who, armed with this knowledge, will be able to shape their strategies more effectively in order to influence purchases. A key element in this is to know which benefits a consumer is looking for when they purchase a product. The motives for buying a lakes and mountains holiday, for example, can vary substantially. Some may be seeking solitude and scenic beauty, perhaps to recover from stress or to enjoy a painting or photography holiday; some will seek the social interaction of small hiking groups or evening chats in the bar of their hotel with like-minded guests; while others will be looking for more active pastimes, such as waterskiing or mountaineering. Only when the organisation arranging the holiday knows which elements of the product appeal to their customers can a sale effectively take place.

EXAMPLE

Niche market segments

In 2013, the travel technology giant Amadeus reported on the future of travel in the Asia Pacific region. This report specifically noted the growing dominance of this region globally while suggesting that the future would see the fragmentation of markets into a greater number of niche sectors. Amadeus proposed that five key segments would experience significant change:

1. The Visiting Friends and Relatives (VFR) travellers, who provide a reason for travel for around one-fifth of tourists in the region.
2. Independent travellers who make their own travel arrangements as they become more experienced in travel and have greater access to the Internet. Solo travel is also expected to grow.
3. Generation 'S' (Senior) travellers will grow in number as the older population make up an ever-greater share of the population. In Australia and Japan, the over-65s already account for one-fifth of leisure travellers.
4. The small- to medium-sized enterprise (SME) business traveller will move cross-border as bureaucracy allows small businesses to expand internationally. Demand for support services such as business centres and budget business travel will expand.
5. The female business traveller market is expanding as more women reach management positions that require business travel. While Japan still has low levels of female business travellers (fewer than 20%), other regions are already seeing greater equity (about 40% of business travellers in China are female).

Consequently, Amadeus concluded that there is greater need to determine which customer groups to target and for travel businesses to develop increasingly tailored offerings.

Source: Amadeus, 2013

CONSUMER PROCESSES

If all consumers responded in the same way to given stimuli, the lives of marketing managers would be much easier. Unfortunately, it has to be recognised that, while research continues to shed more light on our complex behaviour, the triggers that lead to it are still poorly understood. We can make some generalisations, however, based on research to date that can assist our understanding of consumer processes and, in particular, those of decision-making. Marketing theorists have developed a number of models to explain these processes. Perhaps the best-known, as well as the simplest, model is known as AIDA (see Figure 3.4).

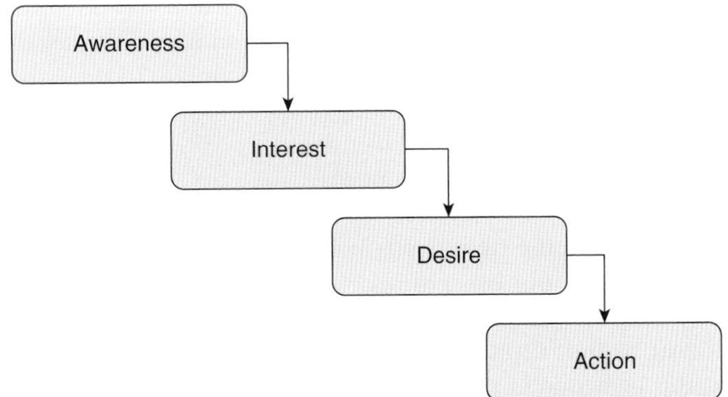

FIGURE 3.4 The AIDA model

The AIDA model recognises that marketing aims to move the consumer from a stage of unawareness – of either the product (such as a specific destination or resort) or the particular brand (such as an individual package tour company or a hotel) – through a number of stages, to a point where the consumer is persuaded to buy a particular product and brand. The first step in this process is to move the consumer from unawareness to awareness. This entails an understanding of the way in which the consumer learns about new products.

Anyone thinking about how they came to learn about a particular destination they have visited quickly recognises how difficult it is to pinpoint all the influences, many of which they may not even be consciously aware of. Every day, consumers are faced with hundreds of new pieces of knowledge, including information about new products. If we are to retain any of this information, the first task of marketing is to ensure that we perceive it; that is, become conscious of it.

Perception is an important part of the learning process. It involves the selection and interpretation of the information that is presented to us. As we cannot possibly absorb all the messages with which we are faced each day, many are consciously or unconsciously 'screened out' from our memories. If we are favourably predisposed towards a particular product or message, there is clearly a greater likelihood that we will absorb information about it. So, for example, if your best friend has just returned from a holiday in the Cayman Islands and has enthusiastically talked to you about the trip, that may stimulate your interest. It may then be more likely that you will spot a feature on the Cayman Islands on television, which may further arouse your interest. If what you see in the television programme reinforces the image of the destination that you gained from your friend, you might be encouraged to seek further information on the destination, perhaps by searching the Web or contacting the tourist office representing the destination. At any point in this process, you might be put off by what you find, for instance if you perceive the destination as being too far away, too expensive or too inaccessible for the length of time you are contemplating going away. If, however, the search process leads you to form a positive image of the destination, you may start mentally comparing it with others towards which you are favourably disposed.

The process of making choices involves constant comparison, weighing up one destination against others, estimating the benefits and the drawbacks of each as a potential holiday destination. As this process goes on, three things are happening, linked to image, attitude and risk.

IMAGE

First, we develop an **image** of the destination in question. Here, it is important to realise that the image may be a totally inaccurate one, if the information sources we use are uninformed or deliberately seek to distort the information they provide. We may then find that we become confused about the image itself. For example, in the early 1990s, the UK media were full of exaggerated reports of muggings of tourists in the Miami area, while the destination itself continued to try to disseminate a positive image and the tour operators' brochures concentrated on selling the positive benefits of Miami, with little reference to any potential dangers faced by tourists.

Images are built around the unique attributes that a destination can claim. The more these help to distinguish it from other similar destinations, the greater the attraction for the tourist. Those destinations that offer truly unique products, such as the Grand Canyon in the USA, the Great Wall of China or the pyramids in Egypt, have an inbuilt advantage, although, in time, the attraction of these destinations may be such that it becomes necessary to 'de-market' the site to avoid it becoming overly popular. In the early 1990s, the Egyptian Tourist Office also faced the problem of negative publicity, associated with attacks made on tourists by Islamic fundamentalists soon after the country experienced a large influx of Western tourists, many of whom failed to conform to the norms of behaviour expected in an Islamic country. A civil uprising in 2011 and further unrest in 2013 and 2014, including terrorist attacks and kidnappings specifically targeting tourists, again affected the image of Egypt as a safe tourist destination. A major objective of tourist offices in developing countries is that of generating a long-term positive image of the destination in their advertising, to give it a competitive edge over its competitors.

EXAMPLE

The influence of YouTube

Historically, tourist boards and tour operators promoted destinations through the use of brochures, advertising in guidebooks and through a variety of PR activities. More recently, the sources used by tourists have shifted to a point where repositories such as YouTube can now hold content liable to influence destination image.

YouTube has expanded from being a site for sharing 'amateur' video to become a gateway allowing organisations to share their promotional videos. Thus, many national and regional tourist boards now have their own YouTube channels to which they upload audio-visual materials.

There has been some effort to move away from traditional promotional films (showing iconic attractions interspersed with images of smiling locals) to create video which is funny, thought-provoking or controversial, and thus more likely to be shared extensively.

Source: Jakopovic, 2015

By contrast with those destinations offering unique attractions, many traditional seaside resorts, both in the UK and increasingly elsewhere, suffer from having very little to distinguish them from their competitors. The concept of the **identikit destination** (explained in Chapter 2) as the popular choice for tourists is becoming outdated, and simply offering good beaches, pleasant hotels and well-cooked food in an attractive climate is no longer enough in itself. In some manner, an image must be developed by the tourist office to distance the resort from others. Then, for example, if changes in exchange rates or inflation rates work against the destination, it may still be seen as having sufficient 'added value' to attract and retain a loyal market.

ATTITUDE

Second, we develop an **attitude** towards the destination. Several theorists suggest that an individual's lifestyle in general can best be measured by looking at their activities (or attitudes), interests and opinions – the so-called **A–I–O model**.

Attitude is a mix of our emotional feelings about the destination and our rational evaluation of its merits, which together will determine whether or not we consider it a possible venue for a holiday. It should be stressed at this point, however, that, while we may have a negative image of the destination, we may still retain a positive attitude towards going there because we have an interest in seeing some of its attractions or learning about its culture. This was often the case with travel to the Communist Bloc countries before the collapse of their political systems at the end of the 1980s, and similarly, notwithstanding the increasing strains in the early twenty-first century on relationships between Western nations and countries with large Islamic populations, interest in their tourist sites and cultures remains high.

RISK

Third, there is the issue of **risk** to consider when planning to take a trip. All holidays involve some element of risk, whether in the form of catching an illness, bad weather, being unable to get what we want if we delay booking, being uncertain about the product until we see it at first hand, or whether it represents value for money. We ask ourselves what risks we would run if we went there, if there is a high likelihood of their occurrence, if they are avoidable and how significant the consequences would be.

Some tourists, of course, relish a degree of risk, as this gives an edge of excitement to the holiday, so the presence of risk is not in itself a barrier to tourism. Others, however, are risk averse and will studiously avoid risk wherever possible. Clearly, the significance of the risk will be a key factor. There will be much less concern about the risk of poor weather than there will be about the risk of crime. The risk averse will book early, may choose to return to the same resort and hotel they have visited in the past, knowing its reliability, and book a package tour rather than travel independently.

Risk is also a factor in the methods chosen by customers to book their holidays. There is evidence that much of the continuing reluctance shown by some tourists to seek information and make bookings through Internet providers can be attributed in part to the lack of face-to-face contact with a trusted and, hopefully, expert travel agent, and in part to the suspicion that information received through the Internet will be biased in favour of the information provider.

Risk and tourist typologies

The extent to which risk is a product of personality is an issue that has been addressed by a number of tourism researchers, most notably Stanley Plog (1974). Essentially, Plog attempted to determine the relationship between introvert and extrovert personalities and holiday choice, and his theories have been widely published in tourism texts (see Figure 3.5).

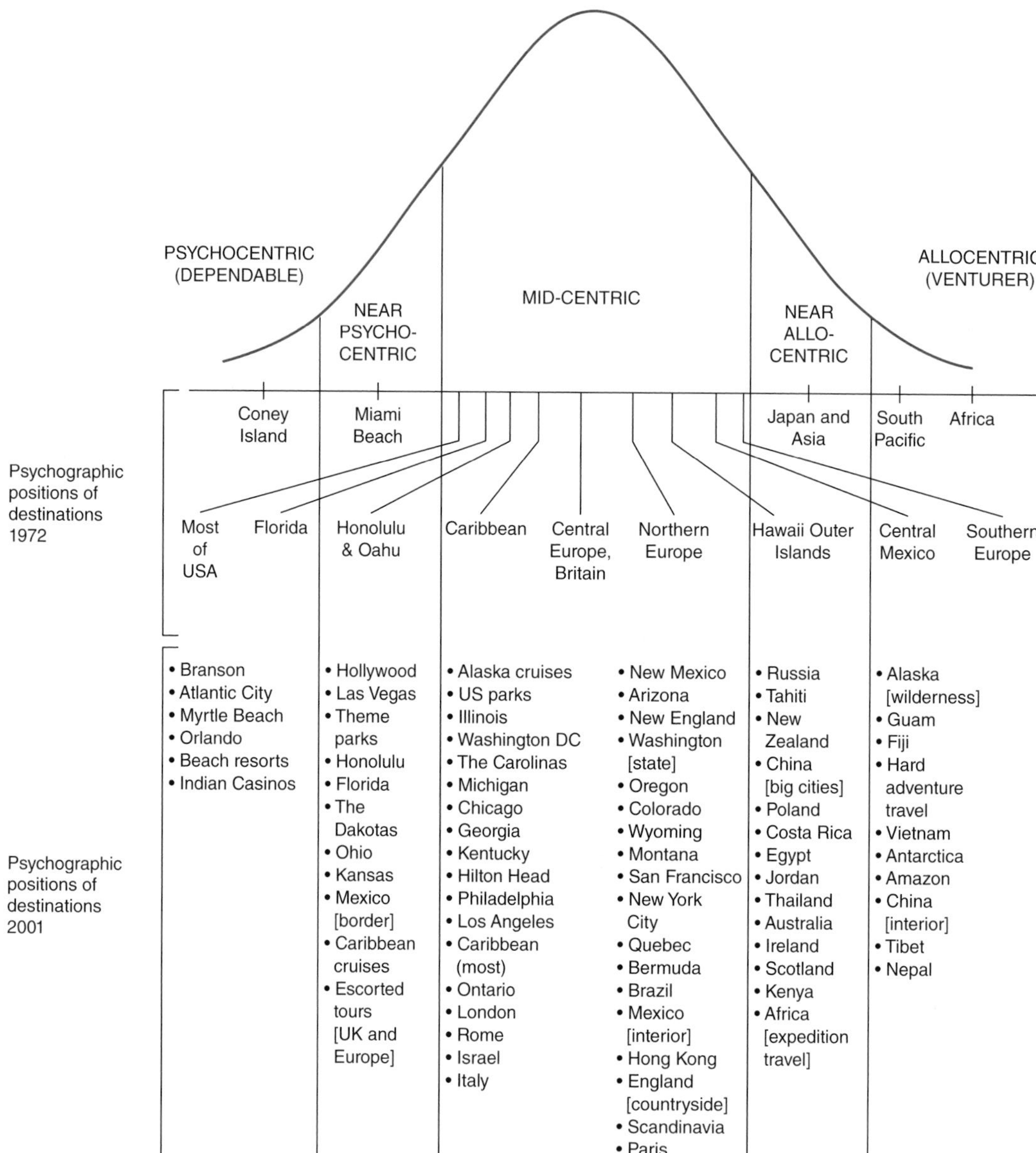

FIGURE 3.5 **Tourist typology and travel destination choice – Plog's allocentric and psychocentric scale**

Source: Plog 1974/2002

Plog's theory attempted to classify the population of the USA by distinguishing between those judged to be **allocentrics** (those seeking variety, self-confident, outgoing and experimental) and those seen as **psychocentrics** (those who tend to be risk averse, thus more inclined to seek security and familiarity). The latter tend to use a package holiday for their travel arrangements. Allocentrics, by contrast, would be disposed to seek new experiences, in more exotic destinations, travelling independently.

Of course, these are polarised examples and, in practice, most holidaymakers are likely to fall somewhere between the extremes – thus, **mid-centrics** make up the largest sector of the market. Furthermore, Plog linked the personality types to destinations most suited to serve their needs. Plog revisited this work in 2001, updating the destinations for each risk sector of the American market.

There has been some criticism of the validity and applicability of this model. Smith's (1990) research questioned whether Plog's findings of American travellers are similarly applicable to European markets. Other researchers noted that travellers may vary in their level of risk, depending on the reason for travel. For instance, a young traveller taking a gap year trip to develop skills and life experience may be prepared to consider more risk than the same traveller taking a short break to alleviate stress after sitting their final exams. Furthermore, financial resources might also influence travel choices.

EXAMPLE

Tourism to the Balearics

Unpublished research conducted during the 1980s found that British tourists visiting the Balearic Islands for the first time were, in many cases, those who had tended to spend their holidays previously in UK domestic resorts. Although by that date Majorca was well established as a popular venue for many British tourists, it was also becoming seen by others as a safe place to enjoy a first holiday abroad. It was observed that the psychocentrics who were holidaying there tended to spend their time at or close to their hotels, venturing further afield only on organised excursions. They also restricted their eating to the hotel restaurant, where they would order only familiar food.

Overcoming initial timidity, these tourists would return, often to the same hotel, for holidays in subsequent years. After two or three such visits, they became bolder, seeking alternative hotels and even hiring cars to tour lesser-known regions of the island (although it took a while for them to adjust to driving on the right). They chose to widen their choice of eating places, too, and began to experiment with their diet by selecting typically Spanish dishes.

Source: Chris Holloway, unpublished research, 1981–83

Plog recognised that personalities change over time and, given time, the psychocentric may become allocentric in their choice of holiday destination and activity as they gain experience of travel. It has long been accepted that many tourists actually seek novelty from a base of security and familiarity. This enables the psychocentric to enjoy more exotic forms of tourism. This can be achieved by, for instance, such tourists travelling through unfamiliar territories by coach in their own 'environmental bubble'. The provision of a familiar background to come home to after touring, such as is offered to Americans at Hilton Hotels or Holiday Inns, is a clear means of reassuring the nervous while in unfamiliar territory.

It is a point worth stressing that extreme psychocentrics (or, indeed, those unable to travel for ill-health reasons) may benefit from the experience of virtual travel. Increasingly sophisticated computers can replicate the experience of travel to exotic locations with none of the risks or difficulties associated with such travel.

MAKING THE DECISION

The process of sorting through the various holidays on offer and determining which is best for you is inevitably complex, and individual personality traits will determine how the eventual decision is made. Some people undertake a process of **extensive problem solving**, in which information is sought about a wide range of products, each of which is evaluated and compared with similar products.

Other consumers will not have the patience to explore a wide variety of choices, so will deliberately restrict their options, with the aim of **satisficing** (a balance between satisfying and sacrificing) rather than trying to guarantee that they buy the best possible product. This is known as **limited problem solving** and has the benefit of saving time.

EXAMPLE

Family holidays: a balancing act

Research by a psychologist at Manchester Metropolitan University revealed that on family holidays one in 14 families end up doing something that *no one* wants to do. With multiple interests and personalities involved in the decision-making process, attempts at family harmony may mean no individual desires are served.

Thus, for family holidays, decision-making can bring difficulties. Sacrificing one's own desires to satisfy others may be necessary. One alternative is to split up. In some cases, this may mean separate holidays, but more commonly it involves engaging in separate activities at the same destination. One benefit is that it can then accommodate different holiday attitudes; for instance, those seeking to relax, sunbathe and read can engage in activities separate from those wanting more cultural or active pursuits.

Source: Wallis Simons, 2014

Many consumers engage in **routinised response behaviour**, in which choices change relatively little over time. This is a common pattern among brand-loyal consumers, for example. Thus, some holidaymakers who have been content with a particular company or destination in the past may opt for the same experience again.

Finally, some consumers will buy on **impulse**. While this is more typical of products costing little, it is by no means unknown among holiday purchasers and is, in fact, a pattern of behaviour that is becoming increasingly prevalent, to the dismay of the operators. Impulse purchasing is a valuable trait, though, where 'distressed stock' needs to be cleared at short notice and can be stimulated by late availability offers in particular.

EXAMPLE

The influence of the digital landscape on the booking process

VisitEngland concluded that there are seven key stages in the holiday booking process:

1. Inspiration
2. Conceptualisation
3. Comparison
4. Price and book
5. Pre-trip defining

6. In-trip
7. Post-trip

At each stage, the digital world is influential. At the outset, social media is now inspiring ideas for trips. Images and comments on Facebook can encourage a trip, although Google remains an important tool in searching for detail to conceptualise the trip characteristics. The comparison process involves the search for deals and discounts (using suppliers such as Groupon). During trips, mobile apps and other travel websites influence decisions on what to see and do, where to eat, how to get around, etc. Finally, when travellers return home, the sharing of images remains an important part of the holiday. Such resources go on to influence the travel decision-making process of others.

Source: VisitEngland, 2012

FASHION AND TASTE

Many tourism enterprises – and, above all, destinations – suffer from the effects of changing consumer tastes as fashion changes and 'opinion leaders' find new activities to pursue and new resorts to champion. It is difficult to define exactly what it is that causes a particular resort to lose its popularity with the public, although clearly, if the resources it offers are allowed to deteriorate, the market will soon drift away to seek better experiences elsewhere.

EXAMPLE

Celebrity destinations

Resorts in the Mediterranean such as St Tropez became fashionable from the 1960s and 1970s onwards after film star Brigitte Bardot chose to reside there. The Costa Smeralda in Sardinia (developed by the Aga Khan) attracted a number of well-known Hollywood stars and thus became popular venues for the star-struck. Similarly, increasing wealth, compounded by the availability of relatively cheap flights, has tended to mean that the celebrity resorts are further afield. In the Caribbean, Barbados (in particular, the Sandy Lane Hotel) attracts many celebrities and others who seek to bask in their light. Travel journalists make a point in their articles of identifying celebrities who have been spotted holidaying at certain resorts, further boosting demand.

Research of 2000 holidaymakers concluded that around 10% of holidaymakers were influenced by celebrity holiday hotspots to the point where they would pay more to head to a destination popular with the rich and famous.

Source: Holiday Hypermarket, 2016

It remains the case, however, that all products, including tourism, will experience a life cycle of growth, maturity, saturation and eventual decline if no action is taken to arrest it. Generally, this will entail some form of innovation or other investment helping to revitalise the product. This change in demand over time was charted by Richard Butler (1980) in his research into the Tourist Area Life Cycle (TALC).

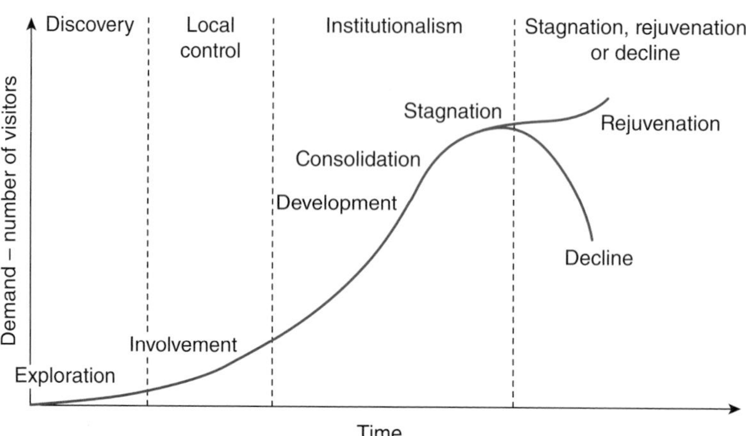

FIGURE 3.6 Tourist Area Life Cycle

THE TOURIST AREA LIFE CYCLE (TALC)

The TALC (sometimes known as the Resort Life Cycle) (Figure 3.6) drew on academic research related to the product life cycle, which recognised that demand changes over time as fashions and new competitors provide greater opportunities for customers to alter their purchase patterns. Butler (1980) created a classic model which visually depicted the changes that occur in demand over time and, while there has since been a range of criticisms regarding its validity, it has been widely used in research to help understand the cycle of destination development.

Each stage of the life cycle reflects different characteristics of demand and supply:

- *Exploration*. At this stage, there are few tourists visiting and interaction with the local population is likely to be high. The visitors who do arrive are likely to be from the 'allocentric' end of the typology scale and are likely to make use of local infrastructure as few dedicated tourist facilities will exist.
- *Involvement*. A small increase in annual visitor numbers will have occurred and, as a consequence, some tourism resources, such as guest houses and restaurants, will have been developed. These are likely to be owned by local entrepreneurs, who will consider some limited promotion of the destination. A tourist season may start to emerge and the local government may be encouraged to provide supporting infrastructure.
- *Development*. A significant number of tourists arrive annually and external organisations (such as global tour operators and international hotel chains) will begin to service the destination. The destination is likely to be attracting the mid-centric tourists.
- *Consolidation*. The number of tourists visiting each year is still growing but now at a slower rate. International chains and franchises are present, which may reduce the power of the local population to control the style and nature of tourism development. Tourists are likely to have limited contact with the local population.
- *Stagnation*. At this stage, visitor numbers are no longer increasing, being maintained by repeat visits from the psychocentric client base. Major efforts in marketing are necessary to maintain demand as the destination may fall out of fashion. Social and environmental problems may be occurring and tourist resources may be rather dilapidated.
- *Decline*. Without new investment, the destination is likely to experience a decline in visitor numbers and tourist facilities may close, unable to maintain economic viability.

- *Rejuvenation (life cycle extension)*. To avoid decline, it is necessary to reinvigorate the destination, often through investment. This may be provided by local government, desiring to maintain jobs and the social wellbeing of the local community. New facilities may be constructed to attract new markets or to encourage existing markets to revisit or stay longer.

There has been some criticism of this model as an effective predictor of development. Critics point out that the 'tourist area' may not be a neatly bounded region, and development (and decline) of resources such as attractions, accommodation and the natural environment may happen at different speeds and times. As facilities age, their fashionableness and perceived quality may also be affected; thus, investment is required continually, not just when nearing the decline phase. It is also important to note that not all sectors can manage the same capacity of visitors – for instance, the capacity of transport arriving at an island may be lower than the potential accommodation provision – so pent-up demand may ensure a longer life cycle than would perhaps otherwise be expected. Finally, it should be noted that demand does not come from one homogeneous market, as business tourism, VFR and leisure tourism all compete for space and use of resources at the destination.

Demand is also influenced by external factors. This may include events such as economic recession or terrorist activity. It may also be influenced by changes in consumer behaviour. Fashion, of course, is one element critical to this process. In recent years, however, there has also been a swing towards improving health and wellbeing, affecting the types of holiday and activities chosen. As a direct consequence, most large hotel chains now incorporate a health centre as an element in their facilities.

FACTORS INFLUENCING CHANGES IN TOURIST DEMAND

It is fitting to complete this chapter by recognising that patterns of demand in tourism are affected by two distinct sets of factors. First, we have factors that cannot be predetermined or forecast but which influence changes, sometimes with very little advance warning. The second set of factors includes cultural, social and technological changes developing in society, many of which can be forecast and for which there is time to adapt tourism products in order to meet new needs and expectations.

In the first category, we must include changes influenced by economic or political circumstances, climate and natural or artificial disasters. Economic influences will be examined more thoroughly in the following chapter, but here it is salutary to look at just some of the factors that have impacted on demand for foreign tourism so severely in recent years.

Undoubtedly, the outbreak of war has been the single greatest threat to foreign travel. Millions of tourists visited the former Yugoslavia every year during the 1980s, but this market virtually disappeared in the 1990s when civil wars broke out. The Vietnam War and its aftermath killed off much tourism to South-East Asia in the 1960s and 1970s. More recently, war in the Middle East curtailed travel there, with long-term significant impact on leisure travel to Iraq. Further upheavals in the Middle East in Tunisia, Libya, Egypt, Syria and Bahrain starting at the end of the first decade of the twenty-first century have substantially discouraged both popular and cultural tourism to the area. Civil war and ethnic strife have similarly inhibited the development of tourism in many African countries.

Recently, it has also been the threat of terrorist attacks, actual or perceived, that has inhibited global travel – both Western fear of travel to Muslim countries and a general fear of travel to cities threatened by Islamic extremism. Terrorism has been a factor with which the tourism industry has had to cope for at least the past 25 years, with some attacks directly targeting tourists and others indirectly influencing either tourism demand or supply.

EXAMPLE

Do terrorist attacks impact tourism demand?

In the immediate aftermath of a terrorist attack, tourism numbers often decline. However, tourists have short memories and often return swiftly. With terrorist attacks affecting cities across Western Europe in recent years (including Paris, 2015; Brussels, 2016; Berlin, 2016; London, 2017; and Manchester, 2017), the region has experienced a downturn in visitor numbers. However, the fall in value of the British pound in 2017, making the UK up to 20% cheaper than previously, led to an increase in visitor numbers despite the attacks. Furthermore, the efficient response of the British emergency services in dealing with the attacks, coupled with a lack of hysterical press reporting, maintained belief in the stability of the region as a tourism destination (Hornall, 2017).

No less serious for global travel has been the threat posed by the rising impact of disease on a worldwide scale. The emergence of more virulent and vaccine-resistant forms of malaria in Africa and Asia has discouraged tourists from visiting infected areas. Countries in Asia suffered the extra blow of a serious outbreak of severe acute respiratory syndrome (SARS) early in 2003, which led to the cancellation of many flights and tourist movements. Indeed, travel to China virtually ceased, apart from its adjacent neighbours, for a period of some six months. During this time, the UK was also severely hit by outbreaks of disease. First, there was the discovery of BSE in UK cattle, which, although with only limited ability to cross the species to humans, scared away many potential visitors. Subsequently, an outbreak of foot and mouth disease, while far less dangerous to human beings, received massive negative publicity in the form of scare stories in the foreign press (to some extent, the result of inept and draconian control measures in the UK that were perceived as actively discouraging tourists from visiting rural areas). The 2009 swine flu pandemic, caused by the H1N1 virus, was believed to have emanated from Mexico and spread by travellers who had visited the region. It created a global concern that deaths would be on the scale of the Spanish Flu epidemic of 1918/19 (which killed more than 50 million people worldwide). While the World Health Organization (WHO) reported 18,000 known deaths from the disease, medical reports have since estimated global deaths from the 2009 H1N1 outbreak in excess of a quarter of a million.

EXAMPLE

An unwanted holiday memento

In 2010, singer and sometime X-Factor judge Cheryl became a high-profile victim of malaria, after contracting the illness while on holiday in Tanzania. Despite taking anti-malaria tablets while travelling, she nevertheless contracted the disease, leading to hospitalisation for several days. It is believed that more than 1700 people return to the UK each year infected, with about 10% of this number dying from the disease (Porter, 2010).

Finally, one must include the issue of climate change, which is contributing to natural disasters affecting tourist destinations globally. Areas already prone to heavy rainfall or hurricanes have witnessed conditions that have been catastrophic for locals and tourists alike, crowned by the disasters of the tsunami in the Far East at the end of 2004 and the impact of Hurricane Katrina on New Orleans and the US Gulf Coast in 2005. The 2011 Japanese earthquake and resulting tsunami impacted on Pacific tourism, and the 2010 volcanic eruptions in Iceland led to the global cancellation of flights in parts of the Northern Hemisphere, with aircraft grounded for weeks, and a resultant huge economic impact on international tourism.

Some low-lying countries, especially islands in the Pacific, are already having to come to terms with the fact that their tourism industries may be doomed by rising sea levels, with the costs of safeguarding their coastlines too great to be practicable. Other developing countries, such as the Maldives, which have invested heavily in tourism in response to the boom in long-haul travel and the demand for active, water-based adventure holidays, face the threats posed by global warming with trepidation.

THE FUTURE PATTERN OF TOURIST DEMAND

Few of these events were predictable in advance. The lesson for the industry has been that, wherever possible, companies must be prepared for rapidly changing circumstances, often at very short notice. They need to build up an organisation and products that are flexible and adaptable so that they can cope with change. The lesson for governments is that the tourism industry is often vital to the economy and the recovery should be supported with public funds if small firms are to remain viable.

In terms of demand for foreign travel, undoubtedly such events compound fears of foreign travel generally, and those most averse to risk-taking – our psychocentrics – are likely to choose to spend their holidays nearer to home or, at the very least, in countries viewed as being safer. Such a trend may even be welcomed by environmentalists, eager to see a fall in the demand for long-haul air travel, but this is to ignore the economic consequences for the destination countries concerned, several of which have no ready alternative means of generating foreign income and investment.

SOCIAL AND LIFESTYLE CHANGES

Social change is easier to predict, as are long-term trends in travel patterns. All too often, however, the industry has been slow to respond to these indicators. We know, for example, that only one family in four in the UK now conforms to the stereotypical pattern of two parents and two children, and increasing numbers of people are living alone or bringing up children as single parents, yet such 'untypical' families are often not welcomed by operators as their pricing structures weigh unfairly against such tourists. Similarly, with increasing life expectancy, the rise in divorce and the fall in marriage rates, there are now more than 7 million single-person households in the UK, yet high additional charges for single tourists in package tours remain the norm and the demand for single accommodation is often difficult to meet.

Other notable changes in society include an increase in the spending power of working women and the earlier maturation of children, leading to a demand for more adult holidays. Children now exert much more influence in the making of travel decisions and are tending to travel more with friends than in the traditional family group.

Perhaps most notable has been the impact of a growing market of senior citizens who are active, have high levels of spending power and are looking for new experiences in their travels. The size and affluence of the senior market may help to sustain some sectors of the industry, in particular the growing demand for cruise holidays.

Such predictions about longevity have suggested that people born today will live longer than earlier (Table 3.4) generations, but it is clear that lifespan is affected by where you live for much of your life. It is also clear that gender is significant, with women living longer than men; in Russia the difference is more than a decade. The UK received more than 5 million seniors (over 55s) in 2009, nearly one-fifth of all visitors and an increase from the one-eighth that this segment contributed in 1993.

TABLE 3.4 Life expectancy at birth (for persons born in 2014)

Country	Life expectancy (years)
Australia	82
Brazil	74
Canada	82
China	76
Denmark	81
France	82
Germany	81
India	68
Ireland	81
Japan	84
Mexico	77
New Zealand	81
Poland	77
Russian Federation	70
Singapore	83
South Africa	57
Spain	83
Sweden	82
Thailand	74
Turkey	75
United Arab Emirates	77
United Kingdom	81
United States	79

Source: United Nations Statistical Division, 2018

Another fast-growing market is the lesbian, gay, bisexual and transgender (LGBT) community, now commonly referred to as the 'pink market'. Members of this group in the UK typically take one domestic and two foreign holidays each year. They earn more – and spend more – than the average traveller. They particularly enjoy travelling to destinations where their sexual orientation is unquestioned, such as Montreal, Bangkok and Sydney. The introduction of laws allowing same-sex marriages in Australia in December 2017 was predicted to bring a $1 million boost to the local economy.

Travellers of all kinds are now both sophisticated and demanding, often being more familiar with world travel destinations and attractions than those selling the products. This produces a new kind of challenge to the industry to provide a professional level of service that it is still a long way from achieving.

There are many other clear social trends in the industry in the opening years of the twenty-first century for which suppliers and agents must learn to cater. Greater choice in consumer purchasing of all kinds is leading to demand for more flexible packages of differing durations. Many will require tailor-made approaches to packaging and companies are establishing divisions specifically for this purpose. This has led to the phenomenon of **dynamic packaging**, where agents and operators put together individual elements of the package, usually by searching websites. This process, however, is labour-intensive and requires extensive product knowledge. This is explained in greater detail in Chapter 19.

Earlier, reference was made to the way in which the mass demand for passive beach holidays has given way to demand for more active holidays of all kinds, even from those in upper age brackets. Special interest holidays now cater for the widening range of hobbies enjoyed by a leisure-orientated society. Adventure holidays, both domestic and foreign, are now packaged by operators to appeal to a range of markets.

In the latter years of the last century, tour operators attempted to gain market share by cutting prices and making budget offers that often fell below the quality levels anticipated by consumers. Selling on price rather than quality became the keynote for the industry. Consumers were encouraged to buy on price and seek out the cheapest. Inevitably, the rising numbers of complaints forced companies to reconsider value for money and quality assurance, although deep discounting remains the bugbear of the industry, for both traditional package tours and the cruise market.

In the format of package tours, we find demand moving in two distinct directions. On the one hand, self-catering has become increasingly popular, partly as a cost-saving exercise but equally as a means of overcoming the constraints imposed by package holidays in general and the accommodation sector in particular. Set meals at set times gave way to 'eat what you please, where you please, when you please'. In reply, the tourism industry provided the product to meet this need: French gîte holidays became popular, and across Southern Europe self-catering villas and apartments flourished, while in the UK demand moved from resort hotels and guest houses to self-catering flats. Hundreds of thousands of Britons invested in timeshare properties in order to own their own 'place in the sun' or increasingly found their own accommodation abroad, while the operators provided 'seat only' packages on charter aircraft to cater for their transport needs.

The other side of the coin is reflected in the growth in demand for all-inclusive holidays. Such packages include accommodation, transport, meals, drinks, snacks and often some activities provided by the local hotel. This particular type of holiday, which allows for careful budgeting in advance for the overall cost of one's holiday, reduces uncertainty and is likely to enjoy growing demand for both short- and long-haul destinations.

The market for short-break holidays of between one and three nights has also expanded rapidly, frequently becoming an addition to the principal holiday. The domestic tourism industry often benefits as many of these breaks are taken within a couple of hours' drive-time of the tourists' home. The choice of short-break destinations abroad has also widened, with the traditional destinations of Paris, Amsterdam, Brussels, Barcelona and Rome being joined by Budapest, Dublin, Prague, Kraców, Reykjavik, Graz, Trieste and New York.

Long-haul traffic has enjoyed a steady rise as disposable incomes have been matched by ever-reducing air fares, especially across the Atlantic. Holidays to the USA have boomed, especially to Florida. Many Britons now own second homes there, not only along the coast but also within easy driving distance of Orlando, where the popular Disney World theme park attracts millions eager to rent self-catering accommodation during their stay.

SECOND-HOME OWNERSHIP

Perhaps the most significant development has been the increase in second-home ownership. Accurate statistics on this trend are difficult to establish, but the most recent government figures for the UK claim that 246,000 people who live in England and Wales had a holiday home abroad in 2011, while 1.6 million residents own second homes within the UK (2.8% of the population). These figures do not include the large number of British citizens who no longer count the UK as their principal place of residence. Some 5.5 million Britons live abroad, contributing to the estimated 232 million people globally who are living in a country different from the one in which they were born. A decision to live abroad does not indicate a willingness to cut off all connections with the mother country, so these changes in country of residence in themselves generate subsequent high levels of tourism mobility in both directions.

Second-home ownership has also been driven by greater media attention. TV programmes such as *A Place in the Sun* and *Wanted Down Under*, both of which help UK residents to find homes in overseas locations, encourage the idea of living abroad, either permanently or as a frequent visitor. So popular has this become that consumer trade shows have been established to further assist those thinking of living abroad.

SUMMARY

All this is not to say that the traditional sun, sea and sand holiday is in terminal decline, but rather that those still loyal to this form of holiday are seeking more activities and cultural visits. Nor are these traditional holidaymakers content merely to seek out the familiar beaches of the Mediterranean; many are now travelling as far afield as Pattaya Beach and Phuket in Thailand and Goa in India to enjoy their beaches in more exotic surroundings.

The traditional 'law of tourism harmony' – every aspect of the tour being of broadly similar standard and quality – has given way to a 'pick and mix' approach, in which savings may be effected in one area in order to indulge oneself in another. Tourists may decide, for example, to choose cheap B&B accommodation while eating out at expensive restaurants; others are booking cheap flights on low-cost airlines and luxury hotels at their destinations, on the grounds that the flight lasts a mere couple of hours, while they intend to stay several days in the hotel, so standards there are more important. By contrast, the term 'Hilton Hippies' has been used to describe those who may want to engage in rough activities such as mountain-biking by day, but look for luxury in their overnight accommodation.

In most developed countries, those in work have been forecast to enjoy increased disposable incomes and a higher propensity to travel abroad. The 2008 global recession affected many tourist-generating countries, and led to a substantial rise in domestic tourism, to the detriment of foreign travel.

Those working in the tourism industry must be familiar with the changing trends and patterns of tourist demand. Some such changes will be generated by tourists themselves, while others will come about as a result of changes taking place in the business environment and in society as a whole. What must be recognised is that the pace of change in the world of tourism is constantly accelerating, requiring entrepreneurs to react faster than they have needed to do in the past. Of equal importance is the requirement for the industry to recognise that protection of the environment and the indigenous populations in the destination countries must also be taken into account. Companies will also have to ensure that any new initiatives do not depart from the obligation to ensure products are sustainable.

QUESTIONS AND DISCUSSION POINTS

1. How can an understanding of the Tourism Area Life Cycle aid long-term decision-making by the manager of a large tourist hotel?
2. Explain the difference between allocentric and psychocentric tourists, as defined by Stanley Plog.
3. Using examples to support your answer, explain the difference between push and pull factors influencing tourism demand.

TASKS

1. Examine the latest copy of the UNWTO Tourism Highlights publication (available online and published annually). For a country of your choice, evaluate the changes in tourist arrival numbers and receipts over the past two decades. Produce a poster or infographic that reports this change in demand and suggest three factors that have influenced this change.
2. Discuss with friends your most recent travel experiences and consider specifically why you took a holiday. To what extent do these reasons match the 11 push factors identified by Ryan (1991), discussed in this chapter? Produce a table that summarises your findings.

FURTHER READING

Cohen, E. (1974) Who is a tourist? A conceptual classification. *Social Research*, 39 (1), 164–82.

Crompton, J. L. (1979) Motivations for pleasure vacation. *Annals of Tourism Research*, 6 (4), 408–24.

Iso-Ahola, S. E. (1982) Toward a social psychological theory of tourism motivation: A rejoinder. *Annals of Tourism Research*, 9, 256–61.

Krippendorf, J. (1984) *The Holiday Makers: Understanding the impact of leisure and travel.* Oxford: Heinemann.

Mansfield, Y. (1992) From motivation to actual travel. *Annals of Tourism Research*, 2, 399–419.

Pearce, P. L. and Lee, U.-I. (2005) Developing the travel career approach to tourist motivation. *Journal of Travel Research*, 43 (3), 226–37.

Ryan, C. (2003) *Recreational Tourism: Demands and impacts*. Clevedon, OH: Channel View Publications.

REFERENCES

Amadeus (2013) *Shaping the Future of Travel in Asia Pacific*. Available online at: www.amadeusapac.com/cmcapac/APACWhitepapers/downloads/Shaping_the_future_of_travel_in_APAC.pdf [Accessed 18 April 2018].

Anderson, S. (2014) *Have You Ever Made a Tactical Holiday Booking?* Available online at: www.sunshine.co.uk/news/have-you-ever-made-a-tactical-holiday-booking-128.html [Accessed January 2019].

Butler, R. (1980) The concept of the tourist area life-cycle of evolution: Implications for management of resources. *Canadian Geographer*, 24 (1), 5–12.

Dann, G. M. S. (1977) Anomie, ego-enhancement and tourism. *Annals of Tourism Research*, 4, 184–94.

Department for Culture, Media and Sport (DCMS) (2013) *Post-Games Evaluation: Meta-evaluation of the impacts and legacy of the London 2012 Olympic Games and Paralympic Games*. London: DCMS.

Driver, C. (2014) Tactical holidays! Majority of Brits time trips abroad to deliberately miss family celebrations and important dates at work. *Daily Mail*, 17 April.

Harrison, E. and Rose, D. (2006) *The European Socio-economic Classification (ESeC) User Guide*. Institute for Social and Economic Research, University of Essex, September. Available at: www.iser.essex.ac.uk/files/esec/guide/docs/UserGuide.pdf [Accessed 7 June 2019].

Holiday Hypermarket (2016) *Do Celebrities Influence Your Holiday Destinations?* Available online at: www.holidayhypermarket.co.uk/hype/celebrity-holidays-cares [Accessed 20 April 2018].

Hornall, T. (2017) Record number of tourists visit UK despite terror attacks in 2017. *The Independent*, 26 December.

Jakopovic, H. (2015) YouTube's role in destination image creation. *Journal of Education, Culture and Society*, 1, 217–26.

Maslow, A. (1987) *Motivation and Personality*. New York: Harper.

McIntosh, R. W., Goeldner, C. R. and Ritchie, J. R. B. (1995) *Tourism: Principles, practices, philosophies*. New York: Wiley.

Plog, Stanley C. (1974) Why destination areas rise and fall in popularity, *Cornell Hotel and Restaurant Administration Quarterly*, 14(4), 55–58.

Plog, Stanley C. (2001) Why Destination areas rise and fall in popularity: An update of a *Cornell Quarterly Classic, The Cornell Hotel and Restaurant Administration Quarterly*, 42(3), 13–24.

Porter, M. (2010) Malaria myths and mistakes; Cheryl Cole is one of the lucky ones – malaria kills half a billion people worldwide every year. *The Times*, 13 July.

Preuss, H. (2005) The economic impact of visitors at major multi-sport events. *European Sport Management Quarterly*, 5 (3), 283–303.

Reid, R. D. and Bojanic, D. C. (2010) *Hospitality Marketing Management*, 5th edn. Hoboken, NJ: Wiley.

Richardson, J. I. and Fluker, M. (2004) *Understanding and Managing Tourism*. French's Forest, NSW: Pearson Hospitality Press.

Ryan, C. (1991) *Recreational Tourism: A social science perspective*. London: Routledge.

Smith, S. L. J. (1990) A test of Plog's allocentric/psychocentric model: Evidence from seven nations. *Journal of Travel Research*, 28 (4), 40–3.

United Nations Statistical Division (UNSD) (2018) *Life Expectancy at Birth*. Available online at: http://data.un.org/Data.aspx?q=life+expectancy&d=PopDiv&f=variableID%3a68 [Accessed 20 April 2018].

United Nations World Tourism Organization (UNWTO) (2017) *Tourism Highlights*. Available online at: www.e-unwto.org/doi/book/10.18111/9789284419029 [Accessed 20 April 2018].

VisitEngland (2012) *The Digital Landscape and the Role of Social Media for the Domestic Visitor*. Available online at: www.visitbritain.org/sites/default/files/vb-corporate/Documents-Library/documents/England-documents/digital_landscape_2012_presentation_-_for_website_tcm30-35206.pdf [Accessed 20 April 2018].

Wallis Simons, J. (2014) On holiday, families are happier when they split up, *The Telegraph*, 25 July.

4

THE ECONOMIC IMPACTS OF TOURISM

CONTENTS

LEARNING OUTCOMES

After studying this chapter, you should be able to:

- identify the economic benefits of tourism for a nation, both nationally and regionally
- be aware of the negative economic effects of tourism for destinations
- understand how tourism is measured statistically
- recognise the limitations of statistical measurement.

> In 2016, travel and tourism directly contributed US$2.3 trillion and 109 million jobs worldwide. Taking its wider indirect and induced impacts into account, the sector contributed US$7.6 trillion to the global economy and supported 292 million jobs in 2016. This was equal to 10.2% of the world's GDP, and approximately 1 in 10 of all jobs. (WTTC, 2017a)

INTRODUCTION

Globally, tourism as an economic activity is important for the many countries that seek to obtain a share of this estimated $8.3 trillion industry (World Travel and Tourism Council (WTTC), 2017a). While it can create jobs, bringing wealth and economic benefits, there are also consequences for those nations and their regions. Therefore, it is important to understand the economic impacts of tourism.

This is a complex topic that can only be touched on in this text. Those who wish to examine the subject in depth are referred to texts designed for this purpose, such as Bull (1995), Hall and Lew (2009) and Vanhove (2011). The aim of this chapter, therefore, is primarily to explore the economic impacts of tourism resulting from national and international tourist flows and the ways in which this is measured. In later chapters, the economics of the firm, the industry and its various sectors will be examined. First, however, we will look at the movement of tourists internationally and some of the economic factors influencing those flows.

THE INTERNATIONAL TOURIST MARKET

Tourism is probably the single most important industry in the world. As the quote at the beginning of the chapter highlights, the global tourism industry (considering international and domestic travel) accounts for 10.2% of global gross domestic product (GDP) and 266 million jobs, representing one in every ten of the world's total jobs (WTTC, 2017a).

According to the most recent estimate by the United Nations World Tourism Organization (UNWTO), 1235 million international trips were taken in 2016. Notwithstanding the occasional dip, tourism numbers have grown virtually uninterrupted from 25 million in 1950 and the UNWTO forecasts for this to reach 1800 million (1.8 billion) by 2030. Worldwide tourism receipts for 2013 were US$1220 billion (see Table 4.1).

TABLE 4.1 International tourist arrivals and receipts, 1950–2016

Year	Arrivals (million)	Receipts (US$ billion)
1950	25	2
1960	69	7
1970	166	18
1980	278	107
1990	434	262
1995	528	403
2000	677	476
2005	807	681

Year	Arrivals (million)	Receipts (US$ billion)
2010	948	931
2015	1189	1196
2016	1235	1220

Source: UNWTO, 2017

The rapid increase in international travel during the early post-war years, exceeding 10% per annum from 1950 to 1960, could not be permanently sustained, of course, as it reflected the pent-up demand that had built up in the war years and the slow economic recovery after the war. It is worth noting, however, that, apart from the odd hiccup, from 1970 to the 1990s, annual growth ran above 4%. Although 2009 saw a decline in international travel, average annual growth since 2005 has been 3.9% (UNWTO, 2017). The good news for the tourism industry, therefore, is that, despite the occasional fall, the long-term trend is forecast to be an upward one.

DOMESTIC TOURISM

The data above relates to international travel and the figures do not include the vast number of people taking trips within their own countries. For many countries, the number of domestic trips far exceeds the level of arrivals from international tourists (see Table 4.2). It is important to recognise, however, that the spending of international tourists may be higher than that of domestic tourists.

TABLE 4.2 A comparison of domestic trips with international tourist arrivals (2016)

Country	Domestic trips (000s) (Euromonitor)	International arrivals (000s) (UNWTO)	Ratio of domestic trips to international arrivals
Argentina	28,297	5559	5.1
Australia	94,338	8263	11.4
Austria	13,982	28,121	0.5
Bulgaria	14,743	8252	1.8
Canada	120,045	19,971	6.0
China	3,762,992	59,270	63.5
Croatia	6558	13,809	0.5
Czech Republic	31,266	12,090	2.6
France	191,908	82,600	2.3
Germany	224,988	35,579	6.3
Greece	14,969	24,799	0.6
Hungary	11,097	15,252	0.7
India	1,653,000	14,569	113.5

(Continued)

TABLE 4.2 (Continued)

Country	Domestic trips (000s) (Euromonitor)	International arrivals (000s) (UNWTO)	Ratio of domestic trips to international arrivals
Italy	48,600	52,372	0.9
Japan	301,670	24,039	12.5
Mexico	226,305	34,961	6.5
Morocco	9093	10,332	0.9
Portugal	18,107	11,423	1.6
Russia	159,340	24,551	6.5
Saudi Arabia	35,726	18,049	2.0
South Africa	45,135	10,044	4.5
Spain	150,299	75,563	2.0
United Arab Emirates	6334	14,910	0.4
United Kingdom	125,199	35,814	3.5
USA	1,091,770	75,608	14.4

Source: based on Euromonitor, 2017 and UNWTO, 2017

TRENDS IN INTERNATIONAL TRAVEL

As controls over the freedom of movement of populations in many countries are lifted, many are seeking the opportunity to travel outside their own borders for the first time, not least residents of China, now the biggest generator of overseas tourist expenditure. Due to increased disposable income and fewer travel restrictions, tourism from this nation alone has increased tenfold since 2000. The UNWTO takes an optimistic view of the long term, with an estimate of 1.8 billion international tourism trips by 2030 (UNWTO, 2018), although the mature regions of Europe and the Americas are expected to experience slower growth than those of Asia, the Middle East and Africa.

International tourism is currently generated, for the most part, within the nations of Europe, North America and China, the result of low prices, frequent flights and large, relatively wealthy populations (see Table 4.3). It is interesting to note that the top ten generating countries are responsible for almost half the total expenditure on foreign travel, while expenditure by the top three countries accounts for well over a quarter of all tourism spending globally.

TABLE 4.3 Leading tourism-generating countries, 2016 (based on provisional tourism expenditure)

Position	Country	Expenditure (US$ billion)
1	China	261.1
2	United States of America	123.6
3	Germany	79.8
4	United Kingdom	63.6
5	France	40.5

Position	Country	Expenditure (US$ billion)
6	Canada	29.1
7	South Korea	26.6
8	Italy	25.0
9	Australia	24.9
10	Hong Kong (China)	24.2

Source: UNWTO, 2017

As the Chinese gain greater freedom of movement, leisure travel has become an aspiration for many urban professionals with the financial means to participate. Although China is a significant tourism-generating country in terms of expenditure, many of the international journeys made are regional. The two special administrative regions of Hong Kong and Macau remain primary destinations, while South Korea, Taiwan, Thailand and Singapore are also popular with this market.

A significant change in recent years has been the decline of the Russian Federation as a source market, whose spend, in spite of its large population, now leaves it as only the eleventh largest globally. The country has been affected by political disputes and trade sanctions that have affected disposable income for many Russians.

Looking at the flow of international tourism over the long term, one can conclude that the tourism business is surprisingly resilient. Whatever short-term problems emerge – acts of terrorism, medical emergencies such as the swine flu pandemic in 2009, the 2004 Asian tsunami, flooding in places such as New Orleans following Hurricane Katrina in 2005 and Thailand in 2011, Iceland's volcano eruption and subsequent ash cloud in 2010, and the earthquakes in Christchurch, New Zealand and Japan in 2011 – tourists eventually return in ever greater numbers.

TOURIST DESTINATIONS

While Western and Southern Europe continue to dominate, the past few years have seen significant growth in arrivals (above 6% between 2005 and 2016) in the Asia-Pacific region (UNWTO, 2017). Simply looking at arrivals, though, will not give a sound picture of the value of tourism to an economy. It is important to consider how much tourists spend – the total receipts (see Table 4.4).

TABLE 4.4 Leading tourism-receiving countries (2017), based on international tourist arrivals in millions and their tourism receipts (US$ billions)

Position (based on arrivals)	Country	Arrivals (millions)	Receipts (US$ billion)	Receipt per arrival (US$)
1	France	86.9	60.7	698.50
2	Spain	81.8	68	831.30
3	United States of America	76.9	210.7	2739.92
4	China	60.7	32.6	537.07
5	Italy	58.3	44.2	758.15

(Continued)

TABLE 4.4 (Continued)

Position (based on arrivals)	Country	Arrivals (millions)	Receipts (US$ billion)	Receipt per arrival (US$)
6	Mexico	39.3	21.3	541.98
7	United Kingdom	37.7	51.2	1358.09
8	Turkey	37.6	22.5	598.40
9	Germany	37.5	39.8	1061.33
10	Thailand	35.4	57.5	1624.29

Source: UNWTO, 2018

In economic terms, the financial value of tourism to a country may be more important than the number of tourists it receives. As can be seen in Table 4.4, the USA earns far more in receipts than France, despite receiving 10 million fewer visitors annually. The average spend of tourists may be influenced by the length of time tourists stay in a country and their average daily spend.

PROPENSITY TO TRAVEL

It is also important to take account of factors likely to lead to the growth or decline of tourism from each country. Residents of countries where GDP is high are perhaps more likely to be able to afford to take holidays, often international, each year. The BRIC countries (Brazil, Russia, India and China) are experiencing a rise in the middle-income classes (although this has slowed somewhat in Russia in recent years), with a correlation between affluence and international and domestic travel patterns. As we have seen in Table 4.3, China is dominating and, with a population of more than 1 billion, a small percentage increase in outbound travel can lead to millions of additional trips.

In spite of the high revenues generated from Americans travelling abroad, only 40% of the population actually possess a passport. However, this is a level that has rapidly increased in recent years (from around 10% in 1994), due to stricter controls that now require American tourists travelling to Mexico or Canada to have a passport. Furthermore, the size and diversity of their own landscape means many Americans are content to take holidays within their own country.

The propensity to take foreign holidays varies considerably within Europe, too. It is high among the Scandinavians, no doubt due in part to the long winters and lack of sunshine, while only four in ten Italians undertake foreign travel. Although Britons have a reputation for travelling abroad, about one-third of the population take no international holidays at all during the year.

It should also be recognised that, while tourism expenditure in aggregate will be highest for wealthy countries having large populations, the high levels of disposable income among the populations of smaller nations with a significant proportion of wealthy residents, such as Switzerland or Luxembourg, will tend to lead to higher levels of participation in international tourism. Where international borders are close to places of residence, as is the case with Switzerland and Luxembourg, this will also significantly increase the propensity to travel abroad.

To help understand the travel habits of particular nations, it is possible to calculate the **travel propensity**, that is, the percentage of the population taking trips.

This can be considered in two dimensions: the **net travel propensity** and the **gross travel propensity**.

Net travel propensity reflects the percentage of the population who have travelled for at least one trip (though many will have taken more). As some of the population will not have taken a trip at all, the net travel propensity will be less than 100%. The Finnish travel market has a net travel propensity of over 90%, although the levels for most countries are likely to be much lower than this (Table 4.5).

TABLE 4.5 Net travel propensity of selected European countries (2016)

Country	Percentage of population participating in tourism (1 night or more)
Romania	24.0
Portugal	25.6
Greece	35.6
Italy	41.9
Hungary	55.2
Poland	56.8
Lithuania	57.3
Malta	59.7
United Kingdom	64.1
Spain	65.7
Slovakia	66.1
France	73.1
Ireland	74.2
Germany	75.4
Austria	76.8
Sweden	78.8
Denmark	79.8
Czech Republic	80.8
Luxembourg	80.9
The Netherlands	85.3
Switzerland	89.8
Finland	91.5

Source: Eurostat, 2017

Gross travel propensity reflects the total number of trips taken in relation to the total population. In areas such as Western Europe, where the local population may take several trips, the gross travel propensity may exceed 100% (as those who have been on multiple trips counterbalance those who have not travelled at all).

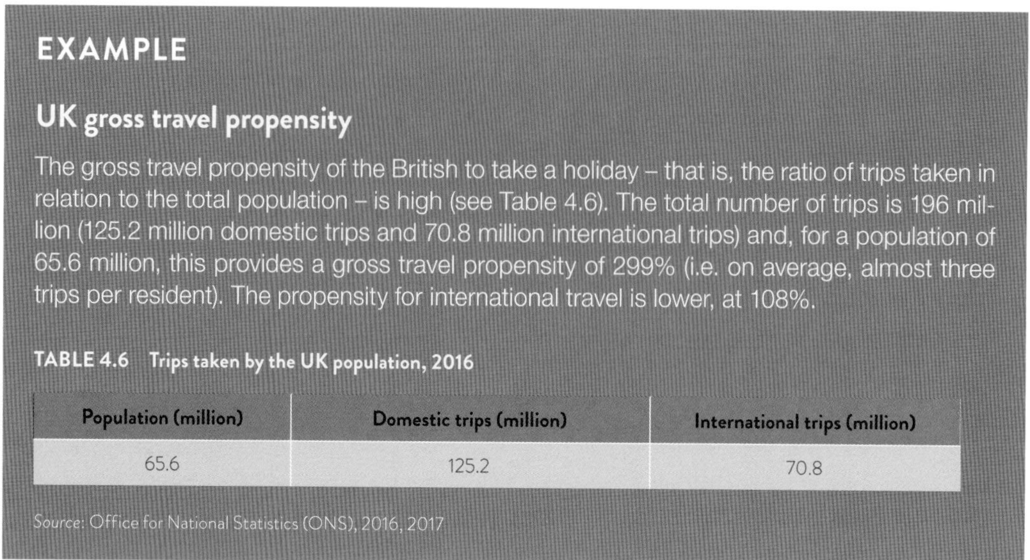

EXAMPLE

UK gross travel propensity

The gross travel propensity of the British to take a holiday – that is, the ratio of trips taken in relation to the total population – is high (see Table 4.6). The total number of trips is 196 million (125.2 million domestic trips and 70.8 million international trips) and, for a population of 65.6 million, this provides a gross travel propensity of 299% (i.e. on average, almost three trips per resident). The propensity for international travel is lower, at 108%.

TABLE 4.6 Trips taken by the UK population, 2016

Population (million)	Domestic trips (million)	International trips (million)
65.6	125.2	70.8

Source: Office for National Statistics (ONS), 2016, 2017

OTHER FACTORS AFFECTING THE ECONOMIC VALUE OF TOURISM

While there are many factors that motivate people to travel abroad, a major one is likely to be the relative cost compared with their income. Since greater demand levels can lead to lower prices, with transport and accommodation costs falling for each additional person booked, there is a direct relationship between cost, price and demand (see Figure 4.1). This helps to explain the vicious price wars in the travel industry, designed to capture market share and increase numbers, which have been so much a feature of competition in the travel industry over the past 40 years.

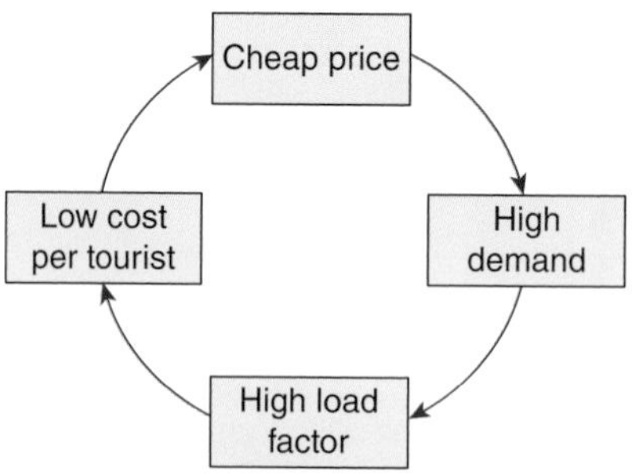

FIGURE 4.1 Relationship between cost, price and demand

One factor to take into account is attitudes to the use of leisure time. In the USA, some 30% of the workforce take less than half the holiday time to which they are entitled, and this is in a country where the average paid holiday is still only two to three weeks, compared with the four to five weeks now standard throughout Europe. The Japanese seldom take their full entitlement. Despite an entitlement of around 30 days (once public holidays are added to work holidays), they typically take just over half of this.

THE VALUE OF ECONOMIC DATA

Gathering data on tourists is a vital task for governments, generating vital information for their own national tourist offices and the providers of tourism services. Governments need to know the contribution that tourism makes to the economy in terms of income, employment, investment and the balance of payments. Concern about regional development requires that these statistics be sufficiently refined to allow them to be broken down by region. Governments will also wish to compare their tourism performance with those of other countries, as well as to establish how well they are doing in attracting tourists to the country over a period of time.

Tourism organisations, whether in the public or the private sector, need such data to enable them to forecast what will happen in the future. This means identifying trends in the market, patterns of growth and changing demand for destinations, facilities or types of holiday.

On the basis of this knowledge, future planning can be undertaken. The public sector will make recommendations and decisions regarding the **infrastructure** and **superstructure** needed to support growth. Infrastructure will include, for example, the building of new airports and seaport terminals or the expansion of existing ones, the provision of new or improved roads to growing destinations and the improvement of other services, such as public utilities, including water and electricity, which will be needed to cope with the expected expansion of tourism. Some of these plans may take many years to implement. For example, the discussions surrounding the building of a fifth terminal at London's Heathrow Airport took place over more than a decade, far longer than the time taken to actually construct the terminal itself.

Superstructure comprises the tourist amenities needed: hotels, restaurants, shops and other services that tourists take for granted when they visit. It cannot necessarily be assumed that these services will be provided by developers in the private sector. If a new destination is being developed, there will be a degree of risk involved while the destination becomes established, so developers may be reluctant to invest in projects such as hotels until there is proven demand at the destination. Governments or local authorities can themselves undertake the construction of hotels, as often occurs in developing countries, or they can encourage hotel construction by underwriting costs or providing subsidies of some kind until the destination becomes established. Similarly, private companies can use the statistics that demonstrate growth or market change, extending or adapting their products to meet the changing needs of the marketplace.

To show how this information can be used, let us take the example of a destination such as London, which attracts a high volume of overseas visitors. The flow of those visitors will be affected by a great many different factors. For example, if tourists can purchase more pounds sterling for their own currency, or air fares to the destination have fallen, or a major event, such as the Olympics, is being hosted, all these factors will encourage tourists to visit the city.

EXAMPLE

The influence of exchange rates

Recessions may hit countries to different extents, so that, in one year, the forecast might be for a reduced number of tourists from the USA, but a growth in the number from Japan.

In the third quarter of 2000, the pound fell sharply against the dollar, while remaining relatively strong against European currencies. This encouraged Americans to travel to the

(Continued)

UK and the British to visit the Continent, while tourists from countries such as Germany and France were dissuaded from coming to the UK and, similarly, fewer Britons visited the USA. In 2004–05, however, the dollar weakened against both sterling and the euro, increasing travel from the UK and the Continent to the USA. In 2007/08, the dollar again weakened against the pound (at times reaching a rate of US$2 for £1). However, 2008 also saw sterling weaken by about 20% against the euro, making Europe a more expensive proposition for UK travellers, and, by the autumn of that year, against a background of threatening recession, sterling weakened against both the dollar and the euro. In 2016, following the Brexit vote, sterling immediately dropped from around €1.30 to €1.13 and similarly lost 20 cents against the dollar. This made the UK cheaper relative to many other countries, resulting in a record number of international tourists visiting Britain in 2017.

This uncertainty about currency movements makes forward planning difficult, adding another element of risk to product pricing, although this can be offset to some extent by the forward purchasing of foreign currencies (in financial terms, this is termed hedging). The tour operator TUI uses currency hedging to reduce the risk for its international operations. Currency hedges are entered into because brochure prices are largely fixed and payment for holiday elements, for example accommodation and ground transfers, are made in a different currency some time during the upcoming tourist season. In the case of TUI, more than 20 currencies are hedged, the largest volumes being in US dollars, euros and sterling.

Negative factors also have an effect. Terrorist activity, wars, medical pandemics or political unrest can all influence travel plans. Negative first impressions, such as air pollution in the city, extensive littering, a decaying and overcrowded public transport system, even large numbers of homeless people on the streets, can all affect tourism adversely, with tourists deciding to go elsewhere or recommending to their friends that they do so.

Companies and tourist offices will have to take all of these factors into account when drawing up their promotional campaigns, possibly needing to consider employing staff with the appropriate language skills to deal with any new, incoming markets. On the basis of the forecasts made, organisations must decide where they will advertise, to whom and with what theme.

International tourism obviously depends on much more than just the tourists' economic behaviour, however. As we noted in the previous chapter, it is also influenced by motivators arising from their efforts to meet psychological or sociological needs.

THE ECONOMIC IMPACTS OF TOURISM

As with other industries, tourism affects the economy of those areas, whether regions, countries or continents, where it takes place. These are known as tourist **destinations**, or **receiving areas**, and many become dependent on an inflow of tourism to sustain their economy. This is especially true of developing countries, some of which are highly dependent on tourism.

The areas from which tourists come to visit these destinations are known as **generating areas** (Figure 1.2 in Chapter 1 summarises this). Of course, as tourists are taking their money with them to spend in other places, this represents a net loss of revenue for the generating area and a gain for the receiving area. We can say that incoming tourist spend is an **export**, while outgoing tourist spend is an **import** (as the tourist is buying services from overseas).

EXAMPLE

Tourism exports and imports

Priscilla is an American tourist who travels from New York to Sydney. While there, she spends money on accommodation, food and attending a concert at the Opera House. Her total spend is AUS$400.

Therefore, this American tourist has bought in these services from Australia, counting as an IMPORT on the US balance of payments. The Australian economy has benefited from selling these services to this foreign tourist and thus the transaction is considered an EXPORT on the Australian balance of payments (Figure 4.2).

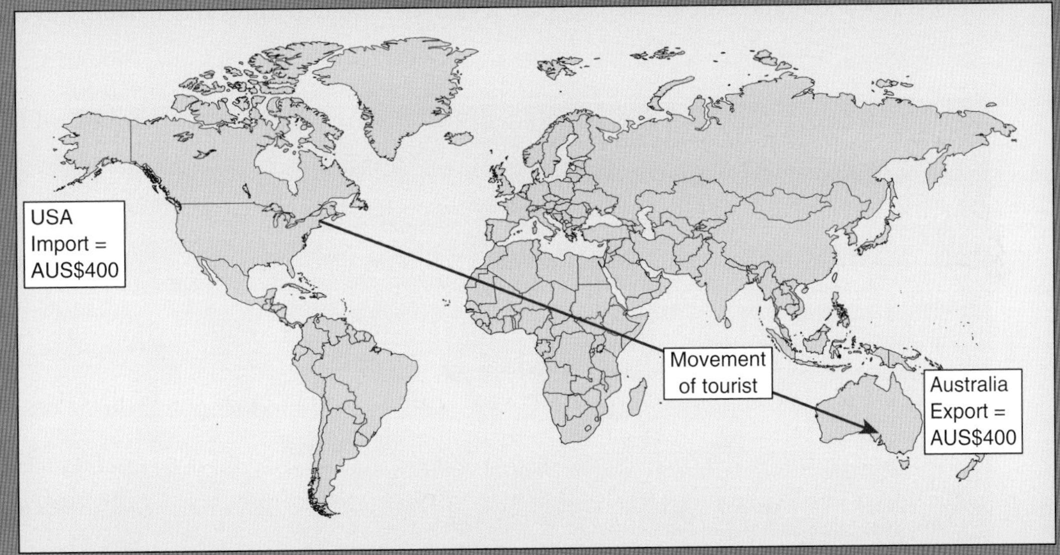

FIGURE 4.2 An American tourist in Australia

The flow of tourists between generating and receiving areas can be measured in four distinct ways. We must examine the effect on **income, employment**, the area's **balance of payments** and **investment and development**. Let us look at each of these in turn.

INCOME

Income is earned from selling goods and services to tourists. While some of this income will pay interest and rent, in a labour-intensive industry such as tourism, the greatest proportion of this earned income is likely to be spent on paying wages and salaries for those working in jobs either directly serving the needs of tourists or benefiting indirectly from the tourists' expenditure. Income is likely to be greater in those areas that generate large numbers of tourists, where visitors tend to stay for longer periods, where the destination attracts an upmarket or more free-spending clientele and where there are many opportunities to spend.

It is essential to recognise that 'tourism is one of the major export sectors of poor countries and the leading source of foreign exchange in 46 of the 49 least developed countries' (Bolwell and Weinz, 2008: 1). Of course, it is also a major income generator in the Western world. In the UK, to take one example, tourism is of prime importance in areas where there is little manufacturing industry, such as in the Scottish Highlands, western Wales and Cornwall. While tourism jobs are often seen as low-paid and seasonal, many are neither seasonal nor temporary. As to low-paid jobs, one must take into account that, without tourism, many workers would have no source of income at all.

Income is also generated from interest, rent and the profits of tourism businesses. These could include, for example, the interest paid on loans to an airline in order to buy aircraft or rent paid to a landowner for a car park or campsite near the sea. We must also count taxation on tourism activities, such as sales tax (for example, value-added tax (VAT) in the UK), room taxes on hotel bills, duty and taxation on petrol used by tourists, and other direct forms of taxation that countries may choose to levy on tourists to raise additional public income. Austria, Belgium, Hungary, the Netherlands and Spain all impose some form of tourist tax. Equally, most countries levy a departure tax on all passengers travelling by air, while in the USA airline taxes are levied on both departing and arriving travellers.

EXAMPLE

Tourist taxes

In 2016, a new tourist tax was introduced by Spain's Balearic islands of Mallorca, Menorca and Ibiza, designed to help fund preservation of the natural heritage and ecosystem. Collected via accommodation providers and ranging from €1 to €2 per person per night, depending on accommodation rating, this is one of many taxes now being introduced by holiday destinations to collect income from visitors. Malta introduced a tax (€0.40 per night with a €5 cap) in 2016, while across Europe many cities charge tax on accommodation. Some examples are as follows:

- Amsterdam – 5% of room rate
- Antwerp – €2.39 pppn
- Barcelona – €1.25 pppn (4* hotel)
- Berlin – 5% of room rate
- Venice – €2.40–€4.00 pppn depending on season (4* hotel).

(pppn = per person per night)

The sum of all incomes in a country is called the **national income** and the importance of tourism to a country's economy can be measured by looking at the proportion of national income that is created by tourism. Some regions of the world, particularly island states, are heavily dependent on the income from tourism (see Table 4.7). Some might see this as an unhealthy overdependence on one, rather volatile, industry.

TABLE 4.7 Total contribution of travel and tourism to GDP, 2018

Country	%	Country	%
Aruba	98.3	Moldova	3.2
Macau	72.2	Uzbekistan	3.4

Country	%	Country	%
Seychelles	67.1	Poland	4.5
Maldives	66.4	Russian Federation	4.8
St Kitts and Nevis	62.4	The Netherlands	5.0
Grenada	56.6	Ireland	6.2
Cape Verde	46.2	United States	7.8
St Lucia	41.8	Germany	8.6
Fiji	38.9	Australia	10.8
Barbados	34.9	UK	11.0

Source: WTTC, 2019

Attempts at measuring the impact of tourism are always difficult because it is not easy to distinguish spend by tourists from spend by others, in restaurants or shops for example. In resorts, even such businesses as laundromats (which we would not normally associate with the tourism industry) might be highly dependent on tourist spend where, for instance, a large number of visitors are camping, caravanning or in self-catering facilities.

Tourism's contribution to the income of an area is also enhanced by a phenomenon known as the **tourism income multiplier**. This arises because money spent by tourists in the area will be re-spent by recipients, augmenting the total.

Tourism multiplier

The multiplier is the factor by which tourist spend is increased in this process of re-spending. This is easiest to demonstrate by way of the following fictitious example.

EXAMPLE

The tourism income multiplier

A number of tourists visit Green Paradise Island, spending £1000 in hotels and other facilities there. This amount is received as income by the hoteliers and owners of the facilities, who, after paying their taxes and saving some of the income, spend the rest. Some of what they spend goes on buying items imported into the area, but the rest goes to shopkeepers, suppliers and other producers inside the area. These people, in turn, pay their taxes, save some money and spend the rest.

From the £1000 of tourist spend, let us assume that the average rate of taxation is 20% and that people are saving, on average, 10% of their gross income, so are left to spend 70% on goods and services (for this example, this would be £700). Let us further assume that, of this £700, the tourist has spent £200 on goods and services imported from other areas, while the remaining £500 is spent on locally produced goods and services, which is money that is retained within the local community. The original £1000 spent by the tourists will then circulate in the local community, as shown in Figure 4.3, in the category 'First circulation'.

(Continued)

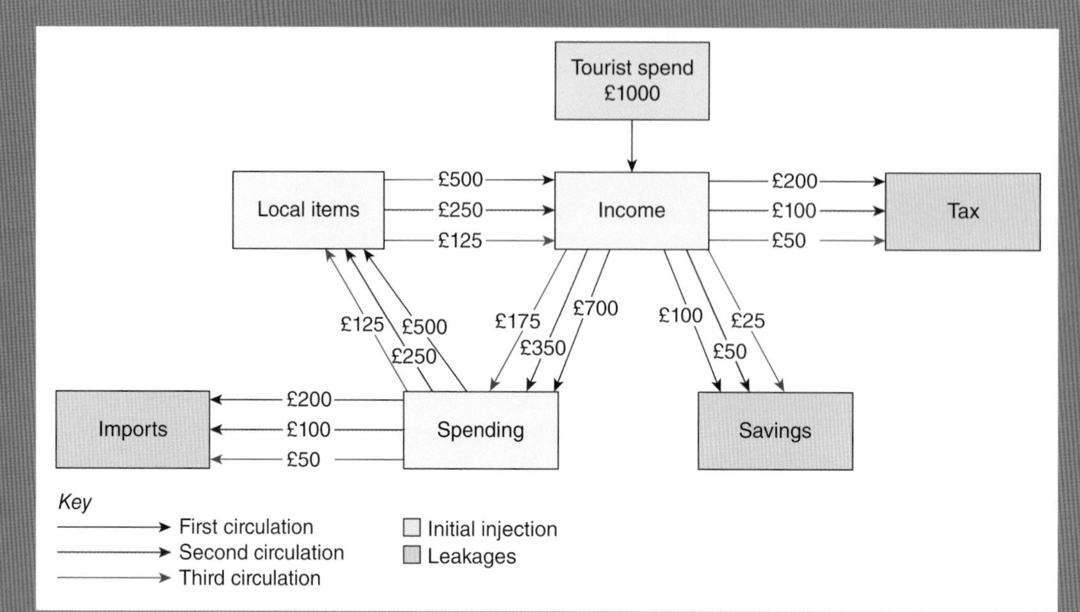

FIGURE 4.3 The multiplier effect of the circulation of income

Of the £500 spent within the community, some will go to tourism businesses, which, in turn, will make payments to their local suppliers for such items as food. The shopkeepers or restaurateurs then pay their employees, who, in turn, shop in other shops locally, although some of what they purchase will have been brought into the region from outside.

This second circulation highlights the further spend by the recipients, including taxation (again at 20%), savings (10%) and leakages due to the purchase of imports.

Once again, the income received by employees and local businesses will circulate through the economy (third circulation) and so the cycle goes on, with a declining level of expenditure at each level of circulation.

The money spent directly by tourists is considered to be the **direct income** received by a destination. This spend goes to tourism businesses, which provide tourists with the goods and services they require for their holiday (for example, accommodation, meals, guided tours). These tourism businesses will then spend some of this earned income obtaining goods and services from their suppliers, which allows them to fulfil their obligations to the tourists. For example, a tourism business providing guided tours may have to pay entry fees to an attraction or the salary for a guide. This secondary spend of income is termed **indirect income**. At this stage, some spend, such as residents spending their pay on food in a local supermarket or a visit to the cinema, may occur. Such spend is known as **induced income**, possible as a result of direct or indirect tourist expenditure.

EXAMPLE

The effect of leakages on the tourism income multiplier

Each time the money is circulated in this way, some will be lost to the area. For example, taxes paid are transmitted outside the area; some savings, similarly, may be removed from the area; and some of the spend has gone on paying for goods imported into the area from other regions of the country or even from abroad.

Expenditures that mean money is lost to other areas are known as leakages from the system. Leakages in this sense can therefore be regional or national, the latter being a loss of revenue to the country as a whole.

So far, how much income has been created? From Figure 4.3, we can calculate this by considering the money entering the field marked 'income'; it is £1000 + £500 + £250 + £125 + ... A progression is developing and, by adding up all the figures (until the circulations become so small that the additional income is negligible) or by using the appropriate mathematical formula, we will find that the total sum is £2000. The original injection of £1000 by tourists visiting the area has multiplied by a factor of 2 to produce an income of £2000.

It is possible to forecast the value of the multiplier if one knows the proportion of leakages in the local economy. The formula for this is:

$$\text{multiplier} = \frac{1}{\text{proportion of leakages}}$$

In the example provided in Figure 4.3, tax was 20/100ths of the original income, savings were 10/100ths of income and imports were 20/100ths of income. Total leakages, therefore, amounted to 50/100ths, or half (0.5) of the original income. The multiplier can be found by applying the formula:

$$\text{multiplier} = \frac{1}{0.5\ \text{(half of original income)}} = 2.0$$

The portion of leakage is 0.5 so the multiplier is 2. Hence, the initial tourist spend of £1000 has led to an increase in income of £2000.

Leakages

So, in an economy with a high proportion of leakages caused by factors such as high tax rates (although we must remember that the government may choose to reinvest this tax money in the local economy, so much of it may not be lost for all time), or where many of the goods demanded by consumers are imported, the tourism income multiplier may be quite low and then the economy will not benefit greatly from tourism. Local hotels may also be foreign-owned, so profits achieved are then transmitted to the hotel chain's head office and lost to the area. This might be true of other tourist facilities in the area, and even local ground-handling agents or coach operators may be owned by companies based elsewhere, leading to further losses in the multiplier effect.

If, alternatively, many firms are in the hands of locals and leakages of these kinds are minimised, the multiplier effect may be quite high and then tourism will contribute far more than the amount originally spent by the tourists themselves.

The principal reasons for leakages include:

- cost of imported goods, especially food and drink
- foreign exchange costs of imports for the development of tourist facilities

- remittance of profits abroad
- remittance of pay to expatriates
- management fees or royalties for franchises
- payments to overseas carriers and travel companies
- costs of overseas promotion
- additional expenditure on imports resulting from the earnings of those benefiting from tourism.

EXAMPLE

Tourism income multipliers

Many studies have investigated the tourism income multiplier in different areas, ranging from individual resorts to entire countries. In most cases, the multiplier has varied between 1 and 2.5, although, in the case of some destinations in the developing world that depend heavily on outside investment and must import much of the food and other commodities demanded by tourists, the figure may be well below 1.

Calculating income multipliers for nations is challenging but the development of Tourism Satellite Accounts (discussed later in this chapter) is helping to gather the necessary data. The WTTC has gone some way to creating benchmarks for this by using input–output data to estimate the effect on GDP of $1 million of spending. The WTTC has also estimated leakages caused by the imports required to service the local travel and tourism industry. While there are some limitations to these approaches, it does allow for national comparisons to be made (Table 4.8).

TABLE 4.8 Effect on GDP of spending and import leakages, 2017

Country	Multiplier effect of spending on GDP	Percentage of leakage through imports
Australia	1.5	12%
China	1.4	8%
France	1.3	12%
India	1.3	10%
Indonesia	1.7	12%
Mexico	1.5	7%
Russian Federation	1.5	9%
South Korea	1.1	18%
United Arab Emirates	1.2	8%
United Kingdom	1.3	15%
United States of America	1.6	6%

Source: WTTC, 2017a

EMPLOYMENT

The WTTC estimates that tourism generates 100.9 million jobs directly, but that nearly three times as many jobs are created when considering the indirect result of tourism. Forecasts indicate that the total contribution of tourism to employment will see levels rise to more than 380 million jobs by 2027 (WTTC, 2017). The industry's importance to many economies as a generator of employment is therefore clear. Several of the leading tourist destinations in the world are developing countries and, in some tourism-dependent economies such as the Caribbean, as many as 25% of all jobs are associated with the industry.

Jobs are created in travel agencies, tour operators and other intermediaries that supply tourist services in both the generating and destination areas. Transport companies such as airlines also employ staff to serve tourists in both areas, but the bulk of employment is in the destination country. The jobs range from hotel managers to deckchair attendants, from excursion-booking clerks to cleaners employed in the stately homes that are open to the public or maintenance staff who keep the rides going at theme parks.

Some of these jobs are seasonal or part time, so tourism's contribution to full-time employment is considerably less than the total employment figures may suggest. While this is a criticism of the industry in economic terms, and one that has resulted in large sums of money being spent in an effort to lengthen the tourist season in many resorts, it is important to realise that these jobs are often being created in areas where there may be little alternative employment. It is also worth making the point that many of the jobs attract those who wish to work seasonally, such as students seeking jobs as resort representatives during the summer or householders who wish to open their homes for summer periods only as holiday accommodation.

For countries that are major receiving destinations or which enjoy a strong domestic demand for tourism, employment figures will be far higher. On balance, tourism as a form of employment is economically beneficial, although efforts must be made to create more full-time jobs in the industry. The extent to which tourism benefits employment can be seen when it is appreciated that, given the figure quoted earlier, roughly one job in ten in the world is ascribed to tourism.

EXAMPLE

Skills shortage

Tourism is one of the world's largest and fastest-growing industries, which can stimulate increased employment opportunities. However, the speed of growth may create both skill and labour shortages.

Research by the Asia-Pacific Economic Cooperation (APEC) Tourism Working Group (2017) identifies skills shortages, particularly related to customer service and business management, as well as some technical skills required of the workforce. Furthermore, a perception that the industry only offers low-paid and part-time work, with poor working conditions and limited career progression, means that attracting and retaining quality staff can be challenging.

Consequently, the tourism industry experiences a gender and age inequality (with employment highest among women and young people) that needs addressing. This might be done through changing perceptions of employment, enhancing training and improving mobility to help meet the needs of the industry and its employees.

Source: APEC, 2017

Just as tourism is globally important, so it is important for regions within an economy. The multiplier that affects income in a region affects employment in the same way. If tourists stay at a destination, jobs are directly created by the tourism industry there. Those workers and their families resident in the neighbourhood must also buy goods and services locally, and their families require education and need medical care. This, in turn, gives rise to jobs in shops, schools and hospitals to serve their needs. The value of the employment multiplier is likely to be broadly similar to that of the tourism income multiplier, assuming that jobs with average rates of pay are created.

Recent developments in technology, however, are threatening labour opportunities in tourism. For example, computer reservation systems (CRSs) have replaced manual reservation systems and, as a result, many jobs in large companies such as airlines, tour operators and hotel chains have disappeared. Similarly, the trend towards online bookings threatens jobs in travel agencies. Call centres are replacing branch shops and, increasingly, these are set up abroad, in countries with lower levels of pay, such as India. Fortunately for the future of the industry, the tourist often seeks a high level of personal service at the destination, the nature of the tourist experience thus ensuring that technology cannot replace many jobs (although, as discussed in Chapter 18, even the key job of resort representative has been sharply curtailed in recent years). The success of tourism in a country, however, will, in part, be dependent on an adequate supply of skilled labour with the right motivation towards employment in the industry and appropriate training.

BALANCE OF PAYMENTS

In a national context, tourism may have a major influence on a country's balance of payments. International tourists are buying tourist services in another country and those payments are noted in a country's accounts as 'invisibles'. A British resident going on holiday to Portugal will be making an invisible payment to that country, which is a debit on the UK's balance of payments account and a credit to Portugal's balance of payments. Similarly, the money spent by an American visitor to the UK is credited to the UK's balance of payments, becoming an invisible receipt for the UK, while it is debited as a payment against the American balance of payments. It is important to remember at this point that, as mentioned earlier, the outflow of British money in the form of spending abroad by British residents counts as an *import*, while the inflow of foreign holidaymakers' money spent in the UK counts as an *export*.

The total value of receipts minus the total payments made during the year represents a country's **balance of payments on the tourism account**. This is part of the country's entire invisible balance, which will include other services such as banking, insurance and transport. This latter item is, of course, also important for tourism. If an American visitor to the UK decides to travel on a UK airline, then a contribution is made to the UK's invisible receipts, while the fare of a Briton going on holiday to Portugal flying with TAP Airlines is credited to Portugal and represents a debit on the UK balance of payments account. Of course, with the demise of national airlines and the growth of global integration, it may no longer be the case that the leading airlines will in the future be so clearly identified with their country of origin and, if the majority shareholding is abroad, ultimately the profits, if not the earnings, will find their way to other countries in the form of leakages.

Some countries, particularly developing ones, cannot afford to have a negative balance of payments as this is a drain on their financial resources and, in such a case, they may be forced to impose restrictions either on the movement of their own residents or on the amount of money that they may take abroad with them. Some countries may suffer severe deficiencies in their tourism balance of payments, which can sometimes be offset by manufacturing exports. Germany and Japan have in the past been examples of countries heavily in deficit on the tourism balance of payments, but which have nevertheless enjoyed a surplus overall through the sale of goods overseas. With both countries now finding it increasingly difficult to compete against low-pay economies in the industrial sector, they are now seeking to boost their own inbound tourism to compensate for this net outflow on the tourism account. By contrast, Spain and Italy both enjoy a strong surplus on their tourism balance of payments as they are popular receiving countries with fewer residents going abroad for their own holidays.

EXAMPLE

Tourism balance of payments for the UK

Throughout the 1970s, the UK enjoyed a surplus on its tourism balance of payments, reaching a peak during 1977, the year of the Queen's Silver Jubilee. Since then, however, spending by British tourists travelling abroad has increased faster than receipts the country has gained from overseas tourists, with the result that, as we have seen, there has been a net deficit since 1986.

The recession that occurred towards the end of the first decade of this century saw more holiday-makers take domestic holidays (often now termed staycations to reflect vacations that involve stays in the local area), which reduced the deficit. However, as the economy strengthened, so the growth in foreign holidays again increased the balance of payments deficit.

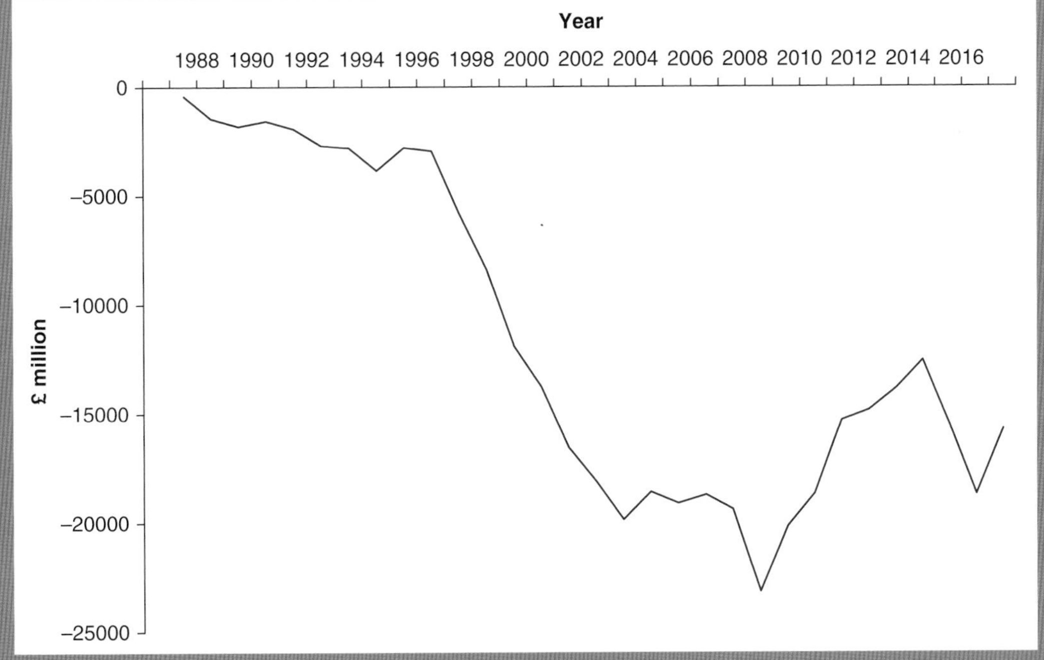

FIGURE 4.4 UK balance of payments – travel

Source: ONS, 2018

INVESTMENT AND DEVELOPMENT

One factor helping to determine the success or otherwise of tourism in a region is the level of investment, whether private or public, in the industry. Unfortunately, tourism has historically been seen by private investors as a high-risk investment. Banks are also reluctant to lend money for tourism projects and developers are not very willing to take investment risks. This often means that tourism cannot take off until the public sector is prepared to 'kick-start' the economy – that is, invest risk capital in order to encourage the development of tourism. This might take the form of grants or low-interest loans to private developers or, in some more centrally operated economies, it may mean that government itself builds and runs facilities such as hotels for tourists.

EXAMPLE

Private investment in tourism

In recent years, private equity firms have turned their attention towards tourism, with an expectation that increased visitor numbers will turn into serious profits.

As examples, Apollo Global Management invested $2.2 billion to purchase Diamond Resorts (a timeshare operator based in the USA), while Carlyle Group invested in CVC Brasil Operadora e Agencia de Viagens, Brazil's largest travel-tour operator. This latter investment was driven in part by expectations for increased demand (and profits) following the 2014 FIFA World Cup and 2016 Olympics. Shares in the Brazilian operator have since jumped by 40%, thus providing profitable returns for Carlyle Group.

In Australia, private equity firm Quadrant purchased luxury train operator Great Southern Rail, the Cruise Whitsundays operation and Rottnest Express marine tourism business, combining these operations to form the Experience Australia Group. This entity now employs 800 people and carries 1 million guests annually.

Sources: Butt, 2016; O'Connell, 2017

Investment is something of a chicken and egg situation. There may be an unwillingness to invest until a flow of tourists to the area can be demonstrated, but the area will attract few tourists until they can see evidence of there being sufficient facilities to attract them. Once tourism is shown to be successful, however, private developers or government agencies are often willing to invest even further in the area; in short, success breeds success. Economists refer to this as the **accelerator concept**.

Areas that have benefited from this phenomenon include Spain and the Mexican East Coast in the 1960s, Hawaii, Tunisia and the Languedoc-Roussillon region of France in the 1970s and Turkey and Greece in the 1980s and 1990s. Naturally, the attraction of these regions to tourists will also attract other industries, which will recognise the benefits to be gained from a large inflow of consumers and a pleasant working environment for staff.

Unfortunately, the relationship between growth in tourism and economic development is uneven, owing to other complicating factors such as the rate of inflation, the ability of an area to diversify, and skills and attitudes among the local labour force, with key workers brought in from outside the area in cases where the local labour force is either unwilling or unable to adapt to the needs of the tourism industry. This may lead to leakages as pay is repatriated, thus reducing the economic benefit to the area. Consequently, the risk for such investment remains high.

BALANCING ECONOMIC DIVERSIFICATION WITH OVERDEPENDENCE ON TOURISM

For some countries or even regions, such as rural areas or declining industrial areas, tourism may offer an opportunity to diversify the economy, increasing the variety of employment opportunities available for the local population. In addition to this, any downturn in one particular sector may be offset by an increase or stability in other sectors.

An example of this is the city of Bradford in the UK, which sought to encourage tourism to the city when it suffered a decline in the textile and engineering industries, the traditional mainstays of its economy. An initiative by the local government in the mid-1980s saw the introduction of initiatives and funding to encourage tourism to the city. By the turn of the millennium, the number of hotel bed nights sold annually in the city had quadrupled, to over 370,000 (Hope and Klemm, 2001).

In some rural areas, tourism is being amalgamated with farming businesses to provide additional income as well as new products for an area. Farm tourism, or **agritourism** (discussed at greater length in Chapter 8), is just one form of rural tourism that can help to bring income and jobs to remote areas.

Such a reliance on attracting visitors must be placed in context, however. While tourism has been used as a catalyst for expanding economies, perhaps in less developed countries or regions, a concern raised is that overreliance on this one sector can bring difficulties. A significant downturn in tourist demand, perhaps through no fault of the destination, will reduce tourist numbers, leaving the destination economically vulnerable. For destinations where tourism is an important component of the economy, attracting tourists from many different source regions as well as different market segments may help to spread the risk. This will not guard against problems experienced in the local destination area, however.

EXAMPLE

Overrun with tourism

The government of the Philippines announced the closure of Borocay, a popular holiday island, due to the damage and pollution caused by an excessive number of tourists. The six-month closure (which started 26 April 2018) was necessary to allow repairs and a clean-up operation to take place. However, this left many tourism operations with no business for half the year.

In 2017 around 2 million visitors arrived on the island, some from cruise ships as day visitors, spending more than $1 billion. Without this spend, the closure would affect more than 17,000 workers on the island.

The Philippines president described the island as a 'cesspool', while the undersecretary for tourism, Fredrick Alegre, described Boracay as 'a world-class island destination with poor services'. Thus, closure was deemed necessary to provide an opportunity for these improvements to be undertaken. However, concerns were raised that the closure would impact tourism in the Philippines more widely as visitors diverted to paradise islands in other countries. Only time will tell as to the extent to which this closure proves successful, based on improvements made and whether tourist numbers return at a sustainable level.

Sources: D'Asis Pamaran, 2018; McKirdy and Quiano, 2018

Although tourism is valuable to many economies, often, as noted, acting as a catalyst for attracting inward investment, the pressures it places on the economy and the environment should also be acknowledged, and tourism should not be relied on to the exclusion of other opportunities.

INFLATIONARY PRESSURES

While tourism can bring money into a tourism destination, creating job opportunities and wealth, the demand for resources (including land and labour) can push the cost of those resources higher as that very demand creates an imbalance in terms of supply. As prices of those resources rise, it can create an inflationary effect: employees seek higher levels of pay in order to be able to afford the higher costs of accessing land or property, food and entertainment and so on. Ultimately, some of the local population may be unable to afford the increased costs and become excluded from accessing their own community's resources.

THE OPPORTUNITY COST OF TOURISM

Further to the key economic impacts discussed above, it is necessary also to consider that, by developing tourism, many resources (such as land, labour and capital investment) are used to support the industry, thus making them unavailable for other industries. This is termed the **opportunity cost**.

Crompton (2006: 75) defines opportunity costs as 'the benefits that would be forthcoming if the public resources committed to a tourism project were (1) redirected to other public services or (2) retained by the taxpayer'. This principle acknowledges the lost opportunities as a result of using such resources for tourism development and those costs should be set against the benefits received.

A further area of opportunity cost to be considered is that of taxation. When governments tax residents in order to be able to invest in tourism projects, they reduce the spending capability of the local population, which can impact the multiplier effect of induced or indirect expenditure. Thus, any positive effect of the tourism project may need to be set against the negative impact on residents' spending.

STATISTICAL MEASUREMENT OF TOURISM

Gathering data on tourism is a vital task for the government of a country. Governments need to know the contribution that tourism makes to the economy in terms of income, employment, balance of payments and investment. Sufficiently detailed figures must be available in order to know how they have affected regional as well as national economies. Governments will wish to examine trends over time, not only within the country, but also in comparison with the performance of other, competing countries. National tourist offices will employ this information to forecast growth and to plan for tourism in their areas.

Information must be both **quantitative** and **qualitative** in nature – that is, data should be provided about not only the numbers and composition of tourists but also their nature and purpose. For example, national statistics on tourism should include:

- the number of international visitors (arrivals) as well as the number of domestic tourists
- how these are distributed over the months of the year
- the countries generating the international tourists and the regions generating the domestic tourists
- the growth, year on year, of those tourists
- their spend – in absolute terms and how they distribute it between accommodation, transport, shopping, catering and so on

- their mode of travel – that is, what form of transport they use, whether they are travelling independently or on an inclusive tour
- the duration of their visit
- the types of accommodation they use
- the purpose of their visit – whether leisure, business or visiting friends and relatives (VFR)
- demographic profiles – age, group composition, social class
- psychographic profiles – personality, lifestyle, interests and activities
- what these tourists seek and the extent to which they are satisfied with what they find.

This is a great deal of information and relates both to inbound and domestic tourism. Data must also be gathered for outbound tourism (residents travelling abroad). Thus, the task of collecting tourism data is daunting, but it is vital that governments undertake it and ensure, as far as is possible, that the data collected are based on commonly defined criteria, so that meaningful comparisons can be made.

If the collection of data allows the nation to know what trends are developing over time, what patterns of growth are taking place and how tastes and preferences are changing over time, this information will enable governments to determine where to site roads and airports, where to make provision for expansion in local government plans and in what countries to increase or decrease the spend on advertising (as well as how to redirect the themes of advertisements when it is found that new types of tourists are being reached).

The private sector will benefit from this information, too, when deciding whether or not and where to invest in hotels or tourist attractions and the forms those facilities should take. Furthermore, the industry requires an understanding of the propensity to take holidays; that is, the proportion of the population choosing to take a holiday each year and, in particular, a holiday abroad or more than one holiday a year, as well as how that propensity is affected by any growth in disposable income.

Public-sector planners must be aware of the multiplier effect, which will call for sophisticated research techniques if the figures produced are to be accurate.

We will next examine the two most commonly used measurements of tourism – international and national surveys.

INTERNATIONAL SURVEYS

Statistics of intra-European and transatlantic tourist flows were collected even before World War II. The systematic collection of tourism data on a global scale, however, dates back to the early post-war years. The methods of measurement have improved in recent years, particularly in those developed countries that have seen tourism expand rapidly.

Global tourism statistics, covering traffic flows, expenditure and trends over time, are collated annually by the UNWTO and the Organization for Economic Cooperation and Development (OECD). A useful, although brief, summary is published as *Tourism Highlights* (2018), freely available on the UNWTO website. While providing a useful overview, these statistics are not always strictly comparable, however, as data-gathering methods vary and differences in the definitions of terms remain.

Other surveys are undertaken to provide additional data on the volume of tourists and their expenditure, although reductions in resources have led to cutbacks in the collection of data by the public-sector bodies, so supplementary information is now largely collected by private organisations. For example, IPK International undertakes more than half a million interviews each year, asking populations of more than 60 countries about their travel behaviour. The results of these interviews are published in the *World Travel Monitor* and *European Travel Monitor*. They also provide businesses with extracts of data, on request, ensuring that they can access the most relevant data for their needs. It should be mentioned that full reports as well as data extracts are often quite expensive to purchase.

NATIONAL SURVEYS

It is important for both national and regional governments to have data on domestic tourism. With this in mind, many governments invest in surveys that can provide details of the travel habits of residents. The EU has also encouraged its member states to extend their statistical data collection related to the tourism market and industry.

EXAMPLE

National Tourism Surveys

Since 1973 the European Commission has been monitoring public opinion in the member states and collects data to collate statistics on tourism. The Tourism Statistics 2016 publication provides information on accommodation types, total number of trips and modes of transport used.

Most countries also commission tourism surveys (although these can vary in level of detail) to inform decisions about their investment in and marketing of tourism. Four examples are outlined in Table 4.9.

TABLE 4.9 Examples of national tourism surveys

Country	Survey	Commissioner
Australia	The IVS and NVS provide information on the characteristics and travel patterns of Australia's inbound, domestic and outbound markets. They cover trip purpose, transportation, expenditure, accommodation type and travel party demographics	International Visitor Survey (IVS) and National Visitor Survey (NVS) (Tourism Research Australia)
Canada	The ITS provides statistics on the volume of international travellers and trip characteristics such as expenditure, activities, places visited and length of stay. The TSRC measures the volume, characteristics (duration, mode of travel, purpose) and economic impact of domestic travel	International Travel Survey (ITS) and Travel Survey of Residents of Canada (TSRC) (Statistics Canada)
The Netherlands	The Continu Vakantie Onderzoek (CVO) report examines the short and long holidays taken by Dutch people. Research examines the extent to which Dutch people go on holiday, destinations selected, accommodation types, modes of transport, use of travel agencies and spending on holiday	Central Bureau of Statistics, The Netherlands (CBS)
UK	The Great Britain Tourism Survey (GBTS) is a national consumer survey measuring the volume, purpose and value of overnight domestic tourism trips. The International Passenger Survey (IPS) collects information about passengers entering and leaving the UK and includes details on purpose of trip, expenditure and length of stay	Great Britain Tourism Survey (GBTS), commissioned by VisitEngland, VisitScotland and VisitWales, and International Passenger Survey (IPS), collected by the Office for National Statistics (ONS)

TECHNIQUES AND PROBLEMS REGARDING MEASUREMENT OF TOURISM

From the descriptions of the methods for gathering tourist statistics outlined above, it can be seen that most research employs quantitative methods in order to provide descriptive information about issues such as when and where tourists travel, where they come from, how long they stay and how much they spend. In some cases, this information is available in considerable levels of detail. For instance, expenditure can be broken down into sectors (shopping, food, accommodation) and data on visits can be identified by tourism region within the country. Although the data collected are not above criticism, by and large there is a sufficient body of information on which to base decisions.

The demand for qualitative research

Research dealing with why people travel is far more limited, however. This situation is beginning to change as organisations become more concerned with understanding the behaviour of tourists – how they choose their destination, what they do when they arrive and why, what satisfies them, and their purchasing patterns (for example having a preference to book directly rather than through an agent, or to book early rather than close to departure time).

None of these factors are easily addressed by the use of structured questionnaires; a more qualitative approach to research is needed. This can involve lengthy interviews in the home or in panels, or focus groups, where consumers talk about their behaviour under the guidance of a skilled interviewer. Some information is best obtained by observation rather than questioning, for example watching how customers visiting a travel agency choose their brochures from the racks.

All these types of research are expensive, and time-consuming to administer. What is more, unlike quantitative methods, they cannot be subjected to tests of statistical probability in order to 'prove' the accuracy of the findings, no matter how carefully and scientifically the information is collected. Many organisations are therefore reluctant to commission research involving qualitative methods, although a growing number of research experts now recognise that they may produce richer and more complete data than the more common quantitative survey. After all, the information provided by the use of questionnaires will only be as accurate as the honesty of the answers, but it is particularly difficult to know whether respondents are answering questionnaires honestly or giving sufficient thought to the questions. This problem is compounded where mailed questionnaires are used.

Some criticisms of quantitative methods

Asking questions of passengers arriving at a destination is, in reality, a survey of their intentions rather than an accurate picture of what those passengers actually end up doing while in the country. Equally, surveys carried out on departing travellers require good levels of recall, so some answers will be, at best, guesswork, especially where the aim is to assess the expenditure that the tourist has incurred.

The categories or definitions used may vary by survey. For instance, the travel survey for Finnish residents limits the sample to adults aged between 15 and 74, which may effectively ignore the unique travel habits of the increasingly significant senior citizen (or grey) market. Age is not the only definitional difficulty. One of the issues of comparing data for different countries as reported by the UNWTO is that some countries may count international tourists by country of residence, while other countries use nationality (determined either by passport or based on immigration forms completed on arrival).

Even if common definitions are used, direct comparisons may be misleading. For example, an international journey may require an American resident to make a trip of several hundred kilometres or cross a stretch of water, which will usually mean forward planning, while a resident of continental Europe may live within a couple of kilometres of an international border and think nothing of crossing it regularly to go shopping or for a meal out. In some cases, it is even difficult to think of border crossings as international. The Schengen Agreement, for example, eradicated border controls between several EU countries, with the result that monitoring visitors has become much harder. Another issue is that some countries still use hotel records to estimate the number of visitors, a system known to be notoriously inaccurate because visitors travelling from one hotel to another are counted twice, while those staying with friends and relatives are omitted entirely from the count.

While some international standards for methods of data collection and definitions of terms have become widely accepted, particularly among the developed countries, small variations continue to make genuine comparison difficult, not only between countries but also within a country over a period of time. Above all, if specific types of tourist activity are being examined, as part of a larger sample of general tourists, limits of confidence may fall sharply. Some survey data in the past have produced results that are accurate only to within 20% either way, owing to the small number of respondents in the particular category being examined.

Accurate measures of tourist expenditure are equally difficult to make. Shopping surveys have problems distinguishing between residents and tourists, and tourists frequently under- or overestimate their expenditure. Above all, much of the real tourist expenditure is not recorded at all, especially in developing countries, because it is not taken into account. This includes secondary spend by recipients of tourist monies and even direct spend by tourists in shops and other outlets. In countries where cash, rather than credit cards, is still the normal means of payment and bargaining is common for even the smallest of items, calculating spending patterns reliably is particularly difficult.

Tourism satellite accounts (TSAs)

In an effort to provide more accurate assessment, the UNWTO has introduced the concept of the **tourism satellite account (TSA)**. This technique attempts to include all such indirect expenditures and their resultant contribution to GDP and employment. The technique was approved as an international standard by the United Nations Statistical Commission in 2000. It created a set of standardised procedures that aim to ensure that all countries are operating similar systems and thus the resulting data are comparable across nations.

The creation of a TSA provides information regarding the economic importance of tourism for a national economy, as well as providing details of both the employment created by tourism and the tax revenues earned as a direct result of tourism activity. Such information can assist with planning tourism resources and may encourage greater awareness of the tourism industry and further investment in the industry.

The implementation of TSAs, however, is fraught with difficulties. It is not only expensive and time-consuming to employ, but accepts all tourism expenditure as beneficial, disregarding the question of sustainability. Neither can the results revealed in one country or region necessarily be transposed to another as each situation is unique and there is no magic formula that will allow estimates of statistical measures to be obtained without full-scale research within the area.

EXAMPLE

Developing regional TSAs

For many years, Tourism Research Australia has collected data to produce TSAs for the nation. However, more recently efforts have been made to apply the TSA framework to develop regional satellite accounts for each of the country's six states and two territories.

Few countries have developed regional TSAs, due to their complexity (above and beyond the existing complexity inherent in developing national TSAs). This could include the lack of available regional data, the cross-state movement of transport and other services, and the accuracy of data related to such things as local employment.

TABLE 4.10 State TSA values 2016–17

AUS$ (billions)	New South Wales	Victoria	Queensland	South Australia	Western Australia	Tasmania	Northern Territory	ACT
Gross State Product	$34.2b	$24.8b	$25.4b	$6.2b	$11.8b	$3.0b	$2.3b	$2.3b

Source: Dwyer et al., 2007; Tourism Research Australia (TRA), 2018

FUTURE ISSUES

Although international travel saw a decline in 2009 to 851 million trips, there was an immediate rebound in 2010, with an estimated 948 million trips having taken place, and the 1 billion mark was surpassed in 2012. During this short downturn, domestic tourism continued to provide a significant contribution to many economies. As highlighted in this chapter, the propensity to travel is often high for developed nations, whose populations still desire holidays even when economies are in recession.

While the economic impact of tourism is of significant interest to local and regional governments, increased interest in the social and environmental impacts of it is now being witnessed. Arguments about the need for sustainability are helping to address the 'grow at all cost' attitude toward tourism development.

The emerging markets of China and India in particular provide interesting opportunities for the tourism industry. With such large populations, the travel propensity does not need to be high for market size to be significant. For example, if just 1% of the Chinese population decided to take an international trip this would account for more than 13 million trips, and similarly if the international travel propensity of the Indian population reached that of the UK this would almost double the existing levels of international tourism. With the potential to serve such large markets, the industry is likely to adapt its provision to meet the demands of these markets.

The collection and dissemination of data related to the economic impacts of tourism have been greatly assisted by computerisation. Both the UNWTO and the WTTC provide online access to parts of their databases, with many reports and statistics available at no charge. This can assist those involved in the planning and development of tourism, informing decisions about new markets, making comparisons between countries and understanding more about tourism in their home countries.

QUESTIONS AND DISCUSSION POINTS

1. This chapter critiques the quality of tourism employment. Summarise the factors to consider when evaluating whether employment in tourism is good for an economy.
2. What is meant by the terms 'leakages' and 'multiplier effect'? How does the former influence the latter?

3. Australian residents took 9,117,692 trips overseas and 97,202,739 domestic overnight trips in 2017. At that time, the population was 24,702,900. Calculate the gross travel propensity for international and domestic overnight travel by Australians. How is this information useful for Australian travel agents?

TASKS

1. Interview ten tourists who have recently booked a holiday. Investigate whether the introduction of a tourist tax at the destination would have deterred them from booking. Does the amount of the tax or the way it is collected (for example, at the point of booking or in resort at the hotel or on departure at an airport) make a difference?

2. Access the latest edition of 'Tourism Highlights' from the UNWTO website (for example, http://marketintelligence.unwto.org/publication/unwto-tourism-highlights-2018). This will provide details of the number of tourist arrivals and the tourism receipts for recent years. For a country of your choice, calculate the average spend per arrival for the latest year and for a period upwards of five years earlier. How has average spend changed over time? What might be the reason for this?

FURTHER READING

Hall, C. M. and Lew, A. A. (2009) *Understanding and Managing Tourism Impacts: An integrated approach.* Abingdon: Routledge.

Mason, P. (2012) *Tourism Impacts, Planning and Management*. Abingdon: Routledge.

Stabler, M. J., Papatheodorou, A. and Sinclair, M. T. (2010) *The Economics of Tourism*, 2nd edn. Abingdon: Routledge.

Tribe, J. (2011) *The Economics of Leisure and Tourism*, 4th edn. Oxford: Butterworth-Heinemann.

United Nations World Tourism Organization (UNWTO) (n.d.) *Tourism Satellite Accounts*. Available online at: www.unwto.org/statistics/tsa/project/concepts.pdf

UNWTO (2017) *Tourism Highlights*. Madrid: UNWTO.

WEBSITES

Organization for Economic Co-operation and Development (OECD): www.oecd.org

United Nations World Tourism Organization (UNWTO): www.unwto.org

REFERENCES

Asia-Pacific Economic Cooperation (APEC) (2017) *Developing the Tourism Workforce of the Future in the APEC Region*. Canberra: APEC Secretariat.

Bolwell, D. and Weinz, W. (2008) *Reducing Poverty through Tourism*. Geneva: International Labour Office.

Bull, A. (1995) *The Economics of Travel and Tourism*, 2nd edn. Melbourne: Longman.

Butt, R. (2016) *Wall Street's Big Investors are Piling into Tourism*. Available online at: http://uk.businessinsider.com/private-equity-firms-piling-into-tourism-investment-2016-7 [Accessed 8 May 2018].

Crompton, J. L. (2006) Economic impact studies: Instruments for political shenanigans. *Journal of Travel Research*, 45 (1), 67–82.

D'Asis Pamaran, M. (2018) Paradise lost? *Manila Times*, 2 May.

Dwyer, L., Forsyth, P., Spurr, R. and and Van Ho, T. (2007) *Developing an integrated suite of regional Tourism Satellite Accounts (TSAs): A case study from Australia*. Paper presented at Travel and Tourism Research Association (TTRA) International Conference: Advancing tourism research globally. Amherst, MA, June. Available online at: https://scholarworks.umass.edu/cgi/viewcontent.cgi?article=1350&context=ttra [Accessed 10 May 2018].

Euromonitor (2017) *Domestic Trip Statistics*. London: Euromonitor.

Eurostat (2017) *Participation in Tourism for Personal Purposes (tourists as share of total population)*. Luxembourg: European Communities. Available online at: http://ec.europa.eu/eurostat/web/products-datasets/-/tour_dem_totot [Accessed 23 April 2018].

Hall, C. M. and Lew, A. (2009) *Understanding and Managing Tourism Impacts*. Abingdon: Routledge.

Hope, C. A. and Klemm, M. S. (2001) Tourism in difficult areas revisited: The case of Bradford. *Tourism Management*, 22 (6), 629–35.

McKirdy, E. and Quiano, K. (2018) *Philippine Riot Police to Keep Tourists at Bay during Boracay Island Cleanup*. Available online at: https://edition.cnn.com/2018/04/17/asia/philippines-boracay-closure-riot-police-intl/index.html [Accessed 8 May 2018].

O'Connell, B. (2017) *Will we see more private equity enter NZ Tourism?* Available online at: www.tourismticker.com/2017/08/04/will-we-see-more-private-equity-enter-nz-tourism [Accessed 8 May 2018].

Office for National Statistics (ONS) (2016) *UK Residents' Visits Abroad*. London: ONS.

ONS (2017) *UK Population Estimates 2016*. London: ONS (released 22 June 2017).

ONS (2018) *BoP: Trade in services – Travel balance*. Available online at: www.ons.gov.uk/economy/nationalaccounts/balanceofpayments/timeseries/fjsr/pb [Accessed 10 May 2018].

Tourism Research Australia (TRA) (2018) *State Tourism Satellite Accounts*. Available online at: www.tra.gov.au/ArticleDocuments/246/State%20summaries_2016-17.pdf.aspx?Embed=Y [Accessed 10 May 2018].

United Nations World Tourism Organization (UNWTO) (2017) *Tourism Highlights*. Madrid: UNWTO.

UNWTO (2018) *Tourism Highlights*. Madrid: UNWTO.

Vanhove, N. (2011) *The Economics of Tourism Destinations*, 2nd edn. Oxford: Elsevier.

World Travel and Tourism Council (WTTC) (2017a) *Benchmark Reports*. London: WTTC. Available online at: www.wttc.org/economic-impact/benchmark-reports/country-results/#undefined [Accessed February 2019].

WTTC (2017) *Travel & Tourism Global Economic Impact & Issues*. London: WTTC.

WTTC (2018) *Travel & Tourism Economic Impact 2018: World*. London: WTTC.

WTTC (2019) *Travel & Tourism Economic Impact 2019: World*. London: World Travel and Tourism Council. Available online at: https://zh.wttc.org/economic-impact/country-analysis/data-gateway [Accessed 24 2018].

5

THE SOCIO-CULTURAL IMPACTS OF TOURISM

CONTENTS

LEARNING OUTCOMES

After studying this chapter, you should be able to:

- understand the various ways in which tourism can impact on the populations of both destination and generating countries
- identify and evaluate different approaches to finding solutions to problems caused by these impacts
- understand the concept, and importance, of sustainable tourism in a socio-cultural context
- recognise the need for adequate planning and cooperation between the private and public sectors as means of overcoming problems.

> Tourism enables interaction between individuals of different nationalities and backgrounds, thus fostering dialogue among cultures and encouraging cultural diversity and creativity.
>
> However, tourism can also cause irreversible damage to culture and the environment if not properly managed. (UNESCO, 2008: vi)

INTRODUCTION

While greater awareness is now given to the reality that mass tourism can place great pressure on host populations, it is still perhaps fair to say that the economic power of the tourism business dominates. It is generally accepted that tourism is, for the most part and with relatively few exceptions, beneficial to both generating and destination countries. Environmentalists, however, are less sure that this is the case and many are arguing for a reduction – or, at very least, a stabilisation – in the volume of global travel as an essential measure to save the planet. In this chapter, we will look at a different and, in many ways, darker side of the tourism business: its impact (other than in purely economic terms) on those who participate in tourism and the residents of those countries subject to tourist flows. This will mean looking at socio-cultural issues affecting both hosts and tourists.

As we saw in the previous chapter, tourism can be a potent force for economic good, creating employment and wealth. Equally, as the UNESCO quote that opens this chapter highlights, tourism provides a basis for widening our understanding of other societies, developing and maintaining links, reducing tensions and even avoiding conflicts. Indeed, in the first half of the twentieth century, tourism was seen, and actively promoted by the authorities in many countries, as a force for good.

While the interplay between tourists and their hosts was seen initially as a means of stabilising relations between nations, it readily became apparent that foreign visitors with a curiosity about other cultures could, through their enthusiasm, ensure the survival of those very cultural attractions that might otherwise have withered away due to lack of support. This book contains numerous examples of the ways in which incoming tourism has benefited the culture and traditions of a particular country or region. With the increasing secularisation of Western societies, arguably it is also tourists who will eventually ensure that great cathedrals survive as the costs of maintaining these buildings for dwindling numbers of worshippers can no longer be borne by the ecclesiastical authorities alone. Similarly, whole inner-city and dockland areas have been restored and developed to make them attractive as tourist sites. Cities such as London and New York would be poorer places without tourists. Around 60% of Broadway theatre admissions are to tourists (one-quarter of which are international visitors and three-quarters domestic visitors) (The Broadway League, 2018). Thus, the variety of theatres available to New Yorkers owes much to patronage by visitors. Furthermore, tourists' use of other public facilities can help fund their provision, thus enabling residents to enjoy a better and cheaper service than would otherwise be possible. In rural areas and small seaside resorts, too, many heritage attractions, such as local museums, art galleries and provincial theatres, would be forced to close without tourist support. Many rural crafts, pubs, even the restoration of traditional pastimes all owe their survival, in part, to the interest in them shown by tourists.

EXAMPLE

How does tourism benefit the city of Virginia Beach?

The Convention and Visitor Bureau (CVB) for this American coastal city has recently reported the benefits of tourism, beyond the $1.49 billion in direct spending to local businesses and the £132 million raised in state and local tax revenues.

The CVB argued that tourists spend money using retail outlets, entertainment venues and transport services. Although they place additional pressure on local infrastructure, such as roads, airports, healthcare and emergency services, the taxes paid by visitors (such as sales or accommodation taxes) contribute more than the additional costs incurred. Furthermore, in recent years the seafront boardwalk and the performing arts centre have both seen revitalisation in part as a result of tourism, while local schools collected around $5 million from the city's general fund (which received $56 million in contributions from tourist taxes).

Such investment means that the local population gets to use upgraded airports, roads and attractions, as well as seeing investment in schools and other community resources. Clearly, the local community gains diverse benefits from attracting tourists to the city.

Source: Virginia Beach CVB, 2018

The rapid growth of tourism during the twentieth century produced problems, however, as well as opportunities on a vast scale for both developed and developing countries. Authorities in these countries came to realise that unrestrained and unplanned tourist development could easily aggravate problems to the point where tourists would no longer wish to visit the destination, and residents would no longer wish to receive them. This is, therefore, not just an environmental issue; a point can be reached where residents feel swamped by the sheer numbers of tourists at peak periods of the year, resulting in disenchantment and, eventually, alienation, with the risk of growing numbers of altercations taking place between residents and visitors.

The breakdown in host–guest relationships can be largely ascribed to the volume of visitors. Doxey (1975) developed an **Irritation Index** (or 'Irridex') model of the relationship between the growth of tourism and community stress (see Table 5.1). In the early stages of tourism development, the locals are euphoric, pleased to see investment and improved job prospects for local people. The comparatively small numbers and the fact that most tourists will belong to the 'explorer' category and accept the norms and values of the hosts mean that tourists are welcomed and even cultivated as 'friends'. As locals become used to the benefits they receive from tourism and aware of the problems that tourism generates as it grows, so they come to accept it and their meetings with tourists become more commonplace and commercial. Further growth leads to a general feeling among locals that tourists are an

TABLE 5.1 Irridex model of stress relative to tourism development

Stages	Characteristics	Symptoms
Stage 1	Euphoria	Visitors welcomed, little formal development
Stage 2	Apathy	Visitors taken for granted, contacts become commercial
Stage 3	Irritation	Locals concerned about tourism, efforts made to improve infrastructure
Stage 4	Antagonism	Open hostility from locals, attempts to limit damage and tourism flows

Source: Doxey, 1975

irritant rather than a benefit, as they note how tourism is changing their community and their cultural norms. In the final stages, locals show open antagonism towards the steady stream of visitors, many of whom will have the attitude that locals are there to meet the tourists' needs, and will not attempt to adapt to local norms.

Naturally, this is a simplified model of the fairly complex relationships that actually develop between tourists and locals. Other factors that must be taken into account are:

- the length of time tourists stay in the community (those staying longer will fit in better and be seen as making a more effective contribution to the local economy)
- the cultural gap between locals and tourists (domestic tourists, sharing the values of the locals, will be less resented than those who have no understanding)
- the dominance of tourism as an industry (in areas where tourism is the main industry, residents may be more tolerant of visitor demands as they are more reliant on the success of this sector)
- the ratio of tourists to locals (where the ratio is high, hosts may feel overwhelmed).

Relatively small destinations that have become the focus of mass tourism are particularly under pressure, and where massive congestion (see Figure 5.1) and cultural differences are both in evidence, local resentment becomes overt, with both locals and visitors suffering in consequence. Where tourism consists largely of short-term visits, the opportunities for misunderstanding are greater and hostility may be stoked by the large numbers of visitors who leave little money in the local economy.

FIGURE 5.1 The iconic Mostar Bridge in Bosnia-Herzegovina is often congested with visitors, many coming from cruise ships visiting the Adriatic

Photo: Chris Holloway

THE SOCIO-CULTURAL EFFECTS OF TOURISM

It is clear that the host population is influenced by their engagement with tourism. The host destination can experience many cultural and social impacts as a result of the influx of large numbers of people, often sharing different value systems and away from the constraints of their own environment.

The socio-cultural impact of mass tourism is most noticeable in less developed countries, but is by no means restricted to them as tourism has contributed to an increase in crime and other social problems in such diverse centres as New York and London, Barcelona and Miami, Florence and Corfu.

Any influx of tourists, however few, will make some impact on a region, but the extent of that impact is dependent not just on numbers but also on the kinds of tourists the region attracts. Those who generally go on mass tourism package holidays are less likely to adapt to the local cultures and will seek amenities and standards found in their home countries, while independent travellers or backpackers will adapt more readily to an alien environment. This has been exemplified in a model devised by Valene Smith (see Table 5.2).

TABLE 5.2 Levels of adaptation of tourists to local norms

Types of tourists	Numbers of tourists	Adaptation to local norms
Explorer	Very limited	Accepts fully
Elite	Rarely seen	Adapts fully
Off-beat	Uncommon, but seen	Adapts well
Unusual	Occasional	Adapts somewhat
Incipient mass	Steady flow	Seeks Western amenities
Mass	Continuous influx	Expects Western amenities
Charter	Massive arrivals	Demands Western amenities

Source: Smith, 1989

According to Smith's model, explorers (tourists whose main interest is to meet and understand people from different cultures and backgrounds) will fully accept and acclimatise to the foreign culture. Such travellers generally travel independently and blend in as much as possible. As increasingly remote areas of the world are 'packaged' for tourists, however, and as ever larger numbers of tourists travel further afield to find relaxation or adventure, they bring with them their own value systems, often expecting or demanding the lifestyle and facilities to which they are accustomed in their own countries.

CRIMINAL ACTIVITIES

At its simplest and most direct, the flow of comparatively wealthy tourists to a region may attract petty criminals, as evidenced by increases in thefts or muggings. In some countries, taxi drivers, tour guides and shopkeepers have been found to overcharge gullible tourists. A familiar anecdote in continental European nations is that the pricing policy of shop goods in resort regions falls into three bands: the cheapest price is available to locals, a slightly higher price is demanded from visitors with sound knowledge of the local language and the highest price is applied to visitors with little or no knowledge of the language.

Where gambling is a cornerstone of tourism growth, prostitution and organised crime often follow. Casino destinations like Las Vegas, Monte Carlo, Sun City and Macao attract domestic and international visitors as their main source of gamblers. However, such developments can bring associated problems such as gambling addiction and unpaid debts.

Furthermore, countries that have more relaxed laws on sexual behaviour than those in the West attract tourists who are in search of sexual encounters, with their governments often turning a blind eye to crimes such as organised child abuse. In some countries, Germany and Japan, for example, tour operators specialise in organising sex package tours to destinations like the Philippines and Thailand. This public promotion of commercial sex, especially where it involves sex with minors, has come under increasing scrutiny and criticism in the Western world from organisations such as End Child Prostitution, Pornography and Trafficking (ECPAT) and Tourism Concern. The UK, along with other members of the G8 countries, has passed legislation to enable paedophiles to be prosecuted in their home countries for offences committed abroad.

EXAMPLE

The Code

In an effort to protect children around the world from sexual exploitation, the tourism industry has signed up to a code of conduct designed to increase awareness of the problems and implement responsible business practices which can help protect children. This can involve:

- training employees to recognise and report suspected abuse cases
- including a clause in contracts with suppliers that sets a zero-tolerance policy throughout the supply chain
- educating travellers to prevent sexual exploitation and report suspected abuse cases
- engaging local stakeholders to prevent exploitation.

Members who have signed up to this code of conduct include global organisations such as airlines (Delta), tour operators (TUI, Carlson and Virgin Holidays), hotels (Hilton and Melia) and trade associations (Schweiz Reisburo Verband (SRV) and the Central Florida Business Travel Association).

Source: www.thecode.org

Crime can be an influential factor on the levels of demand. In areas where crime is perceived to be high, tourists are often deterred from visiting. For some developing countries seeking to build a tourism industry, it is vital to project an image of security and safety for tourists, something which may be difficult to achieve when political instability and poverty are rife. In the summer of 2010, the soccer World Cup was hosted in South Africa. Prior to this event taking place, significant press coverage focused on the need for visiting spectators to consider their own safety during their visit, citing statistics to suggest the country has the highest homicide rate in the world. The South African Tourist Board worked tirelessly to refute this image, highlighting the many events hosted previously without incident. During the event, security was increased and the event passed largely without incident.

DEMONSTRATION EFFECT

There are a number of less direct, and perhaps less visible, effects on tourist localities, including the phenomenon known as 'relative deprivation'. The comparative wealth of tourists may be resented or envied by locals, particularly where the influx is seen by the latter as a form of neo-colonialism, as in the Caribbean or some African countries. Locals can experience dissatisfaction with their own standards of living or way of life and seek to emulate those of the tourists. This is known as the **demonstration effect**. In some cases, the effect of this is superficial, as in the adoption of the tourists' dress or fashions, but in others the desire to emulate tourists can threaten deep-seated traditions in the community, as well as leading to aspirations that are impossible to achieve. The perceived parade of affluence (with tourists flaunting cameras, tablet computers, mobile phones, jewellery and other valuables) can create discontent among the host population. The witnessing of these symbols of wealth can create aspirations within the indigenous people.

It is not just the demonstration of material goods but also social behaviours which can be influential. Tourists away from their home environment may feel more sexually liberated and as a consequence seek out 'holiday romances' or sexual encounters. Similarly, levels of alcohol consumption may be higher when on vacation, as local wines and spirits are tasted. Viewed by the local population, this may give a misconception that tourists are often alcohol-fuelled and promiscuous. This may influence the hosts, especially the younger members of the population, who may feel these are acceptable norms of behaviour.

In some cases, however, tourism can also have a positive influence if it encourages the local population to adjust their actions to enhance their own or their society's wellbeing. It has also been argued that viewing the freedom of tourists has encouraged change, especially in some regions where women, who may have traditionally been restricted to the home, may seek opportunities to establish their own career, and to travel independently.

The demonstration effect concept has also highlighted the fact that in some cases it is the tourist whose behaviour is adjusted. Examples are noted in the clothes worn by some travellers – such as sarongs, salwar-kameez (tunic-length shirts and trousers worn commonly in India) and stetson hats – or tourists return home and try to seek out the variety of cuisines experienced during their travels.

CHANGES IN EMPLOYMENT

Tourism can bring a greater range of job opportunities, which may be coupled with higher levels of pay, when compared to workers from agricultural and rural communities. Therefore, migration to touristic areas such as beach resorts and cities, often by younger sectors of the population, can leave other areas bereft of a balanced workforce. Agricultural regions that experience this out-migration must then rely on the elderly population to sustain their activities. The migrants, freed from the restrictions of their families and home environments, may abandon their traditional values, this in turn leading to a breakdown in traditional family structures and support systems.

Tourism often demands that its employees, especially those in the hospitality industry, work unsociable hours. This may include working on religious days and holidays and can impact on family life as work demands mean that celebrations may have to be deferred. Also impacting on family life are the work opportunities that tourism offers for women. This may take the traditional homemaker into the workplace and requires a restructuring in the roles played within the family.

THE IMPACT OF SECOND-HOME OWNERSHIP

The phenomenon of second homes abroad is due in large part to the increase in travel, which has led to greater awareness of, and desire for, residences in attractive resorts on the European continent, and around the Mediterranean in particular. Where expatriates are willing to learn the language and blend in with the culture, little conflict emerges, but where large groups from one country buy homes within a small region of another, often products and forms of entertainment with which they are familiar are sought out. This can transform the indigenous culture and undermine traditional lifestyles. Many of these homes are bought with the intention of renting, largely to nationals of the same country as the owners, which reinforces both the cultural gap and transitional nature of the interactions between locals and tourists.

EXAMPLE

The impact of second-home ownership on rural Britain

Second homes can bring visitors to an area, spending money in local businesses and providing jobs for the local economy. In some cases, older homes are purchased and renovated to be offered as holiday lets. However, there are some disadvantages of second-home ownership. Demand for property can price the local population out of the market and increase house prices. It can also leave towns deserted when home-owners leave the area to return to their main residence.

To address such issues, the UK government has imposed an additional surcharge (3%) on the purchase of second homes and local councils can increase the annual tax by as much as double on second homes. Other strategies to manage this issue are also being implemented. For example, the popular holiday town of St Ives has such high second-home ownership that the regional council, as part of its neighbourhood plan, has decided to restrict the sale of new homes to local residents. Around one-quarter of houses in St Ives are used either as second homes, or are bought to rent to holiday-makers, meaning the local population is struggling to access affordable homes. Other parishes in popular tourist areas in Cornwall are considering the implications of similar policies.

Source: Rowe, 2018

EXPLOITING LOCAL CULTURE

Sometimes, locals are exploited as 'tourist objects'. In picturesque places, local residents can be annoyed by coachloads of tourists descending on the area to peer through their windows or swamp local bars and pubs in order to 'get a flavour' of the local life.

Exploitation of this kind can result in both sides seeing any contact in purely commercial terms. In Kenya's Masai Mara region, the Masai tribespeople extract payment for photographs, either of themselves or of a 'real' (but purpose-built) village. Charging for photographs has become the norm in many parts of the world and can leave the tourists themselves feeling exploited.

In these situations, the role of the courier or holiday representative as a 'culture broker' becomes vital. These members of the industry hold local knowledge (and may be from the local community), help to avoid misunderstandings, interpret the local culture for visitors and explain what is appropriate and inappropriate behaviour for the guests. Interpretation plays an important role in sustainable tourism, and the guide as interpreter of local customs provides one of the most effective means of communication.

Breaking cultural taboos can produce a backlash; for example, Alassio banned bikinis in the streets, and in the Alto Adige region of the Italian Dolomites in 1993 a local movement erupted spontaneously to prevent the spread of topless bathing in the lakes, although other residents expressed their concern that the publicity accorded this might dissuade some tourists from visiting the area! In Greece, what has become known as the 'Shirley Valentine factor' (after the title of the film dealing with the issue of British women escaping a humdrum life at home to find romance in Greece) has led to a reaction from women in Corfu and Crete, who resent the attention Greek men pay to foreign females and feel that Greek women are now undervalued. It is also true to say, however, that some Greek women have welcomed the increasing liberation from male dominance that tourism has brought.

A lack of understanding of local cultural traditions is common where those traditions appear to be contrary to what the tourist may view as tasteful and appropriate. Thus, tourists who, out of ignorance or carelessness, fail to respect local customs and moral values drive resentment among the local population.

THE CONTROVERSY OF THE PHOTOGRAPH

Photography itself is a sensitive issue for many. Tourists from the West expect to be permitted to take what may often be intrusive photographs at will, yet seldom feel it necessary to seek the permission of their subjects. The growing practice of taking 'selfies' of locals alongside the tourist, using mobile phone cameras, makes such contact even more invasive.

In some cultures, it is viewed as offensive to take any pictures of people, while in some countries care must be exercised to avoid taking photographs of landscapes that include military or quasi-military installations. Some British plane-spotters were arrested, prosecuted and jailed for just such an activity at a Greek airport and released only after the intercession of the UK government; plane-spotting is an unknown, not to say eccentric, activity in Greece. Similarly, birdwatchers have been arrested in some countries when using binoculars close to militarily sensitive areas.

EXAMPLE

Protecting wildlife from intrusive photographs

The booming demand for 'selfies' to share on social media platforms such as Instagram has created additional problems for wildlife tourism. Posing with exotic creatures, such as tigers, snakes and crocodiles as well as the cute and the cuddly, has let to greater exploitation by local operators and facilities that exploit wildlife for profit. As well as a welfare issue, this raises concerns over the conservation of vulnerable species (see Figure 5.2).

The Amazonian rainforest in Brazil has been cited as an example of a region deeply affected by the issue. Wildlife protection groups suggest animals are pulled from their natural habitat and held in unsuitable conditions so that they can be conveniently available for tourists to photograph. The stresses associated with being held and photographed further add to the animal's suffering. Efforts are being made to educate the behaviour of tourists, to reduce the demand for such 'selfies'. There are also efforts to control activities damaging to wildlife, but policing this is not a top priority for many living in a country that wishes to focus its resources on developing its schools and healthcare system for its human population.

Sources: Harpaz and Prengaman, 2017; McIvor, 2017

FIGURE 5.2 Tourist poses with a tiger in Pattaya, Thailand

Photo: Shutterstock

STAGED AUTHENTICITY

Given the constraints of time and place, tourists demand instant culture; an opportunity to sample, even if superficially, the 'foreignness' of the destination. This gives rise to what Dean MacCannell (1989) has referred to as **staged authenticity**, in which a search by tourists for authentic experiences of another culture leads to locals of that culture either providing those experiences or staging them to appear as realistic as possible. In this way, culture is in danger of becoming commercialised and trivialised, as when 'authentic' folk dances are staged for tourists as a form of cabaret in hotels or traditional tribal dances are arranged, often in an artificially shortened form, as performances for groups of tourists.

Tourists will seek out local restaurants not frequented by other tourists in order to enjoy the 'authentic' cuisine and environment of the locals, but the very fact of their discovering such restaurants makes them tourist attractions and, ultimately, the 'tourist traps' that tourists are looking to avoid. Meantime, the locals move on to find somewhere else to eat.

The downgrading of the traditional hospitality towards tourists in Hawaii is exemplified by the artificial welcome to which they are subjected on their arrival at the islands. Traditionally, welcoming natives would place a lei of flowers around the neck of each tourist, but, over time, the cost of this courtesy and the huge volume of tourists have led to the lei being replaced by a plastic garland, reinforcing the impression of a commercial transaction, which this has now become.

The authenticity of souvenirs

Tourists seek local artefacts as souvenirs or investments. In cases where genuine works are purchased, this can lead to a loss of cultural treasures from the country. Many countries now impose strict bans on exports of such items for this reason. Tourists, however, are often satisfied with purchasing what they believe to be authentic examples of local art, which has led to the mass production of poorly crafted works (sometimes referred to as **airport art**), such as are common among African nations and the Pacific islands. An effect of this is that it encourages the freezing of art styles in pseudo-traditional forms, as in the case of the apparently 'mediaeval' painted wooden religious statuary produced in Oberammergau and other villages in southern Germany. In turn, artists and craftspeople are subtly encouraged to change their traditional styles, making their works in the colours that are found to be most attractive to tourists, or reducing the size of their works to make them more readily transportable.

It is perhaps too easy to take a purist stance in criticising these developments. One must also point to the evident benefits that tourism has brought to the cultures of many tourist destinations. Indeed, in many cases it has helped to regenerate an awareness and a pride in local culture and traditions. But for the advent of tourism, many of those traditions would have died out long ago. It is facile to ascribe cultural decline directly to the impact of tourism; it is as likely to be the result of mass communication and technological development.

EXAMPLE

Stealing souvenirs

The historic UNESCO site of Pompeii has, for many years, battled against the light-fingered tourists who take parts of the heritage site home as souvenirs.

In 2018 two French tourists were caught with 13 fragments of terracotta and marble taken from a preserved Roman villa. This follows in the wake of a Dutch tourist caught taking a roof tile, a Georgian tourist caught stealing mosaic tiles and two American tourists hauling away a 30 kg stone artefact as a souvenir of their visit.

However, in recent years the curators of the city of Pompeii have reported that hundreds of packages have been received that contain stolen artefacts, as the thieves assuage their guilt by returning the often-priceless items.

Maintaining local traditions

As Western (and specifically American) culture is the dominant influence around the world, it will inevitably undermine other cultures, particularly those of the developing world. It is equally clear, however, that tourism from the Western nations travelling to such nations has led to a revival of interest in tribal customs in those countries. It is not just in developing countries that this is the case; the revival of Morris dancing in English communities is a direct result of the impact of tourism. Traditional local cuisines in the UK, too, have been regenerated, with the support of the national tourist boards with 'taste of England', 'taste of Wales' and 'taste of Scotland' schemes – a concept regenerated in promotions undertaken by VisitBritain since 2004, emphasising once again the originality and quality of regional dishes in the UK. Dying local arts and crafts have been revived through cottage industries in rural areas that have benefited economically from the impact of tourism.

THE HOSTS' IMPACTS ON TOURISTS

While a considerable amount of research has now been undertaken into the effects of tourists on locals, rather less is available to tell us how locals, in turn, influence the tourists. The seminal collection of research *Hosts and Guests* (1978), edited by Valene Smith in the 1970s, did little to consider this aspect of the relationship and, despite four decades having passed since the publication of this work, still little insight into the host's impact on the guest has been developed.

Early research (Gullahorn and Gullahorn, 1963) proposed that tourists go through three stages when adapting to the local culture of their holiday environment. In the first stage, the tourists are excited by the environment and the novelty of the situation; later, a second stage is reached in which the tourists become disillusioned with, and more critical of, the environment as they become accustomed to the situation. Finally, in what may be a slow process, they learn to adapt to the new setting and, in doing so, may experience 're-entry crisis', where it becomes difficult to adapt again to their home environment when they return.

Other studies have examined the extent to which pre-travel attitudes affect adaptability and whether travel broadens understanding or reinforces stereotypes (see, for example, Sutton, 1967). The evidence suggests that a self-fulfilling prophecy is at work here: that if we travel with the expectation of positive experiences, we will indeed have them.

HOST–GUEST INTERACTION

There can be a problem regarding interactions between hosts and tourists in that any relationships that develop are usually fleeting and superficial, often conducted for commercial ends. A report by UNESCO (1976) identified four characteristics of host–guest relations in tourism:

- relationships are transitory and superficial
- they are undertaken under constraints of time and space, with visitors compacting sights into as little time as possible

- there is a lack of spontaneity in relationships – meetings tend to be prearranged to fit tour schedules, and involve mainly financial transactions
- relationships are unequal and imbalanced, due to disparities in the wealth and status of the participants.

Most tourists visiting a new country for the first time, who may be spending no more than a week there and do not expect to return, will be eager to condense their experiences, which tends to make the interactions brief and superficial. Add to this an initial fear of contact with locals, and tourists' comparative isolation (hotels often being dispersed, away from centres of local activity), and opportunities for any meaningful relationship become very limited. Few relationships are spontaneous; contact is generally with locals who work within the tourism industry or else it is mediated by couriers. Language may form an impenetrable barrier to genuine local contact and this limitation can lead to mutual misunderstandings. The relationship is further unbalanced by the status of the visitors, not only in terms of wealth but the fact that the tourists are on holiday while the locals are likely to be at work, often being paid to serve the needs of those tourists.

Changing languages

One impact of the increased scale of international tourism has been seen in the ability of the tourist and the host to communicate. Historically, the slower pace of travel may have allowed the visitor to learn at least a few words of the language in preparation for their experiences. However, with travel representatives and digital technology available to help the tourist who does not speak the local language, today few tourists would be deterred from visiting a destination because of language barriers.

EXAMPLE

Will technology remove language barriers?

Language barriers may become a thing of the past as more travellers use mobile phones to provide almost instantaneous translation.

For years, the dream of a 'voice translation device' has been limited to science fiction. Back in 1979, author Douglas Adams (in the popular book *The Hitchhiker's Guide to the Galaxy*) created the babel fish, which provided intergalactic translation when placed in the ear of the traveller. At the end of the last century, a website of the same name was developed to provide a basic online translation service, whereby users typed words or phrases into the website and received a text translation. Technology has now moved on sufficiently to provide instantaneous translation more akin to that dreamed of by Adams.

In practice, three technologies are required:

1. a speech recognition system to convert spoken words into text
2. computer technology to convert the text into the second language
3. a speech synthesis function to convert the converted text back to speech.

Technology in all three of these areas has been progressing rapidly in recent years. While there is still some way to go, anyone who has used the Google translate app on a mobile phone will be able to appreciate how close the dream has become. Patents by others working in this area will only serve to refine this technology further.

The arrival of tourists at a destination has often encouraged the local population to learn the languages of their key markets, most commonly English, German and Spanish, although study of Chinese dialects such as Mandarin and Cantonese is becoming more popular. Being able to converse with the tourist provides opportunities to sell their souvenirs, understand demands for food and drink, manage any complaints and attract the visitor to their business. To attract international tourists and enhance the visitor experience, local attractions like museums would then provide interpretation information, such as signs and guides in several languages. It is notable in areas where very large numbers of Chinese tourists are now to be found, for instance in Venice, that shops now not only display window signs in the Chinese language, but are increasingly in Chinese ownership, with Chinese speakers retailing the goods.

This is not to say that developing language skills is a one-way affair. Tourists who regularly visit the same country may well seek to improve their knowledge of the local language in order to enhance their interaction with the local population. Phrase books (often printed, but now also widely available via mobile phone applications) have helped to enhance the interaction between hosts and guests.

CULTURAL TRANSGRESSIONS

The behaviour among a small but significant minority of tourists while abroad has made such visitors unwelcome in several leading resorts on the Continent. Freed from the normal constraints of their everyday surroundings, many young tourists have been attracted to resorts promising unlimited cheap alcohol, 24-hour entertainment and readily available sex, either with fellow tourists or locals. Some of the less responsible tour operators have promoted these resorts to niche markets of youngsters, driving away the family market. This, in turn, has fuelled the growth of bars and discos, while resort reps for the operators organise bar crawls, earning high commissions from favoured bars.

The popularity of such resorts quickly led to their becoming overwhelmed by ill-behaved visitors. Bar and street brawls, open drunkenness and impolite behaviour caused conflicts with locals and, not infrequently, visitors being hospitalised. One after another, resorts such as Benitses and Kavos on Corfu, Ibiza in the Balearics and Faliraki on Rhodes found their more traditional markets drying up. Efforts to change the image of the destinations were often made too late. As local authorities intervened, imposing curfews, licensing bar crawls by groups, employing undercover police and even attempting to quarantine noisy groups within zones, the revellers simply moved on to other resorts, threatening their decline in turn.

This approach to tourism is not easily resolved, although the tour operators responsible for some of the worst excesses have sobered up as a consequence of the bad media publicity they received, and modified their packages and promotions. The problem for the destinations, of how to regain public trust and to reposition their product, is less easily resolved.

IMPACTS ON RELIGIOUS OBSERVANCES

Where cultural differences are tied to religion, conflicts may become greater. Some Islamic countries in the Middle East, such as the United Arab Emirates (UAE), have actively pursued policies to attract Western tourists, but expect them to respect local customs. Dubai, one of the Emirates states, is among those that initially turned a blind eye to inappropriate beachwear or consumption of alcohol by visitors, but flagrant breaches of behaviour reduced levels of tolerance and led to a tightening up of control, notably in the case of two British tourists accused in 2008 of having sex on the beach and insulting the policeman who sought to arrest them. In 2014, another case attracted publicity when the drummer of German rock band The Scorpions was jailed for one month after getting drunk and making an indecent gesture to other passengers while on a flight stopover in Dubai airport.

Tourism can have an impact on the time available to worship and celebrate religious festivals. Furthermore, many religious and sacred buildings are popular attractions for tourists, and managing the demands of visitors with the requirements of worshippers can prove difficult. The visitor may wish to observe, and often photograph, the building as well as the congregation, which can be distracting. However, banning tourists from such spaces is often impossible, and the funding they provide through entry fees often assists maintenance and upkeep.

THE EXPLOITATION OF INDIGENOUS POPULATIONS

Perhaps the most serious accusation that can be made against tourism is the manner in which both members of the industry and destination authorities alike have exploited indigenous populations in their desire to develop tourism in ways that would maximise their own interests. There are countless examples of such exploitation, involving child labour, sexual exploitation and the wholesale removal of locals from their tribal lands to permit the development of tourism. For example, the Masai tribespeople have been removed from their Ngorongoro crater hunting lands in Tanzania in order to allow tourists free movement to photograph wildlife. Botswana has also evicted Gana and Gwi bushmen from their land in the central Kalahari game reserve to open the area to tourism. International opprobrium followed the removal and forced labour of Burmese people to enhance tourist projects in Myanmar.

Tourism Concern and other groups such as Tourism Watch in Germany have been particularly active in drawing attention to the exploitation of porters engaged in trekking and mountaineering tours in several countries. Publicity about their plight led to the formation of an International Porter Protection Group to oversee conditions on Mount Kilimanjaro, Tanzania (where porters were frequently obliged to carry loads of up to 60 kg for low pay, dressed in inadequate protective clothing), in the Himalayas and on the Inca Trail in Peru (Figure 5.3), where official guidelines are designed to ensure that packs do not exceed 20 kg and are weighed by government officials.

FIGURE 5.3 Peruvian porters about to depart for Machu Picchu along the Inca Trail

Photo: Claire Humphreys

Sexual exploitation, especially of minors, has also been a cause of considerable concern in several developing countries, and pressure groups such as ECPAT and the World Council of Churches have encouraged the implementation of legislation to protect minors and prosecute offenders within their own countries for offences committed abroad. The UK reacted in 1997 with the passing of the Sex Offenders Act (UK), including a section that, for the first time, allowed such prosecutions to take place, although the difficulty of gathering evidence in developing countries has hindered the implementation of the Act. As we have mentioned earlier in this chapter, some tourism organisations are pledging a response by signing up to The Code (www.thecode.org).

MANAGING THE SOCIAL IMPACTS OF TOURISM

Sustainable tourism, in terms of the social impacts of tourism on indigenous populations, needs to be managed. It is important that good relations are established between locals and guests, so that guests are welcomed to the region or country and social interactions benefit both parties. There are different approaches to ensuring this and the choice is essentially between two diametrically opposed management methods. Responsible officials can attempt to integrate guests into the local community and control the overall number of visitors so that the local population does not become swamped by tourists. This is really only practical where demand for the destination is limited to comparatively small numbers and the market attracted shows empathy for, and sensitivity towards, local culture. Thus, specialist tourism will allow for this solution to be adopted, but mass tourism will not.

Alternatively, officials can aim to concentrate the visitors in particular districts (sometimes referred to as tourist 'ghettos', often some distance away from residential neighbourhoods) so that any damage is limited to the few locals who will have contact with those guests, usually in the form of commercial transactions. In this way, most locals and visitors will not come into direct contact with one another, though this may also reduce the economic benefit of tourism to the local community. One solution of this kind is the integrated resort complex offering all-inclusive packages. Such resorts are becoming increasingly common at long-haul destinations; examples are found in Cancún, Mexico, Nusa Dua in Bali, Indonesia, Puerto Plata in the Dominican Republic and the Langkawi development in Malaysia. All-inclusive resorts can also be operated sustainably if locals are employed in skilled as well as less-skilled jobs at the site and much of what is consumed at the resort is produced in the surrounding area.

Government policies to attract large numbers of tourists have given way to policies designed to attract particular tourist markets. While this has, in most cases, meant trying to attract wealthy, high-spend visitors, it has sometimes led to a move to encourage visits by those who will have the least impact on local populations – that is, those who will integrate well and accept local customs rather than seek to impose their own standards on locals. Some have gone further, however. The local authority at Alassio, Italy, took rather extreme action in 1994 in an effort to discourage day trippers and *sacopelisti* (sleeping-baggers) who slept on the beaches and brought little income into the town. It asked the railways to provide fewer trains to the resort on weekends. Tourists were also to be accosted and asked to show that they were carrying at least 50,000 lira as spending money. Such approaches are isolated, however, and for the most part, destination authorities have recognised that their obligation is to grow tourism, while ensuring that, as far as possible, whatever impact tourists have on local populations should be beneficial to locals.

BRINGING ECONOMIC BENEFITS TO LOCALS

One other issue is the need to ensure that locals are involved in all stages of the development of tourism at a destination. This means that the onus is on developers and authorities to consult with locals at all levels during the process of development, encourage their participation and ensure that indigenous populations benefit economically from incoming tourism, by the provision of employment at all levels and ownership of facilities. All these activities, however, require a measure of sophistication among the local population, the provision of essential education and training, as well as assistance in raising finance for investment in local tourist businesses. The solution cannot be achieved merely by putting businesses into the hands of local residents. To illustrate this, the example can be given of a tour-operating company in Arnhem Land, Australia, that was originally managed by foreign nationals, but was eventually handed over to local Aboriginal administration. While the new Aboriginal owners were fully capable of handling the operational aspects of the programme, they had little knowledge of, and no contact with, the overseas markets they expected to serve and, in consequence, found it difficult to attract new business. Other schemes, however, have been handled more successfully. One example is the innovation of employing local Bedouin tribesmen to act as escorts for groups of trekkers across the Sinai Peninsula. Similarly, a sustainable village project in Gomorszolos, Hungary, involves tours of small groups (a maximum of 12 people) staying in locally owned hotels, using local guides, and with local conservation projects being undertaken that are partly funded by the income generated by the tours.

EXAMPLE

Tourism ethics and local community benefits

In 2011, the UNWTO hosted a seminar on tourism ethics which specifically discussed the extent to which the social and economic benefits of tourism reached local communities. The seminar concluded that while it is commonly appreciated that tourism can drive job creation and economic development in local communities, less awareness is given to the possibility that it can also increase community access to essential services such as water, sanitation, telecommunications and transport. When not properly managed, however, the positive benefits of tourism run the risk of bypassing local residents.

For over a decade, the UNWTO has promoted a global code of ethics designed to guide the key players in tourism development. The code of ethics has ten key principles, with Article 5 specifically stating that tourism should be 'a beneficial activity for host countries and communities'. Article 5 proposes that tourism policies should be applied in such a way as to help raise the standard of living of the populations of the regions visited, that tourism development should meet local needs and that, where possible, priority should be given to local manpower.

Source: UNWTO, 2014

THE IMPACTS OF TRAVEL ON TOURISTS' HEALTH

An impact is a two-way process and we have examined many of the positive and negative effects of tourism in this chapter. It is notable how the lifestyles of many tourists have changed as a result of their experiences of travelling abroad. They often have more adventurous tastes in food, consume more wine at the expense of beers and hard spirits, and have a wider appreciation of foreign cultural activities, even a greater willingness to master the elements of a foreign language. These are just some of the things that tourists bring back with them to enrich their lives in their home countries. Unfortunately, other things they bring back with them can be less welcome.

SKIN CANCER

Severe sunburn is among the commonest of the ailments afflicting tourists from the generating countries, the result of a desire to maximise exposure to the sun during the brief period spent abroad on holiday. While sunburn is painful, this may be just one impact of spending time in the sun.

The propensity to develop skin cancer has increased as the world's protective ozone layer has been reduced by atmospheric pollution. It is estimated that 80% of all skin melanomas affect fair-skinned people, and those who have experienced sunburn, especially in childhood, are at higher risk. Interestingly, the recent growth in the use of tanning beds to gain and maintain a tan has also influenced statistics on skin cancer. Governments have mounted campaigns to draw attention to the problem. In Australia, for example, the 'slip, slap, slop' campaign (slip on a T-shirt, slap on a hat, slop on suncream) has been highly effective in educating a country of sunlovers.

DIETARY ILLNESSES

Exposure to contaminated food results in other common holiday ailments, ranging from simple upset stomachs to hepatitis and dysentery. The incidence of these kinds of illnesses is increasing as holidaymakers become more adventurous, visiting areas of the world where poor hygiene and inadequate supervision are widespread, and taking more risks when sampling the local food.

INFECTIOUS DISEASES

Tropical diseases are becoming more commonplace, with malaria leading the field; several deaths occur each year among British tourists, many of whom disregard even the most basic recommended precautions. Some forms of malaria are becoming highly resistant to standard prescription drugs, although recent research offers hope of a vaccine within a generation.

Outbreaks of disease such as SARS, avian flu and swine flu also severely impact tourist movements, while the global spread of HIV/AIDS – especially, but by no means restricted to, African and Asian destinations – coupled with lax sexual mores among many travellers, compounds the health threats for tourists.

The solution to most of these problems lies in better education, of both hosts and guests, with the onus being on the travel industry to get the message across to their customers through brochures, websites and on-the-spot resort representatives.

EXAMPLE

Malaria

As the number of international trips taken swells, many to tropical regions that are not malaria-free, so the concern grows for the impacts on tourism. Travellers visiting such areas can reduce the likelihood of catching malaria by avoiding mosquito bites and taking medication that increases immunity. Annually, around 1700 cases of malaria arise in the UK, with most infections occurring among UK travellers (rather than visitors to the UK bringing the infection with them). Similar levels of infection occur in other European nations. This may be influenced by the lack of natural immunity and lack of precautions taken. The latter seems to be a particular problem as frequent travellers become somewhat blasé in their pre-travel preparations and destination research.

Sources: Lalloo and Hill, 2008; Meades, 2016

POLITICO-CULTURAL IMPACTS

Where significant economic benefits are likely to follow from influxes of tourists, tourism can be a force for good politically. This is exemplified by the 2008 Olympics, held in the Republic of China, where the government felt obliged, during the period in which the Games were in progress, to relax (if only marginally and temporarily) some of its authoritarian controls and display a more democratic face to the world. It is almost inevitable that large numbers of tourists visiting a country over extended periods of time will eventually influence the political culture of that country, often for the good.

Controversy inevitably surrounds the question of whether or not tourists should be encouraged to visit more extreme regimes, Myanmar (Burma) being a case in point. The argument favouring visits is that interactions between hosts and guests, however closely controlled, will be of some benefit to locals, culturally as well as economically, while the contrary view is taken by those who believe that tourist revenues flowing into authoritarian coffers benefit and reinforce the regime.

One political issue confronting the global tourism industry, however, is the growth in terrorism, which threatens to undermine both travel and understanding between nations. Attacks directed against Westerners can lead to a dramatic reduction in the flow of tourists to those countries, some of whose economies are heavily dependent on tourism. Local civil wars in some areas of the globe inhibit tourism. Egypt, for example, saw a sharp decline in tourist arrivals because of the civil unrest which followed the 2011 revolution and the ousting of Egypt's first democratically elected president (and now deceased), Mohamed Morsi, in 2013. Government figures suggest that tourist arrivals in 2013 were down on 2012 levels by almost 18%.

The UK foreign office has been frequently accused of ambivalence in the guidance given to tourists, while the industry itself, including travel insurance companies, is obliged to follow its governments' directives in determining whether or not holidays should be withdrawn following attacks. The authorities in the leading generating countries are seldom consistent in tackling these issues, and tourists themselves tend to vary in their reactions. American tourists, for instance, show greater reluctance to travel to countries where there is a perceived threat, however remote, while European travellers appear more resilient.

LEGISLATION AND GUIDANCE PROTECTING THE TOURIST DESTINATION

Awareness of the need for planning is the first step in attempting to control the worst effects of mass tourism. However, in the early stages of such awareness, authorities failed to make the distinction between cultural and environmental impacts, with concern for sustainability initially concentrating largely on environmental issues. The origins of sustainable tourism legislation to cover both cultural and environmental impacts will therefore be examined at this point, while specifically environmental issues will be examined in the next chapter.

Broad awareness of the problems that tourism creates can be traced back to at least the 1960s, but it was another 20 years before they began to be addressed, with legislation introduced to dampen their impact. Influential voices made themselves heard, calling for a new tourism, variously described as 'sustainable tourism', 'ecotourism', 'green tourism', 'soft tourism' and, eventually, 'responsible tourism'. Proponents of sustainability have argued that **responsible tourism** should be defined as underpinning a properly thought-out management strategy, with collaboration between the private and public sectors to prevent irreparable damage before it is too late.

One of the early expressions of concern was manifested when the United Nations World Tourism Organization (UNWTO) and the United Nations Environment Programme (UNEP) issued a joint declaration in 1982 calling for the rational management of tourism to protect, enhance and improve the environment. In the following year, they suggested employing zoning strategies to concentrate tourists in those regions that could best absorb them and disperse them where environments were viewed as being too fragile to sustain mass tourism.

It is important to recognise that not all tourists are seeking the same forms of tourism, just as the terms used above to describe the new tourism are not necessarily synonymous. Ecotourism in its early days was described by the environmentalist Hector Ceballos-Lascurain as 'that tourism that involves traveling to relatively undisturbed natural areas with the specific object of studying, admiring and enjoying the scenery and its wild plants and animals, as well as any existing cultural aspects (both past and present) found in these areas' (1987: 13).

It is arguable that all forms of tourism should be 'sustainable' and not destroy the destination to which the tourist is attracted. Perhaps a better definition is that offered by The International Ecotourism Society itself: ecotourism is defined as 'responsible travel to natural areas that conserves the environment, sustains the wellbeing of the local people, and involves interpretation and education' (TIES, 2015). This definition makes it clear that such tourism includes a responsibility to both the environment and the indigenous populations.

Tourism must be environmentally compatible, as the World Travel and Tourism Council (WTTC) proposed in its ten-point guidelines (see Figure 5.4). It will be noted that only two of the ten points refer specifically to issues that can be defined as socio-cultural.

1. Identify and minimize product and operational environmental problems, paying particular attention to new projects.
2. Pay due regard to environmental concerns in design, planning, construction and implementation.
3. Be sensitive to conservation of environmentally protected or threatened areas, species or scenic aesthetics, achieving landscape enhancement where possible.
4. Practise energy conservation, reduce and recycle waste, practise freshwater management and control sewage disposal.
5. Control and diminish air emissions and pollutants.
6. Monitor, control and reduce noise levels.
7. Control, reduce and eliminate environmentally unfriendly products, such as asbestos, CFCs, pesticides and toxic, corrosive, infectious, explosive or flammable material.
8. Respect and support historic or religious objects and sites.
9. Exercise due regard for the interests of local populations, including their history, traditions and culture and future development.
10. Consider environmental issues as a key factor in the overall development of travel and tourism destinations.

FIGURE 5.4 Guidelines for sustainable tourism

Courtesy of the World Travel and Tourism Council

By comparison, the following ten-point set of principles established by Tourism Concern (Eber, 1992) appears to achieve a more equal balance between socio-cultural and environmental elements:

1. using resources sustainably
2. reducing overconsumption and waste
3. maintaining diversity
4. integrating tourism into planning
5. supporting local economies
6. involving local economies
7. consulting stakeholders and the public
8. training staff
9. marketing tourism responsibly
10. undertaking research.

The issue of sustainability was boosted by the concern expressed by the United Nations General Assembly in the mid-1980s, which established a commission to look in depth at the planet's people and resources and make recommendations on ways to achieve long-term sustainable development. The Brundtland Commission presented its report *Our Common Future* in 1987, adopting the definition of sustainable development as 'development that meets the needs of the present without compromising the ability of future generations to meet their own needs' (Brundtland Commission, 1987).

The influence of this report soon led to the UN organising a major international conference on the topic. The Conference on Environment and Development (the so-called Earth Summit) was held at Rio de Janeiro in 1992. Although tourism neither appeared as an issue in the original Brundtland Report, nor was included in the agenda of the Rio meeting, the industry's planning and development have been heavily influenced by the recommendations emerging from these two sources, most notably by the conference's Agenda 21, a guide for local government action to reconcile development and sustainability regarding the environment.

The year 1992 was a momentous one for sustainability. The hospitality industry launched its International Hotel Environment Initiative (IHEI), designed to reduce the impact of staying visitors on the environment, while, in the same year, the UK-based pressure group Tourism Concern set out its own guidelines (listed above) and began actively to lobby the private sector to take more account of the need for sustainable planning.

By the start of the twenty-first century, the concept had become familiar, both within the industry and among the travelling public. The UNEP introduced its Initiative for Sustainable Tourism, which was aimed at tour operators and adopted in 2000. This was followed by a UN declaration to designate 2002 as the International Year of Ecotourism (IYE). A World Summit on Sustainable Development was held in Johannesburg, also in 2002, and for the first time it took into account the importance of sustainability in the tourism industry. As a direct result of the Johannesburg summit, the UK Foreign Office introduced a Sustainable Tourism Initiative, to which over 40 companies (including the leading tour operators) subscribed. The result was the formation in 2003 of the Travel Foundation, which is strongly supported by both commercial and environmental organisations and industry bodies, such as the Association of British Travel Agents (ABTA) and the Association of Independent Tour Operators (AITO). The Foundation's stated mission is 'to bring together stakeholders to develop practical solutions which maximise the benefits and minimise the negative impacts of tourism in destinations'.

EXAMPLE

EU agenda for a sustainable and competitive European tourism

In 2007, the EU published a communication asserting the need for sustainability in tourism planning and development. This recognised that development of tourist destinations is linked to the natural environment, cultural distinctiveness, social interaction and the wellbeing of local populations (European Commission, 2007).

This report highlighted several challenges to achieving sustainable tourism, including conservation management of natural and cultural resources, the need to minimise resource use and pollution, managing the wellbeing of communities and addressing the environmental impact of transport related to tourism.

Other organisations with links to industry, such as the UNWTO and the WTTC, have added their support for the principles of sustainable development, which aim to minimise damage to the environment, wildlife and local indigenous populations. These organisations have particularly recommended the use of local building materials for tourist sites, the recycling of waste and water, and the recruitment of locals for jobs within tourism. Together with the Earth Council, the two bodies also published a report (and subsequent progress updates), *Agenda 21 for the Travel and Tourism Industry: Towards Environmentally Sustainable Development*, encouraging the industry to take the lead in preserving the environment in the areas it develops.

SUMMARY

In this chapter, we have considered the effects that tourism can have on the host population. The changes that occur may offer positive opportunities to improve the quality of life of the residents and can provide opportunities for self-development and social interaction. It can encourage the local population to value cultural traditions and develop pride in their local area. There are, however, problems caused by an influx of tourists, which can be exacerbated by great differences between the cultures of the host and the guest.

Importantly, it is not just the host who experiences social impacts; tourists themselves can be victims of criminal activity or ill health as an outcome of their travels. On the positive side, tourists can benefit from the interaction between host and guest, as they develop greater understanding of different cultures and places.

As recognition of the socio-cultural impact of tourism grows, it seems that both governments and the tourism industry itself are looking for new ways to protect indigenous cultures and unique destinations.

QUESTIONS AND DISCUSSION POINTS

1. Explain the concept of staged authenticity and discuss what this might mean for the tourist experience.

2. Throughout the chapter, we have discussed many different socio-cultural impacts. What factors are likely to influence the intensity of these impacts?

3. How does Doxey's Irridex help us understand the host–guest relationship?

TASKS

1. In this chapter, we introduced The Code (an initiative to protect children against sexual exploitation). Many tourism organisations have now signed up to The Code and have reported on the activities implemented to protect children. These are available online at www.thecode.org/who-have-signed. Select an organisation and review their latest report on the actions taken to implement the six criteria set by The Code. Summarise these activities in a short report.

2. Obtain a holiday brochure from a travel agent (or download one online from a tour operator). Consider the images used within the brochure and evaluate the extent to which local culture is portrayed to help sell the destination. Deliver your findings in a short presentation.

FURTHER READING

Hall, C. M. and Muller, D. (2018) *The Routledge Handbook of Second Home Tourism and Mobilities*. Abingdon: Routledge.

Krippendorf, J. (1987) *The Holidaymakers: Understanding the impact of leisure and travel*. Oxford: Butterworth-Heinemann.

MacCannell, D. (1989) *The Tourist: A new theory of the leisure class*, 2nd edn. New York: Schocken Books.

Ryan, C. (2003) *Recreational Tourism: Demand and impacts.* Clevedon, OH: Channel View Publications.

Smith, M. K. and Robinson, M. (2006) *Cultural Tourism in a Changing World: Politics, participation and (re)presentation*. Clevedon, OH: Channel View Publications.

Wall, G. and Mathieson, A. (2006) *Tourism: Change, impacts and opportunities*. Harlow: Pearson.

WEBSITES

International Porter Protection Group (IPPG): www.ippg.net

The Code of Conduct for the Protection of Children from Sexual Exploitation in Travel and Tourism: www.thecode.org

The Travel Foundation: www.thetravelfoundation.org.uk

UNWTO Protection of Children in Tourism campaign: www.unwto.org/protectchildren

REFERENCES

Adams, D. (1979) *The Hitchhiker's Guide to the Galaxy*. London: Pan Books.

Brundtland Commission (1987) *The Brundtland Report: World Commission on Environment and Development – Our common future*. Oxford: Oxford University Press. Available online at: www.un-documents.net/our-common-future.pdf [Accessed January 2019].

Ceballos-Lascurain, H. (1987) The future of ecotourism. *Mexico Journal*, January, pp. 13–14.

Doxey, G. V. (1975) *A causation theory of visitor–resident irritants: Methodology and research inferences*. The Impact of Tourism: Travel Research Association Sixth Annual Conference Proceedings, San Diego, CA, Travel Research Association, pp. 57–72.

Eber, S. (1992) *Beyond the Green Horizon: Principles of sustainable tourism*. London: Tourism Concern/WWF.

European Commission (2007) Agenda for a sustainable and competitive European tourism. Brussels, EC, 621 final 19.10.2007.

Gullahorn, J. E. and Gullahorn, J. T. (1963) An extension of the U-curve hypothesis. *Journal of Social Sciences*, 19 (3), 33–47.

Harpaz, B. J. and Prengaman, P. (2017) Controversy over wildlife tourism and selfies in the Amazon. *Seattle Times*, 20 December.

Lalloo, D. G. and Hill, D. R. (2008) Preventing malaria in travellers. *BMJ: British Medical Journal*, 336(7657), 1362–6.

MacCannell, D. (1989) *The Tourist: A new theory of the leisure class*, 2nd edn. New York: Schocken Books.

McIvor, S. (2017) 'Wildlife selfies' aren't cute: They encourage cruelty and animal suffering. *The Guardian*, 3 October.

Meades, S. (2016) Malaria warning: Complacent, unprepared Brit travellers putting themselves at serious risk. *Daily Express*, 25 April.

Rowe, M. (2018) Why does St Ives want to discourage second-home ownership? *Countryfile Magazine*, 23 January.

Smith, V. (ed.) (1978) *Hosts and Guests: The anthropology of tourism*. Oxford: Blackwell.

Smith, V. (ed.) (1989) *Hosts and Guests: The anthropology of tourism*, 2nd edn. Philadelphia, PA: University of Pensylvania Presss.

Sutton, W. A. (1967) Travel and understanding: Notes on the social structure of touring. *International Journal of Comparative Sociology*, 8 (2), 218–23.

The Broadway League (2018) *The Demographics of the Broadway Audience, 2016–2017*. Available online at: www.broadwayleague.com/research/research-reports [Accessed 14 August 2015].

The International Ecotourism Society (TIES) (2015) *What is Ecotourism?* Available online at: www.ecotourism.org/what-is-ecotourism [Accessed 5 June 2018].

United Nations Educational, Scientific and Cultural Organization (UNESCO) (1976) The effects of tourism on socio-cultural values. *Annals of Tourism Research*, 4, 74–105.

UNESCO (2008) *IMPACT: The Effects of Tourism on Culture and the Environment in Asia and the Pacific*. Available online at: http://unesdoc.unesco.org/images/0018/001826/182646e.pdf [Accessed 14 May 2018].

United Nations World Tourism Organization (UNWTO) (2014) *Global Code of Ethics for Tourism*. Madrid: UNWTO. Available online at: http://ethics.unwto.org/en/content/global-code-ethics-tourism [Accessed July 2014].

Virginia Beach CVB (2018) *Virginia Beach Tourism Industry: Frequently asked questions*, January. Available online at: www.vbgov.com/government/departments/cvb/Documents/20180207-CVB-RM-212-FAQs%202018%20_DIAZ%20Tourism.pdf [Accessed 14 May 2018].

6

THE ENVIRONMENTAL IMPACTS OF TOURISM

CONTENTS

LEARNING OUTCOMES

After studying this chapter, you should be able to:

- understand the various ways in which tourism can impact on the environment
- identify and evaluate different approaches to finding solutions to the problems caused by these impacts
- understand the importance of sustainable tourism as it relates to the environment
- recognise how appropriate planning and cooperation between the private and public sectors can help to ensure sustainability.

> The projected sustained growth of the tourism industry will present serious challenges to environmental protection. In general, the tourism industry produces adverse environmental impacts through its consumption of resources, the pollution and waste generated by the development of tourism infrastructure and facilities, transportation and tourist activities. In the absence of proper planning and management, tourism development can create strong competition for the use of land between tourism and other competing uses, leading to rising prices for land and increased pressure to build on agricultural land. (WTO, 1999: 10)

INTRODUCTION

In this chapter, we explore tourism's impacts on the environment and consider the growing awareness of the need to become more sustainable. While the obvious focus will be on how tourism affects the environment at popular tourist destinations, we need to be aware at the same time that the rise in global tourism has environmental impacts that go far beyond those destinations alone. In fact, it is no exaggeration to say that tourism is a major contributor to the despoliation of the environment, notably as a result of transport's contribution to pollution, whether by air, sea or on land.

As tourism expands, so new destinations are put at risk; and twenty-first-century tourists are tending to seek out ever more remote areas of the globe.

EXAMPLE

Tourism in Antarctica

The Antarctic continent has become a regular target for mass tourism, with cruise ships that can carry up to 600 passengers visiting the peninsula on a regular basis and passenger-carrying ice-breakers calling as far south as Scott's and Shackleton's bases. Annual figures for visitors to Antarctica were a mere 6704 in 1992, rising to 12,109 in 2001 and peaking in 2007 at just over 45,000. The following seasons saw levels fall to around 35,000 annually but numbers have grown rapidly in the past five years to exceed 50,000 (Table 6.1). While some visitors only fly over the continent – often taking a flight to reach the South Pole itself – the majority (between 75% and 85% of all visitors) land in order to take part in some form of sightseeing or adventure activity, which may include seal and penguin watching, overnight camping, cross-country skiing or kayaking.

The popularity of the huge penguin colonies (perhaps partly attributable to the film *March of the Penguins*) has meant that some of the colonies are receiving as many as three visits every day, impacting on the birds' behaviour and breeding patterns.

There have also been a number of issues with the vessels themselves. In 2007, the MS NordKapp was involved in a minor accident, and later that year 150 passengers and crew were airlifted from the MV Explorer before it sank in the Antarctic Ocean after hitting an iceberg. In 2009, the Ocean Nova ran aground off the coast of Antarctica, with 65 passengers evacuated

TABLE 6.1 Visitors to Antarctica

Time period	Total	Time period	Total
1999–00	14,623	2012–13	33,962
2003–04	24,318	2013–14	37,044
2006–07	45,652	2014–15	36,271
2008–09	37,573	2015–16	38,069
2009–10	36,642	2016–17	43,915
2010–11	33,438	2017-18	51,707
2011–12	26,003	2018-19	55,764

Source: International Association of Antarctica Tour Operators (IAATO) 2018

for their own safety. The biggest concern is that some vessels were not built to withstand the environmental conditions, making them vulnerable in this inhospitable environment.

Managing these issues is complex. The region is without recognised territorial sovereignty and, as a consequence, regulating tourism has to be achieved through collective agreement. Members of the International Association of Antarctic Tour Operators (IAATO) have adopted a voluntary code of practice to minimise the impacts of visitors, including limiting the number of passengers at any one site to 100, and restricting how close they may approach the penguin colonies. Guidelines to reduce the likelihood of introducing non-native species have also been produced. The difficulty, however, is in policing the many different policies and rulings.

In other ecologically sensitive regions, such as the Galapagos Islands, Costa Rica and Belize, the development of tourism is also controlled, and efforts are made to ensure that all visitors respect the natural environment. The pressures of demand are difficult to resist, however, when the economic benefits to less-developed countries are significant. While in 1974 the authorities set an original target of 12,000 visits to the Galapagos (later revised to 40,000), visitors now number around 225,000 annually, and the ceiling has been to all intents and purposes abolished. The burgeoning tourism industry has attracted residents, mostly from mainland Ecuador, leading to an increase in population level from 5000 in the 1960s to more than 25,000 today. However, despite tourism contributing almost $100 million to the economy, poverty is still a very real issue for many living on the island.

THE ENVIRONMENTAL EFFECTS OF TOURISM

TRANSPORT POLLUTION

Large-scale tourist movement requires the use of mass transportation, particularly by air, and, while aircraft are now twice as fuel-efficient as they were four decades ago, air travel has increased tenfold in that time. In 2010, this resulted in more than 5 billion Revenue Passenger Kilometers (RPK is the number of kilometres flown multiplied by the number of passengers on board), and it is estimated that this figure will increase to 40 billion by 2042 (ICAO, 2016).

Apart from emissions of nitrous oxides (unfortunately, the introduction of quieter, more fuel-efficient and cleaner jet engines has the side-effect of increasing those emissions), these aircraft currently pump carbon dioxide into the upper atmosphere. According to the International Civil Aviation Organization (ICAO), aircraft emissions account for 2%

of all man-made CO2 emissions. The total emission from aviation worldwide is roughly equivalent to that produced by the whole of Germany.

One EU study in 2004 claimed that air travel was responsible for 9% of all global warming, while an article three years later (Gössling and Peeters, 2007) asserted that for European residents, air travel accounted for less than 20% of trips but almost 80% of the greenhouse gases released by tourism-related transport. Emissions are made worse by congestion that leads to stacking over airports and the resultant fuel waste, a problem that is likely to grow as air corridors become more crowded. The rapid expansion of the low-cost airlines, operating on short-haul routes, accounts for a sizeable increase in pollution figures, given that one-fifth of a short-haul aircraft's fuel load is burnt in take-off and landing.

Yet in spite of the clear threat to world health, aviation fuel remains largely untaxed. Fuel taxation was ruled out at the 1944 Chicago Convention in order to boost the post-war airline industry, and even VAT has not yet been applied to airline tickets, in spite of protests from environmentalists. Aviation is specifically exempted from the Kyoto Protocol on climate change.

There has been some success in encouraging the airline industry to take greater responsibility for the pollution created. After years of negotiations, an international agreement has been reached that seeks carbon-neutral aviation growth in the 2020s. This would be achieved through offset activities such as tree planting to soak up the CO2. It would also require airlines to purchase offsets if allowances are exceeded.

Interestingly, the growth of high-speed rail routes across Europe in recent years has led more business travellers to switch from air to train travel, as companies begin to monitor (and offset) their carbon impact.

Other forms of tourism transport make their own contributions to pollution. More than 400 passenger ships now ply world cruise routes, carrying in excess of 28 million passengers each year. The US Environmental Protection Agency (EPA) estimates that, apart from the daily fuel burn, an average cruise ship with 3000 passengers generates some 21,000 gallons of sewage each day – not all of it properly disposed of. Indeed, several leading cruise companies have been prosecuted in recent years for pollution of the seas and rigging instruments to deceive inspections. Waterborne vessels of all kinds, whether on the high seas or on inland rivers, lakes and canals, by cleaning out their tanks or dumping waste overboard, significantly contribute to water pollution, which, in turn, impacts on aquatic wildlife. Even without such illicit dumping, the sheer number of cruise vessels plying popular waterways such as the Caribbean poses a threat through leakages and congestion at key ports. Bermuda is one of several islands now imposing restrictions on the number of cruise ship visits permitted each year.

EXAMPLE

Cruise ship emissions

The expanding demand for cruises has seen expansion in both number and size of ships to serve these markets, and in consequence this sector of the industry is causing ever greater levels of environmental pollution. Maritime fuel is one of the dirtiest and most polluting of all diesels, churned out both at sea and when berthed. While in port and close to US and some European coasts, ships are required to burn low-sulphur fuel; newer ships now include pollution control equipment to further reduce emissions. Despite this, marine pollution analysts in Germany estimate that a large cruise ship burns 150 tonnes of fuel a day and emits more sulphur than several million cars.

Sources: McVeigh, 2017; Vidal, 2016

Inland waterways are, if anything, even more fragile and endangered than coastal waters as a result of excessive use by waterborne leisure transport, whether private or public. Apart from the danger of pollution caused by fuel or oil leaks in rivers, lakes and canals, unless strict speed limits are enforced, riverbanks may be damaged or undermined by the wash from passing boats, causing soil erosion and endangering wildlife.

EXAMPLE

Venice

Venice, with its network of canals, receives up to 20 million visitors every year (Kington, 2009). Most are transported by water during their stay and gondola trips are an expensive but popular form of excursion.

The city is slowly sinking, and its paved areas are subject to frequent flooding. As public transport on the canals is largely motorised, the wash from these vessels is contributing to undermining the foundations of many historic buildings. The Italian government has given Venice the power to limit motorised transport, introduce speed limits and tolls on tourist boats and establish 'blue zones' where transport is limited to gondolas and rowing boats.

It is estimated that 70% of the tourists are day trippers, arriving by bus, car, train and, increasingly, cruise ship. A ban on cruise ships travelling through the lagoon close to the city was overturned in 2014 but the cruise industry has agreed to voluntary restrictions that will keep the very largest of vessels away from this fragile area. However, with 650 ships and 1.8 million passengers passing though the city every year, the environmental impact remains significant.

Finally, account must also be taken of the impact of the many millions of motorists using private and hire cars for their holidays and short breaks. While congestion is the more visible problem arising from the expansion in the numbers of vehicles at popular tourism destinations, pollution resulting from the concentration of exhaust gases in both city and rural tourist destinations can seriously affect the health of tourists and residents alike. The uncontrolled expansion of private vehicles in key tourist cities such as Bangkok can so adversely affect the visitor experience that it threatens to discourage visitors from either travelling there or staying in the city.

A significant proportion of the petrol purchased all over the world is for leisure purposes, whether for touring or day trips; and in some regions the exhaust fumes from these vehicles, when added to those from local traffic, can damage the clean air that is the prime attraction for tourists. This is particularly true of mountainous destinations, where not only touristic appeal but also even plant and animal life can be adversely affected. Some popular mountain resorts, such as Zermatt in Switzerland, have banned non-residential private vehicles from the town, requiring tourists to use park and ride services or rack-and-pinion railways into the resort. The latter provide a picturesque additional attraction to visitors staying there.

The popularity of off-roading with sports utility vehicles (SUVs) is also damaging to the environment in sensitive areas of the world. This sport is popular among American tourists, and some wilderness areas are now under threat, particularly in Utah. Moab, south-east of Salt Lake City, has attracted significant numbers of such vehicles, as have sand dunes in several parts of the world, where these vehicles can destroy sparse scrubland and erode the landscape.

NOISE POLLUTION BY TRANSPORT

All motorised forms of road, sea and air transport can intrude on the calm of a resort by raising noise levels, whether in rural surroundings or in residential areas, and this, too, must be considered a form of pollution.

Aircraft taking off and landing at busy airports severely disturb local residents and tourists alike. Authorities have long recognised the problem of air traffic noise and action has been taken to reduce it. The problem is compounded for night flights, where restrictions are often in force to reduce the problem. Noise limits were first set at Heathrow in 1959 and were applied to Gatwick in 1968 and Stansted in 1993. Although night flights are not banned (except for the noisiest types of aircraft), restrictions are imposed on the number of night departures and arrivals (Butcher, 2017). Noise at airports is an issue for many countries; in India, all airports are still obliged to accept jumbo aircraft throughout the night. Noise-related issues at Zurich airport have also led to heated debates between the Swiss and German governments, as flights into and out of this Swiss airport often follow routes over German territory.

Noise from waterborne vessels is most notable along coasts and in tranquil rural areas where boats using their motors can disturb the peace of the night when travelling along rivers and canals. New waterborne vehicles such as jet bikes and water bikes, often used offshore at popular beach resorts, are particularly noisy, and this (coupled with possible danger to life) has been a factor in attempts to reduce their use offshore at popular Mediterranean resorts.

POLLUTION AT TOURIST DESTINATIONS

Noise pollution that is caused by tourists further compounds the negative impacts of the industry. Tourists visiting national parks and wilderness areas can disrupt wildlife behaviour to an extent that the natural soundscape is hard to appreciate. At the Treetops Hotel in Kenya's Masai Mara National Park, animals visiting the adjacent waterhole at night are driven from the site by the careless loud talk or laughter of a minority of the visitors waiting to see them.

Cities and towns are affected by the cumulative effect of human conversations, shouting and laughter, with the peace of the night also frequently disrupted by late-night music clubs and bars catering to younger tourists. In some resorts, authorities have recognised the danger of negative publicity driving away the family market, and authorised the police to undertake night patrols to combat excessive noise. One such example is Magaluf in Majorca, where police act against pubs or nightclubs registering noise levels higher than 65 decibels. Building construction in fast-developing resorts can also be both visibly and audibly offensive.

EXAMPLE

Noise pollution caused by tourism

The Spanish holiday island of Ibiza has seen protests against the impact of overtourism. In 2017, the island saw the arrival of more than 3 million visitors, far in excess of the 130,000 population. The island is famed for its hedonistic lifestyle and all-night parties, an issue that has concerned local residents because of a parallel rise in crime and noise pollution. One speaker at a protest rally on the island stated, 'We don't reject tourism but we do reject tourism which is unlimited, disrespectful and excessive'. Efforts have been made to curb noise pollution through the introduction of an acoustic protection zone that has set a curfew, requiring outdoor clubs to shut by midnight and other clubs to close by 3am. Restrictions on food outlets also mean customers can only be served inside the premises after 11pm, limiting the use of outdoor terraces late at night.

Source: Dickinson, 2018

The physical pollution of popular destinations poses a growing threat for global tourism. Perhaps the most widespread example is seen in coastal resorts, where beach and offshore water contamination is visible and, in some cases, can be life-threatening to bathers. Across the EU water quality varies, although there have been efforts to encourage improvements across the region. Around 85% of bathing water sites have achieved an 'excellent' rating, with Luxembourg sites achieving 100% at this level, while at the other end of the spectrum only 44.2% of Bulgarian sites have received this rating. Italy, France and Spain have the highest total percentage of sites earning a 'poor' quality rating.

EXAMPLE

Clean water in Europe

The European Union annually reports the quality of bathing waters, both coastal and inland, within the region. Each year, samples of water are taken and countries monitor concentrations of two microbiological factors – intestinal enterococci and Escherichia coli (also known as E.coli). Figure 6.1 shows the percentage of bathing waters meeting excellent standards for each European country.

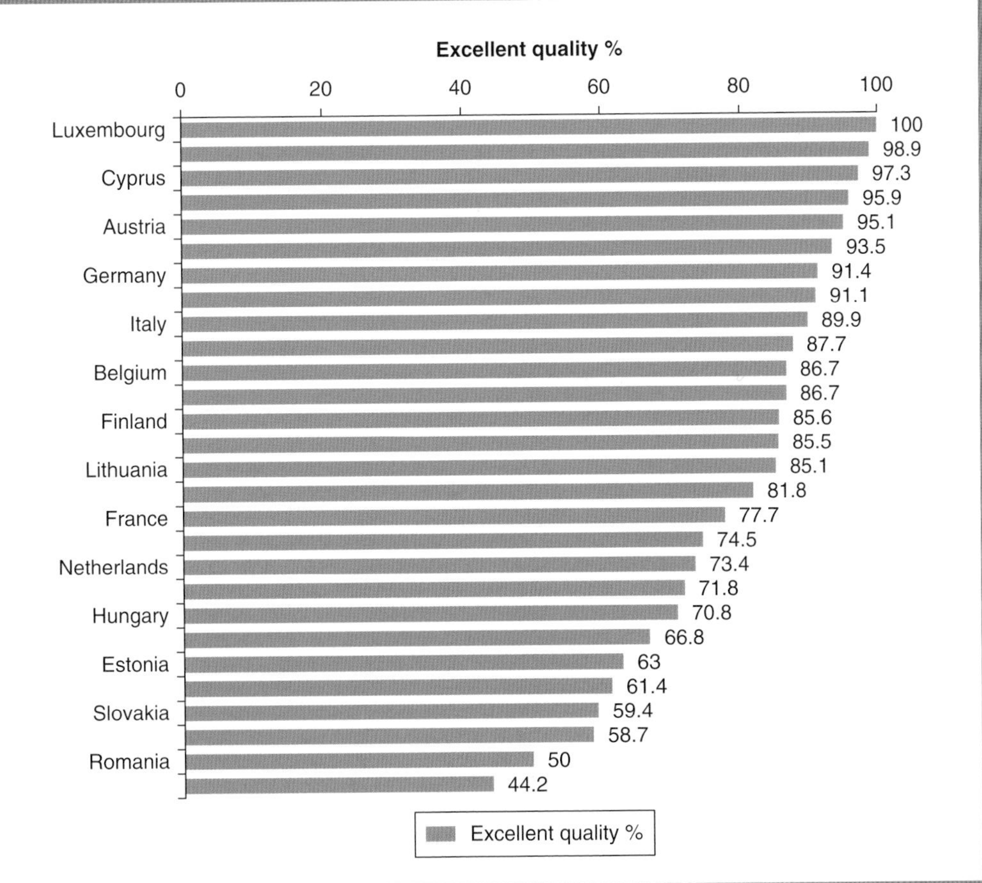

FIGURE 6.1 Bathing water quality

Source: European Environment Agency (EEA), 2018

Beaches in the UK are monitored in several ways. Key certification is in the hands of the environmental charity 'Keep Britain Tidy', awarding blue flags to beaches and bathing water satisfying certain minimal criteria, including water purity and freedom from litter and other pollutants on the beaches themselves. More criteria are applied to beaches qualifying as resorts rather than rural, but both require the beaches to meet at least the mandatory standards of bathing water applied in the EU. The Blue Flag campaign operates in some 45 countries in Europe, Japan, Africa, North and South America and the Caribbean. In 2018, more than 4500 beaches and marinas achieved this award.

VISUAL POLLUTION

Environmental pollution is as much aesthetic as physical. An area of scenic beauty attracts greater numbers of tourists, so more and more of the natural landscape is lost to development, the countryside retreating because of the growth in hotels and other amenities that spring up to cater for tourists' needs. The eventual result is that the site is no longer seen as 'scenic' and the tourists move on to find somewhere more tranquil as well as beautiful. Similarly, without careful control, stately homes that try to meet the needs of visitors provide an ever-expanding range of facilities, such as larger car parks, cafés, shops, directional signposts and toilet facilities, all of which detract from the appeal of the main attraction. Extreme examples of despoliation of the scenery by signposting are readily found in the USA where both countryside and towns can be destroyed by directional signs and advertising hoardings (however, some might argue that, at night, the forest of illuminated signs in towns like Reno and Las Vegas are very much part of the attraction of the resort).

Another aesthetic form of visual pollution is illustrated by the frequent insensitivity in the design of tourist buildings. Lack of planning control is often to blame, as developers prefer to build cheaply, resulting in high-rise hotels lacking character and being out of keeping with the surrounding architecture. In seaside resorts around the world, the concrete skyscraper hotel has become the norm. From Waikiki in Hawaii to Benidorm in Spain, tourists are confronted with architecture that owes nothing to the culture or traditions of the country in which it is found.

Some far-seeing authorities have recognised the potential for this kind of damage and brought in controls to limit it. In some cases, this has led to an insistence that hotels be built using local materials or conform to the vernacular architecture; that is, styles indigenous to the region. Others require that buildings do not exceed a certain height. For example, Tunisia established development regulations which required that new hotel developments in tourist resorts should be no higher than the normal height of the palm trees that surround them. Similarly, the tourism development framework for Oman sets limits on the height of tourism construction in seaside and mountain resorts. Mauritius imposes constraints on both the architectural style and the materials employed in hotel building. While some critics have questioned the rather 'staged' results, with thatched cottages vaguely resembling African kraals, no one doubts the appeal these accommodation units have for tourists. Such legislation clearly must apply to all buildings, not just those for tourism.

EXAMPLE

Visual pollution damaging to tourism in Cyprus

The Larnaca Tourism Board announced that it was having some success in reducing the visual pollution caused by ugly advertising hoardings. The city's strategic tourism plan, which aims to achieve a quality tourism destination, suggests that visual pollution has a direct impact on the Cypriot tourism product. Initiatives across the city have been implemented to upgrade and standardise the design of signage to reduce the cluttered appearance of road junctions and civic squares.

Source: Christou, 2018

Sometimes, planning controls have the effect of restricting innovation in architecture, leaving developers to play it safe by falling back on pastiche or bland designs, attractive only to the most conservative visitor. The attempt to protect local building styles and materials can sometimes have unexpected results, as in Ireland. Roofs traditionally made of corrugated iron have now become such a familiar feature of the landscape that this has been designated a vernacular building material.

Tourists enjoying the landscape of Lanzarote, in the Canary Islands, have much for which to thank local artist César Manrique. He had a major influence on the planning regulations for the island, recognising that tourism's potential could best be fulfilled by sympathetic development. Thus, all housing, apartments and hotels are required to conform to rigorous building regulations imposed by the Department of Tourism on the island. These control not only the style of the buildings but also the colours in which doors and windows may be painted – only white, blue or green paintwork is permitted.

Sometimes, the problem of scale can relate to buildings far smaller than hotels, but it is no less significant. During the early 1990s, the Haworth Parsonage, once the home of the Brontë sisters on the Yorkshire Moors, was threatened with a massive expansion of the visitors' centre, which would have greatly exceeded the size of the original house. The project resulted in an outcry from the public and a rethinking of the plans. The problem of providing sufficient room to accommodate all the visitors – some 80,000 a year in the case of the Bronte Parsonage – at such a small site is a common one and there is no easy, or at least cheap, solution. One plan proposed at Haworth was to conceal the new visitor centre underground, which, although an ideal solution, proved to be too costly for the available funds.

Other common forms of visual pollution by tourists include littering, particularly in areas around picnic sites, and graffiti on buildings. It is a curious fact that even those tourists who come from large cities, where they are so used to seeing litter that they become unconscious of it, immediately become sensitive to litter in a tourist destination.

Resorts that have made the effort to improve their image in recent years tend to start by undertaking a drive against both rubbish in the streets and graffiti on buildings. An important point here is that litter bins should be not only readily available but also attractively designed. Unfortunately, at some sites the fear of terrorist bombs or vandalism has caused rubbish bins to be removed, making rubbish disposal more difficult for tourists.

In environmentally sensitive areas of the world, such as wilderness regions, littering becomes a critical issue because these areas are too far from any public services that could resolve the problem, so the onus is on tourists themselves to safeguard the environment by taking their rubbish with them. This is a very real issue in the Himalayas, now that trekking has become so popular in the region. Many trekkers and organised trekking parties are failing to carry out their litter or dig latrines to hide human waste, with the result that some valleys have become littered with unsightly rubbish, much of which is slow to decompose at the high altitudes there. Environmentalists and enlightened tour operators are encouraging visitors to ensure that their rubbish is either burned or carried out (although local villagers often make use of tins, bags or bottles left behind) and human waste is buried. The authorities are being encouraged to build more permanent composting toilets in frequented areas, using the twin vault principle – each vault being used in alternate years to allow waste to decompose. Nutrients from composted waste can then be used to encourage rapid growth of willow trees, providing a much-needed source of timber for local villagers.

Graffiti has become a common problem in the Western world, with thoughtless tourists desecrating ancient monuments with spray-painted, scratched and even chiselled messages. This, of course, is no new development: the Romans were chiselling their names on Greek monuments 2000 years ago. The sheer scale of modern tourism, however, has forced authorities to take action. In extreme cases this had led to denial of access, as in the case of Stonehenge, where visitors are no longer permitted to walk among the stones themselves, but must be content to view them from a distance.

PROBLEMS OF CONGESTION AND EROSION

Perhaps the most self-evident problem created by mass tourism is that of congestion. In the previous chapter, we considered some of the social implications of overcrowding for tourists and, in this chapter, we will be equally concerned with the effects of overcrowding, in particular on the natural environment. Awareness that the number of tourists in an area was finite led to a consideration of **carrying capacities** – the number of people an area can hold before the impacts caused are beyond recovery. Extensive academic research has explored the concept of overcrowding, especially within recreational settings, and, as a consequence, planning frameworks take into consideration the concept of the Limits of Acceptable Change (LAC). Stankey et al. (1985), in their introduction to the approach, commented that the LAC is a reformulation of the carrying capacity concept, emphasising the conditions desired in an area rather than the total use an area can tolerate. While there has been much criticism highlighting difficulties with the implementation of such an approach, its conceptual ideas have underpinned much of the protection that has occurred since (McCool and Lime, 2001).

Carrying capacity

Congestion is a complex problem because it exists at both a psychological and a physical level. The latter is more easily measured, in terms of the capacity of an area to absorb tourists. Car parks, streets, beaches, ski slopes, cathedrals and similar features all have a finite limit to the number of tourists that they can accommodate at any given time. Theoretically, this is also true of entire regions and countries, although defining the tourist capacity of a city or country has seldom been attempted. Most national tourist offices continue to develop policies aimed at creating an ever-expanding influx of tourists year on year, with little consideration for the ability of the areas to absorb those numbers, although some efforts may be made to divert these influxes to off-peak periods or to less crowded areas of the country. At the urban level, a few cities under extreme pressure, such as Florence and Venice, have taken action to control arrival numbers, including limiting access. This can, of course, lead to disappointment for tourists. In recent years, crowds visiting the Uffizi Gallery and Galleria dell'Accademia (the site of Michelangelo's David) in Florence during peak holiday periods have become so great that the local authorities have had to take the unusual step of temporarily closing the buildings. Indeed, both Florence and Venice face exceptionally heavy demand from international tourists, the latter welcoming 19 million tourists to the Veneto region annually, with about half visiting the city itself. The authorities have responded by reducing coaches to the city from 500 to 150 a day, charging them high fees for the privilege and spot-checking arterial roads out of the city to enforce compliance.

The rapid escalation in deployment of mega-ships calling at popular coastal destinations has made management of such sites critical. Dubrovnik, a key port for these vessels, can witness four or more such vessels daily, disgorging over 12,000 passengers at a time into its narrow streets, resulting in pedestrians squeezing shoulder to shoulder in their efforts to visit shops and restaurants; in Venice, too, the influx of cruise visitors has resulted in massive congestion in the main shopping streets. The inevitable reaction of local populations is a clear indication of stage 4 in Doxey's Irridex model, described in Chapter 5 (Figures 6.2a and 6.2b).

FIGURES 6.2a and 6.2b Antagonism towards big ship cruising is now widely evident in destinations like Venice

Photos: Chris Holloway

EXAMPLE

Manipulating demand at the Taj Mahal, India

Another tourist site suffering from extreme popularity is the Taj Mahal in India, with some 7 million visitors a year. The palace receives up to 50,000 tourists a day, during peak periods. Since 1995, a price differential was introduced, with higher entry charges for foreign visitors; in 2018 the entry fee for foreign tourists was 1000 rupees (around £11), with a reduced fee of 530 rupees (£5.80) for citizens from the South Asian Association for Regional Cooperation (SAARC) and the Bay of Bengal Initiative for Multi-Sectoral Technical and Economic Cooperation (BIMSEC) countries (which includes Bangladesh and Sri Lanka), while Indian tourists pay 40 rupees (less than £0.50). However, such unique sites are highly price inelastic, thus only a rationing system is likely to limit demand.

Further efforts to manage congestion have seen the Indian government impose a three-hour limit to the time who visitors can spend at the site. It is managed through a timed-ticket system, with visitors who exceed the three-hour limit required to buy a new ticket.

Source: O'Shea, 2018

It is also necessary to understand the psychological capacity of a site – that is, the degree of congestion that tourists will tolerate before it starts to lose its appeal. Quantifying this is far more difficult than physical congestion as individual perceptions of capacity will differ, not only according to the nature of the site itself but also the market attracted to it. Expectations of a remote island paradise will mean that a beach in, say, Fiji will be judged overcrowded much more quickly than, say, a beach in the UK at Bournemouth, while in a resort such as Blackpool a much higher level of crowding may be tolerated, even welcomed, as part of the 'fun experience'.

One attempt to measure the psychological capacity of a beach was carried out at Brittas Bay in Ireland in the early 1970s. Aerial photographs were taken of the number of tourists on the beach on a crowded Sunday afternoon and a questionnaire was circulated to those on the beach to receive their views about the congestion that day. It was found that most visitors would accept around 1000 people per hectare (10 square metres per person) without feeling that the beach was overcrowded.

EXAMPLE

Exceeding carrying capacity

Examining tourism carrying capacity can highlight areas that are under pressure, but finding solutions is more problematic. For three beaches in the Brazilian Amazon region – Colares, Maruda and Murubira – the physical and effective carrying capacity was calculated (taking into account physical, environmental and ecological factors as well as the infrastructure and services available). Following this, the actual numbers visiting the beaches were assessed through hourly counts of the central portion of each beach. Findings revealed that while numbers at Colares beach were easily within the effective carrying capacity, and visitation at Maruda beach exceeded levels by approximately 9%, Murubira beach was suffering under the weight of visitor numbers almost three times the level of the effective carrying capacity.

Although the researchers concluded that such excessive visitor numbers means coastal management measures are necessary to address the impact on the environment, experience from other regions of the world suggests that achieving a response is often problematic, because finding a way to limit numbers in a manner that is acceptable to tourists, the tourism industry and the local population is complex; few local governments are likely to have the political will to impose measures that could potentially damage the economic development of tourism.

Sources: Butler, 2010; Sousa et al., 2014

In so-called *wilderness* areas, of course, the psychological capacity of the region may be very low, while areas sensitive to environmental damage may suffer physically even where there are comparatively few visitors. In the USA, Yellowstone and the Everglades National Parks are both physically under severe threat from tourism. Psychologically, too, they are so remote that any mass tourism will greatly reduce their attractiveness. An extreme example is that of The Wave (see Example box).

EXAMPLE

The Paria Canyon-Vermilion Cliffs Wilderness

The Wave is a rock feature situated in one of the most remote sites in the USA, involving visitors in a 3-mile trek across the Colorado Plateau desert region. The sandstone formation is, nevertheless, of enormous appeal to photographers from all over the world; however, the sensitivity of the region is such that access is limited to just 20 visitors a day, ten of whom are selected months in advance by a lottery run by the US Bureau of Land Management. The remaining ten passes are issued daily, starting at 9am, with visitors again chosen by lottery at the site.

Source: 'The wonder of The Wave', *Sunday Times*, 30 June 2013, p. 3

The behaviour of tourists at wilderness sites will be a factor in deciding their psychological capacity. Many visitors to an isolated area will tend to stay close to their cars, so hikers who are prepared to walk a mile or so away from the car park will readily find the solitude they seek. This is obviously a key for tourism planners, as, by discouraging or forbidding car parking and access by vehicle to the more remote areas, they can then effectively restrict entry to these areas to those seeking solitude.

Some authorities have tried to set standards for particular types of tourist activity as a guide to planners. Table 6.2 is based on one attempt, by the UNWTO (then, WTO), to lay down guidelines in terms of visitors per day per hectare.

TABLE 6.2 Visitor capacity of selected sites

Site/activity	Visitors per day/hectare
Forest park	15
Suburban nature park	15–70
High-density picnicking	300–600
Low-density picnicking	60–200
Golf	10–15
Fishing/sailing	5–30
Speedboating	5–10
Waterskiing	5–15
Skiing	100 (per hectare of trails)
Nature trail hiking	40 (per kilometre)
Nature trail horse riding	25–80 (per kilometre)

Source: Inskip, 1991

The *ecological* capacity to absorb tourists must also be taken into account. While too many tourists in a built-up area can detract from tourism, the physical wear and tear on the environment is limited – at least, in the short term. Too many tourists in a rural or otherwise fragile environment, however, can destroy the balance of nature. This can be seen in the increase in tourists visiting African safari parks, where the number of vehicles hunting for the 'big five' at any one time can resemble a car rally in some areas of the parks.

Erosion

Some sites are particularly fragile. Many sand dunes have been destroyed or seriously eroded in the USA by the use of beach buggies and by four-wheel drive vehicles. In the UK, similar problems are thrown up by motorcycle rallying, which can easily uproot the few clumps of dune grass on which an ecosystem depends. It has been reported (European Environment Agency, 2001) that three-quarters of all sand dunes along the Mediterranean coastline between Spain and Sicily have disappeared as a direct result of the growth of tourism.

EXAMPLE

The Dune du Pilat

Located on the Atlantic coast of the south-west of France, this sand dune is the largest in Europe. It is estimated to be over 100 metres high and 500 metres wide, spanning some 2.7 kilometres of coastline. This natural phenomenon is not a static entity. The wind and tidal movements mean that the dune is constantly moving inland, by several meters each year. Consequently, it has eroded large areas of adjacent pine forest, while at the same time swallowing up some nearby camping sites.

In recent years, improved infrastructure, including enhanced highways, expanded car parks and the development of a visitor centre, has made access to the site more convenient. As a consequence, more than a million visitors annually come to see and climb the sand dune. However, the height of the dune means that walking to the top can be physically taxing. Aware of the impact this may have on some, perhaps less fit and mobile, tourists, the managers of the site have installed a staircase which helps ease the climb to the top.

Management of this unique site is the preserve of a public body representing the local commune (La Teste de Buch), the district council (Gironde) and the regional council (Nouvelle Aquitaine). Together, their mission includes the preservation and management of the site as well as ensuring a positive welcome for visitors. Operation of the site is guided by an advisory committee (which includes the Coastal Conservation Authority) and a scientific committee comprising archaeologists, geologists and environmental education groups.

FIGURE 6.3 Tourists climbing the Dune du Pilat

Photo: Shutterstock

An idea of the effect of erosion can be gained from the experiences of the 15 UK national parks, which receive over 100 million visitors annually. The pressure on the land can be immense. Table 6.3 records the number of visitor days per square kilometre. Remember, however, that those using a park do not spread evenly over its area but are often attracted to key locations, termed **honeypots**, as visitors swarm in large numbers to these places. As a result, in some areas footpaths are overused, leading to soil becoming compacted and grass and plants dying. Under some circumstances, the soil becomes loosened and is then lost through wind erosion. A report by the Lake District National Park Authority (n.d.) revealed that a path from Coledale Hause towards Wandope had suffered such extensive erosion that it had formed a gully almost two metres deep.

TABLE 6.3 Visitors to national parks in the UK

National Park	Visitor days per km^2
Brecon Beacons	3720
Broads	51,155
Cairngorms	685
Dartmoor	3253
Exmoor	2882
Lake District	10,161
Loch Lomond and the Trossachs	3753
New Forest	23,684
Northumberland	1622
North York Moors	7531
Peak District	8177
Pembrokeshire Coast	20,934
Snowdonia	4779
South Downs	24,015
Yorkshire Dales	5782

Note: Visitor days takes into account that visitors may stay in a national park for several days and therefore one person coming for a day = one visitor day; one person coming for a week = seven visitor days.

Source: National Parks UK, 2014

This followed similar efforts, made in the early 1990s, to counteract the erosion of footpaths. Across the moors near Haworth, some 25,000 visitors had turned parts of the Brontë Way into a quagmire, making it necessary to set flagstones into the track. Other running repairs have had to be made to long-distance footpaths such as those on the Pennine Way and Cleveland Way. Such artificial landscaping, of course, creates a very different visual landscape from the wild moorland it replaces, but it is a solution that is being used more widely as such footpaths have to deal with greater numbers of visitors each year.

Climbers, too, also damage the parks. With the increased interest in activity holidays, climbing is becoming a very popular pastime. Some 250,000 people climb Mam Tor in Derbyshire every year, for example, and this has so affected the mountain that the summit had to be restored with an importation of 300 tons of rock and soil.

To protect fragile environments, there are often restrictions and regulations introduced. Conflicts between different users, such as walkers, mountain bikers, horse riders and off-road vehicles, can occur and regulations may be needed to ensure that the needs of different groups are met. The impacts from these groups can also differ, thus a variety of protective activities may be needed. There is, however, an inevitable trade-off between protection and economic wellbeing.

Erosion of constructed sites by tourists

Although constructed sites are generally less fragile than natural ones, these too can be affected by erosion in the long term – externally by weather, internally by wear and tear from multiple visitors. Sites exposed to the elements may have to restrict access, especially if they become so dilapidated that they pose a danger to visitors, as is the case with some historic castles.

The Acropolis in Athens has had to be partially closed to tourists to avoid wear and tear on the floors of the ancient buildings, while the wooden floors and staircases of popular attractions such as Shakespeare's birthplace in Stratford-upon-Avon also suffer from the countless footsteps to which they are subjected each year. Stratford, with a population of only 26,000, receives 4.9 million visitors every year, a substantial proportion of whom will want to visit Shakespeare's birthplace. The high numbers led major attractions to construct artificial walkways above the level of the floor to preserve the original flooring. Nearly a million people visit Bath's Pump Rooms and the Roman Baths complex each year and inevitably there are fears for the original stone flooring of the Baths. It may put the problem into context when it is revealed that Roman visitors, wearing hob-nailed boots, did even more damage to the original flooring than do contemporary visitors, though they were far fewer in number.

THE DANGER OF TOURISM TO FLORA AND FAUNA

Wildlife can be an important attraction for some tourist destinations. The Great Barrier Reef in Australia is popular with snorkellers and scuba-divers keen to view the fish and the coral, while destinations across Africa attract safari tourists intent on viewing big game. However, tourism can cause many problems, harming the very wildlife the tourists have come to see.

First, we need to recognise that the construction of tourist infrastructure, such as hotels, bars, restaurants and visitor centres, can reduce the land available to the wildlife. Fencing around developments can influence traditional grazing or migration patterns and can draw key resources, such as water, away from rivers and watering holes. There are also issues with the management of waste products; for instance, some wild animals may become scavengers if food remnants are left in accessible places. Animals may also scavenge through rubbish and be harmed by trying to consume plastic packaging, camera batteries and other such detritus. The construction process itself needs to be carefully managed to ensure that the noise does not scare away the wildlife and that it does not harm nesting grounds.

Even where tourism infrastructure is not adjacent to the wildlife, many tourists will still journey to view amazing flora and fauna. As mentioned at the beginning of the chapter, transport can cause pollution, but we also need to recognise that frequent visits by tourists can impact on the breeding patterns of wildlife as well as their patterns for foraging for food and their natural defence responses to humans. Without careful management, these can lead to a decline in the population size. This has affected loggerhead turtles in Greece and Turkey, as well as in the Caribbean. They become distracted from laying their eggs by the bright lights of tourist resorts or the use of searchlights to observe their coming ashore to lay eggs on the beach.

EXAMPLE

Antarctic seabirds

As we mentioned earlier in the chapter, more than 45,000 tourists travel to Antarctica annually and the tourist ships travelling to the continent can be an issue for birdlife in the region. Birds – especially prion and petrel species – land on ships operating in the Southern Ocean and become stranded. The legs of petrels and prions are not designed to walk, so the seabirds have difficulty in taking off again.

This happens because the birds are disoriented by the lights on the ship, with poor weather conditions such as fog and snow compounding the problem. To address this problem, the International Association of Antarctica Tour Operators has developed a protocol for the ship's crew to minimise the impact on seabirds.

At Philip Island, near Melbourne in Australia, 500,000 people a year come to sit and watch the evening 'penguin parade' of fairy penguins coming ashore to their nests. This event has become highly commercialised and the large crowds are proving hard to control, even though ropes are in place to prevent people getting too close to the penguins. Flash photography is forbidden and wardens caution the audiences against noise or even standing up, all of which disturb and alarm the penguins. In practice, however, the public frequently ignore these strictures.

Animal behaviour can change as a result of prolonged exposure to tourists. In some countries, food lures are used to attract wildlife to a particular locality. For example, in Samburu National Park, Kenya, goats are slaughtered and hung up for crocodiles or leopards. This modifies hunting behaviour and may encourage dependency on being fed by humans. In some wildlife parks, hyenas are known to watch for assemblies of four-wheel drive vehicles in order to take the prey from cheetahs' hunts. 'Bearjams' are created in Yellowstone National Park, USA, as bears trade photo opportunities for offerings of food. The dolphins at Monkey Mia in Australia have long been a popular tourist attraction, with coach tours scheduling their arrival with feeding times (see Figure 6.4).

FIGURE 6.4 Feeding the dolphins in Monkey Mia, Australia

Photo: Claire Humphreys

Tourists who choose to engage with nature by visiting wilderness areas, camping in forests and hiking across mountains will still have an impact on the environment. Campfires can draw on local wood and leave scorch marks on the landscape. While each individual fire may seem to have only a small effect, when large numbers of tourists visit, the overall impact can be unsustainable. Furthermore, uneducated tourists may inadvertently cause wildfires, leading to vast tracts of land, some wildlife and occasionally homes being lost.

EXAMPLE

Protecting Annapurna from the trekkers

Nepal has been renowned for its trekking opportunities for decades and many backpackers head to the Everest region. Yet it is estimated that about 60% of trekkers head to the western area of the country to walk in the Annapurna region – more than 158,000 tourists visited in 2017.

The region now faces many environmental problems exacerbated by this inundation of people. The Annapurna Conservation Area Project (ACAP) was established in 1986 with the goal of encouraging more sustainable tourism. To fund conservation efforts, a fee is charged to enter the area, and checkpoints throughout the trekking area monitor this by ensuring that walkers hold the required permits.

One of its key projects was to minimise the use of firewood, in order to reduce forest depletion. The soaring number of visitors, whose fuel wood consumption is twice that of the local people, has exerted immense pressure on forest resources. Local businesses such as lodges were encouraged to convert to kerosene or fuel-efficient wood stoves, while tourists were informed about the variety of ways that they could reduce their impact; suggestions have included avoiding showers if wood is to be burnt for hot water, not choosing foods that require lengthy cooking times, and eating at times when many others are ordering food so that batch cooking is possible. Since its inception, ACAP has supplied more than 1500 improved cooking stoves and 200 pressure cookers, thus reducing fuel wood consumption by more than 30%.

Another major issue the area faces is waste management. It has been estimated that a group of trekkers creates approximately 1 kg per person of non-biodegradable/non-burnable waste during the course of a ten-day trek. The ideal solution is to require that this rubbish is ported out of the region, but all too often this is left at mountain lodges, and builds up on the edge of villages as no waste-removal system exists. ACAP has funded the development of seven rubbish collection centres, over 200 incinerators and 800 rubbish bins, all of which have helped improve sanitation.

Despite the environmental pressure caused by tourism, in recent years a number of alternative trekking routes have been established and promoted so that 'more trekkers are able to experience greater variety, this while continuing to extend tourism opportunities for other remote communities' (NTNC, 2017: 12). One-metre-wide trails have been constructed to ensure safety and ease of access to these new routes.

Even souvenir hunting can affect the ecological balance of a region. The removal of plants has long given cause for concern (the Swiss were expressing anxiety about tourists' habit of picking gentians and other alpine flowers even before the start of the mass tourism movement) and, in Arizona, visitors taking home cacti are affecting the ecology of the desert. Similarly, the removal, either as souvenirs or for commercial sale by tourist enterprises, of coral and rare shells from regions in the Pacific is also a cause for concern.

The desire to bring back souvenirs of animals seen abroad poses another form of threat to endangered species. The Convention on International Trade in Endangered Species (CITES) imposes worldwide restrictions on the importation of certain animals and animal products from countries visited by tourists. Around 5000 endangered animal and 30,000 plant species have been identified, and the importation of many of these or their byproducts is banned, including ivory, sea turtle products, spotted and striped cat furs, coral, reptile skins and seashells, as well as certain rare plants. Concern is also expressed about the ill-treatment of animals that are kept in captivity for the amusement of tourists. While performing bears have largely been removed from the streets of some Eastern European countries following EU pressure, they are still a common sight in China. Even within the EU, one can still find chimpanzees and monkeys exploited for tourist photographs in countries such as Spain, and, of course, bullfighting remains not only legal but also a popular tourist attraction in that country and the South of France. A number of action groups in the UK have been set up to protect and free these animals.

OTHER ENVIRONMENTAL CONSEQUENCES OF MASS TOURISM

Many popular tourist towns have narrow roads, leading not only to problems of severe traffic congestion but also to potential damage to buildings, as tourist coaches try to navigate through these streets. Increasingly, cars and particularly coaches are restricted in terms of access to the centres of such towns, with park and ride schemes or other strategies employed to reduce traffic. Impeding coaches from picking up and setting down passengers in the centre of towns such as Bath, Cambridge or Oxford, however, can make it very difficult for coach companies to operate as many are on short stopover visits as part of a day trip.

Many developing countries face similar problems of congestion and erosion as the popularity of long-haul travel expands. Goa in India was hailed by many operators as an 'unspoilt paradise', but its wide appeal since the 1990s has caused environmental lobbyists such as Tourism Concern to draw attention to the dangers the region faces. Water shortages in the area are aggravated by tourists' consumption (one 5-star hotel uses as much water as five villages and locals face water shortages while swimming pools are filled) and sand dunes have been flattened. Apart from the environmental impacts, there are also social costs. The private beaches mean access by the locals is denied, and 'Westernisation' of the local carnival dilutes the traditional identity and culture of the region. The problems of Goa have been well publicised in recent years, but this has had little effect on reducing the number of visitors or ensuring that tourism in the area is sustainable.

Sometimes, well-meaning attempts by tourist officials to 'improve' an attraction can have the opposite effect. Historic rock carvings over 3000 years old in Scandinavia were painted to make them stand out for visitors. When the paint eventually flakes off, a process that has speeded up with the effect of acid rain, it takes part of the rock surface with it.

Any development of tourism will inevitably require the sacrifice of some natural landscape to make way for tourist facilities. An extreme example of this is to be found in the demand for golf courses. It has been estimated that there are some 30,000 golf courses in the world. In recent years, new courses have been built in areas where water shortages would normally discourage their construction, such as in Dubai, Tunisia and the Egyptian desert, but the popularity of golf tourism drives their development. Golf as a holiday activity, especially among Japanese tourists, has led to a huge increase in demand for courses in the Pacific region. For example, the island of Oahu in Hawaii, which had already constructed 27 courses by 1985, received a further 30 applications after the Hawaii legislature agreed to allow them to be built on agricultural land. Apart from water use issues, the loss of natural scenery and wildlife habitats also needs to be considered.

EXAMPLE

Sustaining golf in the desert

Las Vegas is renowned as a casino destination. Visitors also head to the desert city for weddings, as a base for their visits to the Grand Canyon and to play golf; but the many golf courses require copious amounts of water, a precious resource.

Southern Nevada Water Authority (SNWA) introduced both incentives and penalties to encourage reduced water usage. Golf courses were set a water budget with punative fines for exceeding this level of use. At the same time, courses were encouraged to remove turf (primarily in areas out of play and on driving ranges) and allow the land to return to desert scrub. As an incentive, $1 per square foot was paid in this 'cash for grass' scheme. The cash received helped cover the cost of remodelling the landscape and ultimately reduced the annual water bill for each course. Estimates suggest that 836 acres of turf have been removed from golf courses, with savings in water usage of 2.7 billion gallons.

Sources: Bennett, 2012; Kanigher, 2014

THE ENVIRONMENTAL IMPACTS OF WINTER SPORTS TOURISM

One fragile ecosystem in Europe is under particular threat: the Alps. Because the system is spread across no fewer than seven countries, collaboration to prevent the worst of the environmental effects of tourism is made more difficult. The Alps receive over 120 million visitors a year and some 7 million passenger vehicles cross them each year. To accommodate the huge increase in winter sports tourism that has occurred since World War II, some 3400 km^2 of ski areas have been constructed. The proliferation of ski-lifts, chalets and concrete villages above 6000 feet and the substantial deforestation required to make way for pistes have led to soil erosion, while the high volumes of traffic crossing the Alps contribute to air pollution. The increased use of snow cannons (providing artificial snow created using water and chemical and biological additives) to augment low levels of natural snowfall further exacerbates the environmental impact (WWF, 2018). Furthermore, a new danger is posed by the introduction of roller skiing on grass and four-wheel-drive car racing in summer.

Lillehammer in Norway, site of the 1994 Winter Olympic Games, took account of the problems already occurring in the Alps when designing its new facilities. Apart from efforts to minimise tree clearance, the authorities also took steps to avoid visual pollution in an area where comparatively few buildings exist. Ski jump runs were moulded into the mountainside to ensure that they did not project above the tree line and similar efforts were made to conceal bobsleigh and luge runs in the forests. The speed-skating stadium was built 20 yards away from the water's edge to protect waterfowl, and leak-proof cooling systems were embedded underground in concrete containers. Private cars were excluded from the town during the period of the Olympic Games. The International Olympic Committee has since produced a 'manual on sport and the environment', designed to offer practical guidance on the sustainable development of sporting facilities.

It is not only sports activities that threaten snowscapes. Glaciers, the ecosystems of which are invariably fragile, attract large numbers of sightseers when located in accessible regions. At the Columbia Icefield in Banff National Park, Canada, giant snowmobiles are employed to bring tourists onto the glacier. The inevitable consequence will be damage to the surface of the site, unless strict control is exercised over the number of trips organised.

POSITIVE ENVIRONMENTAL IMPACTS OF TOURISM

While there has been much discussion throughout this chapter of the negative effects of tourism on the environment, tourism can also play a role in protecting the environment. Conservation and regeneration of historic buildings have been achieved in cases where they have successfully become tourist attractions, with financial support coming from entry fees and donations. Beck and Bryan (1971: xxi) reported that 'many historic houses, villages, old churches and so on could not be kept in a proper state of repair without tourist money'. Entry fees can also help fund museums, galleries and other cultural and heritage resources, providing protection for future generations. There are also many cases where historic buildings have been converted for use as tourist facilities, such as hotels, restaurants and tourist attractions like craft centres and working museums.

Conservation of the natural environment can also be encouraged through tourism. Big game in Africa has been protected though a range of initiatives, such as safaris, which provide the local population with an income, through tourism. There has also been extensive debate regarding hunting tourism as a means of wildlife protection, the justification being that wealthy foreigners will pay significant sums to licensed operators to be allowed to stalk and shoot prey. Advocates argue that, properly managed, it can keep rising animal populations in check, while the high fees providing livelihoods for these tourist businesses generate funding for conservation and breeding programmes and can even benefit the hunted creature by providing a reason to conserve it (Rowe, 2009).

EXAMPLE

Trophy hunting and tourism

Hunting tourism is becoming an increasingly interesting sector for many tourism regions. In October 2012, the Canadian Tourism Commission published a positive assessment of the potential opportunities of developing sport fishing and game hunting in Canada. Similarly, Belarus announced strong demand from this sector, estimating that US$15 million is earned through hunting tourism, predominantly from the Russian, Ukrainian, German, Austrian and French markets.

Views on trophy hunting are polarised, with those seeking to protect animals on one side and hunters (and pragmatic conservationists) on the other (Lindsey et al., 2007), who claim that fees paid by tourists pay for conservation and habitat-protection activities.

Big game hunting is permitted in many African countries with South Africa having the largest share of the trophy-hunting market, bringing in £100 million to the economy. With tourists prepared to pay US$125,000 for a lion trophy and $390,000 for a black rhino, the value of big game is significant. But numbers are limited by the Convention on International Trade in Endangered Species (CITES), which establishes quotas for trophy hunting. The current agreement allows five black rhinos to be killed as trophies annually in South Africa.

However, several African countries – including Botswana, Zambia and Kenya – have banned the practice, primarily over concerns that corruption and poaching are threatening species survival.

Conservation of landscapes has been discussed throughout this chapter, with the funding provided by tourist spending an important element in the continued maintenance of these regions. Importantly, tourism programmes designed to protect the environment can also provide education and awareness of sustainability among the local population.

PUBLIC-SECTOR PLANNING FOR CONTROL AND CONSERVATION

We have now seen many examples of the environmental impact of tourism and a few illustrations of how the problems might be managed. Some argue that it is not enough for individual authorities to tackle the situation – it should be tackled on a global scale. Unfortunately, few governments so far have appeared willing to do so at this level. International designation of an attraction as a World Heritage Site by UNESCO undoubtedly helps, and collaborations between groups with vested interests in the sustainable use of natural resources, as we have seen earlier in this chapter with the example of the Dunes de Pilat, are becoming more common.

In Chapter 5, we looked at some of the moves that have been made since the early 1980s across the globe to embrace tourism sustainability. For the most part, the conferences and resulting papers have focused on making recommendations, leaving the question of mandatory control in the hands of national governments. Nonetheless, 150 countries signed up to the Agenda 21 proposals arising from the Rio Summit in 1992 and the EU has taken an active role in recent years in attempting to control the worst effects of environmental pollution, the Blue Flag scheme being typical of this. Costa Rica can be cited as an outstanding example of a sustainability-aware developing country with a rapidly growing tourism market, issuing Certificates for Sustainable Tourism to tourist companies organising holidays in the country.

The announcement by President Donald Trump in 2017 that the USA would withdraw from the Paris Agreement (an international convention to reduce greenhouse gas emissions) sparked extensive discussion on government efforts internationally to mitigate against environmental pollution. President Trump has also reduced the area of protected public lands by scaling down two national monument areas, leasing public land for mining and impacting other existing conservation activities by reducing National Parks Service budgets.

The creation of national parks to preserve sites of scenic beauty is by no means of recent origin. As early as 1872, the USA established its first national park at Yellowstone, while Europe's Abisco National Park in Sweden dates from 1909. The intention behind the creation of these parks was to ensure that visitors did not destroy the landscapes that they had come to see. Sustainability may be a word of recent origin in tourism, but the concept is much older. The International Union for Conservation of Nature (IUCN) now recognises more than 68,000 protected areas worldwide, covering an area of 5.7 million square miles, nearly 10% of the globe. As sustainability becomes a more important issue each year and, despite the changes occurring in the USA, the volume of protected land swells.

EXAMPLE

Gabon

After an approach by American ecologist and explorer Mike Fay to the Gabon president in 2002, that country's authorities announced at the Rio conference the planned creation of 13 new national parks, with the aim of becoming Africa's leading destination for eco-travel.

The parks extend to over 11,000 square miles, around 11% of the country's land mass. The country has outstanding potential for ecotourism as it hosts marine, island, coral-reef, coastal, lagoon, swamp and rainforest environments (Laurance et al., 2006). Support for these parks has come from organisations such as the Wildlife Conservation Society (WCS), World

Wide Fund for Nature (WWF), Conservation International (CI), ECOFAC and the Smithsonian Institution.

One difficulty in establishing these parks is related to the relocation of the indigenous population. Resettling thousands of people onto new, equally fertile and prosperous, land is an expensive and slow process (Dowie, 2009). The balance between environmental protection and enhancing economic benefits and social wellbeing is always difficult to achieve. The parks have experienced extensive poaching, with 11,000 elephants killed since 2004, fuelled by the demand for ivory.

Of course, most countries and local authorities are generally well-intentioned, but they can also inadvertently become partners in despoliation when putting commercial advantage before aesthetic considerations. Spain, for example, experienced a sudden boom in tourism during the 1960s, but went on to allow massive overdevelopment along its east coast and in the Balearic and Canary Islands, which nearly destroyed its success.

Failure to maintain the quality of the environment in other directions can also lead to a massive loss of tourist business, as the popular Spanish resort of Salou found, following a drinking water scare in 1989. The widespread fall-off in Western European visitors to Spain in the 1980s and 1990s (mitigated to some extent by a rise in Eastern European and Russian visitors), however, caused a reversal of policy and much greater control being exercised over speculative tourism development. A good example of this can be found in the Balearics.

Parliament passed legislation in 1991 to nominate large tracts of land in Majorca, Ibiza and Formentera as zones restricted from further development. In Majorca, only 4- and 5-star hotels were permitted to be constructed, with a minimum of 120 square metres of land per bed, in an effort to drive tourism upmarket. In order for planning permission to be granted for the construction of new hotels, developers have been required to purchase and knock down an existing and deteriorating hotel of inferior status. Badly run-down resorts such as Magaluf were given an injection of capital to widen pavements, introduce traffic-free zones, plant trees and shrubs and install new litter bins and graffiti-free seating. In all, Spain spent over £300 million over a five-year period (ending in the early 1990s) on improving facilities for tourists along its coasts.

In 2003, the Balearics took a further step in sustainability, by introducing an eco-tax that was designed to fund sustainable improvements to tourism in the islands. Unfortunately, insufficient thought went into its implementation. Hotels were expected to collect this from guests themselves, but the resultant discontent led to the tax being scrapped by the new local government, which was elected a year later.

Interestingly, the financial pressures experienced at the end of the 'noughties' led many local governments to revisit the issue of tourist taxation (discussed in Chapter 4), ostensibly to provide funds to manage pressure caused by tourists.

Other countries notable for their failure to provide adequate controls as their tourism industry boomed (and failure to learn the lessons from Spain's experience) include both Greece and Turkey. Among developing countries, Goa in India and the Dominican Republic in the Caribbean were both unprepared for the scale of the mass tourism generated by tour operators in the 1990s and failed to control their development adequately.

Spain's experience is a cautionary one, and the degree to which it has been successful in turning around its fortunes is notable. In general, however, the evidence suggests that, once a resort has gone downmarket, it can be very hard to bring back higher-quality tourists. Simply constructing new, high-price hotels will not lead to success in attracting a new market.

EXAMPLE

Governmental control on visitor numbers

Some countries have taken the view that, where tourism does not already have a strong hold, it is best to control entry to reduce the risk of environmental and cultural despoliation occurring.

The Government of Bhutan only began to open its borders to tourism in the 1970s, but to ensure it protected its traditions and environment, a policy limited the number of foreign visitors to just 15,000 per year. It introduced a high fee to reduce demand (at the time of writing, this is $250 per day, with a $50 per day reduction in the off season), but provided food, internal transport and lodging within this amount. It also includes $65 which goes to fund education, healthcare and poverty alleviation initiatives for the local population. In 2010, with visitor numbers at 30,000 annually, Prime Minister Jigme Thinley announced plans to expand entry permits to allow 100,000 tourists by 2012, an almost threefold increase. This opened the door for further expansion and arrival figures for 2017 revealed that more than 254,000 tourists travelled to Bhutan, with India being the biggest source market (UNWTO, 2018).

At the local level, some form of public control is also essential to ensure that each new building is well designed and all existing buildings of quality are carefully preserved and restored. Heritage is also a sustainability issue, one that goes beyond the interests of tourism alone. It underpins the very fabric of a society and, in nations with a wealth of heritage buildings, each building lost through failure to protect it or enforce its restoration becomes an irreparable loss to the culture of those nations. Europe owes much of its tourism demand to the attractiveness of its traditional heritage and landscape, and destinations, whether rural, urban or seaside, that fail to concern themselves with the sustainability of their attractions cannot expect to retain their tourists.

EXAMPLE

Environmental protection in the UK

In the UK, sensitivity to the impact of tourism on the environment dates back at least as far as the nineteenth century. Concern over possible despoliation of the Lake District, then growing in popularity, led to the formation of a Defence Society in 1883 to protect the region from commercial exploitation. The National Trust was created in 1894 to safeguard places of 'historic interest and natural beauty' and promptly bought four and a half acres of coastal clifftop in Cardigan Bay.

The National Parks and Access to the Countryside Act 1949 led to the formation of ten national parks in England and Wales, each administered by a National Park Authority. The Norfolk Broads achieved the equivalent national park status under the Norfolk and Suffolk Broads Act of 1988. The New Forest on the Hampshire/Dorset borders was raised to national park status in 2004 and the South Downs area followed recently, the latter being formed from two existing Areas of Outstanding Natural Beauty. Scotland created its first two designated national parks – first Loch Lomond and the Trossachs, then the Cairngorms – in 2002 and 2003, respectively.

The National Parks Act also led to the designation of 46 areas as Areas of Outstanding Natural Beauty (38 in England and Wales and eight in Northern Ireland) that merited protection against exploitation. The first of these, the Quantock Hills in Somerset, was so designated in 1957, while the last – the Tamar Valley in England's West Country – was designated as such in 1995. Since then, there have been numerous moves to protect features of historical or architectural interest or areas of scenic beauty from overdevelopment, whether from tourism or other commercial interests. Notable among these are 143 designated national nature reserves and more than 4000 Sites of Special Scientific Interest (SSSI), which contain rare flora or fauna. An EU Wildlife and Habitats Directive gives stronger protection to some of the most notable SSSIs, which were decreed special areas of conservation in 2000. The UK government recognises the threat to these sensitive areas caused by growth in tourism and leisure generally and is attempting to control it, although the countryside remains under threat from the need for more land for the construction of roads, private housing, expansion of airports and similar developments.

THE PUBLIC-/PRIVATE-SECTOR INTERFACE IN THE DEVELOPMENT OF SUSTAINABLE TOURISM

Planning controls, whether executed centrally or regionally, are essential if the inevitable conflicts of interest that arise between the public and private sectors are to be avoided. Private enterprise, unrestricted, will seek to maximise profits, often in the short term, and this can more easily be achieved by concentrating marketing efforts on popular attractions and destinations, rather than investing in the development of new ones. Airlines will clearly find it more profitable to focus on the routes already generating the most traffic, while hotels in a boom resort will build large and relatively cheap properties if this produces the highest margins.

Tour operators and, to a lesser extent, travel agents exercise massive marketing power over destinations through their influence on the decisions of consumers about where to go and what to do. Operators can make or break a destination through their decision to enter or withdraw from it. Sustainability means ensuring cooperation between carriers, hotel companies and operators so that any development is not for short-term gain but in the long-term interests of the locals.

This is by no means a condemnation of the industry as a whole. For every large company that seeks to exploit its market position, there are others that recognise their responsibility to their destinations, as well as numerous small companies, both airlines and operators, actively seeking market gaps – untapped markets and destinations where the opportunity to develop tourism would be welcomed by locals or a focus on superior facilities would be appropriate.

By contrast with the failures in development planning cited earlier, the planning of the Orlando Walt Disney World Resort site reveals a better approach to the protection of a fragile environment. The site chosen, in central Florida, was largely scrubland and a deprived area in need of economic support. Walt Disney Productions took due account of the potentially enormous impact that the theme park would have on the state, including new road networks and airport construction in its plans. Protected sites well away from the park itself and the emerging town were clearly designated and, arguably, the site itself stands as a model of good development. By contrast, the impact that development further south has had on the Everglades National Park, where the wetlands have been significantly affected by engineering to provide water for coastal expansion, including meeting the needs of tourists, has been far less positive.

EXAMPLE

Tourism development in Dubai

The coastline of the United Arab Emirates (UAE) in the Middle East can be cited as evidence of development planning for tourism. Dubai in particular has implemented plans to develop tourism as a strategy to reduce its dependency on oil. The 1980s saw efforts to expand tourism as a catalyst for attracting foreign investment, this focusing on business tourism, leading to a growth in tourist arrivals from 422,000 in 1985 to 1.6 million a decade later.

This success led to the creation of the Department of Tourism and Commerce Marketing (DTCM) as the 'principal authority for the planning, supervision and development of the tourism sector in the emirate' (DTCM, 2011). Alongside its marketing activities, the DTCM works to maintain quality through its licensing role of the accommodation and travel trade sectors as well as through providing skills training to staff of local tourism enterprises. The DTCM also established sustainable tourism initiatives through a 'green tourism award', which encourages the tourism industry to consider the conservation of natural resources and the efficient use of energy and water.

Policies to remove or reduce restrictions on traditional dress, alcohol consumption and visa requirements all helped to expand visitor appeal further, and by 2005 international arrivals were reported to have exceeded the 6 million mark.

Development of the '7-star' Burj-Al Arab hotel and the construction of artificial islands offshore have provided iconic landmarks to create a reputation as an innovative tourism destination (Sharpley, 2008). Importantly, tourism was cited in the Strategic Development Plan 2015 as a key sector to ensure future economic development.

The low-cost airlines have been widely criticised for the air pollution they generate, but, on the plus side, by exploiting opportunities at small regional airports and working in cooperation with specialist tour operators, they have brought prosperity to many regions that previously had only limited access to tourists. Clermont-Ferrand in France, Graz in Austria and Trieste in Italy all have reason to be grateful for their services in making these cities and regions more accessible to tourists. The budget airlines have also been responsible for generating substantial local employment for air crew and ground staff when concentrated at airports such as Stansted and Luton. Of course, the influx of travellers at these regional airports has often pressured local infrastructure, creating additional demands on the natural environment.

The travel industry is continuing to take sustainability more seriously, with greater cooperation evidenced between the public and private sectors. Other notable examples include the Australian Nature and Ecotourism Accreditation Programme (NEAP) and Cooperative Research Centre (CRC) for Sustainable Tourism, South Africa's Fair Trade in Tourism (FTTSA) and the Global Sustainable Tourism Council, supported by the United Nations Environment Programme, the UNWTO and other organisations such as the Rainforest Alliance to oversee sustainable tourism certification.

The World Travel and Tourism Council (WTTC) has worked with the industry since 1994 to develop the Green Globe awards for sustainability (albeit initially with limited success) and promote guidelines for travellers, disseminated in the form of leaflets. The WTTC has also taken on responsibility for the Tourism for Tomorrow awards, initiated by BA, which gain widespread publicity for sustainable tourism enterprises. Finally, in the UK, the formation of the Travel Foundation, referred to in the previous chapter, signals cooperation between the public and private sectors, including some of the largest companies in the industry, reflecting for the first time a real commitment by the industry to the idea of sustainability.

American-owned companies operating globally have been notable for their commitment to sustainability. Walt Disney Enterprises, to take one example, recycles the oils, paints and cleaning materials used on its sites. The Intercontinental Hotels chain undertook a worldwide environmental audit at the beginning of the 1990s, which led to a policy of recycling waste and introducing cruelty-free (not tested on animals) toiletries in guests' rooms.

The accommodation sector has led the way in introducing sustainable approaches, though initially through their desire to save on costs. The now well-established policy of reducing laundry bills by limiting the frequency of washing towels has extended to other cost-saving tactics that offer sustainable benefits. For example, some hotels in Hawaii have installed flow regulators on showers and taps to control water wastage.

The concept of the environmental audit is gaining acceptance among tourism companies, BA being one notable example of a firm having adopted it. While the publication of environmental reports, as an element of the annual report, has become a widespread policy among other industries in recent years, the travel industry is only gradually coming to terms with this innovation.

TECHNOLOGY AND SUSTAINABLE TOURISM

As we highlighted at the beginning of this chapter, technological innovation is improving efficiency in the transport sector for tourism. For example, when taking delivery of the new A380 planes, Emirates Airlines launched a range of initiatives to improve efficiency throughout its operations, including using **on-board navigational technology** that saves time, fuel and emissions.

Another technological advance has been the use of **cloud technology** to increase the efficiency of global operations. In 2013, TUI Group announced its decision to use CloudApps' Sustainability Cloud software to track and analyse sustainability performance across its brands. The online software consolidates environmental data from different parts of the business, enabling TUI to meet its carbon reporting requirements. The system also enables detailed assessment of the sustainability performance of individual hotels, encouraging each premises to monitor and improve its own activities.

While each initiative might seem only a small step forward, when considering the scale of international travel, the use of smartphones and travel apps have the potential to reduce the impact each traveller has on the environment. For a start, no longer needing to print boarding passes – which instead are stored electronically on phones – can reduce the amount of printed paper required. In the same way, hotels are offering electronic records of bookings, with apps storing these centrally in date order, alerting the user as the date nears. Smartphones can also provide access to electronic maps and guidebooks, again reducing the reliance on paper.

As ever, technological innovation is moving at a pace, but we can say with some confidence that technology has the potential to reduce the environmental impact of tourism for businesses and travellers alike.

SUMMARY

The many different negative impacts of tourism are now well reported, leading to awareness of both tourists and businesses. Efforts to reduce the damage caused by tourism have led to many environmental programmes being introduced, although these are often on a local scale. Importantly, some positive impacts of tourism on the environment do exist, and this has helped to ensure that buildings and landscapes are protected and maintained.

There is still scepticism among many commentators as to the extent to which sustainable activities can be viewed as a genuine response to the threat to our environment rather than a public relations exercise designed to win public favour. Many businesses chose to cut back on their sustainable investment when faced with difficult trading conditions in the post-2001 era, and there is little doubt that a number will continue to pay no more than lip service to the concept unless it can be shown to be in their financial interest to do so, based on demand from their customers. While some tourists are believed to actively consider sustainability issues when considering their travel plans, there is still doubt about the majority of the travelling public's willingness to pay more for their holidays if they are designed to be more sustainable.

Nonetheless, what will have started out for many companies as no more than a marketing ploy may later turn into a genuine commitment to improve the environment as lobbying by environmental interests takes effect and public awareness of the issues spreads.

QUESTIONS AND DISCUSSION TOPICS

1. To what extent can national governments reduce the negative impacts of tourism?
2. This chapter reveals that the country of Bhutan controls visitor numbers through a policy that requires a high minimum daily spend on entry. To what extent would a 'high-pricing' approach be possible and/or desirable for tourist attractions already receiving excessive levels of visitation?
3. How can an understanding of carrying capacity assist managers of popular tourist destinations?

TASKS

1. In small groups, produce a video that identifies examples of both negative and positive environmental impacts caused by tourism.
2. Select either a hotel chain or an airline business. Investigate the company's policy on environmental sustainability. Summarise this in a poster and offer suggestions for other actions that could be undertaken by the business.

FURTHER READING

European Environment Agency (EEA) (2015) *Tourism*. Available online at: www.eea.europa.eu/soer-2015/europe/tourism [Accessed October 2018].

Gössling, S., Scott, D., Hall, C. M., Ceron, J.-P. and Dubois, G. (2012) Consumer behaviour and demand response of tourists to climate change. *Annals of Tourism Research*, 39, 36–58.

Mason, P. (2016) *Tourism Impacts, Planning and Management*, 3rd edn. London: Routledge.

UN Environment Program (UNDP) (2012) Tourism in the Green Economy. Available online at: www.unenvironment.org/resources/report/towards-green-economy-pathways-sustainable-development-and-poverty-eradication-15 [Accessed October 2018].

Wall, G. and Mathieson, A. (2006) *Tourism: Change, impacts and opportunities*. Harlow: Pearson.

WEBSITES

Blue Flag: www.blueflag.org

European Environment Agency: www.eea.europa.eu/themes/tourism

Green Globe 21: www.greenglobe.com

International Union for Conservation of Nature: www.iucn.org

Rainforest Alliance: www.rainforest-alliance.org

Responsible Tourism Partnership: www.responsibletourismpartnership.org

Tourism Concern: www.tourismconcern.org.uk

REFERENCES

Beck, B. and Bryan, F. (1971) This other Eden: A study of tourism in Britain. *The Economist*, 240 (6683: xxi).

Bennett, D. (2012) *Golf's Use of Water: Challenges and Opportunities*. USGA Summit on Golf Course Water Use, November. United States Golf Association.

Butler, R. W. (2010) *Carrying Capacity in Tourism: Paradox and hypocrisy?* In D. G. Pearce and R. W. Butler (eds), *Tourism Research: A 20-20 Vision*. Oxford: Goodfellow Publishers.

Christou, J. (2018) Visual pollution damaging to Cyprus tourism. *Cyprus Mail*, 11 June.

Department of Tourism and Commerce Marketing (DTCM) (2011) About the DTCM. Available online at: www.dubaitourism.ae/about/background [Accessed July 2014].

Dickinson, G. (2018) Unlimited, disrespectful and excessive – is the party over for tourism in Ibiza? *The Telegraph*, 24 April.

Dowie, M. (2009) Conservation Refugees: The hundred-year conflict between global conservation and native peoples. Cambridge, MA: MIT Press.

European Environment Agency (EEA) (2001) Environmental signals 2001. Available online at https://www.eea.europa.eu/publications/signals-2001/signals2001/view [Accessed 17 July 2019].

European Environment Agency (EEA) (2018) *European Bathing Water Quality in 2017*. Luxembourg: EEA.

Gössling, S. and Peeters, P. (2007) 'It does not harm the environment!' An analysis of the industry discourse on tourism, air travel and the environment. *Journal of Sustainable Tourism*, 15 (4), 402–17.

Inskip, E. (1991) *Tourism Planning: An integrated and sustainable development*. New York: van Nostrand Reinhold.

International Association of Antarctic Tour Operators (IAATO) (1991) *Protocol on Environmental Protection to the Antarctic Treaty*. Available online at https://iaato.org/documents/10157/19000/Environmental+Protocol.pdf [Accessed 17 July 2019].

IAATO (2018) *IAATO Overview of Antarctic Tourism: 2017-18 Season and Preliminary Estimates for 2018-19 Season*. Available online at https://iaato.org/documents/10157/2398215/IAATO+overview/bc34db24-e1dc-4eab-997a-4401836b7033 [Accessed 17 July 2019].

International Civil Aviation Organisation (ICAO) (2016) *ICAO Long-term Traffic Forecasts: Passenger and cargo*. Montreal, Canada: ICAO, July.

Kanigher, S. (2014) Dominance of resort industry reflected in water use. *8 News Now*, 20 May.

Kington, T. (2009) Who can now stop the slow death of Venice? *The Observer*, 1 March.

Lake District National Park Authority (n.d.) *Path Erosion and Management*. Available online at https://www.lakedistrict.gov.uk/__data/assets/pdf_file/0004/170473/path_erosion_factsheet.pdf [Accessed 17 July 2019].

Laurance, W. F., Alonso, A., Lee, M. and Campbell, P. (2006) Challenges for forest conservation in Gabon, Central Africa. *Futures*, 38 (4), 454–70.

Lindsey, P. A., Roulet, P. A. and Romanach, S. S. (2007) Economic and conservation significance of the trophy hunting industry in sub-Saharan Africa. *Biological Conservation*, 134, 455–69.

McCool, S. F. and Lime, D. W. (2001) Tourism carrying capacity: Tempting fantasy or useful reality? *Journal of Sustainable Tourism*, 9 (5), 372–88.

McVeigh, T. (2017) As British tourists take to the seas, giant cruise ships spread pollution misery. *The Observer*, 8 January.

National Parks UK (NPUK) (2014) National Park Facts and Figures. Available online at: www.nationalparks.gov.uk/students/whatisanationalpark/factsandfigures [Accessed October 2018].

National Trust for Nature Conservation (NTNC) (2017) *Annual Report*. Available online at: www.ntnc.org.np/sites/default/files/publicaations/NTNC%20Annual%20Report%202017.pdf [Accessed October 2018].

O'Shea, R. J. (2018) Taj Mahal to introduce three-hour limit on tourist visits to avoid overcrowding. *The Independent*, 3 April.

Rowe, M. (2009) Cruel to be kind? *Geographical Magazine*, 1 February.

Sharpley, R. (2008) Planning for tourism: The case of Dubai. *Tourism and Hospitality Planning and Development*, 5 (1), 13–30.

Sousa, R. C. D., Pereira, L. C. C., Costa, R. M. D. and Jiménez, J. A. (2014) Tourism carrying capacity on estuarine beaches in the Brazilian Amazon region. *Journal of Coastal Research*, 70, 545–50.

Stankey, G. H., Cole, D. N., Lucas, R. C., Petersen, M. E. and Frissell, S. S. (1985) *The Limits of Acceptable Change (LAC) System for Wilderness Planning*. Ogden, UT: United States Department of Agriculture, General Technical Report INT-176.

United Nations World Tourism Organization (UNWTO) (2018) *Tourism Highlights*. Available online at: www.e-unwto.org/doi/pdf/10.18111/9789284419876 [Accessed October 2018].

Vidal, J. (2016) The world's largest cruise ship and its supersized pollution problem. *The Guardian*, 21 May.

World Tourism Organization (WTO) (1999) *Tourism and Sustainable Development: Report of the Secretary General*, United Nations Economic and Social Council, Commission on Sustainable Development, Seventh Session, 19–30 April.

World Wildlife Fund (WWF) (2018) *Alpine Tourism*. Available online at: http://wwf.panda.org/knowledge_hub/where_we_work/alps/problems/tourism [Accessed October 2018].

PART 2
THE TRAVEL AND TOURISM PRODUCT

7

THE STRUCTURE AND ORGANISATION OF THE TRAVEL AND TOURISM INDUSTRY

CONTENTS

LEARNING OUTCOMES

After studying this chapter, you should be able to:

- identify the integral and associated sectors of the travel and tourism industry
- explain the chain of distribution and how this applies within the industry
- summarise the relationships between each industry sector
- judge the extent of integration within the industry and the reasons for this
- recognise the factors leading to change within the industry and predict the likely directions it may take in the future.

> Two factors interact in the tourism process. There is the tourist, in search of experiences and needing support services and facilities which are also experiential.
>
> Secondly, there is a diverse spectrum of resources which provides the experiences, services and facilities. (Leiper, 1979: 397)

INTRODUCTION

As Leiper (1979) highlights above, the tourist product is a complex amalgam of resources and services, each of which must be brought together and presented to customers by the various sectors of the industry. The demand for tourism is first stimulated, then satisfied by the concentrated marketing efforts of a wide variety of organisers who provide tourist products and services. These together form the world's largest and fastest-growing industry. Because some of these services are crucial to the generation and satisfaction of tourists' needs, while others play only a peripheral or supportive role, defining what is meant by a 'tourism industry' is fraught with difficulties.

Several services, such as catering and transport, obviously serve the needs of consumers other than tourists, too. Other services, such as banks, retail shops and taxis – or launderettes in a resort where a significant number of tourists are in self-catering facilities – may only serve tourists' needs incidentally along with local residents' needs, although at peak periods of the year the former may provide the bulk of their income. Inevitably, what one decides to include in a definition of the tourism industry must be, to some extent, arbitrary. Figure 7.1, however, provides a framework for analysis based on those sectors commonly seen as forming the core of the industry.

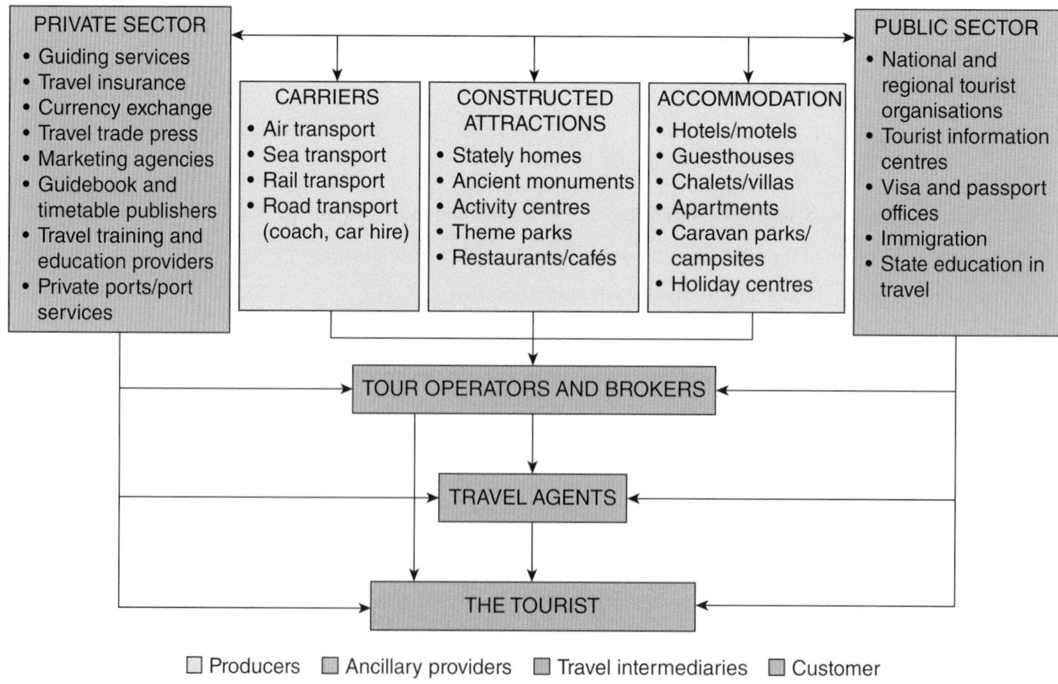

FIGURE 7.1 The network of sectors in the tourism industry

THE CHAIN OF DISTRIBUTION FOR TOURISM

Figure 7.1 is also an illustration of the chain of distribution in the travel and tourism business. This phrase is used to describe the system by which a product or service is distributed, from its manufacturing/creative source to the eventual consumers. The alternative term, marketing channel, can also be used to describe this system. Traditionally, products are distributed through the involvement of a number of intermediaries who link producers or manufacturers with consumers. These intermediaries are either wholesalers (who buy in large quantities from suppliers and sell in smaller quantities to others further down the chain) or retailers (who form the final link in the chain and sell individual products or a bundled set of products, such as package holidays, to the consumer). The structure of the chain of distribution is shown in Figure 7.2.

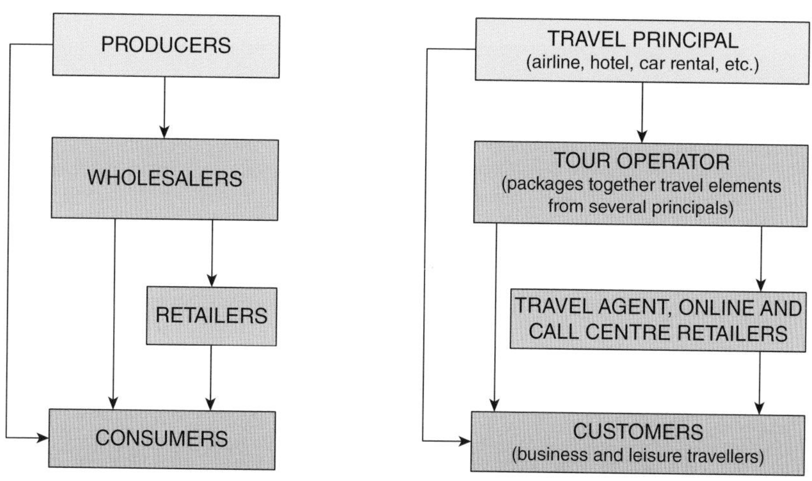

FIGURE 7.2 The chain of distribution or marketing channel

Producers, of course, are not obliged to sell their products through intermediaries. They may instead choose to sell direct to consumers or retailers, thus avoiding some or all of the intermediaries. Wholesalers, in turn, sometimes sell products direct to the consumer, avoiding the retailer.

PRODUCERS

The core tourism product consists essentially of transport, accommodation and attractions, whether constructed or natural. The producers, or 'manufacturers', of these services include air, waterborne, road and rail carriers, hotels or other forms of tourist accommodation and the various forms of constructed facilities designed to attract the leisure and business tourist, such as stately homes or heritage sites, amusement parks, conference and exhibition venues and other, purpose-built activity centres such as ski resorts. These services can be sold to the tourist in a number of ways: direct, through travel agents (still the principal retailers in the tourism industry) or through tour operators or brokers, who could best be described as wholesalers of tourism. Producers are sometimes referred to as principals.

WHOLESALERS

Tour operators can be viewed as wholesalers because they buy a range of different tourist products (such as airline seats, hotel rooms or coach transfer facilities) in bulk, then bundle or 'package' these for subsequent sale to travel agents or to the tourist direct.

By buying a mixture of individual products and services and presenting them as a single product – the package holiday – they are seen by some theorists as *producers* of a *new* product rather than *wholesalers* of an *existing* product. This is a debatable point, but in the authors' view they are best viewed as **intermediaries**, in the sense that their fundamental role is to bulk purchase products, organise them into bundles and sell those bundles off individually (this is discussed in more detail in Chapter 18). The current pattern of trading – in which both tour operators and agents are moving towards dynamic packaging, which involves bundling products to meet a consumer's needs at the point of sale (or 'unbundling the package tour' as some operators express it) – is muddying the distinction between the roles of operators and agents.

EXAMPLE

Expedia negotiates with hotels to offer preferential rates

Online travel company Expedia makes available, 'on a stand-alone and package basis, travel products and services provided by numerous airlines, lodging properties, car rental companies, destination service providers, cruise lines and other travel product and service companies'.

If we particularly focus on the sale of accommodation, this wholesaler earns revenue by using two approaches. The first, and by far the smaller of the two approaches in terms of earnings, is that of commission (known as the agency model). For each hotel room sold on a commission basis, Expedia invoices the hotel – typically, commission rates are around 10% of the room rate.

The second approach, the merchant model, often earns much higher percentage returns and reflects the wholesale role taken on by Expedia. The merchant model operates using a pre-negotiated agreement for Expedia to sell a set number of rooms, provided to them at a net rate lower than the hotel standard. Expedia can then mark up the rooms and sell to customers at levels the market will stand. The mark-up becomes the earnings for Expedia and can be as high as 40% of room rates. Expedia carries some of the risk related to the sale of the room and becomes the merchant, dealing with the customer directly in terms of ticketing, customer services and other matters. Expedia claims that, as the merchant, it generally negotiates supply allocation and pricing with suppliers, enabling a higher level of net revenue per transaction as compared to that provided through the agency model.

Expedia works with affiliates to expand its distribution channel. Travel companies can sell Expedia's hotel inventory, earning a commission from the company. By paying higher commission on merchant hotels, there is greater incentive for affiliates to, where possible, sell this accommodation to their customers. Furthermore, by working with other travel industry producers, Expedia can package travel components together for the customer, increasing the total value of the sale and, in turn, its own earnings. When packaging – often hotel and either flight and/or car components – Expedia makes some of the products available at a price lower than the sale price of each individual component, ensuring the total package price is highly competitive. This also helps to offload the merchant hotel inventory without damaging Expedia's business model for the accommodation sector.

Source: Expedia, 2015

Brokers, who bulk buy tourist products and sell in smaller quantities, are most frequently found in the distribution system within the air transport sector, although others involve themselves in the bulk purchase of hotel rooms or certain other services. As with tour operators, by purchasing aircraft seats in bulk they are able to negotiate much lower prices, which can be sold on to tour operators or travel agents either individually or in quantity at net prices, allowing the other intermediaries to determine their own profit level and the selling price for the seats.

One of the commonest forms of brokering in the travel industry is found in the role of the **consolidator**. These are specialists working in airline brokerage who bulk purchase unsold charter aircraft seats to sell through intermediaries, thereby helping airlines to clear unsold 'stock'.

RETAILERS

Although retailing through the Internet has now become a significant threat to them, travel agents remain an important outlet for selling most travel products within the distribution chain, selling packages and travel services according to client demand. They carry no stock, simply acting as an intermediary between the consumer and the supplier, and their main role is to provide a convenient network of sales outlets for the travelling public.

Traditionally, agents did not charge for their services, as they were remunerated in the form of a commission on each sale they negotiated. One of the most significant changes in distribution patterns in recent years, however, has been the tendency for producers to either reduce commission payments or, in some cases, scrap them altogether, often forcing agents to charge their clients for their services. Airlines were among the first principals to withdraw commissionable sales, mainly in the belief that they could reach the consumer more cheaply by direct contact via the Internet, rather than depending on agents who, for the most part, retain no particular loyalty to any one supplier. This means that many agents are now obliged to add a fee when selling most airline tickets.

EXAMPLE

Hotel chains cut commission on group bookings

Travel agents and meeting planners are feeling the pressure of the decision by both Marriott and Hilton to reduce the level of commission paid from 10% to 7%.

The business models employed by hotel chains such as Marriott International, which now incorporates the Starwood Hotel chain, has shifted in recent years. Marriott and Hilton own few hotels, instead operating as a brand and franchise company that makes its money through fees. Consequently, reduced commissions can lower costs for the owners of the hotels, aiding profitability and enhancing the perceived value of holding a Marriott or Hilton franchise.

At the time of writing, Marriott International is also negotiating with Expedia Group and Booking Holdings (owners of the website booking.com) to lower commission payments in an effort to reduce distribution costs. Consequently, intermediaries will have to respond to these changes in their income stream through an adjustment to their own business models.

Source: Shelvachman, 2018

Some other transport companies and tour operators are beginning to follow suit, although the large operators are unlikely, at least for the foreseeable future, to adopt such a policy. There appears to be a global trend in travel retailing for agents to buy many of their principals' products at market price and add a service fee, but this presupposes there is an adequate level of agency sales expertise and product knowledge that adds value to the process when a customer books through an agent. In fact, the pressure on margins seldom allows retail agencies to provide the salaries and conditions that would enable them to recruit sales staff of the quality and with the skills needed to make this possible. This is discussed in more detail in Chapter 19.

ANCILLARY PROVIDERS

Apart from these core services of producers, wholesalers and retailers, a wide variety of ancillary and support services interact within the distribution system. For convenience, these can be divided into public-sector organisations (those funded, controlled or organised through central or local governments) and those that are privately owned.

The former include national tourism organisations, publicly owned airports or seaports, passport and visa documentation, and other ancillary services such as public education and training institutions offering courses in tourism.

The private sector includes privately owned airports and seaports, services offered by freelance guides, travel insurance and financial services (including foreign exchange and credit card facilities), travel trade newspapers and journals, printers of travel literature and publishers of guides and timetables, as well as a number of specialist marketing services, such as travel consultants, advertising agents and brochure design agencies. In addition, there are private visa agencies that will collect customers' documentation, check it and procure any necessary visas for a fee. This is becoming a more typical pattern for visa procurement as few embassies are willing to mail documents to clients and submission in person is often inconvenient, expensive and time-consuming. Most tour operators now use these intermediaries too, as they have a good rapport with the embassies and consulates they use frequently and provide a dependable service.

The distinction between public and private bodies is not always straightforward. Some national and regional tourism organisations (the USA and the city of Berlin are two examples) are run as private consortia, having been delegated the role by the public sector. Others, while nominally public, would collapse without the financial support they receive from the private sector.

EXAMPLE

Public ownership of tourism attractions

The public sector can be involved in a number of ways in attracting tourists. In some cases, local or national government may have ownership of a building or destination (perhaps a national park, for example) and will operate the facility as a tourist attraction in order to provide public access to the facility or to fund its upkeep and management.

In other cases, governments may provide grant funding to private-sector tourism businesses to support activities that are felt to be in keeping with government agendas. An example of this is the funding provided by the UK government to museums in order to encourage wider access to these cultural resources.

Wollaton Hall, Nottingham, UK

Originally constructed in the sixteenth century, Wollaton Hall passed through several generations of family ownership before being handed to Nottingham City Council in 1925. The council used the building to house the city's natural history museum collections and created both a bird and an insect gallery to display items for public access.

Following renovations completed in 2007 (funded by Nottingham City Council, the EU European Regional Development Fund and the UK Heritage Lottery Fund), visitors can also now access, through escorted tours, the Prospect Room, a vast hall at the top of the house with panoramic views of the surrounding area, and the kitchens in the basement. The grounds include formal gardens, a deer park and, as expected of all tourist attractions today, a café and a shop.

Although entry to Wollaton Hall is free, there are charges made for parking on site. The hall also earns income through venue hire, hosting weddings, and occasionally as a film location, all of which helps to contribute to its running costs.

FIGURE 7.3 Wollaton Hall, Nottingham

Photo: Claire Humphreys

While some countries provide key elements of the travel industry through national or local government, other countries may choose to allow the private sector to provide these facilities. For example, six UK airports were initially owned by BAA, a former public body (the British Airports Authority), which included Heathrow, Gatwick and Stansted, thus largely controlling London's airport provision. The privatisation of airports proved lucrative for BAA, but concern that ownership was not in the best interests of the consumer (or the airlines that use these airports) meant that BAA was forced to sell some of its airports.

For the most part, the tourism industry depends for its success on a close working relationship between the private and public sectors. Many tourist attractions, such as heritage sites, are publicly owned, either by the state or local authorities (as we see above with the example of Wollaton Hall), while public authorities are also frequently responsible for the promotion and distribution of information about tourism (through, for instance, their tourist information centres). This interdependence between private and public sectors, which is an important element in the dynamics of the industry, will be explored in subsequent chapters.

COMMON INTEREST ORGANISATIONS

A feature of the tourism industry is the extent of the association, voluntary or otherwise, that has taken place between businesses and/or public-sector bodies that share similar interests or complement one another's interests in some way. Such associations can take a number of forms, but typically fall into one of three categories:

- sectoral organisations based on the interests of a particular sector of industry (or link in the chain of distribution)
- destination organisations concerned with a specific tourist destination, whether country, region or resort
- tourism organisations based on a concern with travel or tourism activity as a whole.

Each of these can in turn be subdivided according to whether they are trade or professional bodies. The latter are normally composed of individuals whose common interest is likely to be based on objectives that include establishing educational or training qualifications for the industry or the sector, devising codes of conduct to guide members' behaviour and limiting or controlling entry to the industry or sector. Membership of such bodies is often associated with a personal drive to enhance status and prestige.

Trade bodies, by contrast, are groupings of independent firms, the common purpose of which will include such aims as the opportunity to exchange views, cooperation (especially in the functions of marketing), representation and negotiation with other organisations and the provision of identifiable services to their members. In some circumstances, the trade bodies may also take on activities more generally associated with professional bodies, such as restricting entry to the industry or sector and providing or recognising appropriate qualifications.

EXAMPLE

Professional bodies: the Tourism Society

Operating in the UK for more than 30 years, the Tourism Society has over 1000 members, who are employed in the public, private and voluntary sectors of the tourism industry. The aim of the society is to enhance professionalism, knowledge and understanding of the tourism industry.

To work towards this aim, the Society holds a variety of conferences that help to develop the knowledge of its members and provide networking opportunities, which can open up business opportunities for its members. In recent years, the Society has also worked to attract student members as they commence their careers in the tourism industry.

Recently, the Tourism Management Institute (TMI) became a section of the Tourism Society with a specific focus on destination management. The stated mission is 'Supporting and Developing Professionals in Destination Management'. As well as providing and encouraging continuing professional development, the organisation encourages members to advocate for the importance of destination management.

EXAMPLE

Trade bodies: Treasure Houses of England

Many sectoral organisations come together in order to benefit from opportunities to bulk buy at discount prices from their suppliers or sell themselves more effectively and at lower cost. Websites that offer a range of products rather than a single one, for example, will be more effective in reaching the public.

Treasure Houses of England is one such example in the attractions sector of the industry. Composed of ten of the leading stately homes, palaces and castles in the UK, the consortium has its own website (www.treasurehouses.co.uk), produces a joint brochure and offers discounts at partner properties.

The structure of such bodies may vary considerably. In some cases, particularly in the larger organisations, there will be a paid administrative staff, while in the case of smaller bodies (such as local marketing consortia), there may be no full-time staff and administration will often be carried out by volunteers seconded from member companies. A key characteristic of trade bodies, however, is that their membership is made up of autonomous companies or other organisations subscribing to the common purpose of the body concerned.

SECTORAL ORGANISATIONS

Probably the most numerous organisations are those that reflect sectoral interests. As we saw in Figure 7.1, there is a wide range of sectors making up the tourism industry and each of these can be expected to have at least one common interest association. Professional bodies catering for sectoral interests include the Chartered Institute of Logistics and Transport (CILT) and the Institute of Hospitality (formerly the Hotel, Catering and International Management Association). The Chartered Institute of Marketing (CIM) has a section devoted to travel industry members, known as the Chartered Institute of Marketing Travel Industry Group (CIMTIG), while tourism consultants have their own professional body, the Tourism Society Consultants' Network (TCN).

Sectoral trade bodies may be regional, national or international in scope. Some international bodies retain significant influence over the activities of their members. An example is the International Air Transport Association (IATA), which continues in its role of negotiating with international airlines worldwide even though some of its erstwhile power has diminished under the impetus to liberalise this sector of the industry. The European Tour Operators Association (ETOA) was established in 1989 and has 700 members who are tour operators or suppliers in European destinations. This organisation provides networking, trade events and advocacy support at European level to promote Europe as a tourism destination. In the UK, the Federation of Tour

Operators (FTO) amalgamated with the Association of British Travel Agents (ABTA) in 2008 to jointly further activities in the travel sector; since 1959, ABTA has represented both travel agents and tour operators.

The Meetings Industry Association (MIA) and UKinbound represent organisations that make ground handling arrangements for incoming visitors to the UK. Similar bodies are to be found in all countries with a developed tourism industry. The American Society of Travel Advisors (ASTA), for example, fulfils a similar role in the USA to that of ABTA in the UK, but also draws on members from other sectors of industry, as well as overseas members, due to the importance and influence of the USA as a tourist-generating country.

EXAMPLE

American Society of Travel Advisors

Formerly known as The American Society of Travel Agents, ASTA is said to be the world's largest travel association. As well as travel agents, members are drawn from the cruise sector, hotels and tour operators. ASTA's mission is to 'facilitate the business of selling travel through effective representation, shared knowledge and the enhancement of professionalism'.

Founded in 1931, the association has members in 140 countries and continues to fight on behalf of their members against unfair legislation or onerous practices by other sectors of the travel industry. ASTA members must adhere to a code of ethics that promotes integrity and honesty within the travel industry.

Source: www.ASTA.org

Regional bodies will comprise groups such as local hoteliers or tourist attractions. These will often act as pressure groups in their relations with local tourist authorities, but also provide arenas for discussion on issues of mutual interest to members.

DESTINATION ORGANISATIONS

A destination organisation is one that draws its membership from both public- and private-sector tourism bodies that share a common interest in the development or marketing of a specific tourist destination. That destination may be a resort, state or region, a country or even an area of the globe. Membership of such bodies is open to firms or public-sector organisations rather than individuals. These bodies generally share two common objectives:

- to foster cooperation and coordination between the various bodies that provide, or are responsible for, the facilities or amenities making up the tourism product
- to act cooperatively to promote the destination to the travel trade and tourists.

Consequently, they are trade, rather than professional, bodies. Examples range from such globally important regional marketing bodies as the Pacific Area Travel Association (PATA) and the European Travel Commission (ETC), to local marketing consortia made up of groups of hotels or tourist attractions within a particular region or resort.

An example of a national marketing consortium is the Malawi Travel Marketing Consortium. Its members comprise private-sector tourism interests (including airlines, car hire companies, attractions, tour operators and travel agents), which together promote the African country to international travellers. Its efforts have helped to encourage more than three-quarters of a million tourists to visit the country annually. Regional and local tourism consortia also exist; the Bournemouth Hotels and Restaurants Association, the Devon Association of Tourist Attractions, and the Association of Bath and District Leisure Enterprises are all typical examples in England of localised groupings.

EXAMPLE

Regional Tourism Organizations New Zealand

Regional Tourism Organizations NZ (RTONZ) is a membership-based organisation that represents the interests of all 30 Regional Tourism Organizations operating in New Zealand.

The 30 RTOs are:

North Island	South Island
Northland	Marlborough
Auckland	Kaikoura
The Coromandel	Nelson Tasman
Waikato	West Coast
Bay of Plenty	Canterbury
Rotorua	Timaru
Lake Taupo	Mackenzie
Ruapehu	Lake Wanaka
Taranaki	Queenstown
Gisborne	Fiordland
Whanganui	Waitaki
Hawkes Bay	Central Otago
Manawatu	Dunedin
Wairarapa	Clutha Catlins
Wellington	Southland

Each RTO is responsible for promoting their local area to attract international and domestic visitors. In some cases, the RTO is funded by the local council, but in other cases the organisation is financed through membership fees paid by local tourism businesses.

RTONZ, as the overarching association for these organisations, encourages coordination between the 30 RTOs and acts as an advocate to promote their role in New Zealand tourism.

TOURISM ORGANISATIONS

The activities of some bodies transcend sectoral boundaries within the industry. These organisations may have as their aim the compilation of national or international statistics on tourism or the furtherance of research into the tourism phenomenon.

The United Nations World Tourism Organization (UNWTO) plays a dominant role in collecting and collating statistical information on international tourism. This organisation represents public-sector tourism bodies from most countries in the world. The publication of its data enables comparisons to be made of the flow and growth of tourism on a global scale.

Similarly, the Organisation for Economic Co-operation and Development (OECD) also has a tourism committee composed of tourism officials drawn from its member countries and provides regular reports comprising comparative data on tourism developments to and within these countries. Other, privately sponsored bodies have been set up to produce supporting statistics, such as the World Travel and Tourism Council (WTTC), the members of which are drawn from 100 leading travel and tourism organisations. This body also regularly commissions and publishes research data.

Within countries, bodies are set up to bring together public and private tourism interests as a means of influencing legislation, encouraging political action, or sometimes to overcome crises affecting the industry. In the UK, the Tourism Industry Emergency Response Group (TIER) was established to develop crisis plans and manage crisis response for the UK tourism industry, and comprises representatives of VisitBritain, ABTA, UKinbound, UK Hospitality, British Airways and the Association of Leading Visitor Attractions. Wider aims guide the Tourism Alliance, established to act as a common mouthpiece to lobby government and handle future problems affecting the UK tourism industry.

EXAMPLE

ANTOR

ANTOR, the Association of National Tourist Office Representatives, is the principal association representing the world's tourist offices. It provides opportunities for members to meet and exchange ideas, enhance relationships within the travel industry and advocate for responsible tourism. Membership comprises more than 40 national tourist offices across the globe, including such diverse countries as Belgium, Canada, Hungary, Malta, Oman, the Philippines and Trinidad and Tobago.

Many countries with a strongly developed tourism industry establish professional bodies composed of individual members drawn from several or all sectors of the industry. The purpose of these bodies is to promote the cause of the tourism industry generally, while simultaneously encouraging the spread of knowledge and understanding of the industry among members. For example, in the UK there are two professional bodies devoted to the tourism industry generally, although they tend to draw their membership from different sectors of industry. The Institute of Travel and Tourism (ITT) originated as an institute designed to serve the needs of travel agents and tour operators and still draws its membership largely from these sectors, while the Tourism Society, discussed earlier in this chapter, is a more recently formed professional body that attracts members particularly from the public sector, tourist attractions and the incoming tourism industry.

INTEGRATION IN THE TOURISM INDUSTRY

A notable feature of the industry over recent years has been the steady process of integration that has taken place between sectors of the tourism industry. If we refer to our earlier model of the chain of distribution (Figure 7.2), we can identify this integration as being either **horizontal** or **vertical** in character. Horizontal integration is that taking place at any one level in the chain, while vertical integration describes the process of linking together organisations at different levels of the chain (some writers also refer to **diagonal integration** – a term used to describe links between complementary businesses within each level in the chain).

HORIZONTAL INTEGRATION

Horizontal integration can take several forms. One is the integration of two companies offering similar (and, in some cases, potentially competing) products. Two hotels at the same seaside resort may merge, for example, or two airlines operating on similar routes may unite. Alternatively, an airline operating, for instance, between New York and Tokyo might advantageously take over another operating from Tokyo to Seoul, in order to provide an integrated and coordinated service, all the better to compete with a direct service from New York to Seoul. Such **mergers** may result from the takeover of one company by another or simply from a voluntary agreement between the two to merge and obtain the benefits, identified above, of a much larger organisation. **Voluntary unions** can also be established, however, that allow the companies concerned to maintain their autonomy and separate identities while still obtaining the benefits of an integrated organisation. This is the case with a **consortium** – an affiliation of independent companies working together to achieve a common aim or benefit. One example of this affiliation is the marketing consortium, which allows independent companies to gain economies of scale in, for example, mass advertising or the publication of a joint brochure. The Best Western consortium, for instance, among other activities, produces a brochure listing all its member hotels. Alternatively, a consortium may have as its prime benefit the ability to purchase supplies at bulk prices for its members – a feature of groupings of independent travel agents such as the Advantage consortium, which, in this way, can negotiate higher commission levels from tour operators and other principals.

A second form of horizontal integration occurs between companies offering complementary rather than competing products. An example would be the linking of an airline with a hotel chain. As both of these are *principals*, they are at the same stage of the chain of distribution and thus their integration is horizontal. Close links between the accommodation and transport sectors may develop as they are interdependent for their customers. Without hotel bedrooms available at their destinations, airline passengers may be unwilling to book seats, and vice versa. Recognition of this dual need led many airlines to buy into or form their own hotel divisions, especially in regions of high tourist demand where bed shortages were common. This trend was customary in the early years of the jumbo jet, when airlines woke up to the consequences of operating aircraft with 350 or more passengers aboard, each requiring accommodation over which the airline had little or no control. This led to the integration of several major airlines and hotel chains. Rising competition between airlines, which led to huge losses and massive investment in new aircraft, however, obliged many airlines to sell their hotel investments to raise capital in order to survive. Since those days, the more common form of this relationship has been to have closely linked computer reservation systems (CRSs), which allow the airlines a measure of control over hotel bedrooms without having to make a major capital investment in the accommodation sector. The growth of dynamic packaging in the early 2000s reinforced the need for airlines to have access to accommodation, many developing their own websites to include hotel accommodation at prices competitive with specialist hotel websites.

Airlines are increasingly seeking to benefit from liaisons that do not involve competition on the same routes. **Interlining agreements** allow airlines to benefit from connections globally. These are commercial agreements between airlines to provide travel routes for passengers who require the use of multiple airlines. For example, a journey from Germany to the Cook Islands (in the Pacific) may involve flights operated by both Lufthansa and Air New Zealand. Such agreements have been extended to code-sharing, which allows an airline to allocate its own flight number to a service operated by another airline. Close links have also been developed through the global airline alliances that have formed in recent years, such as Star Alliance and Oneworld. Combined, these links can mean that, for example, transatlantic routes can provide 'feeder' opportunities into the US network of domestic routes, allowing foreign airlines to compete with US airlines to carry passengers between two US domestic airports. Such agreements also overcome the problems faced if these airlines were to try to merge – a move often seen as anti-competitive and likely to be challenged by monopolies commissions, which favour open competition.

EXAMPLE

Airline mergers

In the USA, October 2015 saw the completion of the merger of two major airlines, with more than 100,000 employees worldwide. Before the merger, American Airlines was a member of the Oneworld alliance while US Airways was allied with Star Alliance. To gain agreement for the merger, US Airways had to leave the Star Alliance network, and the newly merged airline was then required to surrender slots and gates at key airports in the USA to overcome anti-competitive monopoly concerns raised by the US Justice Department. Such mergers are not unusual in the USA; recent years have seen Delta merge with Northwest, while United has merged with Continental.

In Europe, the International Airlines Group was formed in 2010 through the merger of British Airways and Iberia, although both brands are still operating today. This follows in the footsteps of the merger in 2004 of Air France and KLM.

At the retailing level, integration is also common, but, because the traditional development of travel agencies has led in many cases to regional strengths, integration has tended to be regionally based, leading to the development of so-called 'miniples' – agencies with a significant number of branches within one region of the country only, which may well, within that region, outperform the multiple agents (more detail of this is provided in Chapter 19). The massive growth in the number of branches of the big multiples has tapered off and has even been reversing in recent years.

Tour operating has also experienced growth through integration in the past decade; first, that between large companies in the UK, and later, internationally (see Chapter 18 for more details). The UK's leading holiday company is the German-owned, TUI Group which, following numerous mergers and acquisitions, operates the First Choice and Thomson Holiday brands. While integration in the principal travel sectors is likely to continue, it is unlikely to be as frenetic as it has been in recent years, given the instability of the industry and the fact that most companies are keen to see a return to stable profits rather than chasing expansion.

VERTICAL INTEGRATION

Vertical integration is said to take place when an organisation at one level in the chain of distribution unites with one at another level. This integration can be **forward** (or downward in the direction of the chain), such as in the case where a tour operator buys its own chain of travel agents, or it can be backward (or upward, against the direction of the chain), such as in the case where a tour operator buys its own airline.

EXAMPLE

Is vertical integration a threat to the Canadian travel industry?

Vertical integration is not new for the Canadian travel industry, but it has been given increased attention as Sunwing Travel has extended its expansion activities. In 2011 Sunwing launched Blue Diamond Hotels and Resorts and has since acquired Breezes Grand Negril Resort & Spa in Jamaica. Those voicing concerns about vertical integration argue that because one company exercises control over so much of the inventory, in consequence price and quality can be controlled due to lack of competition.

Although the growth of Sunwing may raise some concerns, it is, by quite a wide margin, in second place in Canada's tourism operations. In first place is Transat, whose vertically integrated operations encompass inbound and outbound tour wholesalers, hotels, airlines and some 600 travel agencies (Figure 7.4). Transat have operations in Canada, France, the UK, the Netherlands, Greece, the USA, Mexico and the Dominican Republic, with sales in excess of CA$3 billion in 2016.

Transat has outlined the merits of its vertical integration strategy, particularly highlighting that it 'ensures better control of costs and helps protect profits which would otherwise go into the pockets of third parties' (Transat, 2017).

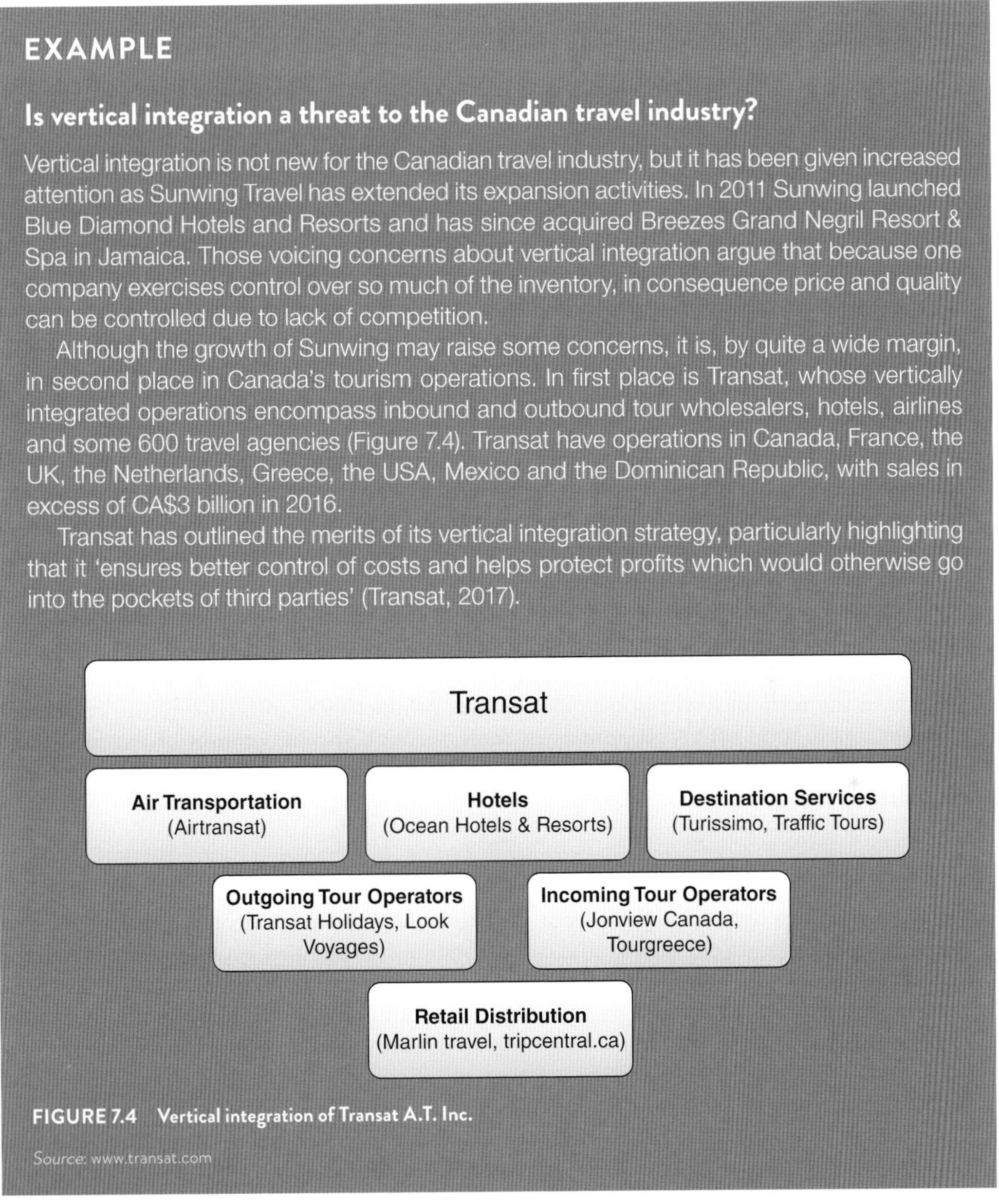

FIGURE 7.4 Vertical integration of Transat A.T. Inc.

Source: www.transat.com

Backward integration in the form of a takeover is fairly uncommon. More frequently in the past, operators have set up their own airlines internally. Forward integration is more typical because organisations are more likely to have the necessary capital to buy businesses further down the chain of distribution, as these require less capital investment than those above them in the chain. It is true to say, however, that, generally speaking, the higher a company is in the chain of distribution, the greater the investment that will be required.

As with horizontal integration, organisations can achieve significant economies of scale by expanding vertically. Whereas total profits in individual sectors may be slight, a reasonable profit overall across the sectors may still be achieved by an integrated business that controls all levels in the chain. Even in a year of intense competition, tour-operating companies owning their own airlines and retail sales outlets (neither of which may be committed to the exclusive sale of the operator's products) may still remain profitable.

BENEFITS OF INTEGRATION

All business is highly competitive and the tourism industry is no exception. Such competition, often encouraged by government policy, has been evident within the tourism industry, especially since the development of the mass market in travel that began in the 1960s. Following policies of deregulation, particularly those in the transport sector affecting air, rail and coach companies, competition became steadily fiercer throughout the latter part of the twentieth century and the early years of the new century. Competition forces companies to seek ways of becoming more efficient in order to cut costs. Integration makes this possible.

Benefits of scale

Horizontal integration enables companies to benefit from economies of scale by producing and selling more of a product. This reduces the unit cost of each product as the fixed costs incurred are spread over a larger number of units, whether these are hotel bedrooms, aircraft seats or package tours. Equally, buyers of these products, such as tour operators, can obtain lower net prices if they buy in larger quantities, just as airlines can negotiate lower prices if they order more aircraft from the manufacturers.

The savings achieved through both these economies of scale can be passed on to clients in the form of lower prices, making the product more attractive to the consumer. Vertical integration offers economies of scale through the integration of executive and administrative functions, as well as increasing leverage on the market through advertising and promotion.

Benefits of supply chain access

Many companies are concerned about ensuring the continuation of their supplies, and vertical integration can address this. A tour operator depending on a continuous supply of aircraft seats and hotel beds, and facing international competition for such supplies, can best ensure adequate and regular supplies by directly controlling them – that is, by integrating backwards, into the airline and hotel businesses.

Today, the World Wide Web is offering suppliers an alternative method of distribution and reducing the necessity of depending on so many links in the chain. For example, hoteliers need no longer depend on granting an allocation of beds to a tour operator, who in turn would make them available to customers via a travel agent. Beds can be sold direct via a website and in any number of foreign languages to meet the world market's needs. Thus, vertical integration can benefit tour operators in that it provides access to hotel stock that may otherwise be sold directly to the customer.

Benefits of size

Large companies offer benefits to both suppliers and tourists. Suppliers, knowing the reputations of the major companies in the field, are anxious to do business with them, in the belief that such firms are less likely to collapse in the face of competition than the small ones (a belief that is not always well founded, as shown by the collapse of the International

Leisure Group (ILG) – the UK's second-largest operator, at the beginning of the 1990s). The tour operator's operational risks are minimised because suppliers, faced with an overbooking situation, will be less likely to turn away clients from the tour operator who brings them so much business. Similarly, hotels uniting into larger groups will be able to negotiate better deals through their own suppliers for the bulk purchase of such items as food and drink, while larger airlines will bring greater bargaining strength to the negotiating table in their dealings with foreign governments for landing rights or new routes.

Most companies, if asked to identify their organisational goals, would cite market expansion as a major objective. Growth in a competitive environment is a means of survival and history testifies to the fact that few companies survive by standing still. Integration is a means of growth, enabling a company to increase its market share and simultaneously reduce the level of competition it faces by forcing less efficient companies out of business.

Greater sales generally mean more revenue, so, potentially, there will be more funds to reinvest in the company to assist with the costs of expansion. This in turn enables the company to employ or expand its specialist personnel. Nowhere is this truer than in those companies whose individual branches are quite small. A small chain of travel agents, for instance, may thus be able to employ specialist sales or marketing staff or recruit its own training staff. Higher levels of revenue also release more money for the marketing effort; a programme of national advertising in the mass media may become a real possibility for the first time.

In addition to these broad benefits offered by integration generally, there are other advantages specific to horizontal or vertical integration, which we will now examine in turn.

INTEGRATION LEADS TO CONTROL

Several of the leading operators have, in recent years, sought to own and operate their own hotels in key resorts abroad to ensure both the availability of rooms and some control over their price. Integration here can be achieved either by direct purchase or by setting up joint venture companies with partners in the hotel industry or other sectors of the industry. Such integration can offer the added advantage of improved control over the quality of the product. This is frequently difficult to achieve otherwise in the case of some international hotels, and it is no easy matter to ensure that standards are uniform, consistent and of the required quality to suit the market. Although operators do own hotels, this has, up to now, been on a limited scale only, with many preferring to exercise control through a franchising scheme or branding, which allows for control of standards while management remains in the hands of the hotel company.

Equally, the production sector will attempt to exercise control over the retailing of its products. Airlines, shipping services and hotels are all multimillion-pound investments, yet, curiously, in the recent past they had to rely to a considerable extent on a fragmented, independent and sometimes inexpert retail sector to sell their products. Travel agents carry no stock and therefore have little brand loyalty to a particular travel company. It was a logical step for principals to try to influence distribution by buying into retail agencies, but the need to compete with existing retail agents for the sale of flight tickets led to airline shops being closed as airlines instead encouraged sales through their websites, or those of online distributors like Expedia and Opodo. The leading UK tour operators have their own retail agency chains and engage in the practice of **directional selling**, in which counter staff are expected to give priority to the sale of the parent company's products. This is discussed in more detail in Chapter 18.

Once again, this forward integration is becoming unnecessary with the growth of the Internet. For *principals*, distribution can be achieved directly to the customer rather than through retailing or wholesaling divisions further down the ladder. The no-frills carriers have depended least on the chain of distribution. Thus, easyJet and Ryanair do not use traditional retail agents; however, both have recently provided access to their inventory on GDS platforms, making their tickets available through travel agents, largely in an effort to attract the lucrative corporate travel market.

CONGLOMERATES AND INTERNATIONAL INTEGRATION

No discussion about the changing structure of the tourism industry would be complete without an examination of the growing role of the conglomerates. These are organisations whose interests extend across a variety of different industries in order to spread the risks incurred by operating within a specific industry such as tourism. Although tourism has the reputation of being a highly volatile industry, the long-term growth prospects for leisure generally have attracted many businesses from outside the industry itself. Breweries, for example, have expanded into hotels and holiday centres. In Europe, conglomeration is well established in numerous countries. Germany, to take one example, invested heavily in travel and tourism businesses through its department stores and leading banks, although various recessions have seen some divestment of such interests.

The travel industry is experiencing rapid internationalisation in ownership. This is a process that has been hastened within Europe by the harmonisation of member countries. Travel businesses have, as a result, been actively expanding their interests in each other's countries. While it is tempting to offer some examples of the current spate in such expansion, the pace of change is now so fast that any examples are likely to date very quickly. Readers are encouraged to keep in touch with the trade press in order to update their knowledge of this process. Suffice it to say that, increasingly, travel companies must look beyond their own national borders to understand the nature of the competition they face.

EXAMPLE

Internationalisation

The European Commission's Tourism Business Portal identified six reasons why tourism businesses should consider internationalising their operations. These include:

1. saturation of the domestic market
2. new competition from abroad
3. access to less competitive markets
4. risk diversification
5. government incentives
6. management interest in operating internationally as a business strategy.

However, tourism businesses are also warned that internationalisation can be bureaucratic, may require significant business adaptation and calls for skills training for existing staff.

To further encourage internationalisation across borders, the European Commission has developed a video tutorial which highlights many of the key structural issues which need to be considered by tourism businesses seeking to internationalise (available at www.youtube.com/watch?v=o0hJEaE7n0Q).

Source: Tourism Business Portal, 2014

SUMMARY

Throughout this chapter, we have discussed changes to the way the tourism product is distributed to the customer. The discussion relating to both horizontal and vertical integration highlights that control over the chain of distribution is important to the success of many producers, as they seek to reach customers in a profitable manner. The Internet is providing new opportunities for distribution, which is correspondingly impacting on the structure of the industry.

We are also seeing increased liaison between the public and private sectors as both seek to maximise the benefits from their spending in areas such as marketing and promotion. Greater awareness of the impacts of tourism has perhaps also contributed to encouraging cooperation and partnerships that seek to ensure wider benefits and long-term sustainability. Reductions in government grants and funding experienced in many developed tourism destinations have also meant that the public sector is dealing with ever tighter budgets, often leading to restructuring and a more commercially oriented approach to their activities.

QUESTIONS AND DISCUSSION POINTS

1. Why might national and local governments be the providers of tourism attractions?
2. In this chapter, we highlighted the existence of professional bodies, many of which are populated by individuals working in the tourism industry. What are the benefits of membership of such bodies for the individual? Does the tourism industry more widely benefit from the existence of such organisations?
3. What is the difference between horizontal and vertical integration?

TASKS

1. In this chapter, we discuss the case of Transat, a Canadian company with operations at different levels of the chain of distribution. For an integrated tourism business of your choice, produce a poster that clearly shows its operations at different levels of the chain of distribution.
2. This chapter identifies many sectoral trade bodies, such as IATA and ASTA. For one such trade body, investigate its purpose or mission. Produce a short presentation that summarises the activities it undertakes on behalf of its membership.

WEBSITES

ASTA: www.ASTA.org

Best Western (consortia information): www.whybestwestern.com

OECD Tourism Department: www.oecd.org/cfe/tourism

Tourism Society: www.tourismsociety.org

United Nations World Tourism Organization (UNWTO): www.unwto.org

REFERENCES

Expedia (2015) *United States Security and Exchange Commission Form 10-K*. Available online at: www.sec.gov/Archives/edgar/data/1324424/000119312516457822/d104083d10k.htm [Accessed January 2019].

Leiper, N. (1979) The framework of tourism: Towards a definition of tourism, tourist, and the tourist industry. *Annals of Tourism Research*, Oct./Dec., 390–407.

Shelvachman, A. (2018) Marriott and Hilton's Group commission cuts put pressure on industry. Available online at: https://skift.com/2018/04/11/marriott-and-hiltons-group-commission-cuts-put-pressure-on-industry [Accessed October 2018].

Tourism Business Portal (2014) What can I do to expand my tourism business into Europe? Available online at: www.youtube.com/watch?v=o0hJEaE7n0Q [Accessed October 2018].

Transat (2017) Transat: Our vertical integration strategy. Available online at www.transat.com/getmedia/cc962e19-9b74-45f5-8a9b-e890f49a74cb/Transat_vertical_integration_strategy-2017.aspx [Accessed October 2018].

8

TOURIST DESTINATIONS

CONTENTS

LEARNING OUTCOMES

After studying this chapter, you should be able to:

- explain the complexity of the destination as a tourism product
- demonstrate the importance of the image and the brand in destination marketing
- distinguish between different categories of destination
- interpret the appeal of each form of destination
- explain why destinations are subject to changing fortunes.

> Defining what actually constitutes a destination is problematic, and there is no agreed definition of the term. Nor is terminology clearly defined: the words 'resort' and 'destination' are often used interchangeably, for example. (Davidson and Maitland, 1997: 3)

INTRODUCTION: WHAT DEFINES A DESTINATION?

At the beginning of this book, we briefly outlined what is meant by a tourist destination. This chapter is devoted to expanding on that explanation, so that we can learn to understand the appeal that different types of destination have for tourists.

As we start to think about destinations, it is useful to briefly come back to a concept we introduced in Chapter 3, that of the Tourist Area Life Cycle (TALC), which described how destinations rise and fall in popularity over time. This concept recognises that, along with changes in demand, at each stage of destination development there are changes in the nature and levels of industry involvement (in the supply of attractions and amenities) as well as changes in government investment and support. Thus, supply influences the characteristics of a destination at any point in time.

Describing all the characteristics that go to make up a destination is one of the more difficult tasks in the study of tourism. It would be easy to say that the desire to visit a particular destination is the underlying reason for all tourism, but in some instances this is far from the case. The destination may be only one element in the appeal of the trip, and sometimes a very minor one. When Concorde was flying, many tourists made it their lifetime ambition to travel on the world's only supersonic aircraft. Where it was flying *to* was of only minor interest to those enthusiasts. Equally, impressive cruise liners such as the *Queen Mary 2* may represent the actual destination for devotees of cruising and the ship's ports of call may be of only passing interest (some enthusiasts of cruising do not even disembark at ports of call en route). Anniversaries are often enjoyed on the Orient Express, the nostalgic rail journey offered by this distinguished train being the prime purpose for the trip; and the attraction of the long rail journey across Russia from Moscow to Vladivostok owes little to the brief stops that the train makes during its epic journey. Sometimes the ambition to drive along a historic route, such as the silk route across Asia, or iconic routes like Route 66 across the USA, outweighs the places visited during the drive. Consequently, we should recognise that, very often, the *transport* selected by tourists can be as important as the destination to which they are travelling.

In other examples, a key *tourist attraction* has become the destination. This is true of many theme parks. Orlando in Florida did not exist as a tourist destination a half century ago, before Walt Disney Productions decided to make it the site of its second development, just as the location of Alton Towers in Northamptonshire in the UK had little to interest the visitor before the construction of this major theme park. Certain hotels, such as Raffles in Singapore, have become famous in their own right as destinations, not because of where they are, but because of *what* they are.

In discussing destinations, we must always bear in mind two important considerations:

- the physical and psychological elements of a destination
- the image and promotion of a destination.

PHYSICAL AND PSYCHOLOGICAL ELEMENTS OF DESTINATIONS

The image of a destination relates to a number of physical attributes: attractions and amenities, buildings, landscapes and so on, together with perceptions allied to the destination, which include less tangible attributes. These can include the hospitality of the local population, the atmosphere generated by being there, a sense of awe, alienation, *Gemütlichkeit* or other emotion stimulated by the place. The sense of awe one experiences in standing on the rim of the Grand Canyon in Arizona can be contrasted with the sense of foreboding experienced when passing through Glencoe in Scotland, the sombre location of the massacre of the MacDonalds by the Campbells in 1692. Visiting the World War II concentration camp at Auschwitz–Birkenau in Poland, now a major visitor destination, generates feelings of shock and revulsion, but underlines the fact that our choice of destination is not dependent on seeking only pleasure or entertainment. At the other end of the scale, different emotions are engendered in a visit to the formal gardens at the Japanese Royal Palace in Tokyo, the Kirstenbosch Botanic Gardens near Cape Town in South Africa or the flower-bedecked balconies of houses in Austria, southern Germany and Switzerland. All of these destinations could be, and often are, marketed to horticultural enthusiasts and all offer a psychologically satisfying visual appeal to the viewer.

Academic research on tourist destination image is extensive (with a summary of research papers on the topic offered by Pike in 2002), providing an evaluation of the way tourists construct their perceptions of a destination. Broadly speaking, however, we can consider two dimensions that shape destination image. The first is driven by the perceptual and cogitative influences whereby an image is developed through an evaluation of attributes of resources such as attractions and facilities. Knowledge of such resources may be gained through first-hand experience of these or from a variety of other sources such as marketing materials, images on films, postcards and TV news items. The second dimension is the affective influence, which is linked to the feelings and emotions evoked by the destination. Combined, these two dimensions influence decisions to visit one destination ahead of others.

THE IMAGE AND PROMOTION OF A DESTINATION

Destinations have very different appeals to different markets. Some people love crowds, while others love isolation and find crowded beaches unbearable. Holidays in the mountains, for some, will awaken thoughts of majestic landscapes, with few visitors apart from the occasional hiker, such as might be found in Tierra del Fuego National Park in Argentina and Chile. Others may immediately think of resorts like Gstaad in Switzerland or Courchevel in France, with their busy ski-slopes and lively social life in the bars and restaurants. It is fortunate that the appeal of destinations is so varied, allowing opportunities for tourism to be developed in almost any country and to almost any region, providing that they are aimed at the appropriate markets.

Destinations depend on their **image** for their success in attracting tourists. Most well-known tourist countries and destinations such as cities and beach resorts rely on the stereotypes that have been built up over the years, and as long as these remain positive, promotional bodies will seek to support such images in their advertising. Thus, the prevailing image of London for the foreigner is of guardsmen riding on horseback through the city, past Big Ben and the Houses of Parliament; Paris, on the other hand, remains forever the city of lovers, with couples embracing on the banks of the Seine with the Eiffel Tower or Notre Dame in the background. It matters little that these images bear little resemblance to real life in these modern cities. The power of an image is the branding iron that drives tourism, and to jettison it in favour of a more modern, but less graphic, image is a far more difficult – and risky – task for marketing than keeping the original.

EXAMPLE

What next for New Zealand?

The massive global success of the Lord of the Rings trilogy, much of which was filmed in New Zealand, provided the National Tourist Board with a global opportunity to promote the natural environment, the bedrock of its '100% Pure New Zealand' campaign.

The campaign predates release of the first film in the series, having been launched in 1999. The term was used in a variety of contexts, including 100% pure relaxation, 100% pure adrenaline and 100% pure welcome. The films provided longevity to this campaign, and with three films being produced from *The Hobbit* book, more than a decade after the initial concept was launched '100% Middle Earth 100% New Zealand' was named best marketing campaign at the 2012 World Travel Awards.

More recently, the campaign came under scrutiny as environmentalists highlighted concerns over the levels of water pollution and greenhouse gas emissions in the country. Consequently, its 20-year-old slogan is undergoing a shift, to focus more specifically on the country's people rather than the physical place.

See www.tourismnewzealand.com/about/what-we-do/campaign-and-activity for more information about the 100% Pure campaign.

Aware of the importance of image in selling destinations, many countries have embarked on a process of **image creation**, with advertisements incorporating quickly communicated slogans and/or readily identifiable logos, often alongside the image of their iconic attraction, as a means of conveying the destination's properties to intending tourists. Slogans are generally emotive as much as informative. Examples include 'Malaysia – Truly Asia', 'Incredible India' and 'Greece – all-time classic'. Others specifically focus on stimulating action. The USA encourages visitors to 'Discover America' and Spain went with 'I need Spain'. Image creation is important in stimulating appeal for a destination.

Destination promotion is of limited benefit unless it is accompanied by other, supporting factors. It is important here to stress the role played by transport companies in this. Budget airlines, for example, have expanded tourism to both existing and newly popular destinations by offering cheap fares and, in many cases, developing new provincial hubs. Many of these are sited in areas of which tourists had only limited knowledge previously. Among destinations to have benefited from the European no-frills airlines in recent years are Turkey, Malta and the Baltic states of Estonia and Lithuania.

CATEGORISING DESTINATIONS

It is convenient to divide destinations into five distinct groupings:

- The **centred** destination is the most frequent – a traditional form of holiday arrangement in which the tourist travels to the destination, where they expect to spend the majority of their time, with perhaps occasional excursions to visit nearby attractions. The classic seaside holiday, winter sports resort or short city break represent the most common types in this grouping.
- Some destinations form a **base** from where the surrounding region can be explored. Some of the UK's seaside resorts have successfully reformulated their marketing strategy to sell themselves as bases for exploring the nearby countryside. Urban locations have also established themselves as the regional tourism base. For example, the city of Cambridge, in the East Anglian region of the UK, has sought to develop its role as

a base for exploring the surrounding area, rather than attracting more visitors to the city itself.

- Multicentre holidays include two or more destinations that are of equal importance in the itinerary. A good example of such a holiday would be that of a tourist with an interest in exploring the new central European countries of the Baltic, buying a package comprising stays in the three capitals of Tallinn, Riga and Vilnius.
- Touring destinations will be part of a linear itinerary, including stops at a number of points. A Caribbean cruise, for instance, will call at several ports en route, while a tour of the American Midwest or Far West or a rail journey across Canada will make stopovers a key element in the itinerary.
- Transit destinations merely provide an overnight stop en route to the final destination. Such stopovers may or may not be pre-planned, but occur at convenient points, particularly for drivers contemplating long journeys by car. Typical examples are tourists driving by car from the UK, Scandinavia or Northern Germany to a Mediterranean destination, who identify useful points at which to stop en route when they become tired. Such a destination may offer touristic opportunities also, but this is not necessarily the case; the principal aim is to break the journey. Location, in terms of driving distances from key generating markets, is therefore a key factor in developing stopover traffic, but an equally important consideration is the availability of suitable overnight accommodation. Singapore, and more recently Dubai, have proved popular as stopover points for air passengers travelling to Australia and New Zealand.

The categorisations above have segmented destinations by their use as a base or a transit location. It is also possible to categorise destinations by their physical or geographic characteristics. Each type of location, whether coastal, urban or rural, will then encourage different forms of tourism to be developed.

COASTAL TOURISM

When we think of coastal destinations, most of us conjure up an image of a typical seaside resort, this being the destination with most popular appeal along any coastline. The attractiveness of a seaside resort is often based on a combination of sun, sand and sea (termed the 3 Ss), which still appeals to the largest segment of the tourist market, either as a form of passive recreation – lying in a deckchair or on the sand and watching the sea – or as a location for more active pastimes, including water sports and beach games.

This form of tourism remains popular, with around 40% of UK residents taking a beach holiday (ABTA, 2018), on a par with city breaks. A similar pattern is seen in Scandinavia, but, for many other nations of the world, the desire to take beach holidays far exceeds that of city breaks (Table 8.1).

TABLE 8.1 Holiday types in 2017 (% of population)

	Beach holiday	City break
Denmark	35%	39%
Finland	32%	46%
Norway	40%	43%
Sweden	46%	39%

(Continued)

TABLE 8.1 (Continued)

	Beach holiday	City break
Brazil	74%	28%
Canada	39%	20%
France	50%	12%
Portugal	64%	27%
USA	48%	22%

Source: Momondo, 2017

Coastal resorts remain popular for international tourists, though cultural and sporting attractions rather than the beach itself may be part of the draw for these destinations. Many seaside resorts in the UK have moved on from their nineteenth-century image and now cater to a variety of different markets. However, it is the traditional resort that has suffered the sharpest decline, due to changing patterns in tourist demand. Above all, this is because these destinations have been slowest to invest in new facilities or renovate their heritage buildings. Many one-time popular resorts, such as Clacton, Cleethorpes, Llandudno, Skegness, Southport and Herne Bay (see Figure 8.1), have remained to a considerable extent frozen in time, with their sweet shops selling candy floss and rock, and their amusement arcades and funfairs, donkey rides and fish and chip shops. The market for these resorts has dwindled as older, loyal, regular visitors have died and their children choose to holiday overseas instead.

FIGURE 8.1 Traditional seafront at Herne Bay, Kent

Photo: Claire Humphreys

A handful of resorts accepted the challenge and invested. Blackpool remains popular simply due to its investment in funfair rides, nightlife amenities and its famous winter illuminations, a light display. Modest investments by towns such as Scarborough have enabled these to survive, if not prosper, while some have striven to change their image by focusing on a single attraction. Bexhill-on-Sea, for example, benefits from the de la Warr Pavilion, perhaps the greatest example of mid-twentieth-century architecture in the country. This was narrowly saved from destruction and now, restored to its former glory, acts as a focus for contemporary art exhibitions. Brighton, with its pebbled beaches, has built on its proximity to London and its cultural facilities to remain an important short-break destination. It has also developed a major new marina to attract yacht owners, while also expanding other non-leisure industries. Margate, trading on its links with the nineteenth-century painter J. M. W. Turner and contemporary artist Tracey Emin, has constructed a modern art gallery as part of regeneration plans designed to attract a new, more cultured market.

A few genteel resorts, such as Eastbourne, Worthing and Deal, have largely resigned themselves to the role of retirement resort, while some larger resorts have diversified sufficiently to be no longer entirely dependent on tourism. Bournemouth, for example, while retaining its tourist market through new investment in attractions and the restoration of its Victorian heritage buildings, is also large enough to have attracted industry (particularly banking and financial services) and education (with its language schools and university). The town is also close to the dense population centres of the south-east.

EXAMPLE

Bournemouth invested in the surfing market

In an attempt to diversify the tourism markets attracted to the town, Bournemouth council invested £3 million in constructing an artificial offshore reef, designed to create great surfing waves.

Sadly, this has been plagued by controversy since it opened in November 2009, with early reports suggesting the quality of the waves created was poor, making it almost impossible to ride. In 2011, routine checks highlighted problems with the construction and positioning of the under-water sandbags, leading to the closure of the reef on safety grounds (*Daily Telegraph*, 2011). Following repairs, the reef reopened in 2014 but still failed to attract significant numbers of surfers. In 2017, parts of the abandoned reef broke away and were washed ashore during a storm.

Despite the lack of success of the surf reef, £100 million of infrastructure investment, improving accommodation stock, transport and entertainment facilities, has helped to improve the image of the destination, which has been particularly successful in attracting the business tourism sector. Arrivals exceeded a million staying visitors and 5 million day trippers in 2015.

The major beneficiaries of changing tourist tastes have been the myriad small fishing ports and seaside villages in the UK, which have largely retained their character and resisted the temptation to expand due to strict planning controls. Some resorts in the south-west, such as Padstow, have been able to build a successful tourist market based largely on the quality of their seafood restaurants. Where there is a strong cultural tradition, such as the colony of artists in St Ives, this has led to a focus on the arts, attracting many galleries, including a notable extension of London's Tate Gallery, which attracts over 200,000 visitors a year, three times the number envisaged when it was constructed. Those with the best marina facilities appeal to the wealthiest members of the yachting fraternity, ensuring that the markets attracted to such destinations remain high-spend.

Many former UK tourist resorts, however, cannot expect to regain their lost markets, given the significant movement of popular seaside tourism over the past five decades, away from the colder, Northern European beaches towards those of the Mediterranean (and further afield), as prices of flights fell and tourists could be assured of sunshine and warm water, something never guaranteed for beach holidays in Northern Europe.

Similarly, the lower fares have enabled Americans to fly to their warmer beaches in Florida or California or even further afield to Mexico, the Bahamas and the Caribbean, abandoning the traditional northern beaches of resorts like Atlantic City and Wildwood, New Jersey or the Long Island beaches of New York State.

Atlantic City fought back by renovating its beachfront, introducing a decked promenade, and developing mega-casinos to attract the high-spend gamblers. This has restored the fortunes of the beachfront itself, but has done little in terms of creating investment behind the foreshore (see Figure 8.2). Miami has successfully rebuilt its market, however, by investing massively in the restoration of its art deco hotels and apartments along Miami Beach, resulting in a regeneration of tourism that has boosted the town economically.

FIGURE 8.2 Beachfront promenade, Atlantic City

Photo: Claire Humphreys

The USA benefits from the exceptional climate and sandy beaches along many of its coasts and, in consequence, has many long-established resorts. Florida and Hawaii, in particular, are noted internationally for the quality of their seaside resorts, although their best beaches are by no means the best-known ones. Research by Florida University's Laboratory for Coastal Research has regularly reported the best US beaches (based on 50 criteria). Estimates suggest that a top ranking can bring a 15–20% boost in visitor rankings. The 2018 top five were:

- Kapalua Bay Beach, Maui, Hawaii
- Ocracoke Lifeguarded Beach, Outer Banks of North Carolina

- Grayton Beach State Park, Florida Panhandle
- Coopers Beach, Southampton, New York
- Coast Guard Beach, Cape Cod, Massachusetts.

(However, note that once a beach has been awarded the coveted number one position, it is removed from the rankings.)

COASTLINES AND ISLANDS

Apart from beaches and resorts themselves, coastlines have an obvious attraction for tourists, whether seen from the land, via coastal footpaths, cycleways or roadways (notable examples of the latter include the Pacific Coast Highway in California, Great Ocean Road in Victoria, Australia and the Amalfi Drive on Italy's west coast), or from the sea (coastal excursions are still popular with tourists, even where no landing is included). In summer, excursion boats sail from Bristol and the Somerset and Devon coasts, circling, and in some cases landing on, the islands of Steep Holm, Flat Holm and Lundy. England's longest coastal footpath, from Minehead to Poole in the south-west, can take up to eight weeks to complete, tempting walkers who may not usually be attracted to the seaside to return time and again in order to undertake the walk in sections. More ambitious visits are made by small cruise ships to islands in Arctic waters around Svalbard and Iceland, where conditions often do not favour landing, yet the bird and other wildlife along these coasts, coupled with the geological formations of the shoreline, still merit observation from seaborne craft of all sizes. Some islands in the Pacific and Caribbean offer little beyond coral atolls or inhospitable beaches, but, even here, cruise ships have organised calls to allow passengers to bathe, snorkel or simply enjoy the unique experience of being on a 'desert island'.

Offshore islands easily accessible by boat or aircraft from the mainland also provide a draw. Heligoland, north of Germany, for example, was a popular destination for German tourists between the two World Wars (and before it was saturation-bombed by the Allies in World War II); it is now a holiday resort, and its natural attractions and tax-free status are encouraging the return of domestic and foreign tourists. Islands such as the Danish Bornholm and the Swedish Gotland also attracted first the domestic tourist and then, more recently, international cruise passengers sailing around the Baltic.

In the Atlantic, the Canaries and Madeira have, of course, attracted tourists for many years, but, more recently, operators have developed tours to more remote destinations, including the Azores and Cape Verde Islands. Often, their appeal is their isolation. They are predominantly rural in character and planning controls are often rigidly exercised to ensure that they remain unspoiled.

Australia is a base for exploring many island paradises and these are now being actively promoted, to a greater or lesser extent, by the tourism authorities. Islands with which we are likely to be familiar include Norfolk Island, Whitsunday Island, King Island, Flinders Island, Three Hummock Island, Cato Island and Rottnest Island.

EXAMPLE

Rottnest Island

This island, located 11 miles off the cost of Fremantle in Western Australia, is a popular getaway for residents of Perth and the surrounding regions. The island covers an area of 1900 hectares and is a class A preserve, the most protected type of public land in Australia.

(Continued)

Attractions include the island's 60 beaches, snorkelling, walking and cycling trails, museums and, perhaps best known, its population of quokka, a small native marsupial.

The island, with a permanent population of around 300 people, welcomes more than half a million tourists each year. Each visitor must pay an admission fee, which is included in the ferry fare to reach the island (private boat owners also pay an annual charge). This funds conservation work as well as education programmes and infrastructure upgrades. The recent desire to take a 'selfie' with a quokka is a growing concern, as these animals' lives are increasingly disrupted by such close contact with tourists (see Figure 8.3).

FIGURE 8.3 Quokka on Rottnest Island

Photo: Shutterstock

More recently, relatively inaccessible islands have become the challenge, especially those without air connections; the more isolated are sought out by specialist travellers. Examples include Pitcairn, St Helena, Tristan da Cunha, Easter Island and the Marquesas. The formerly off-limits Lakshadweep Islands have recently received permits from the Indian government for visits by cruise ships from Goa and are likely to be popular with those who have 'been everywhere and seen everything'.

EXAMPLE

Access restrictions to the Tuscan Archipelago

The desire of many well-travelled tourists to seek out remote and less visited destinations has led to a rise in the appeal of islands. Many of them are underdeveloped, but can be located quite close to heavily populated regions. The Mediterranean offers one example of a region boasting such islands.

While many islands are well known, at least to domestic tourists, there are many others in this part of the world that are little visited, either because they have been seen as having little to attract tourists, or because access has been restricted by the authorities in order to protect the environment.

The Tuscan Archipelago, off the coast of Italy, is an example of the latter. The seven islands that make up the Archipelago are managed by the Tuscan Archipelago Parks Commission. Several are uninhabited and include a state-protected nature reserve and bird sanctuary. The islands have been off limits to all apart from researchers, but the Commission has now agreed to allow access to some of the islands, with a permit required to visit Montecristo (known because of the book by Alexandre Dumas, *The Count of Monte Cristo*), with only 1000 tourists allowed each year.

Although there are many areas with extensively developed islands in the Mediterranean which attract large numbers of international tourists, there are some which have enjoyed long-term popularity with domestic tourists, while others are relatively untouched. France, while boasting well-established beach resorts along its coasts, has also been able to build successfully on the appeal of its many offshore islands and, by carefully controlling development (in one case, by the creation of a national park), has enabled them to retain their natural landscape and seascape charm. On the west coast, the Île de Ré, Île d'Yeu and Belle-Île (near Quiberon) attract wealthy French visitors, as do the French islands off the Mediterranean coast, such as those near Hyères, the Île de Porquerolles, Île de Port-Cros and Île du Levant. By ensuring that supply never meets demand, these islands can select their markets on the basis of price alone. Other islands in the Mediterranean, such as the Italian islands of Ischia and Capri, have long drawn tourists in their thousands, but others, far less well known, have tourism potential for more environmentally sensitive visitors.

THE NEW SEASIDE TOURISM

The fall in long-haul air fares has meant that European sun, sea and sand tourism has now extended to distant destinations like Phuket and Pattaya Beach in Thailand, as well as medium-haul resorts like Sharm el-Sheikh in Egypt and Monastir in Tunis, although political unrest in the region has variously affected travel to these areas over the past decade. Both of the two latter resorts offer the opportunity to combine cultural visits with a traditional beach holiday. The monastery of St Catherine and the landscape around Mount Sinai have become major attractions in Egypt, while the Roman amphitheatre at el Djem and the opportunity to explore the fringes of the Sahara Desert have great appeal to tourists visiting the many resorts along the Tunisian coastline.

Since the turn of the century, new destinations have risen to prominence within the Arabian Gulf, particularly the United Arab Emirates (UAE). Dubai in the UAE has been at the forefront of this development. Recognising that supplies of oil – its major resource – are finite, the state has determined that its future lies in attracting international tourists, and it is investing massively with this in view. Notably, this has involved the construction of a new shoreline, together with offshore artificial islands, offering opportunities for the sale of exclusive second homes alongside luxury hotel accommodation. Its combination of sun, sea and sand with outstanding shopping opportunities and planned museums and art galleries is already seducing many tourists away from their traditional European holiday resorts, although July and August temperatures of 40–50°C in the Gulf may deter visitors in the peak summer periods.

EXAMPLE

The World Islands

An archipelago of 300 artificial islands, forming the shape of the world, is under construction in Dubai. After more than a decade of work, only a few islands had been created, but by 2016 some of these were ready for the construction of accommodation and associated facilities. At the time of writing, it is predicted that 'Sweden' will be the first 'country' to open its doors to visitors, with ten beach palaces nearing completion.

Dubai has built a major international airport in anticipation of receiving up to 15 million tourists annually, a huge increase on the 2009 figure of 6 million. The airport also acts as a key hub for long-haul flights between Europe, the Far East and Australasia. To reach these figures, however, Dubai is now seeking to attract lower-income markets, offering opportunities for other Gulf states, such as Abu Dhabi (UAE), Qatar and Oman, to focus on wealthier holidaymakers by offering not only traditional seaside pursuits but also cultural visits to historic sites and adventure holidays using four-wheel drive vehicles in the nearby desert (see Figure 8.4). Such packages are proving attractive to the new adventure-seeking, middle-income tourists from Europe.

FIGURE 8.4 Four-wheel drive excursion in the Arabian desert, Sharjah, UAE

Photo: Chris Holloway

THE FUTURE OF THE SEASIDE

A question mark hangs over the long-term future of seaside resorts, in the face of the growing threat posed by climate change. Sea levels are rising at such a rate that some estimates suggest they will have increased by about 65 cm by 2100, enough to cause significant problems for some coastal cities (Sharman, 2018). This would also be sufficient to destroy popular resorts in countries like the Maldives and many of the low-lying islands and atolls of the Pacific. Should such a catastrophe occur, holidays to these areas would be the least of our problems, but already such projections are threatening long-term investment in tourist facilities in low-lying locations.

EXAMPLE

A disappearing coastline

The Maldives is a destination portrayed in tourism brochures as a beach paradise, with white sands, palm trees and crystal blue seas. This unspoilt image has helped to make tourism a key industry for the state, accounting for more than 45% of GDP, and in 2017 it welcomed visitor numbers in excess of 1.39 million. The market is dominated by European visitors (47%) but in recent years the numbers arriving from the Asia Pacific region have increased to a level that is almost matching this, at around 44% (Ministry of Tourism, 2018).

However, a perilous fate awaits these shores. Although there are more than 1000 islands, or atolls, the largest is only about 2 miles long and the highest point on the islands is about two metres above sea level. Global warming forecasts anticipate the sea rising above this level and expect these 'paradise islands' to disappear. The tipping point will be when drinkable groundwater will no longer be available. This is anticipated to occur before the middle of this century (Gabbatiss, 2018). In 2008, a proposal was made to purchase land in India, Sri Lanka or Australia where the population of 390,000 could be relocated. However, the government now prefers to resist the rising seas with geo-engineering projects, including the construction of artificial islands at a level higher than the existing natural islands, to which the population can be relocated.

Other islands suffering a similar fate, if climate change forecasts are accepted, include the Seychelles in the Indian Ocean and the Marshall Islands in the Pacific Ocean.

The development of indoor 'tropical' pools at Center Parcs sites has proved highly profitable, and the concept of the indoor beach is a prominent feature in several holiday resorts in Northern Europe. In countries where the appeal of outdoor pools is restricted by poor weather, such domes offer an attractive alternative for swimming and recreation alike.

ARTIFICIAL COASTS

In recent years, Dubai has enjoyed great success with the development of artificial islands as tourist attractions. The Palm Jumeirah, a series of man-made islands in the shape of a palm, was to provide tourist accommodation and attractions as well as luxury apartments for local residents. Around 10,000 people now live on this group of islands, which also provides hotels, beach resorts and retail spaces.

Inspired by the opportunity to develop additional coastline, nearby Qatar has built its own artificial island, the Pearl-Qatar at Doha, the capital. More than 5000 residents have already moved onto the island and several restaurants and luxury shops are open, with more being developed as the local population expands.

The creation of new coastlines and the protection of existing ones are vitally important if coastal tourism is to continue to flourish. However, the demand for traditional sun, sea and sand holidays is changing, with other types of holiday destination offering newer appeal.

URBAN TOURISM

Another category of destination is the **town** or **city**. While seaside tourism has struggled to maintain its historic attraction for visitors in many parts of the world, urban tourism has prospered in recent years. This has been fuelled by a growing interest in cultural activities such as visits to theatres, museums and art galleries, as well as in historical, and even modern, architecture, and the appeal of shopping as a leisure activity. Arts festivals and cultural and sports events have further added to the appeal of many towns and cities.

Most countries have a plentiful stock of towns and cities of both architectural and historic importance. Capital cities have long held a particular draw for tourists (see Table 8.2), and the low fares on no-frills airlines have attracted new markets not only to major cities but also to smaller provincial towns throughout Europe, expanding the short city-break holiday market of one to three nights. Popular cities such as Amsterdam, London, Rome, Vienna and Paris have been joined by Dublin, Prague, Budapest and Bucharest, for example. Barcelona continues to be a leading city for short-break holidays as it has all the benefits required by the short-stay visitor: good shops and restaurants, outstanding architecture (notably by Antoni Gaudí), quality hotels, fine museums and substantial investment in the local infrastructure. It also benefits from competitive prices compared with similar cities elsewhere in Europe. However, this city, along with Rome and Seoul, has now been edged out of the top ten, replaced by two Chinese cities and Kuala Lumpur, the capital city of Malaysia. Interestingly, Beijing, host for the Summer Olympic Games in 2008, received fewer tourists during its Olympic year (3.36 million) than in 2006 (3.59 million) and since (3.44 million in 2009).

TABLE 8.2 Top ten city destinations (by arrivals)

Rank	City	Tourist arrivals 2018 ('000)	Rank in 2012	Rank in 2009	Rank in 2006
1	Hong Kong	29,263	1	10	5
2	Bangkok	24,178	3	2	2
3	London	19,233	4	1	1
4	Macau	18,931	5	11	27
5	Singapore	18,551	2	3	4
6	Paris	17,560	10	8	3
7	Dubai	15,921	13	7	7
8	New York City	13,600	8	6	6
9	Kuala Lumpur	13,434	6	4	15
10	Shenzhen	12,202	7	83	41

Source: Euromonitor International

The growing Asia Pacific market has helped to expand demand for Hong Kong, Macau and Shenzhen, although some other cities in the region have experienced decline in recent years; for example, Seoul saw a contraction in demand of 15% in 2017. Reykjavik, capital of Iceland, has also become a popular short-break destination for Europeans for the past decade, in spite of its relatively high cost of living. Its attractions include its lively nightlife and its unusual surrounding landscape, which offers the possibility of visiting a hot geyser nearby.

The UK is fortunate in that most incoming visitors have as their motivation the desire to see the country's heritage, much of which is found in the urban areas. Apart from London and its myriad attractions, architecturally, historically and culturally, all the leading destinations in the UK are dependent on their heritage to attract the overseas tourist. The university towns of Oxford and Cambridge, the Shakespeare connection with Stratford-upon-Avon, Windsor with its royal castle, the cities of Bath, York, Edinburgh and Chester, all feature on the standard coach tours sold to the package tour market abroad. Apart from their beauty, all these cities benefit from having a very clear image in the public eye and strong associations, making them easy to market as being composed of a complex amalgamation of products, services, natural and artificial resources.

While large cities like Paris, New York and London have the capacity to absorb substantial numbers of tourists, smaller, very popular cities like Oxford and Cambridge in England, Bruges in Belgium and Sirmione on Lake Garda, Italy, suffer from severe congestion in summer, as thousands of foreign tourists visit by coach and car during the peak months, creating major problems of tourist management for the local authorities. Marketing of these destinations has to focus on tight planning and control, coupled with efforts to extend the holiday season, so that tourists can be managed more easily. In Oxford and Cambridge, traffic pressures have become so intense that park and ride has become the norm. Both Sirmione and Bruges have ample parking facilities for cars and coaches on the outskirts of town, but these require visitors arriving by car either to use bus transfers or walk some considerable distance to the heart of the city.

EXAMPLE

Urban heritage

The urgent need for urban renewal in decaying cities, coupled with rising interest in industrial heritage, has led many governments to invest public funds in restoring previously dilapidated buildings as tourist attractions. Former warehouses, woollen mills in the north of England and other important centres of industry during the eighteenth and nineteenth centuries have been converted into museums or other buildings to attract tourists and the leisure market. In some cases, this has extended to entire areas of a city.

An example is the Jewellery Quarter in Birmingham, where tourism has become an economic saviour, attracting residents back into the city centre. Other notable successes include the cities of Bradford and Glasgow, both of which suffered severe decline in the 1980s. They nevertheless contain some fine examples of Victorian and earlier architecture, which has become fashionable again after a long period of falling out of favour.

As with all destinations, urban centres with an established reputation and image attract tourists more readily than those towns having no such clear image. Cities such as London, Paris, Rome, Venice and Amsterdam all have immediately recognisable, clearly differentiated images (although it is interesting to note that, in the 1990s, the London Tourist Board expressed concern that Japanese tourists were diverting to Paris rather than London, the explanation given being that, among Japanese visitors, female tourists are in the majority and they perceived Paris as being gentler and more feminine than London).

Cityscapes are an important element in the appeal to tourists, not least because they have a clearly defined centre, well-established shopping and entertainment districts, attractive enclaves and parks. English towns in particular are noted for their many parks and floral displays; Milan for cutting-edge clothes and furnishing shops; while Stockholm has its Gamla Stan, or Old Town, for historical appeal as well as an attractive waterfront. Some cities, however, suffer from a lack of such a clearly defined centre to provide the focus for a visit. Los Angeles, Moscow and Tokyo have this disadvantage, which reduces their appeal to the independent traveller. That said, the primary appeal of Los Angeles for the international market is Hollywood, while the Kremlin provides a focal point for visits to Moscow, as does the Royal Palace for Tokyo.

CITY WATERFRONTS

Cities that had formerly been important seaports and had suffered from a decline in shipping in recent years were slow at first to exploit the value of their waterfront sites for leisure purposes. Today, many cities have transformed what was formerly a decaying port into an area of recreation for residents and visitors alike. An outstandingly successful example is the Inner Harbour at Baltimore, USA, which, through a combination of private and public investment, was one of the first to become a magnet for tourists due to the wide variety of attractions it introduced along the restored harbourfront. In Australia, Sydney's Darling Harbour has similarly benefited from renewal as a leisure and marine site, as has the Victoria & Alfred waterfront in Cape Town, South Africa. In the UK, more than a dozen waterfronts have been renovated, while retaining the many attractive warehouses and other features of their former port status. London's former Docklands, the Albert Dock area of Liverpool (the site of the Tate Gallery's first provincial art gallery) and docklands at Southampton, Bristol, Salford, Manchester, Swansea, Cardiff, Portsmouth, Plymouth, Newcastle, Gloucester, Glasgow and Dundee have all been developed to attract tourists as well as commercial activity, the latter by the recent construction of a major extension to London's Victoria and Albert (V&A) Museum, on the waterfront adjacent to Captain Scott's *RRS Discovery*, now a maritime museum. Other cities around the world that have landscaped their water frontages to attract tourists are Boston, San Francisco, Fremantle (the port for Perth, Western Australia) and Toronto.

FIGURE 8.5 Excursion boat in Bruges, Belgium

Photo: Chris Holloway

Rivers and canals flowing through city centres can, likewise, add appeal when landscaped attractively. Major capitals, including Rome, London and Paris, have long traded on the appeal of their rivers, but, more recently, disused waterways have also been resurrected to appeal to tourists. A notable example is Birmingham's network of city centre canals, which have become a focal point for locals and visitors alike, with their outdoor canal-side cafés and pubs and narrowboat tours. Similarly, Bruges in Belgium successfully restored its canal network to make it a major feature of one of Europe's most attractive mediaeval cities (see Figure 8.5).

Cities benefiting from a waterfront, but far from the coast, have the added option of creating an urban beach. This is what a growing number of cities have chosen to do, following the lead of Paris, which was the first inland city to create its own 'Paris Plage' in 2002 (see the Example box). The idea was soon copied by other cities, including Berlin, Amsterdam, Rome, Brussels, Vienna and London.

EXAMPLE

The lure of the beach

The feel of sand between the toes can be evocative of glorious summer holidays, and it is felt to be so important that the Paris government creates an urban beach annually alongside the River Seine. By closing the main thoroughfares and providing 3000 tonnes of sand, 50 palm trees, 550 deckchairs and 450 parasols, it attracts Parisians and tourists, who enjoy opportunities to relax, play beach volleyball, listen to open-air concerts, even enjoy an ice-cream.

First introduced in 2002, the Paris Plage covers more than 2 kilometres and operates for two months from early July. Although the original intention was to benefit city residents, tourists soon found this to be another key attraction of the city, and each year the beach regularly attracts 3 million visitors, helping to justify the €5 million it costs to run; this includes activities and events, provided at no cost to users, including tai-chi sessions and numerous family-oriented animations.

RURAL TOURISM

The **countryside** offers a very different holiday experience from seaside and urban tourism. The widespread appeal of the countryside is of relatively recent origin, with an appreciation of nature dating back in the UK only as far as the nineteenth century, and even more recently in the case of other European countries. Initially limited to people in the higher socio-economic groups, its extension to the merchant, and later, labouring, classes emerged only as congestion and pollution made life unbearable in the big cities and escape to the countryside became important for health and tranquillity. Early appreciation of scenery, however, was somewhat artificial. Travellers to the countryside were accustomed to basing their expectations of the landscape on memories of the highly imaginative and frequently hyperbolic paintings by popular artists of the Romantic Movement. In some cases, they even went so far as to observe the scenery by use of a 'Claude' glass, an elegantly framed mirror named after the eminent French landscape painter Claude Lorraine. Observers were encouraged to use these mirrors by standing with their backs to a scene and viewing its framed reflection.

Developing countries, even those with little appeal for the traditional tourist seeking attractive cities or beach resorts, are gaining from the increasing demand by more adventure-minded tourists for holidays 'off the beaten track'. In recent years, large numbers of travellers have discovered such diverse rural gems as the Cameron Highlands in Malaysia, the northern hills of Thailand around Chiang Mai and the tropical heartland of Costa Rica, as well as unusual and attractive landscapes in more developed countries, such as the Cape York Peninsula in Australia and Canada's North West Territories. The popularity of rural beauty has led to regions like Tuscany in Italy and the Ardèche in France becoming popular.

The association of a particular rural area with literary or media connections can provide a powerful draw for tourism, and regional tourist authorities have not been slow to take advantage of this. In England's West Country, Doone Country, set around the village of Oare and based on the North Devon setting of R. D. Blackmore's *Lorna Doone*, led the way for many other regions to promote their links with literature. Until 2012 South Tyneside council promoted 'Catherine Cookson Country' (the region being used as the setting for many of her books), but after 25 years it decided to replace the signs, instead promoting the area for inward investment. Places of birth or residence of famous figures often serve to promote the image of an area and these are frequently available for tourist visits. For example, the home of the children's author Beatrix Potter in Ambleside, Cumbria, is now a National Trust property and has been open to the public for more than 60 years. The nearby village of Hawkshead also has a Beatrix Potter gallery, with information about her later life as well as an exhibition of her paintings, providing further encouragement for tourists to visit this rural area of the Lake District. In some cases, links with historical or famous figures have led to annual festivals being held based on the celebrity's area of expertise, such as a literature festival. A Dylan Thomas trail has been created in Wales that emphasises the use of the Celtic Trail cycle route. Several sites in England have also promoted the association of their district with the mythical King Arthur, most notably the area around Tintagel in Cornwall.

LAKES AND MOUNTAINS

One of the principal draws of rural tourism is lakes and mountains, preferably a combination of the two. Areas offering both have been attracting visitors from the very beginnings of tourism. The Alps and Dolomites in central Europe, stretching through France, Switzerland, Germany and Italy, were catering to British and other holidaymakers as early as the nineteenth century, both for mountaineering and more leisurely pastimes such as walking. The attractiveness of the landscape in each of these countries is certainly heightened by the abundance of nearby lakes.

With a growing focus on activity holidays, mountaineering and high-mountain trekking are gaining in popularity and may well help to offset any decline in winter sports resulting from inadequate snowfall due to global warming. On a more modest scale, England's Lake District, with its combination of mountains and lakes, has special protection as a national park and ranks as one of the most popular tourist destinations in the UK.

The combination attracts distinct markets, with leisure visitors of all ages enjoying the scenery, either passively or on hikes, and younger, more active visitors mountaineering and mountain biking in summer, as well as participating in winter sports at other times, where circumstances allow. Demand for winter sports holidays is putting huge pressure on the Alps, however, which have a fragile environment, easily damaged by overuse. Global warming is affecting Alpine and other mountainous regions, with the snow line receding further up the mountainsides, leaving resorts at lower altitudes without snow for much of the season. This is causing Alpine regions to reinvest to maintain their winter sports. Snow cannons, ski lifts and cable cars are under construction, with France alone investing more than 1 billion euros at the start of this decade in retaining their winter tourism markets. Resorts at lower levels, however, will have to focus on generating warm-weather and other activities in lieu of winter sports.

EXAMPLE

Man-made snow

Lack of snow brings major challenges for winter sports destinations, and as Europe has seen a succession of mild and snowless winters, so increased investment has been made to ensure ski resorts are less reliant on Mother Nature.

One tourist destination now reaping the benefit is the Austrian slopes, which encompass the resort of Saalbach Hinterglemm. Since 2000, investment has seen the construction of large reservoirs across the mountain. Following this, the laying of water pipes and the installation of snow-making cannons has ensured that much of the resort can operate with man-made snow.

The resort now has more than 700 snow-making machines and nine water reservoirs. Snowmaking occurs on all main slopes, ensuring that skiing can occur throughout the winter and into spring. However, Austrian regulations to protect the environment require that no chemicals can be added to the water, so snow-making still requires a minimum temperature of –4° Celsius.

US snow resorts like Aspen and Vail have long been popular for North Americans and Europeans, but other less familiar and more reasonably priced resorts such as Steamboat Springs in Colorado have been discovered by European markets. Packages from the UK have also been launched to still more distant resorts, including Rusutsu and Niseko on Hokkaido Island, Japan, where snow is plentiful and skiing affordable. These two resorts are proving popular with the nearer markets of Canada and Australia, too.

The challenge of climbing major peaks in mountain ranges has moved on from the Alps to more adventurous locations like the Rockies, Andes and Himalayas. For those who do not want to climb, trekking to base camps along trails below the peaks has proved a challenge that is sought after by fit tourists of all ages. Specialist tour companies now organise both climbing and trekking expeditions even to Everest, forcing the Nepalese government to impose high charges for climbing rights in an effort to control numbers. Even though packages can cost in excess of £20,000, this seems to have had little effect on stemming demand; a reported 658 reached the summit in 2013, about half of the total attempting the climb. Overcrowding, leading to delays in reaching the summit, has been cited as contributing to some of the 11 deaths of climbers on the mountain in 2019, although Nepal's Tourism Authority suggests that other factors had also contributed to the year's high death toll (BBC, 2019).

For the less adventurous, simple rambling holidays are enjoyed by countless independent travellers to beauty spots all over the world, and are also packaged for the inclusive tourist.

THE SCENIC COUNTRYSIDE

Although the climate in the UK and Ireland has proved a deterrent to those seeking to enjoy seaside holidays, it accounts for much of the demand for rural tourism. A temperate climate with frequent precipitation creates green fields and abundant woodlands that, coupled with rolling hills and stretches of water, make up the idyll that is the quintessential rural scenery of the British Isles. In spite of its small land mass, the countryside is incredibly diverse, from the meadows and tightly hedged fields in the south and west of England to the drystone walls and bleak moors of the north, from the flatlands and waterways of East Anglia and Lincolnshire to the lakes and mountains of Cumbria, from the wild beauty of the Welsh mountains and the Highlands and Islands of Scotland to the gentle Irish landscape surrounding the lakes of Killarney and the barren historic coastline of the adjacent Dingle Peninsula.

As modern living forces more and more people to live in built-up areas, so the attraction of the countryside grows. Rural tourism attracts international tourists, too, with a growing number of continental visitors coming to tour the UK by car. In turn, many Britons take their cars to France or Germany to take touring holidays. The attraction of contrasts is important here: the Dutch, Danes and Swedes, who have flat scenery and waterways, find the undulating hills and mountains of their European neighbours very appealing.

To protect the vulnerable countryside from development and cater for the demand for rural recreation, the UK has created a network of national parks in England and Wales (as discussed in Chapter 6). Following the passing of the National Parks and Access to the Countryside Act 1949, the Peak District National Park was the first to be created, in 1952, soon followed by nine others. The Norfolk and Suffolk Broads were given similar protected status in 1988 and the New Forest in 2006. There are currently 15 areas (including three in Wales and two in Scotland) with national park status or equivalent. The Cairngorms National Park became the largest in the UK when it was designated in 2003, totalling 1466 square miles, although the exclusion of the highland area of Perthshire adjoining the site was controversial.

TRAIL TOURISM

Hiking or rambling has become a popular pastime, and the UK is fortunate to possess many country footpaths with public rights of way that the Ramblers' Association is anxious to protect as pressures on the countryside grow. In the UK, the Countryside and Rights of Way Act 2000, commonly known as the Right to Roam Act, opened up large areas of the country, giving ramblers the statutory right to ramble on 'access land' in England and Wales in 2005, extended in 2006 to beaches and coastlines. Natural England, the new national countryside agency, intends to open 2000 miles of coastline to walkers over time. The Land Reform (Scotland) Act 2003 offers similar rights in the north. The National Parks and Access to the Countryside Act also created a network of long-distance footpaths, which are enjoying growing popularity with hikers (see the Example box).

EXAMPLE

National trails

The first national trail to be opened in the UK was the Pennine Way, in 1965. The England Coast Path will be the newest (and longest) national trail when it is complete in 2020.

There are currently 15 trails in England and Wales (see Figure 8.6):

- Pennine Way (268 miles)
- Cleveland Way (110 miles)
- Cotswold Way (102 miles)
- Glyndwr's Way (135 miles)
- Hadrians Wall Path (84 miles)
- North Downs Way (153 miles)
- Offa's Dyke Path (177 miles)
- Peddars Way and Norfolk Coastal Path (93 miles)
- Pembrokeshire Coastal Path (186 miles)
- Pennine Bridleway (130 miles)

- The Ridgeway (87 miles)
- South Downs Way (100 miles)
- South West Coast Path (630 miles)
- Thames Path (184 miles)
- Yorkshire Wolds Way (79 miles).

Currently the longest, and perhaps among the most popular, is the South West Coast Path, which extends between the seaside resort of Minehead in Somerset and Poole Harbour in Dorset. It is estimated to take a 56-day walk to complete. In 2010, a European grant of £2.1 million was provided to focus on improving the visitor experience, and to increase the estimated £222 million the trail already brings to the local economy. Additional funding from the UK government has continued to enhance this project.

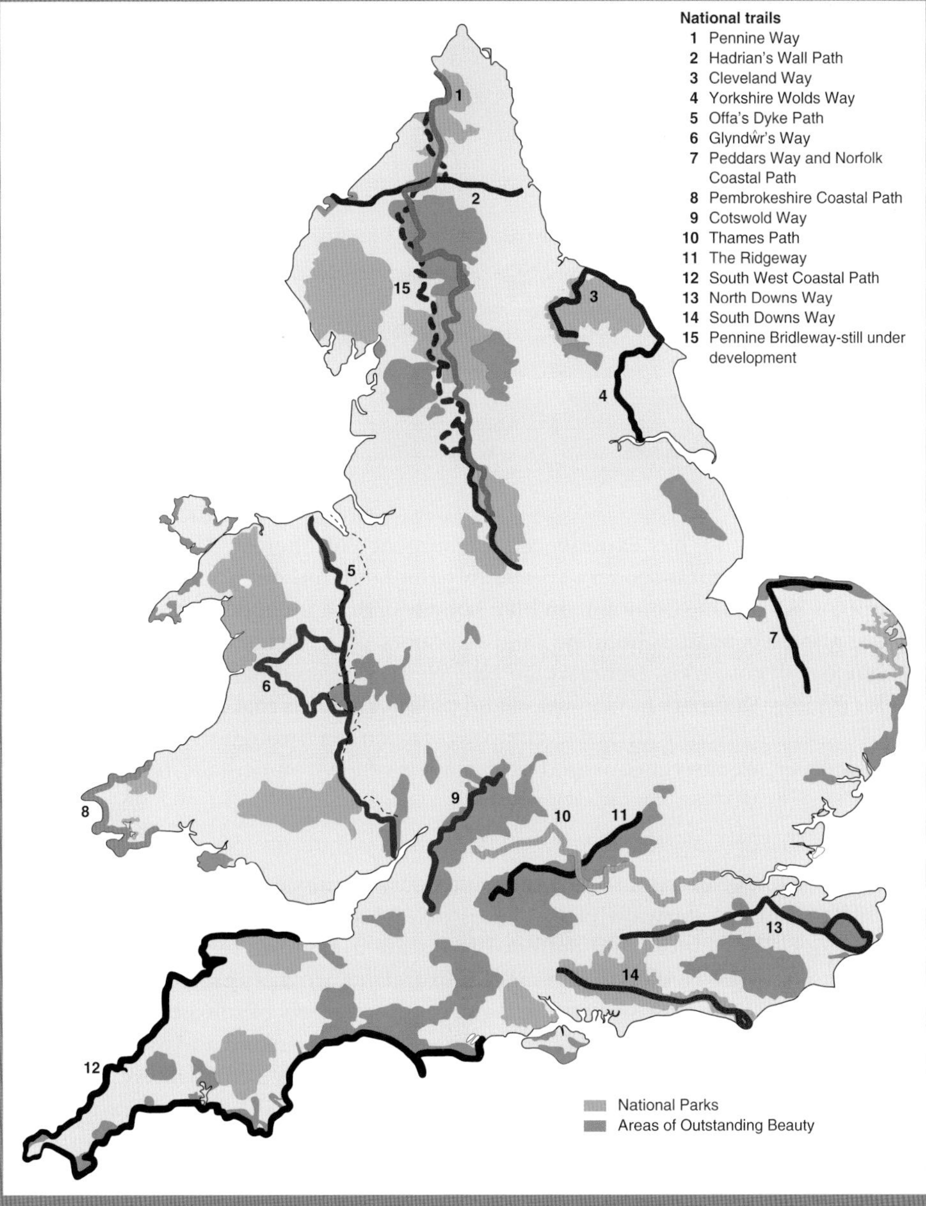

FIGURE 8.6 National trails of England and Wales

An ambitious plan to develop a trail to embrace seven countries in Europe was completed in 2007. The North Sea Trail covers around 3000 miles, running from the north of Scotland, through to Scarborough in England, then extending across to the Continent via the Netherlands, Germany, Denmark and Sweden towards the Arctic regions of Norway. The goal is to extend the trail to 7000 miles of coastal path, drawing on the shared history and culture of the communities that line the North Sea (Rowe, 2011). It is planned to develop cultural and trading links between the regions as well as to improve the economies of the areas adjacent to the trail. Tourism industries are being encouraged to provide supporting facilities and attractions, which will help to enhance the experience of the walkers.

Trails are also popular in the USA (see Example box), where wilderness areas give maximum scope for challenging, long-distance footpaths, as well as a plethora of shorter trails in urban areas.

EXAMPLE

Trails in the USA

The USA is best known for its wilderness trails, often taking weeks to complete, such as the Appalachian Trail. The National Trails System Act 1968 paved the way for federal involvement in rural and city trails and now 11 national scenic trails and 19 national historic trails have been authorised by Congress. In addition to these, more than 11,000 miles of recreation trails exist across the states. More than $19 million has been awarded in grants since 2009 to support some 233 recreational trails across the USA.

The Appalachian Trail, one of the national scenic trails, is over 2000 miles long, with more than 250 shelters and campsites along its route, each approximately one day's hike apart. Each year, over 2 million people hike at least part of this trail.

Cycling, too, has experienced a resurgence of interest. This is a sport that is largely dependent on rural scenery (preferably flat land, although more active cyclists will also opt for hill touring or mountain bike holidays). Both independent and package tour cyclists are attracted to such holidays, and operators offer inclusive tours by bike to a growing number of countries. Denmark and the Netherlands, in particular, offer ideal countryside for cycling, Denmark having woodland trails for cyclists that run alongside certain stretches of coastline, offering attractive glimpses of open sea through the trees. Most of these forms of tourism are also encouraged as examples of environmentally friendly tourism.

RURAL WATERSCAPES

Demand for leisure and recreation using boats has always been popular among the British, and the rural waterways of the UK provide ideal opportunities for water-based tourist activities. The Norfolk and Suffolk Broads are a paradise for both yacht and motor boat enthusiasts. The Netherlands, France and Ireland are just three other European countries with canals and waterways attracting growing numbers of tourists seeking the pleasure of 'messing about in boats', while the countless lakes of Finland and Sweden are also growing in popularity during the short Nordic summer, particularly with domestic tourists and second-home owners. The appeal of water-dependent holidays is fully explored in Chapter 14.

Sites that include major waterfalls are attractive to international tourists. Those that are readily accessible, such as Niagara Falls on the Canadian/US border and Victoria Falls on the Zambia/Zimbabwe border, enjoy considerable popularity and have been built up as key destinations by their countries' tourism authorities. Zambian guides have more recently been escorting intrepid adventure tourists to the Devil's Pool at Victoria Falls, in which, at low water, it is possible (if slightly risky) to bathe on the very edge of the 360-foot drop, an experience promoted as 'swimming on the edge of the world'. More inaccessible falls, including the world's highest, Angel Falls in Venezuela, do not yet attract the numbers of tourists that could be anticipated at such unique scenic attractions if adequate transport and other infrastructure were in place.

WOODLANDS AND FORESTS

Areas of woodland and dense foliage provide yet another appeal for tourism. In the USA, the New England states of Vermont, New Hampshire and Maine and the Canadian eastern provinces attract large numbers of domestic and international tourists to witness the famous 'fall foliage' colours in the autumn.

More exotic foliage is available to tourists in the form of jungle and, in South America, the Amazon has become a popular supplementary tour for those travelling to Ecuador and Peru. Pristine jungle still exists in West Africa, which to date has been little exploited for tourism. Although small group tours are organised to see the gorillas in Rwanda and the Congo, tourism is limited by political instability in these areas of the world. Smaller but more accessible jungles still exist in developed countries, notably El Yunque Rainforest in Puerto Rico and the rainforest in the Cape York area of Northern Queensland, Australia. Countries such as Borneo and Papua New Guinea also offer great potential for exploration of dense tropical forest, if the political and potential health problems can be overcome. The thickly forested tropical landscapes commonly found on the Caribbean islands are also extensively promoted by each island's tourism authorities, and many provide excellent trails for hikers of all ages.

In the UK, there are over 50 historic forests, as well as many further areas of woodland that attract day trippers or walking tourists. Burnham Beeches, near London, is noted for the superb foliage of its beech trees, while forests such as the New Forest (a royal forest and also a national park) and Sherwood Forest (associated with Robin Hood) have close links with history, myth and literature.

Apart from its national parks, the UK has also introduced the concept of national forest parks, the Royal Forest of Dean becoming England's first national forest park in 1938. In the 1990s, the government announced the formation of a new National Forest, covering some 200 square miles of the English Midlands, and in 2018 it unveiled plans to create a new Northern Forest, stretching from Liverpool to Hull. Some limited protection, at least in theory, is also afforded by designating sites as Areas of Outstanding Natural Beauty (AONB) or Sites of Special Scientific Interest (SSSI). There are 46 AONBs in England, Wales and Northern Ireland; and the North Pennines (covering 2000 square kilometres), in recognition of its world-class geological heritage, became the first European Geopark in 2003. This designation by UNESCO is expected to lead to greater interest in nature-based tourism and better protection for the environment. Scotland has a further 40 sites, known as Natural Scenic Areas, which parallel the AONBs.

AGROTOURISM

Rural tourism, as we have seen, has long been popular with independent travellers, and its importance to the economy of the countryside is widely recognised. The concept of agrotourism (or agritourism) was developed in Italy and, from there, spread rapidly throughout the Mediterranean and beyond. Its aim is to develop sustainable tourism in agricultural areas of the countryside, and it has become an important feature of rural tourism planning following the success of the development of gîte holidays in France. French government grants were awarded in the post-war years to help convert decaying farm buildings into rural cottages for tourist accommodation, and the gîte holiday became popular, particularly with independent British tourists. The Portuguese quintas, or rural estates, also attracted a strong following among tourists eager to experience something a little different from the standard forms of holiday accommodation.

EXAMPLE

Agritourism or agrotourism?

The terminology around this sector is yet to be firmly defined. Terms such as agritourism and agrotourism are often used interchangeably. Other terms, such as rural tourism and farm tourism, are also used to denote similar activities. We can look at the some of the definitions brought together by Phillip et al. (2010) to recognise the overlap:

- *agritourism* – 'rural enterprises which incorporate both a working farm environment and a commercial tourism component'
- *agrotourism* – 'tourist activities of small-scale, family or co-operative in origin, being developed in rural areas by people employed in agriculture'
- *farm tourism* – 'rural tourism conducted on working farms where the working environment forms part of the product from the perspective of the consumer'.

What does seem to be clear is whether you consider the term 'agritourism', 'agrotourism' or 'farm tourism', all appear to be a subset of the wider rural tourism industry.

There is now a programme of strong financial support from the EU, with grants that are allowing rural tourism provision to become increasingly luxurious. Recent developments also take account of the interest in adventure sports, many of which are best enjoyed in rural communities, and outdoor sports such as ballooning, horse riding and mountain biking are also now catered for.

Spain, Portugal, Cyprus, Greece and Italy have all invested heavily in agrotourism. Notable developments include those in the Epirus province in north-western Greece and in Sierra Aracena, Huelva Province, in Spain. The USA is also seeing significant expansion in its rural tourism offering.

EXAMPLE

Agritourism in Tennessee

The state of Tennessee has long-established agriculture and tourism industries and is thus well placed to develop agritourism, which is seen as an opportunity to diversify business operations and boost profits. Most farm businesses in the state are small, with perhaps two or three full-time employees, and many farms are often family-run businesses heavily reliant on business revenue. Significantly, research into Tennessee agritourism has revealed that as much as 40% of farm income is derived from tourism-related activities (Jensen et al., 2013).

The activities available to tourists are varied, including fishing, horse-back riding, camping and a variety of farm-based entertainments such as animal exhibits (including petting), pumpkin patches and wagon rides. Farm shops and other sales opportunities (often of locally produced food and wine) provide substantial revenue streams. Some farms even provide facilities to host weddings, conferences and festivals.

The UK has also actively promoted its farming and rural holidays, which have become increasingly important to farmers as a source of revenue due to traditional revenues drying up. Tourist boards and local authorities have helped the private sector to develop new ideas in rural tourism. One example is that of the West Midlands region, which piloted short breaks involving culinary trails – a cider trail in Herefordshire and a pork pie trail at Melton Mowbray – designed to link farmers, food producers and the tourism industry under the banner 'farms, food and peaceful surroundings'. The Department for Environment, Food and Rural Affairs (DEFRA) reports that around two-thirds of UK farmers have diversified their activities (although only 6% offer tourism accommodation and catering), bringing in extra income averaging £7000 per annum (DEFRA, 2018).

Finally, mention should be made of summer camps for children, long popular in North America. Over 7 million children attend summer camps each year in the USA, bringing prosperity to the areas in which they are sited (notably New England). These do not necessarily have to be sited within areas of highest tourist appeal, helping to spread the benefits of rural tourism and avoiding congestion at popular destinations.

EXAMPLE

Summer camps in the UK

Summer camps originated in the USA, but are now prevalent across Europe and are, in some cases, subsidised by local or national government. These camps are often themed, many focusing on adventure and sporting activities.

Having been operating in the UK for over 50 years, PGL is perhaps one of the best-known providers of summer camps (so much so that its company name was rumoured to mean 'Parents Get Lost'*). It operates camps across the UK, France and Spain for children aged between 7 and 17. As well as summer camps for more than 250,000 children, it now offers group activity holidays and school outdoor education courses.

The YHA (Youth Hostel Association), a charitable organisation, also offers a programme of summer camps at three locations across the UK. More than 60,000 young people have participated in these camps, and to extend opportunities to a diversity of markets the YHA offers a 75% bursary for children from low-income families. The camps are all supported by volunteers who give their free time to provide a range of experiences for the participants. Their themed camps include Extreme Adventure, Action Outdoor Pursuits and Future Leader.

Although most residential camps last a week, there is also growing provision for day camps to bring excitement to the long summer holiday. Key UK providers include Camp Beaumont (having devolved its residential camp operations to Kingswood Camps, this company now operates 16 venues in London and the Home Counties), Super Camps, King's Camps and Barracudas.

The cost of participating in residential and day camps can be high, but there is research evidence showing that attendance at camps does help to boost confidence in children, increasing friendship skills, while participation in extra-curricular activities has been shown to enhance academic performance (*Irish Independent*, 2011).

Note: * PGL is actually the initials of the company's founder – Peter Gordon Lawrence.

WILDERNESS AREAS

As open countryside becomes rarer in the developed countries, measures are introduced to protect what remains, especially where this has been largely untouched until recent years. The USA designated the world's first national park at Yellowstone in 1872. This huge park, containing the famed Old Faithful geyser, covers an area of some 2.25 million acres on the borders between Wyoming, Montana and Idaho. Since then, numerous national parks have been created in the USA (see Figure 8.7) and elsewhere throughout

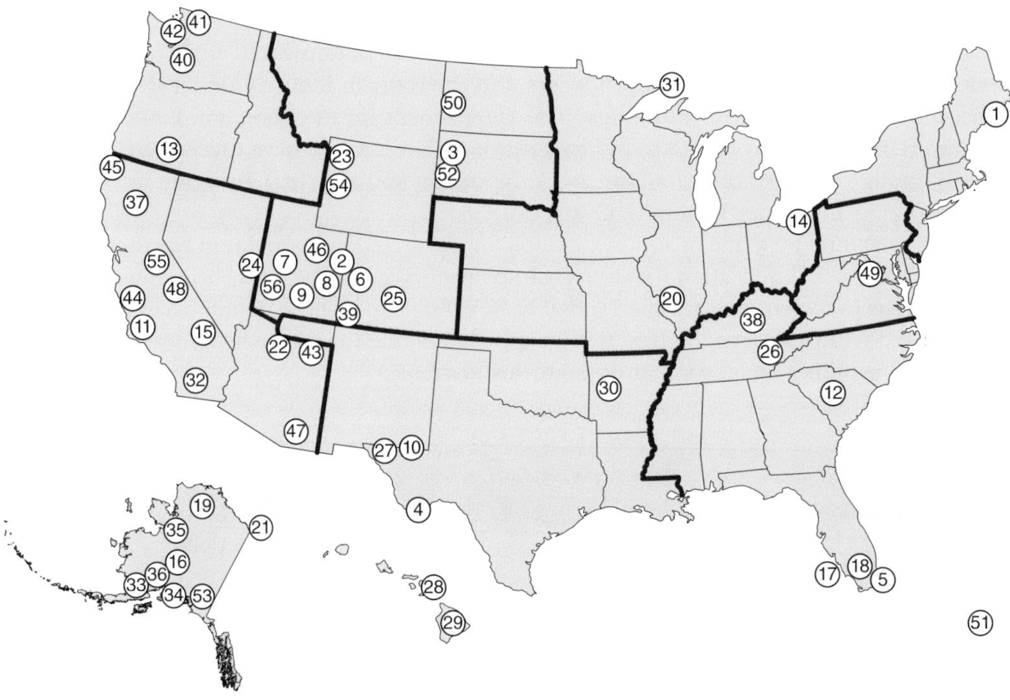

1. Acadia
2. Arches
3. Badlands
4. Big Bend dagger
5. Biscayne
6. Black Canyon of the Gunnison
7. Bryce Canyon
8. Canyonlands
9. Capitol Reef
10. Carlsbad Caverns
11. Channel Islands dagger
12. Congaree dagger
13. Crater Lake
14. Cuyahoga Valley
15. Death Valleydagger
16. Denali dagger
17. Dry Tortugasdagger
18. Everglades double-dagger
19. Gates of the Arctic
20. Gateway Arch
21. Glacier Bay double-dagger
22. Grand Canyon
23. Grand Teton
24. Great Basin
25. Great Sand Dunes
26. Great Smoky Mountains double-dagger
27. Guadalupe Mountains
28. Haleakalā dagger
29. Hawai'i Volcanoes double-dagger
30. Hot Springs
31. Isle Royale dagger
32. Joshua Tree dagger
33. Katmai
34. Kenai Fjords
35. Kobuk Valley
36. Lake Clark
37. Lassen Volcanic
38. Mammoth Cave double-dagger
39. Mesa Verde
40. Mount Rainier
41. North Cascades
42. Olympic double-dagger
43. Petrified Forest
44. Pinnacles
45. Redwood
46. Rocky Mountain dagger
47. Saguaro
48. Sequoia dagger
49. Shenandoah
50. Theodore Roosevelt
51. Virgin Islands dagger
52. Wind Cave
53. Wrangell–St. Elias
54. Yellowstone double-dagger
55. Yosemite
56. Zion

FIGURE 8.7 National parks in the USA

the world. The largest is North East Greenland National Park, covering an area of 373,300 square miles, but new parks are still being developed; for example, the formation of 13 new parks, covering 11,294 square miles, created out of virgin forest in Gabon, which is described in Chapter 6.

Many wilderness areas contain spectacular scenery, drawing huge crowds of tourists in their peak seasons that have to be monitored and managed. Examples include the Grand Canyon, Bryce and Zion Canyons and Monument Valley, where the appeal of solitude and communing with nature, the original concept of the USA's national parks, is soon lost in midsummer due to the sheer number of visitors (see Figure 8.8).

FIGURE 8.8 **Tourists at the Grand Canyon, USA**

Photo: Claire Humphreys

Another way to designate land masses is the safari park, most commonly found in South and East Africa (see Figure 8.9). The Sabi Sabi Game Reserve in South Africa was the world's first designated wildlife park, but, as other African nations started to become aware of the threat to their wildlife resources and the appeal wild animals hold for tourists, the number of parks quickly expanded and rangers were introduced to reduce poaching.

THE SUCCESSFUL DESTINATION

Three important points should be highlighted in relation to tourist destinations. First, the chances of their long-term success will be significantly enhanced if the benefits they offer

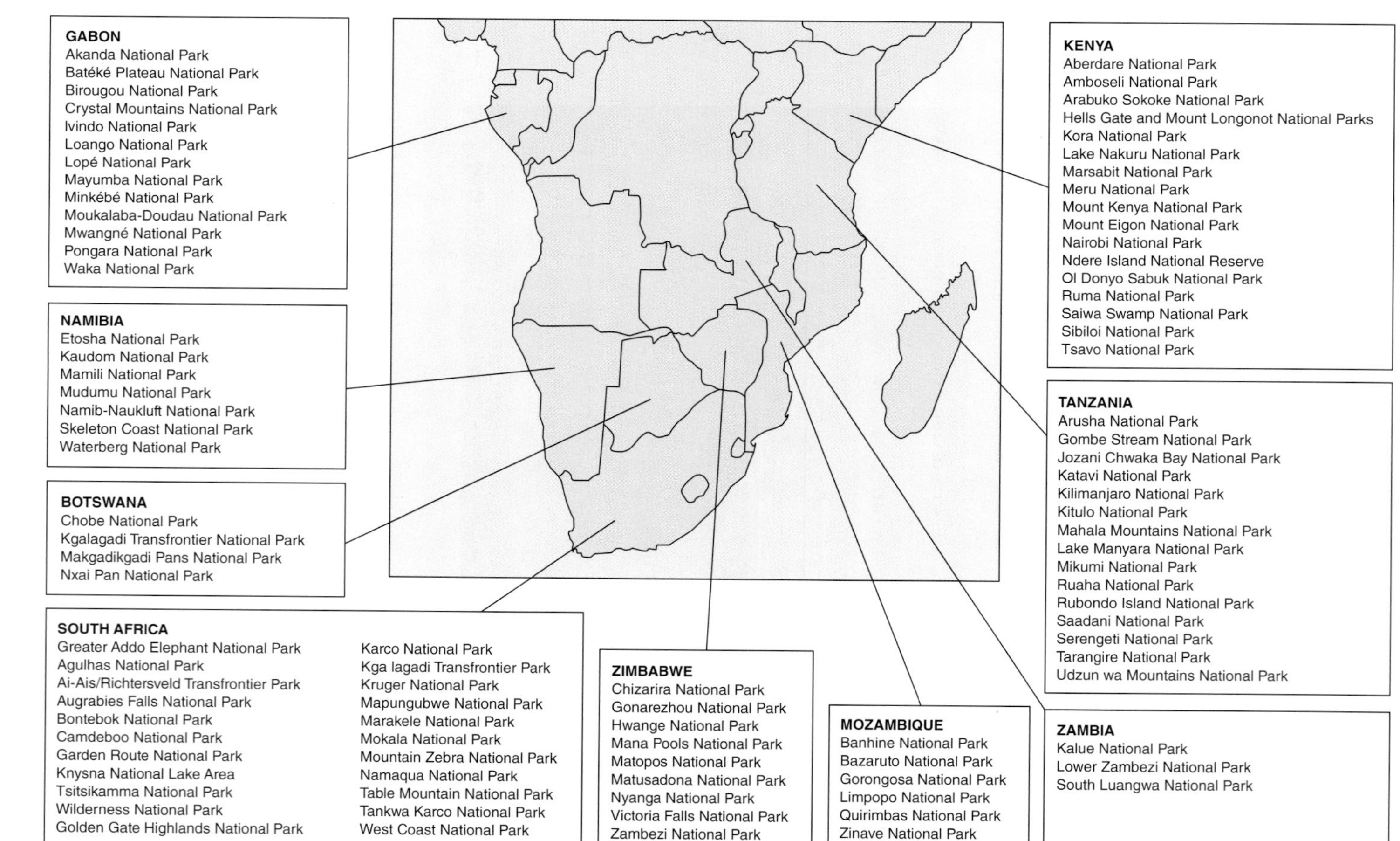

FIGURE 8.9 Major wildlife parks in South and East Africa

are unique. There is only *one* Oberammergau Passion Play, there is only one Eiffel Tower, Grand Canyon or Big Ben, and these attractions can provide the focus for a destination's marketing campaign. These types of destination retain their appeal, even if their prices become less competitive than those of other destinations.

It is true to say, however, that the majority of the mass tourism movement is directed at sun, sea and sand destinations, which the Mediterranean and Caribbean countries provide so effectively. Such destinations are seldom unique and their customers do not require them to be so. They will be satisfied as long as the amenities are appropriate, the resort remains accessible and prices are competitive. Indeed, the similarities in attractions and amenities, as well as the way these destinations are marketed, give rise to the concept of the **identikit destination**. Such destinations have been developed through the activities of multinational tourism organisations. In the development of such destinations, the emphasis changes from an attempt to distinguish the product to one that concentrates on maintaining or improving its image by offering good standards that reflect value for money and ensuring that the destination remains competitive with other similar destinations.

The second point to stress is that the more benefits a destination can offer, the greater will be the attraction of the destination. Multiple attractions provide added value, so the concentration within a specific geographical area of a number of different products appealing to different markets (such as the City of Boston, Massachusetts, which benefits from the seaside attractions of Cape Cod and the rural appeal of New England fall foliage on its doorstep) will improve its chances of success.

EXAMPLE

Duplicating attractions

The government of Christchurch, New Zealand, is supporting plans to create a major new $120 million visitor attraction based on the Eden Project, located in Cornwall, England (which attracts around 1 million visitors a year). The New Zealand attraction will form part of the regeneration of the city, which became necessary following a major earthquake in 2011.

This is not the first New Zealand attraction to draw on the UK for inspiration. On the North Island just outside Wellington is Stonehenge Aotearoa, a full-scale working adaptation of Stonehenge. Drawing on principles allied to its famous namesake in Wiltshire, England, this construction of 24 upright pillars connected by lintels to form a circle uses astronomical principles in its alignment and design. It serves as an outdoor observatory of the night sky, while educational talks, tours and events also attract visitors.

Third, it should be clear that no destination can rely on its past successes to continue to attract tourists. Most depend at least to some extent on visitors returning, so will need to update and augment their range of attractions continually to encourage repeat visits. This means that there is a need for innovation and constant investment. Destinations, like all products that depend on consumer demand, have life cycles; that is, they experience periods of growth, expansion and, eventually, decline, as discussed in Chapter 3. If we examine the history of any well-known resort, we can see the truth of this. Along the French Riviera, Nice, Cannes, Antibes, Juan les Pins and St Tropez have all in turn enjoyed their periods of being fashionable seaside resorts, but, ultimately, their visitors moved on to resorts seen as still more fashionable, often to be replaced by less fashion-conscious, less free-spending tourists. A decline into decay can only be arrested through redevelopment and innovation. In some cases, resorts have been allowed to run down to an extent where the cost of renovation may be beyond the scope of the local authority and decay becomes inevitable.

DESIGN OF THE BUILT AND NATURAL ENVIRONMENT

More recently, attention has focused on the importance of the **public realm** in satisfying tourists once they have been attracted to a destination. The public realm may be commonly defined as the features of a destination that represent the environment in which the tourist stays and moves around, to include public amenities such as parks, squares, gardens, public toilets, litter collection, paved areas, street furniture, car parking and similar features of the built environment that are so important in creating the experience that tourists enjoy, as well as the image that they retain and later communicate to other potential travellers. These features complement the buildings, public and otherwise, that make up the physical characteristics of the tourist product.

Most visitors to a town will explore it on foot, so good street-level design is vital. Use of local materials, whether in modernist or more traditional buildings, is important to create a sense of place. Local building materials are often more expensive to use than, say, concrete, but the additional costs are justified in the long run by enhancing the town's vernacular appeal. In the UK, examples may be found in the use of Bath stone in Bath, black and white half-timbering in the border country, thatch in the West Country and slate in the Lake District or Wales. Even for such mundane features as public toilets, the use of local and natural building materials can greatly enhance the end result; indeed, today it is sometimes insisted on by local authority planning departments. The benefit of using such materials is that they help to reinforce the characteristics of the brand image that the destination and tourist board are trying to create.

No building can be divorced from its setting, and just as thought must go into the design of the building itself, so the site itself must be landscaped attractively to maximise its appeal to visitors. Where a development is on a slope, it becomes even more important to ensure that the buildings blend with the background. If the buildings are to be exposed to view – for example, a group of self-catering chalets high in the Alps – great care has to be taken to integrate them into the landscape. Buildings should not stand out on the skyline, but, if it is essential that they do, then their lines should be broken up with the use of trees and shrubs. On sloping sites, buildings can be 'stepped' or terraced up the hillside to keep their scale in harmony with the environment. Similarly, with waterside developments, buildings should be sited well clear of the waterfront itself, to allow for walkways along the banks that will attract both residents and visitors and ensure that those using the waterway are not intimidated by tall buildings.

Enlightened authorities have come to recognise that the retention of traditional bollards, cranes and other paraphernalia will provide a unique setting, making it even more attractive to visitors, together with the addition of a modest number of trees or shrubs.

STREET FURNITURE

Street furniture is something that we all take for granted, yet it plays an important part in reflecting the national landscape, too. One has only to think of the classic red telephone kiosks (now increasingly disappearing) and the traditional green boulevard chairs and tables still to be found on the streets of Paris, to realise that such items play a part in formulating our picture of townscapes. In the UK, a great deal of attention has been paid in recent years to the design of public seating and litter bins, but any item of street furniture, from litter bins to bus shelters, from public toilets to refreshment stalls, from lamp posts to railings, needs to be carefully designed to be in harmony with the surroundings and reflect the image of the area in which it is sited. Increasingly, these sites must be designed to resist vandalism and, where possible, graffiti, too.

Providing seating in towns and cities is a problem for the planners, as it tends to attract vagrants. The use of simple-to-maintain materials that will provide a brief respite for residents and tourists, but not encourage longer stays, may be the answer to the problem. Individual seats, rather than benches, also reduce their use by vagrants for sleeping.

Local authorities must first determine whether to adopt a classic or modern design for their setting. Heritage sites such as York and Chester are more likely to opt for a traditional and classic design to blend with the architecture of the area. Unfortunately, this has led to the development of a ubiquitous design in cast iron with gold motifs, frequently bearing the crest of the city, which, while tasteful and elegant, does little to distinguish the city's streets from countless others in the same country. These designs are better, however, than some of the products they replace, such as the plastic litter bin (all too often cracked or misshapen), in a choice of battleship grey or garish yellow and still a common sight in urban areas. Litter bins in particular need to be big enough to accommodate the huge amounts of litter created today by takeaway shops, and the council must have a policy of emptying these frequently, otherwise the benefits of good design will be lost as rubbish piles up around the base of the bin. Tourist information, including access to local maps assisting wayfinding, must also be incorporated into the streetscape. As we can see in Figure 8.10, information about local attractions is accompanied by an orientation map as well as the opportunity to purchase a tourist map of the city. The ubiquitous public benches and plastic litter bin, like those mentioned above, are also evident.

FIGURE 8.10 Street signage providing tourist information outside Lincoln Castle

Photo: Claire Humphreys

Cities on the European continent, particularly those whose centres were substantially rebuilt after the war or that wish to promote a modern, dynamic image, often adopt more modern designs. These can work equally well in the appropriate setting. Their cost may be substantially higher than more modest designs, but they not only improve the image of the city but also last much longer without repair or replacement.

PEDESTRIANISATION

Many towns popular with tourists have pedestrianised some of their principal thoroughfares. The result can greatly enhance the atmosphere of a street and encourage visitors to come shopping. Some of the UK's most attractive town centres, such as those of York, Brighton, Bath and Chester, and many continental towns, feature narrow pedestrian walkways that have never been wide enough to support motor vehicles. In such towns, the narrowness of the lanes is their very attraction. Even in towns where such lanes do not exist, virtually all now have areas restricted to pedestrian use. In London, for instance, Covent Garden was redesigned on this basis after the fruit and vegetable market moved away.

Pedestrianising will not in itself be enough to make the area a focal point for shoppers, however. The shops themselves must be appropriate for the setting and the street must be enhanced by well-designed street furniture, tree planting and the display of flowers or shrubs in tubs or other containers. When this is done tastefully, the end result can transform a street. The flipside, however, is that it will also attract much larger numbers of pedestrians, which can lead to congestion and a litter problem that the council must be prepared to tackle.

PUBLIC AMENITIES

Car parks

Car parks are a particular problem for designers as they occupy large areas of land and are often visually intrusive. In the countryside, efforts are now made to ensure that they appear as natural as possible. For example, logs can be used to separate the bays, and the planting of substantial shrubs can help to conceal the cars themselves. Good, but not intrusive, lighting is important too, and the surface can be gravel rather than tarmac. In some small parking areas, it may be possible to use honeycomb concrete blocks that allow grass to grow through them, rendering the concrete surface almost invisible.

Car parks must, of course, be situated well away from any high-grade heritage sites, which may mean that there will need to be special provision for the disabled. In cities, the urban setting will mean that more man-made materials can be used in car parks' construction, but this no longer means high-rise concrete. Designs have become more fanciful, including, in one case, a mock mediaeval fortification. Car parks on open land have proved successful when they have been attractively furnished with decorative modern lamps and plenty of trees to break up the land mass. Given the high prices motorists are now resigned to paying for parking, underground car parks are often economically viable and, of course, have the least impact on the surrounding environment. In Salzburg, Austria, where public parking is at a premium, the local authority went so far as to blast a cavernous car park out of the adjacent cliff faces, underground parking being impractical.

Public toilets

Quality public toilets for tourists are vitally important, despite often being treated as a peripheral issue by planners. Many tourist sites suffer from an inadequate supply of toilets, and in the UK many have had their toilets locked or shut down due to shortages of money for maintenance and supervision. Bath, one of the UK's principal tourist towns, has seen a sharp drop recently in the number of conveniences remaining open for tourists, a common issue across the country, where more than 600 public toilets have been closed since 2010 (Jones and Schraer, 2018). While the UK is not unique in facing this problem, it is interesting to note that, in Japan, architectural competitions are promoted for public toilets, while the Chinese encourage architects to design toilets with the needs of American tourists in mind.

EXAMPLE

The attraction of public conveniences

In recent years, efforts have been made to recognise the best designed toilets, those that attract tourists. The International Toilet Tourism awards were inaugurated in 2017 to further efforts to recognise the unique design of these facilities. Categories include best design, best economic contributor and quirkiest experience.

Another list, compiled by architecture firm Design Cural, identified the appeal of the transparent toilets in Lausanne, Switzerland (for privacy, the glass will frost over at a touch of a button). Also listed were a toilet resembling a sea monster, in Wellington, New Zealand, and a sculpture leading to a circular restroom in Shimodate, Japan.

Utility cables

Telephone and public utility lines can mar the appearance of even the most beautiful town or village. Fortunately, in the UK local authorities have generally taken an enlightened view, hiding these unattractive necessities, but a visit to Spain or Greece will soon illustrate how much visual pollution is caused when overhead wires march along streets, linking into houses (Figure 8.11). Although the cost of burying wires is much higher, in the long run it is worth the investment if it makes the site much more attractive to visitors. The positioning of electricity pylons across the landscape in some of the most scenic parts of the UK, and the more recent intrusion of wind turbines and mobile phone antennae, have also been strongly criticised by defenders of the traditional countryside.

EXAMPLE

Removing the pylons of power

On winning the right to host the 2012 Olympic Games, one of the first tasks facing the Olympic Delivery Authority, the responsible body for constructing the infrastructure at the Olympic site, was to bury ten kilometres of power lines underground. The pylons spanning the site were considered an eyesore, and burying the cables provided an improved public space across the park.

The power cable debate has also affected two other tourist regions in the UK. Campaigns have been launched to keep pylons away from the Cheddar Valley in Somerset, England, as well as the Wallace Monument in Stirling, Scotland. In the latter case, support from local government ministers has been forthcoming, although this has not been enough to force a reversal of plans from the power companies.

FIGURE 8.11 **Visual intrusion of power cables in La Paz, Bolivia**

Photo: Claire Humphreys

HORTICULTURAL DISPLAYS

The use of hanging baskets, floral beds in the centre of main access roads, extensive tree planting along the pavements and similar horticultural displays can make a pretty village outstanding and even an unattractive town bearable. Some of the UK's towns have made such a feature of their floral displays that they have become famous internationally. Bath's hanging basket displays are a highly attractive feature for summer visitors, while the massed floral beds that line the seafronts of towns such as Eastbourne and Worthing draw many older visitors to these resorts year after year. As many flowers bloom in spring, they can be used to attract visitors before the traditional peak summer season. Aberdeen is noted for its display of formal rose beds along its main roads, and on the Continent the sight of flower-bedecked chalets in Switzerland and Austria is indelibly associated with these countries' villages and highlighted in all tourist brochures.

EXAMPLE

Floral towns and villages in France

For more than 50 years, towns and villages across France have bedecked their streets, buildings, public squares and balconies with flowers, as a welcome to visitors, all with the goal of achieving accreditation under the 'Villes et Villages Fleuris' scheme. The accreditation system rewards municipalities who have embellished the streetscape and protected trees and gardens. Juries visit these locations and award ratings from one to four, taking into account the environmental policy and local community engagement as well as the design, landscaping and overall presentation of the flowers.

These costs often have to be met by the public purse, and can be considerable, but at the very least councils need to consider investing funds to make their main approach roads more attractive, both those carrying car traffic to the centre and those providing principal access for pedestrians to the centre from bus or train terminals. First impressions count for a lot when it comes to attracting tourists.

ART AND TOURISM

There is a growing recognition today that art has a role to play in the tourism industry, not just through museums, galleries and arts events organised to attract the tourist, but in the everyday surroundings in which visitors find themselves. Ostensibly, 'street art' is designed to heighten the visual appeal of a town for its residents, but, once again, such embellishment will add to the attraction of the destination for visitors, too. If the work displayed is by artists of international reputation, this will widen the appeal of the destination to international visitors. Sculptures by Henry Moore in Yorkshire or at the Serpentine in London, for example, attract dedicated groups of overseas and domestic visitors. Cities in the USA enforce local regulations requiring a small percentage of the total cost of any new development to be spent on public art at the site, and the prestigious offices of major corporations will also judge it appropriate to enhance their forecourts with sculptures by leading artists of the day. In London, prominent British artists such as Eduardo Paolozzi were recruited to design wall tiles during the renovation of the central London Underground railway stations.

EXAMPLE

Street art attracts tourism

Graffiti has traditionally been seen as an act of vandalism by governments. However, this has become a respected art form in recent years, along with recognition that it has the ability to attract tourists. Graffiti is helping to revitalise run-down areas of cities, with numerous projects that include street art/graffiti elements initiated in North America.

Some European cities are also recognising its value to tourism. Lisbon has developed walking tours that explore the city's street art locations, while in the UK Bristol has established itself as a major site for street art, with a dedicated annual festival, based on the fame of its now internationally recognised street artist Banksy. In Australia, Melbourne has woken to the value of its street art, now promoting itself as the street art capital.

Towns can reinforce their image by the imaginative use of sculpture or art. In Germany, for example, Hamelin has its sculpture of the Pied Piper, while Bremen has greatly enhanced its pedestrian streets with scenes from Grimms' fairy tales. Brussels is famous for the Manneken Pis, the tiny bronze statue of a small boy urinating, copies of which are sold as tourist souvenirs, and photos of him feature on many postcards. Copenhagen's major draw is its Little Mermaid statue, based on the Hans Christian Andersen fairy tale. More recently, the city of Berlin brought back into the town centre a statue of Frederick the Great that had been considered politically unacceptable in East Berlin before the fall of the Wall.

The UK is becoming more aware of the importance of art and the way in which it can serve the interests of the tourist industry. Notable features include two water fountain sculptures by William Pye, 'Slipstream' and 'Jetstream', commissioned by BAA at Gatwick

Airport, and a 130-foot-long sculpture, 'Train', by David Mach, which is a monument to the record-breaking steam locomotive 'Mallard'. Two sculptures, initially rebuffed by those in the locations where they were erected, achieved considerable publicity and, later, support from the local population when their benefits to tourism became clear. Artist Maggi Hambling's 12-foot-high scallop shell memorial to composer Benjamin Britten on the beach near Aldeburgh, Suffolk, was initially vilified, too, as were Antony Gormley's series of Iron Men sculptures in his 'Another Place' setting on Crosby Beach, Merseyside. In the latter case, locals successfully lobbied to keep the sculptures when the council proposed their removal. Both these artists' works have since become iconic symbols for the resorts in question.

Recognising that art is not necessarily restricted to high culture, the Scottish city of Dundee, home of the publishers of nationally popular comics *The Beano* and *Dandy*, has brought to life cartoon figures from these comics as statues in the city centre (see Figure 8.12) as well as renaming some of its streets after the characters.

FIGURE 8.12 **Desperate Dan statue in Dundee**

Photo: Chris Holloway

LIGHTING

External street lighting can play an important role in enhancing a town, both with respect to the design of the lights themselves and to the effect they can create at night. Again, a choice must be made between traditional and modern lamps. Some towns have reinforced their quaintness by choosing authentic gas lighting, which has great popular appeal for tourists. In Norwegian villages in the weeks leading up to Christmas, the shopping streets are illuminated with real flares, giving visitors an impression of warmth and cosiness at a time when the long periods of darkness could otherwise lower the spirits of residents and visitors.

Floodlighting major attractions, a recognised practice for the great monuments in leading cities, has become much more widespread and its use can encourage tourists out onto the streets at night, thus extending the 'tourist day'. One example is to be found in the medieval town of Carcassonne in France, which mounts son et lumière displays to narrate its history. London now offers a winter lights festival in mid-January, displaying interactive artworks that use lighting technology. Similar Lumière festivals also take place in Frankfurt, Brussels and Helsinki.

White lights are normally recommended, the use of coloured lights – apart from settings where a fairground atmosphere is appropriate, such as at the Blackpool illuminations – being best avoided. Many observers feel the use of coloured lights to floodlight Niagara Falls has turned a great spectacle into an example of downmarket kitsch. Limited use of coloured lighting can be helpful, though, in highlighting horticultural displays at night. Care must be taken not to over-light. Strong lights are particularly inappropriate in a village setting, for example.

EXAMPLE

Turn off the lights!

The effects of lighting on the turtle population have been well documented, with concerns that, first, brightly lit beaches dissuade female turtles from coming ashore to lay their eggs and second, any hatching turtles can be disoriented by the lights and fail to quickly find the safety of the water's edge. Campaigners across the globe are trying to protect the turtles by encouraging beachfront hotels and bars to reduce the amount of lighting they use at night.

Another advantage of turning off the lights is the opportunity to attract the 'dark sky' tourism market. Destinations with environments with little or no light pollution make great places to view the stars and planets in the night sky. The UK has more than 100 recognised stargazing sites, including the Brecon Beacons national park, which was granted International Dark Sky Reserve status in 2013. Similar recognition has also been given to reserves in Mont-Mégantic (Canada), Aoraki Mackenzie (New Zealand) and NambiRand Nature Reserve (Namibia).

Finally, mention should be made of the use of firework displays to highlight key events, such as national holidays or other days of commemoration. Independence Day (4 July) in the USA, National Day (14 July) in France and Guy Fawkes Day (5 November) in the UK are all days where fireworks commonly round off the day's events. All over the world, exceptional firework displays have become the norm on New Year's Eve, as cities such as London, Paris, Beijing and Sydney set out to rival one another in spectacular shows appealing to residents and tourists alike.

SIGNPOSTING

All visitors look for signposts, so they become the most visible of all forms of street furniture. These may be directional or informative (and Chapter 16 discusses the different ways they help visitor management). Signs must be easily visible and legible, especially from a distance in the case of signs for vehicle drivers. Generally, standards for road signs are set by local authorities or government departments of transport. Signs may also be subject to local government regulations, limiting their size and placement on safety or visual pollution grounds.

EXAMPLE

Tourist signs in the UK

Following a long period where signposting was arbitrary and often banned from main roads in the UK, the Department for Transport introduced white-on-brown signs in 1986. There are more than 70 different pictographs representing every conceivable variety of tourist attraction and facility (such as hotel or picnic ground). As you can see from the examples provided in the figure below, the images provide a broad association but the nuances are fine (for example, different boat types are used to represent canalside attractions, boat hire and canoeing). Regulations on the use of these and other signs are complex and quite restrictive. Regulation is by the Department for Transport for those attractions accessed from major roads such as motorways, and by the local authority for signs positioned on minor roads.

Sample of tourist sign symbols

Tourist Information Centre

Castle

Museum or Art Gallery

Zoo

Aquarium or Oceanarium

Flower Garden

Agricultural Museum

Air Museum

Historic Dockyard

Motorsport attraction

Battlefield site

Outdoor Pursuits site

Canalside attraction

Boat Hire

Canoeing site

Source: Highways Agency

The use of white-on-brown signs is dependent on the numbers visiting the site (for example, attractions must attract a minimum of 250,000 visitors a year to warrant approval for the erection of a directional road sign on a motorway). Single-carriageway roads require a lower threshold of 40,000 visitors (or a peak month of 8000). This, of course, introduces a catch-22 situation, where already well-established attractions are favoured over newly developed ones.

Politics and the need to cater for foreign visitors can often affect the layout and language of signs. In countries such as Belgium, in parts of Canada and in Wales, for example, bilingualism is the law, so every place name or instruction must be given in two languages. In the Baltic states, although there are many Russian speakers, the continuing resentment towards their former masters means that if any foreign language is to be used on signs, it is English. In China, Japan and Thailand, where many foreigners will drive cars but not understand the local scripts, signs in the large towns are often duplicated in English. However, new apps, including Google Translate, offer technology that allows tourists to point at a Cyrillic sign and see it immediately translated into Roman lettering, a real boon for travellers away from the more popular tourist areas.

THE MEDIA AND THEIR INFLUENCE ON TOURIST DESTINATIONS

One means by which destinations can regenerate their tourism economy or, in some cases, grow one where earlier it had scarcely existed, is through the impact of programmes in the media, whether film, television or radio. The growing interplay between the media and tourism deserves special mention, given the extent to which the tourism industry is now exploiting for its own ends consumer interest in sites associated with 'celebrities'.

EXAMPLE

Seeking celebrities in Hollywood

The density of celebrity homes in the Hollywood hills provides the perfect location for guided tours, to see where the rich and famous live (or perhaps, more accurately, to see the driveways and security gates of their Hollywood mansions).

As well as seeking out celebrity homes, visiting locations favoured by the stars is also a popular tourist pastime in the city. Numerous online resources provide suggestions of the latest in-vogue cafés, restaurants, shops and hotels likely to provide sightings of celebrities. Lists of events likely to attract celebrities are also circulated to increase the chance of success.

A noteworthy aspect of postmodern culture is the fascination that fame, however transient, holds for many people, as witnessed by the appeal of reality shows on television which guarantee minor celebrities instant fame. Tourist destinations have not been slow to exploit opportunities for publicity in the media, especially cinema and television, either by promoting the sites associated with these celebrities or offering inducements to film within their territory. In many cases, governments have colluded with local authorities and the private sector by directly subsidising the media's production costs, well aware that the publicity engendered by global distribution of a film or television programme will generate tourists' interest. In the UK, the National Trust now actively solicits film companies for its sites, following the success of their heritage buildings when used as settings for costume dramas. The TV series *Downton Abbey* (aired between 2010 and 2015) reached up to 10 million viewers in the UK and was hugely popular in the USA, to the extent that Highclere Castle, the principal setting for the programme, saw visitor numbers double to 1200 a day.

Tourist information offices all over the world are producing 'film maps' or 'movie maps' listing sites that appear in popular films or TV programmes. The enormous popularity of the *Harry Potter* films has expanded travel to settings associated with the films in England, helped by a promotional trail entitled 'Discover the magic of Britain', which includes Gloucester Cathedral, Goathland Station (Hogsmeade) and Alnwick Castle (Hogwarts School of Witchcraft), which experienced a 230% increase in visitors over the decade between the release of the first and the last film, generating £9 million in extra revenue for the area (VisitBritain, 2011). The VisitBritain website also identifies locations associated with Braveheart, Miss Potter, Bridget Jones and James Bond films (www.visitbritain.com/us/en/britain-film).

EXAMPLE

Harry Potter and platform 9 ¾

The series of successful wizarding stories claims that the Hogwarts Express departs from Platform 9¾ at King's Cross station in London. Following a major renovation of this transport hub, station managers have created an attraction that allows fans to don a wizard robe and have their photograph taken with a luggage trolley artfully placed so that it seems to be disappearing through the platform wall.

At peak times, the small-scale attraction is managed by staff from the adjacent Harry Potter shop. There is no charge to participate and they provide a professional photo service, similar to that offered on theme park rides, but also allow individuals to take their own photos without charge.

FIGURE 8.13 Platform 9 ¾ attraction at King's Cross

Photo: Claire Humphreys

Other parts of the world have also been quick to cash in on film and television settings as potential sources of revenue. The film *The Italian Job* has a cult following, to the extent that bespoke tours were organised to the locations in Turin where it was filmed. A recent new version of the film boosted further interest. In Australia, *Rogue* – a horror film in which day trippers in the Northern Territory are picked off one by one by a giant crocodile – was followed by another, *Wolf Creek* – in which backpackers (presumably the survivors) are again picked off in turn by a psychopath. Far from discouraging tourists, these two films led to a 10% increase in backpackers to the area, helped by a supporting promotion from Tourism Top End (the board for the Northern Territory).

The popularity of certain cult films guarantees a steady audience of aficionados to the locations where the films were shot. The enduring appeal of the 1945 film *Brief Encounter*, shot at Carnforth railway station in Lancashire, entices many tourists, particularly Asians, to the now restored station with its replica of the famous refreshment room, which is open to the public for the sale of food and drink. This is a classic example of staged authenticity, being a reconstruction of the film set, which itself was modelled on the original. Such lack of true authenticity, however, fails to deter visitors. More recently, the popularity in Germany of the Rosamunde Pilcher novels, set in Cornwall, created a market for package tours to that area, especially the coastal resort of St Ives, a demand boosted by a German television series based on the books. In France, Provence tourist authorities have established a 'Marcel Pagnol route' to popularise the locations at which the French film *Manon des Sources* was filmed.

EXAMPLE

Film tourism overwhelming Cornish beaches

The popularity of the BBC TV series *Poldark* combined with a consistently hot summer sent tourists flocking to the beach locations in such numbers that the area's tourist board warned tourists to stay away. The beaches of Porthcurno and Kynance Cove experienced overcrowding and traffic jams due to a 20% increase in visitor numbers. One consequence was that the tourist board ceased promoting these areas, a decision not without controversy.

The power of Hollywood means that tourists, both domestic and foreign, flock to the locations of scenes in movies filmed in the USA. To cite recent examples of areas that formerly drew few tourists and now, as a result of popular films, attract many: the general store in Juliette, Georgia, which was the setting for the Whistlestop Café in *Fried Green Tomatoes* has now become a tourist attraction in its own right, and North Carolina, especially the area around Asheville, has been blessed by being the setting for numerous films, including *Cold Mountain*, *The Last of the Mohicans*, *Forrest Gump* and *Hannibal*. The state has actively promoted these settings in its marketing campaigns.

Entire regions and countries can be similarly boosted by media exposure. Notable in recent years has been the New Zealand government's exploitation of the *Lord of the Rings* trilogy, with advertising directing tourists to film locations such as Matamata (Tolkien's Plains of Gorgoroth), Tongariro National Park and Nelson (the fact that Tolkien actually based Gorgoroth on the Ribble Valley area in England is conveniently overlooked!). Tunisia, where *Star Wars*, *Raiders of the Lost Ark* and *The English Patient* were filmed, has actively solicited film work and its tourism authority helped to develop an *English Patient* route for tourists. India launched *Life of Pi* tours after the international success of the film.

This is just a handful of examples to demonstrate the power of the media in influencing tourism – a factor that is, for the most part, fully taken into account and built on by tourist information authorities today in their efforts to promote 'cultural tourism'. There are concerns, however, when these films are made in remote beauty spots that subsequently attract large numbers of tourists. Khao Phingkan in Thailand was the setting for the James Bond film *The Man with the Golden Gun*. This ideal setting was rapidly destroyed by the unplanned development of tourism. A similar fate befell Maya Bay on Phi Phi Ley Island, following the popularity of *The Beach*, which starred Leonardo di Caprio (although, arguably, as much damage is done by the film crew at these locations as by subsequent tourism).

DESTINATIONS OF THE FUTURE

What is clear is that the consumers of tomorrow's holidays will be less content with the mundane: the search is on for more adventurous, original forms of holidays to exotic destinations. The search for 'something different' is already beginning to undermine traditional identikit destinations and hotels, which will need to position themselves more clearly and adapt their products to appeal to niche markets. Consumers have control over the transmission of information, too, with websites devoted to exchanging information about destinations and accommodation and making recommendations. Others are devoted to complaints about specific accommodation, resorts or carriers.

This drive for the novel, however, is likely to be tempered by cost. Budget airlines have helped to make some destinations both more affordable and more accessible, stimulating demand for short breaks to urban areas as well as longer holidays spent exploring the surrounding region.

There have been predictions that underwater leisure cities will be built on the seabeds adjoining our coasts, where a controlled climate will make the annual exodus to the sun no longer necessary. Some of these predictions take us into the realms of science fiction, yet we are already on the fringe of developing a **space-tourism** product, so exploiting the untapped resources of the ocean for tourism may well be the next frontier to be explored. Some tour operators are already offering trips in a mini-submarine to the Amundsen Plain, 4400 metres below the sea at the North Pole, a trip hailed as 'the ultimate adventure challenge'.

Space as a destination is very close, with Japanese and American companies planning to build and launch hotels in space once the vehicles are available to get the tourists there. American businessman Dennis Tito became the first space tourist in 2001, having spent eight days with a Russian space crew orbiting the earth. He is understood to have paid $20 million for the trip. In 2004, SpaceShipOne won the US$10 million Ansari X prize, offered to encourage the development of transport capable of taking people into space. To win the prize, the aircraft had to fly to the edge of space twice in a two-week period. Since this success, many companies have entered the market with plans to offer both edge-of-space flights and zero-gravity flights. The tragic loss of the Virgin Galactic spaceship during test flights hindered progress, but the continued investment in space exploration makes such developments feasible. It is no longer a question of if, but of when.

SUMMARY

It is clear that tourists are attracted by a variety of destinations, some that offer unique appeal while others are popular because they can provide a 'familiar' feel. Although tourists may claim to desire more than the traditional beach holiday, seaside destinations, especially in warm-water environments, still attract large numbers of tourists.

Destinations may help to improve their appeal by developing innovative attractions, or linking their marketing activities and place branding to other fashionable products (such as films, books, events or celebrities). What is vital, however, is ensuring that the physical design of the destination – its landscape, amenities and infrastructure – appeals to tourists and encourages them to visit.

QUESTIONS AND DISCUSSION POINTS

1. This chapter identifies numerous examples of destinations made popular by films and television series. To what extent is such appeal sustainable in the long term?
2. What factors influence the demand for urban tourism?
3. Wilderness areas are often popular with tourists. What challenges does this create?

TASKS

1. In this chapter, we highlight the top ten cities for tourism, based on arrivals numbers (Table 8.2). Select one of these cities to investigate. Write a short report that explains the appeal of the destination.
2. This chapter recognises that space tourism is likely to offer a new destination in the not-too-distant future. Using news reports and online sources, create a poster summarising recent activities regarding space tourism opportunities.

WEBSITE

International Dark-Sky Association: www.darksky.org

REFERENCES

Association of British Travel Agents (ABTA) (2018) *Holiday Habits*. London: ABTA.

BBC (2019) *Nepal says overcrowding not 'sole reason' for Everest death toll rise.* Available online at https://www.bbc.co.uk/news/world-asia-48415290 [Accessed 17 July 2019].

Daily Telegraph (2011) Wipe out for Bournemouth's surf city plans as artificial reef splits. *Daily Telegraph*, 18 April.

Davidson, R. and Maitland, R. (1997) *Tourism Destinations*. London: Hodder and Stoughton.

Department for Environment, Food and Rural Affairs (DEFRA) (2018) *Farm Accounts in England: Results from the Farm Business Survey 2017/18*. London: DEFRA.

Euromonitor (2007) *Top 150 City Destinations: London leads the way.* Available online at: http://blog.euromonitor.com/2007/10/top-150-city-destinations-london-leads-the-way.html [Accessed November 2011].

Euromonitor (2011) *Euromonitor International's Top City Destinations Ranking*. Available online at: http://blog.euromonitor.com/2011/01/euromonitor-internationals-top-city-destinations-ranking.html [Accessed November 2011].

Euromonitor (2014) *Euromonitor International's Top City Destinations Ranking*. Available online at: http://blog.euromonitor.com/2014/01/euromonitor-internationals-top-city-destinations-ranking.html [Accessed January 2015].

Euromonitor (2017) *Euromonitor International's Top City Destinations Ranking*. Available online at: https://blueswandaily.com/wp-content/uploads/2017/11/Euromonitor-International_WTM-London-2017_Top-100-City-Destinations.pdf [Accessed January 2019].

Gabbatiss, J. (2018) Rising sea levels could make thousands of islands from the Maldives to Hawaii 'uninhabitable within decades'. *The Independent*, 25 April

Irish Independent (2011) The upside of family downtime. *Irish Independent*, 20 June.

Jensen, K., Bruch, M., Menard, J. and English, B. (2013) *A Snapshot of Tennessee Agritourism*. Available online at: www.uvm.edu/tourismresearch/agritourism/research/tennessee-agtourstudy-6-20-2013.pdf [Accessed January 2015].

Jones, L. and Schraer, R. (2018) *Reality Check: Public toilets mapped*. Available online at: www.bbc.com/news/uk-45009337 [Accessed January 2018].

Ministry of Tourism (2018) *Tourist Arrivals by Nationality*. Available online at: www.tourism.gov.mv/downloads/arrival_updates/2017/December.pdf [Accessed January 2019].

Momondo (2017) International Travel Survey 2016. Available online at: https://c1.momondo.net/assets/press/travel_survey_2017.pdf [Accessed January 2019].

Phillip, S., Hunter, C. and Blackstock, K. (2010) A typology for defining agritourism. *Tourism Management*, 31 (6), 754–8.

Pike, S. (2002) Destination image analysis: A review of 142 papers from 1973 to 2000. *Tourism Management*, 23 (5): 541–9.

Rowe, M. (2011) This coast's so wild they build lighthouses on wheels. *The Independent*, 19 June.

Sharman, J. (2018) Sea levels 'could be rising a centimetre a year' by 2100, say scientists. *The Independent*, 12 February.

VisitBritain (2011) Films continue to draw visitors to Britain. Press release, 18 March.

9

TOURIST ATTRACTIONS

CONTENTS

LEARNING OUTCOMES

After studying this chapter, you should be able to:

- distinguish between a destination and an attraction and define each
- understand what it is that attracts tourists and which attractions appeal to each market
- explain the problem for attractions of changing tastes and fashions and propose solutions to overcome this
- assess the potential for new attractions and how these can be developed.

> Attractions are the raison d'être for tourism: they generate the visit, give rise to excursion circuits and create an industry of their own. (Boniface and Cooper, 2001: 30)

INTRODUCTION

There are some attractions that claim iconic status, requiring all travellers to see them at least once in their lives. Often, these attractions form part of a virtual list to be 'ticked off' as the tourist moves around the world in search of new experiences. Examples will include a visit to the Eiffel Tower when in France, or the Taj Mahal when in India. These tourist attractions may form part of the core reason for visiting the destination.

But what exactly do we mean by a **tourist attraction**? Trying to define it is no easy matter, but to understand the sector and how it operates we have to start with a definition. After all, it is generally the attraction that prompts the tourist to travel in the first place, but the concept of an 'attraction' is a very broad one, encompassing a great many different sights – and sites.

DEFINING TOURIST ATTRACTIONS

Sometimes we use the term synonymously with 'destination', the attraction in this case being the benefits inherent in the destination rather than any purpose-built facility specifically designed to appeal to tourists. The medieval town centre of Dinant in France, Southern Germany's Black Forest and Luquillo Beach in Puerto Rico are all 'attractions', but do not exist primarily to serve tourists' needs.

Authors have defined tourist attractions in a variety of ways, with Dewhurst and Dewhurst (2006) suggesting that this is an aspect with little consensus. In many cases, definitions are quite broad to accommodate the variety of factors attracting visitors to destinations. As an example, Inskeep (1991: 38) defines tourist attractions as 'all those natural, cultural and special features and related activities of an area that attract tourists to visit it'. In his evaluation of numerous definitions of tourist attractions, Edelheim (2015: 14) acknowledges the tendency to 'refer to objects, spaces, places or features of management entities'. However, in some cases it is the non-purpose-built aspects of the destination that provide the appeal. For example, a trip to the seaside may be taken principally for the opportunity to enjoy a swim in the sea at a time when the weather is warm. In such a case, the attraction is the destination but this is not purpose-built to serve the interests of tourism. However, it should be acknowledged that it may have been modified to do so; the beach may have been cleaned up, deckchairs and windbreaks provided for hire.

So, we must accept that no clear definition exists for the term. It is easier just to accept that any site which appeals to people sufficiently to encourage them to travel there in order to visit it should be judged a 'tourist attraction'. It is helpful, however, to make some effort to categorise such attractions.

Swarbrooke (2002), who has considered a number of attempts at definition, splits attractions into four categories (modified here):

- features within the natural environment
- purpose-built structures and sites designed for purposes other than attracting visitors
- purpose-built structures and sites designed to attract visitors
- special events.

Similarly, Leask (2008) distinguishes between built and natural attractions, while also highlighting that distinctions could be drawn by ownership (public, private, voluntary or charity/third sector), intended markets (local, regional, national or international) and entry policy (free or paid admission). Weaver and Lawton (2002: 130) make further distinctions between attractions, suggesting that they are 'mainly natural or mainly cultural', adding that both can be identified as either 'site'-based or 'event'-based. This is summarised in Figure 9.1. Note that Chapter 10 explores man-made, event-based attractions in more detail so this chapter will focus on the other three categories of attraction.

	Site-based attractions	Event-based attractions
Natural	Landscape attractions such as a waterfall or underground cave	Naturally occurring phenomena that occur at particular times, animal migrations or earthly eruptions
	Example: visit to the Iguazu falls, on the border between Argentina and Brazil	Example: travelling to see a solar or lunar eclipse
Man-made	Built attractions such as a theme park or historic building	Events that are developed by humankind for cultural, commercial or other purposes, such as a music festival or spring fair
	Example: visiting Buckingham Palace, London	Example: watching Macy's Thanksgiving Day Parade, New York

FIGURE 9.1 Classifying attractions

Thus, for simplicity's sake, we can conclude that attractions may be defined as natural or constructed (whether or not purpose-built for tourism) and, if not constructed, they may still be, to a greater or lesser extent, 'managed' to suit the purpose of tourism.

Many sites owe their continuing attraction to some event in the past. Liverpool is an example of somewhere that has become a place of pilgrimage for many visitors, due, in this case, to its links with The Beatles in the 1960s – a connection strongly promoted during 2008, when the city became a European Capital of Culture (discussed in more detail in Chapter 10). Also, both John Lennon's home at 251 Menlove Avenue, Woolton, and Sir Paul McCartney's home at 20 Forthlin Road have been bought by the National Trust and are open to the public. Gettysburg in the USA, created as a national military park in 1895, attracts millions of domestic tourists as it was the key battlefield site of the US Civil War in 1863, while Lourdes in France, a place of religious pilgrimage, owes its appeal entirely to events occurring in 1858, when 14-year-old Bernadette Soubirous was said to have experienced apparitions of the Virgin Mary.

One useful listing of different attractions was undertaken by the former English Tourism Council. While not totally comprehensive (its final category is something of a catch-all, while 'leisure attractions' might encompass anything from swimming pools and gymnasia to theme parks like the Walt Disney World Resorts), it does give us some direction for analysis of this sector of the industry:

- historic properties
- museums and art galleries
- wildlife parks
- gardens
- country parks
- workplaces
- steam railways

- leisure attractions
- other attractions.

In all, there are well over 6000 such attractions in the UK for which entrance figures are maintained, a quarter of these being historic properties and a similar number, museums. The Association of Leading Visitor Attractions (ALVA) reported that their top 200 visitor attractions (which include the British Museum, Westminster Abbey and Stonehenge) attracted almost 130 million visits in 2017 (ALVA, 2017). In addition to attractions with monitored visitor numbers, we must add the numerous buildings open to the public for which no attendance records are kept. There are, for instance, 4000 Grade I listed Church of England buildings and 16,000 churches altogether in the UK: it has been estimated that some 40 million visits a year are made to churches and cathedrals annually (Duff, 2009).

New attractions open every year. While a few gain almost instant success, others may struggle to sustain their popularity. For example, Dynamic Earth in Edinburgh estimated, and budgeted for, 430,000 visitors a year, but actually received 500,000 in 1999, its opening year of operation. However, its annual numbers later dwindled to 200,000, and it received a financial bailout from the Scottish Government in 2008. Since then, it has introduced popular new exhibitions to increase numbers, but it is thought unlikely ever again to achieve the estimated 400,000 visitors it originally budgeted for. In 2017 visitor numbers were 245,000. Dynamic Earth is not unusual in failing to reach visitor targets – many other attractions have been hopelessly over-optimistic about their attendance figures and have either struggled to survive or collapsed. The Shania Twain Centre in Ontario, Canada, opened in 2001, with a predicted attendance of 50,000 visitors. This tourist attraction was established with an expectation that it would bring additional tourist numbers into the region. However, even with support from the locally born singer herself, visitor numbers never exceeded 15,000 and the centre closed in 2013.

Most UK attractions host less than half a million visitors annually – if we look at the top 200 ALVA-member attractions, we see that only 67 received more than this number.

EXAMPLE

Everyday items can make fascinating tourist attractions

The Forge Mill Needle Museum, in the town of Redditch, England, provides exhibits related to needles. This humble sewing implement may not seem to be the most exciting of themes to attract the tourist, but the museum tells the fascinating and sometimes gruesome story of needle-making in Victorian times. Models and recreated scenes provide a vivid illustration of how needles were once made and how Redditch came to dominate the industry by producing 90% of the world's needles.

The museum, opened in 1983 by the Queen, contains working machinery, images of the local needle industry and ornate needle cases, as well as extensive collections of needles made by local companies, some dating back almost 100 years.

Funding is by Redditch Borough Council and the museum has a small dedicated band of volunteers who, together with the staff, help to provide the tours, workshops for schools, special events and many other activities on offer. This brings around 20,000 visitors annually – highlighting that even the smallest of household items has the potential to become a successful attraction.

Table 9.1 identifies the visitor numbers of some of the world's top attractions. Note that many of the popular attractions are located in capital cities. The table reveals the popularity of a variety of different types of attraction, including historic buildings, natural parks and entertainment complexes.

TABLE 9.1 Number of visits to a selection of tourist attractions in 2018

Attraction	Country	Visitor numbers (2018) (000s)
Great Wall	China	72,919.5
Tokyo Disney Resort	Japan	32,975.9
V&A Waterfront	South Africa	23,353.8
Magic Kingdom at Walt Disney World	USA	21,063.0
Disneyland	USA	19,203.3
The Forbidden City	China	17,190.7
Universal Studio Japan	Japan	15,604.7
Golden Gate National Recreation Area	USA	15,223.7
Petronas Twin Towers	Malaysia	13,851.2
Ho Chi Minh Monument	Vietnam	13,761.4
Disneyland Paris	France	13,315.0
Sydney Opera House	Australia	13,234.0
Disney's Animal Kingdom at Walt Disney World	USA	12,162.1
Royal Grand Palace	Thailand	10,180.7
Musée du Louvre	France	10,170.6
Giza Pyramids	Egypt	9,750.5
Pantheon	Italy	8,955.6
War Remnants Museum	Vietnam	8,551.7
Taj Mahal, Agra	India	8,524.9
Prague Castle	Czech Republic	8,050.0
Xian Terracotta Warriors	China	7,538.4
Metropolitan Museum of Art	USA	7,361.3
Tour Eiffel	France	6,460.2
Musei Vaticani	Italy	6,427.0
British Museum	UK	5,828.6
The State Peterhof Museum	Russia	5,714.0
Cologne Cathedral	Germany	5,454.8
De Efteling	The Netherlands	5,334.8
Tivoli	Denmark	4,581.8
Sagrada Familia	Spain	3,650.5

Source: Euromonitor 2018

It is important to recognise that many destinations owe their appeal to the fact that they offer a cluster of attractions within the immediate locality. Urban destinations are far less dependent on climate than are rural or coastal sites, and the UK (as with other temperate cities in Northern Europe, North America and Southern Australia) is fortunate in being able to attract year-round visitors to its cities' theatres, galleries and other indoor entertainments. In the UK, the need for a focal point, even in seaside resorts, had already been widely recognised by the nineteenth century – the great era for the construction of piers.

THE FOCAL POINT OR ICON

Contemporary tourism marketing implicitly or explicitly recognises the importance of the focal point – or a synthesis of focal points – at a site, which acts as a magnet, attracting tourists. The focal point may be a historic building, such as a castle or monument, or it may be another type of construction, owing its success to its architectural features, such as a tower, bridge or pier.

A supreme focal point is one that becomes a cultural icon, and the more popular tourist destinations are those blessed with such an attraction. The fame of a cultural icon often extends far beyond the region itself, with the result that the images of the icon and destination are inseparable in the minds of prospective visitors. A few examples of the most successful will reveal the significance of the icon in tourism promotion (Table 9.2).

TABLE 9.2 International tourist icons

Location	Icons
London	Big Ben and the Houses of Parliament, Buckingham Palace
Paris	Eiffel Tower, Notre Dame
New York	Empire State Building, Statue of Liberty
San Francisco	Golden Gate Bridge
Sydney	Sydney Harbour Bridge, Opera House
Kuala Lumpur	Petronas Towers
Copenhagen	Little Mermaid statue
Bilbao	Guggenheim Museum

With the possible exception of the last in this list, none of these buildings were created with the deliberate intention of attracting tourists, yet over time their appeal has widened to a point where tourism flourishes because they exist. In the case of more recent projects (and no doubt boosted by the success of Bilbao, which, prior to the construction of the Guggenheim, offered little to attract tourists), developers and architects have designed either with one eye on the potential for tourism or specifically with tourism in mind.

It is a postmodern irony that many of the visitors attracted to Bilbao by the Guggenheim Museum do not enter the building; its attraction for many is not the artistic contents, but the building itself. Frank Gehry's innovative museum has influenced the design of countless more recent constructions straining for recognition as cultural icons within their communities, including the Kunsthaus in Graz, Austria, and the new Imperial War Museum in Manchester. Recruiting an architectural practice of international standing such as Foster and Partners (responsible, *inter alia*, for the renovated Reichstag in Berlin (see Figure 9.2), London City Hall and the Millau viaduct in France) is now seen as the first step in establishing a landmark building.

FIGURE 9.2 The renovated Reichstag building in Berlin, designed by Foster & Partners in 1999, has become an iconic symbol for the German capital

Photo: Chris Holloway

High towers used to be the icon-to-desire for tourist destinations. Today, it is more likely to be big wheels. Since the Prater fairground in Vienna built its 65-metre Riesenrad (big wheel) in 1897, engineers have sought to find ways to build still bigger ones. The London Eye, a 135-metre big wheel providing aerial views over the city, has proved both culturally and commercially successful, having rapidly become an integral component of Central London's cityscape. Following its success, other cities are striving to compete: Melbourne built a 120-metre big wheel, known as the Southern Star, while the Chinese city of Nanchang has erected a 160-metre observation wheel with a carrying capacity of 480 passengers.

EXAMPLE

The High Roller, Las Vegas

Growing enthusiasm for developing observation wheels saw the opening in 2014 of the High Roller, on the Las Vegas strip. This attraction, when opened, was the highest of its type and has a capacity of over 1000 passengers. The 30-minute ride provides views of Las Vegas Boulevard, the nearby Wynn golf course and surrounding mountains.

The Las Vegas wheel is part of a $550 million development by casino giant Caesars Entertainment. However, its title as the world's tallest observation wheel is likely to be short-lived, with larger ones already planned for New York and Dubai.

That said, not all in the world of observation wheels is successful. The Singapore Flyer, a 165-metre wheel, opened in 2008 (as the world's tallest until the High Roller opened) and went into receivership in 2013 until eventually bought by Straco Corporation, operators of several tourist attractions in China.

It is worth stressing that, while iconic attractions may be crucial in enticing first-time visitors, all important tourist cities need to replenish and complement their stock of tourist attractions from time to time to encourage repeat business. The appeal of cities such as London and Paris is that they can attract so many visitors back again and again because of the wealth of attractions they offer – smaller, less well-known museums and newly constructed attractions alike.

The truly outstanding sites of architectural, cultural or historic importance around the world are recognised as UNESCO World Heritage Sites. In 2019, the 1092 of these sites comprised 845 cultural sites, 209 natural sites and 38 of mixed composition. The UK, with 31 sites, has 3% of the total, while Italy can boast 54 sites, almost double the percentage of the UK's. Other leading countries are China, which has 53 sites, Spain with 47 and France and Germany, both with 44.

TABLE 9.3 Examples of leading UNESCO World Heritage Sites

Cultural sites	Natural sites
Sydney Opera House, Australia	Iguazu National Park, Argentina
Walled city of Baku, Azerbaijan	Great Barrier Reef, Australia
Ruins of Loropéni, Burkina Faso	Okavango Delta, Botswana
The Great Wall, China	Dinosaur Provincial Park, Canada
Mont-Saint-Michel, France	Galápagos Islands, Ecuador
Acropolis, Greece	Komodo National Park, Indonesia
Fatehpur Sikri, India	Namib Sand Sea, Namibia
Padua Botanical Garden, Italy	Sub-Antarctic Islands, New Zealand
Hiroshima Peace Memorial, Japan	Lake Baikal, Russia
Medina of Fez, Morocco	Aldabra Atoll, Seychelles
Lumbini, Nepal	Serengeti National Park, Tanzania
Moscow Kremlin and Red Square, Russia	Giant's Causeway and Causeway Coast, UK
Robben Island, South Africa	Grand Canyon National Park, USA
Tanum Rock Carvings, Sweden	Ha Long Bay, Vietnam
Tower of London, UK	Socotra Archipelago, Yemen

Clearly, there are many different types of attraction, so for simplicity we will group these under some common themes:

- historic buildings and heritage
- museums and galleries
- parks and gardens
- other forms of attraction.

It should always be remembered that those marketing destinations also use events to attract visitors, an issue discussed in more detail in Chapter 10.

HISTORIC BUILDINGS AND HERITAGE

Probably what most of us think of first, when considering the appeal of an urban location to tourists, are its historical and architectural features. Often, these are subsumed into a general 'feel' of the destination, rather than there being an appreciation of any individual building – the sense that the town is old and beautiful, its buildings having mellowed over time and their architecture is quintessentially representative of the region or nation and its people. Thus, old cobbled streets lined with protected shopfronts, gabled roofs and ornamental features, such as those to be found in towns like York in the UK, Tours in France, Rothenburg ob der Tauber in Germany, Aarhus in Denmark and Bruges in Belgium, all convey an overall impression of attractiveness and warmth, inviting us to shop there and enjoy the local food and lodgings. These features are the supreme attraction of the 'old' countries of Europe, to which American, Arab and Japanese tourists alike are drawn when they first visit the country. In spite of an earlier disdain for older properties, the damage wrought by two world wars and the often poor quality of architectural reconstruction in their aftermath, most nations in Europe have retained major elements of their old city centres, even, in some cases (as in Warsaw and Dresden), building entire replicas of the pre-war city centre in an attempt to regain their original character and heighten their appeal to visitors and residents alike.

EXAMPLE

Protecting historic buildings in the UK

To retain and protect their heritage buildings, in 1950 the UK introduced a policy of listing historic buildings (the French had, in fact, introduced a similar but less effective policy at least 100 years earlier). Today, the nation boasts over 500,000 buildings listed as being of special historic or architectural interest.

In England and Wales, truly outstanding buildings fall into the Grade I category, that of 'exceptional interest'. These make up about 2.5% of the total. A further 5.8% fall into the second category of Grade II*, listed as of 'special interest'. Most others are listed as Grade II (in Scotland and Northern Ireland, similar buildings are categorised as A, B+/B or B1/C).

Today, all buildings in reasonable repair dating from before 1700 and most between 1700 and 1840 are listed, with strict controls over any cosmetic or structural changes to their exteriors. Among these, a handful (together with some of those scheduled as ancient monuments, but not necessarily all Grade I-listed buildings) stand out as icons, having sufficient power to draw visitors from all over the world. Castles and cathedrals, palaces and historic manor houses have such power, as do key sites of archaeological interest protected under the Ancient Monuments and Archaeological Areas Act 1979. The Tower of London alone receives over 2.8 million visitors annually, attracted not just by the building itself but also by the Crown Jewels, which are on permanent display there. At the other end of the scale, 'listed buildings' can include post-war prefabricated houses, garden sheds, army camps, pigsties, lamp posts, even toilet blocks.

Apart from key sites, many other important buildings are open to visitors. There are believed to be well over 6000 historic houses, commonly referred to as 'stately homes', with many open to the public. Some are under the care of the National Trust (or National Trust for Scotland), while others are in private hands. The Historic Houses Association (HHA) comprises around 1600 owners of private houses, of whom some 900 regularly open their houses to the public. The particular value of these properties is their location, generally in the countryside, so they become a major support for rural tourism and the coach tour industry.

In continental Europe, historic buildings play an equally important role in tourism for many countries. Notable among these are the châteaux of the Loire in France, Bavarian castles such as Neuschwanstein in Germany and medieval cities such as Florence and Venice in Italy. In Spain and Portugal, former stately homes – known, respectively, as paradores and pousadas – have been converted into luxury hotels, attracting upmarket touring visitors.

Although the history of the new world is shorter, funding is more readily available and early buildings that have survived are treasured. Americans take great pride in their prominent historic buildings, such as Monticello in Virginia, home of Thomas Jefferson, third president of the USA, while the town of Williamsburg, Virginia has been preserved as a living museum of the colonial period. Buildings from the Spanish colonial period are also well preserved, including the missions of San Luis Rey in California, dating from 1789, and what is believed to be the nation's oldest surviving house in St Augustine, Florida.

SEASIDE PIERS

The concept of a pier is a particularly British phenomenon. Very few are to be found in other countries, yet at one time the UK boasted more than 100. These soon proved to be attractions in their own right at many of the UK's most popular seaside resorts.

The first pier was constructed at Weymouth in 1812, soon followed by that at Ryde, Isle of Wight, in 1813. Their heyday, however, occurred between the mid-1800s and early 1900s, with 78 constructed between 1860 and 1910. They were first constructed to serve as walkways to reach the numerous paddle steamers moored offshore to provide excursions for holidaymakers, but were soon used for 'promenading', a popular Victorian pastime. Margate Pier, built in 1853, was the first pier built purely for pleasure.

Piers have now become nostalgic accoutrements to UK seaside holidays and those that remain (around 60 in the UK in varying states of preservation) are currently enjoying something of a revival, with the formation of a National Piers Society to further public interest in their regeneration. Sadly, it was too late to save the dilapidated West Pier in Brighton, a Grade I-listed pier, which collapsed during a storm while efforts were being made to raise funds for its restoration. Hastings Pier, also on the south coast, was closed in 2006 over fears that the structure was unsafe.

EXAMPLE

Herne Bay pier

A pier first opened in this Kent seaside town in 1832. Initially served by London steamers, by 1871 the pier had closed and was sold for scrap. The local council purchased an updated and extended pier in 1909, which include a grand pavilion for theatre shows. In 1968 critical failings in the infrastructure closed much of the pier and the pavilion burnt down in 1970.

This was not the end for this seaside attraction. In 1978 a sports pavilion was constructed on the remaining neck of the pier (see Figure 9.3). Efforts to modernise the pier in 2011 led to the removal of the pavilion, and temporary huts were then installed to provide catering and retail outlets designed to encourage the local population and tourists once again to visit this historic structure. A grant of £50,000 was awarded in 2016 to support regeneration of the pier.

Source: National Piers Society, 2014

FIGURE 9.3 Herne Bay Pier before the removal of the sports pavilion in 2012

Photo: Claire Humphreys

ARCHAEOLOGICAL SITES

Archaeology is the study of human antiquities, usually through excavation, and is generally thought to be concerned with pre- or early history, although much recent research is concerned with industrial archaeology – that relating to study of the industrial relics of the eighteenth and later centuries.

Areas where early civilisations arose, such as the countries of the Middle East, are rich in archaeological sites. Egypt, in particular, attracts visitors from around the world to sites such as the Pyramids at Giza, the burial sites at the Valley of the Kings and the temples at Luxor.

The UK is also rich in early historical sites, such as those at Chysauster prehistoric village in Cornwall, the Roman remains at Fishbourne in Sussex, with some of the richest mosaic flooring in the country, and the Skara Brae Neolithic site in the Orkney Islands.

In the early 1990s, the world's largest collection of paleolithic art, embracing hundreds of Ice Age drawings of animals, was discovered in a remote area of northern Portugal. A fierce battle then developed between those seeking to dam the area as a reservoir and others wanting to conserve the site for tourism. The latter won the day and the Côa Valley Archaeological Park was opened to the public in 1996.

BATTLEFIELDS

Historic battlefield sites are also important tourist attractions, not least because many are situated in rural areas and encourage tourism to what otherwise may be unappealing countryside. A growing enthusiasm for knowledge of military encounters on the fields of battle has been encouraged by the popularity of historical documentaries on television, bringing awareness of these sites to a wider audience. In fact, many battlefield sites in the past have offered little for the tourist to see, the authorities feeling that the events taking place at the sites are best left to the visitors' imagination. As a result, they have remained relatively undisturbed, but this also means that they are often under threat from development and may be compromised by the need for access roads. Local authorities are now making greater efforts to provide interpretation at these sites, using audio-visual displays and, in some cases, organising associated events, such as staging mock battles at these sites on the anniversaries of the original engagements.

On the Continent, the sites of major battles, from the field of Waterloo to World War I and, increasingly, World War II, are attracting tourists in large numbers, as do the war graves. The number of tourists visiting the battlefields of Belgium doubled (to almost 800,000) in 2014, as the centenary of World War I drew great attention to these sites.

The USA preserves and commemorates its battle sites from both the War of Independence and the Civil War. A number of specialist tour operators focus on battle sites in their tour programmes, examples in the UK being Leger, Holts and Bartletts Battlefield Journeys.

INDUSTRIAL HERITAGE

The UK became the seat of the industrial revolution in the eighteenth century, and, over the past half century, interest has been awakened in the many redundant buildings and obsolete machinery dating back to this period. The fact that so many of the early factories and warehouses were also architectural gems has given impetus to the drive to preserve and restore them for tourism. Ironbridge, where the industrial revolution is claimed to have originated in 1709, is now a UNESCO World Heritage Site and has enjoyed the benefit of substantial tourism investment.

Other European countries as well as the USA and Australia have also recognised the tourism potential of such redundant buildings. Lowell, in Massachusetts, where a number of early mills survived intact, received massive federal government funding to be restored as an urban heritage park and, since the conversion of the buildings into museums, offices and shops, it has enjoyed considerable commercial success as an out-of-the-ordinary tourist destination.

The variety of industrial sites is astonishing. Early mining works in the UK have been converted into tourist attractions, as have former docks and manufacturing buildings. The Big Pit Mining Museum at Blaenavon in South Wales and the Llechwedd Slate Caverns near Blaenau Ffestiniog in North Wales have both made important contributions to the local economy of the regions, with tourism helping to replace the former dependence on mining. Former mining sites provide plenty of interest for tourists, not just in terms of their history but also sometimes for the opportunity they present for the tourists to do a spot of mining themselves. Bodie, California, was the site of early gold mining, and is now protected as Bodie State Historic Park. Tip Top, Arizona, was a silver mining area and is now attracting tourists, as is Macetown, New Zealand, an early gold mining area. Kolmanskop in Namibia, an abandoned diamond-mining town, reopened in 1990, offering guided tours of this deserted town.

Derelict textile mills in the north of England, driven out of existence by the importation of cheap textiles from developing countries following World War II, have taken on new life as museums or, in other cases, have been converted into bars, restaurants or new homes.

EXAMPLE

Industrial heritage

In 2014, the Tomioka Silk Mill in Japan joined a long list of industrial heritage buildings registered as World Heritage Sites (WHS). The mill receives a quarter of a million visitors annually, with numbers increasing since its WHS listing.

The Mill was established by the Japanese government in 1872, which sought to modernise the production of silk to meet export demand. The factory was sold into private ownership in 1893, changing hands several times before eventually ceasing production in 1987. Today, the main mill, the warehouse and some dormitory buildings remain.

The local communities were generally supportive of efforts to recognise the mill as a WHS, hoping that it would shore up local tourism. This visitor attraction is popular with domestic tourists and in the Golden Week holiday period following confirmation of its WHS status, local restaurants and souvenir shops experienced a large increase in business; in some cases, sales levels were up by one-third.

The prefecture has since initiated a 'machi-yado' programme that involves the whole town providing lodging and services, to further support the experience of visitors coming to see the attraction.

Sources: ICOMOS, 2014; Japan News, 2018; JiJi Press, 2014

Modern industrial tourism

A number of companies have recognised the possibility of achieving good public relations by opening their doors to visitors, enabling them to visit a workshop or museum of some kind, and in some cases even permit a glimpse of work in progress at the factory. American businesses were the first to recognise the public relations value of this sort of operation, and car companies in particular were soon arranging visits to manufacturing plants where prospective purchasers could watch cars being built. The decline of the motor industry in the USA has considerably reduced these opportunities in recent years, but a handful still exist, including Nissan's Smyrna plant, Ford's Rouge factory near Detroit and BMW's Spartanburg plant in South Carolina. However, several car manufacturers have changed their focus, establishing museums to attract visitors to view their products both old and new, examples being the Volkswagen Autostadt attraction in Wolfsburg and the Opel Museum in Tijnje, the Netherlands. In the UK, MINI, now owned by BMW, offers factory tours at its plant in Oxford, and it is also possible to tour the Ferrari factory in Maranello, Italy, although you have to be a Ferrari owner to be allowed entry – so this could be a rather expensive attraction to visit.

Quite apart from creating good public relations, there are sound commercial reasons for doing this. Watching the production processes of, for example, modern china and glass will stimulate an interest in purchasing it and people can be encouraged to do so from a factory shop. At Cadbury's, the confectioners located in Bourneville, England, chocolates are made by hand and are sold to the public individually by members of staff in traditional costumes. Other museums based on publicising internationally popular products include Guinness in Ireland, Swarovski crystal in Austria and Hershey chocolate, Kelloggs and Coca-Cola in the USA.

China is probably the supreme example of a country where factory visits have been launched to encourage visitors to spend in their shops. What is often a minimal tour of the 'factory' itself is followed by an extended visit to the shop. In other countries where high-value goods are for sale (for example, in precious gem shops in Namibia or South Africa), coffee or wine is served to visitors and they are encouraged to take their time in the shop while perusing the products to encourage sales.

Producers of alcoholic drinks have long tapped tourist markets. Wine producers in both the new and old worlds provide visitors with tours of the cellars and tastings, sherry producers in Spain welcome visitors to their bodegas and, similarly, more than 40 Scotch whisky distilleries allow visits by members of the public.

EXAMPLE

Heritage Open Days

Established in 1994, Heritage Open Days is an event, held annually in September, that allows access to buildings not usually open to the public. The buildings often provide tours, talks and other activities, many of which usually focus on the architecture and local culture. In 2018, around 2000 organisations participated, with 3 million visitors taking advantage of the free entry to explore a variety of unusual properties open to the public, including factories, offices, private homes, windmills, town halls and government buildings.

Heritage Open Days are part of a European initiative to provide access to historical venues; Doors Open Days in Scotland and Wales, Heritage Open Days in Northern Ireland and Open House London all offer similar opportunities.

THE ATTRACTION OF MODERN STRUCTURES

Modern buildings are becoming almost as important as historic ones in their ability to attract tourists. Commercial offices, private houses, bridges, monuments and memorials, towers and many other constructions that represent a fusion of artistic creativity and high technology are all becoming important, when sufficiently spectacular. Often, the appeal of these new constructions is the 'wow' factor – the adrenalin rush that accompanies the viewing of many new spectacles, such as the towering '7-star' Burj al-Arab hotel in Dubai (see Figure 9.4).

FIGURE 9.4 The Burj al-Arab hotel, Dubai, UAE

Photo: Chris Holloway

Tourists have been, and still are, fascinated by the sight of tall towers or other buildings, the Eiffel Tower being an outstanding example and an immediately recognisable icon of Paris. Many destinations still strive to impress their visitors by building the tallest, most impressive towers in the world, with the result that towers of all descriptions are rising ever higher, although few provide access for tourists to visit the summit. An exception is the Shard, which offers visitors spectacular views over London as well as the opportunity to dine in style.

As was the case with the Guggenheim in Bilbao, the significance of modern architecture's appeal is that many of the great buildings are constructed on sites that are not traditionally visited by tourists. The following ten buildings have been cited as 'worth a visit from the international tourist' (Binney, 2004):

- Museum of Fantasy, Bernried, Germany
- Bao Canal Village, China
- Concert hall at León, Spain
- Bodegas Ysios, Rioja, Spain (designed by leading architect Antonio Calatrava)
- Parliamentary Library at New Delhi, India
- UFA Cinema, Dresden, Germany
- 'Aluminium Forest' Visitor Centre, Utrecht
- Tango Ecological Housing, Malmö, Sweden
- Art Museum, Milwaukee, USA (also by Calatrava)
- Modern Art Museum, Fort Worth, USA.

These are hardly mainstream tourist destinations, but several could be described as actively striving to build their tourism markets, and they are using contemporary architecture as one weapon in their arsenal to achieve this.

The bridge is another type of structure that has always found favour with tourists. Indeed, American enthusiasts actually purchased and transported the former London Bridge, re-erecting it on Lake Havasu in Arizona. Tower Bridge in London, the Pont du Gard in France, the Golden Gate in San Francisco and the Sydney Harbour Bridge are all well-established tourist attractions in their own right.

EXAMPLE

Visit the world's tallest bridge

Since its opening in 2004, the Millau Viaduct bridge across the Tarn Valley has attracted many sightseers to the Massif Central region of France. A viewing area, which includes an exhibition space and tourist information point, provides visitors with the opportunity to view this world-class structure. A chargeable short guided tour is also available for those who wish to know more about the bridge.

A million visitors arrive annually and around 60,000 vehicles cross the bridge daily at the height of summer. Local residents, who at first complained about it, are now relishing the inflow of tourists that the bridge has generated.

MUSEUMS AND ART GALLERIES

Both museums and art galleries are visited by huge numbers of tourists each year. Many are established primarily to serve the needs of the local inhabitants – at least initially – but others have quickly gained international reputations. Examples of the latter include the British Museum in London, the Ashmolean Museum in Oxford, the Louvre in Paris, the Smithsonian Museum in Washington, DC and the Museum of Modern Art (MoMA) in New York, all of which receive large numbers of visitors (see Table 9.4). To these can now be added a number of exciting buildings in the Middle East designed by prominent architects, and either recently opened or currently under construction. The significance of these for tourism is that they can act as a catalyst for visiting a destination and, in some cases, become the major reason for a visit to the destination, especially in cases where there are outstanding exhibitions.

TABLE 9.4 Top 20 museums worldwide

Museum	Location	Attendance (000s)
Louvre	Paris	8100
National Museum of China	Beijing	8063
National Air and Space Museum	Washington	7000
The Metropolitan Museum of Art	New York	7000
Vatican Museums	Vatican	6427
Shanghai Science & Technology Museum	Shanghai	6421
National Museum of Natural History	Washington	6000
British Museum	London	5907
Tate Modern	London	5656
National Gallery of Art	Washington	5232
National Gallery	London	5229
American Museum of Natural History	New York	5000
National Palace Museum (Taiwan)	Taipei	4436
Natural History Museum	London	4435
State Hermitage	St Petersburg	4220
China Science Technology Museum	Beijing	3983
Reina Sofia	Madrid	3897
National Museum of American History	Washington	3800
Victoria & Albert Museum	London	3790
Centre Pompidou	Paris	3371

Source: AECOM, 2017

Museums have a very long history, and in the UK date back to at least the seventeenth century, when some private collectors opened their exhibitions for a fee.

John Tradescant's Cabinet of Curiosities provided the foundation for the Ashmolean Museum at Oxford University in 1683. Today, there are six main categories of museum in the UK:

- *National museums*, usually funded directly by the Department for Digital, Culture, Media and Sport (DCMS). These include such famous museums as the British Museum, National Gallery, Tate Britain and Tate Modern art galleries, Victoria and Albert Museum, Imperial War Museum and Royal Armouries, Leeds. Certain national museums are funded by the Ministry of Defence, such as the RAF Museum in Hendon and the National Army Museum in London.
- *Independent (charitable trust) museums*, financed by turnover. The National Motor Museum at Beaulieu is one example.
- *Independent non-charity museums*, such as Flambards Museum in Helston, Cornwall. Collections are funded in a variety of ways, drawing on contributions from both public and private sources.
- *Regional museums*, funded publicly or by a mix of public and private funding. The DCMS also funds museums such as the Geffrye and Horniman Museums in London and the Museum of Science and Industry in Manchester.
- *Local authority museums*, such as the Cotswold Countryside Museum in Gloucester and the Georgian House and Red Lodge Museums owned by Bristol City Council. The recently expanded National Football Museum in Manchester is funded by partners including Heritage Lottery funding, European development funding and Manchester City Council.
- *Small, private museums*, which depend entirely on private funding.

The problem for those who manage museums is that the initial capital investment is not the only financial consideration. Many collections are donated or gifts of money are made in order to establish a museum, but steadily rising operating costs are seldom met by increases in revenue, and after the first two or three years, during which time the museum has novelty value, attendance figures slump. As new museums are opened, so the available market to visit them is more thinly spread. Museums have also been badly hit in recent years by the consequences of the Education Reform Act, which has made the financing of educational visits, a key sector for many museums, more difficult.

Many museum curators argue in favour of subsidies, on the grounds that their museums help to bring tourists to an area and, once there, they can be encouraged to spend. Certainly, clusters of museums and other complementary attractions, such as shops, do give rise to greater numbers of tourists. The Castlefield site in Manchester is a good example of a 'critical mass' of attractions sited close together, making it an attractive day out.

Museums have become increasingly self-sufficient, and their curatorial role is now less significant than their marketing one. The national museums in London were briefly obliged to introduce charges – or, at the very least, they 'suggested contributions' – in the 1990s, resulting in a very sharp drop in attendance. Those that did not introduce charges benefited. Those that did decide to charge, however, were able to invest in refurbishment, which, with government subsidies alone, would not have been possible. Since the obligation to charge has been removed, the galleries have experienced an upsurge in attendance and it is notable that seven of the top ten most visited attractions in the UK are museums or art galleries (see Table 9.5).

TABLE 9.5 ALVA attractions with over 1 million admissions in 2017

Museum	Total visits	Cost of entry
British Museum	5,906,716	Part charge
Tate Modern	5,656,004	Part charge
National Gallery	5,229,192	Part charge
Natural History Museum South Kensington	4,434,520	Part charge
V&A South Kensington	3,789,748	Part charge
Science Museum	3,251,000	Part charge
Southbank Centre	3,232,655	Part charge
Somerset House	3,223,350	Part charge
Tower of London	2,843,031	Charge
Royal Museums Greenwich	2,607,099	Part charge
National Museum of Scotland	2,165,601	Part charge
Edinburgh Castle	2,063,709	Charge
Chester Zoo	1,866,628	Charge
Royal Botanic Gardens, Kew	1,802,958	Charge
Tate Britain	1,777,877	Part charge
National Portrait Gallery	1,703,411	Part charge
Scottish National Gallery	1,600,761	Part charge
Stonehenge	1,582,532	Charge
St Paul's Cathedral	1,571,197	Part charge
Westminster Abbey	1,547,001	Part charge
Royal Albert Hall	1,495,387	Charge
British Library	1,426,433	Part charge
Riverside Museum	1,355,359	Free
Roman Baths and Pump Room	1,318,976	Charge
Kelvingrove Art Gallery & Museum	1,304,072	Free
Old Royal Naval College	1,221,720	Part charge
RHS Garden Wisley	1,143,175	Charge
ZSL London Zoo	1,102,790	Charge
National Museum Royal Navy	1,081,909	Part Charge
Royal Academy of Arts	1,049,962	Charge
Eden Project	1,024,156	Charge
Giants Causeway	1,011,467	Part Charge
Houses of Parliament	1,007,568	Part Charge

Note: 'Part charge' reflects the fact that charges are made for entry to some areas or exhibitions.

Source: ALVA, 2017

EXAMPLE

Free entry to museums

From the information provided in Table 9.5, it can be seen that many museums are free to enter, charging only for entry to special exhibitions or events. There are many reasons why this may be the case, including efforts to broaden access to such resources by all societal groups, regardless of economic means.

Although entry may be free, it is not uncommon for museums to operate a system that seeks a voluntary donation at exit, with an expectation that having enjoyed their experience visitors will make a generous financial contribution to the museum.

This highlights an interesting issue in human responses. In terms of rational economic behaviour, it would be logical that visitors, who have already gained access to the resources required, would give nothing. However, extensive empirical research suggests that most people instead donate a sum which they judge to be fair, with higher levels of satisfaction leading to larger donations.

From the museum's perspective, such an approach provides revenue, is efficient to manage and does not exclude visitors based on ability to pay.

Source: Frey and Steiner, 2012

As a result of the reduction or withdrawal of public funding, museums have been obliged to become increasingly commercial in their approach. Buildings are redesigned to ensure that all visitors exit via the shop, and investigations are made into what sells or fails to sell, and into price sensitivity. Galleries are hired for private functions, and sponsorship is sought to finance exhibitions or even whole galleries. Catering has also become an important money-raiser, with increasing emphasis placed on the location and design of cafés and restaurants. All principal museums in the UK are now expected to engage in fund-raising, both publicly and through their memberships and friends' associations.

Museums not sited close to major centres of population or with poor accessibility generally find it difficult to attract tourists in large numbers. One notable exception, to which reference has already been made, is the Guggenheim in Bilbao, which rapidly became an authentic cultural icon soon after its construction.

EXAMPLE

The Guggenheim museums and their value to tourism

The Guggenheim museums have had particular success in attracting tourists, partly for their contents, but more notably for their architectural merit.

The construction of the Guggenheim in Bilbao was a deliberate move on the part of the local authorities to promote the city as an attractive place to visit. The proposed museum received very strong public-sector support and significant financial aid from the Guggenheim Foundation, which had the foresight to contract an outstanding architect, Frank Gehry, to design the unconventional building.

(Continued)

The result is that tourists beat a path to its door. There were over 1.3 million visitors in its first year, even though Bilbao had never been a traditional tourist destination and had, at least at that point, little else to attract tourists. Bilbao now enjoys success as a strong short-break destination and the museum achieved more than 10 million visits in its first decade of operation, in 2017 alone receiving 1.3 million visitors.

There are currently Guggenheim Museums in New York, Bilbao, Venice, Berlin and Las Vegas, and Frank Gehry was retained to complete a sixth in Abu Dhabi (part of a group of four world-class museums to be clustered on Saadiyat Island). However construction has been suspended since 2013; to date, only the Louvre Abu Dhabi has been opened.

To attract new audiences and bring back previous visitors, many museums are moving away from the concept of 'objects in glass cases' in favour of better interpretation and more active participation by the visitors. New techniques include guides dressed in period costume, audio-visual displays, self-guided trails using recordings, reconstructions of the past and interactive programmes that provide opportunities for hands-on experience.

Some museums are fully interactive, such as We the Curious (formerly Explore) in Bristol, which is designed to explain science to those who do not know too much about it by giving them the opportunity to become involved in practical experiments. At the Big Pit Mining Museum in Blaenavon (mentioned previously), former miners have acted as guides, providing tours that draw on their own earlier experiences in the mines. In a similar vein, former inmates interned on Robben Island under South African apartheid laws now address visitors to the island museum and show them the cell where Nelson Mandela was incarcerated (see Figure 9.5).

FIGURE 9.5 A former political prisoner addresses visitors to the prison where Nelson Mandela was incarcerated on Robben Island, South Africa

Photo: Shutterstock

An example of a 'living history' museum can be found at Llancaiach Fawr Manor, a sixteenth-century fortified house in the South Wales valleys. Here, actor-interpreters (more correctly referred to in mainland Europe as **animateurs**, discussed in Chapter 20), dressed in costumes of the period, act as 'below stairs' staff, guiding visitors around the site, using the language and speech patterns of the time, recreating the year 1645.

Many museums, for example, are the former homes of famous people and the trustees have a curatorial and research role in safeguarding and investigating documents of its famous owner, as well as encouraging tourist trade for commercial reasons. A good example of this is Graceland, the former home of Elvis Presley in Memphis, Tennessee. Long after the star's death, it continues to attract huge crowds of fans who come to see his house, his former possessions and his grave. Graceland has become one of the major tourist attractions in the USA and is listed in the National Register of Historic Places. It is the second most visited home in the USA (after the White House), receiving around 650,000 visitors annually.

PARKS AND GARDENS

GARDENS AND ARBORETA

According to Botanic Gardens Conservation International, there are some 1775 botanic gardens in 148 countries around the world, which admit more than 150 million visitors every year. Key sites, such as Kirstenbosch Botanic Gardens near Cape Town, South Africa, attract visitors from all over the world. The cultivation of gardens has an enthusiastic following, a fact not lost on those organising visits; both private and public gardens, and arboreta, which are essentially museums for living trees and shrubs, are popular. As we see in Table 9.5, the Royal Botanic Gardens at Kew attracted 1.8 million visitors in 2017 and the Royal Horticultural Society Garden at Wisley received 1.1 million that year.

Many gardens popular with visitors are in the care of the National Trust, generally as adjuncts to stately homes. In some cases (as is the case with Stourhead in Wiltshire) the gardens may prove a stronger draw than the houses themselves, and in others only the gardens are open to the public. Great landscape architects of the eighteenth century, such as Capability Brown and Humphrey Repton, built splendid parks to complement great manor houses and as recently as the twentieth century famous gardens were still being constructed. The great garden designer Gertrude Jekyll is a notable example of this.

EXAMPLE

World gardens

National Geographic offers a series of 'Top 10' places to visit. This identifies excellent examples in a number of categories, including ocean views, spring vineyards, beaches and, of particular interest here, gardens. The top ten gardens are:

1. Château de Versailles, Versailles, France
2. Royal Botanic Gardens, Kew, England
3. Powerscourse Gardens, Enniskerry, Ireland
4. Butchart Gardens, Vancouver Island, British Colombia
5. Villa d'Este, Tivoli, Italy

(Continued)

6. Dumbarton Oaks, Washington, USA
7. Gardens of the Villa Éphrussi de Rothschild, St.-Jean-Cap-Ferrat, France
8. Stourhead, Warminster, England
9. The Master-of-Nets Garden, Suzhou, China
10. Sans Souci, Potsdam, Germany.

These gardens are all popular visitor attractions but heading the list are the gardens of the Chateau de Versailles, built for the seventeenth-century French king, Louis XIV. The 250-acre gardens include ornamental lakes, flower beds and a canal used by the king for gondola rides.

Another highly successful attraction in the UK is the Eden Project in Cornwall, which received more than a million visitors in the first three months of its opening. Since opening, more than 18 million visitors have passed through its doors, with 1 million people visiting the attraction in 2017. Initial research indicated that 92% of all visitors stayed in holiday accommodation nearby when they visited, with the Cornish economy anticipated to have benefited by some £1.7 billion since the site's opening in 2001. Its appeal is boosted by its proximity to another garden attraction, the Lost Gardens of Heligan, making it a popular coach trip for garden enthusiasts taking a short-break holiday.

Garden festivals (strictly speaking, these are event attractions) are popular in Germany, France and the Netherlands. A national garden festival is held in Germany every two years and, in the Netherlands, every ten years. France benefits significantly from garden tourism: the formal gardens attached to the châteaux in the Loire valley and Monet's garden at Giverny have become major international tourist attractions, the latter especially so since its restoration. North America also has its share of notable garden attractions. Perhaps the most famous are the Butchart Gardens on Victoria Island, British Columbia in Canada (4th in the National Geographic Top 10 Gardens), but popular and much-visited botanic gardens in the USA include the Denver Botanic Gardens in Colorado and Longwood Gardens, a 1000-acre site founded by the du Pont family at Kennett Square, Pennsylvania, which attracts over 900,000 visitors a year.

WILDLIFE PARKS

Wildlife is a growing attraction for tourists and the tourism industry has responded to this interest in wildlife in different ways. At one time, the most common way for tourists to see wild animals was in the many zoos that exist in most countries around the world. The keeping of collections of animals goes back at least 2000 years, but the present-day concept of a zoo dates back only to the eighteenth century. In the UK, although zoos are known to predate the turn of the nineteenth century, the founding of the Zoological Society in London by Sir Stamford Raffles at the beginning of that century led to the interest that Victorian England took in caged animals.

Today, there are some 1300 established zoos around the world, but attitudes to zoos have changed. People in Western countries have come to consider it cruel to keep animals in captivity. Nevertheless, zoos still enjoy good attendance figures; for example, as Table 9.5 shows, Chester Zoo receives around 1.8 million visitors annually (up from 1.1 million in 2010). Zoos now stress their curatorial role, preserving rare species of wildlife, rather than displaying animals for the purpose of entertainment.

With the growth of long-haul travel, more tourists are taking advantage of the opportunity to see these animals in the wild, usually in safari parks. The best-known of these are situated in South and East Africa, as we saw in Figure 8.9 in the previous chapter. Some of these big game parks have become world famous, including Kenya's Masai Mara, Tsavo, Amboseli and Samburu Parks, Tanzania's Serengeti National Park and South Africa's Kruger National Park. The attraction of these parks lies in the opportunity to see big game, such as lions, elephants, leopards, buffalo and rhino – the so-called 'big five'. All of these parks feature in tour operators' long-haul programmes, although political uncertainty in many African countries and the lack of investment in some have hindered the expansion of tourism to the safari parks in recent years. This has, however, benefited some lesser-known parks in countries like Botswana.

EXAMPLE

Viewing wildlife in Singapore

Despite being a heavily urbanised island of only 275 square miles, Singapore is home to four wildlife parks: Singapore Zoo, Jurong Bird Park, Night Safari and the River Safari. These parks (operating together as Wildlife Reserves Singapore (WRS)) have seen success with their conservation and breeding programmes, including the births of highly endangered orangutans, proboscis monkeys, lion-tailed macaques and Malaysian tapirs.

WRS receives no direct government support, funding its operations primarily through ticket, catering and merchandise revenue. The four parks together receive in excess of 4.5 million visitors annually. Popularity is confirmed by TripAdvisor's Traveller's Choice awards, which rated Singapore as the number one zoo in Asia and third worldwide in 2018.

Source: www.wrs.com.sg

Another form of wildlife park is the wildfowl reserve. Birdwatching is a popular pastime and attracts domestic as well as the specialist international market, with tour operators such as Naturetrek and Birdquest among a number offering specialist holidays for the study of bird life, frequently accompanied by well-known ornithology experts who will lecture to clients en route. Destinations such as Kenya, Botswana, Ecuador and Sri Lanka are all popular birdwatching destinations for international visitors looking to spot birds that cannot be seen in their own country.

Other attractions, for which tourism is a secondary consideration in some cases, include falconry centres and animal sanctuaries. Sanctuaries, of course, exist to protect and tend to wounded animals, but most are open to visitors, who make a useful contribution, through their admission fees, to the running costs of the project. In the Persian Gulf, the popularity of falconry, and the presentation of birds of prey at bird centres, attract both domestic and foreign visitors.

Finally, reference should be made in this section to the popularity of aquariums (now more commonly known as sealife centres). The popular revulsion to keeping animals in cages has not yet generally extended to fish (and, although there are movements to close down entertainments incorporating captive seawater mammals such as porpoises and dolphins, they remain popular in the USA).

On the Continent, the Sea Life Centre in Paris and Nausicaa, le Centre Nationale de la Mer in Boulogne, are two popular additions in this area. Many such centres have also been constructed in the USA, the one at Monterey in California being particularly notable both for the size of the tanks (one of which includes a full-scale kelp forest) and the fact that there is a unique pen with direct access to the Pacific Ocean, allowing sea otters to swim into and out of the setting at will.

THEME AND AMUSEMENT PARKS

Up to now, we have been discussing parks that draw on the natural environment to create the attraction. However, we must also consider parks that draw on a constructed environment to provide the entertainment. Purpose-built leisure parks are, not surprisingly, major attractions for tourists, and they receive the greatest number of visitors of all tourist attractions. It is estimated that total attendance of the top ten theme park groups worldwide was in excess of 475 million visits in 2017 (AECOM, 2017).

The appetite for such parks to entertain the public seems never-ending and, in Europe, they have a very long history. Bakken, in Klampenborg near Copenhagen, lays claim to being the oldest amusement park in the world, having opened in 1583. London's Vauxhall Gardens opened in 1661, followed in the eighteenth century by Ranelagh Gardens and the Tivoli Gardens in Paris. By the nineteenth century, entertainment parks were firmly established, with the Tivoli Gardens in Copenhagen, which first opened in 1843, soon becoming one of the world's leading centres of entertainment. This park continues to attract over 4 million visitors annually. Blackpool Pleasure Beach, the UK's first seaside entertainment centre, opened in 1896 and is still one of the most visited tourist attractions in the country.

The world's biggest amusement park became established at around the same time at Coney Island, in Brooklyn, New York City. The world's first roller coaster was built there in 1884 and, by 1895, an indoor amusement park, Sea Lion Park, had been added. Eventually, three separate parks, Luna Park, Steeplechase Park and Dreamland, opened on this seaside site between 1897 and 1904, with up to 250,000 visitors a day. A succession of fires destroyed two of the parks, but Luna Park remained popular until its decline after the Wall Street Crash in 1929, after which it struggled to survive, finally closing in 1946. Plans to regenerate the area with a $1 billion investment, after its steady decline in the 1950s and 1960s, saw the opening in 2010 of New Luna Park with a beachfront amusement park and, in 2014, a new rollercoaster. Australia emulated the success of Coney Island in its early years with its own Luna Park in Melbourne in 1912, followed by a second in Sydney in 1935.

The 1920s were the heyday of these amusement parks. The Great Depression caused attendances to decline until a new generation of theme parks arrived in the 1950s. Although de Efteling was opened in Europe as early as 1951 with a fairy tale theme, and Bellewaerde Park followed in 1954, it was Walt Disney Enterprises that popularised the concept of the theme park with its development at Anaheim, California in 1955, and it reinvigorated the market. It was followed by a number of Disney developments around Orlando in Florida, the first of which opened in 1971, and these now attract tourists from all over the world.

Today's amusement parks can be classified, according to size, into three distinct categories:

- local parks, catering largely to the day tripper market
- flagship attractions such as the Tivoli Gardens in Copenhagen or the Prater in Vienna, which draw on national markets and attract a significant number of foreign visitors, too
- icon, or destination, parks, such as those of the Disney empire, which have become destinations in their own right and attract a worldwide market.

The USA alone boasts over 750 leisure parks, but the large Disney parks account for by far the greatest number of visitors. Globally, the Disney parks attracted 150 million people in

2017 (The Magic Kingdom at Orlando alone attracted 20 million) and the 11 other Disney parks are listed among the top 25 world attractions. Effectively managing such large numbers is a key part of their success. Universal Studios, also in Florida, attracted 10 million people in 2017, with its Islands of Adventure (also in Orlando) attracting 9.5 million. The US operator Six Flags (which operates 25 parks and entertainment centres across North America) caters for 30 million people. Disney dominates in the USA, and has since developed further sites near Tokyo and Paris as well as in Hong Kong. More recently, Disney has partnered with the Chinese government to develop a new theme park in Shanghai (which receives 11 million visitors annually).

As we can see in Table 9.6, the Disney empire, with over 150 million visitors to its parks, has no direct competition. Its nearest global competitor, Merlin Entertainments, attracted 66 million in 2017, and is expanding rapidly, with turnover now exceeding £1 billion a year.

TABLE 9.6 Major theme park companies

Park owners	Total attendance (millions)	Examples of their parks
Walt Disney Attractions	150.0	Walt Disney World Resort, Florida; Disneyland, California; Disneyland Europe; Tokyo Disneyland; Shanghai Disneyland
Merlin Entertainments	66.0	Madame Tussauds; Legoland; Gardaland, Italy; Earth Explore, Belgium; Heide Park, Germany
Universal Parks and Resorts	49.5	Universal Orlando Resort; Universal Studios Hollywood; Universal Studios Japan
OCT Parks China	42.9	Splendid China; Windows on the World; OCT East Resort; Happy Valley Beijing; Happy Valley Shanghai; Happy Valley Shenzhen
Fantawild	38.5	Zhengzhau Fantawild Adventure, Shifeng Fantawild Dreamland, Ningbo Fantawild Oriental Heritage, and Wuhu Fantawild Water Park
Chimelong Group	31.0	Ocean Kingdom, Hengqin, China, Chimelong water park, Guangzhou, China
Six Flags	30.8	Six Flags: over Texas, Arlington; Magic Mountain, San Francisco; Discovery Kingdom, Los Angeles; Great America, Chicago; New England, Springfield
Cedar Fair Entertainment	25.7	Cedar Point, Ohio; Knott's Berry Farm, California; Canada's Wonderland, Ontario; Kings Dominion, Virginia; Dorney Park, Pennsylvania
Seaworld Parks	20.8	SeaWorld Orlando; Busch Gardens Tampa; Busch Gardens Williamsburg; Sesame Place, Pennsylvania
Parques Reunidos	20.6	Warner Bros. Park, Madrid; Bobbejaanland, Belgium; Mirabilandia, Italy; Bonbonland, Denmark; Kennywood, USA

Source: AECOM, 2017

The clustering and scale of several attractions in one region of Florida, around Orlando, has given the European tourism industry the scope to develop package holidays focused on this region and, as a result, this destination has become one of the most popular in the world for long-haul package holidays. Visitors tend to spend several days visiting the parks, allowing construction of a huge bed stock, approaching 100,000 rooms.

In Europe, theme parks tend to be smaller and have lower levels of investment in both development and marketing than do the Disney parks, and hence do not attempt to compete directly with them, instead drawing mainly on national markets.

The distinction between a **theme park** and an **amusement park** is not always a clear one, although the former is rather loosely based on some theme, whether geographical, historical or some other such concept. Europa Park in Germany has 13 European-themed areas containing more than 100 attractions and shows. In addition to these areas themed around Spain, Scandinavia, Switzerland and others, the park also includes a children's world, an enchanted forest and Minimoys, a kingdom filled with oversized insects. Phantasialand, another theme park in Germany, similarly has themed areas focused on Berlin, Mexico and China as well as areas drawing on themes of fantasy and mystery.

Before the development of such theming concepts, the predominant aim of the leisure park was to entertain by means of the traditional funfair, with stalls, helter-skelters, candy floss and other trappings that have been familiar for many decades. Later, parks began vying with one another to devise new rides and challenge younger visitors by incorporating ever more frightening 'white-knuckle' experiences in their major centrepieces. With the introduction of the new theme parks, while amusement rides remained an important element, the theme (such as associating the park with popular cartoon or TV characters as in Parc Asterix) heightens the attraction for many. Building on the popularity of film and TV characters among younger visitors is important for a market that is composed chiefly of family groups.

Mention should also be made of the success Lego has had in developing its own form of theme park in Europe. The global appeal of this children's building brick toy has enabled the company to expand the brand to its Legoland parks, first in its country of origin, at Billund in Denmark, and, later, to England, at Windsor, Günzburg in Germany, Carlsbad in California, Nusajaya in Malaysia, Winter Haven in Florida and, since 2016, Dubai. The sheer scale of these developments is on a par with the major theme parks and in terms of visitor numbers, they count among the more important tourism attractions in their countries.

EXAMPLE

Legoland: part of a theme park destination

Dubai Parks and Resorts is home to three world-class theme parks: Legoland Dubai, Bollywood Parks and Motiongate Dubai. The resort also includes a water park and Riverland Dubai, a themed retail and dining experience. Six Flags is also constructing a further theme park, with doors scheduled to open in 2019.

Bollywood Parks, opened in late 2016, is the first theme park dedicated to all things Bollywood. It includes a number of live street entertainment shows held in the park throughout the day, including folk dances, cultural performances and Bollywood-themed acts.

Motiongate Dubai is a Hollywood-inspired attraction, which draws on films and characters from the film studios of Columbia Pictures and DreamWorks. This includes franchises such as *Shrek*, *Ghostbusters* and *Kung Fu Panda*. The attraction also includes the Smurf village. The attraction has proved popular, with 2 million visitors in 2018.

On a much smaller scale, there are innumerable other model village-type attractions, usually based in popular tourist destinations to appeal to visitors as impulse visits. These form just one group of small attractions that tourists enjoy but generally receive less prominent attention. Other such forms of tourist entertainment include amusement arcades, model railways, waxworks (including the increasingly popular dungeon settings) and similar small commercial exhibitions. They may be indoor or outdoor attractions and, together, they make up the largest proportion of the attractions business. It would therefore be wrong to ignore their importance within the organisational structure of the industry, even though, individually, their income may be only a tiny fraction of that of the major amusement parks. Like all the smallest museums, their very existence is tenuous, often depending on the commitment of owner-managers and their families and a voluntary labour force.

OTHER ATTRACTIONS

The scope for providing new attractions to feed the insatiable appetites of tourists is never-ending and it would be quite impossible to cover the subject fully in a single chapter. Sometimes attractions are unique to a destination, but share some common features with those in other areas or countries, thus offering scope for creating joint marketing schemes or twinning. An example of this is European Walled Towns (EWT), established as a marketing association in 1992 by a group of European towns that benefit from one characteristic tourist attraction: an encircling fortification wall. Others depend on a unique feature of the district, coupled with an imaginative initiative in marketing it. For example, after the discovery of Cleopatra's sunken city adjacent to Alexandria Harbour, packages were organised to the site to allow tourists to dive and explore the ruins.

Diving, in fact, has immense appeal as an activity undertaken when on holiday. This is in line with the growth in activity holidays generally and some of the more extreme activities associated with it include ice-diving, iceberg wall dives, mine diving (exploring flooded mineshafts) and wreck diving. Examples of the latter include:

- Truk Lagoon, Micronesia, where over 60 shipwrecks from the 1944 Japanese fleet, including the Fujikawa Maru, a 7000-ton freighter, offer ideal opportunities for underwater exploring
- Bikini Atoll, in the Marshall Islands, which has over 40 World War II wrecks to explore
- Pensacola, Florida, where the *USS Oriskany* was deliberately sunk 23 metres off the coast to provide the largest artificial reef in the world
- Vanuatu, in the Pacific, where lies the *SS President Coolidge*, a former liner and troopship.

If all that underwater activity is too extreme, a more relaxing opportunity is provided in the form of undersea scootering, with Bob (breathing observation bubble) trips available to see fish close up, in a number of resorts, including Tenerif in the Canary Islands, St Thomas in the US Virgin Islands, and Cancún, Mexico. No diving experience is necessary!

Early forms of transport are another focus for tourists. In some cases, the equipment can be restored and brought back into service for pleasure trips, such as the many steam railways either in private hands or managed by trusts in the UK. The continuing role of classic modes of transport as tourist attractions is examined more thoroughly in Chapters 14 and 15.

Transport museums are popular attractions in many countries. There are many vintage car and vintage aircraft museums throughout the world. Examples in the UK include the London Transport Museum, National Motor Museum, Beaulieu, and the National Railway Museum, York. Australia offers the National Maritime Museum, Sydney, National Railway Museum in Port Adelaide and St Kilda Tram Museum in Adelaide. Across the USA, museums dedicated to the railroad, automobile and even the cable car (in San Francisco, California) attract tourists.

Historic ships provide unique attractions for local museums. Some of the earliest are the Viking ships which have been found in Scandinavia, and some splendid museums have been created to display them, notably that at Roskilde in Denmark.

The only seventeenth-century warship to survive is the Swedish *Vasa*, which capsized and sank in Stockholm harbour soon after its launch in 1628. Raised in almost perfect condition, it is now a major museum attraction in Stockholm. Still in Scandinavia, Oslo in Norway provides the setting for the *Fram*, the vessel in which Roald Amundsen sailed in 1910, on his way to becoming the first person to reach the South Pole. Similarly, Captain Scott's vessel, the research ship *Discovery*, has now returned to Dundee, where it was built in 1901, and serves as a focal point for the Discover Point museum.

Perhaps the best-known of all twentieth-century ships, the *RMS Queen Mary*, was saved from the breaker's yard and is almost the only modern passenger ship to have been preserved, though sadly much of its original interior has been removed. It now serves as a dry-dock hotel, museum and events space near Long Beach, California, but has proved extremely expensive to maintain. Its sister ship, the *Queen Elizabeth 2*, completed its maritime career in 2008 and since 2018 has operated as a floating hotel in Dubai.

The UK has numerous examples of fighting vessels that have been preserved and are open to the public. *HMS Belfast*, a World War II cruiser, is moored near Tower Bridge in London and attracts some 250,000 visitors each year. Portsmouth is particularly lucky to have three great examples of historical maritime vessels: Nelson's flagship, *HMS Victory*, the nineteenth-century *HMS Warrior*, and the Tudor warship *Mary Rose*, raised from the sea in 1982 and still undergoing conservation (see Figures 9.6a and b). The combination of three vessels of historic value located close together in the same city acts as a powerful magnet for day trippers and helps to account for the large number of visitors who come to see them.

FIGURE 9.6a ***HMS Victory*** **and the band of the Royal Marines, Portsmouth**

Photo: Chris Holloway

FIGURE 9.6b *HMS Warrior*, Portsmouth Harbour

Photo: Chris Holloway

In general, the attractions we have been examining in this chapter up to this point have been permanent sites, available to visitors at any time of the year. We will now turn to examining other factors that help to attract visitors to a destination.

OTHER INFLUENTIAL FACTORS ATTRACTING VISITORS

We have concentrated on sites that attract tourists to destinations, but there are many other factors that motivate visitors to take a trip to a domestic or international destination. There are too many influences to examine them all in this chapter but we will pay particular attention to some key areas, including:

- cultural tourism
- religious tourism
- sports tourism
- shopping
- gastronomy tourism
- medical tourism
- spa tourism
- dark tourism.

CULTURAL TOURISM

In its widest definition, cultural tourism encompasses both 'high' and 'low' culture. The so-called 'fine arts' in all their forms – paintings and sculpture, decorative arts, architecture, classical forms of music, theatre and literature – are matched by 'popular culture' attractions, including music and film, along with traditional forms of entertainment such as folk dancing and handicrafts. In postmodern societies, the former divisions between 'high' and 'low' culture have become increasingly artificial and certainly now have little relevance to the study of tourism, as the industry has become adept at packaging and popularising culture in *all* its forms.

France, noted for its dominance in the fine art field, has packaged art trails covering places Cézanne lived and frequented at Aix-en-Provence, Monet's garden at Giverny and areas associated with Gauguin, Manet, Renoir, Dégas, Pissarro and Sisley. Longer tours, too, such as the 'circuit Pissarro–Cézanne' and 'circuit Toulouse-Lautrec', have proved popular with cultural tourists.

Where a place is popularly identified with an author or artist, tourist interest follows automatically, but where such a link is less well established, it can still be built on. The poet Dylan Thomas' disparaging comments about the town and people of Laugharne have not stopped a steady flow of 20,000 visitors annually to the Boathouse where he lived between 1949 and 1953, despite the locals' preference for playing down this link. By contrast, the towns of Rochester and Broadstairs in Kent have both traded on their links with the Victorian author Charles Dickens.

A discussion of all the different forms of cultural attraction, ranging from 'high' to 'low' culture, would require a level of detail too extensive to be examined here, so you are directed to the many publications (e.g. Richards, 2011; Smith, 2016) that focus on this sector to increase your knowledge of them and the issues arising from each.

RELIGIOUS TOURISM

Travel for religious purposes tends to be grouped among the 'miscellaneous' forms of tourism, falling outside the central purposes of leisure or business. It would be unfair to dismiss it lightly, however, as it represents a key feature in the worldwide movement of tourists. The UNWTO estimates that there are around 300 million visits each year to key religious sites, including Mecca in Saudi Arabia, the Golden Temple of Amritsar in India, Our Lady of Guadalupe in Mexico, Fatima in Portugal and Lourdes in France. All told, religious tourism is thought to contribute around £18 billion annually to these destinations. Religious tourism may take a variety of forms, including:

- pilgrimages
- missionary travel
- faith-based holidays
- retreats
- religious tourist attractions.

Millions who follow the faith of Islam make the obligatory, once-in-a-lifetime pilgrimage to Mecca, the birthplace of Mohammed in Saudi Arabia. While these trips are seen as an obligation arising out of the Islamic faith rather than a pleasure trip, they nevertheless bring substantial financial and commercial benefits to the country that caters to these tourists' needs.

EXAMPLE

The expansion of Buddhist tourism

January 2019 saw the launch of the Buddhist International Travel Mart (organised by the Nepal Association of Tour and Travel Agents), a three-day event which took place at Lumbini,

Nepal, the birthplace of the Buddha. Lumbini is expecting escalating visitor numbers following the construction of the nearby Gautam Buddha International Airport at Bhairahawa. The regional government is planning to develop Kapilbastu, Devdaha, Ramgram and other areas associated with the life of the Buddha to further attract visitors.

Nepal is not the only country that is exploring its Buddhist heritage for tourism. According to the ASEAN Tourism Research Association, Buddhist tourism has strong growth potential across the South-East Asia region, as there are numerous religious ceremonies and festivals that have the potential to attract the 156 million Buddhists living in the region.

Sources: Puvaneswary, 2019; RSS Nepal, 2019

Prominent religious destinations for Christian pilgrims include the Vatican, St Katherine's monastery (often linked with visits to Petra in Jordan for package tours), Assisi and Lourdes (which has one of the highest concentrations of hotels in Europe). Sikhs and Hindus are drawn to Amritsar and Varanasi in India, Buddhists to Shikoku in Japan, while Mount Kailas in China draws both Buddhists and Hindus to its summit in order to shed sins. Other multi-faith sites include Jerusalem, which draws Christians, Jews and Muslims alike, due to its historical importance to all three religions. The political upheavals in that region, however, have discouraged the large numbers that would have been expected in earlier years, with the claimed birthplace of Christ, Bethlehem, particularly affected, being on the Palestinian side of the border.

Specialist operators exist to provide services for religious tourism. Tours are often accompanied by spiritual leaders and, in such cases, could be considered educational tourism, but in other instances (such as pilgrimages to Lourdes, to seek intercession for a cure) the motive comes closer to that of health tourism.

It is open to debate as to which category fits the religious theme parks that are now appearing. One example is the Holy Land Experience, located close to Universal's theme park resort in Orlando. The appeal of religious-themed attractions is spreading; for example, the opening in 2016 in Kentucky, USA of Ark Encounter, an attraction based on Old Testament accounts, has drawn around 1 million visitors annually. Part educational, part missionary, part entertainment and quasi-history, these parks appear to be finding a new market for the curious and the committed alike.

SPORTS TOURISM

The relationship between tourism and sports activities is now so well established that **sports tourism** is recognised as a field of study in its own right, and there are several books devoted to the subject (e.g. Hinch and Higham, 2011; Weed and Bull, 2009).

At its most successful, sports tourism will draw the greatest number of tourists to any one site on the planet. Tickets to the Olympic Games, for example, are in such high demand that sports enthusiasts are attracted from all over the world. Similarly, football's FIFA World Cup, also draws huge crowds. World-class events in golf and tennis also witness demand for tickets well beyond the available supply. The economic benefits of these events to the destinations where they are staged can be enormous.

Of course, sports activities are not limited to events where tourists are merely passive observers. On the contrary, they also seek to participate in rounds of golf on famous courses such as St Andrews, or in improving their tennis with the professionals at coaching schools in Florida and in competitive games around the world. Sports tourists may also choose to visit the numerous sports-related attractions that exist around the globe, examples of which are the Baseball Hall of Fame in Cooperstown, New York, the Wimbledon Tennis Museum in London, the National Football Museum in Manchester and the Berlin Sports Museum, located in the city's Olympiapark.

The Olympics effect

The enormous investment required to mount Olympics events in a country has drawn a lot of media criticism, particularly in the UK, as host of the 2012 Games in London. Doubts arose about the £9 billion cost, and whether this could be justified, with little expectation of making a profit from the event. Montreal, which mounted the Games in 1976, eventually paid off the $1.5 billion debt in 2006, three decades after the Olympic athletes had left town. Barcelona, where the Games were held in 1992, invested £6.5 billion in mounting the events; the cost to Athens in 2004, initially estimated by the government not to exceed €4.5 billion, may actually have amounted to as much as €8.5 billion. Atlanta did better; it spent only $2 billion in 1996 and claimed a profit equivalent to £525 million, but much of the infrastructure needed was already in place before the city won the Games. In 2000, Sydney overspent its £1 billion budget by £300 million, which was underwritten by the country's taxpayers.

In terms of boosting tourism, certainly these international sporting events attract large numbers of visitors to the cities at the time, but even this does not necessarily benefit the cities outside of the venues themselves. The European Tour Operators' Association claims that the Games attract only sports enthusiasts who do not spend money on leisure outside of the venues, and both Los Angeles and Sydney actually experienced downturns in the numbers of people visiting their other regular attractions during the period that the Games were taking place. The different responses from tourists are summarised in Table 9.7.

TABLE 9.7 Movements of visitors during Olympic Games time

Tourist types	Response
Olympians	Persons travelling to the host city specifically because of the Olympics
Extentioners	Tourists who would have visited the host city anyway but decided to stay longer because of the Olympics
Homestayers	Residents who decide to stay in the host city instead of taking a vacation elsewhere
Casuals	Tourists who visit the city, regardless of whether the Olympics are being hosted
Time-switchers	Tourists who want to visit the city but decide to travel at a time when the Olympics is NOT occurring
Changers	Residents who leave the city for a vacation, choosing to travel at the time the Olympics is occurring rather than at some other time
Runaways	Residents who leave the city to avoid the Olympics
Avoiders	Tourists who stay away – but would have come if the Olympics was not being hosted

Source: Adapted from Preuss, 2004

Even the belief that long-term tourism is boosted has been questioned. After 1992, Barcelona was shown to have slower growth in visitor numbers than either Prague or Dublin (all becoming popular short-break destinations), while, in the aftermath of the Sydney event, New Zealand attracted more visitors than Australia (possibly accounted for by the popularity of *Lord of the Rings*, however). Seoul and Sydney both experienced a drop in tourist numbers in the year following the Games. In short, these events will certainly help to put a destination on the map, but may not necessarily ensure significantly large increases in the numbers of visitors thereafter than would be anticipated without the Games. Rather than measuring the impact of tourism as a justification, countries might be better advised to concentrate on the benefits achieved by the reconstruction of impoverished areas. Athens in particular benefited from a vastly improved transport infrastructure. In both Athens and Sydney, however, the specially built venues have been severely under-utilised since the events were held there; attempting to avoid this led to London constructing several temporary venues, which were dismantled and relocated after the Games closed. The UK put great efforts into assuring the maximum success in driving tourism, both inbound and domestic, in 2012, and UK Sport has since estimated that the Olympics generated £19 billion in economic value to the UK economy in the five years following the Games (UK Sport, 2017).

SHOPPING

Shopping plays an important role in tourism. While retailing is not normally considered a sector of the industry, tourist purchases make up a considerable part of the revenue of many shops, and in resorts shops may be entirely or very largely dependent on the tourist trade. Shops selling postcards, souvenirs or local crafts are often geared specifically to the needs of visitors, and out of season may close down due to lack of demand.

Cross-border tourism is fuelled by shopping expeditions and, where large discrepancies in prices are noted on each side of the border, authorities often impose limits on purchases that can be transported back into the home country. For several years, the German and Austrian governments were concerned about cross-border shopping into Poland, the Czech and Slovak Republics and Hungary. Now that these countries have joined the EU, the concern has shifted, with the governments in those countries now being concerned about shopping expeditions into the Ukraine and Russian Federation (although an obligation to obtain a visa for entry into the Russian Federation acts as a hindrance). The EU's limit on the importation of goods from non-EU countries, long limited to £145, increased to £340 in 2009, with a further increase to £390 in 2010. When there is a weak dollar, however, goods bought in the USA may still be cheap, even after paying duty.

Tourist cities like London, Paris, Rome and New York owe much of their popularity to the quality of their shops. Large department stores like Saks Fifth Avenue and Bloomingdales in New York, Kaufhaus des Westens (KaDeWe) in Berlin (claiming to be the largest store in the world) and Harrods in London are heavily dependent on visitors spending their money with them, and of course expenditure on shopping is an important feature in the tourism balance of payments.

EXAMPLE

UNWTO views of shopping tourism

Shopping tourism has emerged as a growing component of the tourism product, and an important part of the tourist experience. The significance of this sector is recognised by the UNWTO, which, in 2014, produced a global report on shopping tourism. The report concludes that cities can use shopping tourism to:

(Continued)

- boost the appeal of the destination
- support economic growth
- where necessary, encourage urban regeneration or revitalisation.

The UNWTO report considers whether shopping drives tourism. Historically, tourists used to go sightseeing to visit the main cultural and natural attractions. Museums, galleries and events remain popular, but the report concludes that demand for retail experiences has strengthened.

Shopping tourism takes into account not only retail in large malls or department stores; it also includes informal shopping interactions with street vendors and hawkers, daily or festival street markets and village shops, many of which exist primarily to serve the local population.

Source: UNWTO, 2014

The downside in small towns popular with tourists is that shops with products appealing largely to tourists can squeeze out those serving the more basic needs of local residents, simply because the former can best afford spiralling rates and rents.

Increasingly, shopping is being combined with other forms of leisure in the development of shopping malls, which have become virtual mini-towns in their own right, attracting huge numbers of visitors prepared to pass several hours enjoying themselves in an environment that encourages people to spend. China contains some of the world's largest shopping malls (the South China Mall in Dongguan, said to be the world's largest, is over 6.4 million square feet in area, while the Golden Resources Mall in Beijing, at 6 million square feet, offers a landscape embracing theme parks, bridges, giant windmills, pyramids, artificial rivers and a copy of Paris' Arc de Triomphe). Those in the West are almost as impressive; for instance, the Mall of America, built in 1992 at Bloomington, Minneapolis, claims to be the second most visited site in the USA, with some 40 million visitors a year. At 4.2 million square feet and offering 500 shops, 45 restaurants, 14 cinemas, a seven-acre amusement park and a sea-life centre, the site provides everything that the leisure shopper could hope for. It attracts a global market and, most notably, brings in shoppers from both European and Asian cities. The enormous West Edmonton Mall in Canada, covering an area of 48 city blocks in downtown Edmonton, vies with this mall to draw consumers from all over the world, boasting more than 800 shops, 100 eating establishments, and nine themed attractions. There are two on-site hotels and events are mounted throughout the year.

Souvenirs

No study of tourist shopping would be complete without a look at the role of souvenirs – essential items for most visitors. The collection of souvenirs as mementos of one's visit has a long history. Certainly, both Greek and Roman tourists were noted for their collections of memorabilia from their journeys, and later, during the period of the Grand Tours, prestigious souvenirs collected by aristocratic travellers would invariably include Italian landscape paintings and archaeological 'finds'. Historians have commented on how souvenirs were collected from the earliest days of travel in North America, when 'items cut from local rock or wood, beaded moccasins, baskets and … miniature canoes' featured prominently (Löfgren, 1999: 86).

Today, we can divide souvenirs into two groups: mementos picked up by tourists (often of little value in themselves but representative of the sites visited) and those bought commercially from shops or local traders. The former includes items such as pebbles and shells collected on the beach, pressed flowers or leaves from jungles and parks, lava from volcanic eruptions or small shards of broken pottery that abound in places such as the area surrounding former Chinese emperors' tombs. For the most part, the collection of these items is harmless, although removing plants, flowers or seeds from parks and gardens is not an act to be encouraged; indeed, it is banned in areas where plants are under threat. Edelweiss in Switzerland and cacti in Arizona, for example, have been protected by laws in this way. Similar laws prevent the collection of rare stones or fossilised trees such as those found in the Petrified Forest in Arizona. It was not uncommon in earlier centuries for travellers to chisel off small chunks of stone from monuments such as Roman amphitheatres and the Egyptian Sphinx or, at the very least, to deface them with graffiti. In our more enlightened times, however, this practice is frowned on and diminishing.

Commercial souvenirs are not only essential items of shopping for many tourists but also for some, such as the Japanese, gifts are culturally obligatory; thus tourists buy souvenirs for themselves and for friends and relatives. This is one explanation for the relatively high spend of Japanese tourists abroad.

Some commercial souvenirs are bestowed on visitors without charge, such as the leis, garlands of flowers placed around the necks of visitors arriving in Hawaii (although mass tourism has resulted in the original flowers being largely superseded by plastic versions today). Visitors to China are often given small souvenirs of their visit, both while travelling within the country and when visiting sites such as the Great Wall of China.

The transmogrification of cheap baubles into indigenous craft items purchased by tourists as souvenirs is characteristic of recent tourism, exemplified by such items as straw donkeys and flamenco dolls from Spain, brass Eiffel Towers from Paris, straw hats from the Caribbean Islands or Bali and bamboo models of cormorant fishermen from China. While widely derided, these mementos still have a place in many tourists' homes, and in the minds and emotions of their purchasers they retain an association with the places from where they originated. The name 'airport art' is frequently used for such debased crafts, which are often on sale to tourists at airports, but the popularity of these items cannot be denied. They do also make a valuable contribution to the economies of the countries where they are purchased.

Finally, the significance of postcards as essential purchases while abroad should be noted. Since the advent of photography, the desire to send home pictures of destinations visited to family, friends and neighbours has become a well-established ritual, the motives for which have frequently been questioned. Whether for social contact, out of a sense of obligation to those less fortunate, to demonstrate one-upmanship or simply to inform, the drive to send cards is universal and, particularly among the developing countries, they are cherished by those receiving them, being pinned up on the walls of homes, offices and bars, signifying to others the possession of a wide circle of well-travelled friends. The permanence of a postcard is also part of its attraction and a consequence has been the introduction of phone applications which allow travellers to submit their images and text, which are then printed in postcard format and posted to the recipient.

EXAMPLE

Technology for personalised postcards

Although modern technology now allows us to send by e-mail or phone digital snaps taken on a mobile phone, there is something reassuring about the continuing popularity of the printed postcard; despite the likelihood that travellers will return home ahead of their postcards, in the UK 130 million postcards are sent each year.

Technology has now made it possible for holiday pictures to be taken on mobile phones and uploaded using specialist postcard apps such as Stannp and Touchnote. These companies print the image and message in the style of a postcard, mailing it directly to the recipient on behalf of the traveller. Because printing and posting frequently take place in the same country as the recipient, arrival is swifter than waiting for overseas post. However, one loss is the experience of receiving mail with international postage stamps.

GASTRONOMIC TOURISM

VisitBritain's research reveals that half of all visitors to the UK cite food and drink as being important to their holiday experience, and this is reinforced in Chapter 12, dealing with the hospitality sector. Of course, eating and drinking have always been part of the enjoyment of a holiday, enhancing it where the food and drink in question are exceptional and/or exotic, as is often the case on holidays abroad. The extent to which Britons have become more adventurous in their eating and drinking habits in their own country can be directly attributed to their experiences as tourists abroad. There are instances, however, where the food and drink become the principal purpose of the trip, whether a short break or longer holiday. The reputation of French food and drink, to take one example, has led to this becoming a key attraction for many tourists of that country. The importance of good, or at least reliable, cuisine abroad is often a priority concern, not least as a measure of health and safety.

Countries with well-established reputations for their food or drink have ensured that these attractions are promoted prominently in their tourism campaigns, whether informally or in the form of package tours. Enhanced awareness of good food has led to more flexibility in packages, allowing tourists to 'eat around', either in partner hotels or associated restaurants.

Stimulated by programmes on television, a much greater interest is taken today in preparing attractive and healthy meals. A number of leading chefs, particularly those having made their names on TV, have established cookery courses, and these attract gastronomy tourists from afar.

There is also a growing association between food and tourism within the UK; the days when sticks of rock and fish and chips were the best-known food products, and the quality of food served in hotels and restaurants was actually a disincentive to visit the country, are long gone. Michelin-starred restaurants, gastropubs, farmers' markets, even English wines, are now gaining a reputation among overseas visitors. Regional tourism bodies, in response, have not been slow to adopt food as an attraction in its own right. At various points in the recent history of tourism, authorities have promoted 'Taste of England/Wales/Scotland' campaigns, culminating in an 'Enjoy England, Taste England' promotion by VisitBritain that prominently features famous British chefs. Similarly, today, no museum or heritage attraction of any size is without its café and shop, many of the latter selling food products grown or manufactured locally, such as Pontefract cakes, Kendal mint cake and local ice-cream.

EXAMPLE

Will street food be banned in Bangkok?

Across Thailand's capital city, street vendors serve a variety of cheap street food; but there have been reports that Bangkok's governor, Wanlop Suwandee, planned to ban street vendors, as part of an initiative to provide improved pedestrian space. Sidewalks are often narrow, and street carts, as well as associated tables and chairs, mean those on foot may end up walking in the street. However, the announcement brought a wave of criticism. Khaosan Road, a street popular with international tourists, saw a daytime ban on stalls which left the area quiet. Gone were the food and souvenir stalls, along with some of the tourists who would have purchased from these vendors. It seems that the chaos of the unregulated street sellers is part of the appeal for visitors. Research has concluded that only about 10,000 street hawkers will remain following all the planned clearances, down from an estimated 240,000 previously selling food and other goods on the streets.

Source: Bemma, 2018; Punyaratabandhu, 2017

Many countries, including the UK, now promote food festivals as key events in the tourism calendar. This is discussed in further detail in Chapter 10.

MEDICAL TOURISM

An increasingly important form of tourism, centred almost exclusively on urban areas, is that undertaken for medical reasons. While health tourism has a long history and is linked to spa tourism (discussed later in this chapter), the term **medical tourism** is now being used to refer to tourists who travel to another country specifically to consult specialists or undergo medical treatment. It has been estimated that 11 million international trips ensured the global medical tourism industry was worth US$45 billion in 2016 (although it should be noted that the World Health Organization warns that most of the available data on medical travel is of poor quality).

British patients have sometimes been referred by the National Health Service for treatment in other EU countries, but others are seeking medical attention privately and often further afield. Private hospitals in Eastern Europe are now openly targeting patients in the UK who cannot afford private treatment in their own country, but could be persuaded to pay the lower fees charged abroad. It has to be acknowledged that British patients are being driven not only by cost but also by NHS waiting lists and quality of care. In addition to surgical treatment, cosmetic and dental treatments add significantly to the total medical tourism sector.

Germany and the USA are leading source markets, while Russia, France and Italy also have substantial numbers of outbound medical tourists. Large numbers of Austrians now travel abroad for treatment, particularly to Sopron in Hungary for dental treatment, and some towns on the Austro-Hungarian border now have economies based largely on dentistry. Many Danes travel to Szczecin in Poland for dental treatment, while the Finns visit Tallinn for eye tests and dental work.

Good medical treatment delivered promptly, cheaply and efficiently is appealing in cases where lengthy waiting lists for operations exist, such as for hip replacements. Over 50 countries actively promote medical tourism and, while accurate figures are difficult to obtain because few countries separate data related to the treatment of foreign nationals generally from those who have specifically travelled for medical tourism, leading medical tourism destinations are Thailand, Malaysia, Mexico, India, the UAE and, for wealthier tourists, Switzerland.

IVF treatment is promoted in medical centres in Kiev, Ukraine, cosmetic surgery in Venezuela, Brazil, Argentina and the UAE, while Budapest in Hungary and Cyprus promote dental treatment for visitors. Thailand, which, like Singapore, has a good record of Western medical training, offers private healthcare to medical tourists in Bangkok, Chiang Mai and Phuket, while South Africa attracts tourists for specialist cosmetic surgery. India has perhaps gone furthest, even taking a stand at the World Travel Market in London to promote its medical tourism. It offers specialist treatment at reasonable prices for dentistry, cosmetic surgery and alternative medicine such as Ayurveda. Organisations are now setting up package tours around such treatment, with accommodation at 4-star hotels included.

EXAMPLE

Medical tourism in Canada

Canada has a world-class government-funded healthcare system. However, many Canadians are now seeking medical treatment overseas, as long waiting lists and a shortage of doctors cause growing concern. Consequently, there is a small but growing market of Canadian travellers seeking medical treatment overseas. Common procedures for these medical tourists include joint replacements, eye surgery, fertility treatments and cosmetic surgery. Popular medical tourism destinations include Costa Rica, Thailand, Mexico and Barbados.

But this is not one-way traffic. Canadian hospitals have regularly treated international patients, although historically these have been on a case-by-case basis, usually addressing specialist issues, for example sick children. However, recently some Canadian hospitals have taken to openly promoting their services to an international market, partly in response to reduced government budgets. This has caused heated debate as Canadian residents fear the erosion of the public healthcare system and growing competition for medical attention, with the potential for ever-longer waiting lists.

Source: Euromonitor, 2014

SPA TOURISM

One important element of **wellness tourism** (now a more commonly used term for this sector of the industry) is treatment at spas. The term 'spa' is said to have originated from the town of that name in Belgium, although some claim that 'Sanitas Per Aqua' – health through water – is the true derivation of the term, which has been applied equally to resorts that provide healthy air (often mountain or seaside resorts) and others offering so-called 'healing' waters. Competing with Spa in Belgium are Vichy and Aix-les-Bains in France, Wildbad and Baden Baden in Germany, Karlovy Vary in the Czech Republic and Bath, Cheltenham, Harrogate, Scarborough and Buxton in the UK.

Back in the seventeenth century, Britain could boast more than 250 active spas. Some were surprisingly urban; Streatham Vale, for example, now a London suburb, was popular for its natural springs as early as 1659. By the twentieth century, though, their appeal had declined to a point where the final ten spa facilities, then under the control of hospitals, had their financial support withdrawn in 1976. The last publicly funded spa, Bath, closed in 1978, but following massive investment and prolonged delays it was re-opened in 2007 and has enjoyed considerable commercial success. Droitwich Spa has also lingered on, providing medical treatment in a private hospital with a small indoor brine bath.

On the Continent, spa tourism remains popular, with an estimated 1200 active spas, and the industry makes a valuable economic contribution to the GDP of several countries. In Germany, Hungary and the Czech and Slovak Republics, thermal treatment, in mud or mineral water baths, still plays an important role in healthcare. Italy's spas are also significant, with a large concentration around the Euganean Hills, south of Padua, notably at Albano Terme and Battaglia Terme, with some 200 hotels in the area being dedicated to the accommodation of spa visitors. North of Vicenza in the Dolomites, the spa town of Recoaro Terme has been noted since the eighteenth century for its mountain spring waters.

EXAMPLE

Health tourism in the EU

A research report for the Directorate-General for Internal Policies for the EU explored numerous aspects of health tourism in Europe. This report highlighted the overlap between wellness and spa tourism as well as the wider association these two sectors have with medical tourism. In particular, it noted the distinction between treatments for illness (which tend to be served by the medical tourism sector) and treatments to maintain or promote wellness (addressed by the wellness/spa tourism sector). The report accepted that some spa tourism also provides treatment for both medical and health components.

Access to spa treatments as part of a national healthcare system varies across the EU, with only Austria, Germany, Hungary and Italy including this in their provision to residents. Furthermore, restrictions on travelling cross-border have also been introduced; for example, no longer can Germans be reimbursed for their spa treatments if they have used spas in Italy or other EU countries.

Source: Mainil et al., 2017

In looking at wellness tourism, Europe dominates in terms of the total number of domestic and international trips (250 million), followed by the Asia Pacific region with 194 million (Global Wellness Institute, 2017). In this latter region, China is experiencing substantial growth in spa tourism, predominantly domestic trips, by an increasingly sophisticated younger generation.

Typical treatments at spa resorts include mud baths, hydrotherapy, saunas, mineral baths, steam baths and beauty treatments. The popularity of spas in other areas of the globe is also well established. More than $6 billion is spent annually at spas in the USA, with hotel resort spas representing two-thirds of total spa sales, while in Japan, onsen (hot springs) such as Ikaho and Shirahone thrive on tourism.

In the past, European spa treatments were often supported by the state health services, but escalating costs led to cutbacks. Nevertheless, some 15 million Europeans daily continue to immerse themselves in thermal waters, in the belief that 'the cure' will alleviate their ailments, and the spas of Europe reap the benefits of this belief.

In the UK, which once attracted many domestic tourists to its spa towns, medical experts became more sceptical about the health benefits of spas in the twentieth century. Recent evidence concerning those with osteoarthritis and osteoporosis, and a growing interest in alternative medicine generally, are causing some medical experts to re-evaluate their former views, which is encouraging some former spas to reopen.

As previously mentioned, much of the research regarding spa tourism is delivered under the banner of health and wellness, a sector that also includes medical tourism. There is also analysis of balneology – the treatment of illness and disease through bathing – which is practised at spa resorts. The European Spas Association (ESPA), representing members from 19 countries, works to promote spas and balneology in Europe. National organisations with an interest in spa tourism include the China Hot Springs Association, the Bulgarian Union for Balneology & Spa Tourism (BUBSPA) and the Hungarian Spa Tourism Association.

DARK TOURISM

The beauty of tourism is that the number of products that can be devised to interest tourists is virtually unlimited. One reads regularly in the press of new ideas that have been promoted, of new, and frequently bizarre, reasons tourists advance for visiting a site. Perhaps our ideas of what it is appropriate to see have changed a little since the nineteenth century, when in England people would travel considerable distances to watch public hangings, and in the USA Coney Island's amusement park displayed 300 dwarfs in 'Midget City' and publicly electrocuted Topsy, a performing elephant, as a tourist attraction.

Although such things would not be sanctioned today, there remains, nonetheless, a fascination, at times bordering on the macabre, with observing scenes such as those exploiting sudden and violent death. Rojek (1993) identifies these as 'black-spots' as he describes the flood of people who came to Scotland to see the scene of the Pan American Airlines crash at Lockerbie in 1988. Similarly, Gray Line offered Hurricane Katrina tours in New Orleans following the disastrous flooding of the city, and the reconstructed area of Ground Zero (the site of the 9/11 attack on New York's Twin Towers) in 2001 is now firmly on the tourist circuit.

The terms **thanatourism** (Seaton, 1996) and, more commonly, **dark tourism** (Lennon and Foley, 2000) have been used to describe such tourists' fascination with death and the macabre. Motives for this may be thought questionable, although travel to 'dark' sites cannot necessarily be ascribed to gratuitous pleasure. Dachau Concentration Camp Memorial Site near Munich in Germany is visited by approximately 800,000 visitors annually, while the Auschwitz-Birkenau memorial, near Krakow, Poland, received more than 2 million tourists in 2017. While the proximity of these sites to major tourist cities may mean a convenient day trip experience stimulating high attendance numbers, for some these visits can take the form of a pilgrimage, while for others the visit is linked to historical interest.

Places associated with the deaths of major celebrities also attract more than their fair share of curious observers. Jim Morrison's tomb at Père-Lachaise cemetery in Paris is said to be the most-visited grave in the cemetery, while those of Oscar Wilde, Edith Piaf, Marcel Proust and other representatives of 'high culture' draw far fewer visitors. The outbuilding in Seattle where Kurt Cobain, of the band Nirvana, committed suicide in 1994 was torn down, but the site is still visited by hundreds of admirers. Graves which, to this day, receive significant numbers of visitors include those of:

- Frank Sinatra (died 1998) – Desert Memorial Park, Palm Springs, CA
- Princess Diana (died 1997) – Althorp Estate, Hampshire, UK
- Elvis Presley (died 1977) – Graceland, Memphis, TN
- Bruce Lee (died 1973) – Lakeview Cemetery, Seattle, WA
- Marilyn Monroe (died 1962) – Westwood Memorial Park, Los Angeles, CA
- Mark Twain (died 1910) – Woodlawn Cemetery, Elmira, NY
- William Shakespeare (died 1616) – Stratford-upon-Avon, Warwickshire, UK.

Whatever the merits or otherwise of dark tourism, the quest for the bizarre features ever more prominently in lists of tourists' motivations. Sometimes this is a reflection of the desire for ever more dangerous activities, particularly among younger tourists. A press listing of the most dangerous streets in the world led to a flurry of interest in visiting those at Snake Alley, Taipei, Khao San Road, Bangkok, Tverskaya Ulitsa, Moscow, and King's Cross, Sydney, while a book appeared in 2006 directing potential tourists to the worst places in the world to visit (Cohen, 2006). *The Sunday Times* (Byrne, 1997) coined the term **terror tourism** to describe the growing trend for tourists to plan visits to countries beset by political disturbances or even civil war. Following the initial end to hostilities in Afghanistan and Iraq, specialist tour operators were quick to arrange visits to those countries for the more adventurous – or foolhardy – in spite of government warnings of the potential dangers, and difficulties faced by those booking in obtaining travel insurance. The problem for the industry is to judge whether such tourist attractions are educationally valuable or merely satisfy the prurient interests of the spectators. Indeed, the very term 'visitor attraction' when applied to sites such as these raises questions. Are visitors expecting to be entertained or does this desire arise from some deeper psychosis in modern society?

EXAMPLE

The nuclear tourist

In 2011, Chernobyl, site of the disastrous nuclear reactor meltdown of 1986, was officially declared a 'tourist attraction'. Visits can now be arranged to abandoned villages like Zalesye and Pripyat (a deserted town which formerly boasted a population of 50,000). Curiosity, and perhaps the sense of adventure through the potential danger of radiation poisoning, plays a part in the attraction of such tours.

In the same way, US visitors travel to Stallion Gate in New Mexico to see Trinity site, where the first atomic bomb was detonated. There are regular tours to the Nevada test site which book up months ahead. Again, the attraction is possible (although largely hypothetical) danger, although doses of radioactivity at the site are, apart from a few avoided hot spots, now less than would be experienced in a single long-haul flight.

Source: Johnson, 2014

The UK has not been slow to trade on the attraction of dark tourism sites, either. Among World War II sites currently open to tourists or being groomed as future sites, one can include the Eden Prisoner-of-War Camp at Malton, North Yorkshire, where some 30

World War II huts house displays commemorating events during the war; air raid shelters in Stockport; the former secret nuclear bunker at Kelvedon Hatch in Essex (which receives 60,000 visitors a year); Hack Green nuclear bunker near Nantwich; and the bunker built during the 1950s near St Andrews, Scotland, to house the regional government in the event of a nuclear war. Also, National Park rangers regularly lead guided walks to the sites of 60 crashed World War II planes in the Peak District. In Belfast, tours are operated to former Northern Ireland trouble spots, including the Falls Road, Shankill Road and the Peace Wall. Numerous museums and attractions that focus on aspects of the Holocaust exist, including the United States Holocaust Memorial Museum in Washington, the Anne Frank House in Amsterdam, Yad Vashem in Israel and an exhibition as part of the Imperial War Museum in London.

Certainly, visits to sites of this nature can be illuminating and instructive, if not entertaining in the traditional sense of the word. Some sites, however, have been heavily restored – perhaps over-restored (as at the Auschwitz-Birkenau death camp, where the original gate and ovens have been replaced with replicas). The extent to which interpretation at such sites is objective is also always open to question, depending as it does on the political colour and viewpoint of the day and those presenting the data. At another death camp, in Buchenwald, Bauhaus university students were recently recruited to design souvenirs and memorabilia to be sold at the site to raise money for its preservation. The intentions were doubtless good, but many critics described the move as 'disrespectful'.

THE SCOPE FOR INNOVATIVE TOURISM

Dark tourism is not always macabre but it can be bizarre, and some examples are of genuine educational interest or may be merely designed to entertain. Here are some of the more curious tourist attractions (not all of them considered 'dark') currently on offer, whether banal, bizarre or both:

- Take a self-guided tour of Adelaide's West Terrace cemetery, which reveals the stories behind the famous and the everyday citizens buried there.
- Corpses displayed as tourist attractions. Perfectly preserved bodies retrieved from bogs in Denmark are on display in museums at Silkeborg and Moesgaard.
- China has opened the site of a hitherto secret armaments factory to allow tourists to practise on the firing range with rocket launchers and anti-aircraft guns. The tour is particularly popular with Americans and Japanese.
- A tour of the nineteenth-century sewers of Paris.
- Walking tours across the arches of Sydney Harbour Bridge have proved immensely popular. A jumpsuit and safety cable are obligatory accompaniments. So successful have these tours been that they have been emulated on bridges in Brisbane and Auckland. In the USA, the Purple People Bridge between Cincinnati, Ohio and Newport, Kentucky – the longest pedestrian bridge in the USA, across the Ohio River – offers the more adventurous an opportunity to don harnesses and climb onto the upper trestles of the bridge, from where they walk out onto a glass floor above the river. The former Millennium Dome building in London has also introduced an attraction, Up at the O2, which allows tourists to walk across the roof of this iconic attraction.
- Two-hour guided tours are on offer in Berlin's red light district, with off-duty prostitutes acting as tour guides. They will answer clients' questions on all aspects of the city, including their own activities.
- In Palermo, Sicily, tourists can be taken on tours to sites associated with the local Mafia, including a visit to a former Godfather's torture chamber.

- Many domestic tourists in the Philippines are attracted to the annual rite of Catholic fanaticism at San Pedro Cutud, where volunteers undergo crucifixion.
- Omanis visit Salalah, on the southern tip of Oman, between June and September each year because of the unusual rainfall in the monsoon season. This is the only area of the Arabian Gulf so affected. Perhaps the only example of rain attracting tourists?
- On a lighter note, in June each year, the Festa do São João in Oporto, Portugal, encourages participants to hit each other over the head with plastic hammers. Overseas tourists are now making enquiries about joining in the fun.

EXAMPLE

Volcano tourists

Special tours and cruises are arranged for visitors to approach active or recently active volcanoes. These include sites in Ecuador, Sicily, Crete, Nicaragua, Iceland and the Azores. The death of more than 40 visitors who were walking on Mount Ontake volcano, Japan, when it erupted unexpectedly in 2014, is unlikely to significantly stem the popularity of such activities.

A report by the Royal Geographic Society warns that emergency services called to assist in the wake of an eruption now have to contend with an influx of visitors trying to experience the heat, smell and sight of this natural spectacle. These tourists then become vulnerable, with the chance of being hit by rocks, inhaling poisonous gases and other threats affecting the safety of both themselves and the emergency services.

Source: Coughlan, 2018

Hoteliers are noted entrepreneurs, and some hotels attract tourists because of the bizarre form of their accommodation. In the USA, tourists can stay at a former research laboratory; while the world's first underwater hotel, Jules' Undersea Lodge at John Pennecamp Coral Reef State Park in Key Largo, Florida, accommodates swimmers only, as guests need to make a 21-foot dive to access the entrance! Tourists can also bed down in railway cabooses at the Featherbed Railroad Company in Nice, California, spend a night in the cell block at the Jailhouse Inn in Preston, Minnesota, or sleep underground in the Honeycombs at the Inn at Honey Run, Millersburg, Ohio. Lower Saxony in Germany offers Hay Hotels, where sleeping bags in hay are provided for visitors. The hotels are said to be popular with cycling tourists, and others have been opened in Poland, Denmark, Italy and the Czech Republic.

EXAMPLE

A topsy-turvy world

In 2010, Gettorf Zoo, in Germany, constructed a wooden house to attract tourists. The unusual thing about this house is that the building, and all the interior fixtures and fittings, including the furniture, is upside down.

(Continued)

This is by no means the first attempt to attract tourists by offering a different perspective on the world. Upside-down houses have previously been opened to tourists in Trassenheide, Germany, Symbark, Poland (see Figure 9.7) and Antalya, Turkey. There are also amusement parks built into upturned venues; for example, the House of Katmandu in Mallorca and Wonderworks in Florida. In 2014, an upside-down house, constructed in a suburb of Shanghai, China, immediately proved popular with tourists.

FIGURE 9.7 Upside-down house in Symbark, Poland

Photo: Shutterstock

SUMMARY

Throughout this chapter, we have discussed the many different attractions that can encourage tourists to visit both popular tourist destinations and less usual places. Effectively marketed, bizarre sites can draw tourists from quite a distance. Although there are too many different types of attraction to discuss them all in detail in such a text, we have highlighted the fact that some attractions, including heritage buildings and natural landscapes, form the basis of much of the appeal of many locations. Many attractions also arrange and promote events, which further add to their appeal. The use of events to attract tourism is discussed in more detail in Chapter 10.

The attractiveness of a destination may be influenced by a variety of factors, some of which may be outside of the control of destination managers; for instance, popularity caused by being the setting for a film or a book, the infamy caused by a tragic event or the sudden rise in success as a gastronomic restaurant is awarded a treasured Michelin star. Alternatively, demand may wane if there is a lack of investment in new attractions, a requirement if repeat visitors are to be encouraged. That is not to say that all destinations may lose their appeal without investment. Some attractions are considered to be a 'must-see' and therefore will always draw tourists, providing other factors such as access and the amenities to support a visit are in place.

QUESTIONS AND DISCUSSION POINTS

1. In this chapter, some examples of tourist attractions at modern industrial operations, such as car manufacturing plants, were identified. Why might tourists decide to visit such places?
2. From a tourism perspective, what are the advantages and disadvantages that should be considered by a city bidding to host a major sporting event, such as the Olympics?
3. Many battlefield sites are visited by tourists. Do you think it is acceptable that such places become tourist attractions?

TASKS

1. Visit a tourist attraction in your local area. Using images and video collected at the attraction, create a short documentary that explains why people would be motivated to visit this attraction.
2. Select one of the major theme park companies identified in Table 9.6. Write an appraisal of the selected enterprise, considering the markets it targets, the themes it employs and any future plans it may have for its parks.

FURTHER READING

Clavé, S. A. (2007) *The Global Theme Park Industry*. Wallingford: CABI.

Frost, W. (2010) *Zoos and Tourism*. Bristol: Channel View Publications.

Hughes, H. and Duchaine, J. (2012) *Frommer's 500 Places to See Before They Disappear*, 2nd edn. Hoboken, NJ: Wiley Publishing.

Jencks, C. (2005) *The Iconic Building: The power of enigma*. London: Frances Lincoln.

Sharpley, R. and Stone, P. R. (2009) *The Darker Side of Travel*. Bristol: Channel View Publications.

UK Film Council (2007) *How Film and Television Programmes Promote Tourism in the UK*. London: UK Film Council.

WEBSITES

Association of Leading Visitor Attractions: www.alva.org.uk

European Spas Association: www.espa-ehv.eu

Historic Houses Association: www.hha.org.uk

Merlin Entertainment: www.merlinentertainments.biz

National Piers Society: https://piers.org.uk

VisitBritain, unusual attractions: www.visitbritain.com/en/Things-to-do/Secret-Britain

REFERENCES

AECOM (2017) *Global Attractions Attendance Report*. Burbank, CA: Themed Entertainment Association (TEA). Available online at: www.aecom.com/content/wp-content/uploads/2018/05/2017-Theme-Museum-Index.pdf [Accessed January 2019].

Association of Leading Visitor Attractions (ALVA) (2017) *Visit Made in 2017 to Visitor Attractions in Membership with ALVA*. Available online at: www.alva.org.uk/details.cfm?p=608 [Accessed January 2019].

Bemma, A. (2018) *Thai Street Food Sellers Battle Bangkok's Clearance Campaign*. Available online at: www.aljazeera.com/indepth/features/thai-street-food-sellers-battle-bangkok-clearance-campaign-181021072146310.html [Accessed January 2019].

Binney, M. (2004) A guide to wonders of the modern world worth visiting. *The Times*, 10 May.

Boniface, P. and Cooper, C. (2001) *Worldwide Destinations: The geography of travel and tourism*, 3rd edn. Oxford: Butterworth-Heinemann.

Byrne, C. (1997) Terror tourists queue up for trips to war zones. *The Sunday Times*, 16 March.

Cohen, M. (2006) *No Holiday: 80 places you don't want to visit*. New York: The Disinformation.

Coughlan, S. (2018) Warning against 'volcano tourism' risks. BBC, 20 December.

Dewhurst, P. D. and Dewhurst, H. (2006) Visitor attractions management. In J. Beech and S. Chadwick (eds), *The Business of Tourism Management*. London: Prentice Hall, pp. 287–303.

Duff, A. (2009) *Unlocking the Potential of Church Tourism*. Available online at: http://cvta.org.uk/wp-content/uploads/2014/11/insights_church_tourism.pdf [Accessed January 2019].

Edelheim, J. R. (2015) *Tourist Attractions: From object to narrative*. Bristol: Channel View Publications.

Euromonitor (2014) *Opportunities and Caveats of Medical Tourism in Canada*. London: Euromonitor.

Euromonitor (2018) *Leading Visitor Attractions*. London: Euromonitor.

Frey, B. S. and Steiner, L. (2012) Pay as you go: A new proposal for museum pricing. *Museum Management and Curatorship*, 27, 223–35.

Global Wellness Institute (2017) *Global Wellness Economy Monitor*. Available online at: https://globalwellnessinstitute.org/wp-content/uploads/2018/06/GWI_WellnessEconomyMonitor2017_FINALweb.pdf [Accessed January 2019].

Hinch, T. and Higham, J. (2011) *Sport Tourism Development*, 2nd edn. Bristol: Channel View Publications.

ICOMOS (2014) *Tomioka Silk Mill (Japan)*. Charenton-le-Pont, France: ICOMOS.

Inskeep, E. (1991) *Tourism Planning: An integrated and sustainable development approach*. New York: John Wiley & Sons.

Japan News (2018) Local businesses band together to make an entire town a hotel. *Otemachi: The Yomiuri Shimbun*, 26 December.

JiJi Press (2014) Tomioka silk mill seen shoring up local tourism. *English News Service*, 4 May.

Johnson, G. (2014) *The Nuclear Tourist*. Washington: National Geographic, October, pp. 122–35.

Leask, A. (2008) The nature and role of visitor attractions. In A. Fyall, B. Garrod, A. Leask and S. Wanhill (eds), *Managing Visitor Attractions: New directions*. Oxford: Butterworth-Heinemann, pp. 3–15.

Lennon, J. and Foley, M. (2000) *Dark Tourism: The attraction of death and disaster*. London: Continuum.

Löfgren, O. (1999) *On Holiday: A history of vacationing*. Berkeley, CA: University of California Press.

Mainil, T., Eijgelaar, E., Klijs, J., Nawijn, J. and Peeters, P. (2017) *Research for TRAN Committee – Health tourism in the EU: A general investigation*. Brussels: European Parliament, Policy Department for Structural and Cohesion Policies.

National Piers Society (2014) *History of Herne Bay Pier*. Available online at: www.piers.org.uk/pierpages/NPShernebay.html [Accessed 21 October].

Preuss, H. (2004) *The Economics of Staging the Olympics: A comparison of the Games, 1972–2008*. Cheltenham: Edward Elgar Publishing.

Punyaratabandhu, L. (2017) *Is Bangkok Really Banning Street Food?* Available online at: https://edition.cnn.com/travel/article/bangkok-street-food-ban/index.html [Accessed January 2019].

Puvaneswary, S. (2019) *Buddhism tourism potential deserves more attention*. Singapore: TTG Asia, 21 January.

Richards, G. (2011) *Cultural Tourism: Global and local perspectives*. Binghamton, NY: Haworth Press.

Rojek, C. (1993) *Ways of Escape: Modern transformation in leisure and travel*. Basingstoke: Macmillan.

RSS Nepal (2019) *Buddhist International Travel Mart Kicks off in Lumbini*. Kathmandu: Rastriya Samachar Samiti, 11 January.

Seaton, A. V. (1996) Guided by the dark: From thanatopsis to thanatourism. *International Journal of Heritage Studies*, 2 (4), 234–44.

Smith, M. K. (2016) *Issues in Cultural Tourism Studies*, 3rd edn. Abingdon: Routledge.

Swarbrooke, J. (2002) *The Development and Management of Visitor Attractions*, 2nd edn. Oxford: Butterworth-Heinemann.

UK Sport (2017) Olympic and Paralympic Sports Worth £19bn to UK Economy. Available online at: www.uksport.gov.uk/news/2017/11/09/olympic-and-paralympic-sports-worth-19bn-to-uk-economy [Accessed January 2019]

United Nations World Tourism Organization (UNWTO) (2014) *Global Report on Shopping Tourism*. Madrid: UNWTO. Available online at: http://affiliatemembers.unwto.org/publication/global-report-shopping-tourism [Accessed January 2019].

Weaver, D. and Lawton, L. (2002) *Tourism Management*, 2nd edn. Milton: John Wiley.

Weed, M. and Bull, C. (2009) *Sports Tourism: Participants, policy and providers*, 2nd edn. Oxford: Elsevier/Butterworth-Heinemann.

10

EVENT TOURISM

CONTENTS

LEARNING OUTCOMES

After studying this chapter, you should be able to:

- explain the concept of event tourism
- distinguish between different categories of event
- understand why destinations are using events as part of their tourism strategy
- identify issues that may influence the future of event tourism.

> Festivals and events are increasingly used strategically to help define and brand places. Hallmark events give identity and positive image to their host community while venues and resorts can also have their hallmark events. (Getz, 2007: 21)

INTRODUCTION: DEFINING EVENT TOURISM

Tourists will often visit a place in order to participate in, or observe, an event. In some cases, the events occur regularly and with some frequency (for example, the Changing of the Guard in London). In others, the events are intermittent, perhaps annually or even less. Examples include arts festivals (the Venice Bienniale occurs every two years), sports events (the Olympic Games is held every four years) and the Floriade flower festival, which takes place in or near a different Dutch city every decade, and in 2012 was held at Venlo (and is due to be held in Almere in 2022). In other cases, there may be ad hoc arrangements to take advantage of a particular occasion. Such arrangements can last for as little as a few hours (a Christmas pageant or street festival, say) or many months (events associated with the cities of culture award or those organised around a historic anniversary, such as Maritime Britain, commemorating the bicentennial anniversary of the Battle of Trafalgar in 1805).

Travel to attend an event (thus **event tourism**) has a long-standing history, but only within the past 40 years has attention focused on using events strategically to develop a tourist destination. The OECD, in their analysis of major events, acknowledged the synergies between the fast-growing events sector and the wider tourism industry (OECD, 2017), and the term event tourism has become widely used in academia since the late 1980s. Since the start of this century, event tourism has grown in importance as 'governments are increasingly utilising events as vehicles for regional development as they continue to demonstrate a capacity to generate positive commercial outcomes for the host regions' (Whitford, 2009: 674).

The effective management of events is vital to their commercial success and to ensuring that events achieve their stated goals. Consequently, there have been numerous academic texts published dealing with this subject, arguably the most notable being those of Bowdin et al. (2012) and Rutherford Silvers (2012). This chapter, however, is not seeking to explain the detailed processes inherent in successful event management, but rather to explore the use of events as a goal in enhancing tourism. It gives particular emphasis to the use of events as part of destination-management strategies. Events are valued by tourism authorities for their appeal as attractions as well as their ability to act as animators of the destination, as image makers and place marketers, as well as their ability to act as catalysts for economic development and in some cases physical and social regeneration (Getz, 2008).

One dictionary defines an 'event' as 'A thing that happens. The fact of a thing's occurring. A result or outcome. An item in a sports programme, or the programme as a whole' (Oxford English Dictionary, 1996: 337). It can be concluded from this that events are both an occurrence and an outcome. One principle applying to events is that they are temporary in nature, with a start point and an end point (Bowdin et al., 2012). Consequently, it is somewhat challenging to distinguish between attractions that operate to the schedule of tourists – for example, a glass-blower providing a display of their skills when tourists arrive as part of a coach tour – and events that operate to a pre-determined schedule, regardless of the arrival timings of tourists. Of course, many attractions schedule events (such as exhibitions) as part of their offering, meaning that there is substantial overlap between the attractions and events sectors.

In defining events, numerous researchers have considered categorisation both by size and by form. When considering event size, it is possible to distinguish between small local or community events, larger major or hallmark events (which by their scale are likely to attract a wider audience and some media interest) and 'mega-events' (which are so large that they attract international media attention and audiences). Using form (or content) has challenges, particularly in trying to fit the many different types of event in existence today into a manageable number of categories. In an attempt to be all-encompassing, three categories – cultural, sports and business events – have been used to create broad groups (Bowdin et al., 2012). To extend understanding of this categorisation, Getz (2005) identified sub-categories for each (Table 10.1). Interestingly, in attempting to span all events, Getz felt the need to reference a separate category, 'Private Events', which encompassed such things as weddings, parties and social occasions.

TABLE 10.1 Typology of planned events

Cultural events	Sports events	Business events
Cultural celebrations: festivals, carnivals, commemorations, religious events	Competitions: amateur/professional, spectator/participant	Business and trade: meetings, conventions, consumer and trade shows, fairs and markets
Political and state: summits, royal occasions, political events, VIP visits	Recreational: sport and games for fun	Educational and scientific: conferences, seminars, clinics
Arts and entertainment: concerts, award ceremonies		

Source: Getz, 2005

With so many different types of event, it is no surprise to learn that the event industry today is vast, with one study estimating that in the UK today events are worth £41 billion and account for around 35% of the visitor economy (BVEP, 2017). Thus, events as a subset of the visitor economy are clearly established; the OECD concluded that 'events (sporting, cultural, business, etc.) are an increasingly important motivator for tourism' (2017: 4). We will go on to explore the different types of event tourism in more detail.

FORMS OF EVENT TOURISM

As previously mentioned, Bowdin et al. (2012) identified three forms of events – cultural, sports and business events. The value of the events industry in the UK is estimated to be around £41 billion (BVEP, 2017), of which business events make by far the largest contribution:

- conferences and meetings – £19.2 billion
- UK exhibitions and trade shows – £11 billion
- global exhibitions by UK organisers – £2 billion
- incentive travel and performance improvement – £1.2 billion
- sporting events – £2.3 billion
- corporate hospitality – £1.2 billion
- music events – £2.3 billion

- outdoor events – £1.1 billion
- festivals and cultural events – £1.1 billion.

BUSINESS EVENTS

As the largest sector, business events include such things as meetings, conferences, exhibitions and trade shows. Such is its scale that this sector, under the broader heading of business tourism, is discussed in detail in Chapter 11. Consequently, we will give limited attention to the business events sector in this chapter, focusing instead on cultural and sporting events.

CULTURAL EVENTS

The sheer volume and variety of cultural events taking place around the world is enormous. Even sites as inhospitable as the Arctic in winter can attract visitors with the appropriate events. In Kemi and Rovaniemi, Finland (both close to the Arctic Circle), an annual Snow Show includes art installations created by leading sculptors, as well as snowmobile and husky riding, while visitors can stay at the Snow Castle, an ice hotel. Staging events in winter to bring in the off-season market is increasingly apparent. Throughout Europe, Christmas markets, a concept that originated in Germany and is still immensely popular there, have spread to a point where numerous similar markets are now organised in towns and cities across the UK and Northern Europe.

EXAMPLE

Christmas markets

Cities across Germany host Christmas markets which attract both local and international visitors. The markets offer handicrafts and Christmas decorations as well as locally produced food and drink. Berlin offers multiple Christmas markets, selling products such as hand-carved furnishings, blown-glass ornaments and unique ceramics. Activities include puppeteers, storytellers, a petting zoo and fairground rides, a toboggan run and ice rinks.

Many cities across Europe host Christmas markets. In France, Strasbourg lays claim to the oldest Christmas market, dating back to the sixteenth century, and today some 300 stalls occupy more than a dozen city squares. London now hosts several winter markets as well as a winter wonderland-themed attraction in Hyde Park, which includes a circus and an ice rink alongside more traditional catering provided as an element of Bavarian village life.

Anniversaries are a crucial catalyst, whether the anniversary is of a past event, as in Trafalgar, or the birth or death of famous figures from the past. Tourism authorities will invariably look towards the 50th or 60th anniversaries or beyond and plan suitable events up to five years in advance. The 60th anniversary of the ending of World War II in 2005 is a case in point, and it was exploited to the full both commercially and politically. The centenary of the start and end of World War I in 2014 and 2018 led to several commemorative events being held across Europe. State events are also cause for celebration; the UK government announced an additional state holiday to mark the Queen's Diamond Jubilee in 2012.

If a centenary or even greater anniversary is involved, and the individual concerned was internationally famous, this provides an excuse for holding a major festival in their home town or country to attract foreign tourists. The 250th anniversary of Mozart's death in 2006, for example, offered scope for worldwide celebrations, not least in his home town of Salzburg.

Some destinations may attract tourists because of cultural or historic events that have occurred there in the past. In most cases, the destination is the permanent base for the event but in some cases the event may be peripatetic, in that it moves location for each celebration of the event. Peripatetic events include the Olympics, World Expos and European Capitals of Culture.

European Capitals of Culture

The EU boosts tourism to certain cities each year that can claim a strong cultural basis by awarding them the title **European Capital of Culture**. It has been offered to two cities each year since 2007 – exceptionally, three in 2010 – with each member country selected in turn for the honour. This award ensures that the chosen towns make substantial investment in infrastructure and superstructure in anticipation of the resulting increased tourist flows during the year of the award and for many years following. In 2008, Liverpool in England (along with Stavanger in Norway) was awarded the title. A diversity of interesting events led to success for the city, with visitor numbers increasing from 63 million to 75 million that year (with day visitors increasing by 20% and staying visitors up by 6%), while the value of tourism to Liverpool's economy rose by 25% (Northwest RDA, 2010). Prior to Liverpool's designation in 2008, the UK last received the award in 1990, when Glasgow gained the title. The city enjoyed a substantial boost in tourism as a result of the designation and it was estimated that the award brought in some £2.5 billion in extra investment, a significant rise in hotel rooms and an increase in the number of tourism-related jobs to some 55,000. Above all, it changed the perception of Glasgow as a dirty, economically depressed city for all time.

The past capitals of culture are shown in Table 10.2. Beyond 2022, the countries to be represented have been identified (Table 10.3) but the specific towns or cities have yet to be selected. What it is important to note when looking at this list of cities is that as time has progressed, so cities that have won the nomination are less likely to be capital cities. For cities less prominent on the international tourist stage, bidding for – and winning – the right to host this event can provide opportunities for their cultural offering to be promoted to a wider audience.

TABLE 10.2 European Capitals of Culture, 1985–2022

Year	City	Year	City
1985	Athens	1995	Luxembourg
1986	Florence	1996	Copenhagen
1987	Amsterdam	1997	Thessaloniki
1988	Berlin	1998	Stockholm
1989	Paris	1999	Weimar
1990	Glasgow	2000	Avignon, Bergen, Bologna, Brussels, Helsinki, Krakow, Reykjavik, Prague, Santiago de Compostela
1991	Dublin	2001	Porto and Rotterdam
1992	Madrid	2002	Bruges and Salamanca
1993	Antwerp	2003	Graz
1994	Lisbon	2004	Genoa and Lille

(Continued)

TABLE 10.2 (Continued)

Year	City	Year	City
2005	Cork	2014	Umeå, Sweden and Riga, Latvia
2006	Patras	2015	Mons, Belgium and Plzeň, Czech Republic
2007	Luxembourg and Sibiu	2016	San Sebastián, Spain and Wrocław, Poland
2008	Liverpool and Stavanger	2017	Aarhus, Denmark and Paphos, Cyprus
2009	Linz, Austria and Vilnius, Lithuania	2018	Leeuwarden, the Netherlands and Valetta, Malta
2010	Essen, Germany, Pecs, Hungary and Istanbul, Turkey	2019	Matera, Italy and Plovdiv, Bulgaria
2011	Turku, Finland and Tallinn, Estonia	2020	Rijeka, Croatia and Galway, Ireland
2012	Guimarães, Portugal and Maribor, Slovenia	2021	Timișoara, Romania, Elefsina, Greece (and Novi Sad, Serbia as EU candidate country)
2013	Marseille, France and Kosice, Slovakia	2022	Kaunas, Lithuania and Esch, Luxembourg

Currently, 2023 sees only Hungary as an allocated country for the nomination of a Capital of Culture city. This is because although the UK was scheduled to nominate a city at that time, one result of Brexit was that the UK was removed from the rotation by the European Commission. This was not without some anger in the UK, as five UK candidate cities had spent not insignificant amounts of time and money on putting together detailed bids (BBC, 2017).

TABLE 10.3 Countries allocated European Capitals of Culture, 2023–33

Year	Countries allocated European Capitals of Culture
2023	Hungary
2024	Estonia and Austria
2025	Slovenia and Germany
2026	Slovakia and Finland
2027	Latvia and Portugal
2028	Czech Republic and France
2029	Poland and Sweden
2030	Cyprus and Belgium
2031	Malta and Spain
2032	Bulgaria and Denmark
2033	The Netherlands and Italy

Source: EC, 2012

Efforts to emulate the concept in the Americas, supported by the Organization of American States, have been frustrated by the financial basis for awards, in which regions are expected to put up funds in advance. UNESCO also sponsors the title of Arab Cultural Capital. While Sirte, Libya was nominated for 2011, the political unrest between the Gaddafi government and rebel forces effectively ruled out any cultural promotion. Baghdad similarly experienced challenges in developing a successful cultural programme. To date, neither the American nor the Arab Capital of Culture awards appear to have developed either the publicity or the economic benefits achieved through the European award. American and Arab Capitals of Culture are listed in Table 10.4.

TABLE 10.4 American and Arab Capitals of Culture

Year	American Capitals of Culture	Arab Capitals of Culture
1996	–	Cairo, Egypt
1997	–	Tunis, Tunisia
1998	–	Sharjah, UAE
1999	–	Beirut, Lebanon
2000	Mérida, Mexico	Riyadh, Saudi Arabia
2001	Iquique, Chile	Kuwait City, Kuwait
2002	Maceió, Brazil	Amman, Jordan
2003	Panama City, Panama and Curitiba, Brazil	Rabat, Morocco
2004	Santiago, Chile	Sana'a, Yemen
2005	Guadalajara, Mexico	Khartoum, Sudan
2006	Cordoba, Argentina	Muscat, Oman
2007	Cuzco, Peru	Algiers, Algeria
2008	Brasilia, Brazil	Damascus, Syria
2009	Asunción, Paraguay	Jerusalem, Palestine
2010	Santo Domingo, Dominican Republic	Doha, Qatar
2011	Quito, Ecuador	Sirte, Libya
2012	São Luís, Brazil	Manama, Bahrain
2013	Barranquilla	Baghdad, Iraq
2014	Colima, Mexico	Tripoli, Libya
2015	Mayagüez, Puerto Rico	Constantine, Algeria
2016	Valdivia, Chile	Sfax, Tunisia
2017	Mérida, Mexico	Luxor, Egypt
2018	Anzoátegui, Venezuela	Oujda, Morocco

EXAMPLE

Quito invests in culture

The Ecuadorian capital, awarded the city of culture in 2011, implemented a $200 million facelift over a seven-year investment programme, encouraged also by celebrations of the 30th anniversary of the award of UNESCO heritage city status.

During the year, a wide variety of concerts, festivals, food fairs and exhibitions took place in the theatres and museums in the city. These were themed across the year, with the first three months focusing on cultural differences, the next quarter themed for religious heritage, the third quarter considering nature and the final three months themed around ancestors, folk and popular culture.

Art festivals and music events

Arts festivals have a long history in many countries, arising out of cultural and traditional festivals that often have local associations. In the UK alone, well over 500 arts festivals are held every year, lasting from two days to several weeks, and they attract some 3 million people, spending over £1 billion. More than half of these have been founded since 1980 and over 60% are professionally managed. Most depend on sponsorship and financial support from the local authority. The leading events in the UK, in terms of revenue achieved, are the Edinburgh Fringe Festival and the BBC promenade concerts (the Proms).

Major art exhibitions draw an international audience of mass tourists. In 1993, 1.1 million visitors attended the Barnes Foundation's exhibition 'A Century of Impressionism' held at the Musée d'Orsay in Paris, while a later showing of the Barnes Foundation's collection in Germany drew such crowds that the museum exhibiting the collection stayed open all night (a practice that later led to longer opening hours in Germany: Berlin has 'Die lange Nacht der Museen' twice a year, when all museums are open until at least midnight). The UK's Royal Academy has followed suit, on occasion opening for a full 24-hour period, thereby dramatically increasing its admission numbers. Blockbuster exhibitions, such as the Venice Biennale, frequently have as much to do with raising the social profile of the institution or city, and encouraging the public to perceive it as a leader in its field, as in directly raising revenue through entry tickets.

Several music festivals in Europe have achieved international recognition and visitors make significant contributions to the economies of the cities where they are held. Berlin, again, is a leader in this field, with three opera houses and seven orchestras, all supported by government funding. It has been estimated that 27% of Konzerthaus audiences are tourists visiting the city (Schmid, 2013). In addition to these, there are countless smaller festivals in the countries concerned, each of which makes an important contribution to local revenues resulting from tourists' visits. While the largest festivals tend to run during the high season, many smaller events are held outside the peak summer periods, especially in places that are subject to heavy congestion at such times.

EXAMPLE

The draw of the Glastonbury festival

The first Glastonbury festival was held in 1970, with 1500 people in attendance. Held at Worthy Farm in Somerset, it has since grown to become a world-renowned music and performing arts event.

Covering an area of 900 acres, with a perimeter almost 9 miles in length and with over 60 performance venues, the festival caters to a diverse audience. The Pyramid Stage attracts top-name bands (Coldplay, Beyoncé, The Rolling Stones, Metallica, Kasabian and Foo Fighters have all headlined in recent years) and can accommodate an audience of almost 100,000 (Figure 10.1). Smaller stages, such as the Other Stage and John Peel Stage, can also cater for audiences in the thousands.

	Licensed attendance	Glastonbury ticket price	Relative price (based on average earnings)
2014	135,000	£225	£225
2010	135,000	£185	£190
2005	153,000	£125	£149

	Licensed attendance	Glastonbury ticket price	Relative price (based on average earnings)
2000	100,000	£87	£127
1995	80,000	£65	£118
1990	70,000	£38	£86.30
1985	40,000	£16	£55.10
1981	18,000	£8	£37.60
1979	12,000	£5	£31.90
1978	Informal event	–	–
1971	12,000	Free	–
1970	1500	£1 (incl. free milk from the farm)	£20.90

It is now so popular that the 135,000 tickets for the 2019 festival (each priced at £248) sold out in just 36 minutes. To reduce the likelihood that tickets are purchased by touts hoping to make a quick profit, all attendees are required to complete a photo registration process, which provides a unique reference number required when purchasing tickets.

On the back of Glastonbury's popularity, hundreds of different music festivals, with themes including jazz, classical, folk, opera, early music, indie and rock, are operating annually across the UK, with Bestival, Latitude and V festival all drawing large crowds. However, the rapid growth in the provision of festivals has seen some struggle to attract enough festival-goers, or meet police security requirements, and as a consequence some find the need to cancel.

FIGURE 10.1 Glastonbury's Pyramid stage

Photo: Claire Humphreys

Apart from music and the fine arts, crafts, drama, dance, literature and poetry festivals are popular. Some commemorate historical occasions and may be highlighted with parades, pageants and *son et lumière* events. Most provide an opportunity for hosts and guests to meet and get to know one another. There is also a growing number of events linked to local food and drink.

Gastronomy events

Whether the focus is on beer or wine tasting, cheese making or cookery masterclasses, an interest in food and drink is driving a growth in the number and size of gastronomy festivals taking place around the world each year. For example, the Melbourne food and wine festival, which has been operating since the mid-1990s, has expanded to a point that it now attracts 350,000 visitors and offers a programme of more than 250 events taking place across the state of Victoria. The event includes talks and masterclasses, tours of vineyards and distilleries, and meals such as the world's longest lunch (the dining table is 500 metres long and seats 1600 people).

In regions noted for particular food or drink products, events are mounted to celebrate their harvest, or simply to provide an excuse to widen their products' appeal. Some examples are:

- Great British cheese festival, Cardiff, Wales
- Feria du Riz, Arles, France, celebrating rice dishes
- Galway Oyster Festival, Ireland
- I'Primi d'Italia, Foligno, Italy, celebrating first courses
- Truffle Festival, Alba, Italy
- Shrimp Festival, Honfleur, France
- Onion Festival, Weimar, Germany
- Chestnut Festival, Mourjou en Chataigneraie, France
- Baltic Herring Festival, Helsinki, Finland.

These are just a few examples of food festivals held in Europe, and it will be seen that the medium gives scope for an almost endless variety of activities centred on food and drink in some shape or form.

Food festivals offer an appeal for the tourist because they provide access to (and sometimes education about) local delicacies. It is also linked to activities undertaken by the local community. For instance, the herring festival is timed to coincide with the migration of this fish to the waters of the Ringkøbing fjord, Denmark. Visitors to the festival get to watch the locals participate in an informal competition to catch the most fish, and then they get to enjoy pickled, filleted or fried herring, a regional favourite. Such festivals often function as a means of maintaining and celebrating community values and provide community-based social functions. Consequently, a growing desire among tourists to engage with authentic experiences drives the demand for access to such events (Hall and Sharples, 2008).

Gastronomy events may be organised to attract industry professionals, local consumers and visitors alike. These can be stimulated by government initiatives (the link with agriculture and rural development often a driver) as well as by local artisan associations and individual producers. Consequently, the commoditisation of local festivals has seen both expansion and increased professionalisation in the event management process, which is helping to drive touristic appeal.

Greater appreciation of the concept of the 'terroir', a French word that represents the natural environment in which produce (typically grapes) is grown and references the soil, climate and topography of landscape, has ensured that the characteristics of products (taste, aroma, etc.) are unique to a district and are therefore inseparable from that place (Cavicchi and Santini, 2014).

EXAMPLE

The benefits of gastronomy events

Hosting gastronomy events that make use of local produce has numerous benefits for both the local region and for the enterprises producing these commodities. These are summarised in Table 10.5.

TABLE 10.5 Benefits of gastronomy events

Benefits for the region	Benefits for producers
Encourage greater levels of economic activity	Build product and brand awareness
Encourage visitors to the region, extend their dwell time and possibly address seasonality issues	Develop relationships between producers by bringing these suppliers together at an event
Increase/maintain employment opportunities	Provide direct sell opportunities (usually with better profit margins)
Enhance destination image	Provide market intelligence through customer feedback
Encourage civic pride	Provide educational opportunities

Source: Adapted from Hall and Sharples, 2008

It is also useful to appreciate the distinction between those gastronomy events that are designed for the food/drink to be consumed immediately and those that offer the product for sampling with an expectation that purchases will be made for later consumption. This can also lead to the purchase of produce as souvenirs to be given to friends and family on returning home.

Finally, it is important to appreciate that the origin of some gastronomy events lies in the seasonal cycles of growth; for example, celebrating the harvest, which means that such events are tied to particular times of the year. Such events can (and this is perhaps more common in Europe) be tied to religious observances which may shape the activities that occur.

Religious events

All over the world, people travel to take part in religious festivals and events. Travel to sites considered sacred has long existed, and religious pilgrimages to sites considered holy, such as the Ganges River or Lumbini, Nepal (the birthplace of Buddha, discussed in Chapter 9), are extensive in their variety and, combined, attract some 300 million visitors annually. However, while there are numerous sacred places to visit, most religions also give worship on sacred dates in the calendar, which can lead to the creation of religious events that also encourage travel.

Perhaps the largest religious event in the world is the Hajj. Millions make the obligatory once-in-a-lifetime pilgrimage to Mecca. At other times of the year, this visit is known as

Umrah, or the Lesser Pilgrimage, but when this is taken at the time of Ramadan, it is known as the Great Pilgrimage, or Hajj. Some 2.3 million Hajj pilgrims visited Mecca in 2018.

In most cases, religious events are held for their spiritual rewards rather than financial ones, although we can consider events such as a church fete to raise money for building repairs or numerous good causes, to be aware of the financial rewards that can be gained from operating such an event. Furthermore, religious buildings are increasingly extending their events calendar beyond core ecclesiastical services to include cultural and community events as well as acting as a space for commercial events, such as graduation ceremonies, awards dinners or conferences (Curtis, 2016).

Large-scale events held as evangelical missions to attract worshippers came to the fore in the UK with the efforts of Billy Graham in the 1950s, attracting more than a million people over a three-month period. Today, similar events exist, predominantly in Africa and India, with speakers such as the German evangelist Reinhard Bonnke and American preacher Joyce Meyer attracting vast crowds (Dowson, 2017).

EXAMPLE

Wembley stadium hosts an open-air Mass

In 1982 Wembley Stadium was the setting for the first outdoor Mass to be held by Pope John Paul II in the UK, attended by some 80,000. The visit was part of a six-day tour timetabling numerous public events, including a service for 24,000 at Crystal Palace National Sports Centre, followed by tours through the streets of Coventry and Liverpool to crowds believed to be in excess of 350,000. Similar numbers turned out at York Racecourse, Manchester's Heaton Park and Bellahouston Park, Glasgow, concluding with a visit to Ninian Park, then home of Cardiff City FC, to celebrate Mass with 33,000 in attendance.

Papal visits still attract vast numbers today. The largest papal event in history is believed to be the Mass of Pope Francis which took place in Manila, in January 2015; attendance was estimated at around 6 million (BBC, 2015).

Such faith events, whether large or small scale, often influence the lives of the individual in attendance. Public holidays associated with numerous religious celebrations may also make available the time to participate in such events.

Political and state events

These events are held by political organisations and by governments. Political events can include party conferences, trade union congresses and organised protests. Such events will inevitably have a political message; for instance, the government may wish to share a policy message with the people, or a protest group may lobby the electorate to change its views.

One challenge that arises particularly from political events is its associated high-profile nature, making it likely to attract significant media attention (Bladen et al., 2018). Political figures are often well known to the public, with opinions that may encourage highly polarised views, calling for high security. Visitors at these events are often passionate in their beliefs and many will have travelled some distance to participate.

State events include those ceremonies required by the nation's laws or held to mark national occasions. These may also include commemorations; for example, the numerous events held on Remembrance Sunday in the UK and other Commonwealth nations, held since the end of World War I, to remember those who lost their lives in the line of duty. Royal ceremonies such as the Changing of the Guard attract many overseas tourists visiting London. The Queen's birthday parade, known as 'Trooping the Colour', also attracts a large number of spectators, each of whom has entered a ballot for tickets (priced at £40 a seat).

EXAMPLE

Windsor benefits from a Royal wedding

The wedding of Prince Harry to American actress Meghan Markle, which took place in Windsor in 2018, was predicted to boost tourism to the town in the years to follow. With a TV audience of around 2 billion, the local tourist industry was predicting a 15% increase in visitor numbers from the USA. Deirdre Wells, head of the British travel association UKinbound, said coverage of the wedding is 'the best free advertising we can wish for as a country and reminds people that they should come to the UK' (Petroff, 2018).

This predicted boost in numbers is in addition to the 100,000 visitors in the town at the time of the wedding. The venue, St Georges Chapel, was opened to the public on the following day so that visitors could view the flowers (Donnelly, 2018).

As well as royal weddings, state events include state funerals. In the USA, these are conducted by the federal government and are usually held in the nation's capital. Most recent state funerals there were for Presidents George H. W. Bush, Gerald Ford and Ronald Reagan and for politicians Daniel Inouye and John McCain. In Australia, there is a distinction between national state funerals (usually offered to prime ministers and long-serving parliamentarians) and those funerals organised by the governments of each of the states and territories, which may be offered to high-profile public figures outside of the political arena, including television and sporting stars.

SPORTS EVENTS

This sector offers some of the largest events in the world, with the Summer Olympics and FIFA World Cup the two biggest in terms of international media coverage and public interest. These events attract very large audiences, with 8.2 million attending the London 2012 Olympics and 3.4 million attending the 2014 Brazilian World Cup. Other sports events that usually attract a substantial numbers of visitors include the Rugby World Cup, World Athletics Championships and Commonwealth Games. In all cases, the right to host the event is determined by a complex bidding process.

When it comes to such peripatetic events, attendance numbers are often dependent on the role that the particular sport plays in the culture or zeitgeist of the hosting country. For example, at the 2018 Winter Olympics, held in Pyeongchang in South Korea, ticket sales were sluggish; six weeks out and almost 40% of tickets were still to be sold. Reasons advanced for this included the lack of alpinism in Korean culture (i.e. there is no historical affinity to winter sports) and the early morning start times for events, convenient for American TV broadcasters (who had paid vast sums for the broadcast rights) but less so for spectators attending (Wharton, 2018).

EXAMPLE

Tour de France event helps Yorkshire tourism

Local governments may pay to host an event because of the benefits it may bring to a region. This can include the opportunity to engage the local population, the economic returns achieved from increased visitor numbers and the positive media attention that a successful event can offer.

Some UK local councils combined to bid for, and then fund the delivery of, the opening stages of the 2014 Tour de France. York City Council paid £500,000 to host the start of day two, with Sheffield paying a £200,000 staging fee to host the finish. Some 2.5 million turned out to watch the two stages that took place in Yorkshire, while tourism numbers increased the following year by 7.5%.

Spectators often have an interest in the sport they are observing and will be prepared to invest the time and money needed to travel to the event. This is also true of those sports events that are designed for public participation. The London Marathon now accommodates more than 40,000 runners and the New York City (NYC) Marathon exceeds 50,000. Application numbers are higher still; more than 100,000 runners applied to run in the 2018 NYC Marathon. Table 10.6 identifies the typology of sports events, recognising the likely distance travelled by participants. It also considers the extent to which events gain media coverage, which can help to attract visitors in the longer term.

TABLE 10.6 Typology of sporting events

Size of event	Example of event	Participant distance	Nature of sponsorship	Nature of media coverage
Local event	School sports day	Restricted to local population	Small-scale sponsorship	Local press coverage
Regional event	Regional football competition	Sourced from surrounding counties/states	Usually by company with direct interest in the sport	Press but might occasionally include television
National event	National Athletics Championships	Open to anyone from the nation/country	Usually by recognised national brand	Some TV coverage and extensive press coverage
International event	London Marathon	Majority of participants from host country and nearest neighbours	Recognised international brand	Media coverage in host country (some coverage might occur in other countries)
Global (Mega) event	FIFA World Cup	Participants from many countries (so considerable distances travelled)	Numerous international brands act as sponsors	Extensive media coverage in many countries

Source: Adapted from Bladen et al., 2018

The increased commercialisation of events has meant that bidding to host smaller sports events is now common, as we can see from the example of the Golden Oldies sports festivals.

EXAMPLE

Golden Oldies heads for Christchurch, NZ

The Golden Oldies movement was created in New Zealand to encourage an older generation of athletes to travel to participate in sporting events, with the focus on 'fun, friendship and fraternity' (New Zealand Tourism, 2018). In order to participate, athletes must be aged over 35, but more commonly participants are 50–60 years old. Teams are asked to declare their level of ability when registering for the event, in order to ensure that teams of similar standards are pitted against each other.

The event started in 1979 with a rugby festival in Auckland that attracted 16 teams. The first Golden Oldies Hockey Festival took place in 1983 with cricket joining the movement the following year. Since its inception, these sporting festivals have taken place in numerous cities across the globe (Table 10.7).

TABLE 10.7 Host cities for Golden Oldies sports festivals

Rugby	Hockey	Netball	Cricket
2020 Denver, Colorado	2019 Vancouver, Canada	2020 Waikiki, Hawaii	2020 Harrogate, England
2018 Christchurch, New Zealand	2018 Christchurch, New Zealand	2018 Christchurch, New Zealand	2018 Christchurch, New Zealand
2017 Lisbon, Portugal	2017 Cape Town, South Africa	2015 Hobart, Australia	2017 Barbados, West Indies
2015 San Sebastian, Spain	2015 Leipzig, Germany	2013 San Diego, USA	2015 Cape Town, South Africa
2013 Prague, Czech Republic	2013 Hawaii, USA	2011 Nadi, Fiji	2012 Adelaide, Australia
PREVIOUS HOST CITIES			
's-Hertogenbosch, Holland; Aberdeen, Scotland; Adelaide, Australia; Auckland, New Zealand; Benidorm, Spain; Bournemouth, England; Brisbane, Australia; Caernarfon, Wales; Campbelltown, Australia; De Bosch, the Netherlands; Dublin, Ireland; Edinburgh, Scotland; Fiji; Funchal, Madeira; Gold Coast, Australia; Heidelberg, Germany; Hong Kong; Honolulu, USA; Moscow, Russia; Perth, Australia; Queenstown, New Zealand; Rarotonga, Cook Islands; Rosario, Argentina; Singapore; Split, Croatia; Trieste, Italy; Vancouver, Canada; Verona, Italy; Victoria, Canada; Zurich, Switzerland.			

When the 2017 Golden Oldies World Cricket festival was awarded to Barbados, it was estimated that around 600 visitors would come to attend the festival. This event was seen as particularly appealing for Barbados, with the head of the Barbados Tourism Marketing organisation commenting: 'What is particularly interesting about having the 2017 Golden Oldies Cricket Festival is that it takes place during the month of May, which allows us to increase arrivals during a traditionally slower month' (*Trinidad & Tobago Guardian*, 2015).

It is noticeable in Table 10.7 that 2018 was unique in that all four sports came together in one city, with each festival operating for one of the weeks of April. Although not reaching the optimistic numbers forecast, it was estimated that some 5000 people were attracted by this series of sporting festivals. The City Council contributed NZ$200,000 towards the festival's costs, with the Ministry of Business, Innovation and Employment putting up an additional NZ$550,000. The economic benefit for Canterbury (the wider region in which Christchurch sits) was calculated to be NZ$15 million (Truebridge, 2018).

The example of the Golden Oldies sports festivals highlights that just as world cities may seek to host mega-events such as the Olympics or World Cup, so smaller towns and cities are also active in their efforts to host events that will bring visitors to the area. Consequently, looking beyond the mainstream sports can open up many more opportunities. The types of sports which attract visitors (to participate or to spectate) are extensive and can be grouped into three categories (Greenwell et al., 2014):

- traditional sports: for example football, rugby, netball, cricket, tennis, hockey, baseball, basketball, gymnastics, running
- niche sports: for instance disc golf, roller derby, kabaddi
- extreme sports: for example mud runs, ironman, extreme lasertag, canyoning.

The existence of such a diversity of sports mean that there are many different events available to be hosted, whether for competition (perhaps the final of a regional or national championship) or for entertainment or spectacle. A conducive climate (snow for ski events, wind for sailing events, etc.) can make some destinations a natural choice to host, while the existence of suitable infrastructure can reduce costs to the destination. Existing infrastructure may include tourist facilities (such as hotels and restaurants), which can ensure participants, officials and spectators alike can all be accommodated.

DEVELOPING EVENT TOURISM STRATEGIES

It is not uncommon for governments around the globe to use event tourism as part of their policy for **strategic regional development** (Whitford, 2009). One major advantage of event tourism is that little additional infrastructure is required and events with tourist appeal may already exist to serve the local community and/or business environment. In some cases, choices can be made to schedule events at times that may help to address seasonality issues. Destination managers can make use of existing resources, such as the history, creative talents and public spaces, to develop their tourism products, with the latter often used as the 'stage' on which events are delivered (Richards and Palmer, 2010). Event locations may also be selected to ensure that crowd management is conveniently possible and that negative environmental and social impacts are minimised (Jago, 1997). Consequently, more and more destinations are including events in their tourism strategy, or developing an explicit event strategy to achieve a coordinated approach to the use of events as a destination-management tool.

EXAMPLE

Scotland: The perfect stage

The tourist board for Scotland (VisitScotland), through its events team, has developed a strategy with a mission to develop the country's reputation as an ideal place to host national and international events. It strives to achieve this through 'a one Scotland approach, a strong and dynamic events industry producing a portfolio of events and festivals that delivers sustainable impact and international profile for Scotland' (VisitScotland, 2015).

The events team acknowledges that the strategic approach undertaken has helped to a build a robust knowledge base and to forge partnerships between the public, private and voluntary sectors involved in delivering events across the nation. To achieve its goals, the strategy has two components:

1. to utilise and develop the assets that Scotland has which make it the 'perfect stage' for events
2. to deliver a portfolio of events that provide world-leading authentic experiences for residents and visitors.

This event portfolio recognises that different types of events achieve varying outcomes in terms of numbers attending, geographical spread, the extent of impacts and the level of global awareness (Figure 10.2).

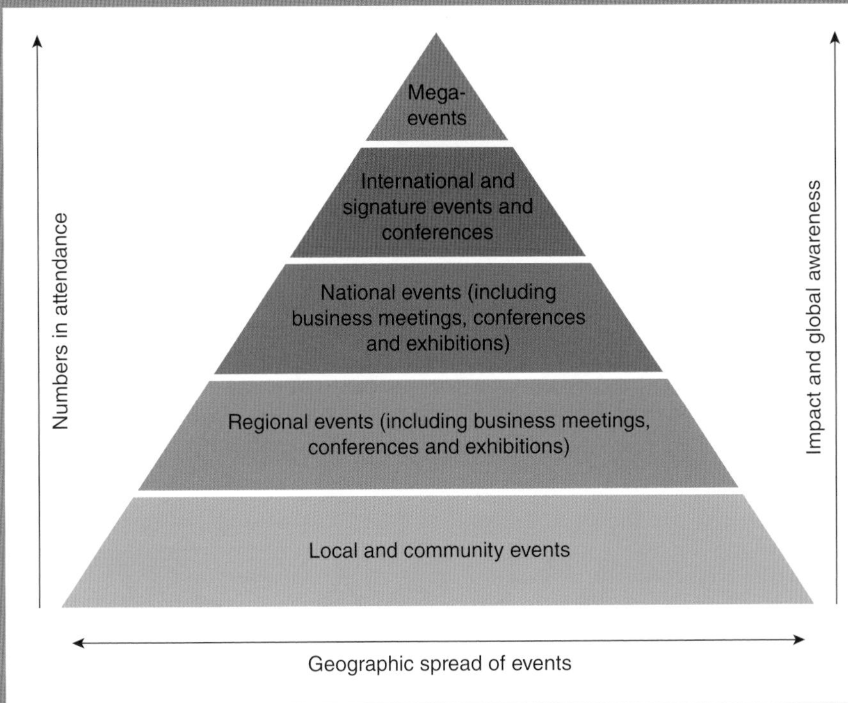

FIGURE 10.2 The changing scale of events

Source: Adapted from VisitScotland, 2015

There is, of course, a direct relationship between the degree of attractiveness of the event and the distance visitors are willing to travel to visit it. Some events, such as finals for sports competitions, will have global appeal, while the appearance of top pop singers and bands at stadiums holding many thousands of fans will be marketed internationally as a package to include travel and hotel accommodation.

Events can also draw people to an area that otherwise may have little to attract them. They may be mounted to increase the number of visitors to a destination or help spread tourism demand to the shoulder seasons. One interesting example of this is the costume events mounted by the Sealed Knot Society in England, a voluntary body with an interest in English history of the Civil War period. This organisation, *inter alia*, recreates battle scenes on the original sites, drawing very large audiences. Consequently, such events can encourage visitors to travel to rural areas or towns off the beaten track for tourists.

Furthermore, an event may still influence the decision to visit long after it has finished. For example, costumes used in the carnival parades in Rio are made available for visitors to try, offering an experience of the event year-round (see Figure 10.3). Similarly, there are numerous examples of Olympic infrastructure being visited by tourists long after the event, including Canada Olympic Park (which hosted events for the Calgary Winter Olympics in 1988), Sydney's ANZ Stadium (built for the 2000 Olympics) and the London Stadium (built for the 2012 Olympics).

FIGURE 10.3 Tourists in Rio dress up in costumes designed for the carnival, even if they are in the city long after the event is over

Photo: Claire Humphreys

Destination managers use events to animate the city (Getz and Page, 2016). Events can add vibrancy and, with significant numbers in attendance, influence the atmosphere of a place – generally for the better, although overcrowding or troublesome behaviour may detract from this. Some football matches at the European Championships or World

Cup have, for example, been disrupted by hooliganism and fighting between rival teams, which can mar the experience for other visitors.

Taking a strategic approach to event tourism often requires destination managers to encourage collaboration between the different stakeholder groups. Stakeholders may include the event rights holder, the venue operators (which may be the government in the case of public spaces), local businesses, the local community, government departments (transport, city centre management, licensing committees, etc.), the police, fire service (for security and safety issues) and many others. Such an approach will also require coordination and communication between the groups to ensure the benefits of hosting the event can be maximised for all (Devine and Devine, 2017). The value of a strategic and coordinated approach is that synergies are achieved, whereby the resulting benefits are greater than would otherwise be experienced. The success of popular events can be jeopardised by greed, however (for example, overcharging by hotels), which can both discourage some visitors and effect long-term damage on the reputation of the destination. Consequently, the strategic use of events requires that all stakeholders consider their role and responsibility in building success for the destination as a whole.

While some destinations are lucky enough to be able to bid for, and win, the right to host a global mega-event, it is also possible for destinations to put together a coordinated programme of smaller events that, combined, attract large numbers. As an example, the Edinburgh Fringe Festival now includes more than 3000 art and culture events that take place in 300 venues across the city over a three-week period in August. In 2017, more than 2.6 million tickets were sold for performances at this festival. It has expanded to such an extent that it is seen to be the world's biggest arts festival. As we can see from this example, events can act as a catalyst for encouraging visits as well as playing a role in destination image development and place marketing (Getz, 2008).

EXAMPLE

When losing can result in a win

Many people are aware that cities bid for the right to host the Olympics, with the winners usually announced about seven years out from the event. However, it is now the case that the rights-holders of small peripatetic events ask destinations to bid for the right to host a future edition.

The cost of bidding for these small events may not be as great as for the Olympics (estimated to be in excess of $100 million), but they still require time and effort to research and submit the document as well as host, at a future point, the bid evaluators. Therefore, the OECD (2017) argues that a strategic approach that determines which events should be bid for is vitally important. Furthermore, a number of benefits accrue from bidding but not winning, including:

- raising the international profile and brand image
- facilitating closer working between public authorities on a range of logistical issues
- accelerating development planning (urban, event-related facilities, transport infrastructure, etc.)
- forcing potential hosts to identify their own metrics for success. (OECD, 2017: 12)

While destination managers may feel that an event tourism strategy may require the introduction of a completely new event, more commonly there is the possibility to grow existing events, though investment, marketing activities or regeneration of the offering. In such cases, a sense of authenticity may be achieved through the use of existing rather than new events, although any effort to expand an event may detract from its association with the local culture and communities. Alternatively, destination managers may choose to bid for the right to host one event or a series that already have an existing image and market appeal. In some cases events can be franchised, with the rights-holder giving permission for the event to happen in several destinations, often at different times of the year. One issue this might raise for destination managers is that, in such cases, events are not exclusively associated with the host location, and consequently the benefits for destination image development may be limited. Regardless of the strategy employed to establish event tourism, the rewards will be dependent on the appeal that the event has for the market, which may or may not be sustained over time.

THE FUTURE OF EVENT TOURISM

Event tourism has really come of age and its strategic use by destinations, whether they are rural areas, cities or entire countries, has ensured that the number of events offered around the globe is rapidly expanding. Offering unique events can be a way of avoiding the 'identikit destination' (see Chapter 2), whereby places are perceived as interchangeable in the minds of tourists.

In times of belt-tightening for the public sector, the money to fund public or community events is becoming harder to find (and to justify to the electorate). Consequently, we are likely to see ever greater efforts to maximise returns on the investment made, perhaps through achieving touristic benefits as well as serving the needs of local communities. The increasing professionalisation of the sector will help to maximise these returns. Coordination between event organisers, government departments and destination managers will continue.

Learning from the experience of places such as Montreal (1976 Olympics) and Sheffield (1991 World Student Games), where the debt caused by the event (construction and operation) was felt by the taxpayers for decades after the event, we are likely to see greater efforts to restrict the long-term debt accrued from hosting large-scale events. Inevitably, more consideration will be given to the post-event use of any facilities or buildings constructed, to avoid the cost of **white elephants** (whereby the costs outweigh the benefits of its existence). The International Olympic Committee has acknowledged that the existence of numerous Olympic buildings that have fallen into disrepair, something both costly and wasteful, is damaging to the Olympic reputation. Paris, due to host the 2024 Olympics, has overtly stated that it will avoid 'white elephant venues that start to decay as soon as the Olympians leave town' (*National Post*, 2017). Time will tell as to whether Paris is successful in its goal.

SUMMARY

Event tourism is now firmly established as a tool for economic development used by destinations. Events can be attractions in their own right as well as acting as a means of animating a destination. They can shape the destination image and are often used in place marketing (Getz, 2008).

It is also useful to note the influence that the size of an event has on its resulting impacts, media attention and its potential to attract tourist numbers in their thousands (and, in a few cases, millions).

The inclusion of events in tourism strategies is no longer uncommon. What we are seeing is the extension of this, with destination organisations now producing detailed event strategies that explicitly focus on the use of events as a tool to attract locals and visitors alike.

QUESTIONS AND DISCUSSION POINTS

1. Why do tourists visit a European Capital of Culture?
2. What is changing in society that is making gastronomy events popular today?
3. Why might a destination manager decide to bid to host a future edition of the Golden Oldies Rugby Festival?

TASKS

1. In this chapter, we highlight the existence of Scotland's events strategy (www.eventscotland.org/stps/the-national-events-strategy) and acknowledge that many other events strategies are now produced. Using this strategy document (or another of your choice), examine the stated goals for the strategy and explore the actions that are planned in order to achieve these goals. Who is going to be involved? Summarise these as an infographic.
2. Write an essay that compares and contrasts three different state events, with particular reference to the reason why it is held, its ability to attract media attention and the likelihood that it will attract international visitors.

WEBSITES

European Capitals of Culture: https://ec.europa.eu/programmes/creative-europe/actions/capitals-culture_en

FIFA World Cup: www.fifa.com/worldcup

International Olympic Committee: www.olympic.org/the-ioc

REFERENCES

BBC (2015) *Pope Francis in Manila: Pope departs Philippines after record-breaking Mass*. Available online at: www.bbc.co.uk/news/world-asia-30875645 [Accessed January 2019].

BBC (2017) *Brexit 'Bombshell' for UK's European Capital of Culture 2023 Plans*. Available online at: www.bbc.co.uk/news/entertainment-arts-42097692 [Accessed January 2019].

Bladen, C., Kennell, J., Abson, E. and Wilde, N. (2018) *Events Management: An introduction*. London: Routledge.

Bowdin, G., Allen, J., O'Toole, W., Harris, R. and McDonnell, I. (2012) *Events Management*, 3rd edn. London: Butterworth-Heinemann.

Business Visits and Events Partnership (BVEP) (2017) *Opportunities for Global Growth in Britain's Events Sector*. Available online at: www.businessvisitsandeventspartnership.com/research-and-publications/research/category/4-bvep-research?download=285:opportunities-for-global-growth-in-britain-s-events-sector [Accessed January 2019].

Cavicchi, A. and Santini, C. (2014) *Food and Wine Events in Europe*. London: Routledge.

Curtis, S. (2016) English cathedrals: Events and spiritual capital. *International Journal of Religious Tourism and Pilgrimage*, 4 (2), Article 3.

Devine, A. and Devine, F. (2017) A strategic approach to international event tourism. In N. Ferdinand and P. J. Kitchin (eds), *Events Management: An international approach*, 2nd edn. London: Sage.

Donnelly, L. (2018) 'Royal wedding effect' will see tourism boom for Windsor, London. *The Telegraph*, 20 May.

Dowson, R. (2017) Towards a definition of Christian mega-events in the 21st century. *International Journal of Religious Tourism and Pilgrimage*, 5 (1), Article 3.

European Commission (EC) (2012) The Commission Proposes Countries to Host European Capitals of Culture after 2019. Available online at: http://europa.eu/rapid/press-release_IP-12-815_en.htm?locale=en#footnote-1 [Accessed January 2019].

Getz, D. (2005) *Event Management and Event Tourism*, 2nd edn. New York: Cognizant.

Getz, D. (2007) *Event Studies: Theory, research and policy for planned events*. Oxford: Butterworth-Heinemann.

Getz, D. (2008) Event tourism: Definition, evolution, and research. *Tourism Management*, 29 (3), 403–28.

Getz, D. and Page, S. (2016) Progress and prospects for event tourism research. *Tourism Management*, 52, 593–631.

Greenwell, T. C., Danzey-Bussell, L. A. and Shand, D. (2014) *Managing Sports Events*. Champaign, IL: Human Kinetics.

Hall, C. M. and Sharples, L. (2008) Food events, festivals and farmers' markets: An introduction. In C. M. Hall and L. Sharples (eds), *Food and Wine Festivals and Events around the World: Development, management and markets*. London: Butterworth-Heinemann.

Jago, L. (1997) *Special events and tourism behaviour: A conceptualisation and an empirical analysis from a values perspective*. Thesis, Victoria University.

National Post (2017) *No More White Elephants: Paris aims to avoid Olympic waste and excess for 2024 Games*. Available online at: https://nationalpost.com/sports/olympics/paris-aiming-to-make-olympic-games-desirable-again-by-2024 [Accessed January 2019].

New Zealand Tourism (2018) *Golden Oldies Comes to Christchurch, New Zealand in 2018*. Available online at: https://media.newzealand.com/en/events/golden-oldies-comes-to-christchurch-new-zealand-i [Accessed January 2019].

Northwest Regional Development Agency (RDA) (2010) Press Release – New Independent Data Confirms Liverpool's Capital of Culture Success. Warrington: Northwest RDA, 11 January.

Organisation for Economic Co-operation and Development (OECD) (2017) *Major Events as Catalysts for Tourism*. Paris: OECD Publishing (Tourism Papers-2017/02).

Oxford English Dictionary (OED) (1996) *Oxford Compact English Dictionary*. Oxford: Oxford University Press.

Petroff, A. (2018) *Royal Wedding: Tourists won't flock to UK for Harry and Meghan*. Available online at: https://money.cnn.com/2018/03/13/news/royal-wedding-uk-travel-tourism/index.html [Accessed January 2019].

Richards, G. and Palmer, R. (2010) *Eventful Cities: Cultural management and urban revitalisation*. Oxford: Butterworth-Heinemann.

Rutherford Silvers, J. (2012) *Professional Event Coordination*, 2nd edn. Hoboken, NJ: John Wiley & Sons.

Trinidad and Tobago Guardian (2015) *Barbados to host World Cricket Festival*. Available online at: www.guardian.co.tt/article-6.2.362502.dd43ce28f1 [Accessed January 2019].

Truebridge, N. (2018) *Golden Oldies Month Labelled Success despite Criticism*. Available online at: www.stuff.co.nz/the-press/news/103465270/golden-oldies-month-labelled-success-despite-critcisim [Accessed January 2019].

VisitScotland (2015) *Scotland the Perfect Stage: Scotland's events strategy 2015–2025*. Available online at: www.eventscotland.org/stps/the-national-events-strategy [Accessed January 2019].

Wharton, D. (2018) Olympics has struggled with attendance: But if it makes billions, does filling seats really matter? *LA Times*, 19 February.

Whitford, M. (2009) A framework for the development of event public policy: Facilitating regional development. *Tourism Management*, 30 (5), 674–82.

11

BUSINESS TOURISM

Prepared in collaboration with Rob Davidson

CONTENTS

LEARNING OUTCOMES

After studying this chapter, you should be able to:

- understand the principal sectors of the business tourism industry and distinguish between them
- explain the objectives of the different types of meetings that may be organised, the various venues in which they take place and the roles of meeting planners
- distinguish between trade fairs and exhibitions and understand the roles of those companies that supply services to this sector of business tourism
- define incentive travel, compare it with other forms of workplace rewards and demonstrate awareness of the challenges of organising successful incentive travel programmes
- understand the principal motivations behind individual business travel and appreciate the factors that companies take into account regarding the features of the business trips made by their employees
- be aware of the main trends that are having an impact on business tourism in the twenty-first century.

> Business travel and tourism is certainly not a new phenomenon. People have been travelling because of their work for many centuries. However, some forms of business tourism, such as incentive travel, are modern inventions. (Swarbrooke and Horner, 2001: 13)

INTRODUCTION

As we see in the quote above, travelling for the purpose of carrying out trade and engaging in commerce was one of the earliest types of tourist activity undertaken by enterprising members of ancient civilisations. Even when those undertaking travel had to contend with the ever-present dangers of attack from bandits, pirates and highwaymen, as well as the severe discomfort resulting from poorly constructed roads or across perilous seas, the business motive was strong enough to drive intrepid merchants and other entrepreneurs to leave their native lands in search of distant markets in which to buy or sell goods and products not found locally.

Today, **business tourism** – principally, travel for commercial, professional and work-related purposes – represents the major non-leisure form of tourism, and business tourists are widely recognised as the highest-spending category of travellers. Modern-day business tourism takes four principal forms:

- travel for the purpose of attending conferences and other types of meetings
- travel to attend an exhibition or trade fair
- incentive travel
- individual business travel.

In the vast majority of cases, each category of business tourism is in some way connected to the traveller's professional life or to their role in the buying and selling process that underpins much of modern commercial life.

MEETINGS

Travelling in order to attend a meeting of some kind is one of the most widespread forms of business tourism. Meetings vary enormously in form, size and purpose, but the meetings that stimulate business tourism are primarily those organised with an objective linked to the attendees' professional activity.

This is most evident when the meeting's attendees all belong to the same profession or trade and are all members of the same professional or trade association. Many of the highest-profile meetings belong to this **association** category. Popular cities for association meetings are Paris, Berlin, London and, most popular in 2017, Barcelona (Table 11.1).

Association meetings can attract many thousands of attendees (or **participants** or **delegates**, as they are also known) and the economic impacts on the destinations in which they are held can be considerable. For example, the conference of the European Society of Cardiology, the members of which are medical professionals specialising in cardiovascular diseases, now regularly attracts over 30,000 delegates. The five-day event provides the delegates with an invaluable opportunity to meet together and exchange ideas and information on new challenges and new techniques related to the field of cardiovascular medicine. It is clear that the collective spending of the delegates on items such as transport, accommodation and catering brings extensive economic benefits to the businesses operating in the cities that host this event.

TABLE 11.1 City rankings by number of meetings organised in 2017

Rank	City	Number of Association meetings in 2017*
1	Barcelona	195
2	Paris	190
2	Vienna	190
4	Berlin	185
5	London	177
6	Singapore	160
7	Madrid	153
8	Prague	151
9	Lisbon	149
10	Seoul	142
11	Buenos Aires	131
12	Budapest	128
13	Hong Kong	119
14	Dublin	117
15	Copenhagen	115

Note: *Data evaluates regular (annual/biannual, etc.) rotating meetings with more than 50 participants

Source: ICCA, 2018

EXAMPLE

Lions Club conventions

The Lions Club is a community service organisation with 1.4 million members in 47,000 clubs globally. Each club meets regularly to discuss activities and projects. Clubs will also arrange to meet with other clubs in their region. However, it is the international convention that draws the largest number of delegates; usually 12,000–23,000 attendees for the five-day event.

The international convention is held in a different city every year (Table 11.2), with cities bidding for the right to host the event.

TABLE 11.2 Locations of the Lions Club conventions, 2010–25

Year and location
2025 – Mexico City, Mexico
2024 – Melbourne, Australia
2023 – Boston, USA

(Continued)

TABLE 11.2 (Continued)

Year and location
2022 – New Delhi, India
2021 – Montreal, Canada
2020 – Singapore
2019 – Milan, Italy
2018 – Las Vegas, USA
2017 – Chicago, USA
2016 – Fukuoka, Japan
2015 – Honolulu, USA
2014 – Toronto, Canada
2013 – Hamburg, Germany
2012 – Busan, South Korea
2011 – Seattle, USA
2010 – Sydney, Australia

The international convention, which includes seminars as well as a presidential address to all members, often takes place in large-scale convention centres. The five-day event also includes a street parade, with attendees, some in their native dress, marching along a predetermined route through the host city. Such is the scale of the event that the bidding process (to win the right to host) takes place six years in advance.

Source: www.lionsclubs.org

Not all meetings are of this magnitude, however. The vast majority are held with colleagues who work for the same company, and these are known as **corporate** meetings.

Companies, large and small, have a number of reasons for organising meetings of their staff, but all are linked to the companies' need to operate effectively in the field of business. For example, many corporate meetings are held for the purpose of training staff in the skills and techniques that they need in order to perform well in the workplace: selling skills, customer relations skills, information technology skills and so on, depending on the nature of the company's business. Other types of corporate meetings may be arranged with the objective of giving managers the opportunity to discuss the company's future strategies, for marketing, expansion, crisis management and so on.

Most such meetings are comparatively small (ranging from a handful of employees to several dozen), so they can be held in the type of small seminar rooms offered for hire by hotels. Indeed, a visit to most 4-star and 5-star hotels will provide information on exactly which corporate events are being held there that day, as such meetings are usually prominently listed in the reception area, for the benefit of the delegates attending them.

All types of company organise meetings for their staff, but some sectors tend to have more meetings than others. The finance (banking and insurance), medical and pharmaceutical, automotive and engineering sectors are the principal markets, in most countries, for the meetings industry.

While association and corporate meetings comprise the largest share of this particular form of business tourism, they are not the only elements. Governments and political organisations at all levels (local, regional and national as well as international legislative bodies, such as the European Commission) also need to hold regular meetings to discuss strategies, choose candidates and announce new initiatives.

Among the most visible of these meetings are the annual conferences of political parties that are held in most countries. In the UK, for example, the Labour Party held their four-day national conference in Liverpool in 2018. These annual events attract upwards of 10,000 attendees, including Members of Parliament, councillors and policy advisers, as well as approximately 2000 representatives from the press and other media, business groups, charitable organisations, think tanks and campaigning organisations.

The other types of organisations that frequently hold meetings are neatly encapsulated in the American acronym **SMERF**, which stands for social, military, educational, religious and fraternal. The SMERF sector of demand for meetings is a useful catch-all category, covering most types of meeting that are not held by professional/trade associations, companies or government organisations:

- *Social meetings*. This segment includes all groups meeting primarily for social interaction, such as collectors, hobbyists, special interest groups and non-military reunions. An example of such a meeting would be the 2019 National Barbie Doll Collectors Convention held in Kansas City, Missouri. The convention brings together collectors of all ages and backgrounds for four days of presentations, competitions and fashion shows, all based on the famous Barbie Doll merchandise.
- *Military meetings*. This segment largely comprises reunions of people who served in the armed forces during periods of conflict. The intensity – and often the tragedy – that can characterise such conflicts means that those who lived through them often find comfort in reuniting with their fellow fighters at regular intervals to discuss their wartime experiences and commemorate their comrades who did not survive the hostilities. Many reunions bring together veteran servicemen and -women with an affinity to a specific section of the military. To give just one example, in September 2018 a reunion for Royal Navy personnel who served on HMS Tiger, a military ship scrapped in 1986, took place at a hotel in Staffordshire, UK.
- *Educational meetings*. Those who attend such events are generally teachers, lecturers and academic researchers who meet in order to share their research in their particular subject area, as well as new challenges and other developments affecting the teaching of their specialist subject. A typical example of an educational meeting would be the annual conference of ATLAS (www.atlas-euro.org), an international association of lecturers specialising in the teaching of travel and tourism.
- *Religious meetings*. Some of the largest gatherings organised in the world's major cities are for the purpose of bringing together, for one or more days, people who share the same faith. At such events, worship and prayer are often combined with debates and workshops during which topical issues relating to the attendees' particular religion are discussed. While many of these events may be small-scale seminars, this is not always the case. For example, in 2018 Denver, USA hosted the American Academy of Religion/The Society of Biblical Literature meeting which attracted 10,000 attendees.

- *Fraternal meetings*. This segment includes primarily meetings of sororities and other fraternal organisations. The attendees at such meetings are often people who went to school or university together and wish to reunite from time to time, to relive the memories of their student days. University alumni reunions are a typical example of a fraternal meeting.

ASSOCIATION MEETINGS AND CORPORATE MEETINGS COMPARED

While government and SMERF meetings display a wide and often colourful variety of themes, the vast majority of meetings fall into either the association or corporate segments, but they differ considerably from each other in a number of important respects. Consequently, it is important to understand the distinguishing characteristics of these two segments and to be able to compare them accurately. Table 11.3 highlights some of the most important contrasts between the association and the corporate segments of the meetings sector of business tourism.

TABLE 11.3 **Association and business conferences contrasted**

Association conferences	Corporate conferences
Delegate numbers can be in the hundreds – even thousands	Delegate numbers tend to be fewer – usually under 100, and often a few dozen
The decision process for choosing the destination can be long and complex, often involving a committee	The decision process for choosing the destination is shorter and simpler – it is often made by one person
Spending per delegate per day can be moderate, as the delegates are usually paying out of their own pockets	Spending per delegate per day can be higher, as the delegates' companies are usually paying
These can last for several days, or even a week in the case of large international association conferences	These are generally shorter and often last for only one day
For associations, conferences represent an opportunity to make a profit, which can in turn be used to pay for the associations' running expenses	For companies, conferences represent a cost that must be financed out of the profits made elsewhere by the companies
Many association events are held in large, purpose-built conference centres	Many corporate events are held in the seminar rooms of hotels
The lead-time for an association conference can be several years	The lead-time for a corporate conference is usually much shorter than for an association conference
Association conferences are rarely cancelled as the by-laws of the association usually state that an annual conference must be held	Corporate conferences can be cancelled more easily, particularly in times of financial hardship for the company
Delegates' partners are usually welcome to attend association conferences, so parallel partners' programmes of events are often planned for them	Delegates' partners are rarely encouraged to attend

THE MEETINGS INDUSTRY

As recently as 25 years ago, the expression 'meetings industry' was hardly ever used, in the sense of an umbrella term describing all of those businesses existing wholly or partly in order to provide the wide range of facilities and services that are required to make meetings possible and ensure that they are run professionally and effectively. Now, the use of this term is widespread and the meetings industry is firmly established as an expanding and vitally important profession in its own right. The principal supply elements of the meetings industry will now be reviewed.

Venues

All meetings require some form of venue in which the attendees can gather for the duration of the event. Derived from the Latin verb *venire* (to come), the word venue is used to denote the building in which delegates come together in order to attend the event. In its most basic form, a venue comprises four walls, a roof and a collection of chairs for the delegates' comfort, but the variety of venues is almost as great as the variety of meetings held within them.

Conference centres

Their city centre locations, sheer vastness and often iconic designs mean that these buildings are certainly the most visible indication that any city is active in hosting large meetings. Many conference centres, such as the harbour-front Hong Kong Conference and Exhibition Centre, have become important symbols of the cities in which they are located. These venues are most often used for meetings requiring large open spaces and are built on a scale that enables them to accommodate hundreds or even thousands of delegates. In addition, they generally offer space for the types of exhibitions that are often run in parallel with large conferences, as well as the high-quality audio-visual and other technical facilities that are essential to the success of such large-scale events.

In their construction, conference centres are either of the purpose-built or converted types. Most are purpose-built – that is, they were originally and solely planned to be venues for conferences (see Figure 11.1). Many of the most interesting and charming conference centres, however, particularly in Europe, were converted into meeting venues from their original, different, function. Prisons, hospitals and factories are just a few of the types of building that have been converted into conference centres to serve the meetings industry. For example, the Mediterranean Conference Centre in Valletta, Malta, was originally constructed as a military hospital, but was converted into an outstanding conference venue in 1990.

Their immense capacity makes conference centres particularly suitable for large meetings of associations. Because, as mentioned, attendees at international association conferences can number in their thousands, conference centres are usually the only type of venue capable of holding meetings on this scale, particularly when, as is often the case with medical events for example, space is required in which to situate a parallel exhibition of products relating to the theme of the conference.

Hotels

Long before the first conference centres were built, meetings were regularly taking place in rooms designed for the purpose in inns and hotels, and to this day they remain the preferred type of venue for most of the world's meetings.

Whether hotels are situated in city centres, suburban locations, airports or rural areas, most depend to a significant extent on the income they earn from renting out their meeting rooms and the conference-related spending on catering and (for residential events) accommodation. Many hotel chains have branded their meeting facilities to ensure that customers using them are assured of a consistent standard of facilities and quality, wherever in the world a particular hotel may be located.

With the notable exception of the 'convention hotels' found in US cities such as Las Vegas, which offer meeting facilities capable of hosting conferences of several thousand attendees, most meeting spaces located in hotels are designed for smaller events of several

FIGURE 11.1 A purpose-built conference centre: Bordeaux Conference Centre, France

Photo: Claire Humphreys

dozen or several hundred attendees. Indeed, many hotel boardrooms are exclusive venues for fewer than 20 attendees. The average size of seminar rooms and other meeting facilities offered by hotel venues makes them eminently suitable for corporate events such as staff training sessions or senior management strategy meetings.

EXAMPLE

Rethinking meeting space

The International Association of Conference Centers (IACC) has researched the changing meeting room, concluding that flexibility in the design of space is becoming ever more important.

As meeting planners seek to engage the five senses of their attendees, to maximise the meeting experience, so they are seeking spaces that have flexible layouts. Easily reconfigured spaces can conveniently allow for three different modes of learning – auditory, visual and collaborative.

Consequently, the furniture used in meeting rooms often includes furniture with wheels, folding tables and soft seating (such as couches and armchairs). The design of breakout spaces (not necessarily entire rooms) remains important, allowing participants the opportunity to move away from the main group for separate conversations – or individual time – which can bring greater productivity and engagement overall.

Source: IACC, 2018

Academic venues

In many countries, universities and other educational institutions are active suppliers of meeting facilities, particularly during student holiday periods and at weekends. With their lecture theatres, classrooms, audio-visual facilities and catering services, such venues offer everything that is required to host meetings, large and small. When such meetings are hosted outside the teaching period, student accommodation may also be used by those attending residential events.

In several countries, universities have created their own marketing consortia to promote themselves as meeting venues. For example, Academic Venue Solutions (formerly Venuemasters) is a consortium that promotes the facilities available for hire to meeting planners at more than 40 venues in the UK and the Republic of Ireland. Members are venues that are either owned by an educational establishment or have as their core business the provision of further, higher or professional education. The consortium offers a venue-finding service for organisations and companies in search of meeting rooms and, if needed, accommodation for their events.

While rarely offering the standards of luxury found in 5-star hotels, academic venues have the advantage of being able to offer their facilities at fairly competitive rates. For that reason, they are often used as the location for meetings where attendees are paying out of their own pockets and costs have to be kept at a moderate level. Certain association events as well as some types of SMERF meetings are therefore natural clients of the academic venue sector of the meetings industry.

EXAMPLE

University of Westminster, London

The University of Westminster has been operating as an educational institution for 175 years. Its location in central London means it attracts clients wishing to host meetings in a conveniently accessible location. The mix of heritage buildings and modern galleries adds to its appeal. Facilities available for hire outside of the academic terms include:

- lecture theatres and classrooms
- exhibition and gallery spaces
- meeting and seminar rooms
- specialist studios and laboratories
- sporting facilities.

Catering facilities are available onsite and audio-visual equipment, installed to meet teaching needs, is thus conveniently available in lecture theatres and meeting rooms. Outside of the academic terms, the university offers delegates accommodation in student Halls of Residence.

(Continued)

FIGURE 11.2 Classroom at the University of Westminster

Photo: Claire Humphreys

Unusual venues

This category includes the meeting facilities offered by a wide range of properties such as museums, stately homes, castles, theatres and theme parks, as well as other tourist attractions such as zoos and aquariums. For most of these, the provision of meeting facilities is an activity that is secondary to the property's principal function, but, nevertheless, an important source of revenue. For example, many sporting venues, such as football stadiums and horseracing tracks, supplement the income they earn from such events by hosting meetings when the facilities are not being used for their original and principal purpose. The world-famous Stade de France in Paris is a typical example of an unusual venue of this type, advertising itself as a meeting venue for events of up to 5000 attendees.

The main motivation for holding a meeting in an unusual venue is to make the event memorable and attractive to attendees. The organisation holding the meeting can also benefit from the reflected glory of the great prestige associated with certain unusual venues. For example, any meeting held in the Victoria and Albert Museum in London will automatically benefit from the considerable cachet associated with such a venerable institution.

Other suppliers

It is clear that, in order to run a successful meeting, much more is required than simply a suitable venue. A wide range of facilities and services is necessary for the smooth running of any such event.

Attendees need to be fed and refreshed at regular intervals during the meeting, so the provision of food and beverages is vital, whether for a simple coffee break or lunch, or the type of sumptuous gala that is often held on the final evening of a grand conference. On such occasions, the decoration of the tables and the dining room can be as important as the quality of the food and wine, particularly for prestigious events.

As well as professional catering, most meetings make extensive use of audio-visual resources to make their events look and sound as good as possible. This is one of the ways in which the production of meetings has changed most in the past few decades. The days of conference speakers making use of a flipchart or overhead projector to communicate with their audiences are long gone. In the twenty-first century, information and communications technology has revolutionised the meetings industry, as it has so many other sectors. Multiple screens, PowerPoint or Prezi presentations and surround-sound quality are now widespread, turning many large-scale conferences, such as those of political parties, into veritable 'shows', characterised by high-quality sound and near-television-production standards.

In an increasingly globalised world, the provision of interpreting services is of growing importance as meetings may well be attended by delegates who speak a variety of different languages. Conference interpreters are those whose considerable skills make multilingual meetings possible and conference centres are generally designed to include interpreters' booths, where professional interpreters can listen to, translate and relay the conference speakers' words simultaneously and accurately – no easy feat.

EXAMPLE

Meetings industry accreditation

The Meetings Industry Association (MIA) is a UK-based organisation with a goal to support and grow the business meetings industry in the UK. It also oversees the UK's only recognised quality standard for the meetings industry (AIM).

AIM accreditation recognises the quality and professionalism of those businesses operating in the meetings industry sector. To gain accreditation, each business is audited against 50 criteria that consider the quality of the facilities, legal compliance, customer service, ethical conduct, accessibility standards and the display of best practice. Currently, more than 500 meetings industry businesses have AIM accreditation.

Source: www.mia-uk.org/AIM

Meeting planners

It is already evident from the above that the planning of meetings today can be a highly complex task. The destination and the venue must be chosen, the attendees' travel and, if necessary, visa requirements must be taken care of and their accommodation arranged, plus topics and speakers for the event must be selected. Some conferences, such as those of associations, must be marketed to prospective attendees and registration payments processed. At the actual event, someone must organise appropriate security measures, particularly if VIP attendees or speakers are involved, and someone must liaise with and manage the providers of audio-visual and catering services.

These tasks, and many more, are the responsibility of the **meeting planner**. In recent years, the role of the meeting planner has increasingly been recognised as a profession in its own right, and its importance in the meetings industry cannot be overestimated. Many now bear the job title 'professional conference organiser' or PCO, although a range of other titles exists, such as events planner, conference coordinator and meetings executive. Many meeting planners are employed by a single organisation, usually an association or a company, organising on a full-time basis all of the meetings, seminars and conferences that their organisation needs.

Others, often called **independent meeting planners**, are self-employed, offering their services to a variety of associations and companies on a consultancy basis, charging a fee for the meetings that they organise on behalf of their clients. This arrangement can be particularly beneficial to smaller organisations that do not hold sufficient events on a year-to-year basis to justify having such a person on their payroll as a full-time, permanent member of staff.

What we have termed the 'meetings industry', therefore, comprises those men and women who earn their living from the provision of facilities and services for the successful running of meetings, large and small. Managing and marketing venues, supplying catering, interpreting and audio-visual services for meetings and taking responsibility for the co-ordination and planning of the actual meetings event – these are the principal functions of those who make successful events possible.

It is worth noting, however, that, while some individuals and companies operate entirely and solely within the meetings industry, for many others, this sector of business tourism represents only a part of their activities. For example, many venues, in addition to providing space for meetings, also hire out their facilities for events such as concerts, weddings and graduation ceremonies. In many organisations, the planning of meetings is only *part* of the job done by the person undertaking the task, a part that may not even be reflected in their job title, as in the case of a training manager or human resources executive who also organises events from time to time. Many airlines and hotels, for example, are hardly aware of the role that they play in supplying vital services to the meetings industry by transporting and accommodating attendees and speakers.

EXHIBITIONS AND TRADE FAIRS

Some of the largest flows of business tourists are to be found where many thousands of people gather in a destination for one or more days to attend an exhibition. As the subject of this chapter is business tourism, the types of exhibition under consideration here are not of a cultural nature, such as exhibitions of paintings or sculptures found in art galleries and museums, but events where the exhibitors hire stands (or, in American English, booths) to present their companies' goods or services to those visiting the exhibition.

Although the word 'exhibition' is often used generically, it is common to distinguish between exhibitions, which attract the general public, and **trade fairs** (known as trade shows in the USA), which are mainly attended by business visitors. The Union des Foires Internationales (UFI), now known as the Global Association of the Exhibition Industry, gives the following definitions:

> Exhibitions are market events of a specific duration, held at intervals, at which a large number of companies present a representative product range of one or more industry sectors and sell it or provide information about it for the purposes of sales promotion. Exhibitions predominantly attract the general public ... Trade fairs are market events of a specific duration, held at intervals, at which a large number of companies present the main product range of one or more industry sectors and mainly sell it on the basis of samples. Trade fairs predominantly attract trade and business visitors. (UFI, 2019)

EXAMPLE

A growing exhibition industry

Research has forecast that the exhibition industry will see steady growth over the coming years. All regions are predicted to see a compound growth rate of around 4% over the five years of 2016 to 2021 (Figure 11.3).

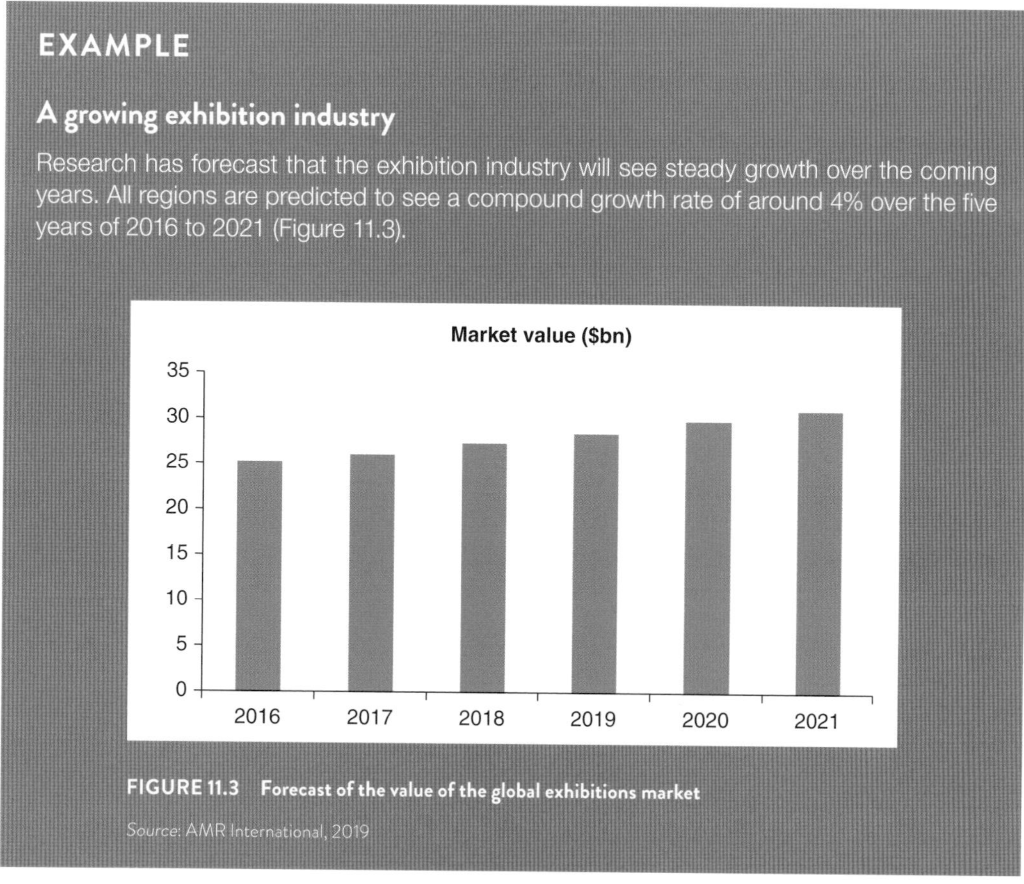

FIGURE 11.3 **Forecast of the value of the global exhibitions market**

Source: AMR International, 2019

In many cases, those who travel in order to attend exhibitions are members of the public seeking to buy, or find information about, goods or services that they need for their own personal consumption. An example of this type of event is the National Wedding Show, held at several UK venues each year, including Newcastle Arena, Olympia London, EventCity Manchester and the National Exhibition Centre in Birmingham. Each show attracts approximately 15,000 visitors, primarily future brides, grooms, bridesmaids and brides' mothers. More than 250 exhibitors display the goods and services they supply for those getting married, including wedding dresses, flowers and honeymoon holidays. There is also a series of workshops on themes such as public speaking (for after-dinner speeches) and make-up and hair-styling for weddings.

Similarly, the organisation International Education Fairs of Turkey (IEFT) runs an annual series of exhibitions that bring together education providers with Turkish students and their families, to promote study options available around the globe. Over the past ten years, this exhibition has grown to a point that 150 educational institutions from more than 25 different countries exhibited during the 2018 IEFT exhibitions, held in hotels in Istanbul, Ankara and Izmir. Almost 20,000 prospective students attended these events.

Those who visit trade fairs are people who are in search of goods and services that are vital to the effective functioning of their businesses. For example, Exposibram is the largest trade fair in Brazil for the mining industry. It takes place biennially over a four-day period, and in 2017 was held in the city of Belo Horizonte, in the mining state of Minas Gerais. Exposibram attracted 50,000 visitors and 500 exhibitors. The exhibitors were companies and organisations specialising in mining equipment and technologies, mining consulting services, mining engineering services, mining software, research and development services, mining maintenance and environmental technologies. During the four days of the trade fair, a mining industry conference, the Brazilian Mining Congress, was held in parallel, attracting 2000 participants.

An industry much more familiar to most people is the cinema sector of entertainment, which also has its own trade shows throughout the world. One such event is CineEurope, held at the Centre de Convencions Internacional de Barcelona (CCIB) in 2019 (www.cinemaexpo.com). Those who travel to this event, from all over Europe and beyond, are mainly proprietors and managers of cinemas in search of information on, and the opportunity to purchase, the latest equipment and services required by their businesses, such as film distribution, seating, staff uniforms, food and beverage kiosks, amplifiers and projection equipment.

EXAMPLE

World Travel Market (WTM) London

This annual business-to-business event attracts buyers of travel products from across the globe. In 2018, total attendance exceeded 50,000, with the first day of this three-day event open only to invited trade. More than 5000 exhibitors represent many different sectors of the travel industry, including airlines, tourist boards, ground-handling services, PCOs and travel technology companies.

WTM London also includes a programme of free educational seminar sessions delivered by influential industry figures, which offer the latest insights, trends and business knowledge. Exhibitor staff and visitors attend these events to further their own professional development.

Having made this distinction between exhibitions and trade fairs, it is certainly not the case that *all* events fall neatly into one or the other category. It is possible for the same event to be both an exhibition *and* a trade show. For example, an event primarily aimed at those running businesses in the construction industry may also be open to members of the general public who are interested in DIY, as both categories of visitors to such an event will be keen to see the vast range of building materials and tools on show. It is common in such cases to have certain days that are reserved for trade visitors only and others where the general public may also attend.

It is clear that each of the thousands of goods and services used in our personal and professional lives may be sold at exhibitions and trade shows, in destinations all over the world. From everyday objects such as shoes, books and mobile telephones, through much more expensive items such as cars, boats and holiday homes, to services such as educational courses, investment products and ski holidays, they all have their specific events, sometimes regional, sometimes national and sometimes international, to which potential customers can travel, in order to obtain information, negotiate and even possibly make a purchase.

Regarding patterns of travel to such events, it is often claimed that travel to exhibitions follows a different pattern from travel to trade shows. As most visitors to exhibitions are members of the public – people travelling with friends and/or family members – they tend on the whole to be making day trips to such events. For example, a family may go to a local exhibition centre to visit a ski show with a view to buying new ski equipment or booking a ski holiday. For the family, this is a pleasant day out, much like a trip to their local shopping centre.

Many trade shows are of such a highly specialised nature that they attract business visitors from other regions and frequently other countries or continents. Such visitors, because of the distances they have travelled, tend to stay longer at their destination, creating valuable business for hotels and restaurants, as well as for the transport companies.

Not only do travel patterns for exhibitions and trade shows differ, but this sector of business tourism may also be distinguished from the other sectors covered in this chapter, in the sense that both exhibitions and trade shows stimulate the travel of not one but two groups of people: the exhibitors and the visitors. So, whether the visitors are families on day trips or business owners who have travelled internationally to attend the event, the exhibitors inevitably remain in the destination for the duration of the trade fair or exhibition, bringing business to the local hospitality industry. At large events, the numbers of exhibitors can be substantial.

THE EXHIBITION AND TRADE FAIR INDUSTRY

The successful planning, marketing, hosting and execution of exhibitions and trade shows call for the concerted efforts and expertise of a wide range of specialist professionals.

Exhibition halls and exhibition centres rent out their facilities to provide the basic shelter and security that are necessary when hosting these events. They also have to provide all necessary utilities such as electricity, water, gas and communication connections (telephone, ISDN, the Internet), as well as a clear signage system. Infrastructure, such as restaurants, parking areas (usually one for exhibitors and another for visitors), toilets and entrance areas, is another integral element of these venues. Moreover, as conferences and seminars are often held alongside these fairs and exhibitions, appropriate meeting room facilities must be included.

As exhibition halls and exhibition centres are often vast buildings (see Figure 11.4), requiring many hectares of space, they are frequently situated in areas where land is

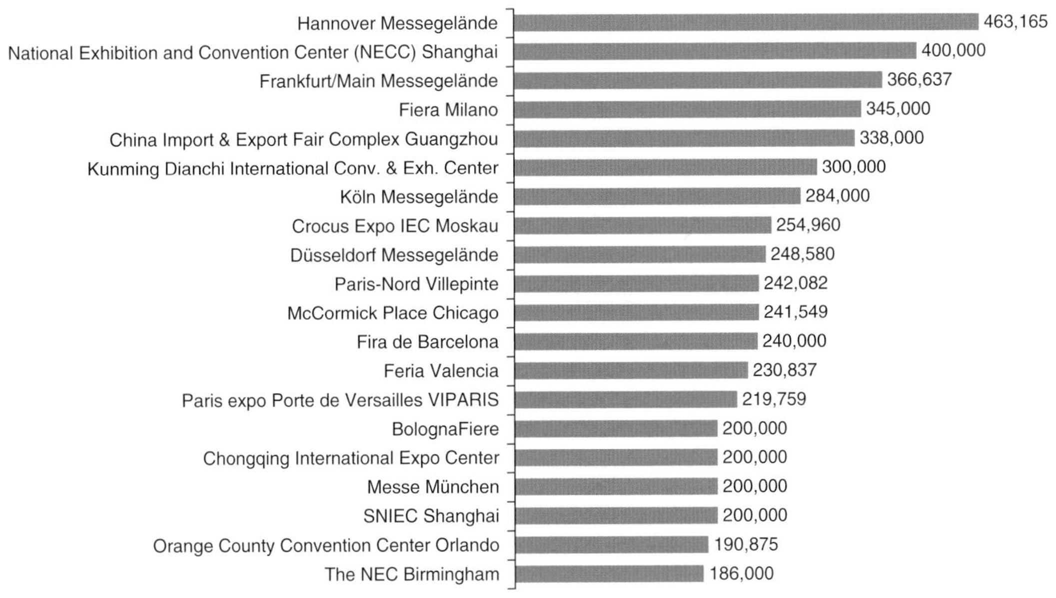

FIGURE 11.4 World's largest exhibition halls by gross hall capacity (in square meters)

Source: Association of the German Trade Fair Industry (AUMA), 2017

cheaper, well away from city centres. Frequently, they are to be found between the city's centre and its airport, where there is ample space for parking and easy access for visitors arriving by air. Venues may be either owned by the local municipality, as is generally the case in countries such as Germany, Italy and France for example, or privately owned and rented out with a view to making a profitable return for their owners.

While large venues such as the Hanover Exhibition Centre are places where the most exhibition and trade shows are held, it is important to remember that many smaller events may be held in hotels or other buildings such as arenas, concert halls or conference centres. Some events, due to the nature of the goods being exhibited, are, in fact, more suited to outdoor venues. Examples include agricultural shows, where livestock and farm machinery are on show, or aviation trade shows, such as the annual Cannes Air Show held at Cannes Mandelieu International Airport on the French Riviera.

EXHIBITION AND TRADE FAIR ORGANISERS

The organisers of these events are the people and businesses who create the exhibition or trade show, rent the venue, then market the event to prospective exhibitors and visitors. They earn a living from identifying opportunities for new exhibitions or trade shows and running these events, usually on a regular basis, for profit. Some of the largest exhibition companies earn revenue exceeding €1 billion (Table 11.4). A considerable amount of research must be carried out initially, to determine whether or not a particular theme for an exhibition or trade show is viable; in other words, are there sufficient numbers of exhibitors who are prepared to pay to have stands at an event dedicated to their industry? In turn, potential exhibitors will only agree to buy space at an event if they are satisfied that sufficient potential buyers will visit it, making their investment worthwhile. Therefore, one of the key tasks of organisers is to market it widely to potential visitors. The mark of a successful exhibition or trade show is when most exhibitors are satisfied with the numbers of visitors coming to their stands and most visitors are satisfied with the variety and range of products on display and, further, that both groups consider it worthwhile returning to the event at a future date.

TABLE 11.4 Revenue for selected exhibition companies (2017)

Company	Country base	Revenue (€m)
Reed Exhibitions	UK	1264.0
UBM	UK	979.0
Messe Frankfurt	Germany	669.1
Informa	UK	631.1
GT Events	France	481.9
MCH Group	Switzerland	421.8
Emerald Expositions	USA	285.2
Fiera Milano	Italy	271.3
HKTDC	Hong Kong	254.1
Fira Barcelona	Spain	187.6
NEC Group Birmingham	UK	182.9

Source: AUMA, 2017

As we pointed out earlier, visitors and exhibitors attend these events not only to buy and sell, but also for the opportunity to attend educational sessions and networking events during the exhibition or trade show. It is another responsibility of the organisers to ensure that an interesting and topical series of seminars is programmed during the event and that there are adequate opportunities for attendees to mix and mingle informally at, for example, opening receptions or after-hours cocktail parties.

STAND/BOOTH CONTRACTORS

Most exhibitors rely on specialist contractors to design and build their stands. In recent years, this task has become an increasingly creative and technical one as stand design has become more imaginative and elaborate, using new materials and new technology to make exhibition stands ever more eye-catching and attractive to visitors.

High visibility is essential at such events, where every exhibitor is in competition to entice visitors to approach their stand and engage with those who are there to sell or provide information on their companies' products. Colour, layout, lighting and prominent display of the company's logo all have a part to play in making a stand attractive and welcoming to visitors. Contractors may also be used to construct the stand before the event and dismantle it at the end.

FIGURE 11.5 Exhibition stand for the Ministry of Tourism and Antiquities, Iraq

Photo: Claire Humphreys

INCENTIVE TRAVEL

One particular type of meeting is usually regarded as being sufficiently distinct from all the others to justify it being given its own separate category. **Incentive travel** is the name given to the travel, usually in groups, of employees who have been awarded a luxury trip, entirely paid for by their company, as a prize for high achievement at work. The practice of using incentive travel to motivate employees to work harder was originally started by American companies in the 1950s, and employers in the USA are still the major generators of this sector of business tourism. Since then, however, the use of incentive travel has spread throughout the industrialised world and is now widely recognised as being one of the most effective management tools for encouraging employees to be more productive and make a greater contribution to their employers' profitability.

Most incentive trips are won by individuals (or teams) who have sold, within a given period, the most units of whatever it is their companies make, whether this is tractors, insurance policies, pharmaceutical products or any other type of manufactured goods or services. For this reason, most of those who travel on incentive trips are members of their companies' salesforce.

Put simply, a company using incentive travel as a reward will announce a competition to their salesforce, informing them that their individual or team sales figures during a particular period (often 12 months) will be recorded for the purpose of determining who sold the most during that time. The prize for being one of the most successful salespeople during that period is the incentive trip, typically of three to five days' duration, which will be described in detail and in the most enticing terms, in order to encourage the sales staff to do their utmost in order to win the trip.

It would be no exaggeration to say that incentive travel is one of the most luxurious, highest-spending and therefore lucrative forms of tourism that exists. In order to motivate employees to work harder to achieve greater results in the workplace, the travel prize they are competing for must be an extremely attractive one. This is particularly the case when those competing to win the prize are managers who travel often, on business and for leisure, and are therefore not easily impressed by yet another flight and another hotel in a foreign destination. Exotic destinations, luxury accommodation and a dazzling variety of exciting and exclusive activities are classic features of incentive travel.

EXAMPLE

Incentive travel trends

Incentive travel experts have concluded that two global trends affecting this sector are the desire for exclusivity and for authenticity. 'Exclusivity' may require that the incentive travel experience developed is not widely accessible to the general public, perhaps because costs prohibit it or because the product is not usually available to be booked. 'Authenticity' may require access to local experiences as part of an overall incentive event.

As incentive planners search for authentic experiences, so corporate social responsibility (CSR) activities are seeing a resurgence in popularity, as participants seek to do some good while on an incentive trip.

Source: Conference & Incentive Travel (C&IT), 2017

Incentive travel winners – those who get to go on these magnificent trips – must be given the impression that they are privileged and greatly valued by their employers, which is why incentive trips must delight and indulge those who are fortunate enough to receive this form of reward for their performance at work. The key word here is 'work' for, although incentive travel participants may look and behave like leisure tourists – dressing casually, relaxing, sightseeing and enjoying sporting and/or leisure activities – the motive underlying their trip is most definitely connected to the participant's working life, which is why this form of travel is firmly categorised within the business tourism sector.

Nevertheless, there are clearly alternative ways to motivate staff to work harder and reward them when they achieve outstanding results. The tool most commonly used by companies to 'incentivise' their employees is not incentive travel but *money*. This usually takes the form of cash bonuses for those who reach specific targets in their work. Gradually, however, more and more employers are beginning to realise that the use of incentive travel as a reward offers them a number of advantages not achieved by simply awarding staff the cash equivalent.

EXAMPLE

Comparing incentive travel with cash as a motive to perform at work

Advantages of incentive travel over cash

- Employees spend time with each other, at leisure. This informal networking offers them the opportunity of getting to know each other better, which in turn can help create a stronger team spirit when they return to work, having shared a number of enjoyable and memorable experiences together.
- For the few days of the trip, the company has an opportunity to inculcate 'company values' into some of its most productive employees. Pep talks are a common feature of incentive trips – motivational speeches praising the incentive travel winners for their hard work and extolling the qualities of the company they work for. This is one of the management techniques employed by companies to reduce staff turnover and, in particular, retain those employees who make the most valuable contribution to their company's profitability.
- Incentive travel is more effective than money at encouraging non-winners to try harder to win the next competition run by their company. The incentive travel winners' absence from work and their subsequent return, full of stories of what they have seen and done on their trip, make this a highly visible prize, as opposed to money, which is far less likely to be discussed with colleagues. Non-winners can be motivated to work harder to win next time when they hear their colleagues recount their incentive trip experiences.
- As incentive trips offer those who participate in them the opportunity to relax and/or engage in physical pursuits, it means that they tend to return to work refreshed and rested, and this boost to their wellbeing can be beneficial to their performance in the workplace.

At the same time, it is undeniable that the use of cash awards offers its own advantages, when compared with sending high-achieving staff on incentive trips.

Advantages of cash over incentive trips

- Low risk. Cash awards are attractive by the very nature of their simplicity. Money is always welcomed by the recipient, but the participant's response to an incentive trip is less predictable. Poor weather, the wrong choice of incentive destination or disappointing accommodation are among the factors that can turn what should be an enjoyable, motivating reward into its opposite.

(Continued)

- No loss of productivity. When some of the company's highest-performing members of staff are absent from work for several days, enjoying an incentive trip, the impact on the company's profitability can be considerable. With cash awards, the winners continue to work and there is no negative impact on the company's sales figures.
- Flexibility. The employee in receipt of a cash bonus for meeting a demanding sales target, for example, can spend the money on whatever he or she wishes or needs. This could be, of course, a holiday or short break, in which case the tourism industry benefits from the spending of this award, but it could equally be spent on home improvements, repairs to the family car or simply invested in a savings account.
- Finally, in an era when attention is increasingly being focused on employees' work–life balance – the balance between the time they spend working and the time they spend with friends and family – it is widely recognised that awarding an incentive trip, however luxurious, as a prize for high achievement at work does mean that the participants are automatically obliged to spend additional time away from home in order to take part in the trip. This may not always be welcomed by employees, particularly those who already find themselves spending evenings away from their family and friends, travelling on company business. Cash bonuses, therefore, can be a more motivating prize for such employees.

THE INCENTIVE TRAVEL INDUSTRY

In our review of the principal elements of the meetings industry, we revealed that a number of specialist suppliers are required in order to make the effective functioning of meetings possible – venues, audio-visual companies, interpreters and so on. By way of contrast, the incentive travel sector of business tourism largely makes use of the same services, facilities and resources that are used by leisure tourists: airlines and other forms of transport, hotel accommodation, tourist attractions, guides, shops, cultural and sports events and so on. Of course, the incentive travel sector does tend to make most use of that end of the tourism market spectrum characterised by 4- and 5-star hotels, exclusive restaurants and privileged, VIP access to tourist attractions and prestigious events.

The one type of specialist agency required in order to facilitate the functioning of the incentive travel industry is the **incentive travel house**. This is the term commonly used for an agency that designs incentive programmes for its clients, those companies using this technique to motivate their staff. Agency staff are professionals who oversee the entire operation, from designing the rules of the competition for employees and the selection of winners, through the choice of the destination and activities for the incentive trip to the planning of the detailed logistics for the trip, including all transport, accommodation and catering arrangements.

While some companies entrust the planning of their staff incentive programmes to high street generalist travel agencies, they are in a small, declining minority. Most companies understand that the planning and execution of incentive trips is so extremely technical and demanding in terms of the high expectations of the winners, that this process is best placed in the hands of specialist incentive travel houses.

One of the many pressures that those employed by incentive travel houses must contend with is the necessity of creating the essential 'wow' factor for every trip they organise. It is often claimed that 'wow' is the most important word in the entire lexicon of the incentive travel sector of business tourism, as any trip that fails to surprise, delight and inspire the participants in this way can fairly be said to have failed in its objectives.

Supplying that 'wow' factor is not simply a case of spending vast amounts of the client's money on extravagant entertainment for its winning employees. Great creativity and imagination are the essential qualities required by anyone wishing to work in this aspect of the incentive travel industry. A vivid, but not particularly unique, example of these qualities at work in the design of an incentive travel programme is the group of incentive winners on a trip to Finnish Lapland, who were given fishing rods and instructed on how to cut a round hole in the Arctic ice so that they could spend the day fishing as the native Lapps do. The cost of this simple activity was minimal, but the impact on the group was outstanding. It fired them with enthusiasm and enchantment – as all good incentive trips should.

EXAMPLE

Educating incentive travel professionals

Inaugurated in the 1970s, the Society for Incentive Travel Excellence (SITE) now has more than 2000 members located in more than 80 countries around the world. The society strives to achieve several goals, including connecting its members to promote relationship-building among this group of professionals, and to drive creativity – important in inspiring those benefitting from incentive travel.

Recently, the Society has introduced a specialist knowledge centre, accessible online, to further support learning and job performance. This is accompanied by training courses on aspects such as 'Selling to the Incentive Market' and 'Managing Incentive Travel Programs'.

Source: SITE, 2017

INDIVIDUAL BUSINESS TRAVEL

The final sector of the business tourism industry identified earlier is that of individual business travel, which may also be termed **corporate travel**. This sector comprises the trips of all men and women whose work obliges them to travel, either regularly or on an occasional basis. These employees are often known by the somewhat tongue-in-cheek title of 'road warriors', due to the time that they spend 'on the road' carrying out company business.

In the modern world, most organisations require some of their employees to travel from time to time in order to conduct some aspects of the company's business. Often, the objective of such trips is to find new customers, in which case a sales or marketing manager may be required to travel in order to present the company's products or services to prospective clients and negotiate prices with them.

As companies expand internationally, with branches in more than one country – and more and more often, as a result of globalisation, in more than one continent – staff find themselves travelling to meet their colleagues in other branches and work with them for a few days to solve a problem or share their expertise. This type of transient movement of staff between different branches of a company is another driver of individual business travel.

Some people, whether they are company employees or self-employed, find themselves travelling regularly on business due to the nature of the job they do. For example, most investigative journalists, whether for the print media, radio or television, could not work effectively without frequently travelling in order to carry out their enquiries. Similarly, those who have highly specialised skills, such as hostage negotiators or opera singers, often find themselves travelling to where their skills are needed at any particular time.

Given, therefore, the number of reasons that exist for employees travelling on company business, it should come as no surprise that individual business travel is a major expense for many firms. For this reason, most companies put into place a number of measures to control and limit their employees' spending on transport and accommodation while travelling on company business. The main technique used for this purpose is the company's **travel policy**. It is rare these days for any company or organisation (except, perhaps, for the smallest) *not* to have a written travel policy giving staff clear guidance on how they can – and, more crucially, cannot – spend their employer's money on business travel. Most such policies will state, for example, which class of air travel the employee is entitled to use when flying somewhere on behalf of the company. Typically, this will depend on a variety of factors, such as the length of the journey to be undertaken (short-, medium- or long-haul) and the employee's level of seniority within their company (junior, middle or senior management). Similar constrictions may be included in the travel policy for other elements of business trips, such as the class of hotel that may be used or the class of vehicle that may be hired. In this way, companies and organisations attempt to avoid the type of anarchic free-for-all that could arise if no controls were in place.

Many companies find it worthwhile employing a **business travel manager** to monitor the travel of employees and ensure that they comply with the travel policy. Business travel managers may also have the responsibility of negotiating with suppliers such as airlines, hotels and car hire companies on behalf of their employer. Large companies, in particular, are in a powerful negotiating position by virtue of the sheer volume of travel their employees undertake each year. So, while members of the general public using hotels only once or twice a year have very little leverage in terms of negotiating rates for overnight accommodation, a company with a salesforce of 50 people, spending between them several thousand nights per year in hotel rooms, is advantageously positioned to bargain with a hotel chain that has properties in the cities visited regularly by its salespeople.

A common task of the business travel manager, therefore, is to negotiate with a limited number of airlines, hotel chains and car hire companies, guaranteeing them a certain volume of business annually in return for preferential rates for the company's employees. When such agreements exist, the employees are generally instructed (in the travel policy) to use those suppliers rather than others with whom the employer has not negotiated preferential rates.

EXAMPLE

Business travel on a low-cost airline?

Historically, low-cost airlines were not a viable option for business travellers who often sought to purchase flight tickets at short notice and required flexibility to meet the changing demands of business meetings, perhaps changing return flight times as meetings overran or additional appointments were added to the traveller's schedule. However, the lucrative business travel market has more recently drawn the attention of airlines such as easyJet.

By offering flexible fares that allow date changes, priority boarding and a luggage allowance, easyJet has made a concerted effort to attract the business travel segment. The airline has also introduced a membership scheme (easyJet Plus), which allows travellers to pre-select seating, use the fast-track security lane at airports and carry an additional bag as hand luggage. The company has also made its flights available for reservation by business travel agents by listing on the main global distribution systems (GDS) such as Galileo, Amadeus and Sabre. Combined, these efforts have proved successful: in the aftermath, easyJet carried more than 12 million business travellers in one 12-month period.

Nevertheless, although companies are constantly seeking the best value for money from travel companies and accommodation providers, it would be a mistake to believe that they always look for the very cheapest fares and hotel rates for their staff who are travelling on business. There are three main reasons for employers wanting to avoid cutting their business travel costs to the bare minimum:

- staff comfort
- staff safety
- staff loyalty and morale.

STAFF COMFORT

Travelling in comfort can be an important consideration when it is vital that staff arrive at their destination fully refreshed and immediately ready to do the job that they have been sent to do.

Managers taking a long-haul overnight flight may save their company a considerable sum of money by travelling in economy class, but the probability that they will be able to sleep well and work at their seat – on their laptops, for example – is much less than if they were travelling in business class, with more personal space and more legroom. If they have not been able to rest and relax, they will hardly be in a fit state to attend an important business meeting in order to make a presentation or negotiate on behalf of their company. They may even need a day to recover from the flight, which means that an extra night in a hotel must be paid for, as well as meals and other expenses. Most importantly, a whole day's work may effectively be lost after both the outward and return journeys, due to the business traveller's loss of sleep.

When all of these considerations are taken into account, the economy-class ticket may seem less of a bargain than it appeared to be at the time of booking.

STAFF SAFETY

Employers have a legal duty of responsibility to do everything within reason to ensure the safety of those travelling on company business.

It is often claimed that business travellers face an even greater range of dangers than those travelling for leisure purposes. They are much more vulnerable, due to the fact that they are likely to be travelling alone, they make more attractive targets for criminals as they may be carrying information in their laptops that could be commercially valuable if it fell into certain hands, and, in some countries, businesspeople may be targeted by kidnappers, who understand that their employers will be prepared to pay a substantial ransom for their safe return.

The safety of business travellers must therefore be of paramount concern to their employers. Accordingly, when a company's employee has to arrange to stay overnight in another city, in order to meet a client for example, the company will usually authorise the booking of a room in a city centre hotel, although it may be much cheaper to book a room in a more distant, suburban hotel. This reduces the business traveller's need to travel around by taxi or public transport in an unfamiliar situation, thereby decreasing risk.

STAFF LOYALTY AND MORALE

Although many claim to enjoy it, individual business travel can be extremely trying at times. It temporarily separates people from their friends and families and can be a source of stress and frustration, in the same way that travel for leisure purposes can. Jet lag, gruelling security measures at airports and loss of opportunities for exercise are just a few of the common complaints of frequent business travellers. If, on top of these privations, business travellers also feel that their companies are cutting travel and accommodation costs to the bare minimum, they are hardly likely to feel positive about the firm they work for.

Resentful and unmotivated members of staff tend to feel very little loyalty to their employers. So, most companies, keen to retain their most valuable members of staff, will avoid adopting a penny-pinching approach to travel expenses and will resign themselves to paying for the occasional in-room movie or mini-bar item enjoyed by their intrepid road warriors.

THE INDIVIDUAL BUSINESS TRAVEL INDUSTRY

Most of the facilities and services used by individual business travellers are also used by leisure travellers. What they need from these suppliers has been discussed in detail elsewhere in this book, so here, a few of the specific needs of business travellers will be considered and contrasted with the requirements of those travelling on holiday or for other leisure purposes.

Transport

A glance at the type of full-page advertisement paid for by airlines targeting business travellers, or at those who book their trips, shows that a major priority for those travelling on company business is punctuality. The expression 'time is money' certainly applies to the countless hours spent each year by business travellers waiting at airports or railway stations for delayed or cancelled flights or trains. Notwithstanding their personal stress levels and frustration, well-paid executives in this situation are (even in the age of wireless communications and laptops) generally far less productive than they would be if they were at their desks working. Punctuality and reliability of service are therefore much sought-after qualities for the individual business travel market.

Frequency of services is also a feature that is taken into account by business travellers choosing which carrier to use. Many individual business trips have to be flexibly timed, due to the uncertainty that can exist over when the work will be completed and the traveller is able to make the trip back home. Negotiations, for example, can run into unforeseen complications that delay the return trip or, conversely, they can go faster than expected, leaving the business traveller free to return to base earlier than planned. In either case, a frequent transport service allows for the flexibility that is required by the traveller faced with an unanticipated change of schedule.

An on-board environment conducive to work is key. Even before the ubiquitous laptop became an indispensable item in the carry-on luggage of anyone between the ages of 17 and 70, those travelling on business tended to work for at least part of their journey, briefing themselves to prepare for their meeting, catching up on work-related reading, working through company accounts and so on. A tranquil environment, good lighting and, on trains, Wi-Fi connectivity and power sources for laptop computers and mobile telephones are examples of the types of facilities required by those who wish to remain as productive as possible while travelling on business.

Accommodation

As with transport, accommodation that offers guests the ability to continue to work productively is at a premium for the business traveller. While leisure guests may be attracted to hotels that promise to be a 'home away from home', business guests tend to seek facilities that turn a hotel into an 'office away from the office', with Internet connection and the possibility of having documents printed, photocopied and even (in some hotel business centres) translated. Lounges in business-orientated hotels are just as likely to be used for one-to-one business meetings as for drinks between leisure guests. There are also a number of other hotel services that are particularly appreciated by the business market, such as early check-in/late check-out, laundry services and the serving of meals in hotel bedrooms.

Business travel agencies

All but the very smallest companies tend to use some form of intermediary to book their business travel services. Some may use their high street travel agency, if their business travel needs are fairly simple and low-volume, but most medium- and large-scale companies make use of specialist business travel agencies, or travel management companies (TMCs) as they have come to call themselves, to make their travel arrangements, including the booking of transport and accommodation, providing advice on visa and vaccination issues and even, in some cases, issuing guidance on business etiquette for the destinations concerned.

In order to keep control of spending on business travel, most companies opt to employ a single TMC, usually chosen following a competitive tendering process and remunerated on a management fee basis. Some TMCs are small- to medium-sized businesses, but others, such as American Express Business Travel and Carlson Wagonlit, are vast companies with a global presence.

To a large extent, the recent evolution of business travel agencies mirrors that of the retail travel agencies discussed in Chapter 19, and the article referred to in the following example analyses some of the challenges facing these intermediaries in the age of information technology.

EXAMPLE

The globalisation of business travel management

In a 2014 White Paper, AirPlus International (www.airplus.com), published background information and key data on the globalisation of travel management. The document was written in cooperation with the Association of Corporate Travel Executives (ACTE – www.acte.org). This White Paper identifies nine reasons why globalisation of corporate travel management programmes has increased:

(Continued)

1. Companies are spending higher proportions of their travel budget outside their local region as they seek suppliers and markets further afield.
2. Consolidation of company travel has occurred to achieve traveller security, particularly in being able to track all employees who are travelling on behalf of the organisation.
3. Gaining cost savings by controlling travel expenditure.
4. Providing transparency in financial expenditure on travel.
5. Containing costs during the economic recession stimulated enthusiasm for systems and processes which could improve cost efficiencies.
6. Travel management companies have extended their supplier range globally.
7. Cloud computing has allowed travellers and travel managers to access computerised booking and travel management tools (such as registering receipt and expense claims) worldwide.
8. Automation has allowed smaller businesses (with limited travel budgets) to globalise.
9. Examples of successful global implementations are encouraging other businesses to follow suit.

This is not to say that globalisation of travel programmes is without its challenges. Local knowledge of appropriate services for each company is needed, while serving local needs and cultural expectations under a single global travel policy can be difficult.

Source: AirPlus/ACTE, 2014: 32

TRENDS IN BUSINESS TOURISM

The rest of this chapter looks at some of the most important trends that will present opportunities and challenges to the global business tourism industry in the years ahead. Many of those trends are already emerging and others may be anticipated because of changes in the wider market environment.

The market for business tourism services and facilities is extremely dynamic and highly sensitive to changes in the political, economic and social environment. This sector is also affected by the accelerating rate of innovation in information and communications technology. On the one hand, it offers significant opportunities for the development of more attractive business tourism products, but on the other, it may also create certain threats to the long-term prosperity of this sector.

ECONOMIC TRENDS

Emerging markets

The rise of new business tourism destinations in many developing economies of the world is a major, and ongoing, phenomenon in this sector. As recently as 60 years ago, North American cities and European capitals had a practical monopoly over the hosting of international association meetings, for example. They were virtually the only places equipped with the infrastructure required to host these large-scale events. The decades since then, however, have seen a burgeoning of destinations entering all sectors of the business tourism market: Australasia, South-East Asia, South America, Central and Eastern European countries and cities in the Middle East have entered the market as vibrant new destinations for the hosting of meetings, trade shows and incentive trips.

At the same time, developing economies create additional demand for business tourism events as their new businesses add to the need for corporate events, and members of the expanding professional classes increasingly have the means to travel to conferences and exhibitions in other countries.

This phenomenon is particularly seen in China and India, two of the world's fastest-growing economies, and countries widely believed to be major sources of international business tourism consumption in the years to come. These two countries represent the two economies that are set to generate the greatest expansion in outbound business travel in the short and medium term. Citizens of these countries are already travelling to other destinations in their own regions, on business, but they will extend their scope to Europe and other long-haul destinations in rapidly increasing numbers in the years ahead. In China, growing levels of personal disposable income, Chinese companies' investment overseas and a fast-increasing number of international air connections with cities in major destinations are factors that will ensure the rapid growth of Chinese outbound corporate meetings and incentive trips, as well as Chinese delegates at international association meetings and exhibitions in the near future.

Growing corporate cost-consciousness

As competition between business tourism venues and destinations intensifies, buyers have become aware that they are purchasing services in a 'buyers' market'. Much of the corporate market in particular has lost no time in reaping the benefits of this situation and meeting planners have quickly learned how to negotiate to their best advantage. With no sign of imminent change in the relationship between supply and demand, corporate buyers are set to become even more cost-conscious in the years ahead.

Almost every survey of demand for business tourism events suggests that corporate buyers expect the number of events they organise to increase in the immediate and short-term future, but there is no corresponding indication that their budgets are going to increase at a proportional rate. On the contrary, most surveys reveal a general reduction in per-delegate expenses as the central issue for many companies becomes that of ensuring better overall value and a higher return on their investment. Therefore, all business tourism destinations, and the venues within them, must constantly look for ways to manage their tariffs and demonstrate their cost-effectiveness. Quality, but at an attractive price, will be a dominant requirement for the foreseeable future, as the majority of businesses now recognise the strengths of their considerable purchasing power.

TECHNOLOGY TRENDS

Information and communications technology (ICT) has already transformed many aspects of the business tourism sector and there is no doubt that further advances in ICT will continue to have a profound impact on how such events are planned, promoted and experienced in years to come. Already a wide variety of smartphone apps exist to assist business travellers: from those that support travel arrangements, such as taxi bookings or holding reservation confirmations and airline boarding passes, to those which record and report travel expenses.

EXAMPLE

Apps to aid the business traveller

New smartphone apps are constantly being developed, so identifying lists of the 'best apps for business travellers' is a popular report offered by the trade press. Below are detailed some frequent entries on such lists:

- TripIt creates a convenient travel itinerary. The user emails reservation confirmations to TripIt and the app records the confirmation numbers by date. Competitors in this market include WorldMate, while, more recently, IOS have introduced Passbook, which provides similar features for iPhone users.
- Flight Board is designed for frequent fliers who wish to minimise the time wasted waiting for planes. It provides access to real-time arrival and departure information for airports across the globe. Similar apps include FlightTrack and Flightradar24. Most airlines have their own apps, while airport apps include the US-oriented GateGuru which provides departure gate numbers.
- Expensify tracks expenditure related to business travel to ease the reporting and reclaiming of costs for corporate travellers. This includes using photo images of cash receipts and GPS technology to track business mileage.

Young people now entering employment in the business tourism sector may never fully appreciate the extent to which the Internet has revolutionised the planning, marketing and execution of events such as conferences and exhibitions. It is rare indeed, nowadays, to find a major conference or exhibition without its own website, where potential participants can read, in advance, full details of the event, register to attend and plan their schedule for the event itself. Developments such as PowerPoint and hand-held devices that allow the audience to respond in real time to conference presentations have enhanced delegates' experience, while radio frequency identification (RFID) makes the tracking and identification of exhibition visitors more efficient. The deployment of Wi-Fi in conference and exhibition venues and in large hotels is expanding fast and is expected by almost all people travelling on business, as a means of keeping in touch with their colleagues and family, and continuing to work while 'on the road'. Social media, such as YouTube, Twitter, Facebook and LinkedIn, are increasingly being used by business tourism destinations and venues as a way of reaching out to potential customers in this market; for example, many conference centres post short videos on YouTube, featuring testimonials from satisfied meeting planners who have used their venue.

SOCIAL TRENDS

More female business tourists

Changes in the profile of the global working population have, in turn, had a very significant effect on the profile of participants in business tourism events. The most prominent of these is the ongoing increase in the proportion of women in professional employment. Women's share of professional jobs continued to increase in the first few years of the twenty-first century in the vast majority of countries, and this trend shows every sign of continuing.

Women are already well represented in a number of professions, such as healthcare and finance, which are expanding rapidly in most countries.

This continuing trend means that there are more women travelling on business, for all work-related purposes, including participation in conferences and exhibitions. The growing presence of female delegates at such events has had a number of impacts on business tourism services, from how conference and exhibition venues are designed (more toilet facilities for women) to the food served during breaks (lighter and generally healthier).

Another indication of the feminisation of the market is the increase in popularity of spas as incentive travel products, and not just for women. Partly through the influence of female participants, the spa has become an amenity that a growing number of delegates expect in hotels and resorts.

More older business tourists

The European and North American working population is ageing significantly and will continue to do so for the foreseeable future, adding to the proportion of those in employment who are in the older age categories. Increasingly, people in their 60s and 70s are remaining in employment, either through choice (they find fulfilment through their work) or through necessity (they cannot afford to retire).

With a significant proportion of workers in the older age groups working in managerial and professional positions, it is highly likely that they will continue to travel on business and to business events, for a number of reasons:

- Because they can! As members of the baby boomer generation start to enter their 60s, it is clear that they are considerably healthier, fitter and more socially involved than the previous generation at that age. Travelling to business events and fully taking part in them present them with none of the physical challenges that their parents would have faced in their 60s.
- Older workers understand that networking is particularly important to them as the type of upper-level management positions they are often seeking are not likely to be advertised. Attending conferences of their professional associations provides them with a valuable opportunity to network.
- There is a positive relationship between older workers staying in the workforce and their need for ongoing training opportunities. Particularly with so many older workers continuing to work in the fast-evolving 'knowledge industries', constant in-service training events are vital to them for keeping their skills up to date. This means that they will be increasingly present at corporate meetings that have a training objective.
- A growing number of retired people are choosing to continue being members of their professional associations; in many cases, for the mental stimulation that profession-based meetings provide, as well as for the opportunity to maintain contact with colleagues.

The challenge of attracting 'Generations X and Y'

Over the next few years, associations will face growing difficulties in attracting attendees to their events. This is partly due to the prevalent phenomenon of people being **time poor**: that is, a growing number of association members have extensive demands on their limited time. It appears, however, that the new and upcoming generation of association members – 'Generation X' (those born between 1964 and 1977) and Generation Y (born between 1978 and 1994) – may also take some convincing that there is value in attending conferences. Generation Xers, unlike their parents, do not so readily see the value of face-to-face events. As they have grown up with electronic media as a primary communication tool, face-to-face events are less attractive to them (this is even more the case with Generation Yers). If this contention proves to be accurate, it presents serious meeting attendance issues for associations, as these two generations, between them, account for a combined demographic of 120 million people in the USA alone.

What can be done to reach this vast and growing section of the workforce and interest them in attending meetings, incentives, conferences and events (MICE)? Understanding their profile, developing strategies and targeting each group with appropriate messages is key to motivating Generations X and Y to join associations and attend their conferences. Both groups have a sophisticated understanding of technology and expect it to be well utilised. The Web wins over traditional media as a primary source of information, and they often select personal fulfilment over monetary rewards, seeking a casual work environment, telecommuting options and time off to enjoy life.

EXAMPLE

Generation Y business travellers

The presence of the Generation Y traveller is shaping the behaviour of business travellers, who approach their trips differently, owing to factors such as access to a variety of digital technology and a desire to explore new places.

It is estimated that three-quarters of Generation Y travellers use mobile devices to plan their travel. There is also a greater likelihood that these business travellers will participate in airline and hotel loyalty schemes, with the desire to gain free travel or discounts (rather than upgrades).

It should also be noted that as the Millennial generation gains more senor positions in the workplace, further changes to the business tourism industry can be expected.

Source: Slate, 2014

As time moves on, the behaviour and preferences of Generations X and Y (the Millennial generation), will come to shape corporate and association life. Therefore, time spent now in understanding their needs and convincing them of the rewards of attending face-to-face events will reap rewards in the future.

Corporate social responsibility (CSR)

The field of corporate social responsibility (CSR) has grown exponentially in the last decade as companies increasingly seek to engage with their stakeholders and deal with potentially contentious issues proactively. Now, more companies than ever are engaged in integrating CSR into all aspects of their business, encouraged by a growing body of evidence that CSR has a positive impact on businesses' economic performance.

The US-based organisation Business for Social Responsibility (BSR) defines corporate social responsibility as 'achieving commercial success in ways that honour ethical values and respect people, communities, and the natural environment' (BSR, 2006: 7). This organisation also says that CSR means addressing the legal, ethical, commercial and other expectations that society has for business and making decisions that fairly balance the claims of all key stakeholders.

The business tourism industry itself is beginning to show increasing awareness of the need to demonstrate its CSR, and this will intensify in future years. All stakeholders in the business tourism industry, from airlines, hotels and venues to intermediaries and the delegates themselves, will need to examine their own commitment to CSR. This will mean that business tourism stakeholders will increasingly be obliged to demonstrate their concern for the natural environment as well as for the host communities that live and work in the destinations where events take place. This is particularly the case when the standard of living of the host community is markedly below that of the business travellers themselves. The apparent luxury and extravagance that characterise certain events can stand out in very stark contrast to the abjectly poor and chronically disadvantaged conditions in which some of the local inhabitants live. For this reason, it is encouraging that a number of conference and incentive travel organisers have begun taking steps to invest in projects that have a positive impact on the communities residing in the destinations where their events are held. Conference delegates raising money for a local charity or incentive travel participants spending a day making environmental improvements to their destination are typical examples of this growing trend.

In the years ahead, more business tourism stakeholders will become aware of the benefits to themselves, and to host communities, of investing time and money in giving something back to the underprivileged people living in some of the destinations where their events take place.

SUMMARY

This chapter has reviewed the elements and characteristics of the business tourism sector, as well as some of the key trends and challenges that the sector is already dealing with and will continue to face in the future. There can be no doubt that the market environment for business tourism will continue to evolve in ways that are perhaps impossible to predict at the present time. It is in this very unpredictability, however, that the challenge and excitement of operating in this sector of the travel and tourism industry lie.

In the complex, volatile flux of market trends and forces, one element that will remain reassuringly constant is human nature itself. Men and women will continue to attend business tourism events, not only for the opportunity to obtain personal and professional development for themselves and business growth for their organisations, but also for the simple pleasure of meeting those with whom they share a common interest or goal. Buyers and participants will be drawn to attractive destinations and venues that deliver efficiently run and memorable events, using state-of-the-art technology, as well as distinctive cultural experiences in a healthy and unique environment.

QUESTIONS AND DISCUSSION POINTS

1. The acronym SMERF is identified in the chapter. Explain the different characteristics of each type of organisation referenced by this term.
2. How is digital technology affecting the different sectors of the business tourism industry?

3. Why might a company choose to use incentive travel to motivate their staff? Are their some limitations that might need to be considered?

TASKS

1. In a small group, arrange to visit a meeting venue in your local area. Create a short video that promotes this venue to the meetings industry. To enhance the usefulness of your video, ensure you give due consideration to a variety of information that a meeting planner might need about the venue.
2. In this chapter, we provide an example of the World Travel Market London (WTM) as a trade fair. Review the website for this event (https://london.wtm.com) to evaluate why a buyer of travel products might choose to attend this event. Include consideration of why sellers of travel products might choose to become exhibitors. Summarise your findings as an infographic.

WEBSITES

Association of Corporate Travel Executives: www.acte.org

Meetings Industry Association: www.mia-uk.org

Society for Incentive Travel Excellence: www.siteglobal.com

World Travel Market London: https://london.wtm.com

REFERENCES

AirPlus/ACTE (2014) *Globalisation of Corporate Travel Programs*. Alexandria, VA: AirPlus International.

AMR International (2019) Global exhibitions market forecast to grow 4% to 2021 with Southeast Asia high on the radar for international organisers. Available online at: www.amrinternational.com/global-exhibitions-market-forecast-to-grow-4-to-2021-with-southeast-asia-high-on-the-radar-for-international-organisers [Accessed January 2019].

Association of the German Trade Fair Industry (AUMA) (2017) *German Trade Fair Industry: Review*. Available online at: www.auma.de/en/media_/publications_/Documents/german-trade-fair-industry-review-2017/auma-review-2017.pdf [Accessed January 2019].

Business for Social Responsibility (BSR) (2006) *Business Brief: Intangibles and CSR*. Available online at: www.bsr.org/reports/BSR_AW_Intangibles-CSR.pdf [Accessed 12 October 2014].

Conference & Incentive Travel (C&IT) (2017) *Incentive Travel Report*. Available online at: www.citmagazine.com/article/1420865/incentive-travel-report-2017-download-full-report [Accessed January 2019].

International Association of Conference Centres (IACC) (2018) IACC Meeting Room of the Future: A survey of meeting venue operators and suppliers. Southam, IACC, June.

International Congress and Convention Association (ICCA) (2018) ICCA Releases 2017 Statistics with another Record Number of Association Meetings. Available online at: www.iccaworld.org/newsarchives/archivedetails.cfm?id=7436 [Accessed January 2019].

Slate, T. (2014) *Generation Y Business Travellers Increasing in Number and Influence*. Available online at: www.tourism-review.com/generation-y-business-travellers-news4210 [Accessed January 2019].

Society for Incentive Travel Excellence (SITE) (2017) Site Knowledge Centre. Available online at: www.siteglobal.com/page/site-knowledge-centre [Accessed January 2019].

Swarbrooke, J. and Horner, S. (2001) *Business Travel and Tourism*. Oxford: Butterworth-Heinemann.

Union des Foires Internationales (UFI (2019) Background and Knowledge. Available online at: http://member.ufi.org/Public/Default.aspx?Clef_SITESMAPS=152#1.2 [Accessed January 2019].

12

THE HOSPITALITY SECTOR: ACCOMMODATION AND CATERING SERVICES

CONTENTS

LEARNING OUTCOMES

After studying this chapter, you should be able to:

- explain the structure and nature of the hospitality sector, distinguishing between the various categories of tourist accommodation and catering services
- describe how accommodation is classified and appraise the problems involved in classification
- understand the nature of demand for accommodation and catering and how the sector has responded to changing patterns of demand over time
- assess the relationship between the hospitality sector and other sectors of the tourism industry.

> In the nineteenth century, hotels became firmly established not only as centres of commercial hospitality for travellers, but often also as important social centres of their communities. Their building, management and operation became specialised activities, with their own styles and methods. (Medlik and Ingram, 2000: 7)

INTRODUCTION

The hotel industry, as part of the wider hospitality sector, is an important part of the tourism industry and can play a major role in the experience of the visitor. In this chapter, we will be principally concerned with the commercial accommodation and catering sector. It must not be forgotten, however, that this sector represents only part of the hospitality business and is often in competition with large non-commercial hospitality suppliers that are no less important to tourism. The visiting friends and relatives (VFR) market is substantial and, in addition, there is a wide variety of other forms of accommodation used by tourists, including the tourists' own camping and caravanning equipment, privately owned boats and – of increasing significance for tourism in the twenty-first century – second homes. There is also a growing market for home exchanges and the swapping of timeshare accommodation, a market facilitated through the establishment of timeshare exchange companies.

It is, in fact, difficult to distinguish between the strictly commercial and non-commercial aspects of the hospitality business. Organisations such as youth hostels and YMCAs, for example, are not necessarily attempting to make a profit, but must cover their operating costs, while it is increasingly common to find educational institutions such as universities and schools hiring out their student accommodation to tourists outside the academic terms. One result of this has been a marked increase in the quality of student accommodation, with en suite bathrooms now the norm in new buildings.

Other forms of tourism that, by their nature, embrace accommodation would include privately hired yachts or bookings on a cruise ship. Operators in some countries provide coaches that include sleeping berths, while in others packages are available using specially chartered trains that serve as the travellers' hotel throughout the trip. Independent travellers can also book sleeping accommodation on rail services and overnight ferry routes. To what extent should all these services be counted as elements of the commercial accommodation available to tourists?

Certainly, any study of tourism must take account of these overnight alternatives and the expansion or contraction in demand for sleeping arrangements that compete with the traditional accommodation sector. The rise in cruise holidays, to take one instance, will have affected demand for more traditional forms of holiday in which travel and somewhere to stay are the norm.

Tourists staying in private accommodation away from their homes, whether with friends and relatives, through private rental arrangements or in second homes, are nevertheless still engaging in tourism and will almost certainly be contributing to tourist spend in the region, as they will tend to use local commercial transport, restaurants and entertainment. Their spend must therefore be included in tourism statistics for the region.

Airlines, recognising that home exchanges can also represent a healthy source of flight revenue, developed and commercialised the home exchange business by establishing directories to assist people in arranging exchanges. Some national or regional tourist offices also keep directories of homeowners who are prepared to make exchanges, and others maintain lists of local householders willing to invite guests from overseas into their homes for a meal (a particular feature of US hospitality). More recently, commercial brokers have been set up to facilitate home exchanges around the world, for a modest fee (www.lovehomeswap.com, www.homelink.org.uk and www.homeexchange.com, for example).

The rental of private homes, whether rooms or entire properties, using online intermediaries to link suppliers with consumers, has seen significant growth in recent years. In Europe, this sector, termed peer-to-peer accommodation; is valued at €15.1 billion (Vaughan and Daverio, 2016). Airbnb is the key player in this market. While local legislation has, in some regions, inhibited growth, we are increasingly seeing destinations introduce legal reforms, which eases the way for more homeowners to enter this market without fear of fine or court action.

EXAMPLE

Airbnb

Founded in 2008, when the economic climate globally was putting pressure on levels of disposable income available for holidays, Airbnb provides an online marketplace for home owners to list accommodation available for short-term hire. This might be a spare room or the entire house, a holiday villa or a castle.

Matching tourists with places to stay has proved popular, and the company has arranged accommodation for more than 400 million guests since its inception. In 2015, the company provided access to 5 million unique places in 81,000 cities around the globe, making it the largest accommodation provider in the world.

This is not without issues, however. Amsterdam, London and San Francisco have all battled with Airbnb over the listing of properties that have not been correctly registered, awarded permits or undergone the required safety checks. Local authorities are also concerned that accommodation hosts are now in competition with hotels, but fail to pay local taxes or adhere to local regulations.

THE STRUCTURE OF THE ACCOMMODATION SECTOR

The accommodation sector comprises widely differing forms of sleeping and hospitality facilities that can be conveniently categorised as either serviced (in which amenities such as room cleaning and catering are included) or self-catering. These are not watertight categories as some forms of accommodation, such as holiday camps or educational institutions, may offer serviced, self-service or self-catering facilities, but they help in drawing distinctions between the characteristics of the two categories. Figure 12.1 provides an at-a-glance guide to the range of accommodation that tourists might occupy.

Hotels are the most significant and widely recognised form of overnight accommodation for tourists. They also form one of the key elements of most package holidays. What constitutes a hotel and distinguishes it from other forms of accommodation, however, is not always clear. VisitEngland has provided definitions for the many different categories of accommodation that it rates as part of its quality assurance scheme (see Table 12.1). We can see from this that there are several subcategories of hotel, all of which are separately distinguished from that of budget hotels.

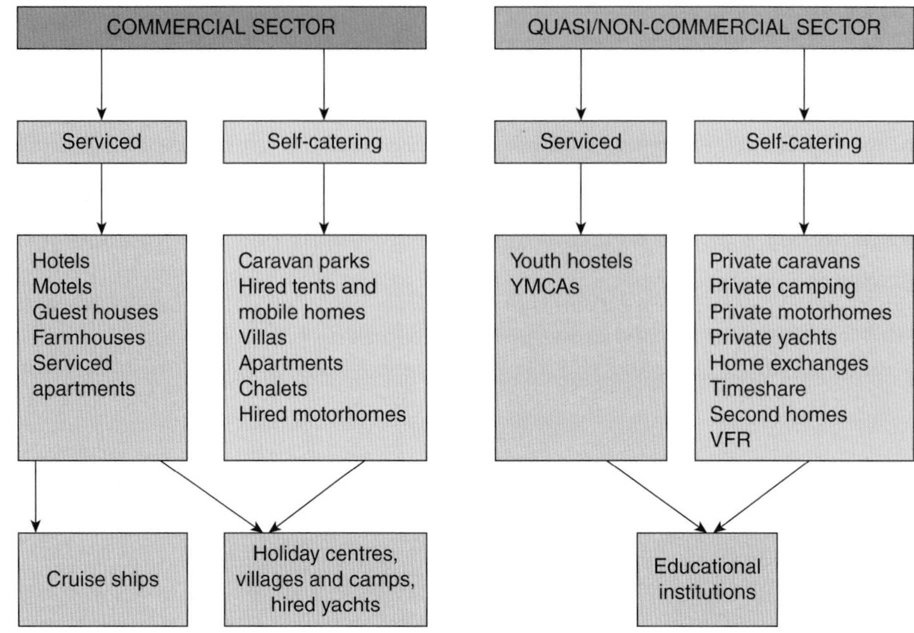

FIGURE 12.1 The structure of the tourist accommodation sector

TABLE 12.1 Accommodation definitions established for the National Quality Assessment Scheme for England

Category of accommodation	Definition
Hotel	A hotel must have a minimum of six bedrooms, be licensed and offer dinner. Also, all bedrooms must be en suite or have a private bathroom. Subcategories include country house hotel, small hotel, town house hotel and metro hotel (which may not offer dinner but is located within walking distance of other restaurants).
Budget hotel	Budget hotels are always part of a large 'branded' hotel group offering clean and comfortable accommodation, with a consistent level of service and facilities across the brand.
Guest accommodation	These properties are likely to be smaller than hotels, with perhaps more of a family home feel and approach, and a less structured service.
Self-catering	All accommodation with its own kitchen and bathroom facilities. Most take bookings by the week, generally from a Friday or Saturday, but short breaks are increasingly common.
Serviced apartment	Often found in big cities, these offer hotel services such as maid service and concierge in addition to a self-contained unit with a kitchen.
Park	This includes parks that cater for touring caravans and/or tents and may or may not include individual caravans (defined below), some of which may be available for hire.
Holiday village	This usually comprises a variety of types of accommodation with the majority provided in custom-built rooms (e.g. chalet, hotel rooms) on a large complex. A range of facilities and activities are also available which may or may not be included in the tariff.

Category of accommodation	Definition
Glamping	Often in unique or quirky locations, this accommodation usually allows the residents to get close to nature, staying in camping-style accommodation (e.g. tepees, yurts, safari tents).
Hostel	Accommodation often in shared rooms with bunk beds, although family rooms may be available. Hostels normally welcome individuals, families and groups, many of whom are staying on a short-term basis. Subcategories may include backpacker hostels, activity accommodation, bothy (camping barn) and bunkhouse.
University/campus	As the name suggests, this scheme applies to educational establishments. In general, campus accommodation is on a college or university site, with some aspects of communal living space.
Caravan holiday home	This includes caravan holiday homes situated on farms, in caravan parks, etc., which are let by the owner as self-catering accommodation.
Hotel boat	This scheme covers narrowboats, cruisers and hotel boats in small and large fleets across England's waterways. Hotel boats are generally narrowboats that are worked by a crew, allowing guests to relax and only help if they want to.
Chalet	A chalet is a building normally constructed in timber, part brick or uPVC and used as holiday accommodation on a seasonal basis rather than as a permanent residence. These properties are often restricted in size and will usually be situated on a chalet park with similar properties. Chalets require individual planning consent and are permanent structures.

Source: VisitEngland, 2018

THE CORPORATE CHAINS

A feature of the industry is that, as mass tourism has developed, so have the large chains and corporations in the accommodation sector. The hotel and motel business has reached a stage of maturity in which a few major companies have come to dominate, if not the markets, then certainly the distribution chain. The policy of these groups is to create an international and uniform marketing image for each brand to assist sales around the world. One benefit of this uniformity is that, as new destinations develop, the existence of trusted brands can help give the consumer confidence to visit a perhaps untested location. For this reason, some governments in developing nations provided financial support to the major chains looking to develop hotels in their key cities and tourist areas.

Economies of scale have allowed the largest chains to increase their spend on international marketing, advertising and sales promotion in partnership with other sectors of the industry, such as transport companies and tour operators, while cutting costs and, in the case of the budget brands, reducing prices to consumers. This expansion has been aided by franchising, whereby hotels and motels are operated by individual franchisees paying royalties to the parent company for the privilege of operating under a brand name. This form of expansion has been used with great success around the world by companies such as Holiday Inn, while the Friendly Hotel group holds European franchises for such well-established brand names as Quality Hotels, Comfort Hotels and Sleep Inns. In order to expand rapidly, the chains have taken not just to franchising but also to entering into management contracts and joint ventures, with actual ownership of the properties declining.

EXAMPLE

Franchising the brand

The business module of InterContinental Hotel Group (IHG) uses three types of operational approach: franchised (by far the most significant sector of their business), managed and owned. Each type of approach requires different levels of resource, summarised in Table 12.2.

TABLE 12.2 IHG hotels

	Franchised (4615 hotels)	Managed (965 hotels)	Owner-operated (23 hotels)
Ownership	Third party	Third party	IHG
Marketing	IHG	IHG	IHG
Staff	Employed by third party	IHG usually supplies general manager (and occasionally other senior managers)	Employed by IHG
Level of capital investment by IHG	None	Low/none	High
Income earned for IHG	Fee – % of room revenue	Fee – % of total hotel revenue plus % of profit	All revenues and profits

Source: InterContinental Hotels Group (IHG), 2017

As we can see, franchising requires little capital investment and no human resource management. As a consequence, it provides an effective way to grow the brand quickly and with limited financial risk. Of course, establishing the brand and developing the franchise guidelines to ensure that consistency and quality are maintained are key responsibilities of the franchisor, in this case IHG.

Leading hotel chains often develop several brands within their portfolio in order to serve a variety of niche markets. These include the following:

- *Marriott International.* In 2016, Marriott purchased the Starwood group (for $13 billion) to establish the largest hotel company in the world, by sales revenue. The combined entity now operates 30 brands so it will be interesting to see whether all of these remain as the integration of the two companies continues. The company now operates around 5800 properties (with 1.3 million rooms) in more than 110 countries, mainly under the Marriott label. The brand portfolio also includes Courtyard, SpringHill Suites and Renaissance hotels. The Starwood brands now in the portfolio include Sheraton Hotels and Resorts, Westin Hotels and Resorts, le Meridien, St Regis, Luxury Collection, W Hotels, Four Points by Sheraton, Aloft and Element. To serve the luxury segment, Marriott operates Bulgari Hotels and Resorts, Ritz Carlton and JW Marriott, while the extended stay market is served by Residence Inn and Towneplace Suites. Three brands are extended to serve the timeshare market: Marriott Vacation

Club, Grand Residences and Ritz-Carlton Destination Club. Marriott launched a range of boutique hotels under the Edition brand and a portfolio of unusual upscale properties branded as the Autograph Collection. It has introduced a new budget lifestyle brand, Moxy, currently with three hotels in Asia, a dozen in the USA and more than 20 in Europe (with this number expected to double by 2020).

- *Hilton Worldwide.* Originally established by Conrad Hilton in 1919, this company now operates nearly 5300 hotels in 103 countries, comprising a mix of owned, leased, managed, timeshare and franchised operations; over 4500 operate under franchise. Prior to the merger of Marriott and Starwood, Hilton Worldwide was the largest hotel company in the world by number of rooms, with 698,000 rooms at the time of writing. The company operates 14 brands, including Hilton, Conrad, Doubletree, Embassy Suites, Hampton Inn, Hilton Garden Inn, Home2 Suites by Hilton, Homeward Suites and The Waldorf Astoria Collection. More recently added brands are Canopy by Hilton, Curio (upscale hotels), Tapestry (boutique) and the Tru (trendy budget) brands. The company also owns the Hilton Grand Vacations timeshare brand. Hilton USA, bought by US investment company Blackstone in 2007, has now amalgamated once again with the Hilton Group UK, reunifying the brand after many years of separate ownership.
- *InterContinental Hotels Group.* In 2017, IHG owned, managed or franchised over 5300 individual properties and 798,000 rooms, spread over nearly 100 countries. Once an offshoot of Bass Breweries, the hotel group is now independent, and in recent years has been active in adding properties to its portfolio. It offers a range of branded products, including top-of-the-range InterContinental and Crowne Plaza Hotels, mid-scale Holiday Inn and Indigo brands and, coming in a little above budget prices, the Express by Holiday Inn/Holiday Inn Express chain. It has also bought into the corporate hospitality market for extended stays, owning, franchising or operating the US brands Staybridge Suites by Holiday Inn (marketed as a 'home away from home' for business travellers) and Candlewood Suites (aimed at the family market). IHG introduced the Hualuxe Hotels brand which focuses on a hospitality style devised to appeal to Chinese travellers and the Even Hotels brand, which is designed to appeal to travellers wanting to maintain a healthy, active lifestyle. It purchased the Kimpton brand (boutique hotels) in 2014 and recently launched the Avid brand, with five hotels due to open at the time of writing (in the USA and Mexico). As we discussed in the example, the company's business model focuses on franchising and managing brands, rather than owning hotel properties outright (IHG, 2017).
- *Accor.* The first non-US-operated hotel chain in this list, this French company operates around 4200 hotels in 99 countries, with a variety of brands ranging from luxury to budget. International brands include Sofitel, Novotel, Mercure, Ibis and Formule 1. In North America, the brand operates under the Sofitel and Novotel brands alongside budget brands Motel 6 and Studio 6 (extended stay hotels). The Sofitel brand has now been subdivided into three formats: Sofitel Luxury Hotels, Sofitel Legend (historic properties) and So by Sofitel (Boutique hotels aimed at the younger market). Existing Sofitel units not fitting any of these categories adequately are rebranded as Pullman Hotels. A new budget brand, All Seasons, was introduced in 2007 but this, along with the Etap brand, has been integrated into the Ibis brand. Accor operates 52% of its hotels under a direct management contract, while 48% are franchised (Accor, 2018).
- *Louvre Hotels.* This group, formed through an amalgamation with Envergure and Golden Tulip, is the second largest European hotel group and operates nine brands; the 2-star Campanile Hotels along with Kyriad, Première Classe, Tulip Inn, Golden Tulip and Royal Tulip. Added to this are the Jin Jiang Inn, Sarovar Hotels

and Resorts and Metropolo brands, the last using a Chinese-European fusion style. Operating more than 2500 hotels in 52 countries, Louvre hotels owns 26% of the portfolio, and operates 27% of hotels under management contract, while 47% of units are franchised.

Further afield, other notable chains include the Mandarin group, concentrated in the Pacific Rim area, while Indian-owned Oberoi Hotels have expanded into Egypt, the Far East and Australia.

These chains market their products aggressively, advertise extensively, work closely with large, tour-operating organisations globally and, in addition to their own websites, provide an effective distribution network linked to the airline CRSs. In total bed terms, their stock is small (perhaps around 10% of the total) compared with the multitude of independently owned facilities, but these, until recently, have had less ready access to both the market and other sectors of the industry. With greater availability of affordable commercial websites, smaller hotels now have greater opportunities to reach their customers directly, even if not on the scale of the large corporations. Some independents have seen the value of coming together as members of a consortium in order to compete more effectively with the large chains.

CONSORTIA

Independent hotels around the world have frequently banded together to form consortia. While this allows the group to obtain some of the economies of scale achieved by the large chains, such as the benefits of mass purchasing, more critically it reinforces their marketing strength, enabling them to improve distribution through a united website and the websites of other leading suppliers. Many of the larger consortia, such as Best Western Hotels, operate on a global scale; others operate on a regional or national scale, as does the Société Européenne d'Hôtellerie (SEH) group, which includes the Qualys Hotel, P'tit Dej Hotel, Inter-Hotel and Relais du Silence brands.

Similarly, some smaller, privately owned hotels have united within a themed consortium in order to market themselves more effectively at home and abroad. This is a highly appropriate strategy when developing a niche approach. For example, Small Luxury Hotels of the World, with over 500 hotels in 80 countries, focuses on building an image of hotels that are of a high standard but personal, while Grand Heritage Hotels, an American-owned consortium that is now drawing members from high-grade European hotels, emphasises luxury and status. Other specialist consortia operating in the UK are Pride of Britain Hotels, Scotland's Personal Hotels and Great Inns of Britain.

EXAMPLE

Hotusa consortia

Grupo Hotusa is an independent hotel consortium, founded in 1977 by a group of hotel managers located in Barcelona, Spain. The expansion of this consortium has moved beyond Europe to include partner hotels in China, Brazil, India and more than 50 other countries across the globe.

Initially, the group was formed to gain enhanced marketing opportunities, but now, with more than 2500 hotels, benefits are improved distribution, quality and computer systems, including:

- an online reservations platform serving travel agents wishing to book rooms in member hotels
- representation on the four main GDS systems (Amadeus, Sabre, Galileo and Worldspan)
- centralised invoicing and commission payment services
- website design and search engine optimisation.

The consortium also promotes an affiliate programme to extend customer-oriented booking opportunities. Affiliates can embed the Hotusa online booking system into their own website in order to gain commission on sales made, earning between 5% and 8% depending on sales volume.

CONSUMER LOYALTY

To encourage repeat business from their guests, most of the major hotel chains operate loyalty schemes. These are similar in operation to the frequent flyer schemes offered by airlines, with guests earning points based on the number of nights stayed and the overall hotel spend. These points can then be redeemed for free nights' accommodation and room upgrades. Frequent guests will often be provided with an upgraded status, receiving additional benefits such as late room check-outs and points bonuses. These programmes generally operate across-brand; for example, Marriott Rewards members earn points for their stays in Marriott, Courtyard or Ritz-Carlton hotels, and now the Starwood branded hotels too. Some examples are:

- Marriott International: Marriott Rewards (due to be renamed when integration with the Starwood Preferred Guest programme is complete)
- Hilton Worldwide: Hilton Honors
- InterContinental: Priority Club Rewards
- Accor: Le Club
- Louvre Hotels: Flavours (linked to the Golden Tulip brands).

These hotel loyalty schemes often work in partnership with airlines. Frequent flyers may elect to have their points added not to the hotel scheme but to an affiliated airline loyalty programme, and the hotel chains often have agreements with several airline partners to make this possible.

The extent to which such programmes are effective in encouraging loyalty has often been debated, but it is helpful to realise that by encouraging their guests to be members the hotel chain can discover customer travel habits and preferences (this can be in some detail – for example, Marriott Rewards members are asked about their preference of pillow) and can undertake direct marketing accordingly.

EXAMPLE

Loyalty programme rewards

Research has revealed that customers increasingly seek enhanced experiences over traditional rewards such as free rooms. Loyalty schemes now offer discounts and perks for the customer, which can include room upgrades, access to unique experiences (paid for in loyalty points) or online shopping opportunities.

In addition to earning points that can be traded for free nights, hotels offer their members additional benefits such as free Internet access, room upgrades and discount promotions. Consequently, to access these rewards travellers are often members of more than one loyalty scheme.

The value of the rewards earned varies from programme to programme. The most generous seems to be the Wyndham Rewards programme, estimated to offer $16.70 in reward value for every $100 spent – double the typical payment range of 5–8%.

Source: Hotelier, 2017

HOTEL DEVELOPMENT

As with other sectors of the tourism industry, there is a growing belief that a handful of mega-chains will in time come to dominate the global tourism market, with independents focusing on niche market opportunities.

A recent development has been the trend to initiate **brand extensions** across products – an example of which we have seen with the move by Bulgari into the hotel sector. The Versace brand has also moved into hospitality, with the opening in Australia of the Palazzo Versace. Several other fashion houses are developing plans to form partnerships with hotel chains that will bear the fashion brand's name, including Armani, Missoni and Moschino, which plan to focus on accommodation in or near prestigious shopping locations. Other examples of brand-stretching include *Maxim*, a men's magazine, which has opened a Las Vegas hotel and casino, while leading catering brands have also moved into accommodation, with the Hard Rock Café developing the Hard Rock Hotel brand.

BUDGET HOTELS

The budget sector of the hotel industry is predicted to see continued growth, with the demand for affordable lodging stimulated by rising middle-class populations in the Asia-Pacific and African regions. Responding to this demand, the large chains have been concentrating on creating or developing their own budget-priced properties, a field formerly left largely to independent organisations or leisure conglomerates.

In the UK, budget branded hotels have increased their market share with occupancy levels over 80% and increased supply (PricewaterhouseCoopers, 2018), thus gaining a stronger foothold in the market. The two leading chains are Travelodge and Premier Inn:

- *Travelodge*. Bought by Dubai Investment Capital in 2006 (but following a financial bailout in 2012 is now owned by investment firms GoldenTree Asset Management, Avenue Capital and Goldman Sachs), Travelodge is one of the leading budget brands, with over 550 hotels and 40,000 bedrooms in the UK. It also operates a few properties in Ireland and Spain. The limited service approach means that rooms do not have telephones, irons or hairdryers, helping to keep overheads to a minimum.

- *Premier Inn*. In 2004, the brewers Whitbread acquired the Premier Lodge and Scottish & Newcastle Hotel brands, merging these into their Travel Inn brand and renaming the group Premier Travel Inn, later simplified to the present brand name. The company operates 785 hotels (with more than 72,000 bedrooms) across the UK and Ireland and is expanding internationally. Premier Inn expects to have more than 30 hotels in China by 2021.

Recent trends are pointing towards a splintering of the budget hotel sector, with luxury budget accommodation at one end of the range, including brands such as City Inn and Big Sleep, while new, super-budget brands like Yotel, Tune Hotels and easyHotel cater for the cheaper end of the market.

EXAMPLE

Would the low-cost model work for hotels?

Tune Hotels, launched in 2009 as part of a group which owns the AirAsia airline, drew on the low-cost airline model to provide limited-service accommodation with a yield-management booking system which encouraged guests to make their reservations early to obtain the lowest prices. In keeping with the low-cost model, services were provided on a pay-as you-use basis, with customers required to pay additional fees for the use of air conditioning, television, Wi-Fi and hairdryers.

However, despite early growth through a partnership with Red Planet Hotels, expanding the chain to 45 hotels, by 2015 the group had slashed the number of hotels in half and had moved to a more traditional business model that ensured key services were included in the price. Tune Hotels currently operates 14 hotels, predominantly in Malaysia.

In mainland Europe, Accor Hotels exploited the deficiency in the super-budget sector by introducing the Formule 1 and Etap chains (now branded Ibis Budget), while others on the Continent have popularised low-budget brands such as B&B Hotels, Mister Bed and Fimotel. These very low-priced hotels have managed to reduce costs by developing a unitary design and automating many of the services provided; reception desks are only manned for short periods of the day, and at other times entry is by the insertion of credit cards into a machine on the external wall. Similarly, breakfast is self-service and highly automated.

THE CHARACTER PROPERTY

The competition between luxury hotels has led to new forms of market segmentation, based on product differentiation. Country house or townhouse hotels place emphasis on giving a personal service in uniquely designed spaces.

The Hotel Vittoria in Florence (one of the Una Hotel chain) has staked a claim to being the most fashionable in the world, with mural portraits on each door and surrealistic decor. Gramercy Park Hotel in New York has original paintings by cutting-edge artist Jean-Michael Basquiat, as well as art pieces by Andy Warhol and Damien Hirst. The Winston Hotel Amsterdam has walls lined with original modern art, while the

Künstlerheim Luise, Berlin, goes one better, offering rooms that, in decor, resemble paintings by van Gogh, Magritte or Edward Hopper.

Other hotels have opted to go for the 'wow' factor, either in relation to their architecture or sheer size. For example, the hotel Puerto America in Madrid, operated by Silken Hotels since 2005, has chosen to have each floor designed by a different famous architect. Size alone had little appeal in the past, as those mega-hotels in the former Soviet Union proved only too clearly, but if sold as luxury resorts in their own right they find a market as readily as the giant cruise ships carrying over 3000 passengers have done. Las Vegas boasts a dozen such mega-hotels with over 3000 rooms.

The Burj al-Arab Hotel in Dubai (see Figure 9.4) is famed not only as the tallest hotel in the world, but also for its self-claimed classification of 7-star status, defining ultra luxury. Within Europe, the Gran Hotel Bali, in Benidorm, at 186 metres and 43 stories high, is the tallest in Spain and offers its own unique appeal. Central atriums with glass lifts, spectacular indoor and outdoor gardens and other eye-catching features all help to reinforce the hotel experience as being something more than just a room and a bed.

Boutique and designer hotels, especially those taking advantage of the fashion for cutting-edge design, have a tendency to attract celebrities. Hotels in this category in London are The Halkin, Blakes, Great Eastern Metropolitan, One Aldwych, St Martin's Lane, the Sanderson and the Trafalgar Hilton, while in the USA one finds the Hudson, Mercer, Morgans and Royalton Hotels in New York, the Avalon in Los Angeles and the Delano in Miami.

EXAMPLE

Celebrity hotels

Several decades ago, the Andaz hotel in Hollywood was the place to stay for rock bands such as *The Rolling Stones* and *The Who*. Often, the behaviour of the musicians was controversial, with numerous rooms being trashed and hotel property damaged. Today, having a celebrity stay at a hotel is less likely to be about dealing with a trashed room and more likely about the challenge in meeting the unique demands of the individual and their entourage. It may also require the hotel to offer discounts or complimentary rooms. But the benefits of having a celebrity stay should be balanced against this. First, there is the possibility of free media publicity, though getting recognition of the celebrity's patronage without compromising guest privacy is a fine balance. Second, the reputational benefits of the association can depend on the celebrity – does their fame and persona match with the brand image of the hotel? Ultimately, if a hotel becomes noted for accommodating celebrities, more regular guests along with other celebrities will also want to stay.

Source: Waga, 2016

The Conrad chain, like many upmarket hotel operators, targets the corporate market, offering all-suite hotels as a principal feature in their luxury product, while hotels which have been converted from buildings formerly used for other purposes have deliberately retained their original character and have therefore appealed strongly to a business market of frequent users jaded by standardisation and uniformity.

A good example of the latter is the small chain known as the Hotel du Vin & Bistro (part of the Malmaison Group), which purchases redundant properties in city centres, such as former warehouses and industrial buildings, redeveloping them as lodgings while retaining their original character. Emphasising its catering strengths, it has succeeded in simultaneously creating some highly praised restaurants. On the European continent, similar aims are shared by Malmaison's Continental hotels, Spain's Melia Boutique and Derby Hotels and Germany's Sorat chain.

Hotels that can offer attributes unique to the country visited are always popular with tourists. The paradores in Spain or the pousadas of Portugal, national chains of state-operated inns located in historic properties, are proving highly successful despite their premium prices. Similarly, traditional haciendas in Mexico and the ryokans of Japan, which offer an authentic flavour of the country's culture, greatly appeal to the independent travel market.

Hotels of character appeal as strongly to leisure travellers as they do to business travellers. In recent years, the country cottage style of accommodation has been popular and has been dutifully incorporated into specialist groupings by tour operators. The Mansions and Manors brand consists of around 200 manor house owners who offer bed-and-breakfast accommodation on a selective basis to the 'right kind of clients', but have no wish to commercialise their product or advertise directly to the public. This group of houses is therefore marketed directly through tour operators overseas. In the USA, the consortium Historic Hotels of America, established with the support of the US National Trust for Historic Preservation, recruits only hotels that are in listed or landmark buildings that are at least 50 years old. Among its members are the 1773 Red Lion Inn at Stockbridge, Massachusetts, and a former Carmelite convent in Puerto Rico, which dates from 1651.

CLASSIFYING AND GRADING ACCOMMODATION

Categorising accommodation units of differing types and standards is no simple matter. As we saw in Table 12.1, there are many different types of accommodation, each providing a variety of facilities and services to suit their market. The process of classification, either for the purpose of legislation or for the systematic examination of business activity, has been attempted on several occasions in the UK in the past (for example, under the Standard Industrial Classification System). These attempts were mainly designed to distinguish hotels and other residential establishments from sundry catering activities, however. Statistics seldom distinguish, for example, between guests staying at hotels and motels.

Within the small independent sector, the problem is even greater. There is a broad spectrum of private accommodation that ranges from the privately owned hotel, through boarding house and guest-house accommodation to bed-and-breakfast establishments. Privately owned accommodation may also include other structures, for example boats and train carriages.

EXAMPLE

The *Edward Elgar*

This hotel boat has three decks, with 11 passenger cabins housed on the lower deck, a restaurant and bar on the main deck and an open air viewing gallery on the upper deck. The vessel can accommodate 22 passengers, and offers week-long and weekend cruises on the canals and rivers around Gloucester. Some cruises are specifically themed

(Continued)

to focus on heritage locations, while other tours provide stops in local towns along the river Severn.

Every cabin includes en-suite facilities, towels and toiletries, razor and electrical sockets, air conditioning, and a housekeeping service is provided. Based on these facilities together with an assessment of the quality of the furniture, flooring, heating, lighting and decoration, this accommodation has been awarded a 4-star rating by the VisitBritain Quality in Tourism Hotel Boat scheme.

FIGURE 12.2 The *Edward Elgar* hotel boat

Photo: Claire Humphreys

Tourists, however, are interested not only in what different types of hotel offer in the way of facilities but also in the *quality* of the accommodation and catering they are being offered. To clarify these features, we need to distinguish between three terms: **categorisation, classification and grading**. Although these terms are often used interchangeably, the following are their widely accepted definitions:

- *Categorisation* refers to the separation of accommodation into types – that is, distinguishing between hotels, motels, boarding houses, guest houses and so on.
- *Classification* distinguishes different examples of accommodation on the basis of certain physical features, such as the number of rooms with private bath or shower and so on.
- *Grading* identifies accommodation according to certain verifiable objective features of the service offered, such as the number of courses served at meals, whether or not 24-hour service is provided and so on.

Readers will note, however, that none of these terms refer to assessments of *quality*, which call for subjective evaluation and are therefore far more difficult, and more costly, to validate, especially when standards, particularly in catering, can change so rapidly over time.

Provision was made under the Development of Tourism Act 1969 for the compulsory classification and grading of hotel accommodation in the UK, but this was widely resisted by the industry itself, and the British Tourist Authority (BTA) made no attempt to impose it at the time, instead relying on a system of voluntary registration first introduced in 1975. The separate National Tourist Boards of England, Scotland and Wales were left to devise their own individual schemes. However, in 1987 the three boards agreed a common scheme that graded hotels into six categories: 'listed', for the most basic property, or from one to five crowns, depending on the facilities offered. The system remained a voluntary one.

Two years later, the boards agreed a unified system of grading quality, additionally designating accommodation 'Approved', 'Commended', 'Highly Commended' or 'Deluxe', in ascending order of quality. This was planned to take into account such subjective issues as hospitality, service, food and decor. Over the years, further attempts were made to harmonise accommodation grading schemes. Agreement was reached between the three national tourist boards and the motoring organisations to adopt a common classification scheme for bed-and-breakfast establishments from the year 2000, and further negotiations led to an agreement on a common star rating (one to five stars) that was introduced gradually over an 18-month period, beginning in 2006.

We should note that the private sector had devised its own schemes for grading hotels, some national and some international in scope; these were often more widely recognised by members of the public than were the public-sector designations. Of the private-sector schemes, the best known in the UK were those offered by the two motoring associations, the AA and the RAC, both of which provided a star rating, the former reaching agreement with VisitBritain to align their classification criteria. In addition to these schemes, there were a number of guides on the market that provided subjective assessments of catering in hotels and other establishments, the best-known being the *Michelin Guide*, *Forbes Travel Guide* and *The Good Food Guide*.

EXAMPLE

TripAdvisor ratings for hotels

The ratings displayed from TripAdvisor are calculated based on the reviews received by travellers. Since its launch, more than 600 million reviews have been provided, assessing more than 1.5 million hotels, B&Bs, specialty lodgings and vacation rentals.

Each review provides a score (with 5 being the highest) for each of the following criteria:

- location
- sleep quality
- room
- service
- value

(Continued)

- cleanliness
- overall rating.

Alongside a score rating, reviewers comment on their experiences of the accommodation and, in some cases, travellers' photographs of the premises. Reviewer comments may offer advice on specific rooms and tips to improve the overall experience.

TripAdvisor ratings are now so widely used that other travel providers embed scores into their own websites. For example, TUI includes the TripAdvisor traveller rating alongside its own hotel rating on the hotel pages of its website. Similarly, Hotels.com includes the TripAdvisor rating as part of the information provided on the hotels it offers.

As far as common systems across Europe are concerned, the harmonisation process within the EU gave an additional boost to these initiatives. There are complications, for example, in the fact that some countries impose higher rates of sales tax on their 5-star properties, making it unattractive for hotels in those nations to give their properties the higher rating even if standards are comparable with a 5-star property elsewhere. Research completed by the European Consumer Centres' Network examined the hotel ratings system across EU member states, as a prelude to considering whether standardisation is possible. The Network's findings are summarised in Table 12.3. Clearly there are many differences between these approaches, and to date introducing a single system has not been attempted. It is also evident that many of the rating systems focus on judging accommodation based on the range of facilities rather than the quality of the service or facilities. Employers and associations are anxious to ensure that 'hospitality assured' standards, as laid down by the European Foundation for Quality Management's Business Excellence model and based on a worldwide model of best practice, can be applied within their own establishments.

TABLE 12.3 Accommodation grading schemes in Europe

Country	Mandatory or voluntary system	Accommodation categories	Classification criteria
Austria	Voluntary	Hotels, guest houses, pensions, B&Bs, apartments	Quality of service, external appearance, hotel entertainment (bars, leisure facilities) and additional facilities (parking, gardens), guest satisfaction
Belgium	Compulsory	Hotels, guest rooms, open recreation terrain, holiday accommodation, motels	Rooms (size, furnishings and facilities), building (rooms and technical facilities, such as elevators, phones) and services (luggage storage, room service)
Bulgaria	Compulsory	Hotels, motels, holiday settlements, family hotels, boarding houses, bungalow and campsites, separate rooms, country houses, houses	Geographic location (sea, mountain, town, etc.), activity (spa, business, etc), building construction, furnishing and staff skills
Cyprus	Compulsory	Hotels, hotel apartments, tourist villages, tourist villas, camping sites, traditional houses, tourist apartments	Size of rooms (and public areas), facilities offered (car park, room service, swimming pool, etc.), staffing levels
Czech Republic	Voluntary	Hotels, motels, pensions, campsites, chalets, walkers' dormitories, botels	Size of rooms, bathroom equipment, facilities, catering

Country	Mandatory or voluntary system	Accommodation categories	Classification criteria
Denmark	Compulsory	Hotels and hostels	Technical facilities and other facilities (radio, TV)
Estonia	Compulsory	Hotels, motels, guest houses, hostels, holiday villages and camps, holiday homes, visitor apartments, B&Bs	Ventilation, en suite facilities, size of beds
Finland	No hotel classification system exists	Since there is no classification system every trader providing accommodation can use their own discretion in regards to the facilities provided	
France	Voluntary	Tourist hotels, hostels, guestrooms	Room size, lobby size, telephones, staff skills
Germany	Voluntary	Hotels, guest houses, taverns, inns, pensions	Two separate schemes cover these categories of accommodation
Greece	Compulsory	Hotels, motels, furnished apartments, mixed-type hotels, camping facilities, rooms to let	Size of bedroom, facilities and services, number of rooms, public spaces near to accommodation
Hungary	Compulsory	Hotels, convalescence hotels, wellness hotels, flophouses, apartment hotels, motels, camping, holiday resorts, tourist hotels, youth hostels	Size and equipment of bedrooms, number and equipment of bathrooms, number of restaurants, lift, reception services
Iceland	Voluntary	Hotels, hotel apartments, motels, rooming houses/hostels, summerhouses, B&Bs	Reception and breakfast provision, night security
Ireland	Compulsory	Hotels, guest houses, holiday hostels, youth hostels, holiday camps, caravan and camping sites, holiday cottages, holiday apartments	Size of bedrooms and public areas, provision of facilities and services (catering, porterage, etc.)
Italy	Compulsory	Hotel establishments, non-hotel establishments (B&Bs, youth hostels), open-air establishments (tourist villages, camping)	Room size, bathroom provision, employee numbers, catering, facilities (TV, telephone, parking, baggage store)
Latvia	Voluntary	Hotels, guest houses, campsites, youth hostels	Building and bedroom size, facilities and services provided
Lithuania	Compulsory	Hotels, guest houses	Size of bedrooms and dining room, availability of rooms for people with a disability
Luxembourg	Voluntary	Hotels and hotel apartments	Bedrooms, bathrooms, washrooms in public spaces, services, cleanliness
Malta	Compulsory	Hotels, aparthotels, tourist villages, guest houses, hostels, B&Bs	Room size, cleaning, furniture, room facilities (TV, safe, minibar), catering, reception services
The Netherlands	Compulsory	Hotels, camping, bungalow parks	Bedrooms, service quality, room functionality
Norway	Voluntary	Hotels, apartments, cabins, hostels, motels	Room size, facilities (bathrooms), catering, services provided
Poland	Compulsory	Hotels, motels, pension/guest houses, camping, houses for tourists, youth hostels, bivouac	Environment outside the building, technical equipment

(Continued)

TABLE 12.3 (Continued)

Country	Mandatory or voluntary system	Accommodation categories	Classification criteria
Portugal	Compulsory	Hotels, hotel apartments, inns, touristic villages, touristic apartments, resorts, holiday villas, rural tourism, camping and caravans	Premises, furniture, services (cleaning, catering, check-in/-out), local environment
Romania	Compulsory	Hotels, hotel apartments, motels, hostels, villas, chalets, bungalows, holiday villages, camping, apartments for rent, ships, guest houses, agrotourism	Building condition, reception services, technical facilities (elevator, air conditioner), room size, room facilities (safe, minibar), leisure and business facilities
Slovakia	Compulsory	Hotels, botels*, guest houses, apartment houses, tourist hostels, holiday villages, camping grounds, campsites, private accommodation	Entrance area, catering, room fixtures and furnishings, communal spaces
Slovenia	Compulsory	Hotels, motels, pensions, inns, camps, apartments, holiday flats, holiday houses, private rooms, farmhouses, accommodation, marinas	Bedroom size, equipment and furnishings, cleaning frequency, accepting credit card payment
Spain	Compulsory	Camping, hostels, hotels, hotel apartments, private rooms, cruises, garni hotels, shelters, spas, holiday resorts, guest houses, motels, botels*, rotels**, boarding houses, rural houses	Room size, number of bedrooms, facilities and services, number of employees
Sweden	Voluntary	Hotels and garni hotels***	Maintenance of public areas, technical facilities, guest rooms (sound proofing, furnishing, bathrooms, TV, telephone)

* Botel – boat hotel

** Rotel – sleeper coach

*** Garni – small hotel offering B&B

Source: ECC-Net, 2009

THE NATURE OF DEMAND FOR ACCOMMODATION FACILITIES

The hotel product is made up of five characteristics:

- location
- mix of facilities (which will include bedrooms, restaurants, other public rooms, function rooms and leisure facilities)
- image
- services it provides (including such indefinable features as the level of formality, personal attention, speed and efficiency of its staff)
- prices charged.

The location will invariably be the first consideration when a tourist is selecting travel accommodation. Location implies both the destination (resort for the holidaymaker, convenient stopover point for the traveller, city for the business traveller) and the location within that destination. Thus, businesspeople will want to be accommodated in a city centre hotel close to their meeting location, while the seaside holidaymaker will seek a hotel as close as possible to the beach, and transit travellers will want to be accommodated at a hotel convenient for the airport or a motel close to major roads.

In economic terms, a trade-off will occur between location and price. The leisure traveller will look for the hotel closest to the beach that still fits the budget, while the transit traveller may well opt for a more distant hotel that is prepared to offer a free transfer to the airport. Location is, of course, fixed for all time. Thus, if the site itself loses its attraction for visitors, the hotel will suffer an equivalent decline in its fortunes. 'Pop-up hotels' can be quickly and cheaply constructed in areas where demand is temporarily increased, perhaps stimulated by a short-term event such as a music festival (Thorpe, 2009). Despite the advantages of reduced time and cost in construction, the extent to which this will influence supply is yet to be proven.

EXAMPLE

A room for London

A boat-shaped structure placed on the roof of the Southbank Centre provided its guests with an exceptional view of the Thames and adjacent landmarks (Figure 12.3). This one-bedroom art installation, designed by David Kohn Architects, was installed in 2012 as a celebratory statement for the Olympics and the Queen's Jubilee, and provided a space where up to two people can spend the night in central London. With views from both the lower and upper deck, this unique space contained an en suite double bedroom, kitchenette and library.

Who got to stay in this unusual accommodation was determined by ballot, usually drawn about two months in advance of the accommodation date. Guests were required to complete a short safety briefing on arrival. Once completed, however, guests were free to come and go, much like any hotel resident.

The accommodation proved so popular that this unique piece of architecture remained in place until 2016, eventually removed to allow for the redevelopment of this part of the Southbank complex.

FIGURE 12.3 A room for London

Photo: Claire Humphreys

The fact that high fixed costs are incurred in both building and operating hotels compounds the risks of running them. City centre sites are extremely expensive to purchase and operate, so the room prices have to be high. The market may resist such prices, but is nevertheless reluctant to be based at any distance from the centres of activity, even when good transport is available. This has been evidenced by the problems facing incoming tour operators accommodating American visitors on budget tours to central London at prices that are competitive with other city centres. One impact of the London 2012 Olympics was the expansion of hotel stock, particularly by budget chains such as Premier Inn and Travelodge, which has helped to expand provision for tour groups.

The demand for hotels centrally located in capital cities, leading to high capacity and profits, has caused those in the hotel business to maximise profits by upgrading their accommodation and appealing to business clients, rather than catering for leisure tourists demanding budget accommodation. Special services were introduced to attract niche customers. The London Hilton, for instance, was among several that introduced a women-only floor, in deference to the increasing number of women travelling alone on business. This included a private check-in facility, increased security cameras and double locks on bedroom doors.

Meanwhile, the French Accor Group was among the first to identify the market gap for low-priced accommodation in big cities as the established hotel chains went upmarket and, as we have seen, launched its Formule 1 and Etap brands to tap into these markets. Major cities also have frequent high-profile events, such as conferences and exhibitions; at such times, the demand for hotel rooms is reflected in every hotel boosting its prices, so that the basic price advertised by budget chains may, in practice, be seldom available.

EXAMPLE

Rio builds hotels for the 2016 Olympics

Every four years, the world's largest sporting event rolls into a city somewhere in the world. For the summer of 2016, it was the turn of Rio de Janeiro, bringing with it hordes of spectators who needed to be accommodated for this 16-day event.

The International Olympic Committee acknowledged that accommodating the visitors would require extensive levels of construction, and Rio increased hotel capacity from 29,000 rooms in 2009 (when the games were awarded) to 56,000 in 2016. Tax breaks offered by the city government encouraged global brands like Accor to move into the market. Thus, one legacy of the Rio Olympics has been a substantial improvement in hotel stock.

While there was a significant permanent expansion in the accommodation sector, the number of tourists arriving in the city has not been sustained. Consequently, occupancy rates are far lower than required for hotels to be profitable and in the two years following the Olympic Games 16 hotels closed, including the Accor Mercure Barra.

Hotels seek to maximise their revenue by offering a wide range of different tariffs to the various market segments they serve. By way of example, one city hotel provides, apart from the normal rack rate (published room rate), at least nine other rates, including special concessions for corporate bookings, conference rates, air crew, weekender traffic and tour bookings. When occupancy levels are low, it has also been possible for clients to negotiate substantial discounts if they book late in the day.

Hotel managers, recognising that any sale is better than none, allow the desk clerks to come to an agreement regarding any realistic offer, which may be as much as 50% lower than rack rate.

Hotel companies may be further constrained by the need to meet building regulations that apply to the location where they are building. Increasingly, concern about the environment and widespread recognition of the damage done to the architectural style of resorts swamped by high-rise hotel buildings have led local authorities to impose stringent planning and other regulations on new buildings. This may mean using local (often more expensive) materials in place of concrete, using a vernacular style in the design of the building, limiting the height to four or five floors (some tropical destinations restrict hotel buildings to the height of the local palm trees) or restricting the total size of the building to ensure that it is in keeping with surrounding buildings.

SOME CHARACTERISTICS OF THE HOTEL PRODUCT

The demand for hotel bedrooms comes from a widely distributed market, nationally and internationally, whereas the market for other facilities that hotels offer will often be highly localised. In addition to providing food and drink for their own residents, hotels will be marketing these services (and sometimes additional services such as a leisure club with swimming pool) to other tourists or members of the local population. Clearly, hotels have to cater to at least two quite different market segments, which calls for different approaches to advertising, promotion and distribution.

Seasonality and periodicity

Another characteristic of the hotel product is that demand is seldom uniform throughout the year or even throughout the week. Beach hotels suffer from seasonality, involving high levels of demand during summer peak periods and little or no demand during the winter troughs, while hotels catering chiefly to businesspeople may find that demand drops during the summer. Care has to be exercised in pricing; while a differential is expected between peak and low seasons, if it is too extreme, competitive destinations will attract visitors away or they will simply not come.

Business hotels also suffer from periodicity, with demand centred on Monday to Thursday nights, while there is little demand for Friday to Sunday nights. The lack of flexibility in room supply, coupled with the 'perishable' nature of the product (if rooms are unsold, there is no opportunity to 'store' them and sell them later), mean that greater efforts must be made to unload unsold accommodation by attracting a variety of markets. However, even the most upmarket hotels well located in big cities are often loath to lose the prospect of high room occupancy at weekends and will feel obliged to take reservations for groups from some operators, but, at the same time, will do their utmost to avoid disruption to their regular business clients. This can result in groups being forced to check into and depart from hotels by back entrances. This, and other forms of distinctive handling, such as the allocation of separate dining areas in restaurants, can result in groups being made to feel like second-class citizens, if not managed properly.

Even with creative marketing and high discounting, many tourist hotels in highly seasonal resorts will find their occupancy levels falling alarmingly in the winter. They must then face the decision as to whether it is better to stay open in the winter in the hope that they will attract enough customers to make some contribution to overheads, or to close completely for several months of the year. The problem with the latter course of action is that a number of hotel costs, such as rates, depreciation and salaries for management staff, will continue whether or not the hotel remains open. Temporary closure may also result in difficulties in recruiting good staff, if jobs are known to be only seasonal.

In recent years, more hotels, especially the larger chain hotels, have opted to remain open and offer enhanced packages for those willing to travel out of season. The increase in second holidays and out-of-season short breaks in the UK has helped to make more hotels viable all year round, although room occupancy remains low out of season in many of the more traditional resorts.

Yield management becomes the criterion in this situation, the aim being to maximise revenue. The hotel sector is heavily dependent on the extent to which the public sector is willing to invest in order to make the resort attractive out of season. For example, Bournemouth, a popular UK tourist destination, through a process of continuous investment and a deliberate attempt to attract the conference and non-seasonal markets, has been able to draw in high numbers of winter tourists, making it economic for many more hotels to remain open all year round. This, in turn, stimulates further business as local attractions and events are also encouraged to stay open throughout the year.

EXAMPLE

Seasonality in the European tourist accommodation sector

The European Commission's research arm Eurostat (2018), reporting the arrivals in accommodation establishments in Europe, concluded that seasonality was high for many European nations, with the two peak months of July and August accounting for one-third of all nights spent in tourist accommodation across the region. The distribution of demand for a select number of European countries is shown in Figure 12.4, which highlights this peak. However, for Austria the demand from winter sports tourists leads to two peaks, with demand in January as high as demand in July.

The extent of seasonality can be evaluated by comparing share of demand in the peak month with that of the quietest month. The data reveal that for Croatia demand is almost 100 times higher in August, the peak month, than in the least popular month, January. In the UK, demand has less extreme fluctuations but the peak (July) is still ten times larger than the quietest month (February).

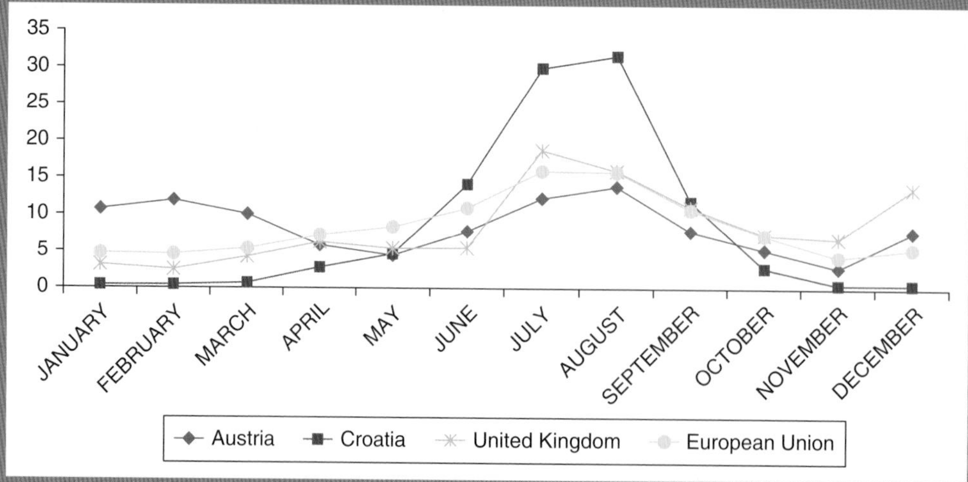

FIGURE 12.4 **Seasonality of demand for European tourist accommodation (%)**

Source: Eurostat, 2018

Atmosphere and attractions

While we have talked chiefly in terms of the physical characteristics of the hotel, the psychological factors that attract visitors are no less important. Service, 'atmosphere', even the other guests with whom the customer will come into contact, all play a role when the choice of hotel is made. More than half of adults have stayed in a hotel in the UK in the last 12 months (Mintel, 2018) and the penetration of chain hotel brands like Premier Inn and Hilton is double that of independent hotels: 44% compared to 22%. Hotel restaurants with a good reputation are particularly influential in attracting customers, with experience and atmosphere, more than just access to a variety of facilities, particularly important in terms of demand.

Factors such as class, age and lifestyle all have a bearing on the choice of sleeping accommodation; some guests may be in search of a quiet night's sleep, while others seek out a lively bar for late-night entertainment. In particular, the nature of, and consequent demand for, large hotels will be quite different from that for the small guest house or bed-and-breakfast unit. A large hotel may well provide attractions of its own, distinct from the location in which it is situated. Indeed, in some cases the hotel may be a more significant influence on choice than the destination. This is often true of large hotel/leisure resorts providing a range of in-house entertainment, as is the case with a number of North American and, increasingly, European hotels.

Similarly, some hotels are so closely linked with the destinations they serve that the combination of stay at hotel/destination becomes the established pattern. This is seen in Canada, where the resort of Lake Louise and the Chateau Lake Louise Hotel are inextricably linked. It is, however, increasingly a characteristic of package holiday hotels, and has been taken a stage further with the growth of the all-inclusive package holiday, in which all food, drink and entertainment are included in the price. The Sandals Hotel chain, based in the Bahamas and the Caribbean, was a major initiator of this development.

The provision of a good range of attractions, as well as a drinks licence, can help to offset the disadvantages that result from the unavoidable impersonality of large hotels. As the chains gain more of a hold on the total pool of hotel beds, an increase in the average number of rooms in each hotel tends to follow, as larger hotels benefit from economies of scale. Hotels with fewer than 100 rooms remain the exception, however, and smaller properties emphasise the personal nature of their service as a feature in their marketing.

Unique designs

Refurbishment of the larger, less attractive hotels is seldom a viable option, the alternative being to pull them down and construct new ones more in keeping with popular taste. In Majorca, the local authorities introduced legislation requiring unattractive mid-twentieth-century hotels to be demolished before new, higher-quality buildings could be constructed. This led to the removal of many 1960s concrete eyesores in ageing resorts like Magaluf, in favour of hotels with greater character.

In countries where change and novelty are features of market demand, hotel companies now 'theme' their properties to distinguish them from others, either in the style of their architecture or interior decoration. This, as was pointed out earlier in the chapter, is now becoming a common approach in expensive hotels around the world. Flamboyant architecture, often reminiscent of gothic fortresses, is springing up in the most unlikely of places, such as Sun City in South Africa. There, a purpose-built resort complex has been designed to provide a simulacrum of 'African culture'; while in the Bahamas is to be found the extravagant Royal Towers of Atlantis on Paradise Island, where 'exotic' describes both the architecture and the prices.

Chain hotels budget for regular changes of decor to update their properties, while older hotels emphasise their traditional values and style. Hotels that can retain the style of yesteryear, while nevertheless offering up-to-date features such as modern bathrooms with good plumbing, can find a ready market for their product. A good example here is the restored Raffles Hotel in Singapore, which, after extensive refurbishment, has successfully blended modern comforts with the traditional architecture of the colonial era.

Increasingly, holidaymakers search for something different and unusual in the places they stay as part of their experience of travel. Specialist operators and independent hoteliers are catering to this need. Long-haul travellers can book into an authentic and traditional native longhouse in Skrang, Sarawak, while tourists to Canada are offered the choice of staying in a North American Indian tepee in Manitoba or an Inuit igloo in the Hudson Bay area.

EXAMPLE

Stay in a jumbo jet

In Sweden, it is possible to stay in a decommissioned 747-200. The Jumbo hostel and café is capable of accommodating up to 76 guests in 33 bedrooms, most with shared bathroom facilities. This alternative to a budget hotel is located close to Stockholm's Arlanda Airport.

The plane was originally built in 1976 for Singapore Airlines and was later flown as part of the legendary Pan American airline fleet. It last took to the skies in 2002 and eventually converted to permanent accommodation in 2008.

A number of different room types are offered, including doubles, triples and a quad-dormitory option which would potentially serve the experience-seeking backpacker market. Perhaps unsurprisingly, luggage storage is in the overhead lockers!

Source: www.jumbostay.com

If a jumbo jet doesn't appeal, why not try an ice hotel? The number of these has expanded in line with popular demand and their appeal has helped to generate a winter tourism market in some most unusual locations, triggered by the construction of the world famous ice hotel at Jukkasjävi in Swedish Lapland. Others can be found in Chena Hot Springs near Fairbanks in Alaska, at Kangerlussuaq in Greenland, in Canada near Quebec City (where a nightclub accommodating 400 is a feature), in Norway and in Switzerland. These pop-up hotels have to be freshly reconstructed after winter thaws each year and are generally open only between January and April.

Other original approaches to accommodation include lighthouses along the Croatian coast, a windmill in Majorca, a police station in Lynton, Devon, a cider press in Abbeville, France, a signal box in County Kerry, Ireland, and converted pigsties in Garstang, Lancashire and Monteriggioni in Italy.

The impulse to do something different and sleep in something unique appears to be growing – the more far-fetched, the better. Treehouses have been constructed at several sites in the UK, France and Sweden. The proprietor of the Dog Bark Inn at Cottonwood, Idaho, promotes his accommodation as the world's biggest beagle, with the sleeping accommodation constructed within a giant carved sculpture of a dog. Another current fashion is underwater hotels. A modest and rather basic prototype, the Utter Inn on Lake Mälaren at Västerås in Sweden, appears to have started the trend, with others following at the

Bahamian island of Eleuthera and in Key Largo, Florida. Undersea dining is also possible in the Maldives and at Eilat, Israel.

These are all attempts at offering more than simply a room to sleep in. Today, adventurous tourists, whether travelling for business or pleasure, seek a package of physical and emotional experiences that together make up the total trip experience, and hoteliers are seeking to satisfy that need. Conversely, some tourists require no more than basic, but clean and comfortable, overnight accommodation. This is particularly true of nature tourists such as trekkers, and backpackers, thus a variety of simple accommodation exists to meet this market's criteria.

CATEGORIES OF ACCOMMODATION

In this chapter, we have, until now, focused much of our attention on hotels, highlighting the many chains that are involved in providing this form of accommodation. This is a competitive sector, and there is constant pressure to adapt to changing trends and demands from the marketplace. However, hotels have not only to compete with each other; they also face competition from other categories of accommodation, which we will now explore.

EXAMPLE

The British seaside holiday has changed

The traditional British domestic holiday based on a one- or two-week stay in a small seaside hotel or B&B is an experience that is today all but dead. Many of these types of establishment have been forced out of business through an inability to respond to modern tourists' needs, the neglected buildings impacting on the overall image of the resort. This has come about largely due to the appeal of holidays abroad, with packages often being no more expensive than those in the UK, and budget flights costing less than domestic transport to the destination.

Overseas resorts have provided much better value for money and, of course, greater likelihood of sunshine. As a result of their experiences in hotels abroad, British holidaymakers now demand similar facilities from hotels in their home country, including improved standards of cuisine, choice of entertainment and en suite accommodation. To survive, hotel proprietors have had to invest to meet these expectations. However, getting a return on investment is difficult while prices remain low to attract the market.

THE B&B

The increasing desire of many tourists, particularly overseas visitors to the UK, to 'meet the people' and enjoy a more intimate relationship with the culture of the country they are visiting has benefited the smallest forms of accommodation unit, such as the guest house or bed-and-breakfast establishment (B&B). These are generally family run, catering to business tourists in the towns and leisure tourists in country towns, rural areas and the seaside.

B&Bs in particular provide a very valuable service to the industry, in that they can offer the informality and friendliness sought by many tourists, cater for the impulse demand that results from holidaymakers touring by car or bicycle and conveniently expand the supply of beds during peak periods of the year in areas where demand is highly seasonal and where hotels would not be viable.

There are estimated to be about 50 million guest-nights in British B&Bs, with around one-fifth of these being taken up by overseas visitors. Most B&Bs have six or fewer guests as this obviates the payment of business rates and neither a fire certificate nor public liability insurance is required in order to operate.

This form of accommodation was virtually unknown in North America until relatively recently, but has boomed since the 1980s as the Americans and Canadians brought back with them the experiences they had gained in Europe. In general, however, these North American properties have moved upmarket, providing much more luxurious accommodation and facilities than would normally be found in their European equivalents (for example, see Figure 12.5).

FIGURE 12.5 **An upmarket B&B at Boothbay Harbor, Maine, USA**

Photo: Chris Holloway

A derivation of the B&B – the home stay – offers a budget alternative that provides opportunities for international tourists to meet and interact more closely with locals in their own homes. Much more time is spent with the hosts, who may organise visits to local attractions or help their visitors to learn the host language. Examples include a stay with a Maori family in New Zealand, a home stay in Santiago, Chile, which comes with Spanish language lessons at a nearby college, or the government-regulated home stays available in a Casa Particular in Cuba. Prices for stays in private homes often work out cheaper than those for a standard B&B.

FARMHOUSE HOLIDAY ACCOMMODATION

Farmhouse holidays have also enjoyed considerable success in recent years, both in the UK and on the Continent. European countries with strong agricultural traditions have catered for tourists in farmhouse accommodation for many years and, as farmers have found it harder to pay their way by farming alone, in part owing to the reduction in agricultural subsidies within the EU, they have turned increasingly to tourism as a means of boosting revenue, particularly in the low season. A study of farm tourism acknowledges that England, France, Germany and Austria dominate supply in Europe, each with about 20,000 operators (Busby and Rendle, 2000).

EXAMPLE

Farm tourism

Tourism has long been recognised as an important opportunity for some agricultural areas. In 1983, the UN Economic Commission for Europe examined opportunities to integrate farming and tourism to aid the development of rural areas. In addition to this, the decline in farm profits, both in Europe and the USA, encouraged owners to expand their tourism activities.

Farm holidays, Denmark

The term 'bondegårdsferie', which translates as 'farm holiday', has been around for four decades, acknowledging the longevity of this form of tourism in Denmark. Research produced in 2007 identified 466 farms (about 1% of all farms) that were providing tourist accommodation, while a further 1214 provide facilities such as farm shops. The National Association for Agritourism provides a website (www.bondegaardsferie.dk) designed to promote farm stays and farm visits to international visitors.

Farm Stay UK

This consortium, established in 1983, currently has 1000 members who provide quality-rated visitor accommodation on farms. The goal is to increase the occupancy rates and income earned from tourism through improving and coordinating marketing activities promoting the concept of farm tourism. Its website (www.farmstay.co.uk) provides an online booking mechanism for these enterprises. The consortium also supports the farmers, by offering workshops and training programmes to help encourage business diversification and business development.

Ranch tourism

Farm stays in the USA are also popular, although they are often promoted as ranch holidays. These are offered in several states, but notably in Arizona, Colorado and Texas. They are often working ranches that provide activities such as riding lessons, cattle herding, roping lessons and rodeos. The accommodation may be in the form of bunkhouse cabins, although some ranches (often termed 'dude ranches') have invested in facilities to move upmarket, charging $250 or more a day for the experience.

The trend towards a healthier lifestyle and the appeal of natural food and the outdoor life have also helped to make farm tourism popular. Within rural areas, tourist boards have provided assistance and training for farmers interested in expanding their accommodation for tourism. Both Ireland and Denmark have been notably successful in packaging modestly priced farm holidays for the international market, in association with tour operators and the ferry companies. In the case of Denmark, this has been a logical development as it attracts tourists to what is generally recognised as an otherwise expensive country for holidays if based on hotel accommodation.

CAMPING AND CARAVANNING

The market for camping and caravanning holidays in the UK is substantial, with around 15 million domestic camping and caravanning trips taking place each year. For international visitors to the UK, the proclivity towards caravanning/camping accommodation is much lower, with only 2% of inbound visitors using this form of accommodation.

While many holidays are, of course, taken in private touring caravans (of which there are around 555,000 in Britain), motorhome holidays are also becoming ever more popular, with 225,000 privately owned vehicles in the UK. Static caravan and mobile homes number some 365,000, located in over 4000 UK holiday parks (see Figure 12.6), of which almost half are star rated.

FIGURE 12.6 Caravan park at Perranporth, Cornwall

Photo: Claire Humphreys

HOLIDAY CENTRES

In addition to the self-catering camping and caravanning sector is the serviced holiday camp or holiday village. This accommodated almost 2% of domestic trips in 2013. Bourne Leisure, the leading firm in the leisure park business, attracts about 4 million holidaymakers a year to its 50 holiday parks, hotels and resorts in the UK, operating under the Haven, Butlins and Warner brands.

Although the Americans were running summer camps for children some years earlier, adult holiday camps as we know them today were very much a British innovation. They were introduced on a major scale in the 1930s and 1940s by three noted entrepreneurs – Billy Butlin, Fred Pontin and Harry Warner. Their aim was to provide all-in entertainment at a low price in chalet-style accommodation that would be largely unaffected by inclement weather.

The Butlin/Pontin/Warner style of holiday camp became enormously successful in the years prior to World War II and the early post-war era, but none are now family owned. Pontins still operates six sites in the UK and Butlins and Warners are, as mentioned earlier, now part of Bourne Leisure. Butlins has retained its focus on family entertainment, but Warner Holidays has changed direction markedly and is now marketed to adults only.

For the most part, the balance of the market is split between large numbers of independent companies, each operating a small number of sites. Some of these operate under franchise agreements to improve their marketing. Hoseasons, to take one example, is a leading holiday site franchisor with 660 sites across the UK and Europe. In 2010, it was acquired by Wyndham Worldwide (who owns multiple vacation rental brands, including Canvas Holidays, James Villas, Cottages4U and Blake's Holiday Boats).

The market for holiday centres remains highly seasonal, with demand occurring almost entirely between May and September. It had been customary for centres to close during the winter months, but improved marketing, including mini-breaks and themed events, has helped to extend sales into the 'shoulder' months of spring and autumn. As a percentage of the total accommodation used in domestic tourism, though, the figure for holiday centres remains relatively small.

Holiday parks entered the tourist boards' grading schemes in 1987 with the introduction of agreed codes of practice for operators, and a trade body, the British Holiday and Home Parks Association (BH&HPA), has been formed to represent the interests of operators.

EXAMPLE

Warner Holiday Villages

Warner hotels and villages offer accommodation only for adults. As a consequence, the range of amenities and facilities are designed to serve this market. Daytime entertainment includes games such as table tennis, snooker, croquet and bowls as well as organised events such as quizzes, tours of historic houses, gardens and local attractions. Evening entertainment, provided most nights, includes live music and dance performances.

(Continued)

Alongside 10 hotels, Warner operates four holiday villages: Lakeside Coastal Village on Hayling Island, Hampshire; Norton Grange Coastal Village on the Isle of Wight; and Corton Coastal Village and Gunton Hall Coastal Village, both in Lowestoft, Suffolk. Accommodation in these villages is comprised of chalets, somewhat reminiscent of the original holiday camps of the Butlin/Pontin/Warner era, although significantly modernised with en-suite bathroom, television and tea/coffee-making facilities provided.

Holiday centres have been affected as much as any other accommodation facilities by changes in public taste. Before the war, they attracted a largely lower middle-class clientele, but in the post-war period their market became significantly more working-class and the canteen-style catering service and entertainment provided reflected the demand of this market segment. Bookings were made invariably from Saturday to Saturday and most clients booked direct with the companies. Each company had a quite distinct image for its clientele, who were strongly brand-loyal and booked regularly with their particular favourite.

More recently, these camps have attempted to move upmarket, a process heralded by a change in nomenclature from camps to holiday centres, villages or parks. Large chalet blocks have given way to smaller units with self-catering facilities. A choice of catering styles has been introduced, ranging from fully serviced through self-service to self-catering, the latter enjoying the greatest rate of growth.

Butlins in particular has made significant investments in redeveloping its remaining three centres to give them a more upmarket image. Additionally, the company has recently moved into the hotel business, operating three hotels adjacent to its Bognor Regis centre. Guests enjoy superior accommodation while still having access to the resort's entertainment and rides. These traditional centres now face strong competition from the new wave of holiday villages.

The new holiday villages

Holiday villages owe their reinvigoration to Piet Derksen who opened the first of a chain of Center Parcs in the Netherlands in 1967, expanding into Belgium, France, Germany and the UK. These offered a very different holiday experience from that of traditional holiday centres, based on a recognition that North European resorts could not compete with sunnier climes and so facilities would have to take account of the inclement weather. This meant that more indoor entertainment was provided as well as fully enclosed swimming pools.

Center Parcs first launched in the UK in 1987. There are now five upmarket holiday villages offering a wide choice of all-weather facilities, most notably vast indoor pools with domed glass roofs and settings designed to resemble a tropical beach. The villages had an extraordinary measure of success in their early years, and maintain this today, with an average 97% occupancy rate. Another company, Gran Dorado, also originating in the Netherlands, developed 40 holiday villages but subsequently merged with Center Parcs to further expand the brand.

In Europe, the market leader Club Mediterranée, which is French-owned and has a worldwide spread of holiday villages, from France to Tahiti. The success of this organisation, which in 1950 was among the first to enter the package holiday business, has been attributed to its unique approach to its clients, who are referred to as *gentils membres*. It had been the practice for beads to be used instead of hard currency to purchase drinks on site, which heightened the feeling for the holidaymakers of being divorced from the commercial world while on holiday. Club Mediterranée experienced a decline in profits after failing to keep pace with holiday centre developments at the end of the 1990s and has been forced into an expensive programme of renovation to restore its position in the market, with many of the old tactics giving way to a more commercial approach. It has reduced the number of properties it runs, now operating 68 villages worldwide, and is seeing improved success, having refocused its activity on high-end, all-inclusive holidays.

SECOND-HOME AND TIMESHARE OWNERSHIP

Second homes

It is appropriate here to discuss the growth of second-home ownership and the effect that this is having on the tourism industry. Owning a second home in the country or by the sea is not a new phenomenon. Since the age of the Grand Tour, the British aristocracy and, later, wealthy merchants invariably had a country seat to retreat to at weekends and through the summer to escape the heat and dirt of the big cities. Similarly, wealthy Parisians owned a second property readily accessible from the French capital. Americans have been buying homes along the north-eastern shores of the USA since the nineteenth century, culminating in the ostentatious residences built as summer homes for the very wealthy along the shores of Newport, Rhode Island, in the 1890s. Later, holiday homes were built on the West Coast and in Florida. Today, many wealthy Americans have two holiday homes: a summer home along the Cape and a winter home in Florida. In Europe, Nordic residents have a long tradition of owning second homes by the sea, even if many are of very simple cottage construction. Löfgren (1999) claims that there were 500,000 such homes in Sweden by the 1970s, owned by a population totalling only some 8 million. A high proportion of these were built for Stockholm residents along the popular west coast of the country, some six hours' drive away. Löfgren estimated that 25% of Swedes and a similar number of other Nordic residents owned second homes by the close of the twentieth century, in comparison with 16% of the French and just 4% of Americans.

These early second homes, however, were almost invariably constructed as summer homes for the owners and their friends. What has marked the big change in more recent times has been the commercialisation of the second-home market. Owners now buy to let, frequently renting out their property when not for their own use through commercial rental agencies who manage the properties for a commission. The holiday homes rental market has soared in recent years as owners purchased property as a principal investment when the share market collapsed.

British residents were rather later in getting into property, but have more than made up for their tardiness in a frenzy of buying since the 1990s. At first, this was confined mainly to the UK, but, as prices soared and restrictions began to be imposed on property construction in the more popular areas of the countryside such as the Lake District, South Devon and the Cotswolds, Britons began to turn to cheaper accommodation in Italy, France, Spain (especially the Canary and Balearic Islands) and Greece. More recently, homes in Florida and the newly admitted countries of the EU, especially Malta, Cyprus and Slovenia, have been in demand. Historically, investment in second homes has been fuelled by both an increase in disposable income among the better-off sections of society and the fall in air transport prices. In the post 9/11 world, transatlantic fares dropped to an all-time low, while the growth of no-frills airlines to smaller regional airports on the Continent has attracted investors to Romania, Bulgaria and Turkey. Although there

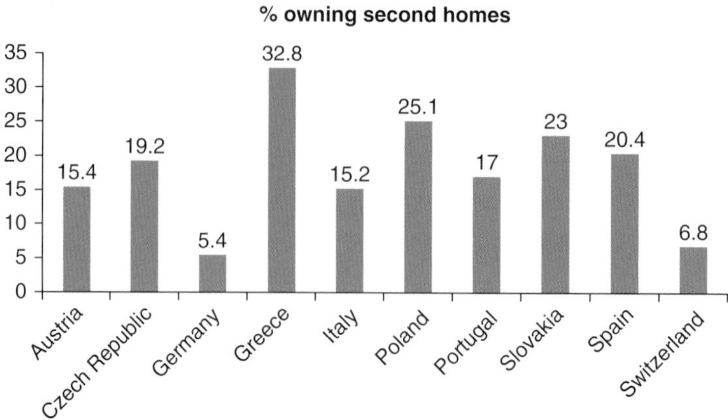

FIGURE 12.7 Percentage of the population owning second homes

Source: RE/MAX, 2015

is limited research on second-home ownership, a recent study by the global estate agency RE/MAX reveals a variation in the percentage of the European population who own second homes. Some of these homes may be used to allow people to live close to their employment during the working week, while others will be holiday homes used more sporadically.

The exact number of second homes owned by British residents abroad is hard to establish and estimates vary wildly. As a guide, the Department of Communities and Local Government (DCLG) estimated that 525,000 UK households owned a second home, with about 47% located outside of Great Britain (Paris, 2011). In terms of the distribution of these second homes, France and Spain dominate for Britons with second homes abroad, with 24% and 33% respectively. The rest of Europe accounts for 22% with the rest of the world making up the remaining 21%.

Timeshare

Where an outright purchase is beyond people's means, the concept of timeshare properties offers an alternative means of enjoying a holiday in one's second home. **Timeshare** is a scheme whereby an apartment or villa is sold to several co-owners, each of whom purchases the right to use the accommodation for a given period of the year, which may range from one week to several weeks. The initial cost of the accommodation will vary not only according to the length of time for which it is purchased, but also depending on the period of the year chosen, so that a week in July or August, for example, may be three or four times the cost of the same accommodation in winter.

The scheme is reported to have been initiated at a ski resort in the French Alps in 1965, although at least one organisation, the Ring Hotel chain in Switzerland, was developing along similar lines some years before this. By the early 1970s, timeshare had been introduced in the USA, and the concept had also arrived in the UK by the mid-1970s. Since then, it has enjoyed enormous success, boosted by schemes allowing owners to exchange their properties for others around the world during their period of ownership. A number of timeshare exchange organisations have been established, of which the largest and best-known are Resort Condominiums International, with 3.7 million members worldwide in 2014, and Interval International (II) with 2 million enrolled members. These companies keep a register of owners and, for a fee, will facilitate home exchanges around the world and organise flights.

Statistics on timeshare ownership are notoriously inaccurate, often being provided by the timeshare industry associations. The Timeshare Consumer Guide, drawing on data published by RCI, Interval International and the Resort Development Organisation (RDO), reported that 20 million households own a timeshare, with 11 million weeks available at 7400 resorts globally. Nearly half of all timeshare owners are Americans, with 6.9% of US households reported to be timeshare owners (ARDA, 2017).

Unfortunately, the extensive development of timeshare properties led to high-pressure sales techniques being used by less reputable organisations, using street touts to approach tourists visiting resorts abroad. This led to some poor publicity for the scheme in the press. The Timeshare Developers' Association was formed to give the industry credibility and draw up a code of conduct for members. The European Union introduced the Timeshare Directive in 1994, with subsequent reviews in 2007 and 2011 striving to further improve consumer protection. Timeshare is not without its problems. It has been found to be difficult to resell such properties due to the amount of new properties coming on to the market and, in some cases, management and maintenance fees have been high.

EXAMPLE

Timeshare and the Millennial generation

Consumers typically buy a one-week share in a holiday property, which is often located as part of a resort. The purchase contract usually lasts 30–40 years and requires the owners to pay a share of the maintenance costs annually. Consequently, the owner is purchasing the right to access the accommodation during the same week every year.

For many of the Millennial generation (born in the 1980s and 1990s), this lack of flexibility is unappealing. It is possible for the owner to join an exchange scheme, which trades the purchased accommodation week for access to other properties at times of commensurate value. However, for a generation seeking authenticity and variety, staying in seven-day blocks at a timeshare resort may not meet their travel expectations.

The industry is responding to the challenge. For example, it has introduced a points-based system that creates the possibility of trading for a short break, extending the stay beyond a one-week block or using the points to access additional lifestyle facilities.

Source: Euromonitor, 2015

The poor image of the timeshare business was marginally improved in the late 1980s when major hotel chains like Marriott, with its Vacation Club brand, Walt Disney and Hilton Grand Vacations all entered the market. In 2018, Marriott purchased US-based ILG to create the largest timeshare operator in the world, with more than 3200 resorts in 80 countries.

EDUCATIONAL ACCOMMODATION

The significance of the educational accommodation sector must also be recognised. Universities and other institutions of higher education seeking to increase contributions to their revenue through the rental of student accommodation during the academic holidays have marketed their accommodation to tour operators and others for budget holidays. Often situated near major tourist destinations, such as Cambridge or York, the universities have experienced considerable success in this venture and have further expanded their involvement with the leisure market by providing other facilities, such as activity centres and public rooms for themed holidays. For some destinations, this form of accommodation can be a significant portion of overall capacity.

The standards of university accommodation have greatly improved in recent years to meet the expectations of students themselves as their standards at home have risen. En suite facilities are now the norm, bringing the standards up to the levels that budget holidaymakers have come to expect, and making them comparable to those of other accommodation for budget conferences and business meetings. This is proving to be a profitable source of revenue for institutions during the academic holidays.

THE DISTRIBUTION OF ACCOMMODATION

Large hotel chains have in the past enjoyed advantages in gaining access to their markets through their links with the airline sector. This close relationship dates back to the early 1970s when airlines, introducing their new jumbo jets, hastily set about establishing connections with hotels to accommodate their increasing passenger numbers. As a result, hotel chains gained access to the airlines' global distribution systems (GDS), the computerised reservation networks that were a key factor in selling rooms to the international market.

While this link remains important, the development of the Internet has changed the nature of distribution, making the large hotel groups far more independent in their interface with customers. Apart from hotel representation on airline-owned (or formerly owned) websites such as Opodo and Orbitz, online agencies such as Expedia and Travelocity, which offer a range of travel products, feature hotels prominently and have become a powerful force in the distribution chain. Websites devoted to accommodation only (such as Booking.com and Hotels.com) have also developed, with rooms at highly competitive prices. Furthermore, the larger hotel groups are increasingly relying on their own websites to reach their customers in an effort to cut costs by avoiding payment of commission to intermediaries.

EXAMPLE

Booking hotels online

There are many travel websites dedicated to the accommodation sector. Perhaps the most well-known for hotels, inns and B&Bs are the two sites of Hotels.com and Booking.com. There are also sites dedicated to other segments such as Cottages4you and Owners Direct, which serve customers seeking the rental of private villas, apartments and holiday homes for short-term let.

To aid the online search for holiday accommodation, there are price comparison sites such as Trivago. This company searches the data published on more than 180 online travel agents (OTAs) to provide travellers with a summary of the prices being charged. Thus, customers can compare the price for a particular hotel from different agents.

Large hotels depend on group as well as individual business, so they must maintain contact with tour operators, conference organisers and others who bulk-buy hotel bedrooms. The tourist boards can play a part in helping such negotiations by organising workshops abroad, to which buyers of accommodation and other facilities will be invited.

All large hotel chains, and most small hotel companies, now have their own computer system to cope with back-of-office and management information as well as providing access to their reservations system worldwide. Some chains maintain their own offices in key generating countries (and, of course, each hotel will recommend business and take reservations for others in the chain), while independent hotels reach overseas markets through membership of marketing consortia.

Increasingly, travellers are prepared to search the Internet for cheap airline seats and hotel rooms. Domestic bookings are traditionally made direct with hotels, and, for reservations abroad, agents are unwilling to get involved unless they hold agreements with the hotels on the payment of commission. Some hotels will pay a standard 10%, while others allow only a lesser rate or restrict commissions to room sales outside peak periods. Many agents are also unwilling to deal with overseas hotels without making a charge for the service. The growth of **dynamic packaging** – essentially, tailor-made programmes put together by an intermediary such as an operator or agent by a search of websites – may provide travel agents with scope to retain their customers' loyalty as they can show that they are offering expertise beyond what travellers can find for themselves. This is discussed in more detail in Chapter 19.

ENVIRONMENTAL ISSUES

All sectors of the tourism industry are becoming sensitised to the issue of ecotourism; that is, ecologically sound tourism that can be sustained as tourist numbers continue to grow. Hotels are in a position to take a lead on this issue. They are also frequently the recipients of complaints by the ecotourism lobby as a result of their practices. For example, hotels in Goa, in India, have been strongly criticised because of their profligate use of water for showers, swimming pools and so on in a region where the local inhabitants suffer from water shortages due to drought.

Many hotels encourage their guests to use water sparingly, taking a shower rather than a bath, restricting water flow rates and taking other measures that reduce waste. Hotel proprietors have recognised that there is unnecessary wastage; for instance, many guests do not require their towels and sheets to be replaced daily, thus savings can be effected by offering guests the choice of having fresh linen (which they may indicate by leaving towels on the floor in the morning) or reusing it (indicated by hanging towels up).

One example of an eco-friendly approach in the industry was the launch of the International Hotels Environment Initiative, referred to in Chapter 5, which set out to monitor the environmental performance of the participating hotels and offer practical advice, especially to small independent hoteliers, on how they might manage their hotels in a more environmentally sensitive manner. This included encouraging the reduction of linen changes, the efficient use of energy, taking into consideration methods of rubbish disposal and even replacing throwaway shampoo containers with shampoo dispensers in the bathroom. Such measures can provide substantial savings on costs for the hotels themselves, as well as helping to protect the environment as a whole and ensuring that, as far as possible, tourism in hotels is environmentally sustainable. This initiative has now been incorporated into the International Tourism Partnership, to encourage the wider tourism industry to consider the practical ways in which members can work towards greater sustainability.

EXAMPLE

Hotels go green

Hotel companies are working towards greater levels of waste reduction, as pressure to be more sustainable – and more cost-efficient – grows. The Green Hotels and Responsible Tourism initiative lists environmental impacts likely to affect key areas of hotel operations, including:

- hazardous waste such as printing cartridges, swimming pool chemicals, garden pesticides and cleaning products
- water and food waste
- consumption of energy and water
- air, soil and noise emissions.

The same initiative encourages hotels to audit their operations in order to reduce impacts. Suggestions to improve procedures include installing energy- and water-saving devices, recycling water and waste products, improving building construction and design to reduce resource use, and adjusting purchasing decisions to reduce packaging and transport requirements. Recommendations also include customer education to improve awareness and influence behaviour.

CATERING

DISTINGUISHING TOURISM CATERING

Catering, often seen along with hotels as distinct from other elements of the tourism product, is nevertheless a vital ingredient of the tourism experience, and, as we saw earlier in the discussion of gastronomy tourism in Chapter 9, it sometimes provides the prime motivation for a journey. A day trip to a famous restaurant or a drive to visit a popular inn at the weekend is a familiar form of excursion that must be included in statistics estimating tourists' expenditure. Similarly, long holidays to France are often taken primarily because of that country's strong tradition of outstanding food and drink.

Catering is, of course, provided to both tourists and non-tourists alike and, as these two markets are seldom differentiated for statistical purposes, the exact contribution made by the hospitality sector to tourism is difficult to gauge. This is even truer of catering than accommodation as most guests staying at a hotel will be tourists, while many choosing to dine at a hotel restaurant or other eatery may well be locals simply enjoying a meal out.

Catering consists of food and beverages, and tourism catering takes place in a range of facilities, to include hotels and motels, campsites and caravan parks, holiday camps and centres, restaurants, cafés, snack bars, pubs, nightclubs and even takeaway food shops.

It will form an important element in many tourism-orientated facilities, including hotels, airports and catering outlets situated in popular tourist destinations such as city centres and seaside resorts. In the latter, takeaways may provide a significant percentage of all food consumed by visitors, especially in the more downmarket resorts serving the needs of day trippers. The beauty of catering as a product is the variety of forms that it can take, ranging from a Michelin-starred restaurant to a humble takeaway, each offering a different experience and catering to very different markets.

EXAMPLE

Record-breaking catering

Visitors to the London 2012 Olympics expected records to be broken in the athletics, cycling, swimming, or in one of the many other sports taking place. But a record was broken before the opening ceremony even took place.

Fast food giant McDonald's, a key sponsor of the Olympics since 1976, announced that one of its restaurants at the Olympic Park (there were four in all) was the biggest it had ever opened. This temporary two-storey outlet accommodated 1500 diners, and was forecast to serve 1.75 million meals during the 29 days of the Olympics and Paralympics (Ormsby, 2011).

While McDonalds experienced good trade inside the Olympic Park, post-event figures reveal that the event came at a big cost for restaurants and pubs generally, with the sector experiencing a net loss of £55 million on what would otherwise have been expected over the same period.

THE MEAL EXPERIENCE

The **meal experience** can be said to comprise four elements:

- food and drink
- service
- decor, furnishing and fittings
- atmosphere.

By juggling these four elements, caterers can direct their efforts to reach a wide variety of niche markets, depending on the type of food served, its quality, the level of service provided, the furnishings and the price charged. A decision will be made as to whether the aim is to move customers through the eating place as quickly as possible, as in the case of many cafés in tourist destinations or hotels catering to tour operators' customers, or allow them to relax over a leisurely meal, as when dining in top-class restaurants, and commonly in many low-budget mainland European eating places; with newspapers and, perhaps now more commonly, Wi-Fi access provided in many cafés. Such facilities are designed to encourage customers to linger over coffee or a meal.

EXAMPLE

Excessive charges

Eating out in resorts popular with tourists has always been relatively price-sensitive, but excessive charges are not unusual. In recent years, Venice has received negative press coverage due to several cases of overcharging by restaurants. In one case, a group of four Japanese tourists were charged €1143 for four steaks, a platter of seafood and a few drinks. A British couple also complained about a €500 bill, stating that waiters brought them expensive dishes they didn't order. Foreign tourists are not the only victims; a group of seven Italians were charged €101 for four liqueur coffees, with the bill including a €42 surcharge because a string quintet was playing in the restaurant at the time.

In line with the rise in disposable income among tourists, the tendency has been to spend a greater proportion of one's holiday money on food and beverages. Just as, at one end of the price range, fast food and drink outlets like Starbucks, Costa, Burger King and the ubiquitous Irish pubs now proliferating all over Europe have benefited from this trend, so too, at the other end of the market, have the higher-priced eating outlets moved to accommodate an increasing demand among tourists seeking new experiences when they eat out. No longer satisfied with full-board or half-board deals that lock them into eating in their hotel, some tourists seek different meal experiences each day. Consequently, some hotels have tried to accommodate this need by allowing their guests to eat at other hotels in the area with which they have links; but the appeal of small, comfortable restaurants where they can eat well-cooked authentic local food is luring many tourists away from the all-inclusive package.

EXAMPLE

Hungry for the familiar

Just as chain hotels offer guests a sense of security by knowing what to expect in terms of the product and service before they enter the premises, so too do large catering chains provide a similar experience. Walk into a McDonald's the world over and the experience will largely be the same, with perhaps the menu offering a slightly different choice to cater for local tastes. This familiarity reassures and draws in the traveller.

Many famous catering brands have expanded by offering franchise opportunities, including McDonald's, Pizza Hut, Subway and Costa Coffee. These outlets are frequently present at transport hubs such as railway stations and airports, catering for the needs of the travelling public.

As profits on food and beverage expenditure will often exceed those on rooms, hotels are keen to do what they can to ensure their customers eat on the premises. Thus, hotels cater for their customers in restaurants, cafés, bars and through room service, and in larger hotels a range of different restaurants is provided, which might include ethnic food, a themed setting (such as a seafood restaurant), separate dining rooms for tour groups and one or more fast food outlets. In the Venetian Macao Resort Hotel, as one notable example, customers are faced with the choice of no fewer than 25 restaurants. Because of a commonly held view that the food in hotel restaurants is inferior to those found in nearby restaurants (a view not entirely without justification, especially in budget hotels where contract caterers may be delivering frozen food for microwave reheating), hotels are now making a greater effort to improve their food and service, as well as offering greater choice to their customers.

EXAMPLE

Are they eating in the hotel?

Some years ago, the CEO of a large chain of corporate hotels in the USA visited a number of the properties incognito, to judge the extent to which customers were using the dining facilities. Addressing the concierges, elevator staff and receptionists, he asked each if they could recommend a good place to eat in the neighbourhood. He received lots of recommendations, but none suggested the hotel! The need to promote its own products was subsequently stressed to staff in the hotel's training programmes.

The problem of providing value for money is increased where group catering in hotels is concerned. Functions of all sizes from weddings to conferences are held in hotels, and the need to serve large groups quickly with a meal of an acceptable quality and still give good service is a challenge. This is frequently best met, in the case of large group meetings, by offering buffet rather than table service.

The widespread desire of people to experiment with new taste sensations is leading to much more adventurous dining out, and higher-priced restaurants are rising to the challenge. Heston Blumenthal, who has introduced highly unconventional food at his now world-famous restaurant The Fat Duck in Bray, Berkshire, has become renowned for such delicacies as snail porridge and mousse created using liquid nitrogen. Sometimes, however, it is the bizarre that strikes a chord with customers, as exemplified by 'dining in the dark' – an idea initiated in 1999 by a restaurateur at Die Blinde Kuh in Zürich. His patrons, having selected their meals, are invited to eat in completely darkened rooms, served by blind waiters. The experience of such a key sense being removed allows diners to concentrate purely on the aroma of their food and its taste, which is said to enhance the experience. A Parisian restaurant, Dans le Noir, soon followed suit, but blindfolded its patrons; this proved so successful that the chain has opened in London, Auckland, Melbourne and Madrid.

In the UK, pubs have taken on a new lease of life as they have had to meet the challenges posed by drink-driving laws and restrictions on smoking indoors. Liberalisation of the licensing laws, permitting alcohol to be served for more extended periods of the day, was one of the few rays of sunshine in an otherwise difficult period for this sector of the industry. This has helped to boost sales in pubs and inns catering particularly to stopover travellers, enabling the industry to compete more equally with its European neighbours. Many pubs have also now chosen to focus on food at the expense of beverages, with a large growth in the number of gastropubs offering high-quality food. The evidence is that the hospitality industry can rise to the challenge of changing circumstances, with the result being greater flexibility and choice in eating out. While the quality and service of food in hotels still has a long way to go in the UK, the food and beverage sector generally is fast losing its reputation among international tourist markets for deplorable food and service.

FUTURE DEVELOPMENTS IN THE HOSPITALITY SECTOR

The recent history of the hospitality industry is dominated by the need for constant innovation to ward off competition by best meeting changing consumer demand for novelty and improved facilities. This pattern will surely continue, with markets broadly split between large chain hotels offering the 'wow' factor, character properties marketed on the basis of architecture and history, fashion hotels, such as art hotels, filling niche markets, and a rapidly growing budget sector selling not just on price but also on brand and image. The more extreme the design of the hotel, the less dependent it is on its location and, in a growing number of cases, the appeal will be the experience offered by the hotel rather than the location.

The growth of Internet-based review sites – one of the largest being TripAdvisor, discussed earlier in this chapter – means that hotels and restaurants are now able to easily monitor the feedback their business is receiving from customers. As other travellers rely more heavily on this electronic word-of-mouth recommendation, so hotels must become more aware of the impact that negative experience can have on demand. TripAdvisor has over 600 million reviews, which include ratings of the service and facilities as well as comments on the stay, and hotels can respond on TripAdvisor to any of the reviews posted, though few hotels today are sufficiently resourced to make the most of opportunities presented by feedback on social media. Adversely, reports in the press have drawn attention to certain hotels paying guests, or upgrading them, for favourable comments, in some cases even posting their own reviews. As with all technology, websites can be open to misuse, making decisions more difficult for clients.

The challenge for the catering industry over the next few years, particularly at the budget end of the business, will be to control costs at a time when food prices are rocketing throughout the world. Good service and quality can, to some extent, compensate if it can be shown that the customer is receiving value for money. While fast food chains will continue to provide an important proportion of tourist meals, notably for younger travellers, there is evidence among older, better-off travellers that the quality of food and service is more important than price and that, if restaurants deliver value for money to tourists, in attractive settings, they can thrive.

The growing number of international tourists coming from the BRIC countries is encouraging hotels to create brands that will meet the needs and cultural expectations of these markets. China, with the world's largest outbound market, has the largest domestic tourism market, so hotel construction in China is now providing extensive opportunities for the major chains.

One area of technology where the hospitality sector is changing is that of electronic payments. Although contactless payment and the technology behind it – near-field communication (NFC) – has been around for a number of years, historically small hospitality businesses would not accept card payment, effectively operating as cash-only businesses (Ducker, 2014). Now the technology required to accept card payments has developed significantly, with devices that can be plugged into a mobile phone or tablet providing a low-budget alternative to the traditional point-of-sale card terminal. Furthermore, the use of mobile phones and digital watches as means of making payment has expanded the demand to make electronic payments.

QUESTIONS AND DISCUSSION POINTS

1. Explain the difference between the categorisation, classification and grading of accommodation.
2. Airbnb has access to more properties than the leading hotel chains. What factors have led to the existence and continued growth of this competitor?
3. Several countries in Europe have a mandatory (rather than voluntary) grading system. What are the benefits of a mandatory system? Are there drawbacks to this?

TASKS

1. Use the Internet to find an unusual place for tourists to stay. Investigate this accommodation to identify the facilities and services it offers. Investigate reviews made by previous visitors and also the cost of staying at the accommodation at different times of the year. Produce a poster that explains the appeal of the place, offering your view of the type of tourist likely to stay.
2. This chapter introduced timeshare accommodation. Buying timeshare properties remains popular, with more than $8 billion spent in the USA in 2015. However, many owners choose to sell or give up their investment, with resale prices much lower than initial purchase costs. Write an essay that discusses the benefits and drawbacks of timeshare ownership.

WEBSITES

Airbnb: www.airbnb.co.uk

European Hotel Design Awards: www.europeanhoteldesignawards.com

TripAdvisor: www.tripadvisor.com

Tune Hotels: www.tunehotels.com

Visit England Quality Assessment service: www.qualityintourism.com

REFERENCES

Accor (2018) A leading hotel operator. Available online at: www.accorhotels.group/en/hotel-development/accorhotels-choice/a-leading-hotel-operator [Accessed December 2018].

American Resort Development Association (ARDA) (2017) *Timeshare Datashare: Number of timeshare owners in the US*. Washington, DC: ARDA.

Busby, G. and Rendle, S. (2000) The transition from tourism on farms to farm tourism. *Tourism Management*, 21, 635–42.

Ducker, P. (2014) Hospitality struggles to keep up when it comes to adopting new technology. *The Caterer*, 24 October. Available online at: www.thecaterer.com/articles/354093/hospitality-struggles-to-keep-up-when-it-comes-to-adopting-new-technology [Accessed 6 December 2018].

Euromonitor (2015) *Looking Below the Surface: Millennials as timeshare's saving grace*. London: Euromonitor.

Eurostat (2018) *Seasonality in the Tourist Accommodation Sector.* European Commission. Available online at: https://ec.europa.eu/eurostat/statistics-explained/index.php/Seasonality_in_the_tourist_accommodation_sector [Accessed December 2018].

Hotelier (2017) How hotel-loyalty programs are evolving to meet the needs of experience-seeking guests. *Hotelier*, 5 December. Available online at: www.hoteliermagazine.com/hotel-loyalty-programs-evolving-meet-needs-experience-seeking-guests [Accessed December 2018].

InterContinental Hotels Group (IHG) (2017) Annual Report and Financial Statement 2017. Available online at: www.ihgplc.com/investors/annual-report [Accessed December 2018].

Löfgren, O. (1999) *On Holiday: A history of vacationing*. Berkeley, CA: University of California Press.

Medlik, S. and Ingram, H. (2000) *The Business of Hotels*, 4th edn. Abingdon: Routledge.

Mintel (2018) *Hotels – UK*. London: Mintel.

Ormsby, A. (2011) McDonald's super-size Olympics plan upsets health groups. *Reuters*, 21 July.

Paris, C. (2011) *Affluence, Mobility and Second Home Ownership*. London: Routledge.

PricewaterhouseCoopers (2018) *As Good as it Gets? UK hotels forecast 2018*. Available online at: www.pwc.co.uk/hospitality-leisure/documents/pwc-uk-hotels-forecast-2018-as-good-as-it-gets.pdf [Accessed December 2018].

RE/MAX (2015) *At Home in Europe*. Available online at: www.at-home-in-europe.eu/home-life/europe/most-people-have-their-secondary-residence-in-their-home-country [Accessed December 2018].

Thorpe, A. (2009) Pop-up hotels set to provide cheap temporary rooms. *The Observer*, 22 November.

Vaughan, R. and Daverio, R. (2016) *Assessing the Size and Presence of the Collaborative Economy in Europe*. London: PricewaterhouseCoopers.

VisitEngland (2018) National Quality Assessment Scheme. Available online at: www.visitenglandassessmentservices.com [Accessed December 2018].

Waga, N.-O. (2016) The Impact of Celebrity Guests on Hotels. *Forbes*, 9 February. Available online at: www.forbes.com/sites/neloliviawaga/2016/02/09/the-impact-of-celebrity-guests-on-hotels/#230cef1f2181 [Accessed December 2018].

13

TOURIST TRANSPORT BY AIR

CONTENTS

LEARNING OUTCOMES

After studying this chapter, you should be able to:

- describe the role that airlines and airports play in meeting the needs of tourism
- explain how air transport is organised and distinguish between different categories of airline operation
- summarise the reasons for air regulation and the systems of regulation in force, both in the UK and internationally
- recognise the dynamic nature of the airline business and appraise the changes that have taken place in recent years
- analyse the reasons for success and failure of airlines' policies.

> Civil aviation is one of the major components of the nation's domestic and international transportation system. It both competes with and is complementary to surface transportation. (Aeronautics and Space Engineering Board, 1968: 5)

INTRODUCTION

The existence of efficient and interconnected transport networks that include aviation, shipping and land vehicles has aided the growth of tourism. A tourist destination's accessibility is the outcome of, above all else, two factors: price (in absolute terms, as well as in comparison with competing destinations) and time (the actual or perceived time taken to travel between the points of origin and destination).

Air travel (with a strong contribution from the no-frills airlines in particular) has, over the past four decades, made short-, medium- and long-haul destinations accessible on both these counts, to an extent not previously imaginable. In doing so, it has substantially contributed to the phenomenon of mass-market international tourism, with all the economic and social benefits and drawbacks that that has entailed. In the UK, consumer spending on air travel was £18.2 billion in 2017; in the USA, spending on air travel was double this amount (at $60.4 billion or approximately £47.4 billion), with the Chinese market spending the equivalent of $57.5 billion (Euromonitor, 2017). Estimates suggest that worldwide spending on air travel exceeds £298 billion, with more than 10 million people employed directly in aviation jobs, and a further 55 million indirectly supported by the aviation industry.

Most forms of transport are highly **capital-intensive**. Building and maintaining airports and regularly re-equipping airlines with new aircraft that have the latest technical advances require massive investments of capital. Such levels of investment are available only to the largest corporations and, in some cases, subsidies from the public sector may be necessary for political or social reasons. At the same time, transport offers great opportunities for economies of scale, whereby unit prices can be dramatically reduced. For example, an airline operating out of a particular airport will have invested a huge amount of money upfront and will have to do so whether that airline operates flights four times a day or once a week. If those overheads can be distributed over a greater number of flights, the cost of an individual seat on a flight will fall.

Caution is advised, however, when considering economies of scale. There comes a point where an organisation's further growth can result in diseconomies of scale, wiping out any former benefits gained as a result of size. The difficulty now faced by larger, traditional airlines attempting to compete with the leaner, more efficient budget airlines highlights exactly this dilemma.

THE AIRLINE BUSINESS

Travel by air has become relatively safe, comfortable, rapid and, above all, cheap, for two reasons. The first is the enormous progress in aviation technology that has occurred, especially following the development of the jet airliner after World War II. The first commercial jet (the de Havilland Comet, operated by BOAC) came into service on the London–Johannesburg route in 1952. Problems with metal fatigue resulted in the early withdrawal from service of this aircraft, but the introduction of the hugely successful Boeing 707 – in service first with Pan American Airways in 1958 – and later the first jumbo jet, the Boeing 747, which went into service in 1970, led to rapid falls in seat cost per passenger kilometre (a common measure of revenue yield). The costs fell in both absolute terms and

FIGURE 13.1 The double-decker Airbus A380

Photo: Shutterstock

relative to costs of other forms of transport, particularly passenger shipping, which up to the mid-1950s had dominated the long-haul travel business.

Both engine and aircraft design have since been continuously refined and improved. The wings, fuselage and engines have been designed to reduce drag, and the engines have also become more efficient and less fuel-hungry. Increases in carrying capacity for passengers and freight have steadily reduced average seat costs, with jumbo jets accommodating up to 500 passengers.

The next phase in this development arrived in 2007, when the Airbus 'superjumbo' A380 (Figure 13.1), a double-decker aircraft seating between 550 and 800 passengers, entered service (initially with Singapore Airlines in 2007), promising further economies of scale. Prices to passengers can only fall, however, if a high proportion of all those seats are filled. In the past, sudden jumps in capacity posed problems for airlines on some routes until seat demand caught up with supply.

EXAMPLE

Operating the A380

The Airbus A380 was once described as the 'new generation in flying' (Chance, 2010). Certainly, the design of this vast jetliner required airports to strengthen runways and build new stands to accommodate the double-deck design and increased wingspan.

Seen as one solution to the increasingly congested skies, the Airbus A380 provided not just greater passenger capacity from one take-off slot, but also improved environmental credentials. The design process also focused on reducing noise emissions, important in meeting airport regulations on night-time landings.

(Continued)

The operational costs per passenger were expected to be lower as, Airbus argued, greater value per departure slot can be achieved with high passenger capacity. However, this is dependent on having the demand to match; the routes operating A380s require significant demand. This has led to concerns in recent years and, consequently, the demand from airlines for the A380 has slowed. In the decade since the first A380 came into service, 217 planes have been delivered, with a further 100 A380s on order. Such low demand from airlines has led to the Airbus construction programme being cancelled, once the final order from Emirates has been fulfilled in 2021.

The plight of this aircraft was evident when Singapore Airlines declined to renew its lease on its two A380s, so, without a buyer for these second-hand planes (with at least ten years of service left), the decision was taken to scrap these for parts (Greenwood, 2018).

The introduction of these huge new aircraft poses other problems to those outlined above. The requirement to load and unload so many passengers for one aircraft within a limited space of time is challenging and requires extensively redesigned terminals. However, on the plus side the increased cabin space allows for greater luxury in higher-grade accommodation, including luxury en-suite cabins and even the introduction of double-bedded cabin suites on some routes.

The motivation behind the development of such large aircraft is not simply efficiency; it also helps to overcome problems caused by growing congestion at airports throughout the world. This is becoming critical at leading hub airports, where there are already acute shortages of take-off and landing slots.

The supersonic Concorde was perhaps the only aircraft whose design ran counter to this drive for economies of scale. Introduced into service in 1976, Concorde carried only 100 passengers at speeds in excess of 1400 miles per hour. Quite apart from the technical problems that have to be overcome when designing an aircraft for supersonic flight, speeds above Mach 1 substantially increase fuel burn, so most current airliners fly at around Mach 0.85, just subsonic. On some key global routes, however, speed was more important than cost, and business travellers, celebrities and other wealthy air travellers were prepared to pay highly for the privilege of cutting their travelling time. With high costs of operation, limited numbers that could be carried, its comparatively short range and the excessive noise (limiting Concorde's use largely to routes over oceans), it was not the most versatile of aircraft. The initial high development costs were written off by the UK and French governments and services were limited to flights between New York (and, initially, Washington) and London or Paris. The crash of a chartered Concorde in France in 2000 led to the grounding of all these aircraft and, despite modifications allowing a relaunch of this plane in 2001, it was removed from regular service in 2003, ending any form of supersonic travel for the foreseeable future.

Replacing the large commercial supersonic aircraft will be a new breed of small executive jets currently under development. One such aircraft, the Cessna Citation X, is already in service and capable of reaching Mach 0.92, very close to the speed of sound. The Gulfstream G500 offers similar speeds and is capable of transporting up to 18 passengers up to 5000 nautical miles on a single fuel load. For the present, the industry is putting its faith in demand for just-subsonic aircraft satisfying the executive market for the next few years.

Periodically, crises have occurred in world oil supplies, resulting in escalating fuel costs. This had a huge impact on aircraft costs from 1973 to 1974 and again following the Gulf War in 1991, the 9/11 crisis in 2001, the subsequent war in Iraq and its aftermath.

These crises have proved to be generally of short duration, but fluctuations in fuel prices have also been a characteristic of the past decade, thus airlines must continue to manage such variations.

Some carriers will hedge by buying up to 80% of their fuel forward, helping to mitigate the worst impacts of escalating prices (Table 13.1). Hedging usually allows an airline the option to buy fuel at a set price in the future, but this option will only be taken if the price of fuel is higher than the agreed price. However, hedging is expensive, as the risk is passed to the insurer, who charges a premium for this peace of mind. The gamble of hedging can be seen by looking at the prices of oil in 2008: it started the year at $90 a barrel and finished the year at $40, having surpassed $140 during the summer period. Although hedging can bring stability to the balance sheet, the cost of this risk reduction may not be justified, and some airlines (for example, American Airlines) have not entered into any hedging arrangements since 2013.

TABLE 13.1 Fuel hedging of European airlines

Airline	Hedging percentage
Air France	55–62% per quarter in 2018
easyJet	73–76% in 2018; 56% in 2019
Finnair	68–73% in 2018
Flybe	73% in 2018/19
International Airlines Group (IAG) – BA, Iberia, Vueling, Aer Lingus	61–79% in 2018; 27–47% in 2019
Lufthansa	76% in 2018
Norwegian Air	27% in 2018
Ryanair	90% in 2019
SAS	83–91% in 2018

Source: Ghaddar, 2018

Of greater concern, however, is the realisation that oil supplies are not infinite. Demand is growing sharply and will outstrip supplies within 20–40 years, even after allowing for new finds (fracking may extend this period, but will not alter the basic premise that new forms of energy are imperative). Moreover, oil prices are unstable, often politically manipulated and can fluctuate rapidly. In general, prices are expected to rise in the future, given demand from new economic powerhouses such as China and India. Consequently, the aircraft industry is searching in the short term for new ways to improve fuel economy, but in the longer term it will be imperative to discover new means of powering aircraft, unless the industry is willing to embrace a sharp drop in the overall number of flights operated.

Many experts believe that the jet engine has now reached a stage of evolutionary sophistication that will make it increasingly difficult to produce further economies, so cost-cutting exercises have replaced technological innovation as a means of reducing prices to the public. To achieve weight reduction, some airlines have reduced the number of beverages carried, withdrawn seat phones, replaced divisions between classes with curtains and even withdrawn or reduced the number of pages in their in-flight magazines.

EXAMPLE

Losing weight can save money

Airlines are now making strenuous efforts to reduce the weight of the on-board equipment and catering. The added weight of each passenger carrying a cell phone is estimated to cost Southwest Airlines $1.2 million annually. Aviation research considered the use of lighter seats, carrying less water for the washroom taps, and swapping the pilot's flight manuals for electronic versions. As an example, Virgin Atlantic has redesigned meal trays, to reduce the weight of the trays themselves and the weight and number of carts needed to transport them.

In a move that has duel benefits for the environment, Singapore Airlines introduced an electronic version of its in-flight magazine, removing the printing costs of production as well as reducing the fuel burn for transporting these documents. Similarly, United changed the paper used for their in-flight magazine, saving one ounce per publication – and saving the company $300,000 a year. Southwest provided pilots with electronic tablets instead of paper manuals, with the reduced weight saving more than 500,000 gallons of fuel across its operations.

Furthermore, airlines have been shutting off an engine during taxiing, cleaning aircraft exteriors more frequently to reduce drag and removing dropped coins from the cabins, all to save fuel. Gaining a confirmed landing time is also important because it can avoid the expense of circling at the destination airport. Finally, in a move also used by ships, cruising at a slower speed is now used to reduce fuel burn.

Airlines are obliged to carry some reserves of fuel for emergencies, but on certain routes they will also carry excess fuel in order to avoid refuelling at airports where fuel costs are high. Airlines facing low profits from competition have to weigh up the advantages of introducing the latest fuel-efficient aircraft against the high capital costs of buying them, a problem that will be discussed later in this chapter.

For a while, aviation research considered liquefied hydrogen, but production challenges have reduced interest in this. Instead, biofuels, which can be produced without competing for water and food resources, are receiving greater research interest. Additionally, while engine technology may have peaked, advances are still being made in lightweight construction materials by aircraft manufacturers: techniques such as ALM (additive layer manufacturing), in which powdered plastic and metal are melted together, are expected to lead to fuselages and wings up to 65% lighter than those made of present materials.

During the 1980s, the technological focus changed to the development of quieter aircraft and aircraft capable of taking off from, and landing on, shorter runways. This originated in the USA, where controls on noise pollution forced airlines to re-equip their fleets or fit expensive modifications to existing aircraft; since the 1970s, a noise reduction of 75% has been achieved through aircraft design. In turn, the airlines press their governments to relax controls over night flying as this enables them to operate around the clock, easing congestion and increasing their productivity. The UK government is under some pressure to reduce night flight frequency and noise levels.

Short take-off and landing (STOL) aircraft such as the de Havilland Twin Otter have been built for commuter services, seating up to 20 passengers, and slightly larger aircraft built for regional services, typically carrying 50–110 passengers, such as the Bombardier and Embraer CRJ and ERJ families, have all helped to revolutionise business travel, allowing airports to be sited much closer to city centres. More recently, the Russian Sukhoi Superjet 100 has also started to compete in this market.

EXAMPLE

London City Airport

London City Airport, situated in the Docklands area, is an example of a development that has been partly dependent on STOL technology for its success. The airport was initially hampered by the lack of good connections to central London and a short-sighted marketing decision to promote the airport exclusively as a business airport, with the expectation that passengers would arrive by taxi. The weakness of this strategy quickly became evident, and public transport connections were encouraged. The airport now operates profitably and surface connections have improved with the construction and opening of a Docklands Light Railway station within the grounds, providing connections to the London Underground service. The result is that services and routes have now expanded substantially. Over 4.5 million passengers departed from this airport in 2017.

Its previous focus on the business traveller has not been ignored, however. With a journey time of 25 minutes from the centre of London to the airport, and with short check-in times (15 minutes for passengers with no hold luggage), BA chose the airport for its London–New York business class-only flights. However, due to the short runway the aircraft cannot carry enough fuel for a transatlantic crossing, necessitating a stop to refuel at Shannon airport, in Ireland. This benefits passengers by allowing them to pre-clear American customs, saving time on arrival at JFK Airport in New York.

Another factor in the development of mass travel by air was the enterprise and creativity demonstrated by both air transport management and other entrepreneurs in the tourism industry. At a time of strictly regulated prices, the introduction of net-inclusive tour-basing fares for tour operators, as well as variable pricing techniques such as advance purchase excursion (APEX) tickets and standby fares, helped to stimulate demand and fill aircraft seats. Later, innovative carriers introduced frequent flyer programmes (FFP), in which passengers are given additional free miles based on the mileage they accumulate with a carrier or one of its partners.

THE BUDGET AIRLINES

By far the most important development in recent years has been the growth of **low-cost carriers**. Prompted by the deregulation of the airline industry in the USA, many regional carriers came into being to fight for a share of the potentially lucrative domestic airline market. Many, such as People's Express, faded quickly, but others, like Southwest Airlines (formed as the first low-cost airline in 1971), maximised new opportunities and went from strength to strength. Southwest carried over 130 million passengers in 2017.

With the liberalisation of air transport in the EU a few years later, an explosion of no-frills carriers emerged, led by Ryanair, which, under Michael O'Leary, sought initially to challenge the hold over the Irish market held by Aer Lingus, later undercutting fares and developing new routes to regional airports throughout Europe. The entrepreneur Stelios Haji-Ioannou followed with the launch of easyJet.

These and other carriers, together with rising seat-only sales on the charter carriers' aircraft, were soon having an impact on the profitability of the major airlines, forcing them to develop their own low-cost offshoots, initially with mixed success. Both BA's and KLM's early attempts to compete via their budget brands Go and Buzz met with failure and they were absorbed into the easyJet and Ryanair empires, respectively.

Inevitably, the leading 'heritage' or **full-service airlines** must decide whether to take the budget airlines on at their own game or distance themselves from this sector of the market by premium pricing. The budget airlines are here to stay, and represent a growing proportion of the overall market for passenger services by air. At the time of writing, there were more than 20 low-cost airlines operating in Europe, with more than 1500 aircraft. Budget carriers have also thrived in Asia and North America, with similar aircraft numbers providing more than 28% of global airline capacity.

Within the USA, competing with Southwest, budget carriers include Frontier Airlines, Spirit Airlines (the first ultra-low-cost airline in the USA), Sun Country Airlines and JetBlue Airways (in which Lufthansa made a 19% investment in 2006). These budget brands serve a wide network of routes throughout North America, including some routes into the Caribbean and Latin America, and carry many millions of passengers. Some of the established North American carriers made efforts to compete by forming their own budget brands, but with only limited success – Delta's Song was absorbed into the main carrier in 2006, and the activities of United's Ted were reincorporated into the operations of the parent company in 2009. Despite growing competition, Southwest leads the way in terms of passenger numbers and is the largest budget carrier globally (Table 13.2).

TABLE 13.2 Leading low-cost carriers worldwide

Airline	Passenger numbers in 2017 (millions)
Southwest	157.8
Ryanair	130.3
easyJet	80.2
Lion Group	51.8
IndiGo	49.2
JetBlue	40.0
Air Asia	39.1
Norwegian Air	33.1
Gol	32.4
Wizz Air	29.6

Source: Ishak, 2018

Specialist niche carriers emerged to attract the top end of the market, creaming passengers from the business and first-class seats of the established carriers. On transatlantic services, ill-fated American operators MaxJet and Eos and UK operator Silverjet introduced all-business-class configurations, with fares aimed at undercutting the lead carriers. With smaller fleets than the budget carriers, however, these premium services do not benefit from the economies of scale available to the lead carriers. MaxJet went into receivership in 2007, followed by Eos and Silverjet the following year.

Low-cost medium- and long-haul airlines have emerged. Early into this market were Zoom, operating primarily on transatlantic routes, and Oasis, which served London and Vancouver from its base in Hong Kong. Both ceased trading in 2008. Norwegian Air has introduced routes between Europe and Thailand as well as Dubai and some transatlantic destinations. Its business model has put it in such a position that it has been pursued by Lufthansa and BA owner, IAG. However, the low-cost long-haul business model has a chequered past, with airlines such as Laker Airways, Tower Air and, more recently, Air Berlin all failing. Scoot (an offshoot of Singapore Airlines operating low-cost short-haul routes) is extending the range of its routes to a point that it is offering long-haul routes, with the Singapore–Berlin route (at 9936 km) its longest. It also operates routes to Athens, Honolulu and destinations in Australia. AirAsia X has also received praise for its operations serving longer routes using a low-fare approach in which customers pay for in-flight entertainment, food and even blankets. Its longest route is Osaka-Kansai to Honolulu (6624 km).

EXAMPLE

Norwegian Air

To improve operating efficiencies on long-haul flights, budget airline Norwegian Air has increased the number of seats it fits into the Boeing 787 aircraft it uses: 291 passengers, compared to more common configurations used by full-service carriers that accommodate around 250 passengers.

The airline also schedules routes and timings to keep the planes in the air for more of the time, perhaps as much as 18 hours a day. Where possible, the airline also uses cheaper secondary airports. However, the biggest challenge for the airline will remain that of filling each aircraft seat to maximise revenue.

Source: The Economist, 2014

The global recession towards the end of the first decade of the twenty-first century changed the travel behaviour of premium-class passengers, with discounted tickets now being expected as part of the corporate agreements for business travel; and, at the top end, passengers who would have considered first-class passage are now giving greater consideration to the use of private charters to meet their travel needs. This has significantly changed the trading landscape for both the low-cost carriers and the full-service airlines.

THE ORGANISATION OF AIR TRANSPORT

It is convenient to think of the civil aviation business as being composed of a number of elements, namely:

- equipment manufacturers
- airports
- air navigation and traffic control services
- airlines.

Each of these is not dependent only on tourists for its livelihood. Apart from non-tourist civilian passengers, they also serve the needs of the military, as well as those of freight and mail clientele, but the tourist market is important for each of these elements so they must be included as components of the tourism industry.

EQUIPMENT MANUFACTURERS

These companies manufacture commercial airframes and engines. The demand for airframes (fuselages and wings) can be conveniently divided between those for large jet aircraft, typically carrying between 130 and 500 passengers, which provide the bulk of passenger services throughout the world, and those for smaller aircraft, seating as few as 18 passengers, which are employed chiefly on business routes or provide feeder services from rural airports. Separately classified are those companies manufacturing private jets, such as the Learjet, typically seating just 4–9 passengers. This last category also has a role to play in business tourism, as these jets are extensively employed in air taxi services, discussed later in this chapter.

The world demand for airframes is dominated by just two manufacturers (Table 13.3), each of which has a roughly equal share of the market: the US-owned Boeing Aircraft Company (which swallowed what was then the second-largest airframe manufacturer, McDonnell Douglas, in 1997) and Airbus Integrated Company (AIC), the consortium responsible for building the European Airbus, 80% of which is built in mainland Europe and 20% (the wings) by BAe Systems in the UK.

TABLE 13.3 Company revenue

Manufacturer	Revenue (2016)
Boeing	$94.6 billion
Airbus	$70.3 billion
United Technologies*	$39.5 billion
Bombardier	$16.3 billion
Embraer	$6.2 billion

Note: * Revenue for the aerospace arm of the business only.

Source: *IndustryWeek*, 2017

The first challenge to the duopoly of these giant manufacturers appeared in 2008 when Canadian-owned Bombardier announced its intention to build a competitive aircraft for the short-haul market: the C-Series. This aircraft is designed to compete with the Boeing 737 and the Airbus A320. However, following a lack of orders for the C-Series, Bombardier and Airbus partnered to allow Airbus to market that aircraft as the A220. Commercial Aircraft Corporation of China (COMAC), established by the Chinese government to reduce dependence on Airbus/Boeing aircraft, launched the ARJ21, a 105-seater regional jet. At the time of writing, six have been delivered with a further 295 on order. A second design, the C919, seating 190 and due for launch in 2021, is expected to compete with the Airbus A320 and the Boeing 737. Finally, Irkut, a division of the Russian United Aircraft Corporation (UAC) is producing the Irkut MS-21, a twinjet with a capacity of 163 seats launched in 2017.

A handful of small companies build airframes, generally for smaller aircraft operating largely on regional routes. The two most important of these are Bombardier, and Embraer of Brazil. Several others have failed (or, in some cases, operations have been subsumed by the larger operators) in recent years, including Fairchild, Dornier, de Havilland, Fokker, Shorts and Saab, while BAe ceased manufacturing regional jets in 2001. There are other potential challengers for the lucrative global markets in the shape of the Russians, who are marketing the Antonov 85-passenger 148 jet; in addition,

Sukhoi (a division of UAC) developed the Superjet 100. Both are specifically designed for short-haul routes. China and Japan are also threatening to compete with the lead manufacturers in the longer term.

Aircraft engines are manufactured quite separately, and three companies dominate this market: GE Aircraft Engines (USA), Pratt & Whitney (USA) and Rolls-Royce (UK). Due to the intense competition for contracts to supply engines to new airliners as they come onstream, these manufacturers, and other, smaller companies, often cooperate in engine design and construction. One consortium set up for this purpose is International Aero Engines (IAE), comprising Pratt & Whitney, MTU Aero Engines of Germany and Aero Engine Corporation of Japan. General Electric and Snecma (of France) cooperate under the banner of CFM International Aero Engines, and Europrop International comprises Rolls-Royce, MTU Aero Engines and ITP Aero (Industria de Turbo Propulsores). As with airframes, we can see that this market, too, is effectively controlled by an oligopoly and the cost of aircraft development and production is now so high that international cooperation between the leading companies has become inevitable.

A single Airbus A320 costs around $100 million before discounts; an A380 around $415 million. From this, one can clearly see the importance of this industry to the countries where they are built and, particularly, the regions in which aircraft frames and engines are constructed. Indeed, civil aviation supported 10.6 million jobs and contributed 5.1% to US GDP (US DoT, 2017). The economic health of Seattle, headquarters of Boeing, is substantially dependent on the aviation industry, as are Toulouse in France and towns such as Broughton (North Wales, where Airbus A380 wings are built). Such demand is subject to global political and economic changes, however, so is extremely volatile. In 2018, Airbus warned that it may cease manufacturing in the UK if the Brexit arrangements would mean increased friction in the movement of parts for aircraft construction (West, 2018). At the time of writing, it is clear that the departure of the UK from the European Union will create new challenges for Airbus, as with many tourism businesses.

EXAMPLE

The demand for commercial aircraft

In 2017, aircraft manufacturers delivered a record number of aircraft (1740), bringing the total fleet of aircraft in operation to 31,000. With predictions suggesting continued growth of air passenger numbers globally, we see a further 15,000 aircraft on order and due for delivery over the next ten years (CAPA, 2018). Forecasts suggest that passenger demand will require a doubling of total fleet size, and consequently there is an expectation for further orders to come. Whether aircraft manufacturers have the capacity to deliver this increase in orders remains to be seen.

One further point to note is that aircraft, wherever they are manufactured in the world, are priced in US dollars, so currency shifts between the dollar and the euro are critical. Airbus costs are mainly in euros, so a hardening of this currency against the dollar (as occurred in 2007–08) is detrimental to Airbus profitability, making it harder to sell aircraft on the world market, while Boeing's task is made easier. Cheaper dollars, however, would make it attractive for Airbus to buy more parts from US sources.

The introduction of the new A380 superjumbo (discussed earlier) represented a significant gamble for the aircraft industry as to whether the future success of airlines would depend on high-frequency, low-volume routes or low-frequency, high-volume routes. Although the aircraft has a potential capacity of 853 seats, no airline has used this all-coach class configuration to date.

Boeing, on the other hand, is convinced that future demand is for fewer trunk routes and more point-to-point services, which require small- to medium-sized jets. Its own forecast is for fewer than 500 superjumbos and it claims that only some 15 routes could support such giants. Thus, Boeing has cancelled proposals to build a superjumbo aircraft, the so-called Sonic Cruiser, but has announced plans for the 777X, which will be capable of transporting 365 passengers for 8600 nautical miles without refuelling.

In the meantime, its strategy is to focus production on the 787 Dreamliner, a 240-/340-seat passenger aircraft with a range of 8000 nautical miles, as a replacement for the current generation of 757 and 767 aircraft. As of October 2018, more than 750 have been delivered, with a further 650 on order. It has proved to be 20% more fuel-efficient than its predecessors, largely due to the lightweight materials used in construction. It has also proved to be one of the fastest-selling aircraft of all time, with 817 orders placed at launch, although enthusiasm somewhat faded while waiting for delivery to come on-stream.

Boeing currently produces the 777-200LR (Worldliner) with a range of 10,847 miles. The longest commercial flight is currently the Singapore–New York route, a distance of 15,344 km and a flight time of just under 19 hours, flying an Airbus A350-900ULR (Ultra Long Range). Several routes of about 17 hours (for example, Auckland–Dubai, Los Angeles–Singapore, Perth–London and Dallas–Sydney) exist. Whether or not passengers are willing to travel even further than this without a stopover is open to question.

Boeing has introduced a new version of the 747-400, called the 747-8. This carries 467 passengers with a range of 14,800 km (similar to the Airbus A380) and the company sees this as filling a gap (in passenger capacity) between the 777 and A380. Reception of the 747-8 has been somewhat muted and airlines have been slow to place orders. By July 2018 (more than eight years after the first was delivered), only 150 had been ordered, and more than two-thirds of these are the cargo, rather than passenger, variant.

Airbus competes with the Dreamliner through the A350. This is designed in three models: the A350-800 will accommodate 270 passengers in a three-class configuration, while the longer-range A350-900 carries 314 passengers. The A350-1000 seats 360 passengers and has a range of 14,800 km. The design of this aircraft is believed to embrace materials that are fully composite in construction; that is, up to 70% of components are to be built of reinforced or hardened plastics. This will substantially cut weight and therefore reduce the amount of fuel burned. At the time of writing, it is the A350-900 aircraft which is proving the more popular, with two delivered and 500 more on order.

After the advent of deregulation in the USA and Europe, as noted earlier, there was a demand for smaller aircraft to provide feeder services from rural (so-called 'spoke') airports into hub airports, where people would then catch their long-haul or intercontinental flights. This demand was met by small aircraft, either twin turboprops or, seating 50 or more, pure jets. Since then, passengers have demonstrated a preference for direct flights between regional airports, even if at slightly higher fares, with a resultant increase in the passenger-carrying capacity of aircraft and the demise of several manufacturers of smaller aircraft.

AIRPORTS

Globally, airport income exceeds $161 billion, which amounts to $13.55 of income per passenger (ACI, 2018). Significantly, around 40% of airport income is derived from non-aeronautical activities such as retail, food and beverage, duty-free concessions and car parking. Aeronautical income is also received from a variety of activities, predominantly passenger charges and aircraft landing charges. A breakdown of aeronautical and non-aeronautical income is outlined in Figure 13.2.

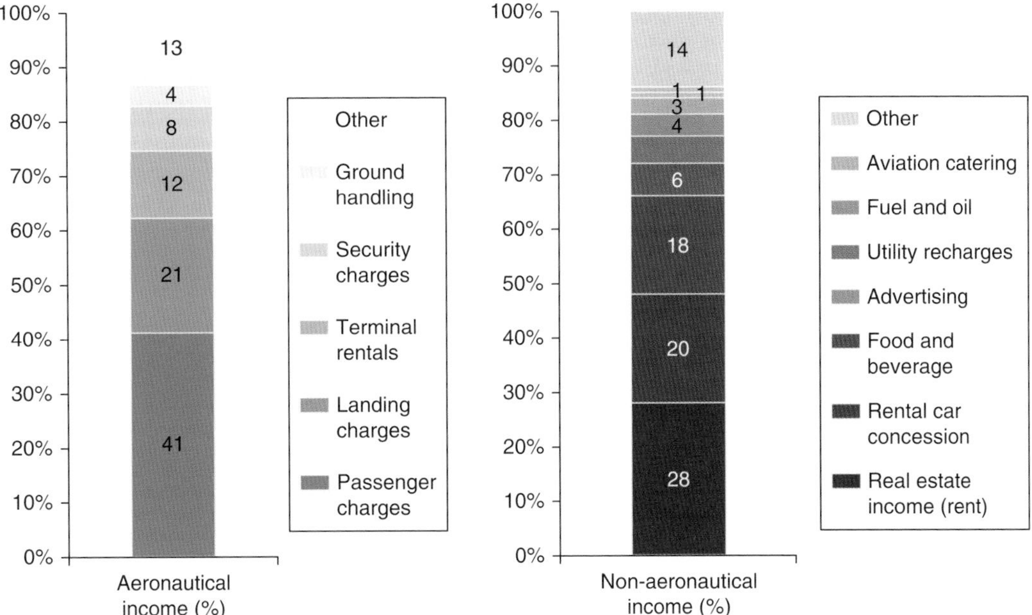

FIGURE 13.2 Airport income

Source: ACI, 2015

Airport ownership varies from country to country. Sometimes airports are state-owned (often by local authorities), but elsewhere they may be in private ownership or else ownership will be split between the public and private sectors. In many German airports, for example, local and state governments share responsibility for running the airport, while in Milan, Italy, control is exercised by a combination of regional and local government and private enterprise. In Spain, the completion of the part-privatisation of Aeropuertos Españoles y Navegacion Aerea (AENA) – the world's largest airport operator, which runs 46 airports – has separated the nation's airports from its air traffic control operations. The French government has reduced its stake in Aéroports de Paris to 50.6%, while, in Portugal, French transport company Vinci has acquired ANA Aeroportos de Portugal (ANA) to take on the management of ten airports including those in Lisbon, Porto and Faro. In Iceland, Finland, Norway, Estonia, Latvia, Luxembourg, Slovakia and the Czech Republic, all airports are in the hands of the government (ACI Europe, 2016).

In the UK, it has been the practice in recent years for local authorities to divest themselves of their local airport ownership and return it to the private sector. Newcastle, Bristol, Leeds-Bradford and Exeter Airports have all been privatised, but Manchester Airport Group (MAG) is a holding company comprising 35% private equity ownership, 35% owned by the city council and 30% owned by nine Greater Manchester local authorities. MAG operates not only Manchester Airport but also Stansted, Bournemouth and East Midlands Airports. Furthermore, a number of local authorities retain an investment in Birmingham Airport. The significance of state ownership is that overheads and direct costs are more easily concealed, enhancing the airport's performance figures – on paper, at least. Under private ownership, however, it is easier to raise money to expand or develop new ventures.

Of the privatised airports, BAA was a dominant player, owning Heathrow, Glasgow, Aberdeen, Southampton and Stansted. Following a Competition Commission ruling requiring it to sell off Gatwick, Stansted and a Scottish airport, there has been a significant adjustment in ownership of UK airports. BAA has been renamed Heathrow Airport Holdings Limited, reflecting its principal interest in this one, critically important, airport. Table 13.4 summarises current ownership of the largest UK airports. Many of these owners are international companies, some of which are investment funds. Several also have investments in other international airports – for example, Macquarie Airports owns a 31% share in Rome Airport and a 57% stake in Sydney Airport, as well as 7% and 5% respectively in Birmingham and Bristol Airports.

TABLE 13.4 UK airport ownership

Airport	Passenger numbers (2017)	Ownership (2014)	Comment
Heathrow	78,012,825	Heathrow Airport Holdings Limited (renamed from BAA following the divestment of its other UK airports)	Owned by FGP Topco Limited, a consortium owned and led by the infrastructure specialist Ferrovial S.A. (25.00%), Qatar Investment Authority (20.00%), Caisse de dépôt et placement du Québec (CDPQ) (12.62%), GIC (11.20%), Alinda Capital Partners of the United States (11.18%), China Investment Corporation (10.00%) and Universities Superannuation Scheme (USS) (10.00%)
Gatwick	45,556,899	Owned by GIP (42%) + a consortium of investors	Sold by BAA following Competition Commission ruling
Manchester	27,826,054	Manchester Airports Group	Owned 64.5% by Manchester City Council and nine regional councils; 35.5% by IFM
Stansted	25,904,450		
East Midlands International	4,878,781		
Aberdeen	3,090,642	Ferrovial (50%) and Macquarie Group (50%)	
Belfast City (George Best)	2,559,846	3i Group	Previously owned by ABN Amro (until 2016)
Belfast International	5,836,735	ADC & HAS Airports	
Birmingham	12,990,303	Owned 49% by local councils, 48.25% AGIL, 2.75% staff	
Bristol	8,239 250	Ontario Teachers' Pension Plan	Sole owner since 2014
Cardiff	1,465 227	Welsh Government	
Edinburgh	13,410 343	Owned by GIP (81%) + a consortium of investors	
Glasgow	9,897 959	Ferrovial (50%) and Macquarie Group (50%)	Sold by BAA following Competition Commission ruling
Leeds Bradford	4,076 616	AMP Capital	Purchased from Bridgepoint in 2017, having moved from public ownership in 2007

Airport	Passenger numbers (2017)	Ownership (2014)	Comment
Liverpool (John Lennon)	4,901,157	Peel Group	Bought out 65% stake held by Vantage Airport Group to take sole ownership in 2014
London City	4,530,439	Consortium led by Ontario Teachers' Pension Fund, with Borealis Infrastructure, AimCo and Kuwait's Wren House Infrastructure Management	Purchased from AIG Financial Products and GIP in 2016
Luton	15,990,276	Operated by AENA	Land and infrastructure owned by Luton Council
Newcastle	5,300,274	Owned 51% by seven local authorities and AMP Capital (49%)	
Southampton	2,069,910	AGS	AGS is a consortium of Ferrovial (50%) and Macquarie (50%)

Airports are experiencing substantial growth, with some 284 million passengers travelling through UK airports in 2017, and even conservative forecasts expect this to increase over the coming years. The UK's largest airport is London's Heathrow with 78 million passengers travelling through its doors. Atlanta Airport deals with the most passengers annually (in excess of 100 million), but Beijing and Dubai Airports have both seen expansion in recent years, now receiving 95 million and 88 million passengers respectively.

Airports require a good balance of passengers to freight to maximise their profitability, but also to boost their revenue and profits through other commercial activities, such as shops and catering services, as well as franchises for supplementary services like foreign exchange and car rental companies.

It has been shown that many travellers enjoy spending time and money on the purchase of goods at airports. One 1997 study found that airport profits rise by 20% for every ten minutes passengers are kept waiting by delayed aircraft, so it is hardly in an airport's interest to reduce congestion! In the mid-1990s, average 'dwell' time at European airports was 94 minutes, a figure that will doubtless have increased as check-in times have been extended to devote more time to screening passengers and baggage in a world beset by terrorist threats. Furthermore, airports can provide environments that trigger impulse buys, whether as a release from the stress of flying or the excitement derived from the holiday atmosphere. The incentive and opportunity to purchase has been shown to stimulate sales, thus the global duty-free industry is expected to grow to about $67 billion by 2020, up from $45.7 billion in 2016 (Atkins and Weinland, 2017).

EXAMPLE

Time to relax

Despite the opportunity to check in online, many travellers are now spending longer at the airport. Queues for the baggage drop and increased security checks have meant that airlines often suggest passengers should arrive three hours in advance of their departure time for an international flight.

(Continued)

So on those days when queues are short and the formalities are processed rapidly, what is done with those extra couple of hours? Airports now provide an extensive range of shopping opportunities to enhance their revenue stream, and with security regulations now restricting liquids in hand luggage, items such as water and toiletries are often important purchases. Once the shopping is over, passengers can also choose to spend their time in the bars and restaurants, also conveniently provided as a revenue earner for the airport. However, passengers today have an alternative place to spend their time. Access was once the preserve of the elite but now some passengers are choosing to pay to use an airport lounge. Historically, these were operated by airlines (usually one for each alliance) and only accessible to business and first-class passengers. Now it is possible to purchase access through membership schemes or on a one-off basis via travel agents and online intermediaries. Companies such as Priority Pass, Serviceair and Airspace Lounges are providing spaces that are not affiliated to a specific airline (or airline alliance group). Instead, consumers can pay per visit and enjoy the comfortable surroundings, catering and work spaces.

In recent years, several credit card providers have included lounge access as a perk of the card. Consequently, more economy-class passengers can access these lounges, creating congestion issues and disruption for premium passengers.

Earnings from the airlines using the airport are based on a complex set of landing charges, which are designed to cover parking charges, air traffic control, landing fees and a per capita fee for passengers carried, so a jumbo aircraft will be charged a considerably higher landing fee than a small aircraft.

Congestion and airport expansion

Congestion at major international airports is becoming so acute that new technology is being pressed into service to improve ground handling. This is becoming even more urgent as the new generation of superjumbos is phased in. Increased automation is helping to speed up the throughput of passengers; e-tickets (electronic tickets) issued against a confirmed reservation, first used widely by the no-frills airlines, have been introduced by all the major airlines to reduce ticketing costs.

The process is further speeded up for passengers who travel with airlines that allow them to undertake the check-in process themselves, using computers at the airport, or increasingly, online in advance of arrival at the airport. The budget airlines employ a system where passengers without baggage can print their boarding passes at home and thus proceed straight to security. Passengers with baggage must still check in online but on arrival at the airport will proceed to a dedicated bag-drop area. Passengers arriving at the airport having lost or failed to print a boarding pass will be charged a fee; for example, Ryanair currently charges a boarding card issue fee of £20.

Regardless of new technology, there are finite limits to the number of passengers that an airport can handle in a given time, with some, such as Heathrow, already close to their capacity. The addition of a further runway and new terminals may postpone the inevitable point where capacity is reached, but air corridors are already overcrowded in many parts of the world and, increasingly, aircraft are forced to 'stack' at busy periods, wasting fuel. This creates a knock-on effect, delaying later take-offs, and the combination of poor weather, lightning air traffic control strikes and the need for increased security have all led to serious problems of congestion at busy airports all over the world.

The pressures on London airports have encouraged the UK government to seek to disperse traffic to regional airports. The importance of major hubs for interline passengers making connections, however, means that delays in expanding Heathrow's capacity have inhibited economic growth. Protests against a fifth terminal at Heathrow, delayed for many years by consultation and lobbying until finally approved in 2001 and opened in 2008, allowed a capacity increase of 50%. A third runway was given the go-ahead by MPs in 2018 (with final planning permission expected by 2021, most likely to include an additional terminal).

There is strong opposition from the environmental lobby to any airport expansion. However, the UK government fears that refusal to develop will simply divert aircraft to Schiphol Airport, Amsterdam (which has six runways). That airport has already benefited from London's congestion by employing the hub-and-spoke system, picking up British regional passengers bound for intercontinental connections. Paris' Charles de Gaulle Airport is another major competitor seeking to become a leading European hub, with a capacity for 80 million passengers.

The UK's regional airports have shown their enthusiasm for expansion, but have not always had the support promised by the UK government. Some airports also face difficulties due to local authorities' unwillingness to expand facilities in the face of opposition from local residents. By contrast, continental airports have actively sought expansion, with the blessing of their central and local governments, and sometimes with financial incentives for the new carriers developing routes. Such subsidies were considered illegal by the EU, which has since modified its stance, deciding to permit subsidies depending on the economic circumstances of the region. Ryanair and easyJet are two of many no-frills airlines that have taken advantage of the relatively low costs associated with regional airports to expand their services.

At popular and congested airports, gaining **take-off and landing slots** for new services is extremely difficult, and in consequence these have been traded in recent years at £10–£30 million per pair. Slots are awarded to airlines through processes of negotiation, which usually take place in November each year, to cover flights in the following year. Scheduled services receive priority over charter, and the so-called 'grandfather' rights of existing carriers (a concept challenged by the EU) tend to take precedence over new carriers – so much so that, at airports such as Heathrow, a new airline seeking to gain slots may find it necessary to take over an existing airline in order to do so. This can give even financially troubled airlines high paper value if they control a large number of slots at significant airports. The 'open skies' agreement, which came into force in 2008, liberalising flights across the North Atlantic, has heightened demand for new services out of Heathrow.

EXAMPLE

The airport slot

A slot is an allocation to take off or land at a predetermined time and airport. Getting access to new slots can be expensive and requires lengthy negotiations. Willie Walsh, when he was head of BA, is reported to have commented that buying Virgin Atlantic would be attractive, just so that BA could obtain their slots (*New Europe*, 2011).

The importance of slots has grown as airports reach capacity. Airlines are able to keep the same slots, providing they make use of them. Any new slots or unused slots are then distributed to new and existing airlines. Rarely do prime-time, prime-location slots come

(Continued)

onto the market for redistribution. More commonly, airlines swap slots to improve operating efficiencies or in response to changes in routes served. Monetary payments may accompany these swaps. As an example, in 2014 American Airlines paid £18 million to Cyprus Airways for a pair of midday slots at Heathrow Airport.

The EU has instigated regulations on slot allocation, concerned over the lack of transparency in these agreements and the restrictions it may place on free trade if new airlines are unable to enter the market. The EU determined that the current system led to inefficient use of capacity, as some slots were under-utilised (EC, 2011). This led to the implementation of regulations, under a 'use it or lose it' threat, that allocated airline slots must be operational at least 80% of the time.

AIR NAVIGATION AND TRAFFIC CONTROL SERVICES

The technical services that are provided on the ground to assist and control aircraft while in the air and on landing and taking off are not normally seen as part of the tourism industry, but their role is a key one in the operation of aviation services. **Air traffic control** (ATC) has the function of guiding aircraft into and out of airports, giving pilots (usually in the form of continually updated automatic recordings) detailed information on ground conditions, wind speed, cloud conditions, runways in use and the state of navigation aids. ATC will instruct pilots on what height and direction to take and be responsible for all flights within a geographically defined area.

At its busiest, around 15,000 flights will be in the air around the world, with this number varying by time of day and season of the year. The USA's Air Traffic Organization (ATO) handles more than 43,000 flights daily, with UK air traffic control (NATS) typically handling some 6200 flights every day. NATS (formerly the National Air Traffic Service) controls take-offs and landings at 14 UK airports, as well as corridors in the skies over the UK and part of the North Atlantic. Formerly a public service, this became a public–private partnership in 2001, with the government currently controlling 49%, a further 42% owned by seven UK airlines, 4% by Heathrow Airport Limited and 5% in the hands of the organisation's staff.

EXAMPLE

NATS' failure closes airspace

NATS controls airspace across much of southern England. However, a technical failure on 7 December 2013 reduced operational capacity for several hours. Following an overnight update to the system software, NATS were unable to operate at full capacity the following day.

NATS responded by re-routing some air traffic to ensure safety. Repairs to the system took much of the day and the outcome was that, while 90% of flights did operate, many were significantly delayed and around 300 were cancelled. Many passengers were left frustrated owing to a lack of information and failure by the airlines to effectively reallocate seats for those passengers whose flights were cancelled.

NATS, in collaboration with airports, reviewed the event and reported on the need to balance the risk of failure with the cost of introducing and maintaining backup systems that are rarely likely to be needed.

It is interesting to note, therefore, that just one year later (12 December 2014) a systems outage again caused the shutdown of UK airspace, directly affecting 65,000 passengers. Flights were again cancelled or delayed, and it took much of the day to get the system restored and operating to its normal capacity.

Improvement in altimeters on board newer aircraft has allowed airlines to halve the vertical distance between aircraft at cruising speed from 2000- to 1000-foot intervals. Initially introduced on transatlantic routes, this ruling was controversially extended to the European mainland in 2002, virtually doubling the flight capacity. The present horizontal distance apart that aircraft must maintain, nose to tail, is 3 miles (at this same cruising height), with aircraft held at least 60 miles apart laterally. If these lateral gaps could also be halved, it would permit an eight-fold increase in the number of flights operating, although the problems of congestion at the airports themselves would still need to be solved. Landing intervals stand at 45 seconds at London's two major airports, Heathrow and Gatwick.

EXAMPLE

Disruption of services

The impact of an ATC strike can be extensive. Over the first six months of 2018, around 22 days of strikes were held by French ATC workers. This meant that any planes due to fly from or land in France would not be able to take to the skies, while any flights scheduled to travel through French airspace en route to their destination would either have to be cancelled or diverted. Consequently, any plane taking off from Amsterdam heading for Barcelona would probably have to divert via Germany and Italy to reach the Mediterranean, a far longer route.

Four airlines (Ryanair, Wizz Air, easyJet and IAG (owner of British Airways and Iberia)) filed a complaint to the European Union, arguing that not allowing flights over the country is unnecessarily restrictive. Eurocontrol (responsible for European air traffic control) revealed that 16,000 flights were affected by these strikes. However, ATC strikes in France are not unusual; of the 423 ATC strike days in Europe since 2004, France has been responsible for 70% of them.

AIRLINES

The services provided by airlines can be divided into three distinct categories:

- scheduled
- charter (in US parlance, supplementals)
- air taxi.

Scheduled services

Scheduled services are provided by some 800 scheduled passenger airlines worldwide, of which around 290 are members of the International Air Transport Association (IATA), these representing most of the world's major carriers (transporting more than 80% of the world's air traffic). They operate on defined routes, domestic or international, for which licences have been granted by the government or governments concerned. The airlines are required to operate on the basis of their published timetables, regardless of passenger load factors (although flights and routes that are not commercially viable throughout the year may be operated during periods of high demand only).

These services may be publicly or privately owned, although there is now a global movement among the developed nations towards private ownership of airlines. Where fully state-owned airlines continue to operate, as in the case of Aeroflot and Qatar Airways, as well as in many developing countries, the leading public airline is often recognised as the national 'flag-carrier'. In the UK, all airlines are now in the private sector, although BA, privatised since 1987, is still seen by many as the national flag-carrier. Privatisation is not always seen as the best solution and, in one case, that of Air New Zealand, the government reversed earlier privatisation by bringing back 80% of the carrier into public ownership after the 9/11 disaster.

Airlines operating on major routes between hub airports within a country are known as **trunk route** airlines, while those operating from smaller, generally rural, airports into these hubs are referred to as **regional** or **feeder** airlines. In the case of the USA and certain other regions, these may also be termed **commuter** airlines, as their prime purpose is to serve the needs of commuting businesspeople regularly using those routes. The growing development of **hub-and-spoke** routes will be discussed later in the chapter.

As was made clear earlier in this chapter, the growth of no-frills, or budget, carriers, more commonly referred to as **low-cost carriers** (LCCs), has been the major development in scheduled service operations in the past decade. These airlines have been successful due to a combination of efficient operations and low overheads and have, as a result, sharply cut into markets formerly held by the traditional full-cost carriers, even where business traffic is concerned.

LCCs will typically employ aircraft like Boeing 737s on high-density, short-haul routes with one class of seats. Virtually all bookings are taken direct, over the Internet. Tickets are generally inflexible and non-refundable. Passengers turning up late or failing to show lose the entire value of their tickets, often even including taxes – a highly profitable ploy by the airlines (although legally taxes should be refundable, many airlines simply impose an administration charge that exceeds the total tax bill, rendering a request for the tax refund pointless). Bookings are usually made well in advance to take advantage of lower prices, providing helpful cash flow to the companies. If routes prove unprofitable, the carriers pull out quickly, as illustrated by Ryanair in the aftermath of fuel price increases and declining demand as the recession hit in 2008.

EXAMPLE

Speed is everything

By operating out of secondary, less congested airports, low-cost carriers can reduce times on the ground and operate more flights per day. One study found that easyJet, for example, could employ its aircraft for 11 hours a day, while BA on comparable flights achieved only eight hours (Tarry, 2002). One factor influencing the amount of time spent on the ground is the time it takes to board passengers.

Research has shown that the order in which passengers are allowed to board a plane determines load time, with methods currently in use unlikely to be the quickest. The slowest method was found to be boarding passengers in zones from back to front. The fastest method was to offer no assigned seats, although the satisfaction level was exceedingly low for this approach. One method, almost as quick and with high satisfaction levels, was to board all passengers in window seats first, followed by those in middle seats and then passengers sitting in aisle seats. This last approach is estimated to cut boarding times by up to 35%, which can translate to profitability; research suggests that for every minute a carrier saves on the ground, operating profit margins can increase by 0.43%.

Source: Fenwick Elliott, 2018

Staff costs are also substantially lower than those of the traditional full-service carriers. For instance, staff costs as a share of revenue earned were almost 21% for BA, compared with less than 10% for Ryanair. Similarly, the costs of marketing, commission and sales and reservations for the two carriers were very different. Such factors influence profitability (see Table 13.5).

TABLE 13.5 Profitability of UK scheduled airlines (2017/18)

	Turnover (£000)	Profit (loss) before taxation (£000)	Number of employees	Salaries as a % of turnover
British Airways	12,226,000	1,744,000	43,125	20.93
Virgin Atlantic	2,663,700	(59,000)	8303	14.56
Flybe	752,600	(9400)	2159	15.94
easyJet	5,898,000	445,000	13,104	14.16
Ryanair	6,265,872	1,411,858	13,803	10.33

Source: Bureau Van Dyke 2018 company annual accounts

The introduction of no-frills flights has resulted in a highly pared-down service where not only are meals and drinks charged for, but airlines also do little to aid passengers in cases of missed flights. Extra charges are made for the carriage of items such as skis, golf clubs and surfboards, and Ryanair was the first carrier to impose a charge even for normal baggage carried in the hold (a policy since taken up by the other budget carriers), and now some of the full-service carriers have started to charge to transport sporting equipment. Additional costs are imposed for priority boarding and the 'privilege' of couples and families being seated together.

EXAMPLE

British Airways introduces hand baggage-only fares

Historically, British Airways flights would include, even on the cheapest of fare classes, an allowance for at least one item of hold luggage. However, in an effort to compete on price in the competitive UK market, BA has introduced into its fare structure a ticket that is designed for those passengers wishing to travel with hand luggage only. This move has allowed BA

(Continued)

to promote lower headline fares on its routes, important in its attempts to compete with the low-cost carriers.

Those who decide after ticket purchase that they do want to take luggage will need to pay an additional fee to check this in. With charges set at £20–£40 per bag, BA hold-luggage rates are comparable with those of the low-cost carriers.

The arrivals and departures of new low-cost carriers are now becoming so frequent that any attempt to list current operators would inevitably date this text before it came to print. By way of example, some 20 global airlines collapsed as a result of the sharp rise in fuel prices in mid-2008. Suffice to say that, throughout the EU, in North America, the Far East and Australasia, new low-cost airlines such as JetBlue in the USA, Virgin Australia, Volaris in Mexico, Norwegian Air (challenging the transatlantic market), as well as Hungary and Poland's jointly owned Wizz Air (Eastern Europe's largest low-cost carrier) have appeared on the scene to take on the longer-established carriers.

Budget carrier easyJet has set a new direction by developing its own holiday website in competition with tour operators and retail agents: www.easyjet.com/en/holidays. It allows its customers to build their own inclusive tours by pairing budget flights with a bedstock of rooms in several thousand European hotels.

Another direction has been taken by new so-called boutique airlines, which focus on niche markets on routes where they can cherry-pick higher-fare-paying passengers. A number of these operate in the USA and one or two, such as LyddAir (operating between Lydd and le Touquet in France), have followed suit in the UK. They appeal chiefly to business travellers, for whom superior service and speedier airport check-ins are important.

Mention should be made of there being a move back to seaplane operations, after a gap of many decades. Although amphibious aircraft have been in use continuously for private charter work (particularly in wilderness areas such as those that exist in Canada, carrying leisure passengers on hunting and fishing holidays to isolated lakes), scheduled seaplane routes were abandoned soon after World War II. Now, both charter and scheduled services are being introduced; for example, Glasgow has constructed a seaplane terminal adjacent to the Science Centre, to provide access to the Scottish lochs and islands, with Loch Lomond Seaplanes providing existing scheduled and charter services.

Charter services

Charter services, by contrast with scheduled services, do not operate according to published timetables, nor are they advertised or promoted by the airlines themselves. Instead, the aircraft are chartered to intermediaries (often tour operators) for a fixed charge and those intermediaries then become responsible for selling the aircraft's seats, leaving the airlines only with the responsibility for operating the aircraft. The intermediaries can change flight departure times or even cancel flights, transferring passengers to other flights.

Major tour operators now invariably have their own charter airlines (a relationship that is examined fully in Chapter 18) and have opened their flights in many instances to bookings on a seat-only basis to increase load factors. This is making the former distinction between scheduled and charter air services less clear-cut.

Air taxi services

Air taxis are privately chartered aircraft accommodating between four and 18 people, used particularly by business travellers. They offer the advantages of convenience and flexibility as routings can be tailor-made for passengers (for example, a feasible itinerary for a business day using an air taxi might be London, Paris, Brussels, Amsterdam and London – a near-impossible programme for a scheduled service), and small airfields, close to a company's office or factory, can be used. There are some 350 airfields suitable for air taxis in the UK alone and a further 1300 in Western Europe (see Figure 13.3), compared with only about 200 airports receiving scheduled services. In the USA, where there are over 5400 small local airports catering principally for private and business planes, 98% of the population are said to live within 30 minutes' driving distance of an airport.

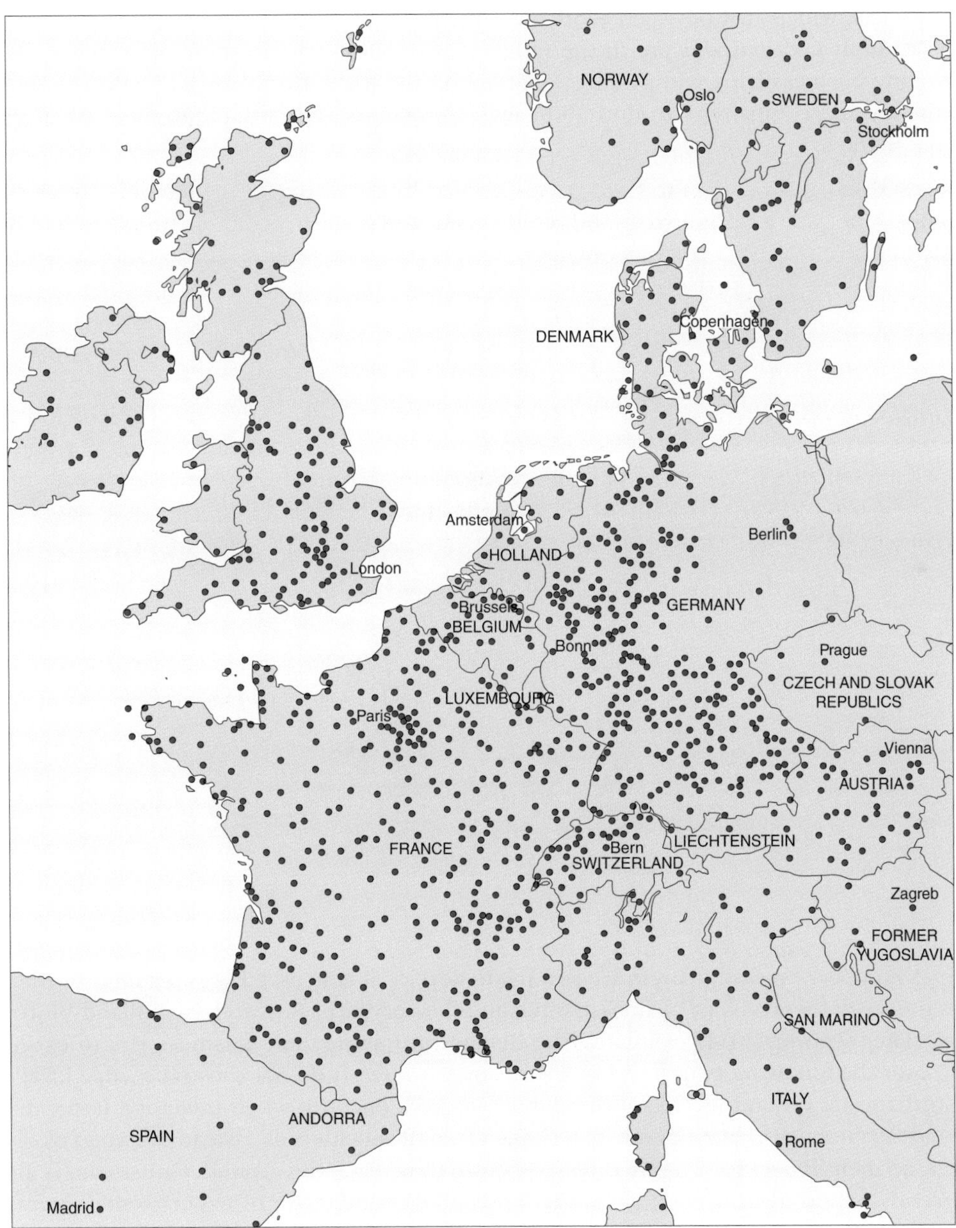

FIGURE 13.3 Airports and airfields in Europe

The attractiveness of air taxi services using these airports is that flights can be arranged or routings amended at short notice and, with a full flight, the cost for chartering can be commensurate with the combined business-class fares of the number of staff travelling.

Aircraft in use range from helicopters such as the Bell Jet Ranger and the piston-engined Piper Twin Comanche (each seating three or four people, with a range of between 350 and 900 miles) up to aircraft such as Embraer's Bandeirante, which is capable of carrying 18 passengers up to 300 miles, and to top-of-the-range Gulfstream V aircraft, costing over $40 million. Larger aircraft can also be chartered as needed. The world's fastest private jet is said to be the Cestna Citation X+, which will cruise at Mach 0.935, just short of the sound barrier. It can hold eight passengers and, with the cost of flying this plane at $4100 per hour (plus crew and airport costs), the hour-long flight from London to Paris would have a minimum operating cost of $513 per person for each leg. This is higher than most private jets, which cost between $250 and $400 per hour to fly.

Most air taxi journeys are in the range of 500–600 miles, so these aircraft are ideal for many business trips within Europe. Many business jets find their way into the fleets of the air taxi companies; around 2000 such companies are available to meet the needs of the market.

EXAMPLE

Bringing air taxis to a wider audience

The demand for air taxi services goes beyond the business traveller. In 2010, Sri Lanka Airlines launched an air taxi service to provide tourists with quick and comfortable access to difficult-to-reach locations. However, the Sri Lankan Air Taxi uses seaplanes, requiring calm, open water as a runway. This inevitably limits the services which can be offered (they provide both charter and scheduled services). Initial promotional fares were set at £30 per person, though this has climbed substantially since; but the opportunity to swap a three-hour car journey for a one-hour plane journey is appealing to many.

Numerous air taxi services exist, and online booking is possible, although more commonly the specific nature of the flight plan means that quotes will be provided by telephone or email. For those with greater flexibility – or who are more price-sensitive – reserving an empty leg flight (using a plane which is either returning from dropping passengers at a destination or flying out to collect them) is substantially cheaper, perhaps by as much as 75%. This does, of course, negate one of the benefits of chartering an air taxi – that the passenger gets to choose the date and time of departure.

A number of manufacturers are looking to develop a new breed of supersonic business jets to satisfy the needs of businesspeople and the very rich. Research by Rolland Vincent Associates (Lehrer, 2014) estimated the demand for supersonic business jets to exceed 600 over the following two decades. These smaller aircraft do not cause the same level of disturbance at ground level as did the much larger Concorde when travelling faster than sound, as their aerodynamics create a ripple of small shockwaves instead of two explosive ones, so their impact has largely diffused before they reach the ground. Gulfstream is also currently experimenting with a 24-foot long spike on the nose of experimental aircraft, which would further reduce noise, producing a sonic boom only one hundredth as noisy as that of Concorde.

Of equal interest is the personal jet or very light jet (VLJ). These minijets, typically seating between four and eight passengers, while not capable of supersonic speeds, are expected to sell at prices up to 30 times cheaper than current business jets, at around £1–£2 million, and will carry far lower operating costs. Examples are the Cessna Mustang and the Embraer Phenom 100, both costing about $230 per flight hour.

Such low-cost aircraft could be marketed to business and leisure tourists as charter transport at a price competitive with commercial scheduled services. One can readily see the marketing opportunities for specialist holiday packages such as the honeymoon market.

One other development is enabling the savvy business customer to cut costs: where it might be difficult to justify the purchase or full-time lease of an aircraft for business purposes, part-ownership may well be considered.

EXAMPLE

Fractional ownership

Fractional ownership is a form of aircraft timeshare that gives a corporation access to a certain number of flight hours each year, dependent on the overall share of the aircraft purchased. This is proving a popular alternative to air taxis for many companies. One company, Netjets Europe, operates a fleet of 130 aircraft, and owners can buy amounts of flight time to suit their needs, the minimum being 1/16 of an aircraft, equating to 50 hours each year. The aircraft range from the six-passenger Embraer Phenom 300 to the 13-passenger Bombadier Global 6000.

AIR TRANSPORT REGULATION

THE NEED FOR REGULATION

With the development and growth of the airline industry, regulation on both national and international scales soon became necessary. First and foremost, airlines had to be licensed to ensure passengers' safety. There are, for example, strict rules on the number of hours that air and cabin crew can work each day. Second, regulations are needed to control noise and pollution. Beyond these two requirements, the question of which airlines are permitted to operate to which airports and in what numbers becomes an issue of public concern, given the finite capacity of airports and air corridors.

As air transport can have a profound impact on the economy of a region or country, governments will take steps to encourage the development of routes that appear to offer prospects of economic benefits and discourage those suffering from overcapacity. While the policy of one government may be to encourage competition or intervene where a route monopoly is forcing prices up, another government's policy may be directed at rationalising excessive competition in order to avoid energy waste or even, in some cases, at protecting the profitability of the national flag-carrier.

Some governments are tempted to provide subsidies in order to support inefficient publicly owned flag-carriers. Private airlines in Europe have long complained of this unfair protection against competition, which is contrary to EU regulations, but still survives in isolated cases within Europe. Another characteristic of such protection is the **pooling** arrangements made between airlines operating on certain international routes, whereby all revenue accruing on that route is apportioned equally between the carriers serving it. This may appear to circumvent competition on a route, but is also one means of safeguarding the viability of the national carrier operating in a strong competitive environment. In developing countries, where governments are anxious to earn hard currency, the support of the national carrier as an earner of that currency through arrangements such as this may be justifiable.

Pooling arrangements are often entered into in cases where the airlines are not of comparable size in order to safeguard the smaller carrier's capacity and revenue. By rationalising schedules, pressure is reduced on peak-time take-off slots and costs reduced. Financial arrangements between the pooled carriers usually limit the amount of revenue transferred from one carrier to the other to a fixed maximum, to reduce what may be seen as unfair government support for an inefficient carrier. Increasingly, such pooling arrangements are no longer acceptable and may indeed be illegal, as is the case in the USA.

In some areas, air transport is an essential public utility that, even where commercially non-viable, is socially desirable in order to provide communications with a region where geographical terrain may make other forms of transport difficult or impossible (New Guinea, Alaska or the Hebrides in Scotland are cases in point). This can result in a government subsidising one or more of its airlines in order to ensure that a service is maintained. Airlines themselves often argue that they provide vital channels of communication for business, trade and investment essential for the wellbeing of communities and that, therefore, even profitable routes should be exempted from tax (aviation fuel, for example, is currently exempted).

EXAMPLE

A case for subsidy

Since 2017, flights operated by BMI Regional between London Stansted and Londonderry/City of Derry Airport in Northern Ireland have received public-sector financial support under Public Service Obligation (PSO) rulings, due to the importance of developing the region and promoting traffic across the border with Ireland. Passengers on these flights are also exempted from the payment of air passenger duty (APD). In spite of these subsidies, however, passenger numbers on this route have shrunk. In 2017, only 54,696 passengers flew this route, a fall of 53% on the previous year.

SYSTEMS OF REGULATION

Broadly speaking, air transport operations are regulated in three ways.

- Internationally, scheduled **routes** are assigned on the basis of agreements between governments of the countries concerned.
- Internationally, scheduled **air fares** are now subject to less and less control and, in both North America and Europe, airlines are free to set their own fares. Governments can still intervene, however, where predatory pricing is involved. In developing areas, the extent of regulation is often far greater, with airlines agreeing fares that may then be mediated through the traffic agreements (known as conferences) of IATA. Agreed tariffs are then subject to ratification by the governments of the countries concerned. Generally, less direct control is exercised over domestic fares.
- National governments approve and license the **carriers** that are to operate on scheduled routes, whether domestically or internationally. In the UK, the Civil Aviation Authority (CAA) has this responsibility and is also responsible for the licensing of charter airlines and of tour operators organising package holidays abroad.

European countries that are members of the EU are now largely subject to its regulations and negotiations regarding the carriage of passengers by air. The EU, for example, has introduced legislation to protect passengers in the event of delays or denied boarding (in the case of an overbooking, for instance), with compensation payable to those affected, but to date the airlines have shown considerable skill in using force majeure rules to avoid payouts.

EXAMPLE

Compensation for flight delays

The rules governing compensation by airlines operating in the EU are complicated. Entitlement to compensation occurs following delays of more than three hours, depending on the flight distance. For flights less than 1500 km, compensation is €250, while delayed flights for routes over this distance will be liable for compensation of €400. For longer flights (beyond 3500 km), compensation for delays in excess of four hours amounts to €600.

If an airline has overbooked a flight and a passenger is 'bumped' onto another departure, the airline must refund that part of the ticket price, as well as making alternative flight arrangements. Compensation is also due, with €125 paid out for arrivals delayed up to two hours on short flights (up to 1500 km) and progressively more as the delay and distance increase. However, compensation is payable only if the delay is the result of an airline fault. Extraordinary circumstances (force majeure), such as bad weather, air traffic management problems or security issues, are considered beyond the control of the airline and thus outside of regulations for compensation.

One final point to be stressed: travellers using airports outside the EU and travelling on airlines that are based outside the EU do not fall under this compensation scheme.

The worldwide trend is to allow market forces to determine the shape and direction of the airline business, so regulation today is less concerned with routes, frequency, capacity and fares and more concerned with aspects of safety. As we mention in Chapter 17, the EU has banned some airlines from its airspace on safety grounds.

EXAMPLE

The world's safest airlines

Several researchers publish rankings for airline safety, including the the Jet Airliner Crash Data Evaluation Centre (JACDEC) in Germany and Airline Ratings in Australia. The latter uses a 7-star system assessing safety certification, blacklisting, grounding and fatalities, while the former considers safety certification and the number and frequency of accidents and fatalities per revenue passenger kilometre (RPK). Table 13.6 identifies the ratings for a selection of airlines.

(Continued)

TABLE 13.6 Airline safety ranking (2018)

JACDEC ranking	Airline ratings
1. Emirates	7 star = 195 airlines including Air New Zealand, Emirates, British Airways, JetBlue Airways, Virgin Atlantic
2. Norwegian Airlines	6 star = 38 airlines including Air France, Malaysia Airlines, Air India Jet Airways
3. Virgin Atlantic	5 star = 19 airlines including Thai Airways, Air Astana, Air India Express
4. KLM	4 star = 71 airlines including TUIfly Netherlands, Norwegian Airlines, Scoot, Ryanair
5. easyJet	3 star = 15 airlines including Southwest Airlines, SpiceJet, Air Panama
6. Finnair	2 star = 7 airlines including Iraqi Airways, AirAsia Thailand, Blue Wing
7. Etihad Airways	1 star = 2 airlines – Yeti Airlines, Nepal Airlines
8. Spirit Airlines	
9. Jetstar Airways	
10. Air Arabia	

Source: JACDEC, www.jacdec.de/airline-safety-ranking-2018; and Airline Ratings, www.airlineratings.com/safety-rating-tool

Air transport regulations are the result of a number of international agreements between countries dating back over many years. The Warsaw Convention of 1929 first established common agreement on the extent of liability of the airlines in the event of death or injury of passengers or loss of passengers' baggage, with a limit of $10,000 on loss of life and similarly derisory sums for loss of baggage (compensation is payable on weight rather than value). Inflation soon further reduced the value of claims, and liability was reassessed by a number of participating airlines, first at the Hague Protocol in 1955, where the figure was increased to $20,000, and again at the Montreal Agreement in 1966, at which time the USA imposed a $75,000 ceiling on compensation for flights to and from the USA. It was also agreed that the maximum liability would be periodically reviewed.

In 1992, Japan waived all limits for Japanese carriers and, in the following year, the UK government unilaterally required UK carriers to increase their liability to a limit of 100,000 SDRs (Special Drawing Rights – a reserve currency operated by the International Monetary Fund and equivalent at the time to about $160,000).

Finally, in 1995, IATA negotiated an **Intercarrier Agreement on Passenger Liability**, which was designed to enforce blanket coverage for all member airlines, whereby any damages would be determined according to the laws of the country of the airline affected. Not all airlines agreed to implement this, however.

THE FIVE FREEDOMS OF THE AIR

Further legislation concerning passenger aviation resulted from the Chicago Convention on Civil Aviation held in 1944, at which 80 governments were represented in discussions designed to promote world air services and reach agreement on standard operating procedures for air services between countries. There were two outcomes of this meeting: the founding of the International Civil Aviation Organization (ICAO), now a specialised agency of the United Nations, and the establishment of the so-called **five freedoms of the air**.

These privileges are to:

1. fly across a country without landing
2. land in a country for purposes other than the carriage of passengers or freight – to refuel, for example
3. offload passengers, mail or freight from an airline of the country from which those passengers, mail or freight originated
4. load passengers, mail or freight on an airline of the country to which those passengers, mail or freight are destined
5. load passengers, mail or freight on an airline not belonging to the country to which those passengers, mail or freight are destined and offload passengers, mail or freight from an airline not of the country from which they originated.

These privileges were designed to provide the framework for bilateral agreements between countries and to ensure that carriage of passengers, mail and freight between any two countries would normally be restricted to the carriers of those countries.

The move to greater freedom of the skies

Other freedoms not discussed by the Convention, but equally pertinent to the question of rights of operation, have been termed the **sixth and seventh freedoms**. These would cover:

1. carrying passengers, mail or freight between any two countries on an airline that is of neither country, but is operating via the airline's own country
2. carrying passengers, mail or freight directly between two countries on an airline associated with neither of the two countries.

These various freedoms can best be illustrated using examples (see Figure 13.4).

While a handful of countries expressed a preference for an 'open skies' policy on regulation, most demanded controls. An International Air Services Agreement, to which more than 90 countries became signatories, provided for the mutual exchange of the first two freedoms of the air, while it was left to individual bilateral negotiations between countries to resolve other issues. The Convention agreed not to regulate charter services, allowing countries to impose whatever individual regulations they wished. Few countries, in fact, were willing to allow a total 'open skies' policy for charters.

The Anglo-American agreement that was reached in Bermuda in 1946, following the Convention, set the pattern for many of the bilateral agreements that followed. This so-called Bermuda Agreement, while restricting air carriage between the two countries to national carriers, did not impose restrictions on capacity for the airlines concerned. This was modified at a second Bermuda Agreement reached in 1977 (and ratified in 1980), however, in line with the tendency of many countries in the intervening years to opt for an agreement that would ensure a percentage of total traffic on a route would be guaranteed for the national carriers of the countries concerned.

A further agreement in 1986 extended the agreed capacities across the Atlantic, the tight control of capacity was relaxed and new routes were agreed, although the concept of **reciprocity** remained in force. The UK government was only willing to concede new routes to American carriers if reciprocal routes would be granted to UK carriers. US legislation also limited foreign ownership of US airlines to a minority shareholding, thus effectively restricting operational control to US ownership.

5th freedom
An Indian aircraft flying from Delhi to New York stops over in London to pick up passengers bound for New York.

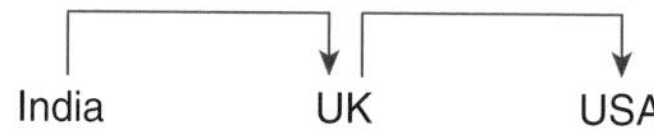

6th freedom
Singapore Airlines flies between London and Sydney, stopping over in Singapore.
It uses rights London–Singapore and Singapore–Sydney to carry passengers through from London to Sydney.

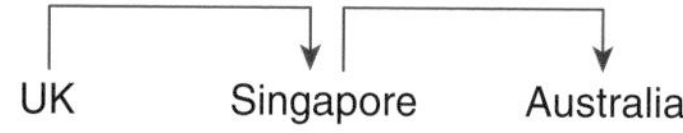

7th freedom
A British aircraft carries passengers between Vienna and Budapest on a shuttle service.

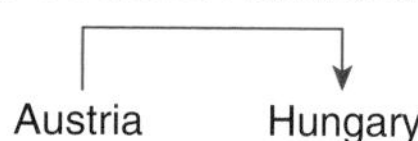

NB: Reference is also made to the possibility of an **8th freedom**, which would allow a foreign aircraft to operate on a cabotage route. An example would be:
A British aircraft is permitted to operate a shuttle service between New York and Chicago.

FIGURE 13.4 Some examples of freedoms of the air

Carriage on routes within the national territory of a country (the so-called cabotage routes) is normally restricted to the national carriers of the country concerned. In some cases, however, this provides opportunities for a country's national carriers to operate exclusively on international routes in cases where these countries have overseas possessions. This was the case, for example, on routes out of the UK to destinations such as Gibraltar or on services between France and Réunion Island or the islands of Guadaloupe and Martinique in the Caribbean.

Under the EU's programme of liberalisation of the air within member countries, the cabotage regulation – the final barrier to total freedom of operation – was dropped in 1997. Any airline of any member country can now file to operate services between cities within another member's borders. While this liberalisation should, in theory, have opened up competition and encouraged a wealth of new services throughout the EU, in practice, the difficulty of getting slots at congested airports meant that it took time for the low-cost carriers to build up competition in some areas and very few are operating out of hub airports.

THE ROLE OF IATA

For many years, control over air fares on international routes was exercised by IATA, a trade body with more than 290 airline members representing most of the leading airlines. The aims of this organisation, which was restructured in its present form in 1945 but traces its origins to the very beginning of air transport in 1919, have been to promote safe, regular and economic air transport, to provide the means for collaboration between the air carriers themselves, and to cooperate with governments, the ICAO and other international bodies for the promotion of safety and effective air transport.

In the past, IATA also had a role in setting tariffs, in effect operating a legalised cartel. Fares were established at the annual tariff-fixing traffic conferences by a process of common agreement between the participating airlines, subject to ratification by the airlines' governments. In practice, most governments merely rubber-stamped the agreements. Critics argued that, as a result, fares became unnecessarily high on many routes and competition was stifled. Often, the agreed fares were the outcome of political considerations in which the less efficient national flag-carriers pushed for prices unrelated to competitive costs.

IATA also controlled many other aspects of airline operation, such as the pitch of passengers' seats, which dictated the amount of legroom they could enjoy, and even the kinds of meals that could be served on board. As a result, the airlines were forced to concentrate their marketing efforts on such aspects of the product as service, punctuality or even the design of cabin crew uniforms, rather than providing a genuine measure of competition.

It was widely felt that this had led to inertia among the participating carriers, with agreements resulting from a desire to avoid controversy. Neither had the cartel ensured profitability for its members as they faced open competition from non-IATA carriers, which successfully competed on both price and added value.

Led by the USA, and soon followed by other countries, airlines chose to withdraw from this tariff-setting mechanism and, as a result, IATA was restructured in 1979 to provide a two-tier organisation: a tariff section to deal with fares, for those nations wishing to maintain this role, and a trade section to provide other benefits that an international airline association offered. IATA's role in tariff agreements has become steadily less important and airlines now largely determine their own service and catering arrangements. An interlining agreement also allowed passengers to switch flights to other member airlines freely. This was an advantage when they were paying full fares for their tickets, but in an age of low-price tickets for all air services, it no longer has the same appeal.

The principal benefit offered by IATA today is its central clearing house system, which makes possible financial settlements between members. Tickets and other documents are standardised and interchangeable between IATA members, while compatibility is established between members in air fare structures and currency exchange rates. Other procedures, too, such as the appointment, through licensing agreements, of IATA-recognised travel agents, are also standardised throughout the world. The computerised Bank Settlement Plan, introduced in the UK in 1984 and now operated globally, permits the monthly settlement of accounts for more than 370 airlines, enabling financial transactions to keep pace with the enormous growth in airline travel.

UK REGULATION OF AIR TRANSPORT

In the UK, the Civil Aviation Act of 1971 led to the establishment of the Civil Aviation Authority (CAA), which has five regulatory functions:

- responsibility for regulating air navigation services (jointly with the Ministry of Defence), through the UK's ATC services
- responsibility for the regulation of all the UK's civil aviation, including air transport licensing, the award of licences (ATOLs) to air travel organisers and approval of air fares
- responsibility for the airworthiness and operational safety of UK carriers, including certification of airlines, airports, flight crew and engineers
- acting as adviser to the government in matters concerning domestic and international civil aviation
- a number of subsidiary functions, including the research and publication of statistics.

Prior to the Civil Aviation Act, no clear long-term government policy had been discernible with respect to aviation in the UK. As governments changed, so did attitudes to the public or private ownership of carriers. With the aim of providing some longer-term direction and stability, a committee of enquiry into civil air transport, under the chairmanship of Sir Ronald Edwards, was established.

EXAMPLE

The Edwards Report: UK air transport in the 1970s

This enquiry recommended that the government should periodically review civil aviation policy and objectives; the long-term aim should be to satisfy air travellers at the lowest economically desirable price and a suitable mix should be agreed between public- and private-sector airlines. The state corporations (BOAC and BEA) were confirmed in their role as flag-carriers, but were recommended to merge and to start charter and inclusive tour operations. The idea of a major second-force airline in the private sector, to complement and compete with the new public airline, was proposed and the suggestion was made that a more liberal policy be adopted towards the licensing of other private airlines. Finally, the report proposed that the economic, safety and regulatory functions carried out by the previous Air Transport Licensing Board, the Board of Trade and the Air Registration Board should thereafter come under the control of a single Civil Aviation Authority.

The Civil Aviation Act, which followed the publication of this report in 1971, accepted most of these proposals. BOAC and BEA were merged into a single corporation – British Airways – while British Caledonian was confirmed as the new second-force airline (following the merger of Caledonian Airways and British United Airways), and the CAA was formed.

Although it was envisaged by the Edwards Report that British Caledonian would compete with the publicly owned flag-carrier, the CAA redistributed routes, giving British Caledonian South American routes and restricting the North Atlantic largely to BA. This limited opportunities for growth; British Caledonian struggled for profitability and was eventually taken over by BA and integrated into its services in 1987.

The CAA is financed by the users of its services, which are mainly the airlines themselves. Any excess profits are expected to be returned to the users through lower charges for its services. The CAA introduced its Consumer Panel, which replaced the Air Transport Users' Council (AUC), to act as a critical friend for the CAA, providing a consumer perspective on the CAA's work, particularly in regards to its priorities and regulations affecting air passengers.

An 'open skies' policy being favoured by both the US and UK governments in the 1980s led to an effective deregulation of fares and capacity across the Atlantic, as well as on domestic routes in both countries. BA was privatised in 1987 and the subsequent redistribution and licensing of routes for smaller UK carriers set the scene for liberalisation throughout Europe.

THE DEREGULATION OF AIR TRANSPORT

Deregulation – or 'liberalisation' as it has come to be known in Europe – is the deliberate policy of reducing state control over airline operations, allowing market forces to shape the airline industry. The USA led the way with the Airline Deregulation Act of 1978, which abolished collusion in air pricing. The US regulatory body, the Civil Aeronautics Board (CAB), progressively relinquished control over route allocation and fares and was itself disbanded at the end of 1984. Market forces were then to take over, the government expecting that inefficient large carriers would be undercut by smaller airlines that had lower overheads and greater productivity.

In fact, the actual outcome was very different, with the opening years of deregulation seeing a rapid expansion of airline operations, with a three-fold increase in new airlines. Among the established airlines, those that expanded prudently, such as Delta, prospered, while others, such as Braniff, became overambitious and committed themselves to a programme of expansion that, as fares became more competitive, they could not support financially. While a few routes saw substantial early rises in fares, especially on long-haul domestic flights, on the whole fares fell sharply, attracting a big increase in passengers. This growth was achieved at the expense of profitability, forcing airlines to cut costs in order to survive. New conditions of work and lower pay agreements were negotiated, with some airlines abandoning union recognition altogether. A few airlines reverted to propeller aircraft on short-haul routes to cut costs, and worries began to emerge about safety as it was believed that airlines were cutting corners to save on maintenance. Indeed, air safety violations doubled between 1984 and 1987.

Within a decade of deregulation, more than 100 airlines had been forced out of business or absorbed as profits changed to losses. Poor morale among airline crew, due to uncertainty about their future job security, led to indifferent service.

Supplementals, as the charter operators are known in the USA, were particularly badly hit as competing scheduled services dropped their fares. They had neither the public recognition nor the marketing skills to compete openly with the scheduled services and many simply ceased to operate. In the longer term, the 'mega-carriers' were the major beneficiaries. They comprised some ten leading airlines, of which the 'big three' – Delta, American and United – held the lion's share of the air travel market. Far from expanding opportunity, deregulation led to smaller airlines being squeezed out or restricted to less important routes by the marketing power of the big carriers. In 2001 (prior to the 9/11 catastrophe), American Airlines took over TWA, which had been operating under America's Chapter 11 bankruptcy rules.

A second consequence of deregulation was the development of **hub-and-spoke** systems of operation: where feeder air services from smaller, 'spoke' airports provide services into the hubs to connect with the onward long-haul flights of the mega-carriers. This is discussed fully later in the chapter. With more liberal policies in force on both sides of the Atlantic, it became clear that renewed talks should take place to negotiate an open skies policy across the Atlantic, too. The Bermuda 2 Agreement having been ruled illegal under EU competition rules and with a further 16 of the 27 EU members having negotiated bilateral agreements directly with the USA, the EU initiated talks with US officials in 2004. The EU pressed for the limitation on foreign ownership of US carriers to be raised to 50% and rights to be granted allowing European carriers to fly on domestic American routes in exchange for opening up inter-European routes to US carriers. US negotiators proved adamant in refusing to accept these terms, however.

Finally, in 2007, after extensive discussion, an **'open skies' agreement** was reached, which came into force in April 2008. The agreement favoured the USA, in that US airlines were now to be permitted to operate on EU cabotage routes by extending their transatlantic operations (New York–London–Athens, for example), while America sacrificed none of its closely guarded cabotage rights and foreign airlines were not to be permitted to secure more than 25% of any US airline's voting rights. The agreement did allow any EU carrier to fly between any EU airport and any US city, however. With these rights, two things become apparent:

- Passengers originating in Africa and the Middle East and using London Heathrow in transit to North America would be likely in the future to use other carriers on the Continent, to the detriment of Heathrow's transit revenue.
- Slots at Heathrow, already in short supply and estimated at the time to be valued at £25 million per pair, immediately become more valuable. To ensure a spread of slots, IAG was required to give up 12 slot pairs at Heathrow as part of its purchase of BMI from Lufthansa. Despite this, IAG still holds more than half of the slots at this major hub airport.

EXAMPLE

UK airport slots

Concern over the effectiveness of the 70-year-old system of slot allocation led to a briefing paper being put to parliament on the possibility of reform. Attempts to improve the system started at the turn of the century but there has been limited progress, with the system still favouring incumbency.

In the UK, slot allocation is only regulated at those airports where capacity would be insufficient to meet demand (Heathrow, Gatwick, Stansted, Manchester, London Luton and London City) and is coordinated by Airport Coordination Limited (www.acl-uk.org). Airlines retain a slot provided they have used it for at least 80% of the time. The remaining slots are pooled and made accessible to other airlines, with new entrants (those with fewer than five slots) getting priority. The 80% rule does create an issue, in that the system creates no incentive for airlines to give up access to a slot they cannot use efficiently.

One step forward for the congested London airports has been the introduction of slot transfer trading, which allows slots to be moved to those airlines that value them most. This is now perhaps the most common way for slots to change hands. In 2016, only 22 slots at Heathrow were made available via the pool, while 224 slots were traded between airlines.

Proposed reform has considered the cessation of grandfather rights and holding an auction of all slots. While this would mean slots would go to those airlines that value them most, there is concern that it would be more difficult for smaller airlines with fewer capital assets to access the busiest airports. There would also be a concern that an airline might buy slots to avoid competitors having them, thus stifling slot use further.

Instead of changing slot allocation, one proposal is to use congestion pricing: increasing airport charges at peak time to encourage the use of quieter times. One drawback of this is that slot times form part of a complex network for airlines. For example, if a long-haul flight is filled by several spoke flights then shifting its departure time is not an option.

As a consequence, little change to the system is likely to occur, although Brexit may free the UK from the EU slot regulation rules currently in place.

Source: Haylen and Butcher, 2017

Air France/KLM sought close cooperation with US carrier Delta (they are part of the same airline alliance programme) to run a joint venture that would include common fares, schedules and capacity. Lufthansa bought out Swiss carrier Swiss International in 2005 and made a substantial investment in US budget carrier JetBlue in 2006 (and still holds 19% of their shares). Lufthansa also has a majority shareholding in Austrian Airlines and a substantial (45%) holding in Brussels Airlines.

BA had also been looking to form closer links with a North American airline and, following abortive talks with Continental Airlines, they renewed talks with American Airlines. BA's first attempt to link with the US carrier dates back to 1997 and further talks were held in 2002, but US anti-trust legislation had inhibited agreements up to that point. In 2010, BA merged with Spanish airline Iberia, the parent company becoming known as International Airline Group (IAG), and European regulators agreed anti-trust principles under which this expanded European airline was permitted to operate jointly with American Airlines.

In 2008, Delta announced a merger with Northwest Airlines, integrating the latter's name into the Delta brand as Delta Air Lines. A merger between United and Continental Airlines followed in 2012, allowing the newly formed organisation, under the United Airlines brand name, to take the title of the world's largest airline. This was an honour only briefly held because American Airlines agreed a merger with US Airways in 2013. The union, through the formation of the American Airline Group, created by far the largest global carrier, with 6700 flights daily and almost 200 million passengers enplaned. To gain government agreement for the merger, the airlines were required to sell off more than 134 slot pairs at Washington Reagan National Airport and 34 slot pairs at New York La Guardia Airport. Airport gates were also relinquished at Boston Logan, Chicago O'Hare and Los Angeles International Airports.

With 'open skies' successfully concluded across the Atlantic, talks were then held between the USA and Australia, to negotiate a similar liberalisation. This led to a similar 'open skies' agreement in 2008 for transpacific routes.

DEVELOPMENTS IN NORTH AMERICAN AIR TRAFFIC SINCE 1990

Since the early 1990s, the North American airlines' struggle to survive has become more acute. Famous names like Pan American (known as Pan Am) disappeared and, between 1991 and 1993, five airlines were forced to operate under America's Chapter 11 bankruptcy code, which permits an airline to continue to operate, although officially bankrupt, while restructuring its finances. The huge losses sustained by even the biggest airlines led to the sale of assets and alliances with major international carriers, a trend that has become of major importance in the twenty-first century. Airline retrenchment also created difficulties for manufacturers of aircraft, which experienced widespread cancellations of orders in favour of leasing or the purchase of second-hand equipment, while the traditional leasing market in turn dried up.

Hub-and-spoke development, after its initial success in the USA, was challenged by new, low-cost regional carriers operating city to city on less significant routes. Southwest Airlines has been particularly successful, offering no-frills flying at budget fares to some 90 destinations and operating medium-sized aircraft spoke to spoke in direct competition with the dominant hub-and-spoke operators. Southwest was the only US airline not to encounter losses after the 9/11 disaster.

By the start of the twenty-first century, some stability had returned, with a pattern emerging of powerful US mega-carriers (which have become known as the 'legacy carriers') on key domestic and international routes, seeking alliances with leading foreign airlines in order to offer truly global air services. Most small airlines opted to concentrate on niche services, but the growth of no-frills airlines in the USA was initially limited, partly owing to effective marketing by the leading carriers, and partly owing to public concern over safety issues (the fatal 1996 crash of no-frills carrier Valujet did nothing to reduce this concern). The big carriers established their own low-cost operations. Delta created Delta Express; American Airlines, its Eagle division; United, Ted. The much-criticised practice of 'bracketing', in which large carriers lay on cut-price flights departing shortly before and after those of rival cheap carriers, also threatened the survival of many of the new airlines. Only where the airline had sufficient resources to pack a route with flights (as was the case with Southwest Airlines) did this tactic prove impractical.

EXAMPLE

Troubled times

The 9/11 terrorist attack on New York's Twin Towers and Washington's Pentagon building in 2001 quickly unseated the airlines' economic recovery. In the aftermath, virtually all the leading carriers sought Chapter 11 bankruptcy protection:

- Delta Airlines in 2004
- United Airlines between 2002 and 2006
- ATA Holdings between 2004 and 2006 and again in 2008 (when Southwest acquired its assets and the company ceased to trade)
- US Airways between 2002 and 2003 and again in 2004 and 2005 (when it was absorbed by America West, subsequently rebranded as US Airways)
- Northwest Airlines in 2005 (subsumed into Delta Air Lines in 2008).

In the period that followed the disaster, the legacy carriers, in their struggle to survive, implemented substantial restructuring and consolidation.

The impact of 9/11 was as keenly felt on European carriers as it was by those in the US, coming as it did on top of an economic downturn that was already depressing airline profitability. Several airlines collapsed, only to return in a new, privatised form, including Sabena, the Belgian flag-carrier (replaced by SN Brussels), and Swissair (now simply Swiss and owned by Lufthansa). Air France and KLM also merged their operations to improve efficiencies.

With the consequent downturn in business following the crisis, the no-frills carriers, led by Southwest Airlines, benefited at the expense of the mega-carriers. The full-service airlines could not raise fares, owing to the competition faced from the low-cost carriers, but, at the same time, they were faced with high staff pay, fluctuating oil prices and added costs for the extra security that has been put in place since 9/11. One result has been a cutting back in service levels, with economy passengers now paying for food and drink on board and the refurbishment of aircraft interiors being undertaken less frequently.

EXAMPLE

Revenue sources for airlines

As intense competition has driven down the price of flights, so airlines have expanded their focus on other revenue streams. United Airlines collected more than $5 billion in ancillary revenue in 2012, earned from fees for baggage, priority boarding and commission earned from hotel and car rental reservations. Over the past five years, other airlines have substantially increased their ancillary revenue to also exceed $5 billion yearly (Table 13.7).

TABLE 13.7 Ancillary revenue

Airline	Revenue (2017)	Revenue (2012)
United Airlines	$5.75 billion	$5.3 billion
Delta Airlines	$5.39 billion	$2.58 billion
American Airlines	$5.27 billion	$1.99 billion
Southwest Airlines	$3.08 billion	$1.66 billion
Ryanair	$2.3 billion	$1.39 billion
Air France/KLM	$1.97 billion	$1.2 billion
easyJet	$1.28 billion	$1.1 billion

Sources: Hetter, 2013; WiT, 2018

A number of joint ventures have allowed airlines to collaborate on routes while overcoming restrictions on mergers. Delta, Air France/KLM and Alitalia agreed a joint venture designed to enhance transatlantic networks, while Delta and Virgin Australia agreed to collaborate to expand network options between the USA and Australia. Lufthansa has a long-established joint venture with Air Canada, and United Airlines, to enhance efficiencies on North American routes, has a joint venture with ANA which sees cooperation on routes between Japan and Europe. American Airlines, British Airways and Iberia (all part of the Oneworld alliance) have also implemented a joint venture initiative to compete on the transatlantic routes.

The likely direction in the future will be continuation of the current process of integration or collaboration. While in the past legacy carriers have been blocked by the competition authorities, extreme fluctuations in demand are likely to mean, inevitably, that fewer airlines will survive and, should the authorities continue to oppose mergers, closer alliances in some shape or form will doubtless be inevitable.

EUROPEAN LIBERALISATION

Elsewhere in the developed world, governments have also supported the steady erosion of state regulatory powers over the airline industry. In Australia, liberalised air policy led to the establishment of new airlines and, for the first time, a competitively priced domestic air service, with JetBlue filling the role formerly occupied by Ansett as Australia's second carrier.

EXAMPLE

The launch and loss of Compass Airlines

Compass Airlines was one of the first low-cost carriers to enter the Australian market following liberalisation of the market in 1990. The company set out to compete with the duopoly of Ansett and Australian, bringing down the price of domestic flights significantly. These steps were marked with initial success, and the airline was said to have 'halved the cost of flying and doubled the number of domestic air passengers' (Yallop, 1992).

However, Compass suffered difficulties, as is the case with so many new airlines, in gaining suitable slots at airports, as well as accessing check-in facilities and other ground-handling services. Ansett and Australian aggressively responded by lowering prices below cost to attract business away from Compass.

Following financial problems at the end of 1991, Compass eventually folded. Nevertheless, it was at the forefront in promoting affordable travel, and thus was popular with the Australian market. Its closure led to street demonstrations and a petition with over half a million signatures was gathered, both efforts seeking to encourage government support for greater competition in the domestic market (see Figure 13.5).

FIGURE 13.5 Street protests in Melbourne, encouraging support for Compass Airlines (December 1991)

Photo: Claire Humphreys

Europe's airlines were also moving towards a 'market forces' policy, although in those countries where the state retained a financial investment in its airlines, the ethos of liberalisation promoted by the EC was resisted. Iberia and Air France, for example, continued to receive public subsidies long after these became contrary to EU regulations. The path to liberalisation had become irresistible, however, with the EU easing the transition by phasing it in three stages between 1987 and 1997, after which all EU carriers became free to fly anywhere within the EU, including cabotage routes, at fares they themselves determined, hindered only by the lack of slots at the major airports. Other European carriers outside the EU – notably Switzerland, Norway and Iceland – followed suit.

Airline deregulation in the UK had preceded that of other EU countries following a number of individual bilateral agreements with fellow EU members, notably Ireland and the Netherlands. This policy led to a substantial growth in the number of domestic carriers, as well as the number of passengers travelling.

No-frills airlines were already springing up in the UK by the 1990s, operating chiefly out of regional and secondary airports, especially Luton and Stansted, which had slots available for expansion and charged lower fees. The less popular regional airports are often keen to subsidise start-up airlines or others developing new routes, with landing charges waived for an initial period and the promise of advertising support. High start-up costs for operators joining dense routes, the big expense of marketing to establish a new brand and the success of frequent flyer programmes among the large carriers constrained small carriers from directly competing. Also, the low prices made levels of commission less attractive to agents, making distribution difficult. All this encouraged the budget carriers to sell their product direct, however, coinciding with the growth in online booking and easier direct distribution. Not all were successful, as we have seen, but the leaders, notably easyJet and Ryanair, were soon undermining even the largest carriers. Irish carrier Ryanair successfully competed with Aer Lingus and then massively expanded its route network throughout Europe, to a point where it overtook all European legacy carriers to become the largest airline in Europe, carrying almost 130 million passengers. Inevitably, the large carriers were forced to retaliate, first by launching their own low-cost carriers and subsequently by slashing the prices of economy tickets on their normal flights.

The potential explosion of passenger traffic resulting from liberalisation has been, as we have seen, severely curtailed by problems of congestion. Government statistics have projected flights from the UK to rise from 238 million in 2005 to, according to some estimates (DfT, 2017), 315 million by 2030, only constrained by the lack of new infrastructure. Mainland Europe, too, is rapidly approaching saturation.

While the introduction of new fast rail services between the European capitals could theoretically offer some help by reducing demand for air travel on routes of up to about 500 miles, the overall growth in demand for air services poses severe problems for the industry in the long run.

One further point must receive a mention: the issue of air safety. Cost competition is driving some airlines to use older aircraft, including some registered outside the UK. While the CAA has imposed restrictions on UK scheduled airlines using foreign aircraft, there are no restrictions on UK tour operators chartering such aircraft to operate into and out of the UK, nor is any firm control exercised over the use of foreign aircraft registered in other EU countries. Pressure to meet targets on air traffic control and the new compensation regulations introduced in 2005 by the EU against delayed flights have led to further concerns about passenger safety within the EU.

THE ECONOMICS OF AIRLINE OPERATION

The development of an airline route is something of a catch-22 situation. Airlines require some reassurance about traffic demand before they are willing to commit their aircraft to a new route, but air travellers look for regular and frequent flights to a destination before patronising a route.

Seat prices are likely to be high to compensate for low load factors (the number of seats sold as a percentage of total seats available) and high overheads (for both operating and marketing) before traffic builds up. When a route has proved its popularity, however, the pioneer airline is faced with increasing competition as other airlines are attracted by the increase in traffic, unless governments decide to control market entry. In an open-market economy, the original airline faces lower load factors, as the market is split between a number of carriers, requiring it to either increase the fares or reduce profit margins, although it may well have kept prices artificially low initially in order to build the market and recoup launch costs later.

Key routes, such as those across the North Atlantic, attract levels of competition that can make it difficult to operate any service profitably, and many airlines that do operate on these routes have suffered losses and low load factors for many years.

THE DEVELOPMENT OF HUB-AND-SPOKE SYSTEMS

Major airlines in the USA recognised that attempting to serve all airports with maximum-frequency city-to-city flights was uneconomic, so developed the concept of the **hub-and-spoke system**. The hub airports provide transcontinental and intercontinental services, while the 'spokes' offer connecting flights from regional airports to meet these long-haul services. The latter services can be provided in aircraft that are smaller and cheaper to operate. Flights are then banked into complexes and, in theory, greater efficiency is achieved. For example, a hub with 55 spokes can create 1500 'city pairs' in this way. Larger aircraft can be used between hubs, and higher load factors and better utilisation of aircraft are achieved.

EXAMPLE

IcelandAir

This airline operates from its hub in Reykjavik and connects 23 airports in Europe with 22 airports in North America, potentially creating 506 paired cities for transatlantic flights (see Figure 13.6).

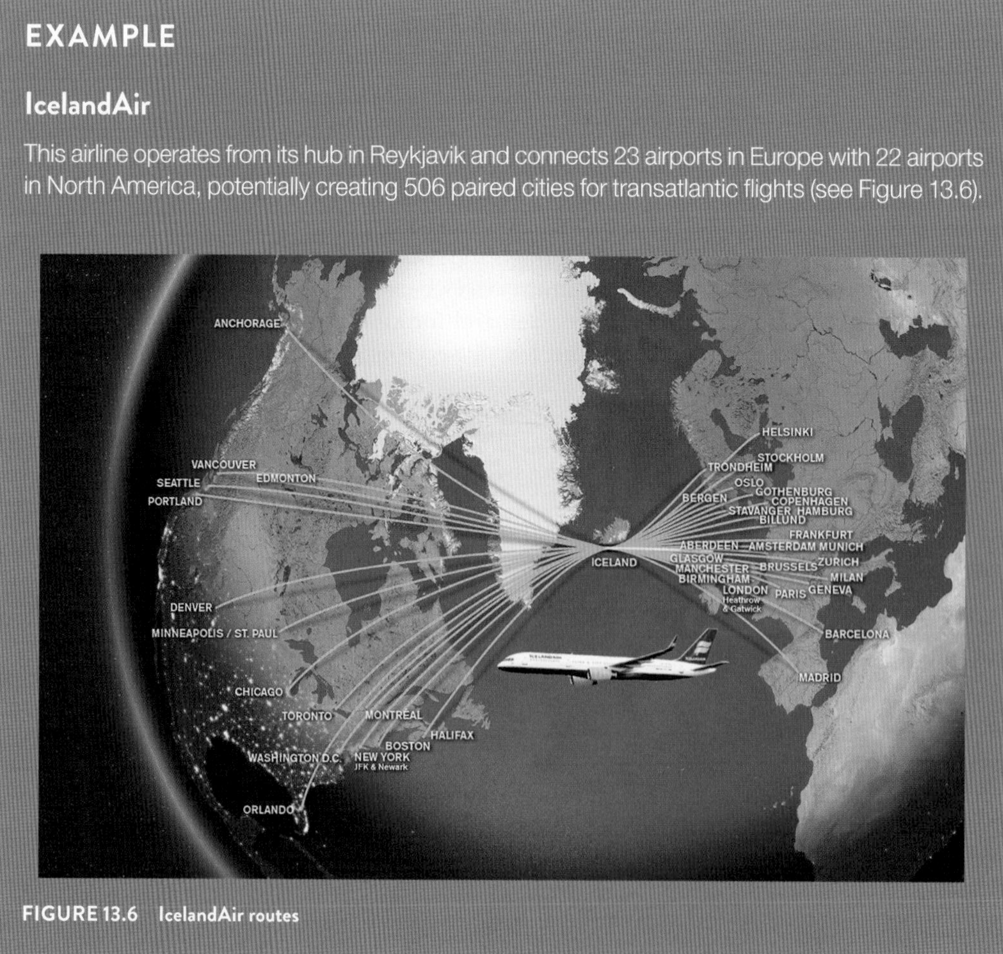

FIGURE 13.6 IcelandAir routes

IcelandAir actively encourages stopovers in the country by allowing passengers to break their journey for up to five nights without paying additional airfare. Additionally, the airline announced plans to codeshare with JetBlue, which would allow passengers to streamline travel between IcelandAir flights arriving in the gateway hubs of Boston and New York onto JetBlue services to Detroit, Orlando, Washington and several other American destinations.

Some 40 hubs were soon established in the USA alone, serving 25 of America's largest cities. Within a few years of their introduction, passengers taking advantage of hub-and-spoke systems accounted for three-quarters of the total at Atlanta airport and half at Chicago, Denver and Dallas/Fort Worth. Similarly, in Europe the hub-and-spoke system was brought into operation by leading airlines, notable among them KLM, which, with Schiphol Airport as its hub, had soon built up some ten waves of spoke flights a day to feed into its European and long-haul services. In this way, the airline was able to attract traffic from UK regional airports to connect with its major routes, in direct competition with long-haul flights from London's airports.

Spokes are generally best suited to feeding long-haul flights, as the additional stopover time is then only a small proportion of the total journey. It later became apparent, however, that there are also diseconomies that accrue from operating these systems. The organisation of hub-and-spoke flights requires frequent waves of closely spaced banks of arrivals and departures to be established, resulting in peaks and troughs at the hub airports, which put further pressure on congested air and terminal space and lead to delays. This also requires large numbers of handling staff on the ground during peaks and involves further peaking expenses. Obviously, on-time performance becomes even more significant under these circumstances, and, if airlines are forced to delay departures while waiting for delayed inbound flights, costs rise.

Some airports are clearly better suited than others to coping with this way of working. Schiphol has benefited from hub-and-spoke flights being based in the same terminal, which means that the time required for passengers to make their connections is shorter.

There is now growing evidence that, in some circumstances, airlines remaining outside the hub-and-spoke system can be more profitable than those within it. They can do this by charging a higher fare for direct services, so even though the demand is not as great, it may still be equally profitable. This applies particularly to business flights, where non-stop services are seen as critical. There are clear limits on the extent to which city-to-city services can be viable, however; this is dependent on passenger demand and the distances to be travelled.

THE GROWTH OF STRATEGIC ALLIANCES

As the problems arising from open competition are obviously going to be long-term ones, the aviation industry has been caught up in a huge global restructuring exercise since the 1990s. European airlines had seen and taken account of developments in the North American market. They recognised that size, which provides economies of scale and scope, would be crucial to survival in the future. They also noted that US domestic carriers were expanding into transatlantic routes and were now benefiting from the five freedoms of the air in Europe, posing further threats to market share. The way forward for the European carriers is seen as lying in either mergers and takeovers or the development of strategic alliances with US carriers.

Alliances are easier to establish, but experience has shown that they can prove less durable. Political differences and differences in management style have frequently hindered effectiveness. The short-lived relationships between BA and United Airlines and between Lufthansa and Air France are cases in point, while the much-vaunted attempt in 1993 to form an alliance between Swissair, Austrian Airlines, SAS and KLM, known as Alcazar, also foundered before being implemented, owing to the failure to agree on a US partner. The movement of airlines between the various alliances in order to gain competitive edge also demonstrates the highly fluid nature of these alliances.

Evidence now points to the success of strategic alliances as being dependent on expansion in three stages. First, there is a need to secure a dominant share in the home market. BA undertook expansion specifically through franchising, absorbing 100% of Brymon Airways, and soon held six franchises in the UK, as well as a further four overseas. Air France absorbed a number of domestic French carriers, as did KLM Dutch carriers.

EXAMPLE

Air Berlin

For airlines, rapid growth is not without its problems. Air Berlin expanded quickly, first by buying DBA (a German domestic carrier first launched by BA) in 2006, followed in 2007 by its purchase of charter operators LTU and a 49% stake in Belair. The company joined the Oneworld alliance and agreed numerous codeshare arrangements with airlines such as Finnair, American Airlines and BA.

At its peak, it was the second largest German airline but, after several loss-making years, the company floundered, filing for insolvency in 2017.

The second step is to gain a strong foothold in the main European countries, especially the UK, France and Germany. This was achieved, for example, by SAS, which controlled 40% of British Midland by the early 1990s, and KLM, which purchased Air UK.

The final stage is the globalisation of the carrier, especially through investments in North America and the Asia/Pacific region. BA became a leader in this strategy, taking a minority investment in Australian carrier Qantas in 1992 and seeking similar investments in US carriers, although this only recently became realised as links with American Airlines came to fruition. The Air France/KLM link-up with Delta is an indication of the achievement of this final step in the process.

It is now clear that global **alliances** are seen as the way forward. These embrace key airlines in Europe, North America and the Asia/Pacific region. While the specific membership of each of these changes quite frequently, the picture in 2018 was as follows:

- *Oneworld* (formed 1998) with current members BA, American Airlines, Qantas, Cathay Pacific, Iberia, Finnair, LATAM, Japan Airlines, Malaysia Airlines, Qatar Airways, Royal Jordanian, TAM, S7, Sri Lankan Airlines together with affiliated regional carriers.
- *Star Alliance* (1997) with Air Canada, Air China, Air India, Air New Zealand, ANA, Adria Airways, Aegean Airlines, Asiana Airlines, Austrian, Avianca, Brussels Airlines, Copa Airlines, Croatia Airlines, Egyptair, Ethiopian Airlines, EVA Air, LOT Polish Airlines, Lufthansa, SAS, Shenzhen Airlines, Singapore Airlines, South African Airways, Swiss, TAP Portugal, Thai Airways International, Turkish Airlines, United Airlines and associated regional members.
- *SkyTeam* (2000) with Aeroflot, Aerolíneas Argentinas, Aeromexico, Air Europa, Air France/KLM, Alitalia, China Airlines, China Eastern, China Southern, Czech Airlines,

Delta Air Lines, Garuda Indonesia, Kenya Airways, Korean Air, Middle East Airlines, Saudia, TAROM, Vietnam Airlines and XiamenAir.

Two other former alliances – Wings and Qualiflyer – have become defunct as airlines merged or were driven out of service.

EXAMPLE

Royal Air Maroc to join the Oneworld alliance

In December 2018, it was announced that another airline was to become a full member of the Oneworld alliance. Royal Air Maroc is expected to gain full membership by 2020. The airline, with a fleet of 55 planes, is tiny in comparison to some other members of the group. However, this is the alliance's first full member (rather than an affiliate) to be based in Africa and means that more than 30 new destinations will be added to the Oneworld route network.

A strategic alliance offers opportunities for rapid global growth, coupled with marketing benefits that cannot be achieved as an individual airline. An effective alliance increases the viability of marginal routes and allows carriers to compete on routes where, separately, they do not hold rights. It also enables companies to reduce costs by using larger aircraft to meet overall demand and sharing operational costs, such as counter space at airports and baggage handling. Marketing costs such as advertising may also be shared. Other operational benefits include control over air terminals. At Heathrow, Terminal 5 has become the BA hub, Terminal 3 is used as the Oneworld hub (alongside a few non-affiliated airlines such as Emirates and Virgin Atlantic), while the newly refurbished Terminal 2 (The Queen's Terminal) has been assigned to 23 Star Alliance carriers.

Alliances may range from the marginal, such as having an interline agreement to accept one another's documentation and transfer of passengers, to marketing agreements, such as joint frequent flyer programmes; or operational agreements, such as blocking space on one another's aircraft to sell their seats. The most common advantage to be gained, though, is that of code-sharing.

CODE-SHARING

Domestic code-sharing was in practice within the USA as long ago as 1967, but was first introduced internationally in 1985, when American Airlines and Qantas agreed to share codes on routes across the Pacific.

Under a **code-sharing** agreement, two airlines agree to share their codes on through routes; for example, between New York and San Francisco and from San Francisco to Sydney. This has the marketing advantage of appearing to be a single through flight, but there are also very concrete advantages for passengers, in that flight timings are coordinated, transfer times between stopovers may be reduced (and carriers will often hold flights for up to 20 minutes for passengers connecting from flights that are code-shared) and baggage can be checked through to the final destination, enhancing passenger convenience. Carriers can sell each other's flights as if they were their own and will frequently block off space to do so. A further advantage is that code-shared flights are featured on computer reservations systems before other connections, as these offer passengers the best value. They may also benefit from multiple listing on the computerised reservation system (CRS) as they will be listed under both carriers' services.

EXAMPLE

Code-sharing

Although there are said to be benefits of code-sharing for passengers, largely related to the convenience in scheduling and baggage arrangements, concern has been raised that such practices can reduce competition on routes. Research (Gilo and Simonelli, 2014) suggests that codeshare flights see elevated airfares, with differences between code-sharing partners and higher fares when compared to other airlines flying the same route.

Typically, airlines collaborate with others in the same alliance, as for instance American Airlines working with other Oneworld members. However, there are a growing number of exceptions to this; to cite one example, American Airlines (a founder member of Oneworld) has announced a code-sharing arrangement with Korean Air, a founder member of the SkyTeam alliance.

AIRLINE COSTS

The selection of suitable aircraft for a route is the outcome of the assessment of the relative costs involved (both capital and operating) and the characteristics of the aircraft themselves.

Capital costs

The global growth in demand for passenger services since the turn of the century has averaged between 4% and 7%, while ACI predicts that it will more than double by 2040, exceeding 20 billion. Airlines must therefore plan for continued expansion and regular renewal, with one eye on operating costs while simultaneously focusing on environmental responsibility and customer demand; for example, newer aircraft appeal to airlines in terms of fuel efficiency and lower emissions and to passengers in terms of both safety and aesthetics.

With even workhorse aircraft like the A320 costing around $90 million each and the latest superjumbos costing in excess of $400 million, investment in new aircraft is a huge commitment. Attractive loan terms are likely to be a key factor in closing sales, and some manufacturers are willing to offer very favourable trade-ins on old aircraft in order to sell their new models. Orders for new aircraft are usually a package, embracing not only the aircraft themselves but also the subsequent provision of spares and possibly servicing. Additionally, there are periods when supply will exceed demand and, when there are many second-hand aircraft on the market, the competition between manufacturers for sales enables airlines to drive very hard bargains when purchasing new equipment.

Airlines also have the choice, of course, of leasing aircraft rather than purchasing them and, although they may incur penalties for doing so, if an airline is hit by recession and a sharp drop in demand, it may well cut back on orders already placed, choosing to lease rather than purchase to keep capital costs down. On occasion, this can result in an airline selling existing aircraft and leasing them back to release capital.

Operating costs

Mile for mile, short-haul routes (of up to 1500 miles) overall are more expensive to operate than are long-haul, although this is not simply due to the cost of the fuel used. While the greater frequency of take-offs and landings on short-haul flights will mean high initial fuel consumption on each leg as aircraft gain height, research (Webster, 2002) has shown that an aircraft travelling long distances in a single hop can consume more fuel than one stopping three times on the same route. The example given was of a 9000-mile flight which, flown non-stop, consumes 120 tonnes of fuel, while an aircraft taking three 3000-mile hops will need only 28 tonnes for each hop, a total of 84 tonnes. The explanation for this is that, ironically, long-haul aircraft use more fuel because they are carrying the weight of the extra fuel needed for the longer journey. When factoring in the additional costs of crewing and landing fees for both forms of travel, however, short-haul costs will overtake those of long-haul and force up ticket prices.

EXAMPLE

The effect of fuel prices

One estimate put the typical fuel burn of flying a Boeing 767 or Airbus A330 between London and New York at 12,800 gallons, reducing to 10,800 gallons for the return flight, due to favourable tail winds (Robertson, 2008). In 2000, with fuel costing just 87 cents a gallon, a return journey would have cost $20,532 in fuel (adjusted for inflation this would amount to about $34,000 today). In 2011, aviation fuel had risen to $3.19 a gallon, putting the round trip fuel cost up to $75,284, almost a four-fold increase. By the end of 2018, the price of aviation fuel had fallen to $1.70, meaning the same trip would cost $40,120 in fuel. Throughout this period, intense competition was forcing airlines to keep ticket prices down.

Of course, over the same period aircraft design has helped to reduce fuel consumption, so airlines investing in new aircraft have the potential to recoup some of their outlay through lower flight operating costs. For example, the Airbus A380 is reported to burn 20% less fuel than the Boeing 747, and the new Boeing 787-800 Dreamliner burns 20% less fuel than a similarly sized Boeing 767.

Long-haul aircraft normally operate at a ceiling of 30,000–40,000 feet (supersonics were operating at 50,000–60,000 feet), while short- and medium-haul aircraft will operate at lower ceilings. While the cost of getting the long-haul aircraft to its ceiling will be greater than that of a short- and medium-haul aircraft, once at these heights, there is little wind resistance and the rate at which fuel is burned falls considerably.

Short-haul aircraft also spend a proportionately greater amount of time on the ground than long-haul aircraft. Aircraft are only earning money while they are in the air and depreciation of their capital cost can only be written off against their actual flying time. For this reason, it is important that they are scheduled for the maximum number of flying hours each day. According to the efficiency of the airline and the airports the airline uses, productivity can be increased without impairing the (legally determined) minimum service and maintenance time required. Routine servicing on a Boeing 747-400 occurs every 600 flight hours and entails 35–60 work hours, with major maintenance (called a C-Check) required after 6000 hours of flying (or 18 months, whichever comes first), taking about 5000 work hours. A heavy maintenance overhaul (a D-Check) takes place every six years and can involve as much as 50,000 work hours.

The American carriers appear to be more successful than the European, with the major US carriers flying at least ten hours per day on short- and medium-haul flights, against a European average of only seven hours (although there are marked differences between the productivity of the various airlines within Europe). In the USA, aircraft turnarounds (time spent on the ground between landing and take-off) can be as little as 30 minutes, while in Europe 45 minutes is the norm. Budget airlines, however, perform significantly better than the traditional carriers, owing in part to their operating out of less congested airports.

EXAMPLE

A week in the life of an aircraft

Research using flight data established the extent to which airlines put their fleet to use by examining the routes flown over the course of a week (in October 2017). During that time, an easyJet A320 flight based in Gatwick completed 29 flights to 14 destinations. It was in the air for 86h 45m and travelled 39,438 miles, equivalent to travelling nearly one and a half times around the world.

During that same week, a Boeing 747 operated by BA travelled 45,487 miles but this consisted of only 12 flights to seven destinations, mostly transatlantic from London. The plane was airborne for 86h 54m to make these journeys. Another long-haul operator, Qantas, flew an A380 for 58,515 miles during the week, travelling to Los Angeles, Dallas and London via Dubai from either Sydney or Melbourne. This aircraft spent 109h 51m – or 65% of the week – airborne.

In contrast, Jet2, a short-haul charter and scheduled operator based at Leeds Bradford Airport, flew a Boeing 737 on 27 flights, spending 48h 17m in the air to cover 23,777 miles and visiting 13 different European destinations.

Source: Morris, 2017

Improving technology is constantly extending the distances that aircraft can fly non-stop. The customer appeal of travelling direct and reducing overall travel time is high, but may be offset by concern over very long, uninterrupted flights and growing awareness of the potential dangers of deep vein thrombosis (DVT). Airlines are countering concern by providing information on simple in-flight exercises, which passengers can perform to reduce the risk.

Costs can be subdivided into the **direct** costs of operating and **indirect** costs. The former will include flight expenses (salaries of flight crew, fuel, in-flight catering), plus maintenance, depreciation, aircraft insurance and airport and navigation charges. Airport charges will include landing fees, parking charges, navigation charges (where these are passed on to the airline by the airport) and a per capita cost according to the number of passengers carried. Navigation charges vary according to the weight of the aircraft and the distance flown over a particular territory. Many of these charges are incorporated into the price of the ticket or are charged as a supplement to the passenger.

EXAMPLE

Surcharges to passengers on a return flight from London to New York

The burden of surcharges is increasing sharply on airline travel. One example, for a Virgin Atlantic round-trip flight from London Heathrow to New York (JFK) in economy class, revealed ten different taxes or surcharges to the basic passenger fare (Table 13.8).

TABLE 13.8 Flight surcharges for London to New York (2018)

Government and airport fees	£
Air passenger duty	78.00
UK passenger service charge – Heathrow	46.62
US custom user fee – JFK	4.60
US transportation tax	29.00
US animal and plant health inspection user fee	3.10
US immigration and naturalisation service user fee	5.50
US passenger civil aviation security service fee	4.40
US passenger facility charge	3.60
Total taxes and charges	174.82
Carrier-imposed surcharge	90.00
Total	**264.82**

Source: Virgin Atlantic website, 2018

Note: Business-class passengers are required to pay a higher UK passenger duty, which adds a further £78 to the ticket price.

After 1998, the notional weight of passengers on EU services was increased, adding to costs. The previous 75 kilos for males and 65 kilos for females have been replaced by a notional weight of 84 kilos per capita for scheduled flights and 76 kilos for holiday charters, in recognition of the trend for people to have increased in body weight internationally.

This higher figure had already been adopted by US and some other carriers, but in fact, the USA opted for a still higher figure in 2005, moving from 185 pounds (84 kilos) to 200 pounds (nearly 91 kilos) for males and a slightly lower figure for females. The USA allows a further five pounds per passenger in winter, in recognition of the need for a higher fuel burn than in summer. These figures, however, include carry-on bags, unlike regulations in Europe. Japanese airlines operate on a notional body weight of 73 kilos (regardless of the nationality of those carried), which enables Japanese carriers to gain advantage over others by providing more seats. The tendency towards obesity among the populations of the developed countries is causing concern for airlines anxious to control their costs as the average extra weight now carried increases fuel costs considerably.

While the no-frills carriers make efforts to improve their slim per capita profits as fuel prices increase, at the other end of the scale equal efforts are being made to reduce aircraft weight in other directions, as we saw earlier in this chapter.

EXAMPLE

Airline policies on transporting persons of size

Samoa Air stimulated a debate on transporting overweight passengers when it announced that it would begin charging passengers by weight. This is a challenging issue for many airlines, which must accommodate heavier travellers while maintaining the safety and comfort of all passengers.

Many US airlines, including United Airlines, Southwest Airlines and Virgin America, require that passengers who are unable to fit into seats, with the armrests lowered, are required to purchase a second seat. In some cases, discounted rates on the second seat are offered. Those airlines that do not require a second seat purchase (for example, Delta) reserve the right to bump passengers to a later flight if suitable or additional seating is not available on the original flight.

In general, the lifespan of an aircraft is estimated at between 25 and 30 years, although there is a tendency today to reduce this period; narrow-bodied aircraft may be sold on after as little as 7–8 years. The purchase price will be written off over the period of service in which the aircraft operates. **Depreciation** is the term used to describe this process, with cost written off on an annual basis against the number of hours it flies. In the case of smaller, relatively inexpensive aircraft, total depreciation time may be as short as 8–10 years, while wide-bodied jets may be depreciated over periods as long as 14–16 years. A residual value of, typically, 10% of the original purchase price is normally allowed for, when the aircraft is disposed of. In some cases, it might be considered prudent to write off aircraft faster than this because obsolescence can overtake their operating life and airlines must keep up with their competitors by re-equipping at regular intervals. With falling profits, however, few airlines find it easy to re-equip and so the tendency is to extend depreciation time. On top of this, insurance costs will be around 3% per annum of the aircraft's purchase price.

Indirect costs include all non-flight expenses, such as marketing, reservations, ground handling, administration and other insurances, such as passenger liability. These costs will vary very little, however many flights are flown, so large airlines will clearly benefit from economies of scale here.

EXAMPLE

Flight costs

Using data sourced from US Airways, it is possible to identify how costs for a flight are proportioned, based on average costs to the business and average fares paid. Using a hypothetical flight with 100 seats, it takes the fares and fees from 99 passengers to cover operating costs. The breakdown can be seen in Table 13.9.

TABLE 13.9 Breakdown of flight costs

Cost item	Proportion of passenger fares and fees
Fuel	29 passengers
Salaries of flight and ground staff	20 passengers
Ownership costs (buying/leasing aircraft, insurance)	16 passengers
Government fees and business taxes (security, airport charges)	14 passengers
Maintenance costs	11 passengers
Other costs (catering, advertising, lost baggage recovery, etc.)	9 passengers
Profit	1 passenger

Source: McCartney, 2012

Fuel costs globally are quoted in US dollars and will therefore vary not only according to changing oil prices but also according to changing currency exchange rates. Other ways to trim costs have included reducing the labour force, while renegotiating levels of pay and conditions of service (often at the expense of good staff–management relations), and moving activities to countries where costs are lower. Several companies have moved parts of their administration functions to India, while others have renegotiated contracts for maintenance or cleaning services with other low-cost countries. Savings can also be achieved by forming low-cost subsidiaries, a move taken by several traditionally high-cost European and American carriers. Above all, distribution costs can be trimmed, given the new means of reaching passengers direct. This will be discussed later on in this chapter.

Aircraft characteristics

These will include the aircraft's cruising speed and block speed (its average overall speed on a trip), its range and field length requirements, its carrying capacity and customer appeal. In terms of passenger capacities, airline development tends to occur in leaps. Thus, with the introduction of jumbo jets, the number of seats on an aircraft tripled, and with the new generation of superjumbos there has been a further sharp increase in capacity. While average seat costs fall sharply as seat numbers are increased, this can only be reflected in lower prices to passengers if sufficient seats are filled.

Carrying capacity is also influenced by the **payload** that the aircraft is to carry; that is, the balance between fuel, passengers and freight. An aircraft is authorised to 'take off at MTOW' (maximum take-off weight), which is its empty operating weight plus payload. At maximum payload, the aircraft will be limited to a certain range, but can increase this range by sacrificing part of the payload; that is, by carrying fewer passengers. Sacrificing both fuel *and* some passenger capacity may allow some aircraft to operate from smaller regional airports with short runways.

Cost savings can be made in a number of ways when using larger aircraft. It is a curious fact that the relative cost of pushing a large aircraft through the air is less, per unit of weight, than a small one (incidentally, this principle also holds true in shipping operations, in that large ships are cheaper per unit of weight to push through the water than smaller ones). Larger aircraft experience proportionately lower drag per unit of weight and can also use larger, more powerful engines. Equally, maintenance and cleaning costs per seat are lower.

ENVIRONMENTAL CONCERNS

Airline operations are facing a growing challenge, politically and economically, regarding the concern over aircraft emissions and their impact on the environment. Greenhouse gases, notably CO2 (carbon dioxide), but also nitrogen oxide and vapour trails that trap heat in the atmosphere when aircraft are flying at height, are now widely acknowledged to add to the problems of global warming. The emissions created by global aircraft movements are estimated to account for around 3% of these gases and are predicted to grow five-fold by 2050. The European Commission has forecast that emissions will have grown by 70% between 2005 and 2020, given the projected increase in flights.

Individual airlines have made some rather half-hearted efforts to offset emissions. BA introduced a 'green fee', ranging from £5 on short-haul flights to £25 for the longest, the money going towards energy-saving projects in developing countries. The disadvantage of the scheme was that it was voluntary and fewer than one in 200 passengers volunteered to pay it when it was first introduced in 2005. Critics have argued in favour of taxation, pointing out that, were aviation fuel to be taxed at the same rate as petrol, a return flight from London to Sydney should attract taxes in excess of £700. The Chicago Convention precludes the unilateral imposition of fuel taxes by one country and there is little likelihood of obtaining a global agreement to tax aviation fuel.

Many environmentalists are putting their faith in an **emissions trading scheme** (ETS). Airlines were required to join this scheme in 2012 and upward of 900 airlines were granted emissions allowances, the majority receiving allowances of approximately 85% of existing levels. The scheme requires organisations, including these airlines, to either reduce their levels or buy carbon allowances at market prices. Air France became the first airline to start trading on the BlueNext emissions exchange (an environmental equivalent of a stock exchange). Airlines now have an incentive to reduce emissions, saving $225 for each tonne of CO^2 avoided. While airlines will reduce emissions, this scheme will result in airlines accepting that they need to purchase additional allowances.

EXAMPLE

Emission controls

When initially announced, the ETS system was to cover all airlines flying into European airspace. However, industry criticism, and threats of retaliatory measures from the USA, China and India, led to long-haul flights outside of the EU being temporarily exempted from the scheme.

In 2016, the International Civil Aviation Organization (ICAO) adopted a global carbon offsetting scheme, CORSIA (Carbon Offsetting and Reduction Scheme for International Aviation), to address pollution levels. This required that, from 1 January 2019, all airlines would need to monitor and report their emissions, purchasing 'emission units' to offset any growth in CO^2. The money raised funds activities that directly achieve CO^2 reductions. The CORSIA scheme has two phases, with the first running to 2026 being voluntary.

Flight frequencies and timings are subject to government controls. For example, it is common to find that governments limit the number of flights they will allow to operate at night. Where long-haul flights and consequently changing time zones are involved, this can seriously curtail the number of flights an airline can operate. In the UK, each individual aircraft is given a quota count (QC) according to the noise it dissipates. The QC of all aircraft flying from an airport at night is totalled and must not exceed the noise quota set by the government for that airport. Boeing 747-400s, for example, are rated at QC2 when landing, while the newer Boeing 777-200s are quieter and rated at QC1, thus making more night flights possible. Airport and route congestion, of course, will have an additional 'rationing' effect. Departure QC is frequently higher, with the 777-200s often rated at QC2 when taking off. To put this into context, the total number of QC points at Heathrow was 9720 in 2012. Since 2017, a new regime has been introduced to progressively reduce the quota level at Heathrow from 9180 to 5150 by 2022.

THE MARKETING OF AIR SERVICES

Aside from economic considerations, the customer appeal of an aircraft depends on such factors as seat comfort and pitch, engine quietness, the interior design of cabins and customer service. In a product where, generally speaking, there is a great deal of homogeneity, minor differences such as these can greatly affect the marketing of the aircraft to the airlines and, in turn, the appeal the airline can make to its prospective passengers.

The recent introduction of flat beds in first and business class on long-haul aircraft is an important factor. Some airlines have configured their aircraft to allow only partial recline, such as up to 160°, while others recline a full 180° to make up into a flat bed. Some first-class flights now even provide double beds in enclosed suites (see Figure 13.7) to offer the ultimate in luxury travel. Such moves are important elements in capturing the key business and celebrity markets.

FIGURE 13.7 Suite-class cabin on Singapore Airlines

Photo: Shutterstock

The marketing division of an airline will play an influential role in determining the destinations to be served, although these decisions are often influenced by government policy and regulation. Marketing personnel must also determine levels of demand for a particular service, the markets to be served and the nature of the competition the airline will face.

Routes are, of course, dependent on freight as well as customer considerations, and a decision will have to be reached on the appropriate mix of freight and passengers, as well as the mix of passengers themselves whom the airline is to serve: business, premium economy and economy class, for example. An airline can be easily panicked into changing routes unless it recognises that circumstances can provide opportunities as well as threats. A good example is seen in the collapse of the so-called tiger economies in Asia at the end of the 1990s. In spite of the economic depression experienced by many of these countries, air traffic to the region actually rose because Western travellers took advantage of the currency collapses to increase their leisure travel to the area.

It is particularly important for business travellers to be able to make satisfactory connections with other flights. To gain a strategic marketing advantage over competitors, an airline will want to coordinate its flights with complementary carriers, with which it must also have interline agreements (these allow the free interchange of documents and reservations). In planning long-haul flights, the airline must also weigh up whether to operate non-stop flights or provide stopovers to cater for passengers wanting to travel between different legs of the journey (known as 'stage' traffic). Stopovers will permit the airline to cater for, or organise, holiday traffic, as well as allowing additional duty-free shopping opportunities. Alternatively, it may dissuade business passengers from booking if their prime interest is to reach their destination as quickly as possible and another, non-stop flight exists. Tahiti experienced a sharp downfall in visitors when the stretched 747-400 was introduced on the transpacific route and it first became possible to fly non-stop between Australia and North America.

YIELD MANAGEMENT

Following the planning stage, the airline must determine its pricing policy. Fixing the price of a seat is a complex process, involving consideration of:

- the size and type of aircraft operating
- the route traffic density and level of competition
- the regularity of demand flow and the extent to which this demand is balanced in both directions on the route
- the type of demand for air service on the route, taking into account demand for first or business class, economy class, inclusive tour-basing fares and other discounted ticket sales
- the estimated breakeven load factor (the number of seats that must be sold to recover all costs) – typically, this will fall at between 60 and 80% of the aircraft's capacity on scheduled routes and the airline must aim to achieve this level of seat occupancy on average throughout the year (budget airlines will set a much higher load factor as their norm).

The last two points are critical to the success of the airline's marketing. The marketing department is, above all, concerned with **yield management** – the overall revenue that is to be achieved on each route. Yield can be defined as the air transport revenue achieved per unit of traffic carried or the total passenger revenue per passenger mile. It is measured by comparing both the cost and revenue achieved per available seat mile (ASM). Balancing the proportion of discounted seats with those for which full fares can be charged, whether in economy or business class, is a highly skilled undertaking as there is a need to ensure that any reduction in full fare will lead to an overall increase in revenue. This is achieved by means of a combination of pricing and the imposition of conditions governing the fares.

Business class, for example, will achieve much higher levels of profit than economy or discounted tickets, so an airline with 10% of its seats given over to business class may achieve 40% of its income from the sale of those seats. The expected demand for the seats on a particular route will call for fine judgement, though. That is because discounted tickets must attract a new market, not draw higher-paying passengers to save money, so they must be hedged with conditions that make them unattractive to prospective business-class passengers. Good yield management can, in some cases, even result in full-service airlines undercutting their budget rivals, as the former can charge much higher fares for reservations taken close to departure times, which helps them to offset the discounts given for early bookings.

EXAMPLE

Changing times and changing cabins

Budget airlines have, for many years, been successfully balancing revenue maximisation and cost reduction through the use of one-class cabins. This has led to a rethink by the full-service carriers. As the business-class market has become both more price-sensitive at the bottom end and more likely to use private jets at the top end, so many flag-carrier airlines have chosen to amalgamate their first- and business-class cabins.

In 2011, American Eagle, the budget arm of American Airlines, introduced two-cabin services on routes serving the business market. This involved providing larger seats and complimentary in-flight catering, and sought to provide superior services for the business and leisure passenger prepared to pay extra for their travel.

Conversely, low-cost carrier easyJet, remaining with a single-class cabin structure, has differentiated to attract the business market by offering flexible tickets (which allow date changes), free hold luggage, advance seat selection and priority boarding, effectively emulating some characteristics of business-class travel on full-service carriers.

One factor that has substantially helped all airlines' yield was the introduction in 2008 of electronic ticketing for all IATA carriers. Eliminating the cost of issuing tickets in favour of an e-ticket (with passengers simply being given a reference number for their flights) has been estimated to save carriers around $3 billion every year.

The growth in bookings using the Internet is a huge bonus for airlines' yield management as, quite apart from avoiding payment of commission, airlines receive payment directly from their passengers when they book, helping cash flow. Previously, payments would be made to travel agents, and payment through the airlines' clearing houses could take up to two months.

Airlines have determined that, in many cases, they can increase yield by downsizing their aircraft, often at the same time increasing flight frequency. This increased frequency can also build new passenger traffic, leading to still greater yield, especially where business traffic is concerned.

BOOSTING YIELD THROUGH FREQUENT FLYER PROGRAMMES

In order to boost overall yield, many airlines have introduced the concept of **frequent flyer** programmes. The idea here is that passengers purchasing airline tickets are entitled to extra free travel, according to the mileage covered. This marketing campaign has been a victim of its own success: over 250 million members worldwide now collect these benefits. One estimate, made in *The Economist* at the end of 2004, claimed that the worldwide stock of airline loyalty schemes, or frequent flyer programmes, was above 14 trillion miles, worth over $700 billion, making them the second-largest convertible currency in the world after the US dollar.

American Airlines was the first to introduce such a scheme in 1981 with its AAdvantage scheme. It is now the biggest scheme in operation, with over 67 million members. Others quickly followed, such as BA's Executive Club, United's Mileage Plus and Virgin Atlantic's Flying Club. The programmes were later extended to allow miles to be accumulated on the value of products purchased at other outlets associated with the airline, such as shops, hotels and petrol stations, as well as partner airlines within the strategic alliances.

The popularity of these schemes has led to so many free seats being offered that airlines are now imposing limitations on their availability. United Airlines, for example, found that, at one point, almost all passengers on its Hawaii-bound flights were frequent flyers, virtually eradicating yield on that route. While frequent flyers can normally only make use of seats that would otherwise be vacant during the flight, each seat occupied costs the airline the price of the food and fuel consumed and, in total, this still adds up to a substantial cost for the airline.

There is some evidence that airline loyalty schemes do change purchase behaviour, particularly when travellers are close to a threshold of earning a higher-status tier. Furthermore, some passengers are willing to pay a marginally higher fare price to gain the benefits of membership (McCaughey, 2014). However, with each point estimated to be worth about $0.013, efforts to collect miles may have limited appeal for less frequent flyers. This may be also be influenced by the restrictions and conditions applied by the airlines to their use.

EXAMPLE

Merging loyalty schemes

The merger of US Airways with American Airlines required the two loyalty schemes – Dividend Miles and AAdvantage respectively – to be amalgamated.

The process allowed a transfer of qualifying miles flown at a rate of one to one from US Airways into the AAdvantage programme. Those travellers holding elite status, such as platinum, gold or silver preferred, were also recognised and, based on qualifying miles, awarded equal rank under the American Airlines programme. Those travellers holding membership of both schemes were allowed to combine their travel accounts, leading to a greater likelihood that a higher travel status would be earned.

In recent years airlines have been reducing the generosity of these schemes, requiring more miles to be traded for each journey. Furthermore, some airlines, American being one example, have introduced significant charges if passengers wish to use their loyalty points to upgrade to a higher cabin class, making this a far less appealing option.

DEEP DISCOUNTING

All scheduled services operate on the basis of an advance reservations system, with the lowest (APEX) fares being available on routes where the booking can be confirmed some time in advance of departure. This allows the airline to judge its expected load factors with greater accuracy.

To fill up seats that have not been pre-booked, the airline offers standby fares, available to passengers without reservations who are prepared to take their chances and turn up in the expectation of a seat being free. On many routes, particularly business routes, the chances of seats being available are good, because business passengers frequently book more than one flight to ensure that they can get back as quickly as possible after the completion of their meeting. Airlines will thus overbook to allow for the high number of no shows (up to 30% on some routes), but must exercise caution in case they end up with more passengers than they can accommodate. If this occurs, they can upgrade them to a better class or compensate them financially and provide seats on another flight, but this may not be sufficient to satisfy an irate passenger. The EU's insistence on high levels of compensation for these bumped passengers has also caused some airlines to rethink their strategy on excessive overbooking and flexible business tickets.

THE AIRLINE DISTRIBUTION SYSTEM

The distribution system consists of two elements: the reservation (or booking) and the issue and delivery of a ticket, where pertinent.

Traditionally, air tickets were sold and distributed through travel agents at an agreed rate of commission, with a proportion also sold direct by the airlines to their passengers. In the USA, the high volume of air travel allowed many more airlines to sell direct, through branch offices in the larger cities, than was possible in the UK. The development of the Internet has now changed this pattern of distribution, with a far greater proportion of sales (and, in the case of some no-frills airlines, all sales) being made through this channel, either direct with the airlines or via Internet intermediaries' own websites.

In the face of many pressures impacting on the airline industry over the past few years, airlines have re-evaluated their distribution systems, seeking to cut costs wherever possible. The first to suffer in this process of re-evaluation has been the travel agent, with commissions first being trimmed, then cut savagely and now largely discontinued, requiring agents to charge their customers a fee for the service they provide. Such a move, however, may further deter customers from booking through intermediaries. As most leading airlines have tended to follow the no commission route, threats by agents to switch-sell air products have had little effect.

Electronic ticketing (commonly referred to as **e-ticketing**) is now an almost universal practice, greatly reducing an airline's costs. This further encourages airlines to push direct sales, with a consequent fall in the number of airline tickets being booked through intermediaries, posing a major threat to agents.

The EC has been monitoring the websites of airlines to check that the prices advertised are a fair reflection of what the customer can expect to pay. Concern was raised that airlines, particularly low-cost ones, were not adhering to rules on commercial practices, which had led to a situation where flight prices advertised did not include compulsory fees and surcharges, thus making price comparisons difficult. In 2009, an EC investigation revealed that 57 airlines now abided by the regulations, while a further 15 examined had agreed to make appropriate changes. In the longer term, it is likely that these monitoring efforts will ensure more transparent pricing for the consumer.

EXAMPLE

Comparing prices

The Internet has placed added pressure on the fare-pricing decisions of airlines, with the growth of flight price comparison sites. These sites, examples of which include Skyscanner, Momondo, Kayak, Hipmunk and Travelsupermarket, search GDS systems and tour operator databases to identify the cheapest flights from a number of providers (sometimes limited to those who have agreed terms with the comparison site).

These Internet sites provide customers with a quick way to evaluate the lowest prices for a given route and offer hyperlinks to the site for convenient booking. The comparison sites will earn a fee for each link used, allowing the service to be offered to passengers for free.

The first step in the introduction of technology to airline distribution systems was the CRS, which provided agents and their clients with a fast and accurate indication of flight availability and fare quotations, coupled with an online reservation service.

The next step was the introduction of the GDS, in which leading airlines themselves held major shareholdings. These rapidly spread to embrace worldwide hotel, car rental and other reservations facilities, and the leading GDSs battled for market leadership in travel agents worldwide. The US systems, notably Sabre and Worldspan, compete against the two leading European systems, Galileo and Amadeus.

The key to dominance in this field lies in the way in which agents make use of the information displayed. Access to a large number of major world airlines is possible using these systems, and 75–80% of all bookings are made using only the first page of information shown. Formerly, bias in the way information was displayed was declared illegal under US and EU law, but the US Department of Transportation ended restrictive regulations on the GDSs in 2004, as the airlines gradually reduced the stock they sold through this system in the wake of the 9/11 disaster, preferring to sell direct via their own websites.

In the following year, it became EU policy to allow airlines to have commercial agreements with the GDSs that resulted in their favouring certain carriers. The GDSs are, in turn, having to face the challenge of new websites; either those of the airlines themselves, or intermediaries such as expedia.com, ebookers.com and travelocity.com selling their services. These electronic retailers, the so-called **e-tailers**, have become a major force in the distribution system, particularly for the sale of late availability tickets.

The GDS companies argue that the establishment of websites by intermediaries is unnecessary, given that they themselves are utilising the Internet to provide the same range of travel products, but the intermediaries have successfully challenged these well-established and proven systems.

Apart from their own websites, airlines have also come together to organise joint websites for interactive reservations and information. The US website Orbitz was established in 2000 by five US carriers – American, Delta, United, Northwest and Continental – while the European Opodo network (initially launched by nine European airlines) followed in 2001. These offer access to hotels and car hire, in addition to airline flights. Both companies have since moved out of airline ownership and into the hands of other travel companies; at the time of writing, Orbitz is a subsidiary of the Expedia Group, and Opodo is part of eDreams ODIGEO, a group specialising in online travel.

Future developments in the technological field are likely to involve expansion into social media, with several airlines already providing customer support services through channels such as Twitter. Other initiatives have included mobile phone applications dedicated to providing quotes, taking bookings and managing the online check-in process. These mobile applications have also removed the need to print boarding passes, with tickets stored electronically on the phone and placed on scanners at security and departure gates to be read. This has a particular advantage to passengers returning home from holiday in that they no longer have to find a printer through which to produce their boarding pass after online check-in. One concern, however, is that phone failure, perhaps through lack of battery power, would render it impossible to read the pass. Still, this system does seem to be growing in popularity with passengers.

THE ROLE OF THE AIR BROKER

One comparatively little-known role in the airline business is that of the **air broker**. Air brokers act as intermediaries regarding the control of seats rather than merely their sale between aircraft owners and their customers. They provide a level of expertise to business clients, travel agents or tour operators who may have neither the time nor the knowledge to involve themselves in long negotiations for the best deals in chartering aircraft seats. They maintain close contact with both airlines and the charter market and can frequently offer better prices for charters than tour operators could themselves.

They play an important role in securing aircraft seats in times of shortage, and in disposing of spare capacity at times of oversupply. The broker takes charge of the entire operation, booking the aircraft and taking care of any technical requirements, including organising the contract and arranging any special facilities.

In their role as so-called **consolidators**, they purchase seats on scheduled airlines on demand, at discounted rates, and can sell these on to agents at the usual rates of commission. Leading companies in the UK are Gold Medal Travel, Travel 2 and Travel 4. Flight-only operators buy blocks of seats or a whole aircraft to sell wherever they can find a market. These roles are all ones that may be challenged by electronic direct booking systems.

WHAT IS THE FUTURE FOR AIR TRANSPORT?

In looking to the future, one must take into account both the short term and the long term. The short term is dominated by the need to reduce operating costs, particularly focusing on fuel efficiency.

Aviation experts agree that the development of jet aircraft has reached a plateau, with productivity and efficiency being unlikely to improve substantially.

There is growing pressure to reduce the environmental impact of flying, and pressures from the European Commission to stem the growth in total carbon emissions using a monetised trading system may go some way to stimulating further change, but this will require global agreement if it is to have substantial impact on total emission levels. Pressure on businesses to assess, limit and offset their own carbon emissions may encourage business travellers to consider alternative methods of transport, such as rail, for short journeys. However, price, speed and comfort levels on rail travel will need to improve considerably before business, and much leisure, travel is likely to make a substantial shift away from flying.

Perhaps the most interesting area of speculation is progress towards the development of hypersonic flight. The reality of space flight is with us, albeit still with a substantial cost attached. Virgin Galactic initially proposed to start scheduled suborbital flights from the Mojave Desert in 2013, carrying passengers into space for a one-hour flight, at a cost predicted to be $250,000. Even at this fare, Virgin claims that 700 customers have paid to reserve seats and many thousands more have registered their interest to fly. However, delays and accidents, including the crash in 2014 of Virgin Galactic SpaceShipTwo, with the loss of life of one of the two pilots, pushed back the start date. Some progress has been made, with a test flight taking place in December 2018, paving the way for passenger flights in

2019. Construction of a specially designed spaceport in southern New Mexico, USA, has supported the development of this new travel product.

Although few would be prepared, or able, to pay the huge sums involved to undertake these trips, research carried out by US aeronautical company Futron revealed that, while only 50 people a year would be willing to spend the equivalent of $20 million for a week in space, a further 15,000 a year would be prepared to invest $100,000 for a 20-minute suborbital ride, supporting the applications waitlisted for Branson's project. The space tourism market is predicted to be worth $1.2 billion by 2023.

EXAMPLE

The first space tourists

There is some controversy about how many non-scientists/astronauts have actually travelled into space up to the time of writing.

The American Dennis Tito is unchallenged as the first tourist into space, in 2001, followed by Mark Shuttleworth, a South African-born Briton, in 2002. American Greg Olsen took the trip in 2005 and Daisuke Enomoto, who is Japanese, followed in 2006.

Those space travellers are thought to have paid between £11 million and £20 million for the privilege. Others to have made the journey, however, include Anousheh Ansari, the first female space tourist, Toyoshiro Akiyama, a journalist for the Tokyo Broadcasting System, who did so in 1990, and Prince Sultan bin Salman, the head of the Supreme Commission for Tourism in Saudi Arabia.

In 2018, Space X (a competitor of Virgin Galactic) announced the name of the first space tourist being awarded the opportunity to fly around the moon: Yusaku Maezawa, a Japanese billionaire entrepreneur and art collector. Although originally scheduled to take place in 2018, technical challenges have delayed the planned departure date.

There are other organisations also working to enter the space tourism market, despite the huge capital investment costs required and the safety hurdles to be overcome. Investment, encouraged by the Ansari X prize, a $10 million competition for the first non-governmental, reusable manned spacecraft (won in 2004 with the successful launch of SpaceShipOne), has been made by Blue Origin, Space X and Space Adventures, the latter two having announced plans to offer travellers a lunar visit.

QUESTIONS AND DISCUSSION POINTS

1. Manufacturers of the Airbus A380, commonly configured for fewer than 600 passengers, have struggled to find airlines willing to operate this aircraft. Have we reached a peak in terms of aircraft size?
2. How can airport capacity be increased to meet the growing demand for air travel?
3. Why might a company choose to use the services of a private jet hire company rather than send their senior management on business-class flights?

TASKS

1. Interview ten people who have booked a flight over the past 12 months. Investigate the factor that influenced them to choose one flight ahead of others, particularly considering choices made regarding departure/arrival airport, flight times, full-service or low-cost carrier, price, loyalty schemes and method of booking. What can be concluded from your findings?
2. After years of research and development, space tourism is reaching a point whereby regular flights may soon commence. Investigate the latest news for this sector, to consider the different types of space tourism product offered. Summarise your findings in a poster.

WEBSITES

Airport Operators Association: www.aoa.org.uk

Civil Aviation Authority: www.caa.co.uk

International Air Transport Association: www.iata.org

REFERENCES

Aeronautics and Space Engineering Board (ASEB) (1968) *Civil Aviation Research and Development: An assessment of federal government involvement*. Washington, DC.

Airports Council International (ACI) (2018) *Airport Economics Report*. Brussels: ACI.

Airports Council International (ACI) Europe (2016) *The Ownership of Europe's Airports*. Brussels: ACI.

Atkins, R. and Weinland, D. (2017) Airport retailers look to make every minute count. *Financial Times*, 4 August.

Bureau Van Dyke (2018) *FAME: Key financials and employees*. Available online at https://fame4.bvdinfo.com/version-2019626/fame/1/Companies/Report/seq/0 [Accessed December 2018].

Centre for Asia Pacific Aviation (CAPA) (2018) *Record Global Aircraft Deliveries in 2017: Boeing ahead of Airbus again, but behind on order backlog*. Available online at: https://centreforaviation.com/analysis/reports/record-global-aircraft-deliveries-in-2017-boeing-ahead-of-airbus-again-but-behind-on-order-backlog-393914 [Accessed December 2018].

Chance, K. (2010) Aviation has evolved with Airbus's ultra-quiet titan. *Business Day* (South Africa), 3 March.

Department for Transport (DfT) (2017) *UK Aviation Forecasts*. October. London: DfT.

Euromonitor (2017) *Consumer Expenditure on Air Travel*. London: Euromonitor.

European Commission (EC) (2011) *Impact Assessment of Revisions to Regulation 95/93*. Brussels: EC.

Fenwick Elliott, A. (2018) How long does it take to turn a plane around – and what's the fastest way to board? *Daily Telegraph*, 27 March.

Ghaddar, A. (2018) *Jet Fuel Hedging Positions of European Airlines*. Available online at: https://uk.reuters.com/article/airlines-fuel-hedging/table-jet-fuel-hedging-positions-of-european-airlines-idUKL5N1T144K [Accessed December 2018].

Gilo, D. and Simonelli, F. (2014) The price-increasing effects of domestic code-sharing agreements for non-stop airline routes. *Journal of Competition Law and Economics*, 11 (1), 1–15.

Greenwood, M. (2018) *Two Unwanted Airbus A380s to Be Scrapped*. Available online at: www.engineering.com/AdvancedManufacturing/ArticleID/17016/Two-Unwanted-Airbus-A380s-to-Be-Scrapped.aspx [Accessed December 2018].

Haylen, A. and Butcher, L. (2017) *Airport Slots: Briefing paper no. CBP488*. London: House of Commons Library.

Hetter, K. (2013) *Airlines Collect $27 Billion beyond Ticket Revenue*. Available online at: http://edition.cnn.com/2013/06/05/travel/ancillary-revenue-fees-airlines [Accessed February 2015].

IndustryWeek (2017) The *IndustryWeek* 1000. Available online at: www.industryweek.com/industryweek-1000/2017-industryweek-1000?full=1 [Accessed December 2018].

Ishak, S. (2018) World airline rankings. *Flight Airline Business*, July/August.

Lehrer, A. (2014) *Aerion Corporation makes flying crazy easy with supersonic business jet*. Available online at: http://hauteliving.com/2014/07/aerion-corporation-makes-flying-crazy-easy/507023 [Accessed December 2018].

McCartney, S. (2012) How airlines spend your airfare. *Wall Street Journal*, 6 June.

McCaughey, N. C. (2014) *'Not just a pie in the sky': An investigation into the cash-equivalent value of loyalty currency and the impact of a frequent flyer program on its members*. PhD thesis, Victoria, Monash University.

Morris, H. (2017) 58,000 miles and 46 flights: A week in the extraordinary life of a modern aircraft. *The Telegraph*, 13 October.

New Europe (2011) The slot machine. *New Europe*, 14 March.

Robertson, D. (2008) European airlines facing profit squeeze. *The Times*, 25 April.

Tarry, C. (2002) Airline analyst at Commerzbank, reported in 'Flights of fancy'. *The Times*, 3 December.

The Economist (2014) Making Laker's dream come true. *The Economist*, 29 November.

US Department of Transportation (DoT) (2017) *Economic Impact of Civil Aviation on the US Economy*. Washington, DC: Federal Aviation Administration.

Web in Travel (WiT) (2018) *Airlines Flying High with Rising Ancillary Revenue*. Available online at: www.webintravel.com/airlines-flying-high-with-rising-ancillary-revenue [Accessed December 2018].

Webster, B. (2002) Long-haul flights on way back to Earth. *The Times*, 17 January.

West, K. (2018) Airbus 'in a holding pattern' waiting for the nuts and bolts of Brexit. *The Observer*, 14 July.

Yallop, R. (1992) People come to rescue of the people's airline. *The Observer*, 19 January.

14

TOURIST TRANSPORT BY WATER

CONTENTS

LEARNING OUTCOMES

After studying this chapter, you should be able to:

- identify each category of waterborne transport and the role each plays in the tourism industry
- explain the economics of cruise and ferry operations
- identify the markets for cruising and how cruise companies appeal to each
- recognise principal world cruise routes and state the reasons for their popularity
- be familiar with other forms of waterborne leisure transport and their appeal to tourists.

> In the cruise ship sector, vessels with over 4000 passengers and almost 1500 crew require supply chains able to service their supplies needs, carefully aligned to set itineraries, and onboard tactical planning to ensure day-to-day operations run smoothly. (Page, 2009: 212)

INTRODUCTION

The increasing size of cruise ships, along with the introduction of new routes, has led to the construction of complex support networks spanning the globe. The launch of vessels designed to reach new destinations, offering a wider variety of on-board experiences, means that the operation of the cruise industry is increasingly intricate. The industry is also designing cruise products to cater for the requirements of a younger or more active market. No longer are cruise holidays just for honeymooners, the old or the rich.

Although air travel has become by far the most popular means of travel for tourists, very few passengers treat it as anything other than the most convenient means of getting from A to B. Certainly, the frustrations that accompany this form of travel, such as airport delays, queuing and the relative lack of comfort while airborne, tend to detract from the idea that flights are an enjoyable part of a holiday. Transport by water, on the other hand, *can* be enjoyable in its own right, and for many it will be the dominant element in the holiday. When cruising, for example, the intention is not necessarily to arrive at a particular destination, but to enjoy getting there. Recent years have seen continued expansion in cruise capacity, the cruise industry now having the ability to accommodate around 500,000 passengers on more than 300 ships. Add to this the large number of passenger ferries and those vessels offering day trips or longer cruises on rivers and lakes, and it becomes evident that, whether travelling by sea or on lakes, rivers and canals, waterborne holidays have never been more popular, and shipping in all its forms is playing an ever more important role in the travel industry.

Travelling by water is inherently relaxing and cruising requires the luxury of free time, whereas air transport's appeal is largely that of speed – often critical when travelling to a long-haul destination. Although cruising has historically been seen as a more expensive form of holiday than air travel, the wide range of prices available today makes it attractive to most markets and comparable in price to many foreign holidays when the all-inclusive nature of a cruise is taken into consideration.

In recent years, cruising has staged a revival after several decades of decline, and now enjoys a level of popularity not seen since its heyday in the first half of the twentieth century. The advantages of this form of travel are total relaxation and a price that includes all accommodation, food and entertainment (and some cruises now even include drinks, excursions and gratuities – the equivalent of the all-inclusive holiday at sea). Cruises allow the passenger to be carried from one destination to another in comfort and safety, in familiar surroundings and without the need constantly to pack and unpack. Short sea (ferry) vessels have also achieved high levels of comfort and speed on many routes, to a point where they now attract tourists not just as a means of transport, but as an enjoyable 'mini-cruise'.

Technological developments have helped to reduce high operating costs, while new forms of waterborne transport have been developed, such as the hovercraft, jetfoil and twin-hulled catamaran ferry. These have provided rapid communication over short sea routes and sometimes, as in the case of the hovercraft, across difficult terrain.

The pleasure that people find in simply being afloat has spawned many recent tourist developments, from yacht marinas and self-drive motor craft to dinghy sailing in the

Mediterranean and narrow boat holidays in the UK and on the European mainland. The continuing fascination with older means of propulsion has led to the renovation and operation of lake steamers in the UK and on the continent of Europe, with purpose-built and often classic river boats operating on the Rhine and Danube in Europe, the Nile in Egypt and paddle steamers plying the Mississippi River in the USA.

In this chapter, we will investigate the appeal and operation of these various forms of water transport. It is convenient to divide them into five distinct categories:

- line voyage shipping
- cruise shipping
- short sea shipping, more familiarly known as ferries
- inland waterway and excursion vessels
- privately chartered or owned pleasure craft.

THE OCEAN LINERS

Line voyage services are those offering passenger transport on a port-to-port basis rather than as part of a cruise. Ships travelling these routes are known as **liners**. This form of transport has declined to a point where very few such services exist any longer and those that do tend to be operated on a seasonal basis. The reasons for this decline are not hard to identify.

From the 1950s onwards, advances in air transport enabled fares to be reduced, especially on popular routes across the Atlantic, to a point where it became cheaper to travel by air than by ship. The shipping lines, which, until the advent of aircraft, had no competition from alternative forms of transport, could not compete: they faced rapidly rising costs for fuel and labour. The gradual decline in numbers of passengers as they switched to the airlines led to losses in revenue for the shipping companies, which made it impossible to consider renovating ageing fleets or replacing them with new vessels.

By 1957, more passengers were crossing the Atlantic by air than by sea and the demise of the worldwide passenger shipping industry appeared imminent. Leading routes such as Cunard Line's transatlantic services, P&O's services to the Far East and Australia and Union-Castle and British India Lines' services to South and East Africa were either withdrawn or reduced to a skeleton service.

The resulting shake-up in management led to attempts to regenerate passenger demand, mainly by employing the same ships on cruises; but vessels built for fast line voyage services are not ideally suited to alternative use (many were built for the emigrant trade from Europe and offered four- or six-berth cabins without private facilities), while at the same time the appeal of cruising was beginning to decline. A small but loyal demand for sea transport remained among those (usually older) passengers who feared flying or enjoyed sea voyages and were willing to spend time getting to their destinations. Few lines were able to continue operations to serve such limited markets.

Today, only Cunard Line, among the major carriers, continues to provide a regular summer service across the Atlantic between Southampton and New York; the liner *RMS Queen Mary 2* was introduced in 2005 for this express purpose. The company launched a new vessel in 2008 – a new *Queen Elizabeth*, following the withdrawal of the earlier *Queen Elizabeth 2*. This would have enabled Cunard to reintroduce a two-ship service across the Atlantic, if demand had grown sufficiently to profit from this; however, the latter vessel, like her companion ship *Queen Victoria*, has been found to operate more profitably by undertaking cruises. Outside of the summer months, *Queen Mary 2* also cruises, although the size of all three ships limits the ports at which they can call.

Apart from this transatlantic service, line voyages devoted purely to passenger services technically no longer exist. **Positioning voyages**, in which cruise ships are moved across the Atlantic in the spring and autumn to transfer cruise operations between the Caribbean and the Mediterranean for the season, however, do allow these sailings to be sold as line voyages between Europe and Florida or Caribbean ports. Additionally, a handful of other cargo–passenger liners operate around the world, such as the Mauritius Shipping Corporation's *m/s Mauritius Trochetia*, carrying 108 passengers, which connects Mauritius with the islands of Reunion, Madagascar, Rodrigues and Agalega. Other services operate from Tahiti carrying up to 60 passengers to the Marquesas islands and Tuamoto atolls in the South Pacific, and vessels operating under subsidy from the Indian government, which connect the Indian mainland to the Andaman and Nicobar Islands.

There are a number of cargo vessels operating around the world that also accommodate up to 12 passengers. This limitation is imposed because the International Maritime Organization (IMO) requires a doctor to be carried as a member of crew if this number is exceeded. Some vessels take as few as two passengers, accommodated in the 'owner's suite', but all are clearly designed for lovers of sea travel for its own sake. Table 14.1 lists publicised routes, but freight demand means that neither departure dates nor ports of call can be guaranteed, nor can it even be certain that passengers will be allowed to disembark at the destinations en route. Entertainment is limited – in some cases, non-existent – on board and passengers dine with the ships' officers. This is not a cheap alternative for long-distance travel – on the contrary, fares on cargo–passenger vessels will be comparable to those on cruise ships – but it nevertheless attracts an enthusiastic market and passengers frequently have to 'waitlist' their requirements a year or more in advance.

TABLE 14.1 Passenger services on cargo ships

Company	Route	Capacity
PZM Polish Steamship Company	Amsterdam (the Netherlands) to Cleveland (USA)	3–5 passengers
Independent Container Line	Antwerp (Belgium) to Liverpool (UK) to Philadelphia (USA)	3–5 passengers
NSB Freighter Cruises	Felixstowe (UK) to Bremerhaven (Germany) to Le Havre (France) to Freeport (Bahamas) to Veracruz (Mexico)	5 passengers
Rickmers Linie	Houston (USA) to Philadelphia (USA) to Hamburg (Germany) to Antwerp (Belgium) to Genoa (Italy)	6 passengers
CMA CGM French West Indies Line	Rotterdam (the Netherlands) to Tilbury (UK) to Rouen (France) to Fort de France (Martinique) to Pointe a Pitre (Guadeloupe)	12 passengers
CMA CGM Australia Line	Tilbury (UK) to New York (USA) to Kingston (Jamaica) to Manzanillo (Panama) to Papeete (Tahiti) to Sydney (Australia)	6 passengers
Hamburg Süd	Long Beach (USA) to Tauranga (New Zealand) to Sydney (Australia)	4 passengers

THE DECLINE OF LINE VOYAGES

The decline of line voyages was not due solely to the rise of air transport. Enterprise was for many years restricted by the so-called 'conferences' (industry agreements) – notably the Transatlantic and Transpacific Passenger Conferences – that governed the operation of fleets worldwide and restrained open competition. Shipping management must also bear much of the blame for its failure to adapt the product to meet changing needs. Ships were built without air conditioning or adequate numbers of cabins with en-suite facilities, both essential requirements if ships were to attract the American market. The vessels' specifications and size made them inflexible and unsuitable for routes other than those for which they were built, and little was done to adapt them for other purposes.

Traffic conferences were not finally swept away until the 1970s, by which time the market was to all intents lost, and the negative image of cruising, as appealing only to the old and infirm, had become firmly ingrained in the minds of the new generation of travellers. Whether the long-term decline of line voyages can ever be reversed is debatable, although research is under way to test the feasibility of developing jet ships, capable of travelling at 40 knots or more, allowing transatlantic crossings to be completed within 90 hours. The Cat Link V catamaran made the West–East journey in 1998 at an average speed of 41.3 knots, covering the total distance in 68 hours. The reality is, however, that nothing tangible has emerged that would be capable of sustaining such speeds over these periods of time in the years since jet ship technology was first mooted.

CRUISING

Although line voyages were also in popular use for leisure trips, and P&O were marketing their ships for Mediterranean cruises by the mid-nineteenth century, the concept of the purpose-built cruise ship did not arrive until the beginning of the twentieth century. The first such ship, Hamburg-Amerika Line's 4400-ton *Prinzessin Victoria Luise*, went into service in 1900, but had a lifetime of only six years.

The cruise market emerged gradually, to a point where the ultimate cruise aspiration was a round-the-world voyage. The 42,300-ton *Empress of Britain* was launched in 1931 specifically to attract passengers to out-of-season round-the-world voyages, but the intervention of the Depression restricted demand. Shorter voyages from US ports became popular around this time, with the advent of Prohibition, as demand was created by the fact that alcohol could be consumed legally once the ship entered international waters. Later, these sailings were extended to Bermuda, Nassau in the Bahamas and Havana, Cuba.

EXAMPLE

Measuring the size of a ship

The size of all vessels is based on their gross registered tonnage (GRT), but it is inaccurate to refer to the 'weight' of a ship. That is because 'gross tonnage' refers to the volume of the vessel's enclosed spaces rather than its weight or displacement. One ton is equal to 100 cubic feet (a measure formally laid down in the Merchant Shipping Act, 1854). Net registered tonnage is the internal volume devoted to passenger and cargo space only, excluding any non-revenue-earning space, such as the engine room, crew accommodation and so on.

As examples, Cunard's *RMS Queen Elizabeth* has a gross registered tonnage of 90,900 and can carry 2068 passengers, and her sister ship *RMS Queen Mary 2* is 151,400 GRT, accommodating 2620 passengers.

The growth of cruising was delayed by World War II, but in the immediate aftermath cruising again became popular. From the 1950s onwards, the passenger shipping industry shifted its emphasis from line voyages to cruising. However, this was not without some difficulty, as vessels were for the most part too large, too old and too expensive to operate for cruising purposes.

During the 1960s and 1970s, the most popular size of ships built for cruising were between 18,000 and 22,000 tons, capable of carrying some 650–850 passengers. However, changes in demand and advances in marine technology have enabled cruise ships to be purpose-built in a variety of sizes, and, providing there is sufficient demand, optimum profits can be achieved by employing larger vessels. These burn relatively little extra fuel and, proportionally, no more crew, so adding extra passenger capacity lowers the cost per passenger. The trend since the 1980s has therefore been to build ships of steadily increasing tonnage, first in the range of 50,000–70,000 tons and later in excess of 100,000 tons, capable of carrying as many as 4000–6000 passengers. After the 1970s, it also became popular for companies to return older ships to the shipyards for 'stretching' – that is, cutting the vessel in half and inserting a new section to increase capacity.

More recently, a polarisation of cruise ships has developed, between, on the one hand, very large vessels and, on the other, much smaller vessels, often operated by niche companies. The trend towards larger sizes is putting a strain on port facilities and requires significantly increased investment, especially in the Caribbean, the cruise market's most important destination.

EXAMPLE

The explosion in the global cruise market

In 2018, 27 new ships of substantial size were introduced to serve ocean, river and other speciality cruising. This raised the global fleet (those lines with membership in the Cruise Lines International Association (CLIA), the official body promoting cruising) to 449 ships (up from 410 in 2014). A further 54 ships, adding over 170,000 beds, are scheduled to join this fleet during the period of 2019–26. The phased withdrawal of older vessels, coupled with a growing demand (an estimated 28 million passengers cruised in 2018, up from 19.1 million in 2010), will help to compensate for this increase in supply.

Of the 28 million passengers selecting cruises, 35.4% chose the Caribbean as their destination, 15.8% the Mediterranean, 11.3% other European destinations, 6.0% cruised the Australasian region, 6.0% visited China, 4.4% Asia (excluding China), 4.3% chose Alaska, 2.1% South America and 14.7% other destinations.

The cruise market is now dominated by only a few players, with two companies serving two-thirds of the global cruise market: Carnival Corporation and Royal Caribbean International (RCI). These are followed, in terms of passenger numbers, by Norwegian Cruise Line, MSC Cruises and Genting Hong Kong

Source: CLIA, 2018a

In fact, as the example above confirms, cruise companies have enjoyed exceptional market growth in recent years, and, with forecasts at the time of writing suggesting further global growth, reaching 39 million passengers by 2027, prospects remain generally healthy.

More than half of all cruises operate out of US ports, and Americans represent the majority of cruise passengers globally (see Table 14.2). However, the Western European market comprises over 6 million passengers cruising each year and the increase in demand for cruising is predicted to come principally from the European and Asian regions.

Among European passengers, the typical length of a cruise is 7–14 days, with an average cruise length of eight days (CLIA, 2018b), many choosing routes in the Mediterranean, Canary Islands or Baltics. Barcelona (Spain) and Civitavecchia (close to Rome, Italy) both received more than 2 million cruise passengers in 2016, while 1.6 million visited Venice, and Marseilles, Naples and Dubrovnik all received in excess of 1 million passengers. In Northern Europe, St Petersburg, Tallinn and Stockholm received around half a million cruise passengers each.

TABLE 14.2 International cruise passengers, 2016

Country of origin	Passenger numbers
USA	11.5 million
China	2.1 million
Germany	2.0 million
UK	1.9 million
Australia/New Zealand	1.3 million
Canada	0.8 million
Italy	0.8 million
France	0.6 million
Brazil	0.5 million
Spain	0.5 million

Source: CLIA, 2018a

The majority of cruise ships built today are constructed by just four companies: Fincantieri in Italy, STX Europe (with its principal base in Saint-Nazaire, France), Meyer Werft, whose principal base is at Papenburg, Germany, and Mitsubishi in Japan (although this latter shipwright has announced it will stop constructing large passenger vessels). Other yards in Finland, South Korea and Japan are responsible for most of the rest of the world's fleet. With building costs that can go as high as $1 billion, more than twice the cost of a superjumbo aircraft, these ships represent a huge capital investment for their owners.

The whole concept of a cruise holiday has changed from its traditional image. Cruise ships are coming to be seen as floating holiday resorts that conveniently move from one destination to another, offering new scenery every day and non-stop entertainment on board. The very large tonnage not only allows a vast range of public rooms, which on the newest ships include facilities for climbing walls and ice-skating rinks, but also ensures that passengers have the widest conceivable choice of acquaintances to meet and make friends with on board.

EXAMPLE

Cruise ship innovation

On its maiden voyage from Barcelona in March 2018, the Royal Caribbean International's *Symphony of the Seas* became the largest passenger ship ever, at 362 metres. With a gross tonnage of 228,000, it is capable of transporting 6680 passengers and has 2200 crew. To entertain passengers, the ship includes the following:

- two surf simulators
- glow-in-the-dark Laser Tag
- a zipline
- ice skating
- a children's adventure science lab
- a dual water slide
- a rock climbing wall
- mini-golf
- a fairground carousel.

In addition, the cruise ship contains more than 40 bars and restaurants, more than 20 pools and jacuzzis, two theatres, a spa and gym, a casino and extensive shopping opportunities.

In keeping with this desire to differentiate the product, shipping lines are focusing on novel forms of interior decor. The Norwegian Cruise Line, to take one example, has restyled its freestyle ships with cabins that more closely resemble rooms found in modern art hotels, with curved walls and open bathrooms.

At the other end of the scale, a market has opened up for vessels of typically 3000–10,000 tons, carrying around 60–250 passengers. Many of these are aimed at the luxury end of the market, including vessels such as *Le Levant* (90 passengers), the *Clipper Odyssey* (128 passengers) and, slightly larger at 8000 tons, *Le Diamant*, which carries 226 passengers. In 2018, two smaller cruise companies, MSC and Silversea (the latter now owned by Royal Caribbean), typically carrying fewer than 1000 passengers, placed orders for seven vessels of this size for delivery after 2020.

Many of the smaller ships provide a yacht-like form of cruising for those who are prepared to pay the higher prices these vessels need to charge. They frequently attract wealthier over-55s who seek more adventurous destinations such as Greenland, Antarctica and the Amazon, and often do not accept young children. Many of these ships are able to enter harbours far smaller than would be possible for the traditional cruise ships, opening up new ports of call for cruising, such as Seville on the Guadalquivir River in Spain, Chicoutimi on the Saguenay River in Canada or the further reaches of the Amazon River and Iquitos in Peru. Small ships can also negotiate constricted canals, such as the Corinth Canal in Greece and the Panama Canal, neither of which is navigable by the larger cruise vessels. Small ships with ice-strengthened hulls can also penetrate deeper into Antarctica, visiting the Ross ice shelf.

There is another important issue relating to the size of cruise vessels and that is the question of their **sustainability**. It is debatable whether building ever larger cruise ships is an appropriate strategy for the tourism business, even if they are profitable. In purely practical terms, the effect on small island economies of vessels disgorging up to 5000 passengers simultaneously at a port and within a strictly limited time period, must be judged against any possible benefits of the visitor spend for the local economy there. Furthermore, the logistics and viability of putting such large numbers of people ashore and organising shore excursions for them is another factor that must be weighed up carefully. Passengers are reluctant to queue up for two hours or more in order to go ashore or return to their vessels. Some of the more popular ports like Dubrovnik and Venice can experience four or more of these vessels arriving on the same day, with up to 20,000 passengers engulfing the town, making normal sightseeing almost impossible. Notably, the Venice authorities have decided to ban larger vessels from the Grand Canal after 2020, diverting them to dock at nearby Marghera, an industrial town of little appeal to tourists.

EXAMPLE

Cruise ships descend on Orkney

This comparatively remote Scottish group of islands has seen the number of cruise ships calling at its ports increase in recent years, with more than 168 scheduled to arrive in 2019. This would mean total passenger numbers reaching some 125,000. This is a substantial increase on the 36,000 arriving in 2011.

In 2017, every three weeks between June and September saw the arrival of the *MSC Preziosa*, en route from Iceland to Hamburg, with up to 4345 passengers on board. The ship was in dock for ten hours, and during that time local tourism agencies and businesses would collaborate in their efforts to ensure that the attractions, restaurants, cafés and souvenir shops maximised their benefits from these visitors, while trying to ensure that the islands were not overwhelmed by this short-term arrival of cruise passengers; but an influx of such proportions is not without its challenges.

CRUISE ROUTES

Broadly, the world's major cruise routes are located in seven regions of the globe (see Figure 14.1). These are:

- Florida, the Caribbean, Bermuda and the Bahamas, including the coastal towns of North, Central and South America
- the West Coast of Mexico, the USA (particularly Alaska) and Canada, plus Panama Canal transit
- the Mediterranean, divided between the western and eastern sectors
- the Pacific islands and the Far East
- the Baltic Sea, Northern European capitals and the west coast of Norway as far north as the North Cape – extensions to Svalbard, a Norwegian island territory north of the Arctic Circle, are rising in popularity, as are cruises to Arctic regions such as Iceland and Greenland, which are easily accessible from both Europe and North America
- West Africa and the Atlantic islands of the Canaries, Madeira and, increasingly, the Azores – occasionally, this is extended to the Cape Verde Islands
- round the world (usually permitting short-leg bookings).

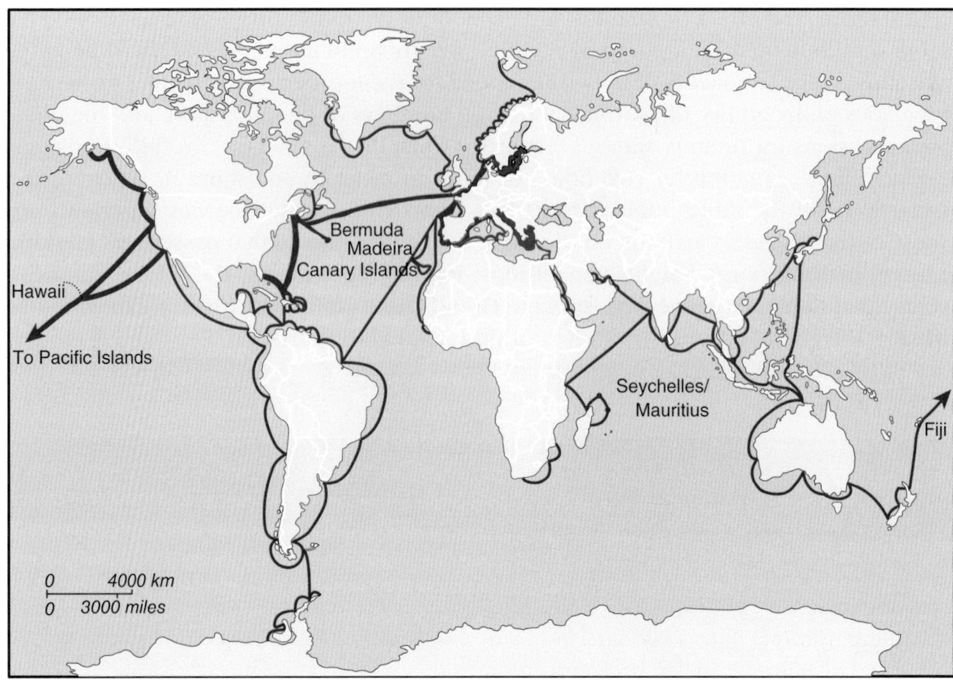

FIGURE 14.1 The major cruise routes of the world

Fly-cruises have enabled long-haul routes to become popular for those with more limited time to spare. These allow the development of routes from the East Coast of the USA to Central America, especially Costa Rica and the Mexican East Coast, the East Coast of the South American continent and cruises around New Zealand (the latter being a popular route for the Australian market). Dubai has successfully developed its cruise port facilities, handling round 625,000 passengers annually, while Cape Town is a popular starting point for cruises around southern Africa. Singapore is promoting itself as a major shipping hub for cruising, with interest rising in ports along the Indian coast, Hong Kong and the Indonesian 'spice islands'. River cruises in the USA, Europe and Africa are also gaining in popularity, as are the Antarctic, the Middle East and Trans-Pacific itineraries.

EXAMPLE

The Chinese cruise market

As previously noted, China has become the world's second-largest market for cruise travel. The market grew some 70% between 2013 and 2016 and now exceeds 2 million passengers annually, with 96% of Chinese cruise passengers choosing itineraries that visit Asia.

Ten Chinese ports, including Shanghai, were departure points for nearly 1000 tours in 2016. Consequently, global cruise operators are striving to capture the market opportunities here. Costa Cruises (part of the Carnival Corporation) started offering tours to the Chinese market in 2006 and RCI has based the *Quantum of the Seas*, built in 2014, in Shanghai, to capture a share of the growing middle-class market in this country.

Several ships have been redesigned to provide amenities to meet the demands of Chinese consumers. However, recent turbulence in the market has seen global cruise operators shift some of their fleet away from China. Of substantial impact, the political dispute with South Korea in 2017 resulted in a travel ban that stopped cruises visiting this country, popular on many itineraries. Consequently, the *Norwegian Joy* and *Majestic Princess*, both constructed specifically to serve the Chinese market, are no longer based in China year-round.

Source: Weissmann, 2018

The Antarctic Peninsula is experiencing strong growth, often as an extension to South American ports of call and combined with calls at South Georgia and the Falkland Islands. Vessels bound for Antarctica are expected to meet the requirements necessary for the extreme conditions they will encounter (although these cruises are limited to Southern Hemisphere summer periods), with specially reinforced hulls. Ushuaia in Argentina has become the principal base for these vessels and is now of economic importance as a tourist destination, both as a port of departure for Antarctic-bound ships and as a gateway to the Tierra del Fuego National Park.

In the UK, round-Britain cruising has also achieved a measure of popularity in recent years. In addition to calls at the mainland and Ireland, these sailings often include visits to Shetland, Orkney, the Hebrides and the Faroe Islands, with occasional forays to remote outposts such as St Kilda, a group of islands now without permanent residents.

Most routes are seasonal, which means that shipping companies may be obliged to move their vessels from one region of the globe to another to take advantage of peak periods of cruising demand. These positioning voyages, as we have noted, are then sold as long cruises or even as line voyages where transatlantic sailings are involved, although they might include a call at mid-Atlantic islands such as the Azores or Cape Verde islands, both of which are rapidly developing a tourism infrastructure in their own right. Baltic and North Cape cruises are operated during the Northern Hemisphere's summer period, with visits to the North Cape programmed to coincide with the high summer when passengers can experience the midnight sun. Alaskan cruises are similarly programmed through the summer months.

American cruise passengers are generally cautious about foreign travel and have always shown a preference for cruising in their own waters or those nearby. The on-board culture and currency are often US-orientated and Americans, until recently, were not required to carry passports for cruises to the Caribbean – an important selling point when only a small minority of the population owned a passport. The Caribbean also benefits from the proximity of the islands to the American mainland, as well as a climate that allows year-round cruising, although the winter's more temperate climate attracts the highest level of demand. Ports in Florida, such as Fort Lauderdale, Miami/Port Everglades and Port Canaveral, have become key bases for cruise ships, with Port Canaveral embarking a record 4.5 million passengers in 2017. Demand from Europe, too, is such that charter flights from Europe now provide connections with many of the vessels sailing from Florida's ports.

Fly-cruising has made a significant contribution to the growth of cruising from European countries. Passengers are carried by the cruise company on chartered aircraft to a warm-water base port from which they can directly embark on their cruise or spend a few days at a nearby resort before or after the cruise. This ensures that passengers can be enjoying the sunshine and calm seas of the Mediterranean or Caribbean from day one of their cruise holiday. In recent years, however, the demand for direct embarkation has remained strong enough within Europe for several companies to position their vessels at ports such as Southampton or Bremen, at least for the summer season. In 2015, 840,000 of all UK cruise passengers chose a cruise that sailed directly from a UK port against a total of 949,000 choosing a fly-cruise holiday (Mintel, 2016). This is a ratio of 47%:53% UK port departure versus fly-cruise departure, a significant change from 2008 when the ratio was 38%:62%.

The search for new destinations has led to the opening up of ever more adventurous cruise routes. Emulating American adventure cruises, companies such as Noble Caledonia and Jules Verne pioneered Pacific inter-island cruises and voyages in the Arctic and Antarctic regions, often using smaller, purpose-built vessels. They and other specialist operators also charter Russian vessels with specially strengthened hulls to penetrate further south along the Antarctic shores.

Such cruises are still largely aimed at the top end of the market, though, with prices starting as high as £500 or more a day. 'Ultra luxury' cruises, categorised using criteria that include passenger capacity (between 100 and 1000), a crew to passenger ratio of 1:2 and at least 40 square metres of space for every passenger, has seen an increase in market size over the past five years. In the UK, almost 2% of cruise customers fall into this category, often paying over £5000 for their cruise. Recently, the large mainstream cruise operators have been acquiring these luxury brands to gain access to this high-spending market; for example, in September 2014 Norwegian Cruise Line purchased Prestige Cruises International, parent company of the luxury Oceania Cruises and Regent Seven Seas Cruises.

EXAMPLE

Ultra-luxury cruising

The World – a £182 million investment project by ResidenSea – represents a new departure for the cruise industry. This 43,500-ton ship (see Figure 14.2) was built in 2002 as a floating apartment block, with individual apartments priced between £1.5 million and £5 million sold off to wealthy investors as second homes (plus operating fees for apartment owners believed to be in the region of $20,000 per month). The original intention was that these were to be used mainly for their own pleasure, with the owners joining the ship at any point during its itinerary.

Initial sales were slow, so it was decided that some of the apartments would be sold for short legs only, while others would be made available for commercial rent to cruise passengers. Prices were set at the highest end of the scale, but resident owners were disappointed at the resultant mix of private ownership and commercial rental. The original financial backers were bought out by the owners, who now administer the ship's operations themselves. Over 100 families, from 45 countries, own the 165 apartments and decide on the itinerary for the vessel. *The World* has transited the Northwest Passage though the Arctic as well as breaking the record for the most southerly navigation in the Antarctic's Ross Sea.

FIGURE 14.2 ***The World* – cruising into London**

Photo: Claire Humphreys

Two further luxury residence ships have been announced. The first project, Quintessentially One, involves construction of a 45,000-ton, 220-metre luxury super yacht that will provide 12 triplex apartments and a 500-room luxury hotel. The development was promoted as a members-only cruise ship. The second project, Utopia, is to become a 108,000-ton vessel with 190 residences and a 206-bedroom hotel. However, meeting the original planned launch dates (2013 and 2016 respectively) have proved impossible, with lack of funding for these vessels holding up construction.

For further information, see: www.aboardtheworld.com; www.quintessentiallyone.com, www.utopiaresidences.com

THE NATURE OF THE CRUISE MARKET

The thought of a cruise still carries, for many holidaymakers, two distinctly negative images. On the one hand, cruise ships are thought to be peopled by conservative, rather elderly passengers who choose to spend their days at sea playing bridge or sitting on steamer chairs covered with blankets, while on the other hand, at the cheaper end of the market, the image is one of ships as floating holiday camps, peopled by hyperactive, extrovert middle-aged passengers propping up the bars, looking for non-stop entertainment and enjoying five-times-a-day opportunities to eat, in between shipboard romances. While undoubtedly such stereotypes exist, and some shipping lines cater for each of these, such images are far from being an accurate general picture of cruising today.

The key factors that determine cruise demand can be identified as price, length of cruise and ports visited, but there are a number of other factors contributing to people choosing one cruise over another, not least the efforts made by the shipping companies to appeal to niche markets through their ship design, on-board activities and brand image. Unlike other sectors of the travel industry, cruising is a product that enjoys strong brand loyalty, providing a high proportion of repeat bookings, many of which are rewarded by deep discounts.

Cruise companies

Three distinct forms of cruise company have emerged to cater for this global demand:

1. There are, as we have noted, major international cruise companies that draw on global markets and are tending to dominate the industry. The US-owned Carnival is by far the world's largest cruise company with a 44% market share, having taken over many leading cruise brands, including the former UK companies P&O and Cunard. Its nearest competitor, RCI, serves 24% of the market. These two companies focus largely on the North American and European markets. Next in terms of market share are Norwegian Cruise Lines, now with nearly 9% of the market (having incorporated both Oceania Cruises and Regent Seven Seas Cruises into its portfolio), and MSC cruises with 7% of cruise passengers. The fifth player in this market is Genting Hong Kong (4% market share) operating the Star, Dream and Crystal Cruise brands (*Cruise Industry News*, 2018). This latter cruise company has a 20% share of the Asian/Pacific market.
2. There are a handful of long-established lines with few vessels, such as Hapag-Lloyd and Fred Olsen, which are strongly dependent on their home markets and tend to attract brand-loyal cruise passengers. Customer commitment may be to companies, but in some cases it may be to individual ships. This category also includes the four Disney cruise ships, aimed particularly at the family market, and a cluster of companies operating super-luxury vessels that have a more international appeal. It also includes the two ships run by Saga, which have been largely aimed at the senior citizen market. These carriers operate large vessels, but they are not behemoths, and do not seek to offer the range of activities and entertainment on board that are to be found on ships operated by the leading carriers. Their survival is due in part to the strong financial support they receive from their parent organisations. For example, the Disney Cruise Line is part of the Disney entertainment empire and Hapag-Lloyd is owned by the TUI travel empire.
3. There are niche cruise operators, generally operating much smaller vessels and with a narrower focus. Typically, these offer more adventurous destinations or activities, designed to appeal to particular markets. These operators also have intensely loyal passengers. Examples include Noble Caledonia's *Island Sky* and *Serenissima* (see example below), Voyages of Discovery's *Discovery*, Silversea Cruises' *HAS Prince Albert II* and Hebridean Island Cruises' *Hebridean Princess*. Sailings are aimed at the more sophisticated traveller and are frequently sold as cultural cruises, accompanied by experienced guides and lecturers. Smaller vessels are well suited to itineraries such as summer cruises in the Baltic, with destinations that appeal to upmarket audiences with an interest in culture. Expedition cruising, offering more adventurous destinations such as the Chilean fjords and Antarctica, in which landings are made by Zodiac tenders, calls for a more energetic (although not necessarily younger) market. These ships are often chartered or part-chartered to specialist tour operators that search out and organise ever more adventurous holiday destinations.

EXAMPLE

Noble Caledonia's *M/S Serenissima*

Serenissima provides us with a good example of niche marketing in the cruise industry. Launched as the *Harald Jarl* on the Norwegian Hurtigruten route in 1960, she is one of the oldest cruise vessels still serving, having had two complete restorations in her lifetime. Bought by Elegant Cruises of Croatia in 2002 and placed back into service as the *Andrea* following a major refit, she was transferred in 2012 to Noble Caledonia, whereupon she was given a further refit and renamed *Serenissima* (Figure 14.3).

A small ship of 2632 tons, carrying just 107 passengers, with relatively shallow draft and a strengthened hull for her former service in sea-ice waters, she has proved ideal for coastal cruising and entry into ports and estuaries not accessible by larger craft. Her small passenger capacity, however, requires high fares, and thus appeals to an upmarket and largely elderly clientele. To meet the needs of the market, the ship's focus is on cultural and wildlife cruising, with entertainment based largely on on-board lectures. Ticket prices include gratuities, excursions, unlimited free bottled water, tea and coffee and virtually all drinks.

At many landing points, and for viewing scenery or birdlife along the coast, passengers are obliged to make use of zodiacs, and this can pose a problem for the less fit among the passengers, with sea swells forcing cancellation of some calls or risking possible injury.

FIGURE 14.3 A study in contrasts: The Noble Caledonia's *Serenissima* (107 passengers) ties up alongside the jumbo cruise ship *Independence of the Seas* (over 5000 passengers)

Photo: Chris Holloway

THE ECONOMICS OF CRUISING

The present variation in the size of cruise vessels is a natural development, arising from the competition that emerged during the late 1980s as cruising once again became a popular form of travel. The losers in this competitive market were the higher-cost companies, particularly those US-owned. High labour costs and expenses incidental to flagging vessels in the developed countries have led to the demise of a number of carriers, among them Regency, Dolphin, Premier, Commodore, Crown, Renaissance, Royal Olympic and American Classic Voyages. Through growth, mergers and acquisitions, the current market leaders came to dominate the global cruise market, taking advantage of economies of scale, typically flagging their vessels in countries offering substantial tax benefits, such as the Bahamas, Panama or the Marshall Islands, and recruiting cheap labour from low-cost developing countries (the International Transport Workers' Federation estimates that more than half of all the world's cruise fleet is now registered under flags of convenience, where taxation is either low or, in some cases, nil). The huge investments that these giant corporations can make in new vessels have led to a new form of cruising holiday – the ship itself becoming the destination, with an ever-widening range of activities and attractions on board, so that calls at ports en route become almost incidental to the shipboard experience.

Cruising appeals on a number of levels: the all-inclusive nature of a cruise, in which unlimited, and often excellent, food is on offer; the general ambience on board; the attraction of travelling with 'like-minded people' with whom it is easy to make friends; the amount of baggage that can be carried; and the level of security that isolation on a ship can provide. Indeed, for those with a real fear of, or medical need to avoid, flying, cruising directly from home ports provides one means of travelling to far-flung places abroad.

Great care goes into the design of a modern cruise liner, in order to create the illusion of greater space, while still including all the facilities that maximise the revenue-earning opportunities for the shipping company, in the form of shops, hairdressing facilities, casinos and bars. The design also takes account of the preferences of the nationalities of those travelling. Cruise ships aimed predominantly at the US market, for example, tend to make greater use of plastics, gilt stairways, mirrors, neon lights and bright colours, while the more traditional European, and particularly British, market will expect greater use of wood (although safety standards at sea encourage the use of more fire-retardant materials today) and quieter, more refined decoration.

The image of cruising as an older person's holiday has faded as companies like Carnival and TUI target the traditional cruise market and reach a younger group of holidaymakers. However, the average age of British cruise passengers in 2015 was 55 years; almost two-thirds of those cruising were aged 55 and over, and only 12% were under the age of 35 (Mintel, 2016). Vessels appealing to the family market, such as those operated by the Walt Disney Company, are undoubtedly encouraging a younger market, while the more price-sensitive ships operated by the large tour operators such as TUI also attract a younger market. In the USA in particular, cruises are marketed as just another form of package holiday, comparable to an all-inclusive holiday on land. According to research, this has led to some 24% of all Americans having taken a cruise at some point in their lives (Cruise Market Watch, 2018).

Shipping companies have recognised the difficulty of appealing to varied markets and varied nationalities on the same vessel, however appealing this might be economically. Multinational passenger mixes call for multilingual announcements and entertainment on board, which will not be an attractive selling point. Passengers from different countries have differing habits and preferences in on-board food and entertainment. Those from Latin countries, for instance, prefer to take dinner later than those from the UK or USA. These differences lead cruise companies to separate markets, whether by price, brand or type of cruise offered. For example, P&O's vessels *Adonia* and *Arcadia* are reserved for adults only, while their *Oceania* was designed to appeal to passengers new to cruising, both in its style and routes. *Artemis*, introduced in 2005, is a smaller vessel of 45,000 tons with more traditional décor, designed to appeal to a conservative market.

Competition encourages shipping companies to emphasise product differentiation, while striving to build the newest ships, and to offer the latest on-board facilities to meet the expectations of an increasingly sophisticated cruise market. Entertainment has become increasingly varied, with Cordon Bleu cookery courses, acting classes, wellness at sea programmes and golf academies. One trend is to provide greater variety in catering on board. P&O's *Oriana*, for example, has introduced a pizzeria on board, while Crystal Cruises offers a choice of Italian, Japanese and Chinese restaurants on its vessels.

EXAMPLE

Themed cruises

For special events such as a product launch, it is possible to charter an entire vessel and introduce on-board activities focused around a particular theme. Frequently, however, the theme is developed by the cruise companies themselves, being designed to attract specialist audiences who will book to share the experience with other 'like-minded' passengers.

Some themes for 2019 sailings are the following:

- Star Wars cruise aboard *Disney Fantasy*
- Golf around the British Isles aboard *Crystal Serenity*
- Monsters of Rock music cruise aboard *Mariner of the Seas* operated by RCI
- World Space Week cruise aboard *Queen Mary 2* operated by Cunard.

Past themed events have included Holland America Line's Alaska Knitting Cruise and the same company's History and Genealogy cruise, RCI's Film Festival at Sea and Crystal Cruises' Forbes Cruise for Investors. This last event provides an example in which external providers and cruise companies can work together for mutual benefit.

In spite of the rise in popularity of cruising, it remains a highly volatile market and is quickly affected by adverse events, such as terrorist activities or political unrest. Cruise companies can then be obliged, in such circumstances, to reposition their vessels to other, often already congested, regions which, even with rising demand, can lead to oversupply.

Cabotage rights (controlling companies from transporting passengers within a foreign territory) extend to shipping operations as much as they do to airline operations (although these rights have been abandoned within the EU, with cruise companies of member states being free to determine their own routes within the EU). In other parts of the world, vessels of foreign registry are not permitted to carry passengers between two ports within the same country, nor in some cases to carry passengers from and back to the same port without an intermediate port of call in a foreign country.

American legislation governing cabotage originated with the Passenger Vessel Services Act 1886, and later this was reinforced by the Merchant Marine Act 1920, better known as the Jones Act, which extended the ruling to cargo vessels. Briefly, non-US-registered vessels are prohibited from carrying passengers or freight between two US ports without a call at a 'distant foreign port' (Canadian ports are close and therefore not counted as foreign for the purpose of the Act). The Acts also require ships travelling on cabotage routes to be US-flagged, US-crewed, US-built and subject to US domestic labour laws (although the Act has been amended to exempt certain routes and industries). Because of the high costs associated with US flag-carriers, it has proved difficult to provide a service between points such as the US West Coast and Hawaii, or an inter-island service within Hawaii. More than 40 countries around the world still continue to enforce cabotage rules, including Canada, Mexico and Japan.

Managing costs

Cruising is both capital-intensive and labour-intensive. A modern cruise liner can easily cost more than $250 million to build, with some, such as the *Queen Mary 2*, costing in excess of $500 million (costs for a 222,000-ton vessel such as the *Oasis of the Seas* exceed $1.3 billion). The life expectancy of a cruise ship is fortunately far longer than that of an aircraft and, allowing for some rebuilding and complete interior renovation, a 50-year productive life would not be unusual. The *Queen Elizabeth 2* enjoyed a life of more than 40 years before her withdrawal from service in 2008.

Fuel burn is obviously an important consideration in overall operating costs, although perhaps not as critical as one might expect, thus efforts have been made to increase operational efficiency. RCI's Celebrity Cruise Line has repainted the hulls of its vessels with a low-drag silicone coating, reducing fuel use by 3%. New, more efficient marine engines are making an appearance, burning liquefied natural gas (LNG), which emit much lower levels of carbon dioxide and nitrous oxide. Of course, only half of the fuel used is for propulsion; the rest is used to provide electricity for air-conditioning, catering and other on-board necessities. Consequently, fluctuating oil prices can seriously affect cruise companies' profit levels.

Further economies are obtained by calling at a greater number of ports on any one itinerary and spending more time in port, both of which help to reduce fuel burn, while at the same time increasing the passengers' satisfaction. A reduction in speed also saves on fuel, but, if vessels are to travel slowly and call at numerous ports, it is essential that the ports are grouped closely together. For this reason, the Caribbean, with its many islands of differing nationality, makes an ideal cruise destination.

EXAMPLE

The bottom line

Carnival Cruise Line is by far the largest cruise company, with brands that include Princess Cruises, Costa Cruise Lines, Holland America, Cunard, Seabourn Cruise Line, P&O Cruises and AIDA. In 2017, it declared a profit of $2.6 billion on revenues of over $17.5 billion, having carried 12 million passengers. Its operational costs and revenue are broken down in Table 14.3.

We can see from this the importance of on-board revenue (adding over £4 billion) and the impact of staffing costs, accounting for 14% of operating expenditure. Improvements to fuel efficiency, as well as moderately low oil prices, meant that this accounted for about 8% of operating costs, far lower than the 14% experienced in 2014, when oil prices were close to an all-time high.

TABLE 14.3 Consolidated statement of income for Carnival Corporation

	2017 ($ million)	%
Revenue		
Passenger tickets	12,944	74%
On-board revenue	4330	25%
Tours, excursions and other	236	1%
Total revenue	**17,510**	
Costs		
Commission and transportation	2359	16%
Fuel	1244	8%
Food	1031	7%
Other on-board costs	587	4%
Tour costs	163	1%
Payroll	2107	14%
Sales, marketing and administrative	2265	15%
Other shipping costs	3010	20%
Depreciation/amortisation	1846	13%
Goodwill and trademark impairment	89	1%
Total costs	**14,701**	

Source: Carnival Corporation, 2018

The global political situation requires that ships and seaports now need heightened security, just as do aircraft and airports. Passengers and their luggage have to be checked more carefully as they board and the vessels must be guarded around the clock while in port and under way.

Vessels also need a substantial number of crew, both in passenger service and below deck; a 4- or 5-star cruise ship would carry as many as one member of crew for every two passengers, and a ratio of one to one is not unknown for the ultra-luxury cruises. As we can see with the example of the Carnival Corporation, this leads to high labour costs. As mentioned previously, cruise companies have trimmed costs by registering their fleets in developing countries and recruiting crews from countries where labour costs are low. A study completed in 2000 reported that more than half of cruise ship employees were earning less than $1000 a month (Klein, 2006). Some large companies have also reduced the ratio of crew to passengers, aiming to deliver a 3-star, rather than 4- or 5-star, service.

EXAMPLE

Cunard's transatlantic service

One example of effective cost reduction in shipping operations was demonstrated by Cunard, which, in 1996, took the decision to extend the journey time for its *Queen Elizabeth 2* between the UK and New York from five to six days.

While this achieved significant savings in terms of fuel burn, reducing the average speed from 28.5 knots to 23 knots, it also offered other advantages, in marketing terms. A higher on-board spend was encouraged, while the passengers themselves saw an additional day's cruising as an added benefit. It also allowed the ship to arrive at a more convenient time of day for those with onward travel arrangements. This policy remained in force with the introduction of the *Queen Mary 2*, and its economic success encouraged Cunard to add a further day to some crossings from 2010 onwards, making all crossings seven-night voyages.

Costs can be reduced by putting passengers ashore by tender (ship's launches), rather than tying up alongside. This may be a cheaper alternative when ports are pushing up mooring fees, but it does delay disembarkation and is a less attractive selling point. Furthermore, competition has forced the leading companies to speed up their turnaround times at their home ports between cruises. Some turnarounds have been reduced to as little as 12 hours, although concern has been expressed that such tight scheduling does not allow for adequate cleaning between cruises, risking the spread of on-board diseases such as the Norovirus, which has plagued the shipping companies in recent years.

Companies operating large fleets can also obtain some economies of scale by reducing the cost per unit of their marketing and administration. It is also more economical to operate large ships rather than small ones. For 5-star operators such as Silversea Cruises, this highlights the challenge: high levels of profitability are hard to achieve when capacity is low, but any increase leads to difficulties in delivering the expected high standards of service. Thus, optimum viability for the luxury end of the market is believed to be achieved with vessels of around 25,000 tons, carrying a maximum of 400 passengers.

The largest ships are able to pare costs by providing smaller cabins, with larger areas given over to public use. This provides space for shopping and other sales opportunities that, together with shore excursions, make up around one-third of a cruise line's revenue. Dining rooms accommodate large numbers within relatively confined spaces, either by having two sittings for meals or providing only large tables (tables for two are rare on board many ships). Some companies have capitalised on this, however, by designing their ships to permit *all* passengers to be accommodated in the restaurant at a single sitting – an attractive marketing advantage.

Earning revenue

One feature that the cruise industry shares with the airline industry is the highly fluid pricing structure that it has adopted. Deep discounting has become the norm for nearly all cruise lines, with discounts for early bookers, last-minute bookers, loyal clients, even for readers of certain newspapers and magazines. Identical cabins will be sold at different fares in the UK, continental Europe and North America – the result, the shipping companies insist, of market conditions, although website searches by passengers are reducing this differential. Most cruises are sold through travel agents and they, in turn, may offer discounts and incentives to secure the booking, on top of any discounts offered by the principal; however, shipping companies are in many cases now resorting to selling cruises to agents at the full retail price, limiting opportunities for the agent to undercut direct sales. With a wide variety of cabin types, and only minimal distinction between each, opportunities for 'up-selling' are provided if lower-quality cabins are unavailable.

One impact on the total revenue earned from cabin sales is set by the lifeboat capacity. Occupancy rates for cruise ships often exceed 100% because cabins are designated as holding two people, yet often children are accommodated in the same cabin. However, every ship is allocated a maximum capacity based on lifeboat seats. This means that if large numbers of cabins are reserved with more than two adults, the capacity can be reached well before all cabins are sold. This is factored into the design of the ship; for example, the *Disney Magic* ship has 877 cabins and 2713 lifeboat seats (Biehn, 2006) – this must also be factored into the fluid pricing calculations.

Cruise lines have to ensure that their ships are used for the maximum amount of time during the year (just as airlines do), although this does not necessarily mean that they are used only for cruising. Some companies charter cruise ships to tour operators, while others have successfully chartered ships for use as floating hotels when accommodation pressures force tourist destinations to find alternative accommodation for special events. The German passenger ship *Deutschland* was berthed in London during the 2012 Olympics to accommodate guests of the German Olympic Sports Confederation. This represents a substantial saving on operating costs for the companies concerned as the period of charter requires no use of fuel.

As we can see from the Carnival Corporation example above (Table 14.3), on-board sales can account for a quarter of revenue earned by many cruise companies. Predominantly, this is achieved through bars and casinos. The latter, now a frequent addition to ships, are often operated by a concessionaire, who pays a fee and a percentage of the profits to the cruise operator. Historically, the prices of drinks on board were kept low as companies passed on the duty-free discounts, but now it is more common for prices to be in line with those found in hotel bars. Estimates have put profits as high as 80% on the price of drinks, and this is maximised by the ban many cruise lines set on passengers bringing aboard their own refreshments. The high prices have also stimulated a market for all-inclusive cruise holidays, as we noted earlier, which address passenger concerns that on-board spend will add significantly to total trip cost.

On-board sales will also be made in the shopping malls now common on the large ships, many of which are also operated as concessions. Revenue also comes from providing communications (such as telephone and Internet access), spa facilities and some leisure activities which charge a fee, using golf ranges or rock climbing walls, or participating in cookery lessons, for example. Some ships have also introduced 'extra tariff' restaurants and coffee bars, which can also encourage passengers to spend on board.

One other important income stream is shore excursions. It is common for more than half of passengers to disembark at ports, and many take pre-arranged excursions booked on board prior to arrival. The cruise companies, working with the providers onshore, will charge a premium rate for the convenience of tying into the schedule of the ship. Anecdotal evidence suggests that the cruise company's share of the profits can be as high as one-third of the excursion price.

EXAMPLE

Buying excursions

Shore excursions are considered such a profitable element within the cruise industry that competition is entering this sector, too. Passengers will often take an excursion at each port of call, adding significantly to the overall cost of the holiday.

(Continued)

To provide an alternative to those excursions offered for sale on board ship, a new online company – Cruising Excursions – has been established. Cruise passengers can visit its website prior to the start of their holiday and view a range of excursions specifically tailored to fit with their ship's itinerary. The company claims that prices will be up to 60% lower than on-board prices. This is not the first company to venture into this market; in the USA, several companies already exist to provide a similar service both for travel agents and to travellers directly.

To compete with this emerging sector, Carnival Cruise Lines announced a Shore Excursion Best Price Guarantee for its cruises departing from North America. This guarantee promises to provide an on-board credit for the difference if passengers find the same tour advertised at a lower price.

Finally, one other revenue stream for the large cruise lines is from the destinations visited. Ports have been known to pay bounties for landing passengers ashore. One example was Panama, which announced in 2000 that it would pay cruise companies a fee for every passenger, with the amount per head escalating as more passengers were landed. This five-year scheme resulted in more than a dozen ships introducing a stop in their itinerary. Schemes in the Bahamas and Puerto Rico have also operated along similar lines (Klein, 2006).

THE CRUISING BUSINESS

A useful rule of thumb in judging the relative luxury and spaciousness on board ship is to ascertain the size to passenger ratio (SPR), sometimes referred to as the **passenger space ratio** (PSR). This is based on the vessel's gross registered tonnage divided by the number of passengers carried. If this amounts to 20 or fewer, the ship is likely to appear crowded, while a figure approaching 60 would be considered luxurious and command high daily rates (see Table 14.4). Tonnage alone is not always an accurate guide as to the relative luxury, however. *World of Cruising* magazine points out that the *Lirica*, at 60,000 tons, has a PSR of 25.42, while the *Discovery* at 19,900 tons offers a PSR of 32.6, yet both are classed as 4-star ships.

TABLE 14.4 Comparing size and comfort of some leading cruise ships

Ships	Tonnage	Star rating	Space ratio	Passenger to crew ratio
Grandeur of the Seas	74,137	★★★★	38.00	2100/760
Oriana	69,000	★★★★	37.80	1830/760
MSC Lirica	60,000	★★★★	25.42	1600/760
Island Escape	40,132	★★★	26.50	1600/612
Black Watch	28,500	★★★★	37.45	761/310
Emerald	26,431	★★★	26.60	1100/420
Marco Polo	21,000	★★★★	24.10	800/356
Discovery	19,900	★★★★	32.60	600/325
Braemar	19,900	★★★★	26.10	727/320

Source: Modified from Voyages of Discovery brochure, 2005, based on September 2004 edition of *World of Cruising*

Distribution is all important in this competitive sector, and, although cruise operators have made full use of the Internet to market their products, the complexity of cruising makes it difficult for sales staff to acquire adequate knowledge of the variety of types of accommodation and ships available without gaining first-hand experience. In past years, the Passenger Shipping Association (PSA), the marketing arm of the passenger shipping business in the UK, has attempted to overcome this problem by mounting special campaigns to train agents through CLIA UK (Cruise Line Industry Association UK).

The larger cruise companies tend to receive greater support from travel agents, who find it easier to deal with companies owning a greater number and variety of ships and, therefore, a larger choice of both sailings and destinations. A growing number of agents, seeking ways to specialise as the commission received for other services has reduced, have switched their focus to the cruise sector, developing their competence in selling to the cruise market.

Although demand has been rising strongly for more than a decade, it has barely kept pace with the growth in supply, in terms of both the number of vessels and their overall size and capacity. This has maintained competition in the industry, with artificially high 'brochure prices' allowing the maximum price flexibility and deep discounting to clear unsold accommodation. Over-tonnage in American waters has forced cruise companies to turn to Europe to fill ships, and several companies now offer free flights to the Caribbean to join their cruise ships based there.

Carnival, in particular, has been able to attract a much younger than average market for its major division, Carnival Cruises, which offers relatively cheap cruises of short duration, using large vessels of, typically, 100,000–130,000 tons or more. They are sold as 'fun cruises', offering a wide range of on-board facilities, including shops and casinos.

Niche markets are being tapped by both the shipping companies themselves and specialist operators around the world, often using chartered vessels. Even the largest vessels find their specialist markets. For example, in 2006, the *Ocean Majesty* was chartered by Just You, for single passengers only. In the USA, operators Atlantis and RSVP offer exclusively gay cruises, while Alternative Holidays caters to a similar market in the UK. Olivia, an operator in San Francisco, has chartered ships exclusively for lesbian passengers. The *Queen Mary 2* was sold as a gay transatlantic crossing for one sailing in 2007.

EXAMPLE

Cruise ships for hire

Windstar Cruises operates a number of itineraries with its fleet of six small ships, each accommodating between 150 and 310 passengers. Their comparatively small size makes them attractive for private charter.

In 2015, the *Star Breeze*, at 9975 tonnage and 134 metres, was docked alongside many mega-yachts in the crowded harbour of Monte Carlo for the Formula 1 Grand Prix; but for this week the vessel served as a private residence, chartered by a wealthy client to share with 200 friends. The weekly cost for this charter was around $500,000.

With vessels of such size, port taxes would usually add around $70,000 to the cost but food, drink and on-board entertainment are usually included in the charter price. This is a growth market to such an extent that new vessels are now being specifically designed to allow for private charters.

Source: Ellwood, 2016

HEALTH, SAFETY AND THE ENVIRONMENT

Health and safety issues are controlled by the International Maritime Organization (IMO), which requires ships and ports to conform to internationally set standards. The International Convention for the Safety of Life at Sea (SOLAS) (1974) is the principal regulation governing standards for ships and their crew, and its directives are widely adhered to throughout the world, but the dominance of the Americans in the world cruise market and American concerns about both safety and hygiene have also resulted in strict standards being imposed on all foreign flag-carriers operating out of, or calling at, US ports. All such ships are subject to unannounced inspections by the US Vessel Sanitation Program. Vessels are rated for the quality of their water, food preparation, cleanliness, storage and repairs. An acceptable rating is 86 points out of 100, but it is not uncommon for even leading cruise ships of the world to be given grades considerably lower than this. Owners are then required to raise their standards. Scores from assessments are reported publicly at wwwn.cdc.gov/InspectionQueryTool/InspectionResults.aspx, and adverse publicity in the press is a further incentive not to fail these tests. Over the past decade, there have been numerous outbreaks of contagious diseases on board cruise ships, ranging from viral gastroenteritis to the Norwalk virus (Norovirus), and such outbreaks get maximum publicity in the world's press.

EXAMPLE

Sea sickness

The RCI cruise ship *Explorer of the Sea* broke an ignoble record in January 2014 for having the highest number of sick people on any cruise ship in two decades. With 629 passengers and 54 cruise workers ill, the planned ten-day cruise was cut short and the ship returned to port, Cape Liberty in New Jersey, USA. The ship has a maximum capacity of 3114, consequently 20% of the passengers became ill within days of sailing.

Officials from the Centers for Disease Control and Prevention (CDC) boarded the ship six days into the journey to study the outbreak and the response by the inboard medical team, with early reports suggesting symptoms consistent with Norovirus, such as diarrhoea and vomiting.

All passengers on board this abbreviated trip were offered a 50% refund and 50% discount off a future cruise. Those who were quarantined due to illness were also offered additional credit of one future cruise day for each day in confinement. Of course, these credits and discounts will require passengers to travel with the same company again, if they have the stomach for it.

Source: Karimi and Hudson, 2014

New regulations governing environmental protection are also affecting the shipping industry. Global shipping emissions of greenhouse gases are estimated to be some 1 billion tonnes a year (although this figure, of course, includes all maritime craft – container ships, tankers and so on) (Olmer et al., 2017). This represents around 2.5% of all global CO2 emissions. In North America and Europe, **Emission Control Areas** (ECAs) have been introduced, requiring the use of low sulphur fuel which reduces pollutants and emissions. Other regions are also looking at introducing restrictions to encourage the use of less polluting fuels.

EXAMPLE

The impact of sustainability legislation on Antarctic cruises

In 2011, the International Maritime Organization (IMO) introduced important new legislation to regulate ships' emissions. The International Convention for the Prevention of Pollution from Ships requires all ships built after 2013 whose tonnage exceeds 4000 to improve fuel efficiency by 10%. This is to increase to 20% by 2020/24, and by 30% thereafter.

The ruling has had a significant impact on vessels sailing to Antarctica, and led to Saga and Voyages of Discovery abandoning their calls, while Hurtigruten reduced its services to the region, and Swan Hellenic, operating just one vessel, was shortly to withdraw all its services.

Since then, the Polar Code, in force since January 2017, has extended requirements of ship design, construction and equipment to improve safety and reduce environmental pollution when operating in the inhospitable polar regions.

Illegal cleaning of tanks at sea, discharge of oil and pumping of raw sewage into the oceans has been of increasing concern in terms of their effect on the environment. The waste produced on board ships is extensive; typically 1200 tons of liquid and solid waste are produced daily on board a cruise ship (Honeywell, 2017). Cruise companies are responding by making investments in their waste treatment systems, recycling initiatives, engine efficiencies and energy-saving devices.

The original International Convention for the Prevention of Pollution from Ships, adopted in 1973 and modified in 1978 (now known as MARPOL 73/78), laid down strict controls governing the disposal of waste at sea, and these were adopted by 136 maritime countries. Further rulings on environmental pollution came into force in 2004 and 2010–11. These changed again in March 2018, amending regulations on waste disposal. As a result, ship operators will increasingly be expected to upgrade older vessels, or failing this, to invest in newer ones to address pollution and waste emissions. In 2018, the IMO agreed new emissions targets for vessels to meet by 2050; one means by which shipping companies may seek to attain these new targets is to reduce speed: a 10% reduction in speed, for example, can equate to a 20% reduction in fuel consumption.

More recently constructed vessels, designed to achieve higher standards of safety, can attract lower insurance premiums. These vessels are also more technically advanced and have lower operating costs, resulting in older ships finding it difficult to compete. On top of this, owners are also required to be bonded against financial collapse, adding to costs. In this respect, the shipping and airline businesses face similar problems. Medium-sized operators are likely to be absorbed over the next few years by the five largest companies, leaving only the niche market cruise operators to remain as independents in the field.

The expansion of the cruise business has been welcomed for the benefits it can bring to holidaymakers, shipping companies and cruise destinations alike, but there can be less attractive consequences for some popular cruise ship destinations. Responsible cruising suggests not only environmental concern but also the need to ensure that destinations receive adequate financial rewards from ships' visits. The large operators, however, are stressing on-board spend, and the construction of ships that have become virtual leisure complexes in their own right has resulted in many port destinations experiencing a decline in onshore spend, which parallels the problem faced by other destinations that have experienced expansion by tour operators of the all-inclusive holiday concept. Bigger on-board spend equates to less money being spent ashore – less expenditure in local shops, bars and transport companies. Some shipping companies have purchased their own, frequently uninhabited, islands on which they can land their passengers for barbecues and lazy beach days, ensuring, once again, that no revenue goes into the local economy. Private islands that are either owned or rented include:

- Great Stirrup Cay (NCL/Star Cruises)
- Coco Cay (RCI)
- Half Moon Cay (HAL/Carnival)
- Princess Cay (Princess Cruises/Carnival).

Larger ships also tend to attract passengers with lower incomes, resulting in a further reduction in the per person spend at ports of call, while the growth in size of cruise vessels, as we have seen, threatens massive congestion at small island ports.

Health and safety issues affect the carriage of disabled passengers, too. In 2006, the US Supreme Court ruled that the Americans with Disabilities Act applied equally to US and foreign cruise ships operating within US waters (contrary to UK regulations, where the Equality Act does not yet apply to shipping). As is the case with hotels, in order to comply with the Act, some cabins must be equipped to meet the needs of physically disabled passengers, including wider doorways for entry to the cabin and bathroom, while gangways have to accept wheelchairs. Currently, not all cruise lines accept guide dogs for the blind and some insist on disabled passengers being accompanied by fare-paying, fully able-bodied escorts to look after them. There are ample lifts on large cruise ships, but this is not always the case where river cruising is concerned, making these vessels far from ideal for disabled passengers, even though this is a form of travel likely to be favoured by both disabled and elderly tourists. Further complications arise in the case of cruise ships if landings have to be made by tender or zodiac, as we discussed earlier (the latter, large rubber dinghies, become hazardous even for the able-bodied in sea swells). Encountering rough seas can pose a threat to the disabled, whether or not they are wheelchair-bound. The question of compensation in the event of injuries then arises and whether or not exclusion clauses in contracts can overcome such threats.

BUDGET CRUISING

Although cruises are sold as package holidays in the USA and tour operators there have also played their part as intermediaries in bringing the product to the notice of the travelling public, UK tour operators, on the other hand, were in general slower to move into the cruise market. Some early attempts were made during the 1970s, when operators, including market leader Thomson Holidays, started to charter or part-charter cruise ships that they incorporated into their programme of inclusive tours, but efforts to bring down the overall price of cruising led to dissatisfaction with standards of service and operation. Two decades later, Airtours, one of the leading operators at the time, introduced its own ship, *Carousel*, with low lead-in prices and, for the first time, cruises were marketed as just another package holiday, with all meals and entertainment thrown in. Other leading operators soon entered the competition and, in 2000, RCI bought a 20% stake in tour operator First Choice to form a joint cruise company, Island Cruises, with the clear intention of using the operator's retail outlets to push cruise sales in the UK.

The entrance of these tour operators into the mass-market cruise business changed the face of cruising in the UK. Not only did the average age of cruise passengers come down, but also a whole new market was introduced to cruising. One budget cruise company, Ocean Village, claimed that 60% of its passengers were first-time cruisers. Undoubtedly, the budget cruise companies helped to account for the fact that by 2010 one in nine of all foreign package holidays booked in the UK was a cruise. Tour operators also helped to popularise the short cruise in the British mass market, which brought down cruise prices, and the seven-day, or shorter, cruise has since enhanced the appeal of this form of holiday for both European and American passengers. A major player among the tour operators is TUI, operating four ships aimed at the German market, and a further five ships operated for the UK market under the Marella Cruises brand.

THE FUTURE OF THE CRUISE BUSINESS

For all the contributions made by the mass-market tour operators, it is anticipated that most cruising will retain its upmarket image, at least within Europe. Both luxury and middle-priced cruising have been experiencing sharp rises in demand and it is these that are seen as offering the best opportunity for long-term profitability. The market for this price bracket is very loyal; both P&O and Cunard have claimed that 60–70% of their market is repeat bookings. Loyalty programmes, similar to the frequent flyer programmes offered by the airlines, also help to encourage this by offering repeat customers discounts on future trips and on-board amenities and facilities.

The future of the cruise industry in general also looks healthy in terms of growth in demand, but perhaps less so in terms of profitability, with long-term uncertainty over the cost of fuel, wages and changes required as a result of environmental protection regulations.

As we have noted, brand loyalty is strong among cruise passengers and great efforts are now made to differentiate individual ships as well, rather than depending on discounting to sell unsold cabins. Certainly Carnival, with its niche marketing to the younger holidaymakers in the USA, has led the way in this direction, while other companies have focused on theme cruising to survive. Some shipping operators have experimented with new types of vessel. Radisson, for example, introduced twin-hull catamaran vessels, while both Windstar Cruises and Club Mediterranée offer luxury sail-assisted ships to widen the appeal of cruising. Small luxury ships are also in vogue. Society Expedition Cruises offers luxury cruising for around 100 passengers to exotic destinations such as the Amazon and the Antarctic, while the similarly small (4260 gross tons) Sea Dream Yacht Club ships offer unparalleled luxury to more traditional destinations in the Caribbean and Mediterranean for just 110 passengers, with a crew of 90 and a retractable platform at the stern from which passengers may swim, snorkel or sail while the ship lies at anchor. Diving holidays from even smaller ships are also growing in popularity.

Looking to the longer term, research is continuing on designs for more fuel-efficient craft. Marine research in the short term is focusing on improving designs and finishes to reduce drag. The pressure must also be on to develop new forms of energy to propel ships, given the efforts to reduce oil consumption. As we saw earlier, liquefied natural gas is already in use for ships on short sea routes, but, unlike the automobile industry, the development of hydrogen power for seagoing vessels does not appear to be imminent.

The appeal of cruise ships that resemble floating hotels with a full range of leisure facilities has led to the construction of ever larger vessels, such as *Oasis of the Seas* and *Allure of the Seas*, with a capacity of over 6000, but whether this trend will taper off is debatable. One prediction (by Tillberg Design – the company responsible for designing the *Queen Elizabeth 2* and *Queen Mary 2*) was to see even larger vessels, carrying up to 7000 passengers, who would be carried to shore in smaller vessels, as the mother ship would be too large to enter most existing ports. Currently, however, there seems to be little enthusiasm to take this step up in size. Such ships would indeed be veritable floating hotels, with gardens on the top deck and a range of environmentally friendly additions, including solar panels to generate hot water on board.

Proposals have also been advanced for much larger catamarans and trimarans (twin-hulled and triple-hulled vessels) than those currently in existence, capable of transporting large numbers of passengers at high speed and with far more comfort, without the customary problems of motion sickness experienced with single-hull ships. It is conceivable that the construction of such vessels would allow transatlantic crossings to be completed in under 48 hours.

Finally, the impact of piracy will continue to be an issue for many cruise companies. Attacks on cargo vessels in the Gulf of Aden, off the coast of Somalia and increasingly further south off the African coast, have led to the payment of ransoms, encouraging yet further attacks. The failed attack on the *MV Seabourn Spirit* off the coast of Somalia in 2010 drew global attention to this issue, with several attacks occurring since. The cost of security for ships passing through such vulnerable areas and the impact on company image can be devastating when attacks on passenger ships occur. Some UK cruise ships travelling through the area have now armed themselves with high-pressure water canons to prevent pirates boarding.

There is another rising problem for those at the luxury level of the market. The sophisticated cruise passengers in this field are older, have travelled extensively and are seeking new destinations, while the possibilities of such destinations become fewer as political upheaval around the world and issues of security impact on carriers' choice of routes.

FERRY SERVICES

The term 'ferry' is one that embraces a variety of forms of short-distance waterborne transport. This includes urban transport in cities such as Stockholm, where people travel from the city centre to outlying suburbs and surrounding towns by water. Ferries of this type also attract tourists, who use it as either a convenient form of local transport or an original way to view the city. Some ferries, such as the Staten Island ferry, which links Manhattan with the borough of Staten Island in New York, and Hong Kong's Star Ferry, have become world famous and a 'must do' for visitors. Other notable ferry rides that serve the needs of both locals and tourists are the Bosporus ferries linking Europe and Asia in Istanbul, the many island ferries in Greece and Indonesia, the Manly ferry between Sydney and Manly in Australia, the Niteroi ferry crossing Guanabara Bay in Rio de Janeiro, the Mersey ferry in Liverpool (immortalised in various songs), the Bainbridge Island ferry in Seattle, the Alameda–Oakland ferry in San Francisco, the Devonport and Waiheke Island ferries in Auckland, and the Barreiro and Cacilhas ferries crossing the River Tagus in Lisbon. Most of these, of course, have been designed primarily to provide essential links for local commuters, but, inevitably, such transport also provides an important attraction for tourists either wishing to get a different view of a city or planning to visit more remote areas of a country, where convenient links by air may not be possible. Examples of the latter include the Greek islands, the Hebrides off the west coast of Scotland, the Isle of Wight off the south coast of England and crossing the Strait of Messina, between Italy and Sicily.

The key ferry routes for tourists, however, are those that are major links between countries separated by water, such as across the English Channel, between countries in the Baltic Sea, between Corsica and Sardinia and across the Adriatic between Italy, Greece and the Balkan countries. These routes may be vital for those wishing to take their car on holiday, but also provide an attractive alternative to flying for those with time to spare. Additionally, there are many places in the world where transport is dependent on good national ferry services, owing either to the number of islands belonging to the territory or the difficulty of reaching coastal destinations by air or land. A notable example is the west coast of Norway, where small towns cut off from land routes and air connections depend on the Hurtigruten, or express route, where daily ferries call at dozens of ports between Bergen and the North Cape. This itinerary has become so popular with tourists that full-size cruise vessels now ply the route. Other popular routes include the west coast of Canada and Alaska and the Hebridean islands off mainland Scotland's western coast.

EXAMPLE

Dubai introduces ferry services

Traffic congestion has become problematic in Dubai. To ease the problem, public transport infrastructure has been developing at a rapid pace, with a second Metro line and the Palm Monorail constructed. But to further serve local commuters and tourists to the city, Ferry Dubai has been launched. Although it is operated by the RTA (Roads and Transport Authority), the ferry is more of a tourist service operating from five termini: Dubai Marina, Al Ghubaiba, Dubai Canal Station, Al Jadaf and Sheikh Zayed Road Station. The route between Al Ghubaiba and Dubai Marina Mall station is promoted as travelling from 'the heart of old Dubai to the heart of new Dubai' (RTA, 2014). A circular trip to Burj al Arab and back runs from Dubai Marina, while a 1-hour tourist trip around Dubai Creek departs once daily from Al Ghubaiba.

Marine transport is not new to the Emirate. Dubai has long been served by Abras, long narrow wooden boats, which can each carry about 20 passengers. The boats, of which there are both motorised and rowing versions, while fairly basic, contribute to the 13 million passengers a year taking water-based transport. To manage safety issues, Dubai Roads and Transport Authority has provided official boarding stations and Abra operators must be licensed.

The significance of the short sea ferry market can be appreciated when it is learned that, by the end of the last century, some 2150 ro-ro (roll-on/roll-off) ferries were estimated to be in operation worldwide, and demand shows no sign of slackening. More than 19 million international ferry passengers travelled to and from the UK in 2017 (DfT, 2017). Of course, not all these passengers will be counted as tourists, an important point to remember. Typically, ferry services are designed to provide a communication network for local populations, while taking advantage of visitors to boost numbers and become profitable. In 2017, more than 44 million passengers travelled on domestic water routes, of which around half are river services.

In Europe, passenger ferries are concentrated in three regions: the Baltics, the North Sea and the Mediterranean, the latter providing more than half of the routes. The Mediterranean region also outnumbers the other regions in terms of operating capacity, transporting more than 450,000 passengers in 2014 (European Parliament, 2016).

In the UK, the demand for ferries over the past half century can be partly attributed to the general growth of tourism and trade in the region, especially between EU countries, but the growth of private car ownership and independent travel have also played a significant part in raising demand. There has also been a steady rise in coach transport between the UK and the Continent, as coach companies introduced long-distance coach routes linking London with the capitals and cities of continental Europe. Despite the challenge offered by the Channel Tunnel linking the UK and France since 1994, Dover remains by far the most important of the ports serving the Continent, with DFDS and P&O currently offering cross-Channel services from this port (see Table 14.5). Since the end of the last century, when passenger numbers peaked at 36 million, there has been a steady decline in passenger numbers, perhaps partly as a result of the abolition of duty-free shopping in 1999, which reduced the number of passengers taking day trips.

Good marketing by the ferry companies has played a part in stimulating traffic over the years. New routes have been developed to tap regional markets and provide greater choice, so passengers have been able to choose to travel to the Continent from a variety of ports along the south coast of England (Figure 14.4). Not all new routes have proved viable, as price competition attracts tourists to the most popular routes even if they are not the most convenient. The generally high prices charged by ferries out of Kent to the Continent (claimed to be the highest

TABLE 14.5 Ro-ro ferry journeys from UK ports

Port	Passenger numbers, 1980	Passenger numbers, 2000	Passenger numbers, 2010	Passenger numbers, 2017
Dover	10,965,000	16,078,000	13,125,000	11,698,000
Portsmouth	722,000	3,176,000	2,212,000	1,845,000
Holyhead	1,142,000	2,518,000	2,073,000	1,920,000
Hull	484,000	972,000	950,000	838,000
Harwich	1,669,000	1,335,000	620,000	667,000
All short sea routes	**23,395, 000**	**28,517,000**	**21,883,000**	**19,468,000**

Source: DfT, 2011, 2017

fares per mile anywhere in the world) were challenged by Danish company Speedferries, which undercut the prices of the established lines operating across the Channel but foundered in the economic recession experienced in the early part of this decade. Eurotunnel, too, reduced prices to attract more passengers to the land link with the Continent.

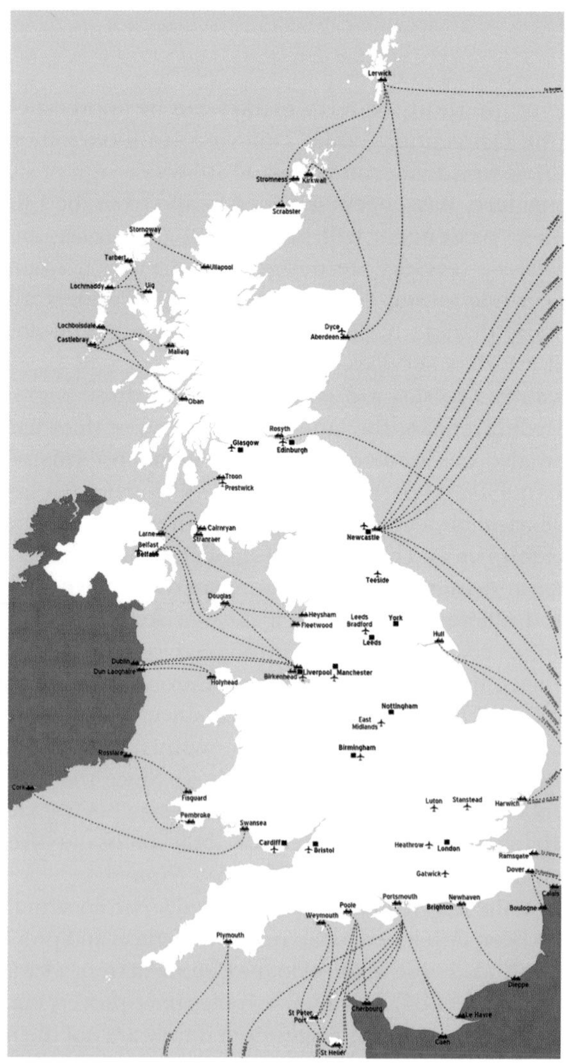

FIGURE 14.4 UK ferry routes

From the UK, routes can be conveniently grouped into four geographical regions:

- English Channel (short sea crossing) routes, including services from ports such as Ramsgate, Dover, Folkestone and Newhaven
- Western Channel routes, including services from Portsmouth, Southampton, Poole, Weymouth and Plymouth
- North Sea routes, including services from Newcastle/North Shields, Hull, Felixstowe, Harwich and Sheerness
- Irish Sea routes, including services from Swansea, Pembroke, Fishguard, Holyhead, Liverpool, Stranraer, Cairnryan and the Isle of Man.

It should be stressed that, while these have been identified as key ports, services operating out of them do vary from time to time as competition forces out some companies and others attempt to operate new routes in their place. The expectation that a route, once announced, will continue to operate for many years is no longer true. Recent years have seen a number of companies' routes fail, while others have withdrawn services or reverted to alternative ports. Even one of the oldest ferry routes, that between Newhaven and Dieppe, with a history of service stretching back to 1825, was briefly without a ferry connection until new services were introduced earlier this century.

In addition to the UK's ferry connections to the continental and Irish ports, a number of important smaller ferry services provide internal links to the Hebridean islands of Scotland, the Orkney and Shetland islands, and to the Isle of Wight, the Isle of Man, the Scilly Isles and Lundy Island in the Severn Channel.

THE ECONOMICS OF OPERATING FERRIES

As with cruising, operating short sea ferry routes is expensive, in terms of both capital investment and direct operating costs. Modern ferries on many routes are now nearly as large and sumptuous as cruise ships (see Figure 14.5) and building costs can run into hundreds of millions of pounds. Within the EU, ferries are expected to be written off over a 27-year timespan, although Greece has traditionally operated its ferries for as long as 35 years.

FIGURE 14.5 Interior of *Stena Hollandica*, operating on the Harwich–Hook of Holland route

Photo: Chris Holloway

Profitability is achieved through a combination of maximum usage of equipment and on-board sales. The termination in 1999 of duty-free sales within the EU had a significant impact on cross-Channel revenue (it had accounted for up to 50% of ferry companies' turnover), so ticket prices were forced up. Rapid turnarounds in port at the end of each journey are essential, as are round-the-clock sailings, with, ideally, an even volume of business all year round and a balanced flow of demand in both directions. In practice, this is, of course, impossible to achieve. In winter, when much of the pure holiday traffic dries up, the ferry services become very dependent on freight to contribute to their costs. Despite transporting almost 3 million passengers annually, Seafrance was declared bankrupt and ceased operations in 2012.

EXAMPLE

The importance of vehicle transportation

Ferry companies can either transport foot passengers only or they can decide to transport passengers and vehicles (which includes passenger vehicles such as buses and cars as well as vehicles carrying freight). Passenger-only ferries must earn their revenue from the sale of passenger tickets along with any on-board spend that can be encouraged, while passenger-vehicle ferries are able to charge a far higher ticket price when transporting commercial freight vehicles.

Ticket prices will depend on the level of competition (influenced by the availability of alternative routes or other ferry service providers), the type of passenger accommodation offered (cabin or seat) and the season. The size and type of any accompanying vehicle also influences price. In recent years, online ticketing has led to greater flexibility in pricing, more in line with low-cost airlines, and good marketing management has increased total revenues for many ferry operators in Europe.

However, passengers generating a low level of revenue are costly to serve; comfort, space, safety and crewing requirements lead to higher costs. By comparison, transporting vehicles often requires little more than suitable deck space in the hull and can add significantly to the revenue earned.

Sources: Kay, 2011; European Parliament, 2016

From the UK, the shorter sailings to France, Belgium and Holland attract greater market demand than the longer routes to Scandinavia, Germany and northern Spain, although some ferry companies have achieved considerable success in marketing the longer (24 hours or more) sailings as mini-cruises. Their success is modelled on the enormously popular service between Stockholm, Sweden and either Turku or Helsinki, Finland, which, in addition to providing one of the most scenic routes anywhere in Europe for a ferry service, also attracts customers through the sale of relatively cheap on-board drinks in a region where alcohol is expensive. As a result, the ferry market between these two countries has grown to a point where the two major carriers, Silja Line and Viking Line, can support a string of superferries, the largest of which, at 58,000 tons, is capable of carrying almost 3000 passengers. By including a stop at the Finnish-owned Åland Islands, which have special status within the European Community, duty-free goods can continue to be sold on board these vessels, maintaining their popularity with the short-break market.

Off-peak sailings on shorter routes can be boosted by low fares, aiming a wide range of discounted prices at differing market segments. Quick round trips on the same vessel or short stopovers of one to three nights have expanded.

At extreme off-peak periods and for night sailings, which attract fewer bookings, some ferry companies will price their sailings to make only a small contribution to fixed costs rather than attempt to cover all costs on every crossing. Some ferries offer accommodation in en-suite cabins, which provides an opportunity to earn revenue additional to the passenger fare (for example, Stena Line makes it compulsory to book a cabin on the Stena Britannica and Stena Hollandica for overnight services on the Harwich–Hook route). As well as the longer, overnight services, such facilities can be sold as ticket upgrades on mid-length routes (for example, the 4–5-hour crossing from Pembroke in Wales to Rosslare in Ireland), particularly if sailing times are in the late evening or early morning. Low fares enticing more passengers to travel will also increase on-board spend, making a useful contribution to total revenues. The ferry companies have increased the shopping facilities in their newer ships in order to boost on-board sales.

Leading ferry companies have made strenuous efforts to cut their operating costs in recent years, particularly labour costs. New labour practices were introduced to increase the efficiency of crewing, but only after serious confrontations with the seamen's union. As with cruising, many staff from developing countries are now recruited. At the same time, SOLAS regulations, which came into effect at the end of 2004 following the Stockholm Agreement signed in 1997 between the UK and six Northern European countries, have substantially added to increasing costs.

The objective of these regulations was to increase the safety and stability of ro-ro ferries, following the *Herald of Free Enterprise* disaster (it sank at Zeebrugge in 1987 and nearly 200 people died), and the subsequent sinking of the ferry *Estonia* in the Baltic in 1994, with the loss of a further 850 lives. The Stockholm Agreement requires vessels operating into and out of ports to be capable of remaining upright in waves up to 4 metres high and with 50 centimetres of floodwater on the car deck. It called for transverse bulkheads to be fitted on all ships to improve stability in rough seas, but these obligatory modifications can reduce car capacity and slow down the loading and unloading of vessels, affecting turnaround times.

Regulations controlling emissions mean that alternative forms of energy for marine vessels are receiving attention. One interesting development is that of the *Solar Sailor* – a 100-passenger catamaran ferry that was in service in Sydney Harbour between 2000 and 2010. This vessel operated with solar and wind power, with a backup electric motor running from batteries that store the energy the craft collects while running on the alternative energy sources. It is silent, smooth, creates no pollution whatsoever and its photocells are boosted 20% by the sun's reflection in the water. An innovative solar-powered catamaran, *MS Turanor*, pushed forward this technology to circumnavigate the globe, although it did take 584 days, somewhat longer than the record 45 days for sailing round the world. Since 2013 a small hydrogen-powered ferry, the *Hydrogenesis*, has been undergoing test runs in Bristol Harbour, and in 2018 it was announced that Scotland's Ferguson Shipbuilders have received EU funding to build the world's first sea-going ferry running on fuel cells.

EXAMPLE

MF Ampere

In Norway, the first ever all-electric powered vehicle ferry was launched in 2014, with commercial operations beginning in 2015. The vessel, *MF Ampere*, operates on a 5.7-km crossing between the villages of Lavik and Oppedal.

(Continued)

Its owner, Norled, which operates 80 vessels to serve routes along the Norwegian coastline, has also commissioned the construction of three hybrid ferries, which will charge batteries while in port loading freight and passengers. Once launched, these ferries will serve the company's short-sea routes. The use of battery power (supported by diesel power as backup) will substantially cut emissions on these routes.

A decade ago, only six 'electric' ships existed worldwide; now more than 200 are either in operation or under construction. This reflects the changing attitude to the environmental impact of shipping. The market for electric and hybrid vessels is expected to reach $20 billion by 2027.

Source: Stokes, 2018

THE CHANNEL TUNNEL AND FERRY SERVICES

The Channel Tunnel was viewed initially as the single greatest threat to cross-Channel ferries since their inception. Opened to passenger traffic in 1994, the Tunnel has attracted the lion's share of the cross-Channel market, but has failed to drive the ferries out of business. Over the years, it has even come close to financial collapse itself, due to the huge burden of capital debt it bears. The background to this problem is described more fully in Chapter 15, but here we will take account of the impact of this land link on ferry services.

Groupe Eurotunnel (at the time of writing being rebranded as 'Getlink' in anticipation of Brexit), which operates the Channel Tunnel, suffered a number of setbacks in building and operating the Tunnel, including repeated delays in opening, delays in obtaining equipment to run through the Tunnel and a disastrous and costly fire in a freight wagon at the end of 1996. Eurotunnel's original estimates of passenger numbers proved wildly optimistic, but nonetheless the company achieved a 51% share of the Dover Straits traffic (Dover/Folkestone to Calais/Boulogne) within its first five years of operation. Eurostar, which offers rail connections between London, Lille, Paris and Brussels via the Tunnel, has also been successful in diverting a substantial number of air travellers back to rail between these destinations.

The ferries were quick to retaliate. P&O and Stena invested heavily in their short sea operations and merged their services on the route between Dover and Calais, following investigation by the Monopolies and Mergers Commission (now merged into the Competition and Markets Authority). Improvements in passenger-handling facilities at Dover were introduced, allowing passengers to check in just 20 minutes before sailing. A 'turn up and go' service obviated the need for reservations, while, curiously, Eurotunnel itself moved to encourage more of its passengers to hold a reservation before arrival at the terminal. New, faster ferries were introduced, with the travel time between Dover and Calais reduced from 90 minutes to 75 minutes. The emphasis of its marketing shifted, selling the crossing as part of a holiday, with time to relax and unwind on board. The Tunnel was disparaged as offering no more than 'a toilet and a light bulb'. Larger, more luxurious ships on the route helped reinforce the concept of a mini-cruise, with the result that the short sea routes have held up well, although the other, longer routes suffered badly from the competition.

On the medium-distance crossings, a new generation of fast ships and catamarans came onstream. This resulted in the crossing time from Portsmouth to Cherbourg, for example, being reduced from five hours to two hours 45 minutes. Today, analysis of international arrivals reveals that the number of holidays originating at all the seaports in the UK combined is broadly equivalent to those arriving via the Channel Tunnel (see Figure 14.6).

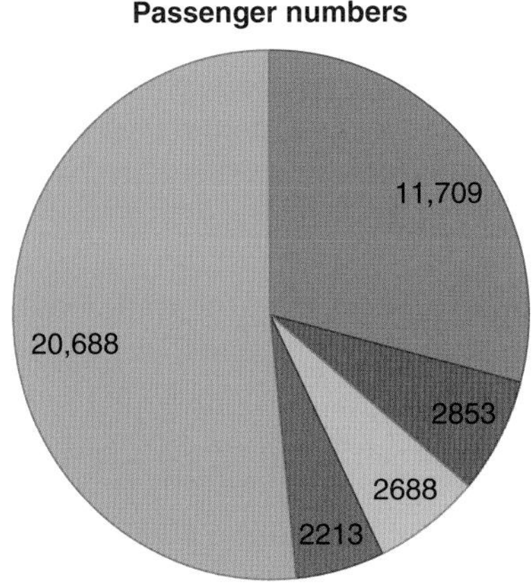

Thames & Kent – Dover and Ramsgate
South Coast – Newhaven, Plymouth, Poole, Portsmouth and Weymouth
West Coast – Fishguard, Holyhead, Liverpool and Milford Haven
East Coast – Felixstowe, Grimsby, Harwich, Hull and Tynemouth

FIGURE 14.6 Arrival of international sea/Channel Tunnel passengers to the UK

Source: DfT, 2017

EXAMPLE

Contrasting fortunes

Competition between Eurotunnel and the Port of Dover has been intense, ever since the Channel Tunnel opened. While tourists travelling abroad in their own cars are important, equally so is freight traffic. The port also received 94 visits from cruise ships in 2017.

TABLE 14.6 Operating data for Eurotunnel and the Port of Dover

	Eurotunnel (2017)	Port of Dover (2017)
Cars	2.6 million	2.2 million
Lorries	1.6 million	2.6 million
Revenue	€1 033 million	£65.2 million
Operating profit	€526 million	£10.2 million

Source: Company Annual Reports

Any comparison of these two entities should note that Eurotunnel acts both as port and as transport operator, while the Port of Dover relies on ferry and cruise companies to provide the sea crossings.

NEW MODES OF CROSSING

Alongside the introduction of the new fast ferries, alternative and still faster forms of water transport have become popular on many short- and medium-range routes. First hovercraft, then hydrofoils and, finally, catamarans entered service, with the benefits of speed and a certain degree of novelty.

Hovercraft were used to initiate the first fast ferry services across the Channel as early as 1968. They offered several advantages over the traditional ferries. Riding on a cushion of air just above the surface of the water and able to travel over land as well as water, they avoided the usual capital costs associated with dock facilities, as the craft could simply be beached on any convenient and obstacle-free foreshore. Unfortunately, they also offered their passengers a somewhat bouncy and noisy ride by comparison with the more traditional ferries, and could not operate in seas with waves greater than 2.5 metres. The vessels also suffered many technical problems in their development and throughout the years of their operation, so were finally withdrawn from service in 2000, being replaced by catamarans.

The hydrofoil offers better prospects for future development, even though it, too, suffered initial teething problems. This vessel operates with a conventional hull design, but when travelling at speed the hull is raised above the surface of the water on blades or 'foils'. This enables the vessel to travel at speeds of up to 60 knots. Recent models have been powered by jet engines (jetfoils), but their unreliability on open waters and inability to contend with high waves have hindered their adoption more widely.

The most promising recent development in ferry operations has been the high-speed, wave-piercing catamaran. These began operating on cross-Channel services in 1991, replacing the hovercraft. They are mainly twin-hulled vessels, large enough to accommodate cars, travelling at speeds of up to 40 knots. This type of vessel has now proved reliable in most weathers, operating successfully from the UK to Ireland and the Continent, as well as on routes such as Dover–Calais and Newhaven–Dieppe. Catamarans have also proved popular on routes across the Baltic Sea and other key European routes.

The high-speed, twin-hull ferries introduced by Stena at the end of the last century stretched capacity, carrying up to 1500 passengers and 375 cars. The downside, however, was that some constraints remained on their operation in rough weather; waves above 4 metres led to cancellations, a serious constraint in the winter months. Additionally, the higher fuel burn of these craft impacted running costs more severely than on other forms of ferry. As a result, Stena Line took these vessels out of service, the last operating in 2015.

OTHER EUROPEAN FERRY OPERATIONS

While the focus here has been primarily on connections between the UK and its continental neighbours, the continuing importance of other routes, especially within Europe, must be recognised. In the Mediterranean, ferries provide not only vital connections to travellers on a port-to-port basis, but also the opportunity to package these routes as mini-cruises, calling at a variety of different countries. By way of example, services are available in the eastern Mediterranean between Venice, Dubrovnik, Piraeus, Iraklion and Alexandria or between Istanbul, Piraeus, Larnaca, Lattakia (Syria) and Alexandria. Other important routes include those between Patras (Greece) and Ascona (Italy) and between Nice and Corsica. Tourists who traditionally think only of travelling by air to Majorca may be unaware of the alternatives – Trasmediterranea, for example, offers services from Barcelona or Valencia to Palma.

Greece is considered to have the largest ferry market in the EU, with 34 million passengers using ferries to travel around the 114 inhabited islands and to the mainland (European Parliament, 2016). Of course, not all of these journeys are made by tourists. The significance of marine travel to Greece was such that EU cabotage restrictions were permitted to remain in place until 2004. The disastrous sinking of the poorly maintained and elderly ferry *Express Samina* in 2000, however, led the Greek government to withdraw the licences of some older vessels and bring deregulation forward by two years. Vessels from other countries are now allowed to operate freely in Greek waters. This has spurred Greek shipowners to invest heavily in new equipment, as well as expanding their own activities outside the country.

Ferry operations in the Baltic call for special mention. Services here connect the Scandinavian countries and, in turn, provide vital connections for travellers between these countries and Germany. Independence for the three Baltic states of Latvia, Estonia and Lithuania, the entry of these countries into the EU, the rebuilding of the historic port of Gdansk (formerly Danzig) in Poland and the reunification of Germany have all renewed interest in these destinations for tourists, and both cruise ships and ferry crossings have achieved considerable growth in this area. The benefit of having St Petersburg in Russia as a major port in the Baltic has further stimulated interest in the region. With the enormous popularity of Tallinn as a tourist venue since EU accession and the short ferry journey between Helsinki and Tallinn – just one hour and 40 minutes by fast ferry – it has become a key route in the Baltic. It provides tourists with the opportunity for an attractive mini-cruise, coupled with bargain-priced shopping. Reference has already been made to the equally popular route between Stockholm and Helsinki. An overnight sailing can be treated as a mini-cruise, the 60,000-ton superferries carrying up to 2800 passengers at a time. The obvious success in this region of selling what were originally merely transport connections as luxury mini-cruises has established a trend that other ferry operators have been keen to emulate.

THE FUTURE OF FERRY OPERATIONS

Work on still more advanced vessels is under way. *Airfish 8*, to take one example, operates by generating a stable cushion of air under the wing as the craft 'flies' close to ground or water. By travelling on this dense layer of air, the craft benefits from reduced drag and increased lift, thus achieving high levels of fuel economy. Exceptionally high speeds are anticipated at one-fifth of the normal fuel cost of a ferry. It is expected that the craft should be capable of carrying between 80 and 150 passengers over distances of up to 250 miles. An added advantage of such a vessel is that it requires neither runway nor port in the accepted sense of the words. Registered in Singapore in 2010, it has a speed of 90 knots and travels 6 metres above the surface of the water. The nature of the design does, however, limit its operations in high winds or over seas with high waves.

COASTAL AND INLAND WATERWAYS TOURISM

The attraction of water offers many other opportunities for tourist activity, both independently and in forms that have been commoditised and packaged for visitors. Inland waterways, in particular, lakes, rivers and canals, provide exceptional opportunities for recreation and tourism, and across the globe the renovation of former canals, run-down ports and similar watersites have added in recent years to the many opportunities for recreational activities.

The major waterways of the world have long attracted tourists. The Nile river in Egypt has provided inland waterway cruising for many decades, with the popularity of this stretch of waterway leading to an enormous expansion in the number and size of cruise ships operating as part of package holidays up to the early years of the 1990s. The volatility of the tourism business is well illustrated by the collapse of the Egyptian inland cruise market in the mid-1990s, when the country was hit first by terrorism in which tourists were targeted explicitly, and then drought, which caused navigational difficulties in the upper Nile region. In 2000, the Nile came back into favour briefly, until the advent of 9/11, and then the Iraqi war once again discouraged tourists from travelling to the Middle East.

Civil uprising in 2011 and the overthrow of the Egyptian government, subsequent civil unrest and imposed Foreign Office travel restrictions all led to further questions over the viability of tourism to the area.

Some popular European river cruises are the Rhine/Danube (between Amsterdam, the Netherlands and Passau in Germany, thence to Constanta in Romania), the Douro in Portugal and the French rivers Seine and Rhone. Elsewhere, rivers with strong tourist appeal include the Mississippi in the USA (where traditional paddle steamers offer a nostalgic cruise experience) and the Yangtze and Li rivers in China, while the Volga and Russian waterways linking St Petersburg with Moscow, the Italian River Po and the German Elbe are all increasing in popularity. The Guadalquivir River in Spain allows small passenger craft to travel from the port of Cadiz as far inland as Seville and this has become one of the more recent innovations in river cruising. In South America, the Amazon River is sufficiently large to allow ocean-going ships to navigate as far inland as Iquitos in Peru. All of these river journeys have been packaged as tours and sold to tourists throughout the world.

Public craft are employed on coastal trips as well as on inland waterways. The popular excursion boats *Waverley* (one of the few remaining paddle steamers in the world) and *Balmoral* carry tourists on trips along the coast in the UK during the summer from ports in Scotland, South Wales and the West Country.

Others travel across the Scottish lochs and along the Caledonian Canal (Figure 14.7). The lake steamer remains a familiar sight in many parts of the world, providing an important tourist attraction in the US and Canadian Great Lakes, the Swiss and south German lakes, the islands of southern Sweden around Stockholm and the Scottish lochs and English Lake District in the UK. Many of these are elderly craft that have been restored and are kept in tiptop condition because of their appeal to tourists. The Swiss, for instance, have restored their classic (1909 built) *Stadt Rapperswil* and *Stadt Zürich* operating on the Zürichsee, while the Bodensee (Lake Constance) has 34 lake steamers owned by five different companies operating between ports in Germany, Switzerland and Austria. Both these lakes employ steamers essentially as regular transport for residents, but, because of their appeal as iconic tourist symbols, they are just as important to tourism.

FIGURE 14.7 Steamship *Sir Walter Scott* transports tourists across Loch Katrine, Scotland

Photo: Claire Humphreys

It is the growing attraction of rivers and canals for the independent boating enthusiast that perhaps holds the greatest potential for development over the next few years. The networks of rivers and canals in countries such as the UK, Holland and France have been redeveloped and exploited for tourism, and canals such as the Burgundy and the Canal du Midi in the South of France, as well as the Gota in Sweden, are being discovered by tourists in growing numbers. In 2011, it was announced that Italy plans to reopen its inland waterway between Locarno in Switzerland, on Lake Maggiore, and Venice, via Milan, a distance of some 500 km.

EXAMPLE

River cruise numbers are growing

Like ocean cruising, there has been a growth in recent years in the number of tourists taking river cruises. Research has revealed that more than 210,000 UK holidaymakers took a river cruise in 2017. Almost 90% of bookings were for itineraries along European rivers, with the Rhine and Danube dominating. Russian waterways and trips along the Douro river on the Iberia Peninsula were also seeing significant growth in demand. As alternatives to the European rivers, UK tourists were heading for the Mekong in Vietnam and the Irrawaddy in Myanmar.

Perhaps unsurprisingly, the UK market for river cruises is currently dominated by seniors and retirees. However, research suggests that the Millennial generation shows a greater fondness for river cruising than sea cruises, suggesting a potential to attract a younger market.

Sources: Gibson, 2018; Mintel, 2016

The UK itself is particularly well endowed with canals and rivers suitable for navigation. In the mid-1800s, the nation could boast of some 4250 miles of navigable inland waterways, many of which had been developed for the movement of freight. As these became redundant with the advent of the railways, they fell into disrepair until many stretches became no longer navigable. In the past few decades, however, British Waterways (superseded in 2012 by the Canal & River Trust) encouraged the development and use of these waterways for pleasure purposes, and, in partnership with private enterprise, aided by voluntary bodies, helped to restore and reopen many formerly derelict canals.

Today, some 2000 miles of navigable waterways are open (Figure 14.8) and maintained through the Canal and River Trust, which licenses 35,000 boats to use its network. Visitors use the waterways and its towpaths for recreational purposes, whether for angling, walking or cycling. The Canal and River Trust has charitable status, and funding for its activities comes from donations, sponsorship and, increasingly, commercialisation of its activities.

Additionally, the Norfolk and Suffolk Broads offer 125 miles of river and lakes cruising and have been catering for thousands of holidaymakers in private or hired vessels every year since the early twentieth century. The reopening of many formerly derelict waterways has made it possible for boat hire companies to organise packages that allow enthusiasts to follow a circular route during a one- or two-week holiday, without the need to travel over the same stretch of water twice.

Boat rental is a highly competitive business, and in the UK the season is relatively short. Most pleasure boat companies are small, family-run concerns, achieving low returns on capital invested and generally low profits. Effective marketing, especially to overseas tourists, is a problem when companies' budgets for promotion are small and the destination being sold is linear (the Kennet and Avon Canal, for instance, runs through a number of different regions, making unified marketing difficult).

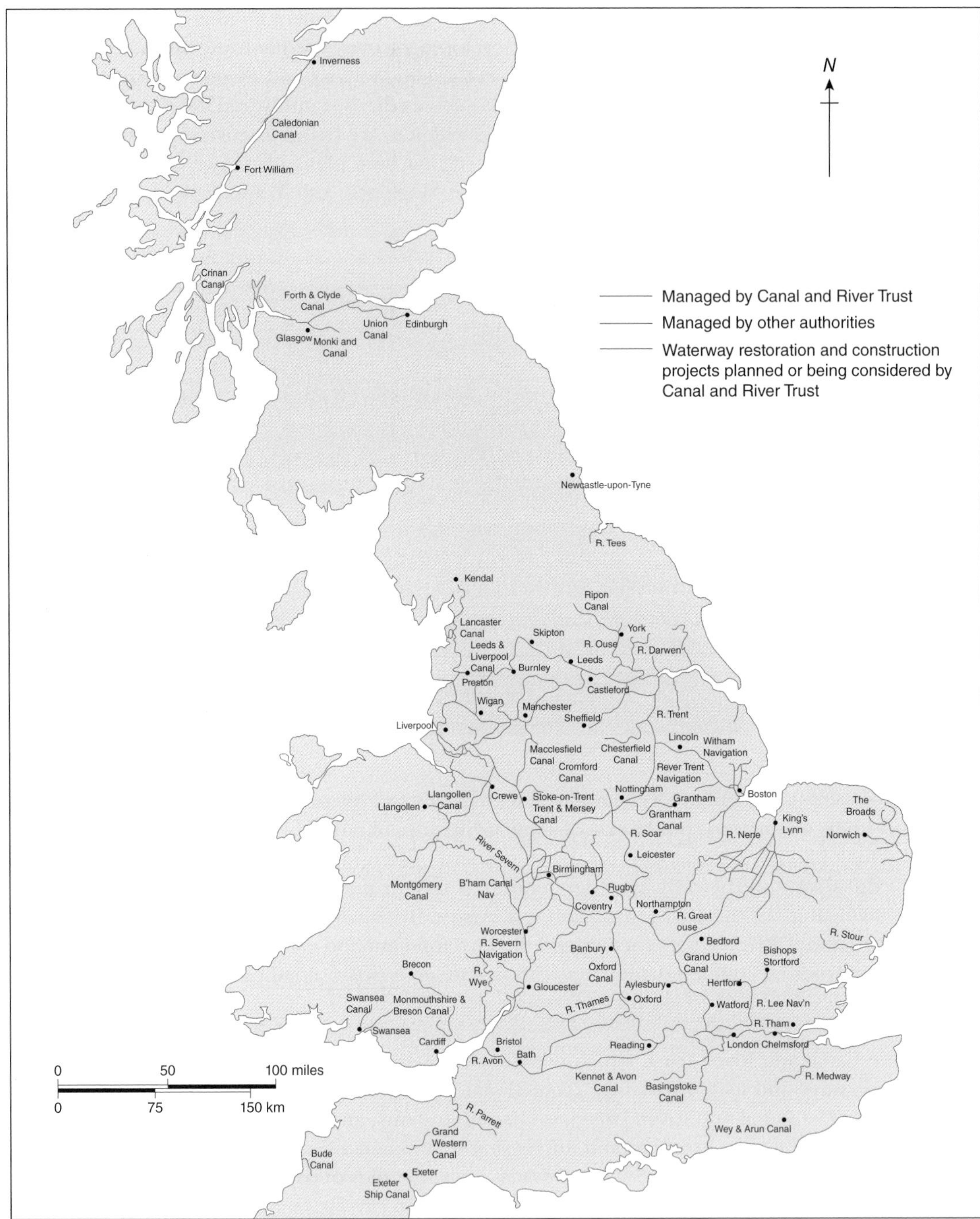

FIGURE 14.8 The inland waterways of the UK

Courtesy of Canal and River Trust (formerly British Waterways)

In such circumstances, cooperative promotion between the small boat companies themselves, working with other private-sector interests, is generally the best solution. A star rating for boat hire companies, along similar lines to that used for hotels, has been introduced in the UK, helping direct boat-hire customers to their preferred products. Consortia like Blakes and Hoseasons offer the power of centralised marketing for small companies and, for others, the Internet is making direct selling easier. Some tour operators have also taken an interest in this sector and are packaging holidays on inland waterways across Europe and in the USA.

EXAMPLE

Sightseeing cruises

While much of the discussion of river cruises has considered longer trips, which include overnight accommodation, we also need to consider the large number of sightseeing river cruises, perhaps lasting only a couple of hours, which allow visitors to see different views of a town or city.

In London, these trips are offered by companies such as Bateaux London and City Cruises. The latter is the largest operator, with more than 4 million passengers boarding their vessels annually, either on scheduled sightseeing tours, dining cruises, special events or as part of a group on board a private charter. Together, City Cruises transports almost half of all passengers transported on the river.

Since the start of its operations 30 years ago, City Cruises has seen significant improvement to the environmental quality of the river Thames, and the company has ensured that its fleet of river boats are designed to minimise their environmental impact.

Sustainability is an important factor for inland waterways, too. Apart from the dangers of pollution from fuel and oil leaks in sensitive freshwater areas, the erosion of riverbanks caused by powerboats and sheer congestion on popular stretches of waterway create additional problems. The introduction of solar-assisted boats on the Norfolk Broads, mentioned above, may help, in time, to reduce the impact of private boats on this most environmentally sensitive region.

SEAGOING PLEASURE CRAFT

This chapter would not be complete without some mention of the growing demand for holidays aboard seagoing pleasure craft, a demand that is now being met by the travel industry. It has been estimated that there are over a million households owning a boat in the UK (Arkenford, 2017), with some 4 million people taking part in a boating activity in 2017. This is naturally leading to people seeking boating holidays. Specialist operators and hire companies are now offering package holidays aboard small chartered sailing ships or steamboats, with facilities ranging from the luxurious, where the passengers are guests, to the more basic, where passengers play an active part in crewing the boat. Tour operators also cater for this growing demand for boating holidays with flotilla cruising holidays, especially in areas with numerous small islands where sheltered anchorage and fair weather conditions can be found. The Greek islands and certain Caribbean islands, such as the Windward and Leeward groups, offer ideal conditions for these types of package, in which individually hired yachts sail together in flotilla formation from island to island. In this manner, tourists have the benefit of independent use of the yacht while also enjoying the social life of the group when together at anchor.

EXAMPLE

Sailing holidays

The variety of sailing opportunities is extensive, as is demonstrated in this example of programmes organised by Neilson, a UK tour operator:

(Continued)

- First, Neilson offers yacht training courses, where holidaymakers can learn the complexities of sailing and marine navigation. The culmination of this might be certification by the Royal Yacht Association (RYA). Such courses are designed either for the individual enthusiast or as a family holiday.
- Alternatively, Neilson offers flotilla holidays, where each group of holidaymakers can rent their own craft and sail in a group between ports, with a lead crew in a separate boat to offer guidance and assistance. This provides the opportunity for sailors to travel at their own pace and join with others only when they feel the desire for company.
- A third option – one designed for the more experienced sailor – is a bareboat holiday. Neilson provides the boat, marine equipment and a briefing on the local routes, but the rest is down to the sailor. This gives a freedom to sail unfettered by the itineraries of others.
- Finally, again for the experienced sailor, is the Neilson Delivery Trip. This offers a two-week sailing experience, moving the fleet of yachts between their winter home and their summer flotilla base.

The influential factor in selecting the type of holiday is likely to be the level of sailing experience and the desire to balance independence with group interaction.

For further information, see: www.neilson.co.uk/sailing

A phenomenon of the early twenty-first century has been the rapid expansion in ownership of superyachts around the world. These are categorised as vessels exceeding 30 metres in length, and it has been estimated that around 10,000 such vessels were in service in 2016. There is a substantial economic benefit to ports harbouring these vessels, including mooring fees, labour, maintenance and leisure spend ashore by owners and their guests, although estimates have yet to be made of the contribution this business makes to local economies.

Many superyachts are used only by their owners, but some are purchased specifically for the charter market while others are available for rental from the owners for part of the year. Costs of renting a superyacht can be as high as £500,000 for a week, but typically will be between £50,000 and £250,000 per week.

Fractional ownership is now emerging as a new means of owning leisure craft for holidays. Luxury yachts cost many millions and require expensive upkeep, but owning a *share* of one will cost only a fraction of the price and enable the owner to buy one or more weeks each year to enjoy holidays on board a luxury yacht with a full crew. One company, for example, offers a one-eighth stake in a £7 million yacht and owners may rent out some or all of their weeks to earn income.

WHAT DOES THE FUTURE HOLD FOR WATER TRANSPORT?

Research is under way, as we have noted, on more advanced forms of sea transport, much of it focused on improving efficiencies in order to reduce operating costs and damage to the environment. Increasing speed is also a focus as it becomes clear that, for a great many holidaymakers, faster transport times to reach their holiday destination become important.

The appeal of cruise ships that resemble floating hotels with a full range of leisure facilities is leading to the construction of ever larger vessels, providing activities, some of which are often more suited to onshore holidays. At the same time, the demand for holidays that appeal to particular niche markets is encouraging the development of smaller vessels able to access more remote locations. It is likely that this sector in particular will see significant growth.

Finally, inland waterways will provide further opportunities for newly developing destinations as the desire to develop river tourism is incorporated into the activities of destination marketing organisations. One example is that of Vietnam, where the Ho Chi Minh City Tourism Association has established the Vietnam Yacht Club with the aim of facilitating the development of river tourism in the city. The infrastructure required, such as dock facilities and marinas, although substantial, may well be justified by the typically higher spend of this type of tourist. There are many existing tourism destinations also looking to reinvigorate their river tourism to boost earnings from visitors. Australia's Murray River has long been a popular holiday spot for domestic tourists, but improvements are now being encouraged in order to attract the international visitor. Whether this sector experiences significant growth may well be determined by the ability to link the attraction of the riverside with the quality of the facilities on board the riverboat and market this to a receptive audience.

QUESTIONS AND DISCUSSION POINTS

1. In this chapter, we highlighted that the Millennial generation has a greater fondness for river cruises than sea cruises. Why might the younger generation prefer river cruises?
2. There are many hundreds of cruises available to the market today, to an extent that deciding one ahead of others may require a complex decision-making process for the tourist. What factors may influence their decision?
3. What are the negative environmental and socio-cultural impacts of water-based tourism?

TASKS

1. Cargo ships sometimes offer to transport passengers between destinations en route. These vessels are designed to haul goods, so offer a very different range of facilities and experience from a traditional cruise ship. Investigate the facilities provided on cargo ships (several operators act as booking agents; for example, www.cargoshipvoyages.com or www.freighterexpeditions.com.au) and provide a short report that summarises the difference between these two types of product. Consider a variety of factors, including the on-board facilities offered, prices charged and routes scheduled.
2. The trade magazine *International Cruise & Ferry Review* (which includes a section called 'Ferry Business') is published twice yearly. You can read the current and archive copies of this magazine online at www.cruiseandferry.net/magazines. Examine the 'Ferry Business' section of the past two editions to identify:

   i. two issues currently affecting the ferry industry

   ii. one way in which technology is changing the ferry industry.

   Report your findings in a short presentation.

FURTHER READING

Chin, C. B. N. (2008) *Cruising in the Global Economy: Profits, pleasure and work at sea*. Aldershot: Ashgate.

Dickinson, B. and Vladimir, A. (1997) *Selling the Sea: An inside look at the cruise industry*. New York: Wiley.

Prideaux, B. and Cooper, M. (2009) *River Tourism*. Wallingford: CABI.

WEBSITES

Canal & River Trust: https://canalrivertrust.org.uk

Cruise Lines International Association: www.cruising.org

IMO podcast on sustainable shipping in Polar waters: www.imo.org/MediaCentre/Multimedia/AudioPodcast/Pages/Default.aspx

Seatrade magazine: www.seatrade-global.com

Staten Island Ferry: www.siferry.com

World Shipping Council: www.worldshipping.org

REFERENCES

Arkenford (2017) Watersports Participation Survey 2017: Summary report. Available online at: www.rya.org.uk/SiteCollectionDocuments/sportsdevelopment/2017-watersports-study-final-summary.pdf [Accessed December 2018].

Biehn, N. (2006) A cruise ship is not a floating hotel. *Journal of Revenue and Pricing Management*, 5 (2): 135–142.

Carnival Corporation (2018) *Annual Report 2017*. Available online at: www.carnivalcorp.com/phoenix.zhtml?c=140690&p=irol-reportsannual#collapse1 [Accessed December 2018].

Cruise Industry News (2018) *2018–2019 State of the Industry Report*. New York: *Cruise Industry News*.

Cruise Lines International Association (CLIA) (2018a) 2018 *Cruise Industry Outlook*. Available online at: https://es.cruiseexperts.org/media/2848/clia-2018-state-of-the-industry.pdf [Accessed December 2018].

CLIA (2018b) *Regional Report Europe: Full year overview 2016–2017*. Available online at: https://cruising.org/news-and-research/research/2016/december/clia-regional-report-europe-full-year-overview-2016-2017 [Accessed November 2018].

Cruise Market Watch (2018) *Growth of the Ocean Cruise Line Industry*. Available online at: https://cruisemarketwatch.com/growth (Accessed December 2018).

Department for Transport (DfT) (2011) *Sea Passenger Statistics*. London: DfT.

DfT (2017) *Sea Passenger Statistics*. London: DfT.

Ellwood, M. (2016) *Renting Giant Cruise Ships is the New Wave in Private Yachting*. Available online at: www.bloomberg.com/news/articles/2016-02-17/renting-giant-cruise-ships-is-the-new-wave-in-private-yachting [Accessed December 2018].

European Parliament (2016) *The EU Maritime Transport System: Focus on ferries*. Brussels: European Union.

Gibson, R. (2018) *Record Number of UK Passengers took River Cruises in 2017*. Available online at: www.cruiseandferry.net/articles/record-number-of-uk-passengers-took-river-cruises-in-2017 [Accessed December 2018].

Honeywell, J. (2017) What happens when you flush the loo on a cruise ship? *Daily Telegraph*, 1 February.

Karimi, F. and Hudson, W. (2014) Royal Caribbean cruise ship headed home – with a sickness record. *CNN Wire*, 29 January.

Kay, N. (2011) *Some Simple Economic Realities of Ferries*. Available online at: www.brocher.com/Ferries/reality.htm [Accessed December 2018].

Klein, R. A. (2006) Turning water into money: The economics of the cruise industry. In R. Dowling (ed.), *Cruise Ship Tourism*. Wallingford: CABI, pp. 261–9.

Mintel (2016) *Cruises – UK*. London: Mintel.

Olmer, N., Comer, B., Roy, B., Mao, X. and Rutherford, D. (2017) *Greenhouse Gas Emissions from Global Shipping, 2013–2015*. Washington, DC: International Council on Clean Transportation.

Page, S. (2009) *Transport and Tourism: Global perspectives*. Harlow: Pearson.

Roads and Transport Authority (RTA) (2014) Marine transport modes. Available online at: www.rta.ae/wpsv5/links/marine/Ferry_Marina_Ghubaiba.jpg [Accessed December 2018].

Stokes, R. (2018) First steps towards electrification of shipping. *Energy World*, November.

Weissmann, A. (2018) Stuck in the doldrums, Chinese cruise lines plan for growth. *Travel Weekly*, 17 September.

15

TOURIST TRANSPORT ON LAND

CONTENTS

LEARNING OUTCOMES

After studying this chapter, you should be able to:

- understand the role and scope of railways and their place in tourist travel
- explain the significance of the coach industry in tourism
- recognise the importance of the private car to tourist travel
- appraise the function of car hire in domestic and foreign tourism
- identify the growing importance of tourist travel by bicycle and on foot.

> Transport plays an important role in the successful creation and development of new attractions as well as the healthy growth of existing ones. Provision of suitable transport has transformed dead centres of tourist interest into active and prosperous places attracting multitudes of people. (Kaul, 1985: 496)

INTRODUCTION

In this chapter, we explore the different forms of land transport that help tourists reach their destination, while not forgetting that, as we highlighted in Chapter 8, some transport can form part of the attraction of a destination because it can offer visitors a unique and memorable experience. Typical examples of this would be a rail journey on the *Orient Express* through Europe or the *Blue Train* through the African countryside.

THE ROLE OF THE RAILWAYS IN TOURISM

During the second half of the twentieth century, railways played a somewhat limited role in serving expanding mass-market tourism. This is surprising when one considers the important role played by the railways in their 100 years of existence up to that point, when rail transport was the principal means by which people took their annual holidays, travelling either to the coasts of their own countries or across Europe to the Mediterranean. Rail transport's decline in popularity contrasted with the rise in ownership of private cars, and rail companies appeared content to focus on what they saw as their prime markets – commuters and business travellers – and, of course, freight. Even before the outbreak of the 1939–45 war, the decline in tourist travel by rail had become noticeable.

Across Europe, improvements in coach transport, as public road vehicles became more comfortable, faster and more reliable, and the significant gap in price between road and rail, encouraged those without private vehicles to switch to road transport for their holidays, while the better-off made increasing use of their private cars. A similar pattern occurred in the USA, where the switch was to domestic air travel alongside the growth in private car usage.

Instead of fighting back, the railways retrenched, cutting services and routes and concentrating on the main intercity routes. The US railway companies switched their focus to more remunerative freight, with passenger services largely restricted to a handful of well-established intercity routes – a strategy that continues to this day, despite the formation of Amtrak as a public service railroad system, with government subsidies to encourage regeneration of the rail services.

Unprofitable branch lines were closed, especially in the UK following the Beeching Report in the 1960s, and, as a result, many smaller UK coastal resorts and other rural destinations that attracted tourists became inaccessible by rail. The alternative of coach services linking with rail termini made tourist travel inconvenient and time-consuming, and this, coupled with continuing disparities in fares and the relative decline in the cost of car travel, soon made the railways an unattractive choice for many destinations.

Privatisation of the railways in the UK in the late twentieth century, which resulted in higher fares and inferior service, and the previous long-term lack of investment in track and signalling under public ownership, all made rail travel still less attractive for tourists. This was in contrast to developments on the Continent, where investment in high-speed rail over the past two decades has brought many tourists back onto the trains.

EXAMPLE

Rail travel to European destinations

Residents of Europe made more than 200 million tourism trips to other EU member states in 2016. The vast majority of these trips were by road or air, with only 5% being by rail, on average. However, such statistics hide the disparities in use of rail to reach some destinations. For example, one-fifth of arrivals in Belgium reach the country by train. This is comparable with arrivals by air (also 20%), but both are outweighed by arrivals to this country by road. Table 15.1 highlights the railways' share of arrivals for selected European countries.

TABLE 15.1 Share of arrivals at selected European countries by mode of transport in 2016

Country	Share (%) of arrivals by rail	Share (%) of arrivals by car or bus	Share (%) of arrivals by air
Belgium	20	53	20
Switzerland	17	51	30
France	15	46	30
Slovakia	13	73	9
Czech Republic	12	58	29
Denmark	7	58	29
UK	7	15	74
The Netherlands	7	60	28
Germany	6	58	32
Sweden	4	30	35
Italy	3	53	41
Spain	1	14	84

Source: Eurostat, 2018a

There are several factors that will determine whether rail is used as the choice of travel mode, including ticket price, the distance to the destination country, the availability of high-speed train services and the existence of train routes to the holiday destination.

High-speed rail provision has expanded across Europe, with France, Spain, Germany, Poland, Austria and the UK all planning additions to their high-speed network. Today, rail travel can no longer be dismissed as insignificant to tourism; within Europe, the rail companies themselves are now actively pursuing tourist markets over distances of up to 500 miles, and in some instances further, in open competition with the airlines.

Improvements in rail services within the UK are gradually enabling the railways to win back tourists from air and from other surface transport, aided by growing road congestion and crowded airports. Some services in the UK remain popular, transporting domestic tourists from the major conurbations to key English resorts like Brighton, Bournemouth and Torquay.

Faster services with Eurostar, which uses the Channel Tunnel high-speed rail link to connect London with the high-speed network on the Continent, are attracting British tourists not just to Paris and Brussels, but also to other popular tourist destinations such as Cologne, Lille and even the Côte d'Azur in the summer. Direct services also operate to the French and Swiss ski resorts in winter.

Rail companies have become more marketing orientated, often partnering with specialist tour operators to target tourists. Rail and hotel packages in the UK have proved popular for the short-break market, particularly to London and capital cities on the Continent. Efforts to entice rail travel enthusiasts have also met with some success, even though this is on a limited scale. Nostalgic day trips and excursions using old steam engines are popular, as are packages aimed at the over-55s. Recognising that unsold off-peak seats represent substantial lost revenue, the railways have used variable pricing policies and promotions to attract tourists and excursionists back to rail travel.

Tickets offering unlimited travel by train, sold to inbound tourists only before their departure from their own countries, are yet another means of boosting rail travel. These include the Britrail pass within the UK and Eurailpass on the continental mainland, while a Scanrail pass provides unlimited travel within the Nordic countries, coupled with a 50% reduction on interconnecting ferry services. Such schemes are aimed at tourists, particularly those from the USA and Australia visiting Europe independently or on tailor-made itineraries, and appeal to the young backpacker market. Similar Railpass schemes are on offer on Amtrak services in the USA, and in Australia; however, the distances involved, some less than adequate services and budget transcontinental air fares make rail travel in these countries less attractive to tourists.

THE PRIVATISATION OF RAIL TRANSPORT IN THE UK

Towards the end of the twentieth century, it became clear that action would have to be taken to improve the railway systems in both Europe and North America. Heavily subsidised and lacking adequate investment over many years, railways were in a parlous state. Two alternatives presented themselves: either the state could move railways out of public ownership or it could agree to a programme of massive state investment to increase the appeal of the railways as a form of public transport.

In the UK, the Conservative government then in power took the decision to denationalise the railways. Private companies were to be allowed to bid to run parts of the British Rail system, while the maintenance and operation of all track, signalling and stations were to be hived off to a separate company called Railtrack. The government's belief was that a privatised railway system would become more efficient, ending the drain on government funds through subsidies, and competing more effectively with other forms of transport through new private investment that would attract travellers back to the railways. Privatisation was initiated in 1993, and by early 1997 25 train-operating units in the UK had replaced the former monolithic rail system and a further three companies were formed to control rolling-stock.

While passenger traffic did increase on most services, partly as a result of better marketing, passengers became confused about the range of choice and fares facing them, and journeys involving the services of more than one railway company became more complex. Concern rose over the lack of promised investment by the rail companies and the impact of cost-cutting by some companies in order to boost profits, which, in some instances, led to safety violations and even accidents.

Distribution systems for rail tickets also suffered. Travel agents were already abandoning the sale of rail tickets as unprofitable before the advent of privatisation, and this was hastened by the additional complexities of dealing with a score of different rail companies.

A computerised reservations and ticketing system, ELGAR, was developed, initially to handle bookings for the Channel Tunnel's Eurostar service, and later extended to all members of the Association of Train Operating Companies (ATOC).

Eurostar's marketing and distribution were strongly criticised. Onward bookings beyond Paris and Brussels could no longer be made to any European destination, but were instead limited to major railway stations. Systems to sell tickets to the public via the Internet replaced the role of many travel agents, with companies such as thetrainline.com (owned by Virgin Rail and the National Express bus group) acting as electronic intermediaries for the sale of rail tickets. In 2008, agents' rail commission was cut from 9 to 5% and, at the same time, Eurostar abandoned the ELGAR distribution system, further disincentivising the retailing of rail tickets.

Continued criticism of rail services in the UK led eventually to changes in the structure of the organisation. Network Rail replaced Railtrack as owners of track, signals and stations, with 27 train operating companies gaining franchises to control the rolling-stock, usually under contracts of five to eight years, although some were extended up to 20 years. (Curiously, these sometimes fell into public ownership once again. For example, Deutsche Bahn, owned by the German state, bought the franchise for Chiltern Railway in 2007, and East Coast was established as a subsidiary of the Department of Transport, when the route was re-nationalised after failure of the National Express East Coast company to operate this route profitably.) By 2018, financial failures, mergers and acquisitions had led to a reduction in the total number of train operating companies.

EXAMPLE

UK extending high-speed rail services

The only truly modern high-speed rail line in the UK is the Channel Tunnel rail link, now rebranded as HighSpeed One, developed to provide Eurostar with high-speed services between London and the Channel Tunnel at Folkestone. This track is also used by Southeastern to provide high-speed services between St Pancras and major towns in Kent.

Due for construction in the near future, although subject to controversy on the grounds of escalating costs and environmental concerns, a second high-speed line (HS2) is planned for the UK. Planned to open in 2026, this will connect London to Birmingham, with a second phase linking to Sheffield and Leeds. Additionally, a link from Birmingham to Manchester is scheduled for completion by 2033.

HS2 is expected to cut the London–Birmingham journey time from 81 to 49 minutes.

Although the potential exists for a greatly expanded market for rail travel within the EU, the full potential of this is only just beginning to be tapped. Marketing agreements between the European train operators and the interest in high-speed trains are changing attitudes to rail travel. An agreement between Eurostar and the Thalys international rail network helped boost rail travel between London and Amsterdam, and this was followed by the establishment of a marketing alliance of the high-speed railways in the UK, France, Belgium, the Netherlands, Germany, Switzerland and Austria, under the brand name Railteam. Train timetables throughout the region are now synchronised, a single timetable produced and common regulations (such as for children's fares) introduced. Most importantly, a single website provides access to all these integrated services.

THE CHANNEL TUNNEL AND THE RAILWAYS

In Chapter 14, we examined the impact of the Channel Tunnel on ferry operations from the UK. Here, we must examine its impact on, and relationship to, land transport services elsewhere in the UK and in mainland Europe.

The Channel Tunnel is one of the great engineering feats of the twentieth century. With 37.8 km of its 50-km length under water, it takes pride of place as being the longest underwater rail tunnel in the world. While Japan's Seikan Tunnel between Tappisaki, Honshu Island, and Fukushima, Hokkaido Island, has the honour of being the longest rail tunnel at 53.8 km, the section underwater is shorter, at 23.3 km.

The first direct rail link between the UK and France was completed and opened to traffic in 1994, after frequent delays. It offers passengers the choice of two forms of transport: passenger travel on Eurostar from London to either Paris or Brussels, calling at Ebbsfleet (and, less frequently, Ashford in Kent) and Lille in northern France (with opportunities to transfer to high-speed trains for onward travel in Europe); and Eurotunnel's vehicle-carrying flatbed rail service, operating between Cheriton (near Folkestone) and les Coquelles (near Calais). Cars are driven onto double-decker carriages (see Figure 15.1 – note that taller cars, those with trailers, and coaches are accommodated in single-deck carriages). These are then transported across the Channel and passengers can drive off to connect directly with the French motorway system in a little over 30 minutes after leaving England.

FIGURE 15.1 Inside of the Eurotunnel double-deck car carriages

Photo: Claire Humphreys

Rail connections between London and the Continent have been firmly pitched at the business traveller. Eurostar is programmed to operate at speeds of up to 186 mph, reducing the journey time between London and Paris to just two hours and 15 minutes (and around two hours to Brussels). This compares with closer to four hours by air, when allowance is made for check-in times and the inevitable security queues, making journeys by rail a viable alternative for the business traveller as well as leisure tourists. To expand its market, Eurostar now offers a twice-daily route direct to Amsterdam, launched in 2018, that delivers a journey time of under four hours.

Annual passenger numbers for Eurostar exceeded 10 million in 2017, while overall this passenger rail service has carried some 185 million passengers since the Tunnel's opening. The owners of Eurotunnel, Getlink (formerly known as Groupe Eurotunnel), reported that in 2017 over 21 million passengers were carried on all services, and Le Shuttle holds around 55% of the cross-Channel car market. Rail is now a viable option for travel between London and both Paris and Brussels. A two-hour trip from London St Pancras to Lille also enables the leisure tourist to connect with the French TGV high-speed trains for onward travel to southern France or adjoining European countries. Lille itself, heavily promoted as a destination in its own right, has become an important city-break market for British tourists to France. Routes such as London to Amsterdam or Frankfurt take almost the same time by train, city centre to city centre, as by plane.

At the insistence of the Conservative government, the Channel Tunnel was privately financed, with no public contribution. Its construction involved leading-edge technology and the project ran into delays and huge cost overruns, leaving Eurotunnel with debts amounting to some £9 billion. Overambitious estimates of traffic and revenue were not realised, but this is not to say that the Tunnel has been a failure. Within two years of operation, it had made sufficient inroads into the share of the short sea market to badly worry the ferry companies (discussed in Chapter 14), which were obliged to slash their prices to compete. A fire in the Tunnel in 1996 was a serious setback, but despite this, Eurostar holds some 80% of market share on the London–Paris route (Martin, 2016).

When it was established, control of the Eurostar rail services was the responsibility of each national railway (SNCF in France, SNCB in Belgium and Eurostar UK in the UK). Since September 2010, a separate business entity, Eurostar International, has been responsible for operations. This entity is owned by three shareholders: SNCF (55%), SNCB (5%) and LCR (40%), although in 2015 LCR (originally under the control of the UK government) sold its stake to Caisse de dépôt et placement du Québec (CDPQ) (30%) and Hermes Infrastructure (10%) for £585 million.

The minimum usage charge paid by Eurostar to Eurotunnel, agreed in the initial contract with the company, ended in 2006; but despite this, Eurotunnel has succeeded in taking control of its finances, paying off some of its huge burden of debts and increasing load factors to a point where it had become operationally profitable in 2007.

RAIL TRAVEL ON THE CONTINENT

Railway investment on the Continent is in marked contrast to investment in the UK's railways, whether under public or private administration. Continental rail companies and their governments recognised that investment in high-speed rail would encourage regional investment, giving rise to increased property prices and at the same time boosting tourism. In 1990, the EU approved the formation of a Trans-European Network for Transport (TEN-T) of high-speed road and rail links, the bulk of which were to be in place by 2005 (with the full network to be completed by 2020). The first European railway directive, designed to encourage competition across national borders, came into force in 1993, with subsequent updates in 2001, 2004 and 2007. Yet, in 2018, the

European Commission's Directorate-General for Mobility and Transport acknowledged that an integrated network is still a long way off (Smith, 2018), despite €23.7 billion of investment since the turn of the century.

In France, SNCF, the publicly operated rail service, and SNCF Réseau, which is responsible for building and maintaining tracks, operate more than 30,000 km of lines, of which over 2600 miles carry high-speed trains. This is set to expand further following the announcement in September 2018 by French President Emmanuel Macron that €13.4 billion will be invested over the next decade to deliver five new high-speed lines.

Germany found £54 billion to build its own network of 280-kph ICE (Intercity Express) trains, with an even faster route between Cologne and Frankfurt, allowing the ICE3 330-kph train to halve the previous journey time. Italy introduced its Pendolino 250-kph tilt-body train on the Milan to Rome route, while Spain's AVE (Alta Velocidad Española) offers a high-speed (2 hours and 15 minutes) service between Madrid and Seville.

In 2008, Renfe, the Spanish railway operator, also brought into service a high-speed line for the Madrid to Barcelona service. The VelaroE travels at speeds of up to 350 kph, cutting the 410-mile journey to just two and a half hours. High-speed routes from Madrid to Málaga opened in 2007, and in 2011 the Spanish network linked with the TGV (Train à Grande Vitesse) services at Perpignan. There are further ambitious plans for a total of 10,000 km of high-speed track by 2020, with better signalling, which will allow for speeds of up to 220 mph.

The Koralm high-speed railway linking the Austrian cities of Klagenfurt and Graz has been under construction since 2006. Once complete, it will reduce journey times from three hours to one hour. This €11 billion project is part of a trans-European network linking the Baltic and Adriatic seas, from Gdansk in Poland to Ravenna in northern Italy. The prospect of comfortable, reliable, high-speed trains running continuously between Northern Europe (including the UK) and the Mediterranean is a tantalising one for the future of tourism.

Within Northern Europe, Thalys, a Belgian–French high-speed train, serves the route between Paris and Brussels, as well as Amsterdam and Dortmund (via Cologne). Sweden's hugely successful X2000 high-speed train has reduced the journey between Stockholm and Gothenburg to less than three hours, increasing rail's share on this route from 30% to over 50% and leading to the extension of the service to other Swedish cities as well as to Oslo, in Norway. In the latter country, the Signatur tilting train, introduced between Oslo and Kristiansand in 1999, gained sufficient popularity to ensure other routes were opened up throughout Norway. High-speed services of NS HiSpeed, the Netherlands rail company, joined the network in 2007.

The advent of these high-speed networks is changing the face of European transport. Even allowing for the success of the budget airlines, rail services are finding that, if they can provide reliability, comfort and speed at the right price, they can attract markets from other modes of transport. There is no uniform agreement that these new high-speed rail services can force airlines to withdraw from the routes, however.

EXAMPLE

A rail alliance

In 2007, European high-speed rail operators launched an alliance to enhance their rail product. With a common goal to make rail the first choice for travel across Europe, Railteam is a cooperative venture between Deutsche Bahn (Germany), SNCF (France), Eurostar (UK,

France and Belgium), NS Hispeed (the Netherlands), ÖBB (Austria), SBB (Switzerland), SNCB (Belgium) and their subsidiaries Thalys and Lyria.

Established to coordinate rail links that will stretch from London to Hamburg in the north, Vienna in the east and Perpignan in the south, the alliance aims to ensure a smooth journey when using connecting rail networks, the booking and ticketing covering the entire journey (if one part of the service is delayed, then tickets will still remain valid on connecting journeys). The alliance has also introduced a 'frequent traveller' scheme, providing reward tickets and access to business lounges.

A mobile app has been developed that provides a timetable and real-time platform information for all European trains. However, the work of the alliance has not been without issues. Plans for a centralised Europe-wide common booking system were abandoned because of increasing costs due to the complexity this required.

As high-speed networks expand across Europe over the next decade, so the possibility of travelling by rail to ever greater numbers of destinations will see demand increase. By 2016, 124 billion passenger kilometres had been travelled on high-speed lines, a substantial increase from just 15 billion in 1990 (European Court of Auditors, 2018).

Minimum travel times by rail between key European city destinations are now given as:

- Brussels to Paris 1 hour 20 minutes
- London to Brussels 2 hours 1 minute
- London to Paris 2 hours 16 minutes
- Frankfurt to Basel 2 hours 49 minutes
- Paris to Geneva 3 hours 5 minutes
- Cologne to Paris 3 hours 14 minutes
- Paris to Stuttgart 3 hours 39 minutes
- Vienna to Munich 3 hours 55 minutes
- Frankfurt to Amsterdam 3 hours 56 minutes
- Brussels to Avignon 4 hours 17 minutes.

It is likely that other factors are at work to determine modes of transport, including status, place of residence and attitudes within the business world – even habit. It is certainly the case, however, that demand from tourists, both business and leisure, for the new high-speed services has increased, paralleling a rise in demand for new budget air routes.

Booking times may act as a barrier in the use of rail as a means of leisure travel. While airlines usually open the booking window 330 days ahead of departure, purchasing rail tickets may only be possible from as little as 60 days (in the case of Eastern Europe) or 90 days (in Western Europe) in advance of the travel date. This means many travel arrangements (for example, accommodation) may need to be made long before transport arrangements can be confirmed.

Where formerly water acted as a barrier to fast surface transport, new bridges have helped to increase demand for the European rail networks, especially in Scandinavia. In Denmark, bridges across the Great Belt and the Øresund between Denmark and Sweden have opened up continuous rail travel between London and Stockholm for the first time. The surface link that brought Copenhagen and Malmö closer together has led to a partnership between the regions, encouraging international tourism to what was formerly a somewhat isolated and economically deprived region of southern Sweden.

Where bridge construction is impracticable, tunnels are opening up other fast-track routes through Europe. Under development is the 18-km long Fehmarnbelt Tunnel; originally scheduled to open in 2018, it is now due to be completed in 2028. This will replace the ferry operating between Germany (Puttgarden) and Denmark (Rodbyhavn), speeding travel between the cities of Hamburg and Copenhagen. Other notable tunnels are being constructed through the Alps. In 2006, work started on the world's longest tunnel, which will link Innsbruck in Austria with Fortezza in Italy, following the EU's plan to provide a continuous link between Munich and Palermo. The Brenner Base Tunnel will be 63-km long (the length of the existing Gothard Base is just 57 km) and is planned to cut the 2 million vehicles currently travelling every year from Germany and the North to the Mediterranean resorts (however, this flow of traffic is said to account for substantial increases in pollution as it makes its way through the mountains). The new twin tunnels through the Alps, due for completion in 2025, will be capable of carrying up to 400 trains a day.

Improved equipment and service, rapid connections between major cities and the avoidance of delays in congested airports are making European rail services appear increasingly attractive to the tourist market, and there is little doubt that rail services will figure prominently in the future of European tourism. Moreover, under EU liberalisation rules, present train companies within the member countries now face open competition, with non-EU companies being permitted to run international train services anywhere within the Community.

EXAMPLE

Train versus air travel

Supporters of high-speed rail travel have frequently touted the benefits of this form of travel for short-haul journeys as an alternative to air transport. Frequently, this has focused on cross-border routes such as London to Paris, where no change of train is required.

However, in August 2010, a geography lecturer at Saarland University of Applied Sciences challenged students to make a comparison of the two modes, with a race from St Ingbert (Saarland, Germany) to Piccadilly Circus in London. One team took the train while a second team travelled by low-cost airline. Assessment of the journey took into account not just total time taken but also price, comfort, booking process and environmental impact.

Overall, the students' results favoured the train journey in three respects:

Journey time:	train – 6 h 25 min;	air – 6 h 45 min
Price:	train – €101.58 per person;	air – €105.96 per person
Environmental impact:	train – 22 kg per person;	air – 144 kg per person

Air travel was, however, assessed to be better in terms of comfort and booking.

The comparison between train and air travel is heavily influenced by proximity to airports serving the destination. For those cities not accessible through a direct flight, train travel can provide a competitive option.

Source: Rail-news, 2010

RAPID TRANSIT SERVICES IN THE FAR EAST

In Japan, the Shinkansen (popularly known as the **bullet train**) has changed the face of high-speed transport, and its reliability and high levels of service have proved immensely popular with tourists. The journey between Tokyo and Osaka, for example, usually takes less than three hours from city centre to city centre by train, compared with an hour's flying time between airports, so 80% of all passengers now use the train for this journey.

Japan takes immense pride in its bullet trains; any delays are counted in seconds rather than minutes, and the technical specifications of the trains are constantly improved. The E7 series, introduced to the network in 2014, is designed to travel at 260 kph, slightly slower than the earlier E6 series which operates at a maximum speed of 320 kph. While faster trains exist, with capabilities of 360 kph, trials have revealed problems with long-term wear to power cables and noise issues, so these have yet to be introduced.

Despite Japan's record, the award for fastest train service in the world now goes to the high-speed Maglev rail service built by the Chinese to link Shanghai's international airport to the city's central metro system (discussed later in this chapter). Speed on this 19-mile track peaks at 431 kph (267 mph). China's new Fuxing trains have become the world's fastest bullet trains, shaving an hour off the 1318-km journey between Shanghai and Beijing. With 27,000 km of track, China has the world's largest high-speed network, with planned investments expecting to lead to further expansion. In 2017, passenger numbers exceeded 1.7 billion across the network. Concern regarding the safety of these services was raised, following the serious derailment of a train in 2011, which led to reductions in the maximum operating speed. Conversely, safety has always been a priority for Japan and the inclusion of seismometers averted disaster when an earthquake hit the region in March 2011. These seismometers sensed the impending shock and sent warnings to the system 12 seconds before the earthquake hit, triggering emergency brakes and cutting power supplies to the 650 conventional trains and 26 bullet trains on the track. Despite significant damage caused by the earthquake and subsequent tsunami, parts of the train system were up and running the following day.

CLASSIC RAIL JOURNEYS AROUND THE WORLD

There remains a strong body of transport enthusiasts throughout the world for whom the 'romance of steam' remains a major attraction, and they are willing to travel anywhere in the world for the privilege of taking a journey on one of the few remaining steam trains. Some of these have been reconditioned, with lines re-laid or reopened to cater to tourist demand, although others are often mere shadows of their former selves, nevertheless continuing to appeal either through their exotic routing or due to nothing more than their romantic titles. Consequently, we now have two distinct forms of 'nostalgic rail' journey – on classic trains or on classic routes. In rare cases, the two coincide.

Classic train journeys are generally provided in reconditioned or reconstructed period coaches and are sometimes still drawn by steam engines. The *Venice Simplon-Orient-Express* is a leader in such nostalgic journeys, drawing on the appeal of its name and the image of ultimate luxury. The company now trades on that name, operating not only on the Continent, but also in the UK, the Far East and Australia.

At the top end of the market, such luxurious journeys in reconditioned trains or carriages are very attractive to tourists, who will build their itinerary around their rail journey. An example is the *Al Andalus Express*, a vintage train comprising 12 carriages built in the 1920s and 1930s, operating between major tourist centres in southern Spain, including Seville, Jerez and Granada, during spring and autumn. This itinerary and others like it are featured in the upmarket programmes of specialist tour operators like Great Rail Journeys

FIGURE 15.2 Vietnamese hawkers serve food and other wares to train passengers as they stop at a passing point between Saigon and Hanoi

Photo: Claire Humphreys

of the World and Travelsphere. Hungary has introduced the *Royal Hungarian Express*, employing carriages built originally for the use of high-level party members under the communist regime, as a feature to attract tourists to destinations outside Budapest. The *Danube Express* is a recent introduction, operating between Budapest, Prague and Venice.

Further afield, countries in which steam engines still operate, such as India and China (although these are being phased out), attract both independent travellers and package tourists. Regular steam services in India may be mostly a memory, but *The Palace on Wheels* keeps that memory alive for those still anxious to experience the classic trains of imperial India.

In the Far East, a few steam-hauled trains still operate in Cambodia's highlands, while luxury trains designed to cater for the growing flood of tourists to Vietnam include the *Victoria Express* between Hanoi and Sapa and the *Reunification Express* from Hanoi to Saigon. The single-line track, running for over 1700 km, means that the train journey is interspersed with waits at key passing points for the train service running in the opposite direction (see Figure 15.2). These all add to the journey experience.

In South Africa, the famous *Blue Train* continues to cater to the top end of the market, while Rovos Rail's *Pride of Africa*, a train with 1930s carriages, is chartered out to tour operators to provide an equally luxurious service between East and South Africa, via Victoria Falls. Namibia, emulating the success of its neighbour, introduced its own luxury train, the *Desert Express*, operating out of the capital, Windhoek, to the coast and Etosha National Park.

Australia has extensively promoted its famous trains: the *Indian Pacific* (a three-day service across the country between Perth and Melbourne) and *The Ghan* (from Adelaide across the red centre to Darwin via Alice Springs), while the tilt train between Brisbane and Rockhampton is also proving popular with tourists visiting the resorts of the East Coast and the Great Barrier Reef.

Longer rail journeys across the continents of Europe and Asia, while far from luxurious, fulfil the ambitions of true rail aficionados, who can choose between the *Trans-Mongolian Express*, *Trans-Manchurian Express* and *Rossiya*, or *Trans-Siberian Express*, and these too have been incorporated into programmes by specialist operators.

A recent introduction is the trans-Asia railway route, from Istanbul to Dhaka, linking in with European tracks. A tunnel across the Bosporus, replacing the ferry, opened in 2013, completing one more link in this 7000-mile route.

EXAMPLE

The highest railway in the world

In 2006, China completed the highest railway in the world, between Qinghai and Lhasa in Tibet. At its highest point, the Tanggula Pass, the train reaches a height of 5070 metres (over 16,000 feet) and at this height the carriage compartments are pressurised, owing to the thin air. Oxygen cylinders are also carried on board to cater for emergencies, which are not uncommon.

The construction of the rail track was in itself a major engineering feat, as much of the route is across permafrost, requiring the track to be laid on causeways raised above the unstable ground. The diesel engines were specially designed so they could operate efficiently at this 3-mile-high altitude.

Curiously, to date no iconic name has been chosen for the train, but this has not stopped a surge of bookings from intrepid passengers from all over the world, and the journey has been rapidly incorporated into specialist operators' rail itineraries.

RAIL SERVICES IN NORTH AMERICA

In North America, rail travel in the 1960s and 1970s declined in the face of lower air fares and poor marketing by the railway companies themselves, which chose to concentrate on freight revenue at the expense of their passenger services. The continuing losses suffered by most US rail companies, and the importance of the rail network in social communications, led the government to integrate rail services in the country into a centrally funded public corporation known as Amtrak. This organisation has achieved some success in reversing the decline of passenger traffic and achieved some benefit after a rise in bookings by Americans nervous about flying following the 9/11 disaster, although additional security measures, commensurate with those in place on airline flights, have added to the journey times. In 2017, Amtrak carried 31.7 million passengers, the largest annual total in its operating history.

The Obama administration was vocal about investing in high-speed rail, but this was followed by calls by the Trump administration for budget cuts to the rail industry. Currently, Amtrak operates 21,000 miles of routes, but only about half of its trains operate at speeds of 100 mph (160 kph). Three routes in the north-east operate at speeds of 125 km, but nothing matches the high-speed lines (speeds at or above 250 kph) of China, Japan and Europe. Amtrak operates 15 long-distance services including the Texas Eagle, which operates from Chicago to Los Angeles, travelling a distance of some 2700 miles with a total journey time of about 65 hours.

While many of the famous names of the past, such as the Santa Fé *Superchief* and the *20th Century Ltd*, have gone forever, the mystique of rail travel is maintained, at least in name, by others that *have* survived, including the *Lake Shore Ltd* on the Boston–New York–Chicago route, the *South West Chief* from Chicago to Los Angeles, the *Capitol Limited* from Washington to Chicago, the *California Zephyr* between Chicago and San Francisco, the *Empire Builder* between Seattle/Portland and Chicago, and the *Coast Starlight* between San Francisco and Los Angeles. The only fully transcontinental service, the *Sunset Limited*, operating from Florida to California, was severely disrupted by the flooding in Louisiana in 2005 caused by Hurricane Katrina. Although the section of the route from Florida to New Orleans has been reconstructed, political and managerial wrangling impacted a return to coast-to-coast services. However, demand for the New Orleans–Los Angeles route is still popular, with 91,600 passengers carried on this thrice-weekly route (Amtrak, 2017).

North American railways pass through some of the finest scenery in the world, and both the USA and Canada exploit this in their rail journeys. Rail journeys to the Rockies already form an important element in excursions for those booking cruises out of North American ports on the west coast. The *Rocky Mountaineer* provides an opportunity to package scenic local transport when visitors travel to this region, while *The Canadian*, operating between Toronto and Vancouver via Jasper, has been restored to its original 1950s style, with an observation dome on the rear carriage giving tourists spectacular views of the passing scenery.

Tourists are also attracted to the restored or reconstructed nineteenth-century trains operating within the regions, notably in the Far West, such as the Silverton and Durango Railroad's steam train to Durango and the steam-hauled Grand Canyon Railway's trains. GrandLuxe Rail Journeys has introduced vintage Pullman carriages for its luxury scenic tours of the mainly western states.

EXAMPLE

Survival of a heritage railway

There are heritage railways and railroad museums in almost every state of the USA. One example, the Durango and Silverton narrow gauge railway, was listed in the top ten railway trips by *National Geographic*. Opened in 1882, the line hauled passengers and freight from the mining regions of south-west Colorado. With spectacular views along its route, it remains a popular tourist attraction today, using a coal-fired steam locomotive to pull the carriages along 45 miles of narrow gauge railway (although work to convert the locomotives from coal to oil-fired power is under way). At each terminus are museums housing railroad memorabilia.

In 2018, the operation of this heritage railway was hampered by the outbreak of wildfires in June and mud slides in July, restricting the route that could be used by the trains. It was estimated that passenger numbers were reduced by about 60,000, corresponding to a loss of about $10 million in ticket and shop sales. While the peak summer season was badly hit, the trains were back in action in time for the winter running of the *Polar Express*, a promotion that usually sees about 34,000 riders annually. It was predicted that total passenger numbers would still reach 200,000 in the following year (Romeo, 2018).

By no means period or traditional, but nevertheless offering tourists memorable transport experiences, the *Talgo* tilting express travels from Seattle down the west coast, while on the eastern seaboard the *Acela* high-speed rail link between Boston, New York and Washington cuts the journey between Boston and New York from five hours to just over three (although even these services can be affected by the priority given to freight, which can lead to delays to passenger schedules).

Mexico has entered the market for tourist passengers, the privately run *Maya Express* in Yucatán taking tourists between Cancún and other popular coastal resorts.

RAIL NOSTALGIA IN THE UK

In the UK, nostalgic rail enthusiasts are being given the opportunity to enjoy rail services that conjure up a period when travel by train was, in many cases, a luxury for the well-heeled. Among others on offer in recent times have been the:

- *Shakespeare Express*, between Birmingham and Stratford
- *Belmond British Pullman*, between London and Bath (operated by Orient Express)
- *Cathedrals Express*, between London and Salisbury (and other cathedral cities)
- *Jacobite*, between Fort William and Mallaig (operated by West Coast Railways).

In Scotland, another successful venture has been the introduction of the *Royal Scotsman*. Although without the benefit of a genuine pedigree, the 1920s-style train has been packaged with success in the American market, offering a very upmarket tour of the Scottish Highlands. These enterprises demonstrate that market niches exist for unusual rail programmes, which can undoubtedly be emulated in other tourist regions.

The continuing appeal of steam trains has led to a new steam train, built in 2008 by the A1 Steam Locomotive Trust, to operate classic rail excursion services on the national rail network in the UK.

THE 'LITTLE RAILWAYS' AS TOURIST ATTRACTIONS

With the electrification of the railways in the UK, nostalgia for the steam trains of the pre-war period has led to the re-emergence of many small private railways. Using obsolete track and former British Rail rolling stock, enthusiasts have painstakingly restored a number of branch lines to provide one more type of attraction for domestic and overseas tourists.

In the UK alone, there are over 250 railway preservation societies and more than 50 private lines in operation. Some of these depend largely on tourist patronage, while others principally serve the needs of the local community. Their profitability, however, is often dependent on a great deal of voluntary labour, especially in the restoration of track, stations and rolling stock to serviceable condition. As these services are generally routed through some of the most scenic areas of the UK, they attract both railway enthusiasts and tourists of all kinds and undoubtedly enhance the attractiveness of a region for tourism generally.

Notable examples are the Ffestiniog Railway in Wales and the Romney–Hythe service in Kent. A route now devoted exclusively to serving the needs of tourists is the Snowdonia Mountain Railway, which has been in continuous service since the nineteenth century, transporting tourists to the highest point in England and Wales.

THE FUTURE OF RAIL TRAVEL FOR TOURISTS

The future holds the promise of trains travelling at much higher speeds than even the fastest in operation today. Magnetic levitation (Maglev) offers the prospect of rail journeys at speeds of up to 360 mph, but the cost of building these is prohibitive. This form of propulsion offers high speed coupled with exceptional quietness, the track consisting of a metal trough generating a magnetic field that repels magnets on the train, causing the vehicle to ride 10 cm above the track. There is therefore little wear and tear and, in consequence, the cost of maintenance is much reduced.

The Germans and the Japanese have led the research into developing Maglev propulsion, and the first working line, constructed by a German engineering firm for the Chinese government, is the 270-mph route between Shanghai's Loyang Road Station and Pudong International Airport, covering the 19 miles in just eight minutes. The company estimated that 20% of its passengers in the initial years were coming aboard purely for the ride.

In Japan, the Central Japan Railway's Maglev MLX-01, when it was tested, achieved a top speed of 361 mph (581 kph) in 2003. The 9-km Linimo line opened in 2005 in Aichi. This has been followed more recently by the opening in 2016 of the Incheon Airport Maglev, in South Korea. Several others are under construction or have been proposed, so the development of this form of rail travel is expected to take a leap forward over the coming decade.

In the USA, more prosaic schemes are being researched. Rail authorities have tested the CyberTran – a cross between a high-speed train and a light railway system – designed to provide fast, non-stop services at speeds of up to 150 mph between US cities.

Russia and America have previously held talks to discuss the construction of a 50-mile tunnel under the Bering Strait and a 4600-mile rail track to provide a surface transport link between the two countries. More recently, discussions have included China, which has proposed building a rail track (with a tunnel across the Bering Strait) to connect North Eastern China with Alaska and onwards through Canada into western states of the USA. While designed primarily as a means of competing with shipping across the Pacific for the carriage of freight, it would also enable the rail enthusiast to travel by rail between London and New York in 14 days. However, the cost of all these developments is substantial (the US–Russian project alone is estimated at $99 billion) so they are unlikely to materialise until much later this century.

Efficient rail travel provides strong competition for short-haul air services, as we have stressed, particularly on major business routes. In view of the existing congestion of many air routes and growing concern about aviation's pollution of the atmosphere, the development of alternative high-speed land routes is vital if trade, and tourism, are to prosper.

COACH TRAVEL

The term **coach** is used to describe any form of publicly or privately operated road service for passengers, other than local, scheduled bus services (although Americans still use the term 'bus' to apply to their long-distance vehicles). It thus embraces a wide range of tourist services that are sold to the public, both directly and through other sectors of the travel industry, and these may be categorised under the following headings:

- express coach routes, both domestic and international
- private hire services
- tour and excursion operations
- transfer services.

Long-distance coach services provide a cheap alternative to rail and air travel, and the extension of these services to include cross-border routes has drawn an increasing number of tourists at the cheaper end of the market, particularly those in the younger age groups. Younger passengers have also been attracted to adventurous transcontinental coach packages that provide, for a low all-in price, both transport and minimal food and lodging en route (often under canvas). These long-distance services were curtailed to some extent owing to political problems in the Middle East and beyond, but some have since been reintroduced, skirting major trouble spots, while others have been diverted to the African continent. Another form of cheap coach tourism is the Rotel sleeper coach (Figure 15.3), an innovation scarcely known in the UK, although on the Continent, particularly in the German market, this is a popular form of budget long-distance coach holiday. In this form of transport, the coach either has built-in sleeping berths or pulls a sleeper trailer that, at night, can accommodate all the passengers in sleeping bunks.

Apart from these exceptions, for the most part coach travel remains the mode of transport of the older traveller, despite efforts by coach companies to widen their market. In the UK, most coach holidays are taken by those aged between 55 and 64, with over-65's nearly three times more likely to take coach holidays than under-65's (Mintel, 2014). This is perhaps unsurprising, given the advantages that coach services offer to the older

FIGURE 15.3 A Rotel sleeper coach in India

Photo: Chris Holloway

market; not just low prices (reflecting low operating costs vis-à-vis other forms of transport), but also the convenience of door-to-door travel when touring, overcoming baggage and transfer problems, and courier assistance, especially overseas, helping to avoid problems of language and documentation handling. Additionally, coach operators frequently make arrangements to pick up and drop off passengers at points convenient to their homes. One result of this is that coach companies traditionally benefit from high levels of repeat business, often supported by loyalty rewards such as discounts or special treatment like preferential hotel rooms.

Coach companies now tend to the view that their marketing efforts are best spent on raising the frequency of sales to the older market, rather than trying to attract a new, younger market, given that the former market is expanding rapidly, as more people retire early. The most popular holiday destinations for British clients are Germany's Rhineland and Bavarian regions, the Austrian Tyrol and the Swiss Alps.

The operation of coach tours is a highly seasonal business, however, and companies are often forced to lay off drivers and staff out of season, unless they can obtain sufficient ad hoc charters or contract work (such as school bussing, useful for the coach companies as these commitments do not coincide with their busy holiday periods). Other out-of-season opportunities have been successfully marketed, however, notably Christmas market trips for British tourists to the Continent, pre-Christmas shopping trips to major cities and across the Channel, pantomime visits in the early part of the New Year and, of course, bank holiday trips.

Most coach companies specialise in certain spheres of activity. While some operate and market their tours nationally, others may concentrate on serving the needs of incoming tourists and tour operators by providing excursion programmes, transfers between airports and hotels or complete coach tours for overseas visitors. These coach companies must build up good relations and work closely with tour operators and other intermediaries abroad or in the home country.

COACH REGULATIONS IN THE UK

Coach operators are now governed by EU directives, which are designed to ensure adequate safety provisions for passengers. The concern with safety has been highlighted by incidents in the coaching industry, most notably accidents on the Continent involving holiday coaches. The maximum number of hours' driving permitted for each driver per day is stipulated for all express journeys by coach, with stages over 50 km. A tachograph (a device fitted to a vehicle that records its speed and distance, together with selected driver activity) provides evidence of the hours of operation and vehicle speeds of individual drivers. However, accidents, often involving fatalities, are a feature of coach travel in some developing countries where regulations are less strict or inadequately enforced.

While there can be little doubt that implementation of regulations has led to higher safety standards in the industry, the effect has also been to increase the cost of long-haul coaching operations, making it more difficult for them to compete with rail or air services. To permit through-journeys without expensive stopovers, two drivers must be carried or, more commonly (as rest periods must be taken off the coach), drivers are exchanged at various stages of the journey. With the constraint of a limited number of seats on each coach, this has the effect of pushing up the cost per seat.

In the UK, under the terms of the Transport Act 1980, coach operators must apply to the Transport Commissioners for a licence, which will normally remain in force for five years and limit the operator to a specific number of vehicles. Applicants must have a good financial record and demonstrate adequate resources, including professional competence based on management experience and appropriate educational qualifications, for example membership of the Chartered Institute of Logistics and Transport (CILT).

EXAMPLE

The dominance of National Express in the UK

The 1980 Transport Act in the UK ended many of the restrictions on express coach services on routes of more than 30 miles. This led to a spate of new coach services of all types being introduced in 1981. A period of intense competition followed, in which the National Bus Company (NBC) (originally state-run) emerged as the chief beneficiary, using the National Express brand name. Its dominant size offered an advantage over its rivals as it was able to offer greater frequency of services and flexibility. With its huge fleet of coaches and a national network of routes, it was able to replace a defective vehicle at short notice with little inconvenience to its passengers – an advantage denied to its smaller rivals.

The newly privatised National Express established a partnership with continental operators to create Eurolines (which it purchased in 1993), operating long-distance services between the UK and major cities in mainland Europe. The company also invested in the UK railways (including a share in Eurostar) and in North American and Spanish coach operations.

Competing with National Express is Stagecoach, a private company that, through aggressive acquisitions, became one of the UK's leading bus and coach companies, with interest in trams and ferries as well as the largest rail franchise in the UK, South West Trains. In 2003, the company also launched a popular low-budget coach service, Megabus, in the UK, later expanded to the USA. A third company, First Bus (later renamed FirstGroup), acquired prominent local bus companies and also successfully bid for train franchises, including the operator First Great Western, to become the third member of the triumvirate. All three have interests in overseas transport services.

Two other medium-sized operators, Go-Ahead and Arriva, have joined the triumvirate and, combined, they now effectively control the scheduled bus and coach industry in the UK. The privatisation of transport in the UK has been watched with interest by companies and governments abroad, several of which have their own plans to move transport to the private sector. In common with the US airline industry a decade earlier, deregulation of the bus and coach industry appears to have had the opposite effect of that intended, with the growth of a handful of powerful oligopolistic scheduled carriers. Other coaching companies have found it easier to specialise in the inclusive tour markets, rather than compete openly with the leading carriers.

COACH TOUR-OPERATING COMPANIES

Despite its rather archaic image, the coach tour remains popular with British travellers. Operators best known for organising package tours by coach have also tended to amalgamate since deregulation. Initially, two market leaders emerged from the string of takeovers – Wallace Arnold and Shearings – and these, in turn, merged in 2005, to form WA Shearings (since 2007 the company has been known simply as Shearings Holidays), which is now by far the largest coach tour operator in the UK. The company provides holidays for well over a million passengers (principally the over-55s) each year. The company packages tours throughout Europe and in North America, Australia and New Zealand and, in addition to its fleet of 240 coaches, it owns 50 hotels, operating under the Bay Hotels and Coast and Country brands. This is typical of the movement towards horizontal integration among the coach companies, and vertical integration between the coach companies and the hotels they use. Smaller companies are finding it ever more difficult to compete and will have to find niche markets if they are to survive.

EXAMPLE

AATKings

For more than a century, AATKings has been providing tours of Australia. The company is an amalgamation of AAT, which started out offering guided sightseeing tours around the Sydney area, and Bill King's Northern Safaris. Today the company provides guided coach holidays and small group tours using mini coaches or four-wheel-drive vehicles, servicing more than 250,000 passengers annually.

The guided coach holidays are overseen by a travel director who will provide local information to the guests on aspects such as local culture, history or flora and fauna. They will also provide information on things to see and do during free time at tour stopping points. Travel directors also assist guests with hotel check-in, oversee luggage handling and help arrange additional activities and excursions.

While having the assistance and support of the travel director can make coach holidays appealing for less mobile tourists, AATKings includes activities that can appeal to the more adventurous traveller, including white water rafting, camel rides, hiking and scuba diving.

Some specialist coach operators have chosen to move upmarket rather than attempt to compete directly with the market leaders. Coach charters are a popular means of achieving this. By purchasing luxury vehicles and fitting these out with videos, bar and catering facilities, more luxurious seating and an accompanying host, the coach companies can target niche markets for business routes, charters or long-distance luxury travel to compete with trains.

Some operators have opted to provide coaches with sleeping accommodation. Unlike the Rotel coaches, these are used for charters, principally by the music and entertainment industry, for artists and crews touring to play gigs. Typically, they have sleeping facilities for between eight and 16 passengers in comfortable, curtained-off bunk beds, with seating areas at the rear; some also include catering facilities.

At the other end of the market, many independent operators are engaged in small-scale enterprises that include transfers between airports and hotels, local excursions and city tours.

International long-distance scheduled operations form another sector of the budget coach market. The growth of shuttle services between the UK and the Continent, led by the Eurolines service, has been a prominent feature of budget travel for tourists within Europe. These international stage journeys travel as far afield as Bosnia, Poland, Hungary, Greece, Finland, Turkey and the Ukraine, their success varying according to the relative strength of sterling against other European currencies and the differential between air and coach fares.

Coach operations in North America have become equally concentrated. For many years, two powerful coach companies, Greyhound Lines and Trailways, dominated the domestic coach market, and their low fares enabled them to compete successfully against both the huge network of domestic air services and the private car. In 1982, however, road passenger transport was also deregulated in the USA, leading to a flood of small, low-priced coach companies, against which, in marked contrast to events in the UK, neither of the two giants seemed able to compete. Trailways cut services in an effort to remain profitable, but ultimately merged under new management with Greyhound in 1987. Despite this move, the amalgamated company went into bankruptcy three years later. After further restructuring and the introduction of new vehicles, including minibuses, Greyhound emerged from bankruptcy to face new challenges from other small companies, notably US Bus, launched in 1998 with smaller, more comfortable vehicles.

Greyhound's problem was its dependence on low-budget travellers and the fact that many of its city termini were in run-down and depressed areas of the cities. Although now out of bankruptcy and under the ownership of the UK's FirstGroup, the company has been forced to cut services, having to compete not only with budget bus companies but also with no-frills budget airlines (notably Southwest) and the Amtrak rail services, which are locally subsidised and have become more attractively priced. Updates to the brand and to the coaches, which included providing more leg room, power sockets and Wi-Fi, has helped address company issues. Furthermore, in 2014 a yield management system was introduced, allowing better monitoring of ticket sales and dynamic adjustment to prices.

The proliferation of small, low-priced bus companies over the past decade is a phenomenon of US travel. Stagecoach's Megabus, with its minimum $1 rides, has made an impact since its introduction to the USA, while other companies, such as Chinatown Bus, have arrived on the scene to take on the national carrier on key routes. Also, online ticketing agency Gotobus has enabled passengers to book their tickets on the Web, so they can choose on the basis of price from a range of bus companies. All these companies operate in the heavily travelled north-eastern corridor of the USA.

Finally, mention should be made at this point of the Gray Line organisation, an American franchise offering coach excursions and tours not only within the USA and Canada but also in many other countries. Franchising globally on this scale is relatively uncommon within tourism, but offers a pointer to the possible direction the industry will take in the future, as large companies go multinational.

It must not be forgotten that, in many countries, vehicles in common use for local residents are attractions for visiting tourists, too. Just as some ferries across the world are must-see attractions, so famous local services will attract tourists just to sample the experience. Examples include London's double-decker buses and the vintage buses in countries such as Malta and the Philippines, but this phenomenon is by no means limited to buses and coaches. The San Francisco cable cars, the tram and gondola rides to mountain tops in Hong Kong and Cape Town, black cabs in London, yellow cabs in New York, tuc tucs in Bangkok, tricycles and rickshaws in the Far East (and now spreading to Europe) – these are all essential elements of the tourist experience of the destination and contribute to tourism revenue as well as forming an ideal way in which to see the sights of the city.

For every country with a well-developed tourism market, however, there are many others that make little effort to bring their local bus and coach services to the attention of visitors. Buying bus and tram tickets can be a daunting experience for those visiting a foreign city for the first time, where tickets often have to be purchased in advance from kiosks, then punched in a machine on board the vehicle, yet all too often instructions are only available in the local language. Visitor passes and pre-purchase tickets, often available online, all help to make this process simpler. One example is Eurostar's sale of Paris Metro tickets at the St Pancras terminal in London, reducing the need to queue for tickets on arrival in France and thus speeding the onward journey of passengers.

Promoting public transport encourages tourists to stay longer as they can be told how to visit attractions away from the town centre; transport costs are often very cheap, so they need never fear being overcharged. In Finland, Helsinki has successfully marketed the internationally renowned Arabia ceramic factory, museum and showroom located out of town at the end of a tram route. By contrast, visitors to Tallinn in Estonia are offered little guidance in other languages on how to use public transport, despite the rapid growth in their numbers. Similarly, visitors to Beijing in China receive little guidance on the use of local buses, even though they are cheap and frequent.

EXAMPLE

Tourist ticket to explore Reykjavik

The marketing office for Iceland's capital city is actively promoting the use of a travel card as an affordable, convenient and eco-friendly way for visitors to see the sights. The card, which can be purchased to cover a 1-, 2- or 3-day period, provides entry to museums, galleries, the zoo and the thermal pools as well as providing unlimited use of public bus transport. It also includes the ferry ride to neighbouring Videy Island.

The ticket can be purchased online, although this means that the visitor must first head to City Hall to swap their purchase receipt for the physical ticket. Alternatively, the card can be purchased at many of the hotels and museums in the city. Information about the bus network is conveniently available online (in Icelandic and English) to allow tourists to plan routes and access timetables.

The perceived value offered by this ticket is important for a city considered to be the world's most expensive tourist destination, largely as a consequence of the strength of the Icelandic krona (it gained 40% against the euro between 2009 and 2018).

In some countries, the **postbus** fulfils the need for public transport where traffic is too limited to sustain a scheduled bus route. These are postal delivery vehicles that are also equipped to carry a limited number of passengers. They have long been popular in mountainous areas such as Austria (where they are operated by the Austrian Railways) and Switzerland, but are also used extensively by adventure tourists and backpackers travelling independently.

The UK introduced these passenger-carrying vehicles for the first time in 1967, serving the community around Llanidloes in Wales, and, over time, some 200 postbus routes were established, principally in the less-populated communities in Scotland. Sadly, they have been phased out, the last, in the Scottish Highlands, withdrawn from service in 2017.

In Australia, similar services are provided by the mail planes. Tourists are finding these useful means of getting about where other forms of public transport are limited or non-existent and, in turn, these services are learning to attract visitors as well as locals. Indeed, the mail services in Australia have gone as far as packaging tours around their mail runs in the remote Flinders Range, including accommodation and meals.

Finally, mention must be made of the curious, not to say bizarre, use to which some vehicles are put to give rides to tourists. While they are too numerous to list extensively, a few good examples will serve the purpose. In San Francisco, among other exotic transport modes such as duck boat trips in the harbour and antique car tours, visitors can take a

75-minute ride over the Golden Gate Bridge on an authentic antique fire engine, dressed in firefighter gear. More demure transport is on offer in Australia, where wine lovers can tour the wine-growing area of Margaret River, Western Australia, in chauffeur-driven classic Bentley cars.

THE PRIVATE CAR

Undoubtedly, the increase in private car ownership has done more to change travel habits than any other factor in tourism. It has provided families in particular with a new freedom of movement, increasing opportunities to take day excursions as well as longer trips. From the 1950s onwards, the costs of motoring have been falling in relative terms, and car owners also tend to take into account only the direct costs of a motoring trip, rather than the full cost, which would include depreciation and wear and tear. Thus, car transport has long been favoured over public transport.

The effect of this preference on the travel industry has been considerable. Over the years, the hotel and catering industries responded by building motels, roadside cafés and restaurants, while formerly remote hotels and restaurants suddenly benefited from their new accessibility to these tourists. Car ferry services all over Europe flourished, and countries linked by such services experienced a visitor boom. France remains, for the British, the leading holiday destination, being seen primarily as a destination for the independent and mobile tourist.

Camping holidays also boomed, and tour operators reacted by creating flexible self-drive car packages, including packaged camping holidays in tents or mobile homes. The rented cottage industry took off, the gîte holidays in France soon being followed by cottage and villa rentals in many other countries. Fly-drive and rail-drive packages were introduced. The railways, too, adapted to meet the needs of motoring tourists, introducing motorail services that allowed people to take their cars with them on longer journeys, such as to the south of France and Spain.

In the twenty-first century, the desire for greater flexibility has to be weighed against the burden of a rapid escalation in the cost of motoring, particularly in terms of fuel. If relative travel costs continue to rise, a reduction in demand for motoring holidays may be seen. Many British-owned second homes, for instance, are in fairly isolated regions on the Continent, so access would be difficult without personal transport.

A decline in car usage may be beneficial for some aspects of tourism. The construction of car parks and new roads catering for mass travel causes environmental damage to the countryside and the expansion of motoring and private car ownership is leading to enormous problems of pollution and congestion. Car ownership across Europe has continued to increase over the past 25 years (see Table 15.2), but this may change in the future as the Millennial generation appears to have less enthusiasm for car ownership (Euromonitor, 2015), renting access to cars through the commercial or sharing economy as required.

TABLE 15.2 European car ownership

Car ownership per 1000 residents	1990	2000	2010	2016
Belgium	387	456	480	503
Bulgaria	152	245	353	443
Czech Republic	234	336	429	502

(Continued)

TABLE 15.2 (Continued)

Car ownership per 1000 residents	1990	2000	2010	2016
Denmark	309	347	NA	NA
Germany	385	532	527	555
Estonia	154	333	416	534
Ireland	227	344	424	439
Greece	169	295	469	479
Spain	309	429	475	492
France	404	460	487	479
Croatia	166	261	355	374
Italy	483	572	619	625
Cyprus	305	384	551	595
Latvia	125	237	307	341
Lithuania	133	336	554	456
Luxembourg	499	622	659	662
Hungary	187	232	299	338
Malta	302	483	581	615
The Netherlands	367	409	464	481
Austria	388	511	530	NA
Poland	138	261	453	571
Portugal	256	509	444	470
Romania	54	139	214	NA
Slovenia	289	437	518	531
Slovakia	240	237	310	390
Finland	388	412	535	604
Sweden	419	450	460	477
United Kingdom	361	425	451	469

Source: Eurostat, 2018b

A growing interest for ecologically friendly tourism will inevitably discourage motorists from taking their cars to such destinations. Greater control can be expected in the future in the form of developments such as park-and-ride schemes, provided in many congested cities, where visitors are encouraged, and sometimes required, to park their cars at car parks on the outskirts and either walk or use public transport to travel in to the centre. Rationing by charging high prices for car parking (as has been introduced in both Oxford and Cambridge) or limiting access or denying facilities for car parking (as occurs at the more popular US national parks and is now finding favour in some of the UK's national parks) will inevitably become a characteristic of future tourist destinations when demand rises to a point where there is insufficient physical space to accommodate all who wish to arrive in their private cars. Many towns in the UK now adopt a variable pricing policy for parking, with comparatively low prices for parking up to two or three hours, to encourage shoppers and short-stay visitors, but rising sharply thereafter to discourage commuter parking. Prices then drop in the evening to encourage leisure visitors after the business traffic has left. On the other hand, pressure to raise revenues at local authority level is encouraging some communities to impose meter parking charges even during evening hours and on Sundays.

Some cities, notably London and Stockholm, have introduced congestion charging schemes to encouraging greater use of public transport. While many such schemes target commuters, the impact on tourism also has to be taken into account. To what extent is private car usage vital to either domestic or inbound tourist markets? Are tourist car rentals largely restricted to use to reach rural areas? Do inbound tourists actually consider changing their holiday destinations on the strength of the congestion problems they might face? These are highly relevant questions for the industry, but they have been inadequately researched.

The next development to discourage car use is likely to be road pricing, with drivers paying a set fee per mile of the roadways they drive on. Road pricing for motorway driving is common in Europe, with tolls on French motorways, for example, costing about €1 for every ten miles. Tolls for bridges and tunnel crossings also add to the cost of road travel. Again, little is known about the possible impact of such a move on tourism.

EXAMPLE

Road tolls in the UK

Paying tolls for travelling on UK roads is limited largely to charges imposed on a few bridges, toll roads and for travel within the London congestion zone. Historically, payment has been via a manned toll booth at the entrance or exit of the zone. However, the London congestion zone changed this approach, with number-plate recognition cameras identifying vehicles within the zone and payment being made in shops or online.

In 2014 the heavily used Dartford crossing, taking the London orbital road (M25) across the Thames between Kent and Essex, replaced toll booths with a digital system using number-plate recognition and predominantly online payment, though advance payment by post is possible. Regular users can create an account and hold a sum in credit to allow automatic deductions to occur when the crossing is used. However, unawareness of the system by tourists may lead to big fines, while payment issues with foreign credit cards have made travelling this section of motorway a further concern for international visitors, many of whom have already had to acclimatise to driving on the opposite side of the road.

CARAVAN HOLIDAYS

Caravanning has always been popular in the UK, since the manufacture of the first leisure caravan, the Bristol Carriage Company's 'Wanderer', in 1880. Today, there are some 2000 licensed caravan parks in the UK, 365,000 caravan holiday homes and over 550,000 privately owned mobile caravans. The National Caravan Council (NCC) estimates that around 2 million people take caravan holidays every year. For the most part, caravan holidays have been falling relative to other forms of holidaymaking. However, there was a spike in demand during the recession that occurred at the end of the last decade. Furthermore, since 2014 there has been marked increase in sales of caravans and motorhomes across Europe, with Italy, Spain and the Scandinavian region showing particularly strong markets (ECF, 2018).

In the USA, sales of trailers (the American term for caravans) have declined as motorhomes or campervans (motorised caravans) have found favour. These vehicles are widely known in the USA as recreational vehicles (RVs). Originating with the invention of the Curtiss Aerocar in the 1930s, they have steadily grown in popularity to a point where, today, more than 25 million Americans make use of them each year.

The industry responded by providing new and more luxurious camping facilities, with the franchise company Kampgrounds of America ensuring water and electricity were available at all its sites. RVs are widely available for rental too, and are popular among European visitors touring the USA, especially in the far west. While not cheap to rent, they are luxurious by any standards, with amenities that compare well with many hotel rooms, including en suite showers. While some have been imported into the UK, their sheer size makes them unsuitable for use on most of the UK's roads. There are, however, specialist holiday companies that rent out motorhomes and they are popular on the Continent where, in many countries, the roads are not too crowded and there are adequate facilities to park overnight.

THE CAR RENTAL BUSINESS

It has been estimated that there are over 1000 car hire companies operating in the UK, with more than 130,000 cars available for hire (many being fleet cars on hire to private companies). The car rental business owes a substantial proportion of its revenue (and, in many resorts, virtually all its revenue) to tourists. While in total only 30–40% of car hire is associated with leisure, small companies and local car hire operators get a disproportionate share of this, while the large corporations have the lion's share of the business travel market.

Car rental companies for tourists can be divided into two categories:

- large international companies or franchise operators
- small, generally locally based, independent hire companies.

The traditional model for car hire has been challenged by the introduction of car-pooling companies that connect passengers with drivers with empty seats. There is also the rapid growth of car-sharing services, such as Zipcar, which has 10,000 cars located across the UK (and has operations in the USA, Spain, Canada, France, Austria and Turkey). However, because such services require membership registration, such services are often used by local residents.

Most of the larger car hire companies charge broadly similar prices, but offer a choice of cars, hiring locations and flexibility (for example, the ability to pick up a car at one location and drop it off at another). This flexibility and convenience make them attractive to business travellers, who are less sensitive to price but insist on speed of service, reliability and a more luxurious standard of car. Contracts with suppliers generally tie them to favouring a particular make of car, on which they are given advantageous prices. Several of the large international chains now offer a home-delivery service.

The largest car rental agency in the world is Enterprise Holdings, which operates the Alamo, Enterprise and National brands. Hertz is second largest with over 10,000 outlets, while Avis, which also owns Budget Rent-a-car (and, since 2013, Zipcar), is the largest car hire company in Europe. Ownership of these two companies has changed frequently over the years and their operation now appears secondary to the perceived value of the asset. Hertz was sold in 2005 to a group of private equity firms, while AvisBudget Group was purchased by travel conglomerate Cendant and separated into an independent entity. In 2011, AvisBudget Group purchased Avis Europe, a separate organisation which has purchased the franchise rights to operate under the Avis and Budget brands in Europe, the Middle East and Asia. This will bring the two organisations under one worldwide operation. In the UK, Europcar and Enterprise Holidays dominate the market, each earning almost one-third of the total sales revenue.

As to the second category, there are literally hundreds of small, local car rental companies that generally offer limited choice but low price and the convenience of a local pick-up, although perhaps from only one or two locations. Because of their reliance on the leisure market, these companies work in a highly seasonal business, where they may be unable to maximise their opportunities for business in summer because they have insufficient vehicles. In addition, there are some specialist car hire operators that provide very luxurious vehicles, high-powered sports cars or even classic vehicles, for a small upmarket leisure or business clientele.

The competitive nature of the industry has once again resulted in good marketing playing a key role in the success of individual car rental companies. The expansion of outlets has been greatly aided by the introduction of franchising in the 1960s – a means of distribution now used by all the large companies. Three other factors have been critical:

- *Contracts with airports and railways.* These allow car rental companies to maintain a desk at airport or rail terminals. The opportunities for business that are provided by having desk space in these locations make these contracts very lucrative and they are fought for by the major companies, occasionally changing as competitors offer higher bids at the termination of a contract agreement.
- *Links with airlines and hotels.* This establishes good relations with (and hence referrals from) hotel chains and larger airlines, generates huge volumes of business and is critical for maximising sales opportunities for business travel bookings. Large hotel chains may also offer desk space for the car rental company in reception areas. The independent travel behaviour of many of their passengers has meant that budget airlines have provided direct links from their website to their car hire partners, receiving a small commission on every rental.
- *Computer reservation systems (CRSs).* The development of a good CRS (and, increasingly, global distribution systems, GDSs), together with accessibility via the websites of major airlines or intermediaries, plays an important role in the success of the larger car rental companies, which cannot afford not to be linked to such major systems. Equally, these information providers need car hire as an adjunct to their flight and accommodation sales via the Web. One company that has recognised this is online agency lastminute.com, which acquired the fast-growing leisure rental company Holiday Autos to complement its website operations.

Historically, car rental companies have also courted travel agents, which provide a good proportion of advance sales for business and leisure travel. Attractive rates of commission of 15% or more are still on offer to gain agency support. Mintel (2017) reports that 58% of car hire by UK residents travelling abroad was booked online pre-travel, while 10% was booked with a travel agent. The growing 'seat only' airline reservations market helped to expand the demand for car hire overseas, as has the huge demand generated by second-home owners travelling to their holiday homes across Europe.

EXAMPLE

Low-cost fly-drive

Low-cost airlines are increasing their revenue through links with car hire companies. For example, easyJet provides direct links on its website to car hire opportunities at the destinations it flies to. It also includes car rental options as part of the flight-booking process.

Through its collaboration with Europcar, it can encourage travellers to include car hire at the time of booking flights. The partnership, established in 2003, has seen several million rentals arranged though this link. Mintel (2017) reported that 18% of UK car hire bookings were made via airlines.

Trading conditions for the car rental companies are particularly competitive, with profits thin for the leading franchises. This is further challenged by the development of companies organising private transfers. With the growth of independent travel, more holidaymakers are putting together their own packages by searching the Web, and this includes arranging transfers to their hotel abroad. Specialist companies are arranging transfers by taxi, mini-coach, private limousine, even helicopter, for customers on their arrival at airports abroad. These services can also be incorporated into dynamic packaging programmes by agents.

CYCLING AND TOURISM

Over the past three decades, holidaymakers have shown a much greater interest in cycling holidays than in the past, partly on the grounds of their ecological sustainability. CTC (formerly the Cyclists' Touring Club) boasts some 65,000 members in the UK, and several specialist holiday firms have been established in recent years to cater for those seeking organised cycling holidays in the UK, on the Continent and even further afield. These include both leisure and sporting (off-road) pursuits, reflecting the growth in ownership of equipment such as mountain bikes. Tour operators like Cycling for Softies, which specialises in cycling holidays in France, provide vehicles for the transfer of cyclists' baggage between accommodation stops, leaving their clients to travel light. Germany, Austria, Denmark, Switzerland and France are the most popular European cycle tourism destinations (CBI, 2015).

Rural destinations, particularly those in relatively flat but attractive landscapes, have recognised the growing popularity of cycling as an activity for visitors and encouraged cyclists by providing suitable trails and informative leaflets about the surrounding countryside. Small businesses, such as cycle hire companies, have sprung up to serve these visitors. An example is that of the village of Worpswede, north of Bremen in Germany, which is a popular venue for domestic cycling tourists. The village lies on the edge of the famed Teufelsmoor, a nature reserve, and the Worpswede Radtour offers five themed cycle rides through the region, ranging in length from 19 to 45 km.

France, too, has long popularised holidays by bicycle. The Loire à Vélo, for instance, offers an 800-km cycle route between Cuffy (near Nevers) and St Brevin-les-Pins on the Atlantic coast, combining heritage sites, gastronomy and wine tourism, and visiting Nantes, Angers, Saumur and Fontevraud in the Loire Valley, in part a UNESCO World Heritage Site.

The interest in off-road biking has led to tour programmes catering for mountain bike tours in distant countries. Morocco, South Africa, New Zealand, the USA,

Kyrgyzstan and Kazakhstan are just a few of the countries now offering mountain bike adventure tours.

EXAMPLE

Cycle routes in Europe

Having successfully gained funding from the European Commission in 1997, plans for a trans-European network of cycle routes was launched. There are now 15 long-distance cycle routes agreed, extending over more than 70,000 miles of cycle paths and existing road networks:

- Eurovelo 1: Atlantic Coast Route: North Cape–Sagres, 8186 km
- Eurovelo 2: Capitals Route: Galway–Moscow, 5500 km
- Eurovelo 3: Pilgrims' Route: Trondheim–Santiago de Compostela, 5122 km
- Eurovelo 4: Central Europe Route: Roscoff–Kiev, 4000 km
- Eurovelo 5: Via Romea Francigena: London–Rome and Brindisi, 3900 km
- Eurovelo 6: Atlantic–Black Sea: Nantes–Constanta, 4448km
- Eurovelo 7: Sun Route: North Cape–Malta, 7409 km
- Eurovelo 8: Mediterranean Route: Cádiz–Athens and Cyprus, 5888 km
- Eurovelo 9: Baltic–Adriatic: Gdansk–Pula, 1930 km
- Eurovelo 10: Baltic Sea Cycle Route (Hansa circuit), 7980 km
- Eurovelo 11: East Europe Route: North Cape–Athens, 5984 km
- Eurovelo 12: North Sea Cycle Route, 5932 km
- Eurovelo 13: Iron Curtain Trail: Barents Sea–Black Sea, 10,400 km
- Eurovelo 15: Rhine Route: Andermatt–Hoek van Holland, 1320 km
- Eurovelo 17: Rhone Route: Andermatt–Mediterranean, 1115 km

At the time of writing, only Eurovelo 15 has been completed to an extent that it has met the formal certification criteria for a Eurovelo route. The route starts in Switzerland and then travels for 900 km through Germany, into France for 180 km, and onwards to the Netherlands to finish at the coast.

Source: www.eurovelo.com/en/eurovelos

The UK is now following the lead of other European countries like the Netherlands and Denmark, in providing dedicated paths for cyclists in and around towns, and new traffic-free, long-distance cycle routes are also being established. Work is under way to complete the National Cycle Network, consisting of 16,000 miles of dedicated cycleways (coupled with walkways) throughout the UK. There is clearly high demand for this amenity as, according to Sustrans, over 786 million trips were made on the National Cycle Network in 2017, with 377 million of these being cycle trips.

Cycling has been encouraged in cities and towns through the introduction of convenient cycle hire points, which do not require the user to return the cycle to the start point. London introduced these in 2010, although non-residents were unable to use the system for

FIGURE 15.4 Danish train with carriage equipped to carry bicycles

Photo: Chris Holloway

the first six months of its operation, as computer and docking stations were trialled. The London system offers a low daily rate for the occasional user (currently £2) with additional hire costs based on the length of time the cycle is used, the first 30 minutes being free. Similar schemes are in operation in Paris and other provincial cities across France as well as Barcelona, Copenhagen and New York.

Efforts are also being made to improve opportunities for cyclists to take their cycles on trains, which would encourage rural tourism by bike. Integrated transport planning can facilitate this opportunity – for example, the Danish railways are noted for the facilities they offer cyclists, with most routes offering special carriages equipped to allow cycles to be carried (see Figure 15.4).

TOURISTS ON FOOT

In examining the role of transport, one must not forget tourists who travel mainly on foot. Walking holidays in the mountains have a long tradition, and hiking and trekking have both grown in popularity in recent years. Ramblers' associations represent the interests of these long-distance walkers, working to ensure that rights of way over both public and private land in the UK are protected. The European Ramblers' Association was established in 1969, and, since that time, 12 European long-distance paths have been defined, often using refurbished long-existing routes. The longest, at 12,000 km, runs from Tarifa in southern Spain to Larnaca in Cyprus, via Grenoble (France), Budapest (Hungary) and Sofia (Bulgaria). Some of the 12 routes, such as the E2 Grande Traversée des Alpes or the five pathways through the Austrian Alps, are well maintained and extensively used, while others, such as those in southern Italy, Romania, the Ukraine and Turkey, have far lower levels of usage.

Tourism on foot is also important to towns and cities. In the most popular urban destinations, trails are often marked out by means of symbols on pavements or signposts, just as markers on trees enable visitors to find their way along forest trails.

Apart from the obvious attractions identified by these trails, promotional bodies are recognising that walking tours provide the opportunity to introduce tourists to little-known regions of the town, allowing poorer districts to benefit from the influx of visitors. Liège, in Belgium, offers a ten-day Festival de Promenade for tourists visiting the city in August, with more than 40 different walks of varying lengths, appealing to a variety of different tastes.

EXAMPLE

The New York High Line

A 1.5-mile linear park was created along the disused section of the elevated freight rail line running up the western side of Manhattan island. This provides a promenade space, with seating areas and views overlooking the city streets. Planting alongside the walkway provides a beautiful landscape for visitors. The park also includes temporary exhibitions and performance spaces to encourage visits.

It is estimated that more than 7.5 million visitors walk the High Line annually, but the park has not been without controversy as local neighbourhoods struggle to adjust to the influx of visitors and private investment from property investors. *The New York Times* (Moss, 2012) described the park as a 'tourist-clogged catwalk' responsible for rapid gentrification of the local area.

FIGURE 15.5 The High Line

Photo: Claire Humphreys

FUTURE DEVELOPMENTS IN LAND TRANSPORT

In terms of future development, the railways in particular are making substantial progress. Trains increasing in top speed, improving interconnectivity and efficient ticketing could certainly pose a major threat to air routes of distances over land of up to 1000 miles.

The cost of fuel and the environmental impact of creating and burning fuel for transport are frequently in the news. Attention is turning to transport making use of biofuels, and the development of hybrid systems, and it is likely that investment in this area will continue to grow. The introduction of electric systems, especially in situations where journeys are short and don't require high speeds, has already been seen, for example in the shuttle buses taking tourists up the mountain to Machu Picchu from the base at Aguas Calientes in Peru.

Growing awareness of the health benefits of exercise is encouraging more tourists to be active, and to include walking and cycling as part of their holiday. The EU, among others, is promoting such exercise as part of a healthy lifestyle, and, as demand increases, we may see a greater variety of facilities conveniently available to tourists.

Finally, there has been much improvement in information about transport, for instance the electronic noticeboards at bus stops that detail the arrival of the next bus. Moves are also afoot to ensure that all transport networks will eventually be linked by global positioning software, enabling travellers to track the current location of any form of transport using smartphone technology. Mobile apps also provide convenient booking for transport such as taxis, rail and coach tickets.

QUESTIONS AND DISCUSSION POINTS

1. In what ways are the railways changing to offer greater appeal as a mode of transport for tourists?
2. What factors are influencing the demand for different forms of car hire today?
3. To what extent is the development of electric bicycles likely to change cycle tourism in the future?

TASKS

1. You are to research the following five travel routes between capital cities in Europe:
   - London to Berlin
   - Paris to Amsterdam
   - Brussels to Rome
   - Copenhagen to Stockholm
   - Budapest to Warsaw.

   Identify the time it takes to travel between these destinations by train and by plane. Ascertain the cheapest ticket available (for travel in five weeks' time) for both plane and rail travel. Produce an infographic that reports your findings. What conclusions can you draw from this study?
2. Select a coach touring company and examine the different tours that they offer. How do the tours offered by the company change at different times of year?

REFERENCES

Amtrak (2017) Amtrak FY16 Ridership & Revenue. Available online at: https://media.amtrak.com/wp-content/uploads/2015/10/Amtrak-FY16-Ridership-and-Revenue-Fact-Sheet-4_17_17-mm-edits.pdf [Accessed November 2018].

Confederation of British Industry (CBI) (2015) *Cycling Tourism from Europe*. The Hague: CBI Market Intelligence.

Euromonitor (2015) *Millennials and Car Ownership*. London: Euromonitor, July.

European Caravan Federation (ECF) (2018) Another Significant Increase in Newly Registered Leisure Vehicles in Europe. Available online at: www.e-c-f.com/fileadmin/templates/4825/press/262018_Neuzulassungen%20Freizeitfahrzeuge_Europa%201.HJ%202018_ENG.pdf [Accessed November 2018].

European Court of Auditors (2018) *A European high-speed rail network: Not a reality but an ineffective patchwork*. Special Report No. 19. Available online at: http://publications.europa.eu/webpub/eca/special-reports/high-speed-rail-19-2018/en/ [Accessed November 2018].

Eurostat (2018a) Tourism Statistics – Intra-EU Tourism Flows. Available online at: https://ec.europa.eu/eurostat/statistics-explained/index.php/Tourism_statistics_-_intra-EU_tourism_flows#Aeroplane_most_common_for_travelling_to_another_EU_count [Accessed November 2018].

Eurostat (2018b) Passenger Cars per 1000 Inhabitants. Available online at: http://appsso.eurostat.ec.europa.eu/nui/show.do?dataset=road_eqs_carhab&lang=en [Accessed November 2018].

Kaul, R. N. (1985) *Dynamics of Tourism: A Trilogy – Volume 3: Transportation and Marketing*. New Delhi: Sterling Publishers.

Martin, A. (2016) It's the Eurostar test: A sure way to tell if we're heading for exile in Europe. *The Guardian*, 28 October.

Mintel (2014) *Coach Holidays – UK*. London: Mintel, March.

Mintel (2017) *Holiday Car Hire – UK*. London: Mintel, June.

Moss, J. (2012) Disney World on the Hudson. *The New York Times*, 21 August.

Rail-news (2010) Railteam Prevails in Race vs. Low-cost Airline. Available online at: www.rail-news.com/2010/08/13/railteam-prevails-in-race-vs-low-cost-airline [Accessed November 2018].

Romeo, J. (2018) Durango & Silverton Narrow Gauge Railroad rolls again. *The Durango Herald*, 22 September.

Smith, K. (2018) Hololei – rail must show it is worthy of further EU investment. *International Railway Journal*. Available online at: www.railjournal.com/in_depth/hololei-rail-must-show-it-is-worthy-of-further-eu-investment [Accessed November 2018].

PART 3

INTERMEDIARIES IN THE PROVISION OF TRAVEL AND TOURISM SERVICES

16

THE MANAGEMENT OF VISITORS

CONTENTS

LEARNING OUTCOMES

After studying this chapter, you should be able to:

- explain the concept of visitor management
- identify different techniques employed to manage tourists
- understand the role of interpretation in visitor management
- summarise the controls that can be implemented to protect the physical environment.

> Tourism relies upon the natural and built environment. The protection of this environment is vital for the success of the tourism industry and as visitor numbers increase there is a need to develop and apply planning and management solutions which address the problems of over-development, congestion and pollution. (Office of the European Communities, 1995: 11)

INTRODUCTION

As can be seen in the quote at the beginning of this chapter, natural landscapes and the built environment require management strategies to protect against tourism demand. The pressure of excessive numbers of visitors has long caused concern in locations across the spectrum – from remote wilderness areas to the biggest of cities. Managers of those places popular with tourists need to control the ensuing impacts, ever mindful that global growth of the tourism industry further exacerbates this problem. As tourists seek new experiences, so the frequency of both short and long breaks has increased and the numbers of leisure tourists have increased. Destinations not traditionally seen as tourist resorts are becoming popular places to visit, and consequently pressure to respond to an influx of people lies at the heart of visitor management.

Visitor management involves finding ways to regulate visitors in order to minimise negative impacts and, where possible, maximise the benefits of tourism (Mason, 2005). This chapter examines some of the techniques that can be employed by tourist businesses and destinations in order to control and manage visitors and, in consequence, their impacts. These impacts extend beyond placing pressure on the physical environment – large numbers of tourists can also impact on the host community and its way of life. Furthermore, large tourist numbers can place pressure on infrastructure and superstructure, impacting on the economic balance of the destination.

CONTROLLING THE IMPACTS OF VISITORS

A great deal has been written over the past few decades in acknowledging the diverse impacts of tourism and, importantly, considering the ways in which negative impacts can be prevented. Visitor management can help to ensure that the expectations of tourists are balanced against the demands of the host environment, community and tourist businesses. Successful visitor management requires a clear understanding of the demands of these groups and the compromises organisations are prepared to make to achieve a balanced outcome for all stakeholders.

EXAMPLE

Encouraging visitor management

The United Nations Environment Programme (UNEP) has explored visitor management as part of its guidance on achieving sustainable tourism. It suggests that there are four strategic approaches to reducing the negative impacts caused by visitors:

1. Manage the supply of opportunities by controlling the time and space made available to visitors.

2. Manage the demand for visitation by influencing length of stay, who might visit and the types of use demanded by such visitors.
3. Manage the resource capability by adapting the site (in all or part) to better withstand visitor pressures.
4. Manage the impact of use by dispersing or alternatively concentrating use to specific areas best designed to cope.

Such actions might include closure of all or parts of the site at some times, or setting a limit on visitor numbers through a ticketing system. Education and information provision can also assist in adjusting visitor demand and on-site behaviour.

Source: UNEP, 2002

A variety of visitor management strategy models have been employed over the years, including the Recreation Opportunity Spectrum, Visitor Impact Management model, Visitor Experience and Resource Protection model and Visitor Activity Management Program (Richardson and Fluker, 2004). The approaches of these models are underpinned by an appreciation of the need to control negative impacts by establishing limits for tourism, embracing two key principles – carrying capacity and the limits of acceptable change.

CARRYING CAPACITY

This concept (introduced in Chapter 6) proposes that there is a finite capacity for a tourist facility or destination, which should be identified and not exceeded in order to restrict any detrimental impacts. Specifically, this can be defined as 'the maximum use of any site without causing negative effects on the resources, reducing visitor satisfactions, or exerting adverse impacts upon the society, economy or culture of the area' (McIntyre, 1993: 23).

The origins of this concept derive from wildlife management, where it has been recognised that plants and animals require certain physical conditions in order to survive. Once an environment has been altered to a point where those conditions no longer exist, the wildlife populations cannot be sustained. This principle makes the assumption that impacts are likely to be relatively gradual, until a point is reached at which intense changes occur. For the principle of carrying capacity to be effective, clearly the limiting point should be set somewhere before such changes happen. One critique of this approach takes the view that intense impact on environments occurs when use of them first begins, with increased use only adding marginally to that impact. If that is the case, unless all tourists are banned, an increase in visitor numbers will cause little marginal distress to the landscape. While both perspectives may have validity, it is achieving an understanding of the impacts of use that is the underlying principle here.

Although initially carrying capacity focused on damage to the physical environment, there is now greater awareness of other carrying capacities. Richardson and Fluker (2004) identify five subtypes of carrying capacity:

- *physical* – the number of visitors that the site was designed for or has the ability to accommodate
- *economic* – the level at which the tourism business can operate before other industries are squeezed out by the competition for resources

- *perceptual* – the level of use that can be accommodated before the psychological experience of visitors is negatively affected
- *social* – the numbers of visitors that can be tolerated by the host community
- *ecological* – the numbers of tourists that can use an area before damage is done to the natural or biological environment.

For some attractions, such as a staged Wild West show or a city bus tour, the maximum capacity may be fairly easy to determine, based perhaps on the number of seats in an auditorium or on the vehicle. For many other attractions, however, such a finite number is often difficult to establish. It is worth adding that it can be difficult to establish one numerical carrying-capacity point, as various stakeholders are likely to have different perspectives on where the limit lies. For the planners and managers of popular tourist destinations, the objective to protect animal and plant life will need to be balanced against the objective to maintain an environment acceptable to the host community, the tourists and those businesses seeking to profit from visitors. This may lead to conflicting pressures when considering maximum capacity.

Finally, even if an exact number is precisely established, it may then be hard to control numbers so that they remain within that capacity limit; for example, attractions such as national parks may have several entry points, which makes restricting numbers difficult. Furthermore, fundamental principles such as the right to access national parks may make closure or restrictions unpopular or unenforceable in law. In such cases, a range of more subtle visitor management techniques, discussed in detail later in this chapter, may help to control demand.

As it may be impossible to establish and implement an exact carrying capacity, an alternative approach may be to determine the level of impact or alteration that is acceptable to these user groups, through compromise and negotiation, accepting that some change to the environment will occur.

THE LIMITS OF ACCEPTABLE CHANGE

This principle acknowledges that humans' use of the natural environment will ultimately lead to change. Therefore, the aim is to manage the destination or attraction through this change, acknowledging that impacts beyond a pre-established level will not be tolerated and responses will be implemented to ensure that the limits of acceptable change (LAC) are not exceeded. The management challenge 'is not one of how to prevent any human-induced change, but rather one of deciding how much change will be allowed to occur, where, and the actions needed to control it' (Stankey et al., 1985: 1).

The LAC approach requires that the nature of different types of impacts is identified as well as noting where those impacts occur. Managers of the destination or site must then determine the levels of impacts that are acceptable and introduce initiatives to ensure that actual impacts remain within these boundaries or limits. Stankey et al. (1985) propose that the LAC process consists of four major components:

1. the specification of acceptable and achievable resource and social conditions, defined by a series of measurable parameters
2. an analysis of the relationship between existing conditions and those judged acceptable
3. the identification of management actions necessary to achieve these conditions
4. a programme of monitoring and evaluation of management effectiveness.

Over the years, this approach has been implemented at a variety of destinations and tourist sites, especially in wilderness areas in the USA.

MEETING THE COST OF VISITOR MANAGEMENT

Both the strategic process of creating a visitor management plan and the implementation of operational methods to control visitors have an inherent cost. For example, there are likely to be significant costs involved in adapting the physical environment, such as constructing paths, a visitor management centre or signage, to control the behaviour of tourists. The costs may be passed on to visitors, borne by the host community or met by local tourism businesses. In cases where tourists are expected to meet (or pay a contribution towards) the cost of managing the impact of their activities, a direct charge for access may be made, perhaps in the form of an entry charge. Many popular heritage sites charge entry fees that contribute towards the cost of maintaining the site and making it accessible to visitors. In order to ensure that the local population is not excluded from accessing its local heritage site, a reduced charge or discounted annual fee may be offered.

EXAMPLE

Entry fees for Canterbury Cathedral

The historic city of Canterbury, located in the south-east of England, is home to this popular tourist attraction, now receiving around a million visitors annually. To help manage visitors, an entry charge is levied. First introduced in 1995, this charge was seen as a means to address two problems: the overwhelming visitor numbers (believed to be in excess of 2 million at the time) and the limited financial resources available, leading to a deficit. Today, the money raised from this charge helps to maintain the upkeep of the building as well as providing information and other facilities for tourists.

To ensure that this does not exclude the local population, entry is free to those who work in the old city or live within 4 miles of the cathedral.

As an alternative to entry fees, tourists may be required to purchase a licence to gain access to a destination. Limiting licences will control the number of tourists accessing the protected area. For example, a trekking permit is required to enter the Annapurna conservation area in Nepal. More than 25,000 trekkers visit this area annually, with the permit fees estimated to improve the living standards of around 40,000 local people, as well as funding environmental protection and sustainable tourism initiatives. Trekking permits are also required for the popular trail to Machu Picchu, Peru. Passes are limited to around 400 permits per day to trek the Inca trail to the site. Since 2017, timed tickets have been required for all visitors (not just trekkers) in an attempt to control congestion.

The host community may cover the costs of managing local resources, perhaps through the level of state or council taxes that they are required to pay, while businesses may be required to make a contribution through their business rates. Tourism companies may foot the bill for visitor management through demands to adapt their operations, perhaps by constructing supporting infrastructure, funding information provision, marketing campaigns or other similar activities.

While many tourist attractions are commercially operated businesses, some resources are under the control of governments. Natural environments, such as national parks and wilderness areas, as well as some built heritage sites, may be the responsibility of the national government, which must provide the funding to protect, maintain and manage them. In such cases, governments may open such resources to the public and tourists as part of a remit to provide access. The cost of implementing effective visitor management is likely to be borne by the public purse.

OPERATIONAL APPROACHES TO VISITOR MANAGEMENT

The operational techniques employed to manage visitors and their impacts can be broadly separated into two categories: 'hard' and 'soft' management. The **hard management** techniques are those methods that restrict tourist activities, perhaps through financial or physical controls. **Soft management** techniques focus on encouraging a change in behaviour, through design or subtle persuasion.

While hard techniques have been a common approach employed to protect the environment and resources from the pressures of tourism, the use of soft techniques can help to balance the need to protect with the need to provide a positive experience for the visitor. For example, educating visitors about the impacts they cause and the ways in which these effects can be minimised can serve not only to encourage improved behaviour but also to provide a greater engagement with the activities undertaken to protect resources from demand pressures.

TABLE 16.1 Examples of hard and soft visitor management techniques

Hard techniques	Soft techniques
Closure of attraction or areas within an attraction	Marketing
Zoning	Directional signage
Permits and licences	Limited infrastructure development
Vehicle bans	Codes of conduct
Entrance fees	Education and information provision

More than 20 years ago, the Department of Employment and the English Tourist Board (DoE/ETB, 1991) produced a report, 'Tourism and the environment: Maintaining the balance', designed to encourage improved management of tourism resources. This identified the following three key areas for managing visitors:

- *Controlling demand* may be achieved by attempting to spread the arrival of visitors throughout the year. Furthermore, it may be possible to control the areas that are accessed by visitors. This can ensure that tourism is more evenly spread across the area (reducing the intensity of pressure). An alternative may be to contain visitors in one location that, while intensifying the pressure in that specific location, allows for the protection of other areas left untouched by the tourists. Ultimately, control may be achieved by limiting total numbers or the amount of time that tourists can spend at a location, or banning access altogether.
- *Altering visitors' behaviour* may be possible through increased awareness. Encouraging tourists to understand the impact of their presence and to take responsibility for this may lead to improved behaviour, thus reducing the impact. Codes of conduct are often designed to encourage such responsibility.
- *Adapting supply* can ensure that resources are better placed to cope with demand. This may include developing supporting infrastructure, such as roads and paths, toilets and information centres.

These areas are interlinked, and employing initiatives that consider all three areas can provide greater benefits than just attempting to address one aspect alone. Therefore, the techniques identified in the following sections recognise the effects on all three realms.

CONTROLLING DEMAND AND FLOW OF VISITORS

All too often, discussion relating to visitor management at a destination only arises when problems start to emerge, yet it is vital that policies and the actions required to successfully manage the impacts of tourism should be introduced as soon as visitor flows begin. As demand levels change, so the strategies for managing visitors should be revisited. A variety of initiatives can be implemented to adjust the flow of visitors.

Pricing policies and strategies

As previously highlighted in the example of Canterbury Cathedral, price mechanisms are often proposed as means of controlling tourist demand, with an increase in prices expected to reduce the number of visitors attracted. As prices are often relatively inelastic where major tourist attractions are concerned, however, this may not always have the desired limiting effect.

The benefit of employing a pricing policy is that it raises revenue that can help to finance the implementation of visitor management. Selective taxation on hotel accommodation or higher charges for parking can also be imposed, but some criticise this as a regressive tax, affecting the less well-off but having little effect on the wealthy.

For some attractions, the use of pricing as a means of controlling demand can be controversial. Several religious buildings (including St Paul's Cathedral in London and St Basil's Cathedral in Moscow) have introduced entry charges, often using the funds to assist with the costs of maintenance, but the charge does not sit easily with many, who feel that places designed for religious worship should not be limiting entry only to those who can afford the charge.

Controlling access through ticketing and licensing

Limiting entry through some form of permit or **licence** is another practical alternative. Requiring prior application can allow destination managers or tourism businesses the chance to deter arrivals. As we saw in the earlier mention of Machu Picchu, the number of licences can be restricted, both in total and across time periods – the latter helping to manage congestion and, in some cases, seasonality. Thus, control by licence simultaneously restricts tourists and provides the government with useful revenue, directly and indirectly.

EXAMPLE

Timed tickets for Harry Potter studio tour

The studio location where all eight Harry Potter movies were filmed opened its doors to the public in 2012 (Figure 16.1). Visitors take a tour of the sound stages – viewing costumes and props from the film – as well as the backlot which houses sets of Diagon Alley, Privet Drive and the Knight Bus. The attraction is immensely popular, with dates during school and summer holidays often being sold out weeks in advance. The attraction manages demand by offering only timed tickets, whereby approximately 250 visitors can enter the attraction every 30 minutes during daily opening hours. Average dwell time is two and a half hours, but with no maximum visiting time congestion can build through the day.

(Continued)

FIGURE 16.1 **Entrance to the Harry Potter studio tour in Leavesden, Hertfordshire**

Photo: Claire Humphreys

Timed tickets, which allocate visitors to a particular time of day, help to spread demand for the resource, while providing tourists with an opportunity to participate in other activities in the meantime. This can significantly enhance visitors' experience as well as benefiting the destination – visitors can see other attractions in the area as well as using the time to eat and shop, which can substantially increase their spend.

Restricting activities

In order to control the impacts of tourist demand, it may be necessary to set regulations or policies that restrict the use of resources. There are various ways in which restrictions can be implemented. Failing to expand supporting infrastructure is an option sometimes chosen by local authorities in an attempt to discourage visitors. This can be effective, but unfortunately it can impact on local residents equally, whose frustrations with, say, inadequate road systems may lead to a political backlash. Additionally, it may be considered appropriate to control the length of time tourists spend at a destination. This may be necessary in popular locations, where keeping the visitors flowing is vital. Linked to this is a management approach that can restrict the use of sites at particular times.

In addition to restricting the time spent at an attraction, it may be helpful to restrict access by groups or the range of activities allowed at particular sites. For example, camping and campfires may be banned in the fragile forest areas of some national parks.

Marketing

Another form of control can be achieved through marketing, concentrating publicity on less popular attractions or geographical regions and promoting the low season. For example, the national tourist board VisitBritain might stress the appeal of the north-east of England in its marketing abroad, making little reference to the south-west, which already attracts a high proportion of domestic tourists.

Attempts to do this may be frustrated by private-sector promotions, however. Airlines, for example, may prefer to concentrate on promoting those destinations for which they already have strong demand, although credit must be given to the no-frills carriers, which have opened up new areas by flying to small provincial airports. There is always a danger that if the public-sector strategy is too successful and tourists are siphoned off to the new regions, the amenities and attractions at more popular sites could suffer a downturn in business. These popular sites may be better able to cope with large levels of tourism, while the diversion of visitors to other areas less able to cope with a large influx may cause new problems for both the established and the new destination.

Niche markets

To ensure a consistent demand for tourism all year round, it may be advisable for marketing efforts to try to attract specific niche sectors. For example, the conference market may be sought by a seaside resort destination, as these events tend to take place outside the traditional summer holiday period. Thus, a large conference can fill bed spaces and use restaurants, transport and meeting venues at a time when other holiday markets are scarce.

Alternatively, marketing activities may focus on encouraging traditional holidaymakers to visit at less popular times of the year. In some cases, external factors, such as school and public holidays, mean that some people cannot be encouraged to alter the time they travel, but other travellers may not be restricted by such factors. To take one example, retired or childless travellers may be encouraged to adjust their travel plans to the shoulder season, spreading demand and reducing congestion.

Changing the behaviour of the more flexible traveller may be achieved by offering lower prices, but, importantly, this can also be achieved through marketing and information provision, making the traveller aware of the benefits of travelling to the destination at a quieter time or to a less popular area of the destination. While the benefits for the traveller may include less congestion, fewer queues, lower prices and improved service as staff are less pressured, it is also useful to highlight that such a shift in behaviour can help to protect resources, limiting pressure on the natural environment, reducing the likelihood of accidents and reducing pressures that may affect the quality of life for the host community. In this way, tourists may be encouraged to adjust their travel patterns to protect the destination.

Demarketing

It may seem unimaginable to some businesses or destinations, but there are several examples of places that too many tourists wish to visit, leading to marketing activities being undertaken to deter visitors. Efforts may focus on trying to discourage visitors during peak times or dissuade those tourists who will be less profitable. Kotler and Levy (1971: 75) defined the concept of **demarketing** as 'that aspect of marketing that deals with discouraging customers in general or a certain class of customers in particular on either a temporary or permanent basis'.

A variety of adjustments to the marketing mix can be employed in demarketing, including increasing the price for some or all of the market, reducing promotional activities and limiting sales outlets offering access to the product. Such actions can be controversial, however. Restricting access to those who can afford the higher price may be perceived as elitist, while a reduction in promotional efforts by a destination management organisation (DMO) may not be popular with local tourist businesses.

ALTERING VISITOR BEHAVIOUR

While acknowledging the benefits of reducing the impact of tourism through restrictions on demand, we can appreciate that the management of those tourists who do visit will also help to reduce the pressures caused. This will improve tourists' experience, as it can minimise conflict between different stakeholder groups.

Interpretation, information and education

Information can be provided in a variety of ways, both prior to visiting and on reaching the attraction or destination. One reason for providing information to visitors may be to meet obligations to educate – often an important remit for attractions funded by governments, such as galleries and museums. Providing an interpretation of exhibits or information about landscapes and buildings can help to fulfil this obligation.

Adequate information can also help to change the behaviour of visitors. For example, telling them about the pressures caused by tourism and the ways in which such pressures can be reduced may encourage visitors to develop an awareness of their responsibility and the impact of their activities, but it is important to stress that the majority of tourists do not set out to harm or damage the destination they visit. Cole (2007: 443) reports that 'while some tourists may be open to learning, they are often unaware of appropriate behaviour and have little guidance on how to behave'. Signage can also help ensure visitor safety (see Figure 16.2).

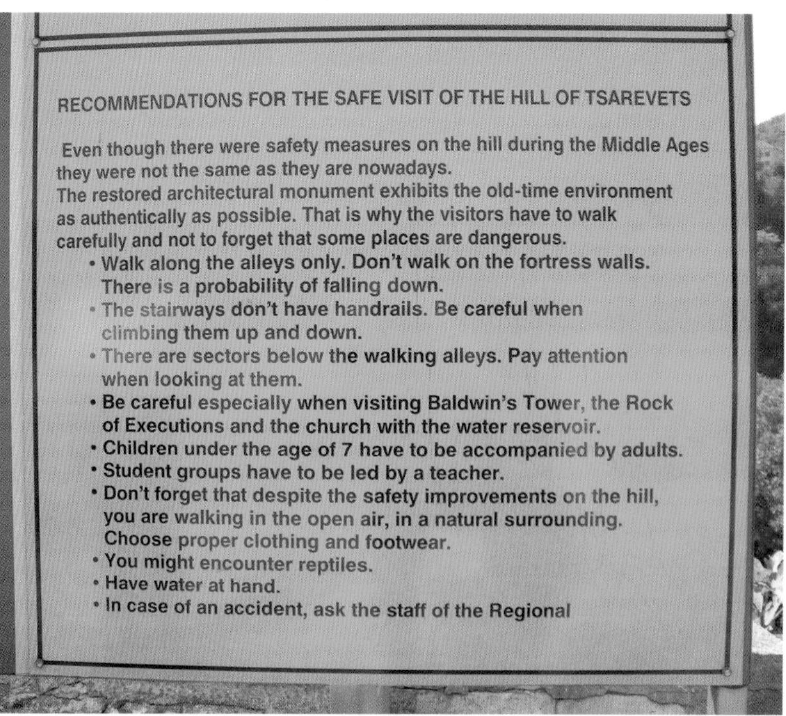

FIGURE 16.2 Managing tourist safety and protecting the historic medieval stronghold of Tsarevets, Bulgaria

Photo: Chris Holloway

It is often the combined activities of tourists *en masse* that cause significant pressures and problems for destinations. It is possible to adjust the behaviour of each tourist, however, through education and information, leading to considerable adjustments to the overall impact for the destinations. There are a variety of ways in which visitors can be informed, including signage, guides and codes of conduct.

Signs and guides

There is an extensive diversity in the signs and guides available to inform and educate tourists. The reasons for their provision are also varied, and they may be funded either by tourism businesses or governments at local or regional level. Signposting can fall into two categories: **informational** or **directional**. Informational signs can provide interpretation of a particular point of interest or act as a marker, pointing it out. An example of this may be a blue plaque on a building identifying a location as the place of birth of a noteworthy person in history. Informational signing is used to add to the knowledge of visitors, thus enhancing their experience.

Directional signposting is used to assist tourists to navigate, perhaps finding their way to a tourist attraction or locating particular amenities or facilities, such as toilets. Directional signage needs to be clear, consistent in style and suitably positioned.

Early warning is vital for car drivers navigating unknown routes, so signs must be positioned well in advance of junctions, and repetition of signs may be needed. Directional signs may not necessarily take car drivers on the shortest or most direct route. Often, routes are designed to encourage the use of bypass or ring roads, as well as keeping tourist traffic away from commonly congested areas. The growing popularity of satellite navigation systems, however, may lead to many of these diversionary tactics becoming ineffective.

Signs aimed at pedestrians must generally provide the most convenient and safest routes, taking into consideration the needs of those with pushchairs, in wheelchairs or less stable on their feet. Directional signs may also be provided for specific groups, such as walkers, cyclists or horse riders, each having their own requirements for convenient routes.

For a less well-known destination or visitor attraction, it may be necessary to provide guides to help interpret the nature and importance of the place. These are often provided in multiple languages. Guides can play a very important visitor-management role, however, so even well-known or established destinations use them to inform visitors, seeking to influence their behaviour.

Perhaps the commonest type of guide is the **tour guide** – a person who takes on an explanatory role, providing information about the heritage and history of a destination (see Figure 16.3), as well as describing the operation of machinery at an attraction, or topics relating to the local population. An example may be seen in the case of the guide who takes a small group on a factory tour of the Ferrari car plant in Italy, explaining the equipment or processes en route. Alternatively, an explanatory guide may be tasked with explaining the different stages of a religious service to observers witnessing it for the first time.

Guides may also take on the role of wardens, controlling the behaviour of tourists at the destination. In such cases, the guide may inform the visitor of expected modes of behaviour and remove or chastise tourists who do not conform. In that way, the guide acts to protect the resources by reducing or removing threats caused by those tourists who may be ignorant of the effects of their actions. While the role of such a guide may sound severe, in reality it may only require him or her to ask and visitors will respond. For example, guides will commonly ask visitors to dress suitably when entering religious buildings, be quieter when walking through areas where rare animals may be spotted and avoid entering buildings if they are residences of the local population. In such cases, only when tourists ignore the advice is there a need for the guide to take more severe action.

FIGURE 16.3 **Tour guide educating visitors at Machu Picchu, Peru**

Photo: Claire Humphreys

EXAMPLE

Tour groups are too big in Cambridge, England

Cambridge, England is a popular tourist destination. In 2018, Visit Cambridge and Beyond, the city's official tourism service, said it wants to slash tour group sizes because some streets become 'impassable at peak times'. This continues a long-held strategy of demarketing the city to day visitors, in an attempt to gain the more lucrative overnight tourist. City managers also moved the coach drop-off/pick-up locations away from the congested city centre. The result is further inconvenience for those hoping for a quick visit while en route to tourist cities elsewhere in the country.

The recent announcement has acknowledged that the large groups of up to 50 tourists can lead to a poor experience for residents and visitors alike, while the city's narrow streets and small central area further exacerbate congestion issues. The local tourism organisation wants arriving tourists to use local tour guides who are better placed to manage the behaviour of groups to reduce visitor impacts.

Source: Lumby and Pengelly, 2018

A guide can also take the role of a director or leader, selecting routes that can take tourists to less congested areas or less well-known attractions, helping to relieve pressure on the destination. The guide can also determine the length of time spent at particular sites, which may be vital at popular sites as it ensures that a turnover of visitors is achieved. The guide who acts as a group leader may also be able to divert tourists to other attractions.

There have been many examples of tour groups being taken to 'attractions' that offer little more than shopping opportunities (for which the tour guide may be provided with a financial reward for bringing the group there). While many tourists have negative reactions to such actions, the practice remains widespread.

A final role for the tour guide may be that of public relations. Given that guides have tourists in their company often for an hour or more, they have an extensive opportunity to provide positive information in order to enhance the image of a destination.

Travel guidebooks conveniently provide tourists with details about the destinations they are visiting. Books can include information on the history, attractions, facilities and amenities in the area, as well as some key phrases or words in the local language. The German publisher Baedeker set the standard when it started to print travel books over 150 years ago, providing accurate, detailed information in its travel guides; since then, companies like Lonely Planet, Rough Guide, Frommer's, Fodor, Insights and numerous others have produced their own city and country guides covering the globe.

Information provided to visitors in the form of guides can have an impact on their behaviour at destinations. **Written guides** can be designed to highlight the range of facilities or attractions in an area, which can in turn encourage a longer dwell time. Guides can also be published to provide information about a specific attraction, detailing the history and enhancing visitors' interpretation of exhibits. They can also act as a souvenir of a visit.

Difficulties faced when deciding to publish guides are extensive. If guides are to be sold to tourists, then the amount of information included must justify the price to be paid. Major attractions or destinations will need to consider several versions in different languages to serve their most popular markets. Adaptations for different markets may involve adjusting the content by identifying relevant areas of interest. If guides are to be provided free to visitors, then the costs of their production may need to be controlled, which may limit the size and quality of the guide. If free guides are to be offered, it may be necessary to consider how these complement any other guides available for purchase.

The use of human and written guides has been discussed above, but here we need to consider pre-recorded commentaries available in places such as museums, tourist attractions and now, more commonly, on city bus tours.

Audio guides can provide an extensive range of information on specific topics, but, unlike a human guide, offer no opportunity for questions to be asked. They are often available in a variety of languages and can be programmed to provide segments of information at particular locations. In museums, signs close to exhibits can show codes that can be entered into an audio guide for the visitor to hear the relevant segment of explanation. Technology thus allows pre-recorded guides to offer a level of control over the information provided to visitors.

The rapid growth in popularity of digital music players (including iPods and telephones that can play MP3 audio recordings) has also provided visitors with the opportunity to download files containing information designed to enhance their visit.

EXAMPLE

Digital guides to download

As more and more travellers take their music players (and smartphones) with them on holiday, so the online market for downloadable audio guides of city destinations has taken off. There are many different companies offering pre-recorded information, frequently

(Continued)

structured as a walking tour of the city with a charge being made for each download. Examples include Tourist Tracks (www.tourist-tracks.com), Audio Steps (www.audiosteps.com) and RickSteves (www.ricksteves.com/watch-read-listen/audio/audio-tours). In the UK, several local tourist offices now provide digital walking tours for their area, including Bath and Bristol.

Codes of conduct

The creation of codes of conduct can place responsibility for the impact and problems caused by tourism on those who cause them or have a role to play in reducing them. The existence of such codes is about more than just the regulation of behaviour; it also plays a role in education, raising awareness of the problems and issues. While codes of conduct are often aimed at tourists, there are many cases where host communities and tourism businesses are encouraged to agree to codes of conduct to ensure that their actions and operations are responsible. To take one example, the United Nations World Tourism Organization, together with ECPAT and UNICEF, introduced a code of conduct for the travel industry that is designed to protect children from commercial exploitation, especially in the sex tourism industry. This is explained in more detail in Chapter 5.

Codes of conduct are suggested as being relatively easy to introduce, as well as effective (Cole, 2007). This is especially true in cases that include considerable levels of restriction, which, if implemented through local legislation, may take years to reach the statute books (Garrod and Fennell, 2004).

EXAMPLE

Code of conduct for tourist guides

The Travel Industry Council of Hong Kong requires all accredited tourist guides to abide by a code of conduct, the objectives of which are to ensure professional standards are maintained in terms of service quality, as well as upholding the reputation of the destination. Specifically, the code encourages:

- high standards of service
- a spirit of cooperation with others working in the tourism industry
- obedience to the law
- ethical behaviour
- a professional image (including displaying the tourist guide pass)
- promotion of the tourism industry
- adherence to policies on accepting commission, gratuities or tips
- protection of the tourist in relation to shopping activities
- awareness of safety issues
- protection of confidential information and data.

This code is designed to protect the tourist. It also protects the tourism industry from rogue behaviour which can create a negative impression of the destination.

Source: www.tichk.org/public/website/en/guides/code/html

The disadvantage of voluntary codes of conduct, however, is that they may have limitations, such as being unable to effectively penalise offenders when the regulations are breached or ignored. To be successful, such codes rely on a moral consensus being reached to abide by principles in order to achieve the desired goals. As more companies are being encouraged to consider their social responsibility roles, so greater pressure to abide by codes of conduct may be felt.

ADAPTING SUPPLY

In order to protect attractions such as natural and heritage areas, there is often a need to make changes or adaptations to the supporting infrastructure. This can help to ensure that the demands of tourists are best served, while reducing negative pressures on the resource itself.

Queuing

In many areas of life, there is the need to queue – perhaps in a post office, a supermarket, to be served in a bar or café, or while waiting for a customer service assistant on the telephone. Unsurprisingly, queues are every bit as evident in the tourism business. While there are many initiatives aimed at reducing or dispensing with them, in some cases queues can be seen as a sign of popularity, attracting attention and thus, on occasion, they may even be encouraged. However, when insufficient resources are assigned to handling queues, the result can be frustration, and even downright anger, when customers are forced to wait for lengthy periods for something as simple as paying for and collecting a ticket.

EXAMPLE

The longest queues and 'skip the line' entry

TripAdvisor has identified those tourist attractions that have the longest queues. Perhaps unsurprisingly, many are in popular tourist cities such as London, New York and Rome.

To address the long waits – which can be up to four hours in peak times – the TripAdvisor report highlights that many of these busy attractions offer the opportunity to pay for a premium ticket which includes priority access, thus allowing tourists to 'skip the line'. The additional costs of priority access may not be that great or may come with additional benefits that enhance the visit. Often, it is achieved through advanced booking for a timed entry ticket.

TABLE 16.2 Standard versus 'skip the line' prices for popular attractions

Attraction	Standard entry price	'Skip the line' price
Colosseum	€14.00	€18.00
Empire State Building	$37.00	$65.00
London Eye	£28.00	£34.20
Paris Catacombs	€13.00	€29.00
Sistine Chapel	€17.00	€21.00

Note: Prices correct as at October 2018.

Source: Travel Weekly, 2017 and authors' own research

Queues form when the arrival rate is higher than the time taken to service those arrivals. For example, passengers on a plane landing at an airport will disembark at the same time and reach customs together. As it takes time for the border security staff to process each of these passengers, the outcome will be the formation of a queue.

Having to queue can create a negative impression, affecting the visitor's experience. There has been extensive research into ways to shorten wait times as well as understanding attitudes towards waiting. Three decades ago, David Maister (1985) explored the psychology of waiting and suggested eight propositions:

- occupied time feels shorter than unoccupied time
- an 'in process' wait feels shorter than waiting to get started
- stress and anxiety can make the wait feel longer
- uncertain waits feel longer than finite, known waits
- unexplained waits can appear longer than explained delays
- unfair waits appear longer than equitable waits
- waiting alone seems longer than waiting with a group
- the more valuable the service, the longer the customer will wait.

These propositions give insight into strategies that can be introduced to manage the experience of waiting visitors. They can be commonly seen in the activities of those tourist operations where queues are prevalent – theme parks, airports, catering establishments and hotel receptions, for example. The following are some responses to managing queues:

- *Entertain visitors while they wait.* This can be achieved through a range of distractions, such as providing entertainers to amuse a queue waiting for a theme park ride. This does not necessarily have to be expensive or high-tech – for example, a wall of mirrors that distort the image can entertain visitors as they move slowly along in the queue. A restaurant may ask customers to wait in the bar while their table is prepared, or peruse the menu. While distracting customers from the wait, this can also provide the impression that they are in process, that their presence has been acknowledged and they will be seated in the restaurant in due course.
- *Start the process.* It is useful to greet customers and assess their needs. This can ensure that customers have not waited only to discover later that they are in the wrong place or that they need not have joined the queue. This can help service providers identify VIP customers – the business may have a policy to service these customers in a different manner. For example, airlines usually board first- and business-class passengers ahead of economy-class travellers.
- *Use customers as a resource.* Asking customers to complete paperwork while they are in the queue or even prior to arrival may reduce the time needed to service each customer, thus shortening the length of queues. Car hire company Avis offers frequent customers the opportunity to complete a hire agreement form in advance that can then be applied to all their rentals. This reduces the need for paperwork for each occasion and lets these customers bypass the hire desk, going straight to the parking lot to collect their pre-booked car. This benefits both the frequent traveller and other customers, as it reduces the queue at the service counter.
- *Inform customers of the length of time they can expect to wait.* This is an important factor in enhancing customers' experience. While many flyers may be happy to wait an hour or more at an airport, often being entertained by the duty-free shopping or

restaurants, once their expected departure time has passed, only short waits will be tolerated before their level of satisfaction is affected. Keeping customers informed of delays can allow each individual to make a choice about how the time is to be spent. For instance, advising that the plane will be delayed by an hour may allow the customer the chance to go to a bookshop to purchase reading matter, check e-mails or make business calls, have something to eat or grab a last-minute gift from a souvenir shop. While companies are encouraged to be honest about waiting times, there are occasions when expected delays are exaggerated so that customers are pleasantly surprised when they experience a shorter delay than they had prepared themselves for. Restaurants, especially, may employ this tactic. Many theme parks, too, manage their queues by informing visitors of the time it will take to reach the front of the line.

- *Use equitable queuing systems.* Confronting customers with several queues requiring them to make a decision can cause anxiety that other queues will move faster or the queue joined may be the wrong one. A common resolution to this problem is to create one long queue, with customers being allocated to a service agent only when they reach the front. This can encourage a sense of fairness. Signs are also important. Customers need to know that their particular need can be addressed by the service agents once they reach the front of the queue.
- *Introduce separate queues for those customers who can be serviced quickly.* Cafés may create a separate counter for takeaway service, separating these customers from others who may need to wait for a table. Ski resorts and theme parks often employ a similar system for 'singles' or customers prepared to ride the ski-lift or rollercoaster without their friends alongside them. Such an initiative allows every seat to be filled, thus moving more passengers through the system, shortening the waiting time for all customers.
- *Consider the use of booking systems.* Allocating fixed time slots can spread the arrivals of customers, but it is vital that the time between those slots is appropriate. If the slots are too far apart, then resources may be left idle, but if it is too short, then a backlog will build, frustrating later arrivals. Booking systems may also fail if customers do not show for their appointments, so it may be necessary to impose penalties on customers who fail to come at their allocated time. Applying penalties may be problematic, however. The causes of delays or missed appointments may be beyond the control of customers, who will have already suffered stress, so penalising them still further can create antagonism towards the business. Flexibility regarding imposing penalties may be needed.

While businesses should evaluate *actual* waiting times, analysing what may cause congestion points within their operations, using a range of strategies to reduce the *perceived* time spent queuing to be served, can be an important factor in enhancing customer satisfaction and effectively managing visitors.

Zoning

For popular destinations that receive large numbers of tourists, it may be beneficial to group together those who have similar expectations or patterns of behaviour. For example, those tourists who wish to relax and sunbathe on a beach may be separated from those who wish to play ball sports. This can be achieved by providing volleyball nets, goals and other such facilities in one area, making it attractive for those playing sports to move to that location. Similarly, at seashores or lakes, areas allocated to sailors, windsurfers and so on may be separated from those allocated to swimmers.

While zoning is an effective tool for managing a variety of demands for resources and reducing the potential for conflict between users, it is also used to balance the demands of users with conservation ideals, protecting the natural environment. This has been seen in relation to the protection of marine parks as well as national parks (Geneletti and van Duren, 2008).

Zoning has also been used to balance the conflicting demands of tourists and the host population. This may be achieved through planning policy and is used in urban as well as rural locations. Tourist zones are often prevalent in cities, where attractions, accommodation, amenities such as bars, restaurants, currency exchange facilities and so on are clustered together, all benefiting from the large numbers of tourists drawn to these areas.

Closure

While zoning areas for particular use can help to balance the conflicting demands of users, in some cases protection and visitor management can only be achieved by means of closure. One approach may be to close an area by erecting fences and security, refusing entry to the site. This can achieve a maximum reduction in access and ensure that an area is protected from the demands of tourists. Refusing entry to all visitors, including the local population, however, may be seen as extreme and a more moderate form of restriction may be desired.

Protection of some attractions or destinations may be achieved by restricting opening hours – perhaps only allowing afternoon visits or access just at weekends. This can significantly reduce the impact of visitors. If such an approach is to be employed, it is necessary to provide tourists and tour operators with information about the restricted hours. This ensures that tourists are not disappointed by arriving and finding that the attraction is closed. In such situations, marketing efforts should focus on explaining that the closure provides a means of protection.

The pressure caused by the excessive demands of tourism may also be managed by the use of selective closure. This may restrict access to particular parts of the destination or attraction, perhaps by means of a zoning policy, marketing efforts to divert attention or changes to the infrastructure. An example of limited closure to protect a site from the impact of visitors can be seen in the case of Stonehenge, a World Heritage Site in the south-west of England. The site introduced a rope fence around the stones, keeping tourists some distance from these historic stones. This has reduced the amount of erosion previously resulting from visitors touching and walking through the circle.

Pedestrianisation

In recent years, it has become increasingly common to protect the central areas of towns and cities by restricting access by cars: in effect, pedestrianising the area. Changing road systems is a complex and expensive task, but the rapid increase in car ownership has required cities – especially those with historic centres not designed to cope with modern-day traffic – to impose measures to control traffic flows. This has the added benefit of enhancing the experience for both locals and visitors, who no longer have to compete with the traffic for space. The absence of cars parked in historic city centres also enhances the visual experience of the site.

While it is common for pedestrianisation to be a permanent feature, in some cases the closure may be for only short periods of time. For example, there are several provincial towns in France that close their central streets in order to allow street markets to take place. Temporary pedestrianisation may also be implemented to accommodate increased visitor numbers during events and festivals. For instance, streets around Castlehill in Edinburgh close nightly in August to accommodate tourists attending the Royal Edinburgh Military tattoo.

When implementing pedestrianisation, it is important to ensure that the improved environment also addresses health and safety demands. This may mean ensuring that emergency vehicles can gain access to the enclosed area if required. Areas must be made safe for all users, especially those who may have visual or mobility impairments. Pedestrianised areas can be used as social and event spaces for the local community, but, however used, it is vital that such areas are perceived to be safe and free from crime.

EXAMPLE

Pedestrianisation in Paris

France's capital city is implementing measures to make the city more pedestrian friendly. The Marais, with its narrow medieval streets, is being pedestrianised to substantially reduce the number of vehicles coming into the area. This follows the closure of a 3-km stretch along the right bank of the Seine, making it accessible for cyclists and pedestrians only. For several years, the area has been used for the 'Paris Plages' beach project each summer, so this stretch of highway is not new to traffic restrictions.

On the first Sunday of every month, the Champs Elysée, a main thoroughfare linking the Arc de Triomphe to the Place de la Concorde, is closed to motorised vehicles. The street is popular with tourists visiting its boutique shops and renowned restaurants. Car-free Sundays see this iconic street used by locals and tourists alike, to stroll, shop, sit and have picnics. Public film screenings and other events have also made use of this car-free space.

Research into pedestrianisation schemes in a selection of German and UK cities (Hass-Klau, 1993) revealed that, while the pedestrianisation of areas can lead, in the short term, to a downturn in trade for local shops, in the longer term it can lead to improvements in turnover. Thus, pedestrianisation can gain great support from local enterprises, as well as being beneficial for locals and visitors who use the area.

Gateways

It is possible to manage the pressure caused by the influx of tourists by creating gateways. These are convenient routes providing access to popular areas, directing demand through those areas best able to cope with it, and they are designed to manage the impacts of that demand. Encouraging tourists to use specific gateways to tourist areas can be achieved by effective signs, marketing, the location of convenient coach drop-off points and the creation of facilitating resources, such as visitor centres and parking spaces.

Visitor and tourist information centres (TICs)

Visitor and tourist information centres can play many roles: they can be used to educate visitors, perhaps affecting their behaviour, granting protection to the resource, and they can become an attraction in their own right.

In this way, visitor centres may provide convenient parking points for visitors, attracting tourists in a way that can then be appropriately managed. For example, in areas of natural beauty they may act as a gateway or starting point for tourists' exploration of the area, perhaps on foot or by other transport. This role as a hub means that trails (walking, cycling and driving routes) can be constructed, influencing the behaviour of visitors.

Trails and pathways

Trails may be used to disperse tourists, relieving pressure on an area and encouraging less well-known areas to be accessed. Alternatively, trails may be designed to cope with large numbers of visitors – perhaps by constructing surfaced paths, informative signs and toilet facilities. While such approaches may *increase* various impacts on these routes, they also serve to protect those areas that are less able to cope with such influxes of visitors. They can often be controversial, however, as the amount of construction necessary to hard-surface paths to manage the footfall of the many visitors can mar the landscape, affecting its natural beauty. This has to be balanced with the fact that, in many cases, constructing such paths can control erosion of the land, as well as control the spread of damage. Furthermore, the surfacing of paths can create an environment that is better able to cope with increased numbers of tourists. The downside is that this ultimately makes access easier, further stimulating an increase in demand (Mason, 2005).

EXAMPLE

Hiking trails in the Grand Canyon, USA

This iconic natural attraction receives in excess of 4 million visitors a year, many of whom take hiking tours to enjoy the scenic beauty. However, 250 people have to be rescued annually from the canyon. To reduce such problems, the National Parks Service identifies a variety of trails that are designed to encourage visitors to hike in the area safely.

Two locations, one each on the north and south rims of the canyon, act as hubs to service the needs of hikers and the many other, less active visitors who come to view and photograph the canyon. These areas provide a tourist information centre, car parking, shuttle bus access, catering and accommodation facilities.

Along the south rim, multiple viewing points, accessed via tarmac paths, are available, encouraging visitors to take a short walk, or cycle, along the edge of the canyon.

FIGURE 16.4 Signage at the South Rim Visitor Center, Grand Canyon National Park

Photo: Claire Humphreys

Transport links

Gateways can be linked with supporting transport services. This may include park-and-ride options, which can provide mass transport services to sensitive areas. These may exist in both urban and rural areas. Many historic cities have set up park-and-ride facilities to cope with the demand for access from the local population as well as visitors, while in rural locations, including national parks, such schemes can limit the need for car journeys into wilderness or natural areas. To cite one example, in the Grand Canyon National Park shuttle buses provide a park-and-ride facility into the park from the nearest town as well as around South Rim village. It is estimated that, over the 30 years of their operation, more than 75 million passenger journeys have been completed.

TECHNOLOGY THAT CAN ASSIST IN VISITOR MANAGEMENT

Many tourist businesses have employed a variety of technological methods to examine visitor behaviour in order to improve the experience for their customers. To take one example, Alton Towers, one of the largest theme parks in the UK, provided selected visitors with an electronic badge that used tracking technology to monitor the time they spent in particular areas of the park and the routes they took. This provided the park managers with information that could help them decide where to site new rides or catering facilities. Badge monitoring is often used at business events such as conferences and exhibitions, to track the movements of visitors. Camera technology is also used to monitor visitor behaviour, identifying areas where queues might build up or tourists are reacting negatively to particular resources.

The Internet can provide a variety of opportunities to enhance visitor management, including the dissemination of information and the means to conveniently pre-book timed-entry tickets, thus allowing the flow of visitor arrivals to be managed. An example of this is the use of the Internet by airlines to manage visitors through the provision of online check-in. This can help to speed visitors through the airport system.

FUTURE ISSUES

With ever-growing visitor numbers, the need to manage the pressures caused by tourism is significant. It is important, however, to recognise that many tourists' expectations are also changing. As more visitors demand 'experiences' that can provide special memories, so there is a need to ensure that the management and control of visitors do not detract from the overall encounter. This may require excellent communication to inform and establish expectations.

The rapid development of mobile technology may offer an opportunity here. The provision of information and opportunities to reserve tickets conveniently using dedicated phone software or 'apps' may help to ensure that tourists are able to plan their travels with greater convenience. Furthermore, GPS systems on phones can also provide updated information about attractions in the immediate vicinity. For example, Alton Towers, the theme park mentioned earlier, has developed an app that allows visitors to obtain real-time updates of queue time for rides in the park.

Finally, as budgets tighten for many attractions, the cost of visitor management may become a greater issue. It is vital to recognise that successful visitor management can ensure that resources are protected, reducing the likelihood that costs will be encountered at a later date to repair damaged facilities. Furthermore, an improved visitor experience may well increase dwell time as well as enhancing positive word-of-mouth reviews, both of which can potentially increase visitor spend.

QUESTIONS AND DISCUSSION POINTS

1. Under what circumstances might closure of a popular tourist site be an acceptable visitor management strategy?
2. What are the visitor management benefits of providing a human tour guide instead of an audio tour guide?
3. Does visitor management enhance or detract from the tourist experience?

TASKS

1. Visit a tourist area or attraction of your choice. Consider whether any or all of the visitor management techniques identified in Table 16.1 have been implemented. Produce a poster that summarises your findings.
2. Many audio guides are freely available to download or listen to online. Select an audio tour for a city or tourist attraction of your choice. Evaluate whether you think visitor behaviour would be altered as a result of listening to the guide. Summarise your views in a short report.

FURTHER READING

Beunen, R., Regnerus, H. D. and Jaarsma, C. F. (2008) Gateways as a means of visitor management in national parks and protected areas. *Tourism Management*, 29 (1), 138–45.

Butler, R. W. (2010) Carrying capacity in tourism: Paradox and hypocrisy? In D. G. Pearce and R. W. Butler (eds), *Tourism Research: A 20-20 vision.* Oxford: Goodfellow Publishers.

Leask, A. (2016) Visitor Attraction Management: A critical review of research 2009–2014. *Progress in Tourism Management*, 57, 334–61.

Richardson, J. I. and Fluker, M. (2004) *Understanding and Managing Tourism*. French's Forest, NSW: Pearson Hospitality Press.

WEBSITES

United Nations Environment Programme (UNEP), Tools for Visitor Management: www.unep.fr/shared/publications/other/3084/BP8-7.pdf

Wilderness.net, Visitor Use Management Toolbox: www.wilderness.net/visitoruse

REFERENCES

Cole, S. (2007) Implementing and evaluating a code of conduct for visitors. *Tourism Management*, 28, 443–5.

Department of Employment and English Tourist Board (DoE/ETB) (1991) *Tourism and the Environment: Maintaining the balance*. London: DoE/ETB.

Garrod, B. and Fennell, D. A. (2004) An analysis of whalewatching codes of conduct. *Annals of Tourism Research*, 31 (2), 334–52.

Geneletti, D. and van Duren, I. (2008) Protected area zoning for conservation and use: A combination of spatial multicriteria and multiobjective evaluation. *Landscape and Urban Planning*, 85 (2), 97–110.

Hass-Klau, C. (1993) Impact of pedestrianization and traffic calming on retailing. *Transport Policy*, 1 (1), 21–31.

Kotler, P. and Levy, S. J. (1971) Demarketing? Yes, demarketing! *Harvard Business Review*, 49 (6), 74–80.

Lumby, T. and Pengelly, E. (2018) Cambridge slashing tour group sizes to tackle 'problem' visitors. Available online at: www.cambridge-news.co.uk/news/cambridge-news/cambridge-tourists-group-council-city-15260940 [Accessed October 2018].

Maister, D. (1985) The psychology of waiting lines. *Harvard Business School, Note* 9, May, 2–3.

Mason, P. (2005) Visitor management in protected areas: From hard to soft approaches. *Current Issues in Tourism*, 8 (2–3), 181–94.

McIntyre, G. (1993) *Sustainable Tourism Development: Guide for local planners*. Madrid: World Tourism Organization.

Office of the European Communities (1995) *Official Journal of the European Communities: Information and notices*, 38, C106, pp. 1–13, 27 April.

Richardson, J. I. and Fluker, M. (2004) *Understanding and Managing Tourism*. French's Forest, NSW: Pearson Hospitality Press.

Stankey, G. H., Cole, D. N., Lucas, R. C., Petersen, M. E. and Frissell, S. S. (1985) *The Limits of Acceptable Change (LAC) System for Wilderness Planning*. Ogden, UT: United States Department of Agriculture – Forest Service.

Travel Weekly (2017) Where you'll find the longest queues for tourist attractions. *Travel Weekly*. Available online at: www.travelweekly.com.au/article/where-youll-find-the-longest-queues-for-tourist-attractions [Accessed October 2018].

United Nations Environment Programme (UNEP) (2002) *Sustainable Tourism in Protected Areas: Guidelines for planning and management*. Available online at: www.unep.fr/scp/publications/details.asp?id=3084 [Accessed October 2018].

17

THE STRUCTURE AND ROLE OF THE PUBLIC SECTOR IN TOURISM

CONTENTS

LEARNING OUTCOMES

After studying this chapter, you should be able to:

- explain the part played by local, regional and central governments and their agencies in the planning and promotion of tourism in a country
- recognise the growing importance of the public sector in all aspects of tourism and its role in public–private partnerships
- define the term 'social tourism' and understand its significance for disadvantaged populations
- explain how governments and local authorities in the UK and elsewhere supervise and exercise control over tourism
- assess the changing role of public-sector tourism in the UK.

> For the sector to thrive, and for travel and tourism to develop in a sustainable manner, governments need to provide a supportive physical, regulatory, fiscal and social environment – one which is also conducive to business development. This means adequate infrastructure, incentives for private sector investment, easy access – including good transport connectivity and visa facilitation – and intelligent taxation, as well as the appropriate policies to encourage growth in demand. (WTTC, 2017: 8)

INTRODUCTION

Tourism often plays an important part in a nation's economy by providing opportunities for regional employment, contributing to the balance of payments and stimulating economic growth. Countries that experience an influx of large numbers of tourists, however, also suffer the environmental and social consequences of mass tourism, unless care is taken to plan for and control the flow of tourists. As we can see from the quote at the beginning of this chapter, the involvement of government is not insignificant. Any economy that has become overly dependent on tourism can be massively weakened by a single political or natural disaster that dissuades tourists from visiting. Furthermore, it does not necessarily benefit a country to switch labour and other resources away from, say, agriculture towards tourism. For both economic and social reasons, therefore, governments cannot let market forces alone rule – they must take a direct interest in the ways tourism affects their country. The more dependent a nation becomes on tourism, whether domestic, inbound or outbound, the more likely it is that the government will intervene in the industry's activities.

THE NATURE OF GOVERNMENT INVOLVEMENT

A country's system of government will, of course, be reflected in the mode and extent of public intervention. At one end of the scale, **centrally planned economies** may choose to exercise virtually complete control, from policy-making and planning to the building and operating of tourist facilities, the organisation of tourist movements and the promotion of tourism at home and abroad. Since the collapse of the Soviet Union, such central control has been limited to a very few countries, and even some of those nations still ostensibly operating centrally planned economies recognise and accept the importance of private enterprise, and the benefits of private investment, in their tourism planning. China, for example, co-operates with privately owned American hotel interests to establish chains of hotels in popular tourist destinations throughout the country, and accepts the independent movement of tourists on itineraries tailor-made by Western operators. Even Saudi Arabia, which for cultural and political reasons had restricted tourism, is easing its constraints on visas to attract more visitors. Only North Korea and Turkmenistan still control tourism so rigidly that independent travel around either country is impossible.

Most other nations have **mixed economies**, in which public and private sectors coexist and collaborate in the development of tourism within their borders; only the balance of public versus private involvement will vary. The USA, with its belief in a free enterprise system and a federal constitution, delegates much of the responsibility for overseas promotion of the nation either to individual states or even to private organisations created for the purpose. Central government intervention in the USA is limited to measures designed to protect the health and safety of its citizens (such as aircraft safety and air traffic control). It even disbanded its public tourism body, the US Travel and Tourism Administration, in 1996, allowing private enterprise to fund overseas marketing. The public body was replaced by the privately sponsored US Travel Association, which now represents the many different components of the travel industry in America. A destination marketing organisation, Brand USA, was created to market the USA abroad, funded annually by destinations, private-sector tourism organisations and some government funds derived from the visa waiver programme.

Public ownership of transport is also generally declining, as rail and air services are denationalised, but in some developed countries widespread examples are still to be found. The French government, to cite one example, owns 100% of SNCF, the French rail network, and 14.3% of Air France–KLM, while many French airports have some proportion of public ownership (ACI Europe, 2016).

The system of government is not the only factor dictating the extent of state intervention. If a country is highly dependent on tourism for its economic survival, its government is likely to become far more involved in the industry than would be the case if it were of minor importance. The government department to which the responsibility for tourism is allocated can highlight the perspective and importance placed on tourism by its government (see Table 17.1).

TABLE 17.1 Government departments responsible for tourism in a selection of countries

Field	Country	Government department
Tourism	Brazil	Ministry of Tourism
	India	Ministry of Tourism
	Malaysia	Ministry of Tourism
Industry/economy	Peru	Foreign Commerce and Tourism
	Germany	Economic Affairs and Energy
	Hong Kong	Commerce and Economic Development Bureau
Environment	Namibia	Ministry of Environment and Tourism
	Tanzania	Minister for Natural Resources and Tourism
	Austria	Ministry for Sustainability and Tourism
Art and culture	Ghana	Ministry of Tourism, Arts and Culture
	Korea (Republic)	Ministry of Culture, Sports and Tourism
	UK	Department for Digital, Culture, Media and Sport
Other fields	France	Europe and Foreign Affairs
	Ireland	Department of Transport, Tourism and Sport
	Romania	Ministry of Regional Development and Public Administration

Source: C. Humphreys, author's own research, based on Ministry of Tourism websites, 2018

The relative importance attached by government to tourism in the UK can be judged by the amalgam of responsibilities assigned to the Department for Digital, Culture, Media and Sport. Not only does tourism not appear in the title of the department, the job title of the minister within the department is Minister for Arts, Heritage and Tourism.

Countries where tourism has only relatively recently become a significant factor in the economy, and where that sudden growth has become problematic, are likely to exercise stronger control over the development of tourism than are those where tourism is either in its early stages of development or has developed slowly over a long period of time. Mauritius, for example, recognised that the wave of visitors it experienced in the early 1980s could soon lead to the country being swamped by tourists, destroying the very attractions that had brought them to the islands in the first place, unless the government were to take steps to control such key activities as hotel construction. Tunisia, too, learned this lesson, introducing control over hotel and other construction relating to tourism early in the development of mass tourism to that destination.

Unfortunately, the potential for quick riches can exercise a greater influence than the long-term interests of the country, and there are all too many examples of countries that have suffered from a lack of sufficient control over building and development, leading eventually to a drop in visits as tourists turn to less exploited destinations. Overbuilding in Spain was held up as an example in the late 1960s and could have influenced subsequent development in other Mediterranean countries to which tourists turned en masse somewhat later. Nevertheless, the 1980s and 1990s witnessed overdevelopment in some key regions – first in Greece, then in the Portuguese Algarve and, later (despite initial efforts to control hotel-building), in Turkey. Corruption and nepotism – the significance of having influential 'connections' to overcome planning controls should never be underestimated – are very real enemies of sustainable tourism policies.

EXAMPLE

Nepotism in Northern Cyprus

Research completed in 2006 revealed the existence of nepotism in staff recruitment to hotels in the tourist regions of Northern Cyprus. In particular, the research identified cultural, political and educational circumstances pushing inhabitants to be more tolerant of nepotism in small countries; the hospitality industry, a labour-intensive sector which includes many small, family-owned enterprises, is likely to demonstrate this characteristic.

The findings of the research concluded that nepotism can restrict access to work for new recruits, limit promotion opportunities for ambitious workers who lack connections, and demoralise existing employees who are left to feel they are working in an unfair environment. One consequence of this is that employees are more prone to speak critically about their organisation in word-of-mouth communication. If staff are demoralised, or recruitment is based not on their talents but on their connections, then the delivery and quality of service experienced by guests may be poorer than would otherwise be the case.

Source: Arasli et al., 2006

All countries require reliable supporting infrastructure in order to attract tourists initially, and this will inevitably require local and/or central government involvement. Adequate public services, roads, railways, harbours and airports must all be in place before the private sector will be interested in investing in the equally necessary superstructure of hotels, restaurants, entertainment, attractions and other facilities that will bring in tourists.

Developing nations may have a further incentive for involving government. Private developers may be reluctant to invest in speculative tourist ventures, preferring to concentrate their resources in countries where there is already proven demand. In this case, it may fall to the government to either aid private developers (in the form of grants or loans for hotel construction) or even to build and operate the hotels and other tourist amenities that will first attract tourists. Where the private sector can be persuaded to invest, it is often companies from the generating countries that first show interest, with the result that most of the profits are repatriated instead of benefiting the local economy. There is also the danger that private speculators will be more concerned with achieving a quick return on their investment rather than the slow but secure long-term development that will benefit the country most.

The state is often called on to play a coordinating role in planning the provision of tourist amenities and attractions. Supply should match demand as closely as possible, and only the state can ensure that facilities are available when and where required and that they are of the right standard.

As tourism grows in an economy, so its organisation, if uncontrolled, can result in the domination of the market by a handful of large companies. Even in a capitalist system, the state has the duty to restrict the power of monopolies, to protect consumers from malpractices such as unfair constraints on trade or exorbitant prices.

Apart from these economic reasons for governments becoming involved in tourism, there are also social and political reasons. In many countries, especially in developing nations, national airlines are state-owned and operated. While, of course, the income accruing from the operation of the airline is important to the state, there is also the political prestige of operating an airline, even if the national flag-carrier is not economically profitable. Furthermore, while certain airline routes may be unprofitable, they may provide a vital economic lifeline to the communities they serve, and thus are subsidised by the government.

EXAMPLE

Connecting the regions

Across the European Union, there are more than 160 airline and ferry routes that operate to provide a lifeline for local communities as well as encouraging regional development. Such routes are often unprofitable and therefore are supported by government grants under EU Public Service Obligations (PSOs). EU countries that operate PSOs include Croatia, Cyprus, Estonia, Finland, France, Greece, Ireland, Italy, Portugal, Spain, Sweden and the UK.

In the UK, PSOs exist to connect rural areas of England to London, the Isle of Anglesey (in Wales) to Cardiff and some of the islands of Scotland to its regional towns and cities. The Anglesey–Cardiff air route was established in 2007 to provide connections for North Wales, and has seen demand fluctuate between 8500 and 14,700 annually. However, this route has proved challenging; the operator in 2015, LinksAir, having its licence revoked by the Civil Aviation Authority. The route was subsequently operated by Van Air (whose fleet was grounded in 2017), swiftly followed by Eastern Airways, which also operates PSO routes in France.

Since 2016, the Welsh government has completed a number of reviews of the operation of this route, as well as examining the possibility of the development of other PSOs to further improve connectivity across Wales. However, with a subsidy of almost £2 million for the Anglesey route alone, there are some concerns regarding the affordability of further expansion for the Welsh government.

Governments also have a duty to safeguard a nation's heritage. Buildings of historical or architectural interest (particularly UNESCO World Heritage Sites and others of international importance) have to be protected and maintained, as must landscapes of exceptional merit. The state will therefore fund national heritage agencies (such as Historic England, Historic Environment Scotland and CADW in Wales) and establish national parks to protect sensitive sites and buildings.

We can sum up by saying that a national government's role in tourism can be manifested in the following ways:

- in the planning and facilitating of tourism, including the provision of financial and other aid
- in the supervision and control of the component sectors of the tourism industry
- in direct ownership and operation of the components of the industry
- in the promotion of the nation and its tourist products to home and overseas markets
- in supporting key tourism interests in a time of crisis.

This clarification of the range of activities that need to be undertaken by national governments is helpful when they are considering their own responsibilities in relation to the provision and management of tourism.

PLANNING AND FACILITATING TOURISM

Any country in which tourism plays a prominent role in national income and employment can expect its government to devise policies and plans for the development of tourism. This will include generating guidelines and objectives for the growth and management of tourism, both in the short and the long term, and devising strategies designed to achieve those objectives.

It may be the case that the government feels the need to invest in the tourism industry in order to **pump-prime** or stimulate investment, development and growth in a sector of the economy. For example, UK government policy on tourism has favoured investment in tourism to create employment opportunities, although the cost to the public purse was a concern. While support for tourism was initially through grant aid, by the 1990s the government took the view that the industry was now 'mature' and further investment should be left to the private sector.

VisitBritain, as a quasi-autonomous national government organisation with the responsibility to promote the UK abroad, has as its aims not just to increase the total number of tourists to the UK but also to spread visitors more evenly throughout the regions and across the months, to avoid the concentration of demand in the south and during the summer months. In Spain, as demand had already been created by the private sector for the popular east coast resorts and the Balearic and Canary Islands, its national tourist office policy has focused on promoting the less familiar north-west coast and central regions of the country, while coastal development has become subject to increasing control.

Tourism planning calls for research – first, to assess the level of demand or potential demand for a particular region; second, to estimate the resources required in order to cater for that demand; and, finally, to determine how those resources should best be distributed. As we have seen, demand is unlikely to be generated to any extent until an adequate infrastructure and superstructure are in place, but it is not sufficient simply to provide these amenities. Tourists also need staff to service the facilities – hotel workers, travel agents, guides – trained to an acceptable level of performance. Planning therefore implicitly includes ensuring the availability of a pool of labour, as well as the provision of apprenticeship schemes or training through hotel, catering and tourism schools and colleges to provide the skills and knowledge the industry requires.

In some cases, providing the facilities that tourists want can actually have a negative impact on tourism to the region. To take one example, while the building of airports on some of the smaller islands in Greece opened up these islands to larger flows of tourists, it made the islands less attractive to upmarket, high-spending tourists, who preferred the relative isolation that existed when accessibility was limited to ferry operations.

GOVERNMENT CONTROL OVER ENTRY

Accessibility is a key factor in the development of tourism. It relies on both adequate transport and the absence of any political barriers to travel. If visas are required for entry to a country, this will discourage incoming tourism.

EXAMPLE

Entry to the USA

In 1988, the USA abandoned the requirement for visas for many visitors from Western Europe (albeit with some limitations that continued to hinder the free flow of tourism), having recognised the barrier that this bureaucratic constraint created at a time when other factors, such as relative exchange rates, were favouring the rapid expansion of tourism to North America. The political panic that followed the 9/11 disaster changed attitudes, however, and the US government tightened entry requirements, including the need for computer-scanning of passports. Biometric data (including fingerprinting and iris scans) were taken on entry, and visas, where required, became more difficult to obtain, with prospective tourists having to travel long distances to attend interviews at US embassies.

Since October 2005, the Department of Homeland Security has mandated airlines and cruise ships to provide details of their passengers, prior to arrival. The information required includes each passenger's full name, date of birth, gender, citizenship, passport details, country of residence, address while in the USA and arrival and departure transport details. This has raised debate regarding the rights to privacy, as well as concerns over protection and security of the data provided.

In addition to information provided by the airline, from 2009 all visitors using the visa-waiver scheme had to apply for travel authorisation prior to arrival. This operates through an online system called ESTA (Electronic System for Travel Authorization) and, although this service was initially free, a charge of $14 was introduced in September 2010 – $10 of which was used to fund promotional campaigns to attract more visitors to the USA.

The difficulty in obtaining a visa and concern that the increased security will cause problems for arriving travellers have combined with other factors to influence arrival figures. Despite a weak dollar, international arrival figures (excluding those coming from Mexico and Canada) took until 2010 to reach the levels that existed prior to the terrorist attacks of 2001, despite global international tourism arrivals increasing by almost 40% over the same period.

The ending of visa requirements for trips to the Baltic states following the collapse of communism in Russia and the satellite countries led to a substantial increase in tourist visits. Russia, by contrast, continued to insist on visas. The predictable result was a drop in the number of visitors to Russia, while the Baltic states enjoyed a significant rise, which accelerated after their entry into the EU.

Maximising revenue from inbound tourism flows is always a temptation for governments, but it is a practice that backfires if visitors can simply switch to alternative destinations offering similar attractions. Arguably, long-haul travellers will be more willing to accept reasonably high visa costs when travelling extensively in a country, but such costs are off-putting for short-break visits or calls by cruise liners.

China restricted access to leisure travel for its citizens by granting visas only for selected destinations, with only six countries having approved destination status (ADS) by the end of the 1990s. The list of countries gaining ADS has since expanded rapidly, however; at the end of 2007, the USA became the 95th country to be added, and there are now over 140 countries and territories holding ADS. With 135 million Chinese trips overseas in 2016, countries gaining ADS seek to receive a significant share of this massive market. Importantly, although ADS allows Chinese companies to offer tours to the overseas country, travellers still require entry visas and these are not always easy to obtain.

EXAMPLE

The EU's Schengen agreement for non-EU visitors

The Schengen zone has been significantly expanded since its introduction — eight Eastern European countries and Malta were added in 2007 and Bosnia and Albania were included at the end of 2010 — so the Agreement now covers travel across 26 European countries. Border controls have eased for travellers between these countries. While EU travellers and visitors from the USA and Japan can travel without a visa in the EU zone, other travellers moving around Europe historically would have required a separate visa for each country they entered. Now, a single Schengen visa can provide access to all 26 countries, saving money as well as making travel across Europe more convenient, thus making Europe a more attractive destination for some international tourists.

Recently, there has been political concern regarding the Schengen area arrangements, raised because of a spate of terrorist attacks and concerns over the influx of refugees. As a consequence, Schengen visa arrangements are being threatened as internal border controls have been reintroduced in some areas in France, Austria, Germany, Denmark, Sweden and Norway.

Negotiations for the withdrawal of the UK from the European Union have included some political rhetoric regarding the reintroduction of visa requirements for UK citizens wanting to visit EU member states. At the time of writing, no agreement has been confirmed regarding whether a visa will be required but, given the scale of travel between the UK and EU countries, such a move would add a layer of bureaucracy on an unprecedented scale. Furthermore, this would appear as a highly political move, given that residents from the USA, Canada, Australia, Japan and several other countries do not require a visa to holiday in EU countries. As Brexit arrangements continue to be determined, so it is expected that issues such as visa requirements will become clearer.

In summary, the cost of obtaining visas, together with the complexity of applications, can have the effect of encouraging travellers to choose to visit countries that do *not* require a visa.

TAXATION POLICY

Government policies on taxation can impact on tourism, whether the taxes are applied directly to tourists (such as an entry or exit tax), to the industry (such as on hotel accommodation) or indirectly (such as VAT or sales taxes, which can discourage shopping). It may even encourage day trips across national or state borders to shop in areas where taxes are lower.

The UK government's imposition in the 1993 Budget of an airport departure tax (air passenger duty (APD)) of £5 in the EU and £10 elsewhere was widely criticised in the press, and the decision to double this rate from November 1997 provoked fury in the trade. A further increase followed in February 2007, and by 2013 APD was calculated by using four bands, based on distance and class of service. Band A (2000 miles) incurred a levy of £13, while at the top end of the scale band D (over 6000 miles) cost the passenger £94. Continual lobbying of parliament by the transport and tourism industry led to a shift in policy on APD, and 2015 reform led to the four bands being reduced to two (Band A for flights below 2000 miles and Band B for journeys over 2000 miles). This meant that the cost in 2018 for economy-class passengers was £13 for Band A and £78 for Band B. Business-class passengers pay double this figure; however, a change to the rules now means children under the age of 12 are exempt from the tax.

If the revenue raised by such taxation were to be reinvested in the tourism industry, there would perhaps be less of a sense of outrage, but when it is introduced purely as a convenient means of raising taxation, travellers often feel that it is an injustice.

EXAMPLE

The Balearic Islands' eco-tax

In 2002, the Balearic Islands' government, composed of a coalition of socialist and green parties, introduced an eco-tax as a means of discouraging low-spending visitors and funding enhancements of the islands' infrastructure to attract more upmarket visitors. The local government was concerned that the islands were attracting some 7 million visitors a year, swamping the resident island population of 600,000. The tax was imposed on hotel accommodation, ranging from €0.25 to €1.00 per night for hotels up to the 4-star category and €2.00 for the 5-star category.

There was an immediate negative reaction from the tourist trade abroad, which argued that sales for flights and package tours would drop and it had been introduced too quickly for tour operators to add to their brochures. There were also complaints that the tax was unfair as it applied only to hotels, not unlicensed accommodation, villas, B&Bs or privately owned second homes. As a direct result, it was eventually agreed that the tax be collected directly from travellers at their hotels.

(Continued)

A year later, the tax was scrapped, when a new centre-right government was voted into power. During the time in which it was in operation, however, it is estimated that the tax raised more than £25 million to help fund tourism projects. While the overall number of visitors to the Balearics did drop by 7% compared with the previous year, this could not be ascribed solely to the effect of the tax; visitors to the Canary Islands dropped by a similar amount, while those from the UK actually increased by some 8%.

In July 2016 the tax was re-introduced, again with concerns raised by the local tourism industry that this would impact visitor numbers. The local government aimed to bring in more than €120 million through the levy. The tax was then doubled in 2018 which, coupled with some anti-tourist campaigns led by local activists, has led to a decrease in visitor numbers from the main markets of Germany and the UK.

FACILITATING TRAINING

Another important factor determining tourism flow is the attitude of nationals in the host country towards visitors in general and those from specific countries in particular. Governments in countries heavily dependent on tourism must mould the social attitudes of their populations, as well as ensuring that those coming into contact with tourists have the necessary skills to deal with them. Customs officers, immigration officials, shopkeepers, hotel staff, bus and taxi drivers must not only be competent at their jobs but also trained to be polite and friendly, as first impressions are vitally important for the long-term image of a country.

The USA is one of several countries that have found it necessary to mount campaigns to improve the politeness and friendliness of officials dealing with incoming visitors, while some Caribbean governments have run training programmes to reduce xenophobia among the local populations and make residents aware that their economy depends on incoming tourism. In the UK, the government has supported industry moves to improve social and personal skills in handling foreign tourists, with training programmes such as Welcome Host and WorldHost. Encouragement has also been given to learning foreign languages – a major weakness among personnel in the UK's tourism industry.

THE RESPONSIBILITIES OF CENTRAL AND LOCAL GOVERNMENT

The very complexity of tourism makes its administration difficult as it does not sit easily in any one sector of government. For example, although responsibility for tourism in the UK lies with the Department for Digital, Culture, Media and Sport (DCMS), there are clearly other departments with a direct interest in the industry, including the Department for Environment, Food and Rural Affairs (DEFRA), the Department for Transport (DfT) and the Department for Business, Innovation and Skills (BIS) (its responsibilities including consumer affairs, employment relations and higher education). In practice, coordination between these various departments is difficult to achieve, hindering the effectiveness of the overall planning of tourism initiatives within the country. It is further hindered by the fact that the Scottish Parliament and the Welsh Assembly have responsibility for tourism within their own regions.

The responsibilities of central and local government will also differ with respect to issues affecting tourism. Local government may be responsible for planning, policy and infrastructure and, as a consequence, have to address a number of issues that directly affect visiting tourists, including the provision of car and coach parking, litter control, maintenance of footpaths and promenades, public parks and gardens and, where appropriate, beach management and monitoring of seawater for bathing. These responsibilities are, to some extent, split between city and regional councils, and conflicting views may surface between local authorities, as well as between local and central government. Local authorities are, of course, greatly influenced by the views of their local taxpayers, who are often unsympathetic to the expansion of tourism in their area. In countries where tourism is not a statutory obligation of local authorities (and the UK is one such example), they may not legally have to include tourism in their plans. This issue comes to the fore in times of cutbacks, when the funding of non-statutory activities is often closely reviewed.

FINANCIAL AID FOR TOURISM

Governments contribute to the growth of tourism by financing the development of new projects. On a massive scale, tourist resorts have been constructed around Cancún on Mexico's eastern coast, while in the 1970s the Languedoc–Roussillon area in the south of France was the subject of development that included draining swampland and eradicating mosquitoes in order to build five new tourist resorts, including the now well-established Cap d'Agde and la Grande Motte. The success of these ventures demonstrates the effectiveness of large-scale private/public-sector cooperation in building new tourism resorts from scratch, with the public sector providing the huge funds necessary to acquire land and build the necessary infrastructure.

On a smaller scale, governments may also provide assistance to the private sector in the form of financial aid, offering loans at preferential rates of interest or outright grants for schemes that are in keeping with government policy. One example of the way in which such schemes operate in developing countries is for loans to be made on which interest only is paid during the first few years, with the repayment of capital postponed until the later years of the project, by which time it should have become self-financing. Other forms of government aid include subsidies such as tax rebates or tax relief on operating expenses.

EXAMPLE

Nigeria announces tax relief for tourism investors

In November 2018, Nigeria announced that it would offer a three-year tax exemption for those looking to bring tourism investment to the country. The Ministry of Information and Culture, leading the initiative, confirmed that fiscal benefits would be given to those initiatives that align to the national tourism policy.

Further advantages include providing land at concessionary rates and import/export incentives to support the investment. Work permits for foreigners with relevant specialised skills would also be supported.

Source: Journal du Cameroun, 2018

Government support is also necessary at a time of catastrophe. The recovery of popular Asiatic resorts following the disastrous tsunami in 2004 depended on a programme of massive international government aid, supported by direct contributions from millions of ordinary people around the world. Similarly, in the UK, after the devastating outbreak of foot and mouth disease in 2001, the government stepped in to offer financial aid to small tourism businesses in rural areas; these were granted 95% tax relief, while the Welsh Assembly extended 100% rate relief to Welsh businesses with higher rateable values. Central government grants were also made available in the affected areas for marketing and investment in information technology.

Apart from financial aid from a country's own government, public-sector funds are also available from sources overseas. Within Europe, the European Investment Bank (EIB) provides loans at commercial rates of interest to small companies (normally those employing fewer than 500 staff). Such loans have been provided for up to 50% of fixed asset costs, with repayment terms of up to eight years, and the interest rates may be slightly lower in the EU's designated 'Assisted Areas'.

EXAMPLE

Ghana obtains World Bank loan for tourism

In 2018, the World Bank agreed a US$40 million loan for the Ministry of Tourism, Arts and Culture in Ghana, with an expectation that this will be used to enhance its tourism sector.

The money is to be used to improve the existing tourism environment, in an attempt to bring facilities and attractions up to international standard. It will also provide financial support to tourism enterprises for capacity building. This would have a particular focus on education and skills training. Some of the funding is earmarked for enhancing branding and marketing to entice international visitors.

The overall goal of the loan is to improve the performance of tourism in targeted destinations in Ghana, which will, in turn, trigger economic transformation through jobs, local enterprise and investment.

For further Information, see: http://projects.worldbank.org/P164211/?lang=en&tab=overview

The European Regional Development Fund (ERDF) offers financial assistance for a range of initiatives, including many tourism projects. Between 2000 and 2006, funding was provided based on three objectives: focusing on promoting development in impoverished areas, supporting areas facing structural difficulties and supporting the modernisation of training and education. The 2007–13 plans focused on convergence, regional competitiveness and employment and territorial cooperation. The 2014–20 key priority areas are:

- innovation and research
- the digital agenda
- support for small- to medium-sized enterprises (SMEs)
- the low-carbon economy.

Alongside the ERDF projects, the EU provides other funding streams that can offer grant support for tourism businesses. Table 17.2 summarises these for the 2014–20 period.

TABLE 17.2 Most relevant European programmes for the tourism sector

Area	Financial programme
Cohesion	Structural funds: • European Cohesion Fund • European Social Fund • European Regional Development Fund • European Territorial Cooperation
Environment, Agriculture & Marine and Fisheries Policy	LIFE (L'instrument financier pour l'environnement) European Agriculture Fund for Rural Development European Maritime and Fisheries Fund
Research, Innovation and Competitiveness	Horizon 2020 (Framework Programme for Research and Innovation) COSME (Programme for the Competitiveness of Enterprises and SMEs)
Culture and Education	Creative Europe programme Erasmus for All programme
Employment	EaSI (EU Programme for Employment and Social Innovation) PROGRESS (Programme for Employment and Social Solidarity) EURES (European Employment Services) PROGRESS Microfinance Facility

Source: European Commission (EC), 2016

It is worth noting here that the UK's departure from the European Union will see access to such funding being withdrawn for the UK tourism industry. Whether the UK government replaces this with its own funding schemes will only be determined over time.

SOCIAL TOURISM

One aspect of public-sector support for tourism is to be found in the encouragement offered by way of **social tourism** – little-known, at least in the UK, but now receiving greater attention in academic literature and tourism education (McCabe et al., 2012).

The concept of social tourism has been used in several contexts, so it is difficult to provide one specific definition. In some cases, this term is used to propose the idea that the opportunity to take a holiday is a human right and there should be provision by the welfare state for those unable to afford to take a holiday. From a supply side, the term is often used when considering circumstances in which governments encourage tourism to specific areas in order to promote economic development. To provide an encompassing definition, Minnaert et al. (2006: 9) suggest that 'social tourism is about encouraging those who can benefit from tourism to do so. This may represent a wide variety of groups, such as the host population of an exotic destination, tourists on a cultural holiday, persons with disabilities, their carers, the socially excluded and other disadvantaged groups'.

Economic support to encourage social tourism may be offered in the form of finance (grants, low-interest loans and the like) or direct support, such as the provision of free coach trips or holiday accommodation. Several countries have been active in providing subsidised tourism for their deprived citizens, led by Belgium, France and the southern countries of the EU. Indeed, the Brussels-based International Social Tourism Organisation (ISTO) – formerly the International Bureau of Social Tourism (BITS) – has been active since 1963 as a base for the study and debate of social tourism issues and maintains a data bank, issues publications and conducts seminars on the subject.

There are well-established programmes of aid on the European continent for holidays for the mentally, physically and socially handicapped, although financial pressures are reducing these opportunities. The French government, for example, terminated its programme of welfare-funded spa holidays in 1999 – a severe blow to the spa tourism industry, which hosted over 600,000 French visitors who had been able to recover up to 70% of their costs through the social security system. Other now well-established programmes of social tourism remain in place, however.

Little support of this kind is provided in the UK for the disadvantaged, although the UK has over 6 million registered disabled people. Responsibility for providing this service is delegated to local authorities (the Chronically Sick and Disabled Act 1970 imposed a statutory duty on local authorities to fund holidays for the disabled). Many authorities used to provide coach outings for the elderly and other disadvantaged groups, but, over the past 20 years, cutbacks in local authority funding have sharply reduced these services, and the number of those receiving financial help from local councils has slumped. The result has been that social tourism has largely become the responsibility of the private or voluntary/third sector.

Sponsored by the then English Tourist Board, and with the full support of the travel industry in the UK, the Holiday Care Service was set up in 1981. Essentially, it provided information about holiday opportunities for the disadvantaged; later, this was expanded to include training programmes for members of the tourism industry. A number of specialist operators then turned to catering for the needs of these groups or providing discounted holidays for those with limited means. These responsibilities are now vested in Tourism for All, which is a national charity. The Travel Foundation also provides help for disadvantaged holidaymakers with financial support from the industry.

EXAMPLE

The Family Holiday Association

A UK national charity, the Family Holiday Association (FHA), promotes holidays for disadvantaged families. It suggests that holidays benefit individuals as well as wider society, through:

- improving wellbeing and reducing stress
- increasing self-esteem and confidence
- strengthening family communication and bonding
- providing new skills, widening perspectives and enhancing employability
- giving long-lasting, treasured memories
- resulting in happier, stronger families and a more inclusive society.

Poverty is the principal reason for one out of three people in the UK not going on holiday at all. The FHA was set up in 1975 to provide grants that would make a holiday possible for this group. The FHA receives donations and legacies amounting to some £1.3 million annually, enabling the FHA to provide holidays for around 4000 families.

For further information, see: www.fhaonline.org.uk

Holidays are also organised by trade unions in the UK, which have established holiday homes and subsidise holidays for their members. Other bodies arranging holidays for the disadvantaged include Mencap, the Red Cross, the Multiple Sclerosis Society and the Winged Fellowship Trust. Both SCOPE (formerly the Spastics Society) and the Spina Bifida Association also own holiday homes where holidays can be provided for those suffering from these illnesses.

The UK government's involvement in helping the disadvantaged in this area is largely restricted to ensuring there is adequate access to tourism attractions, hotels and so on for the disabled. The Disability Discrimination Act 1995 (DDA) had a profound effect on tourist facilities in the UK, necessitating their making substantial investments to meet the conditions of the Act. In 2010, the Equality Act replaced most of the DDA, further extending the rights of people with disabilities and their carers.

EXAMPLE

Understanding accessible tourism

ABTA has launched an online (e-learning) tool designed to develop the knowledge and skills of those working in the tourism industry as they encounter those with accessibility issues. The training tool highlights ways to best support those with visible and non-visible disabilities, as well as developing the confidence in staff to respond consistently and clearly to meet the needs of all customers.

The tool has been developed to accommodate the demands of the 2010 Equality Act as well as changes in package holiday and GPDR (data protection) regulations, which also affect the way in which customers are served.

ABTA stresses that meeting the needs of those with disabilities will make travel easier for these groups, thus stimulating further demand – and with 14 million disabled people in the UK, this is not an insignificant market group. As well as training the industry, ABTA provides information for the traveller, including a checklist to help the traveller identify their needs to travel suppliers.

For further information, see: www.abta.com/tips-and-advice/accessible-travel

SUPERVISION AND CONTROL OF TOURISM

The state plays an important part in controlling and supervising tourism, as well as helping to facilitate it, where it is deemed necessary. It will, for example, intervene to restrain undesirable growth or unfair competition or, alternatively, help to generate demand by improving infrastructure or encouraging the building of hotels (as the Development of

Tourism Act did in the UK in 1969). Governments also play a role in maintaining quality standards and protecting all consumers (in this case, tourists) from business malpractice or failure.

Local government may introduce visitor management policies (details of which are provided in Chapter 16) to control both the numbers visiting destinations and their actions and behaviour there. Visitor management may be enforced by local government, but it is often implemented both by government initiatives and the activities of private-sector tourism businesses.

A government can act to restrain tourism in a number of ways, whether through central directives or local authority control. Refusal of planning permission is an obvious example of exercising control over the development of tourism. This is seldom totally effective as a mechanism, however, as when an area is a major attraction for tourists, the authorities will be unlikely to dissuade visitors simply by, say, refusing planning permission for new hotels. The result of such actions may simply be that overnight visitors are replaced by excursionists, or private bed-and-breakfast accommodation moves in to fill the gap left by the lack of hotel beds.

Up to a point, planning for the more extensive use of existing facilities can delay the need to de-market certain attractions or destinations, but it is undoubtedly true that some tourist destinations are victims of their own success. Only in extreme cases are tourists totally denied access to destinations or attractions. In France, the prehistoric cave paintings at Lascaux have been so damaged by the effect of countless visitors' breath changing the climate in the caves that the French government has been obliged to introduce a total ban on entry to the site. A replica has been built on an adjacent site, however, which continues to attract many visitors.

In recent years, the UK has debated the need to follow the example of some of its other European neighbours in attempting to stagger holidays, by means of legislation. However, even though holiday periods vary across Europe, it is clear from Table 17.3 that July and August will always see demand peak.

TABLE 17.3 School holidays across Europe

Country	School summer vacation period
Austria	9 weeks between early July and early September
Denmark	6 weeks between end of June and early August
England and Wales	6 weeks between mid-July and early September
France	9 weeks between early July and early September
Germany	6 weeks – staggered – between end of June and mid-September
Greece	12 weeks between mid-June and mid-September
Italy	12 weeks between June and September
Portugal	12 weeks between mid-June and early September
Spain	11 weeks between late June and mid-September

Source: Loveys, 2011

The staggering of school holiday periods is expected to help avoid the worst peaking problems of the summer months. On the Continent, not only educational holidays but also industry holidays are staggered. In Germany, the *Länder* (individual states) are required to take their holidays on a cyclical rota basis, thus avoiding the holiday rush that is common in the UK at the end of the school summer term. Factories, schools and businesses all plan their closures in keeping with the rota. France, too, divides the country into three zones, each of which takes the summer holiday at a different time. While this helps to avoid national peaking, it is not without drawbacks – for example, the mass exodus of German holidaymakers clogging the motorways from their particular *Land* when their turn arrives!

Sometimes governments exercise control over tourism flows for economic reasons. Governments may attempt to protect their balance of payments by imposing currency restrictions or banning the export of foreign currency in an attempt to reduce the number of its citizens travelling abroad. The last significant control of this kind in the UK occurred in 1966, when the government of the day imposed a £50 travel allowance, while France also imposed restrictions on the amount of currency that could be exported in the early 1980s. There is little evidence to suggest that such controls are particularly effective in preventing the outflow of foreign currency and, since the advent of the free movement of currency within the EU, the right of its members to travel within the EU can no longer be restricted. The euro has benefited tourists, including the British and others who remain outside the common currency agreement, who no longer have to change their holiday money as they move from one eurozone country to another.

EXAMPLE

Currency controls during Greek debt crisis

In June 2015, the Greek prime minister announced that currency controls would be introduced, restricting the amount of money that people could withdraw from the country's banks. This also restricted access to foreign currency and overseas transfers of cash, meaning that Greeks planning to take a holiday outside the eurozone would have little access to holiday money.

Not wanting to limit money coming into the country from overseas, tourists visiting Greece were able to use their credit and debit cards without restriction, albeit finding a cash machine with money available could be a challenge.

The restriction was initially set at an amount of €60 a day. While there was some easing of this restriction, it took almost three years for the withdrawal limit to be substantially increased from €2300 per month to €5000. At the same time, the amount of foreign currency that could be taken abroad was increased from €2300 to €3000.

Source: Smith, 2018

Concern over safety is a government responsibility and all governments will take measures to enforce standards of safety, prosecuting breaches of safe practice. Transport companies are obliged to meet the necessary criteria to obtain licences to carry passengers, and tour operators are also subject to certain controls through the imposition of air travel organizers' licences (ATOLs). In many countries (although not yet in the UK), travel agencies are required to have a government licence to operate, and in others tour guides are licensed by the government or a local authority. In France, motorboats must also be licensed, even in the case of visitors from abroad, following a spate of accidents caused by poor navigation.

EXAMPLE

Airline safety a priority

Europe has an excellent aviation safety record because it insists on high standards of aircraft maintenance and operation. To improve safety further, the European Commission restricts or bans some airlines from operating in European airspace if safety procedures do not meet internationally recognised safety standards. The airlines affected are too numerous to list here but can be identified online at: https://ec.europa.eu/transport/sites/transport/files/air-safety-list_en.pdf.

EU legislation protects tourists in a variety of ways, taking precedence over national laws. Legislation introduced in 2005, for instance, requires airlines to pay compensation to passengers for delayed flights, with the extent of compensation varying according to the length of the flight. Prosecution is enforced in Britain through the CAA.

Governments will intervene where it is thought that the takeover or merger of large companies could result in the emergence of a monopoly. In the UK, the Competition Commission exists to investigate such situations, but, in general, it has taken a relaxed attitude towards horizontal integration (explained in Chapter 7) on the grounds that tourists have not been disadvantaged by the moves. The EU, however, has tended to take a stronger line on this issue and has interceded in a number of cases in recent years, notably that of the proposed merger between BA and American Airlines.

Perhaps the most common form of government supervision within the tourism industry in all countries is to be found in the hotel sector. Apart from safety and hygiene requirements, many governments also require hotels to be compulsorily registered and graded; prices must be displayed, and buildings are subject to regular inspection. Camping and caravan sites may also be subject to inspection to ensure consistent standards and acceptable operating conditions.

Finally, the government's concern with quality will lead to setting up systems of inspection, where safety is concerned, or training programmes and other means to enhance quality where it is seen as sub-standard. Again, the UK has recently promoted schemes leading to publicly recognised standards of quality, including the National Quality Assurance Schemes (NQAS) and Visitor Attraction Quality Assurance Schemes (VAQAS). The growth of self-catering accommodation provided by second-home owners renting out their properties to holidaymakers in resorts has also resulted in the need for annual checks, to include certificates of inspection for gas and electricity provision and checks on individual electricity appliances.

THE ORGANISATION OF PUBLIC-SECTOR TOURISM

Having looked at the various ways in which public-sector bodies concern themselves with tourism, we can now usefully summarise their main activities. For the most part, government policies and objectives for tourism are defined and implemented through national tourist boards, although in many cases other bodies directly concerned with recreation or environmental planning will also have a hand in the development of tourism. These boards are normally funded by government grants and their functional responsibilities are likely to include all or most of the following:

- planning and control functions
    - product research and planning for tourism facilities

  - protection or restoration of tourism assets
  - human resources planning and training
  - licensing and supervision of sectors of the industry
  - implementation of pricing or other regulations affecting tourism;
- marketing functions
  - representing the nation as a tourist destination
  - undertaking market research, forecasting trends and collecting and publishing relevant statistics
  - producing and distributing tourism literature
  - providing and staffing tourist information centres (TICs)
  - advertising, sales promotion and public relations activities directed at home and overseas markets;
- financial functions
  - advising industry on capital investment and development
  - directing, approving and controlling programmes of government aid for tourism projects;
- coordinating functions
  - linking with trade and professional bodies, government and regional or local tourist organisations
  - undertaking coordinated marketing activities with private tourist enterprises
  - organising workshops or similar opportunities for buyers and sellers of travel and tourism to meet and do business.

National tourist boards will generally establish offices overseas in those countries from which they can attract the most tourists, while their head office in the home country will be organised along functional lines. This is demonstrated in Figure 17.1, taking the example of the Singapore Tourism Board. It has structured the responsibility by theme of activity, highlighting the many different activities undertaken by the organisation.

This chapter now provides a snapshot of public-sector tourism structure and operations by looking at the UK as an example, but it is important to note that the picture is not dissimilar in many other developed countries. It considers government involvement at national, regional and local levels.

THE UK GOVERNMENT'S INVOLVEMENT AT NATIONAL LEVEL

The illogical nature of the UK's tourism policy has been a feature of UK governments for a number of years. The promises of support and a recognition of the contribution that tourism makes to the UK economy, coupled with simultaneous cuts in government funding, lack of development grants for tourism in depressed regions and the decline in support for an English national board vis-à-vis the other national boards, all suggest a failure on the part of successive governments to think through rational policies that would give full support to tourism. As evidence, we need to go no further than a speech given by the then recently elected prime minister, David Cameron, highlighting the importance of tourism in the UK as the third biggest export earner for the UK. Said Cameron,

> For too long tourism has been looked down on as a second class service sector. That's just wrong. Tourism is a fiercely competitive market, requiring skills, talent, enterprise and a government that backs Britain. It's fundamental to the rebuilding and rebalancing of our economy. (No. 10, 2010)

Yet just two months later, the government announced that the national tourism organisation, VisitBritain, would lose more than a quarter of its funding over the next four years.

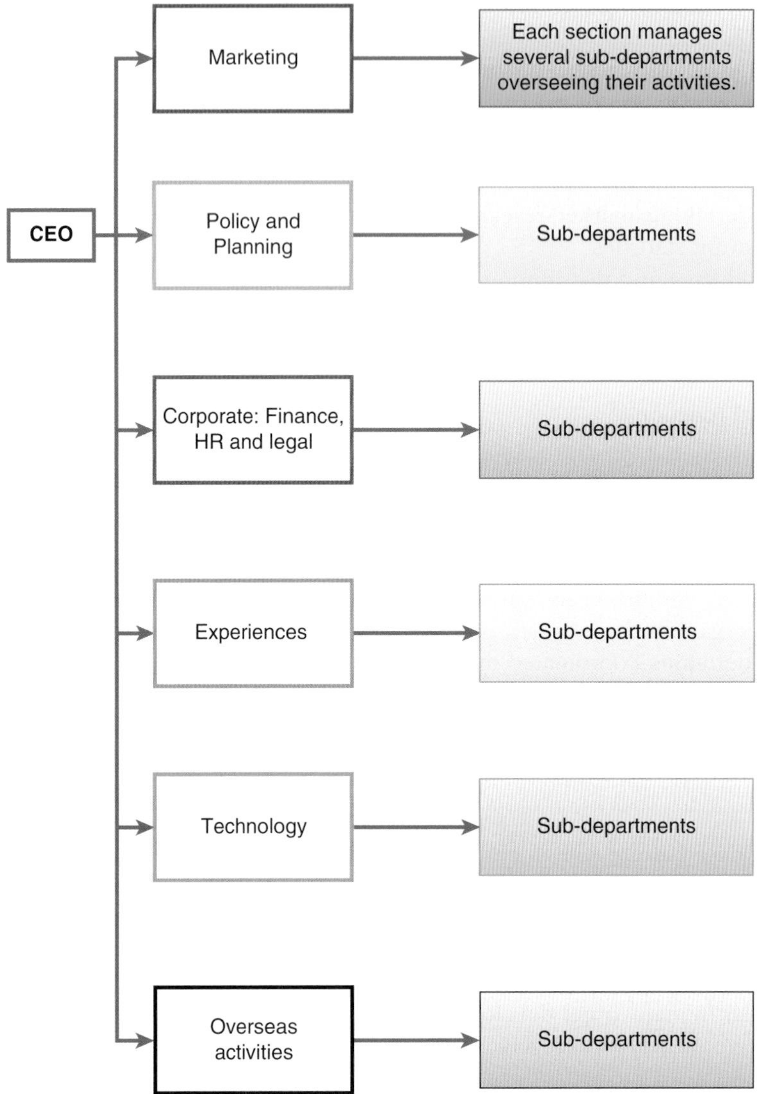

FIGURE 17.1 Organisational chart for the Singapore Tourism Board

Further damage is imposed on the industry by the unfavourable rate of VAT on restaurant and hotel accommodation in the UK in comparison with that in other countries; the imposition of air passenger duty (discussed earlier in this chapter); an inadequate transport infrastructure (notably the railways and London Underground); and the continued failure to provide an integrated transport policy that would facilitate tourism.

Against these failures, however, one can point to one clear success achieved through a public–private partnership (PPP), that of the awarding of the Olympic Games to London in 2012. Against what were seen as overwhelming odds favouring Paris, the PPP was able to make an effective case, based substantially on the benefits that would accrue to a deprived area of London, the new sports facilities that would become available to the population and the increase in permanent employment for locals resulting from the construction of the facilities. The long-term rejuvenation of one of the most impoverished regions of London has been viewed by many as sufficient justification for the enormous expense that was incurred to develop the facilities needed to host the Games.

Before 1969, tourism played little part in UK government policy-making. Prior to that time, some funding was provided to establish the Travel Association of Great Britain and Northern Ireland in order to encourage travel to the UK from overseas. During the interwar years, this evolved into the British Travel Association (BTA), which was given the additional task of promoting domestic holidays for British residents, but no clear policies were laid down for its activities and its powers were limited. Voluntary tourist boards were established in Scotland in 1930 and in Wales in 1948, the same year in which a board was first established in Northern Ireland. It was more than 20 years later, however, before a coordinated framework for public-sector tourism was established in the UK as a whole.

The Development of Tourism Act 1969 provided the first statutory legislation in the country specifically concerned with tourism. It dealt with the organisation of public-sector tourism, providing financial assistance for much-needed hotel development and a system of compulsory registration of tourist accommodation.

National tourism boards in the UK

The first part of the 1969 Act called for the establishment of four national boards to be responsible for tourism and defined the structure and responsibilities of each of them. Initially, both the BTA and the English Tourist Board (ETB) were responsible to the Board of Trade, while the Scottish and Wales Boards were responsible to their respective secretaries of state.

All four bodies were established by the Act as independent statutory bodies and were to be financed by grants-in-aid from central government. Later, responsibility for the BTA and ETB passed to, first, the Department of Employment, and subsequently, in 1992, to the newly created Department of National Heritage, which absorbed a number of other related interests, including the royal parks and palaces, arts and libraries, sport, broadcasting and the press, as well as heritage sites. This department became known as the Department for Culture, Media and Sport when the Labour government came to power in 1997 (adding 'Digital' to the title in 2017).

In 1999, the ETB's title was changed to the English Tourism Council, and in 2003 it was abolished as a separate entity altogether, its functions being integrated with those of VisitBritain, the new brand name for the BTA. Finally, it was again recreated in 2009 as a separate entity, VisitEngland.

EXAMPLE

The role of VisitBritain

With general responsibility for tourism throughout the UK, VisitBritain acts as an adviser to the government on tourism issues and is financed by an annual grant-in-aid from the Treasury, channelled through the Department for Digital, Culture, Media and Sport (DCMS). In justifying the funding, VisitBritain claims that for every £1 invested in VisitBritain/VisitEngland, visitor spending amounts to some £25. In 2017–18, its grant from the DCMS amounted to £26.5 million. In addition to this funding, the organisation has, at the time of writing, been granted £22.1 million from the Department for International Trade, the British Council and the Foreign and Commonwealth Office to operate the 'Britain is GREAT' marketing and branding campaign.

In addition to marketing activities, VisitBritain also carries out market research, provides an advice hub for tourism businesses and liaises with the other tourism bodies in the UK.

In August 2016, the government published a Tourism Action Plan to enhance the tourism offering of Britain and expand domestic and international tourism. Priorities included enhancements to the tourism landscape, improving human resource skills, addressing regulatory issues affecting the industry, enhancing transport for tourism and ensuring a GREAT welcome though aspects such as improving the visa application process. This plan supported an earlier initiative, which came with £40 million of funding, focusing on enhancing the competitiveness of England as a tourism destination though improvements to its tourism product.

Following the devolution of power to Scotland and Wales, responsibility for tourism in these parts of the UK was placed directly in the hands of the Scottish Parliamentary and Welsh Assembly governments. In Ireland, following the 1998 Good Friday Agreement, The Northern Ireland Tourist Board, which reports to the Northern Ireland Office, united in 2002 with its opposite number south of the border, the Irish Tourist Board, to form Tourism Ireland for marketing purposes.

THE UK GOVERNMENT'S INVOLVEMENT AT REGIONAL LEVEL

The changes in structure outlined above heralded even greater upheavals that were to affect the UK's public-sector tourism in the twenty-first century. One of the most significant changes was the rerouting of DCMS funds for the English board direct to the regional development agencies (RDAs), which were responsible for all economic strategy in the regions. However, government funding cuts led to a decision to abolish the RDAs in 2012, the government asserting that 'tourism, previously the responsibility of regional tourist boards within RDAs, will be passed to new Destination Management Organisations, which will be formed through existing tourism support bodies, councils, local business networks and new local enterprise partnerships' (Sandford, 2011).

In the wake of the closure of the RDAs, several regional tourist boards were closed. Today, responsibility for regional tourism is being encouraged through local enterprise partnerships (LEPs). At the time of writing, 38 LEPs exist and all recognise tourism as an important economic activity. Those LEPs established to date vary in size, with some focusing on a county (Dorset LEP), while others span multiple counties (South East LEP comprises Essex, Kent and East Sussex) or share a transport corridor (Enterprise M3 covers areas adjacent to the M3 motorway in Hampshire and Surrey).

Like the RDAs which preceded them, LEPs cover more than tourism in their activities. Within the work of these entities has been the development of **destination management organisations** (DMOs). Several sub-regional DMOs, already in existence at the time of the closure of RDAs, have remained in existence, becoming more prominent in tourism marketing and development of their local area.

EXAMPLE

Destination management organisations in England

At the time of writing, VisitBritain lists more than 150 DMOs covering areas of England. Some of the DMOs focus on a town or city, while others work to attract tourism to the county as a whole. Alternatively, the DMO may focus on an area defined by a common destination theme, which can often span the political borders of counties (see Table 17.4).

TABLE 17.4 Examples of English DMOs

Towns and cities	Counties	Cross-county/destination theme
Bournemouth Tourism	Cumbria Tourism	Shakespeare's England
Destination Colchester	Destination Staffordshire	Cotswolds Tourism
Destination Hartlepool	Experience Bedfordshire	English Riviera Tourism Company
Huntingdonshire Association for Tourism	Destination Worcestershire	Discover Yorkshire Coast
Basingstoke Together	Welcome to Yorkshire	New Forest Destination Partnership
Visit Greenwich	Visit Nottinghamshire	Tourism South East
Visit Leeds	Marketing Lancashire	White Cliffs Country

Note: A current list of English DMOs can be accessed online at: www.visitbritain.org/destination-management-organisations-england

VisitWales, located in the Welsh government's Ministry for Culture, Tourism and Sport, acts as the country's tourist board, responsible for the promotion and development of tourism. It works with four regional tourism partnerships. These are:

- Tourism Partnership North Wales
- Tourism Partnership Mid Wales
- South West Wales Tourism Partnership
- Capital Region Tourism.

The principal role of these four organisations is to improve the competitive performance of tourism in Wales so that it better contributes to the economic and social prosperity of the area. Each organisation works in partnership with VisitWales, local authorities and tourism businesses to market their respective destinations, while encouraging new product development and the enhancement of existing resources.

In Scotland, 15 tourism areas exist to address local tourism priorities on an integrated basis. Each region brings together representatives from the private and public sectors, such as tourism operators, local tourism groups, chambers of commerce, local authorities and VisitScotland. The regions are:

- Aberdeen and Aberdeenshire
- Argyll and the Isles
- Ayrshire and Arran
- Dumfries and Galloway
- Dundee and Angus
- Edinburgh and The Lothians
- Fife
- Greater Glasgow and The Clyde Valley
- Loch Lomond, The Trossachs, Stirling and Forth Valley
- Orkney

- Outer Hebrides
- Perthshire
- Scottish Borders
- Shetland
- The Highlands and Moray Speyside.

These regions are expected to design and implement plans that focus on the development and marketing of tourism in their region. These plans should work in alignment with the national tourism strategy. Funding these activities is achieved by encouraging the private sector to invest in initiatives that will ultimately assist in enhancing the profitability of their operations. The area partnerships also act as a lobby group, to actively voice the interests of tourism in the area.

Northern Ireland, in addition to its forming one region within the all-Ireland marketing consortium Tourism Ireland, also has regional-level organisations. Following a review and reduction in funding, the number of regional tourism partnerships (RTPs) has reduced, with Visit Belfast, Visit Derry, Fermanagh Lakelands Tourism and Flavour of Tyrone remaining (Northern Ireland Assembly, 2015).

THE UK GOVERNMENT'S INVOLVEMENT AT LOCAL LEVEL

We have provided examples of how tourism is structured at national and regional levels, with particular reference to the structure in the UK. We now examine the third tier in this structure, that at local authority level, where towns and district councils also have statutory responsibilities and interests when it comes to providing tourist facilities – or, at the very least, in encouraging inbound tourism where the potential for it exists, as part of the economic development plans for the area. This will generally include the provision of TICs.

In the UK, the Local Government Act 1948 empowered local authorities to set up information and publicity services for tourism. This Act was reinforced by the Local Government Act of 1972, giving local authorities the power (but not the obligation) to encourage visitors to their area and provide suitable facilities for them.

Historically, the organisation of tourism at local level in the UK has been piecemeal. Councils at county or district level on the whole relegate responsibility for tourism to departments that are also concerned with a range of other activities, with the result that it is seldom given the significance that its economic impact on the area merits. Up until 30 years ago, fewer than half of the local authorities in England included any strategy relating to tourism in their planning. This has now changed. Research published in 2002 revealed that 80% of local authorities surveyed had a written tourism policy, with nearly all (98%) having a tourism strategy (Stevenson, 2002).

Such strategies should take into account the impact of tourism and the resultant need for car and coach parks, toilets, information centres, tourist attractions and local accommodation. The principal responsibilities of county and district authorities that have a bearing on tourism are as follows:

- provision of leisure facilities for tourists (such as conference centres) and residents (theatres, parks, sports centres, museums and so on)
- planning (under town and country planning policies) – note that district councils produce local plans to fit the broad strategy of the county council's structure plans and those plans are certified by the county councils
- powers to control development and land use

- provision of visitor services (usually in conjunction with tourist bodies)
- parking for coaches and cars
- provision of caravan sites (with licensing and management the responsibility of district councils)
- production of statistics on tourism, for use by the regional tourist bodies
- marketing of the area
- upkeep of historic buildings
- public health, including food hygiene and safety issues, as well as litter disposal and the provision of public toilet facilities.

EXAMPLE

Managing Edinburgh tourism

At the start of 2018, Edinburgh's Culture and Communities Committee published a dossier revealing the issues associated with tourism in the city. The issues highlighted include:

- pavement congestion for residents and visitors trying to move around the city; this is particularly prevalent on Princes Street, one of the main thoroughfares
- an increase in litter that needs to be cleared
- pinchpoints when crowds gather at busy bus stops, and to watch street performers and buskers
- noise pollution caused by traffic, open-top bus tours, amplified walking tours and open-air concerts.

Visitor numbers to Edinburgh swell during the August festival season, with the International Festival, Royal Military Tattoo, the Art Festival, the Book Festival and the Festival Fringe (renowned particularly for its comedy offering) all taking place during this busy month. For example, footfall counters recorded an average of 45,000 people per day on Princes Street in August, more than double the level seen in June. Consequently, managing the pressures caused by tourism during this time is particularly challenging.

Source: Culture and Communities Committee, 2018

Local authorities may also own and operate local airports, although increasingly these are now partly or wholly in private hands. The provision of visitor services will normally include helping to fund and manage TICs, in cooperation with the regional tourist boards, which set and monitor standards. Local authorities will also fund tourist information points (TIPs), as well as information boards found at lay-bys, car parks and city centres. They may also encourage the creation of a DMO as a public–private partnership.

Any DMO established is likely to act as a coordinator for tourism in the area, advising on development and grant-aided opportunities, to and carry out research related to local tourism. It may become involved in the provision and training of tourist guides, and provide training in areas such as service quality and business development for SMEs, especially small businesses such as guest houses or cafés.

The DMO will also undertake a range of promotional and publicity functions, including the preparation of publications such as guides to the district, accommodation guides, information on current events and entertainment, and specialist brochures listing, for example, local walks, shopping, restaurants and pubs. The cost of most of these publications will be met in large part by contributions from the private sector, either through advertising or, as in the case of the accommodation brochures, through a charge for being listed.

DMOs may also organise familiarisation trips for the travel trade and the media, and, if the resort shows sufficient potential, may invite representatives of the overseas trade and media. They frequently play a part in setting up and operating the local TIC, which may include a local accommodation-booking service. DMOs may also produce a trade manual, aimed at the travel trade and giving information on trade prices, conference facilities and local attractions.

Tourist information centres (TICs)

TICs play a particularly important role in disseminating information about tourism. There are now around 200 official VisitEngland TICs, a significant decline in numbers over recent years, while in 2017 VisitScotland announced the closure of 39 of its 65 centres. Across the UK, those that remain are being forced to become more commercial, reflecting government policy and the decline in funding from local authorities (which do not, in any case, have a statutory duty to provide these services). Now, TICs are increasingly introducing commercial products for sale within their shops, while seeking ways to cut costs to remain viable. Cafés and shops have been combined with exhibition and interpretation galleries in many TICs to attract tourists and encourage them to spend money in the centres.

It should also be stressed that TICs can make a valuable contribution to tourism through the buildings they occupy. In many cases, TICs are housed in buildings of outstanding architectural or historic interest in a city, and their careful preservation and adaptation for this purpose has ensured that the buildings are not only put to good use but also provide an additional point of focus for visiting tourists, who are able to see the interior of a building that might otherwise be restricted (see Figure 17.2). Increasingly, local authorities have come to recognise the important role that the TIC can play in drawing attention to modern design as well, whether in the traditional style and materials of local buildings, or in a more modern concept where the new building can itself become a stimulus for tourist interest.

INFORMATION TECHNOLOGY INITIATIVES IN THE PUBLIC SECTOR

One means of providing tourist information cheaply is to have tourist information points (TIPs): unattended stands providing information about local facilities. These may well be located in TICs, but in some cases they are placed in popular tourist spots and can include sophisticated booking systems for local hotels, either using telephone connections or via computer.

The computer-linked accommodation reservation system used by TICs was just the first step into IT taken by the public sector. The UK tourist boards have moved steadily towards developing and expanding their websites and now provide the public with a

FIGURE 17.2 TIC at Colle val d'Elsa, Italy

Photo: Chris Holloway

comprehensive package of information and booking services. The BTA devised its first VisitBritain website in 1997, incorporating details of tourist attractions, events and hotels, with accompanying advertisements. These have been complemented by the extensive websites provided by DMOs.

Few can doubt that websites are one of the most popular means of accessing information about tourism products and making accommodation bookings. Both national tourist boards and DMOs are developing smartphone apps that provide access to tourist information, including details of local attractions, accommodation, maps and transport options. Although national tourist boards frequently act as a gateway to provide information for the tourist, it is likely to be the newly emerging DMOs that provide up-to-date information on attractions, accommodation and local events, all of which will encourage tourists to visit.

THE WIDER INFLUENCES OF THE PUBLIC SECTOR ON TOURISM IN THE UK

While departments with a specific responsibility for tourism play a major influential role in the development and management of the industry, the diverse nature of tourism and its impact on so many different facets of the economy mean that there are often other government departments that have a vested interest in the way in which tourism is planned and managed. Furthermore, there are also public or quasi-public bodies that, owing to their roles, impinge in one way or another on tourism.

EXAMPLE

Transport and tourism

The Department for Transport (DfT), quite apart from its public transport responsibilities, exercises control over certain types of signposting, and the signposting of attractions is of immense importance to the success of tourism. In January 1996, the relaxation of control over brown and white road signs for tourist sites led to information about these sites becoming far more readily available to passing tourists, enhancing tourist spend.

In 2005, the Peak District National Park, concerned about the increasing numbers of visitors it received each year (22 million at the time), proposed an environmental levy on cars visiting the park, but this was rejected by the DfT.

The water authorities offer just one example among many non-government interests that relate to tourism, as water-based recreation has come to play an important part in leisure and tourism planning. Local authorities and water authorities are now fully aware of the commercial leisure opportunities associated with open expanses of water. In this respect, it is interesting to note the extent to which tourism was taken into account in the planning and development of the Kielder Reservoir in Northumbria compared with earlier reservoir development. Opened in 1982, Kielder is the largest man-made lake in Europe, with a shoreline 27 miles long, and is set within the largest man-made forest in the UK, Kielder Forest (which is managed by the Forestry Commission). Accordingly, the area, which attracted 410,000 visitors in 2016, planned its tourism assets from the outset, including picnic areas, campsites, water sports, fishing and mountain bike hire.

Other quasi- or non-governmental bodies with interests that touch on tourism include Natural England (incorporating the former Countryside Agency and English Nature), the Forestry Commission, the Arts Council, the National Trust and SportEngland; yet there is no common coordinating body to bring these interests together.

National heritage bodies

Heritage plays a particularly important role in tourism; monuments, historic homes and cathedrals make a substantial contribution to many areas' tourist attractions. Although many of these resources remain in private hands or are the responsibility of bodies such as the Church Commissioners, a number of quasi-public organisations exist to protect and enhance these heritage sites. These bodies, therefore, fulfil an important role in the tourism industry. Even when heritage buildings are not open to the public, they still form an attractive backdrop to any townscape for passing tourists.

Internationally renowned UNESCO World Heritage Sites draw people from all over the world, and are carefully protected. UNESCO works to protect sites of international importance, encouraging management plans to be developed to ensure the protection and conservation of its recognised sites (at the time of writing, in 2018, more than 1000 have been recognised). It also provides around $4 million annually in funding support.

PUBLIC-/PRIVATE-SECTOR COOPERATION

Due to the sheer complexity of tourism, there is frequently a lack of coordinated tourism policy at government level, while, at the same time, financial constraints are restricting public expenditure on tourism. As we have seen in the case of the UK, increasingly, the view is being taken that the public sector can best assist a country's prospects for tourism by reducing its role in development and focusing on entering into partnership with the private sector for marketing, promotion and other activities.

The desire to turn national tourism promotion over to the private sector or develop partnerships with the private sector has been led, as we discussed earlier, by developments in the USA, with the introduction of the privately sponsored US Travel Association. Individual US states have also gone down this road: Visit Florida is a **public-/private-sector partnership** that is funded in part by taxation on car hire within the state, and in 2017 raised more than $128 million in private-sector sponsorship from the local tourism industry.

Regions, sometimes transnational, are also opting for a collaborative approach. An interesting example is that of the Øresund region, where Denmark is geographically separated from southern Sweden. The construction of a bridge linking the two countries has led to the formation of a joint marketing organisation – the Øresund network – to promote the Danish islands of Zealand, Lolland-Falster, Møn and Bornholm and the Swedish region of Skåne. One notable effect of this marketing drive has been the economic improvement resulting from tourist flows into Malmö and southern Sweden, an economically depressed region. This exemplifies a general move to introduce DMOs that work to encourage partnerships between the public and private sectors in order to promote tourism to a region more effectively.

It should be stressed that public funds for private tourism projects have not ceased entirely. Many countries still offer subsidies in the form of grants, loans or other financial incentives that help to reduce costs for entrepreneurs in tourism. For example, Visit Florida, mentioned previously, awarded $459,000 in grants, contributing towards, among other things, small business development and cultural, heritage and rural tourism initiatives. Where the state remains keen to see the development of private tourism, and funding for such development would not be forthcoming without direct public assistance, both central and local governments will still offer some measure of help.

TOWN TWINNING AND TOURISM

No discussion of public-sector tourism can be complete without exploring the development of town twinning, even though the impact of this relationship between towns is seldom considered as an element of the tourism business.

The concept of town twinning emerged in the aftermath of World War II, as a means of overcoming hostilities between the warring nations and forging greater understanding between communities in different countries. Usually, the selection of a twin town is based on some common characteristics, such as population size, geographical features or commercial similarities. Local authorities and chambers of commerce arrange for the exchange of visits by residents of the twinned towns.

Although conceived as a gesture of friendship and goodwill, the outcome has commercial implications for tourism, as visitor flows increase between the twinned towns. While accommodation is normally provided in private homes, expenditure on transport, shopping and sightseeing can have a significant impact on the inflow of tourist revenue for the towns concerned, some of which may have little other tourist traffic. Friendships formed as a result of these links also lead to subsequent demand for travel. So far, no studies appear to have been made as to the financial contribution resulting from these links, but it is likely to be considerable overall.

EXAMPLE

European twinning

Town twinning has been in existence for many decades and today there are 20,000 European links in existence, with French and German municipalities leading the way (each country having more than 6000 established). The UK has around 2000 European links and many others further afield. Recently published research (Diebold, 2018) on the French–German agreements reveals that, for two-thirds of cities, twinning arrangements are either stable or growing in intensity of activity. Most commonly, this involves student exchanges or trips to attend festivals or local events.

Much of the enthusiasm for links is maintained within Europe. Supported, and partially funded, by the EC, through its 'Europe for Citizens' programme, towns and cities are uniting with a partner to encourage cross-border cultural connections. To help in the search for a suitable partner, the EC has developed a website – www.twinning.org – which lists more than 600 requests for partners.

THE ROLE OF THE EUROPEAN UNION (EU)

By contrast with some EU nations where tourism makes an equally important contribution to the economy, the UK has chosen, largely, to allow the free-market economy to operate in the tourism field, with little attempt to centralise policy-making. As the UK integrated more closely with the EU, however, UK travel and tourism interests became subject to EU legislation. Most importantly, since harmonisation came into force at the beginning of 1993, any constraints of trade have been largely abolished, allowing travel firms to compete within the EU on an equal footing and without legal hindrance.

The UK's withdrawal from the European Union (commonly termed Brexit) it expected to reduce the control that Europe has over legislation in the UK. However, any changes are likely to be slow in coming as the UK seeks to maintain trading relationships with EU countries that may demand a protection of the rights and safety of their citizens when they travel to the UK.

Currently, within the EC, almost half of directorates-general (the Commission's departments) have some responsibilities that impact on the tourism industry, although the Tourism Unit itself is allocated to the Directorate General for Enterprise and Industry. Of course, there is no system for coordinating tourism interests across the directorates-general.

In 2010, the EC announced efforts to develop a new political framework to support tourism across member states. The EC (2010) identified four priorities for action:

- to stimulate competitiveness in the European tourism sector

- to promote the development of sustainable, responsible and high-quality tourism
- to consolidate Europe's image as a collection of sustainable, high-quality destinations
- to maximise the potential of EU financial policies for developing tourism.

THE FUTURE ROLE OF THE PUBLIC SECTOR IN TOURISM

It seems that there is greater recognition today, by governments across the globe, of the economic benefits of tourism. However, the economic downturn at the beginning of this decade left many governments seeking to make cutbacks, and for nations with a mature industry especially, funding the support for tourism now is an endeavour they wish to share with the private sector. There are, of course, still examples where governments are providing extensive financial support, often to develop a fledgling industry; the Chinese government, for instance, is offering financial support in order to both develop its domestic industry and attract the international inbound visitor.

Security and cross-border travel remain important issues for many nations, as immigration and anti-terrorism legislation heightens awareness of homeland threats. Increased security at airports has lengthened the time required to reach the departure gate and this may, in the short term, lead to some travellers choosing domestic rather than international travel. Complex and expensive passport and visa requirements can deter travellers, leading them to choose alternative destinations with fewer restrictions, or to refrain from travelling at all if the problems are created by their home government.

The continued expansion of the EU may make cross-border travel more difficult to monitor; research into international tourism in countries with open borders has often had to rely on the accommodation sector for estimates of international tourism arrivals. Whether the borders continue to be truly open remains to be seen. A recent move by some European governments has seen the reintroduction of border checks, though these are claimed to be only 'spot-checks' designed to restrict illegal importing, to avoid falling foul of EU regulations on the free movement of European citizens.

SUMMARY

Governments across the globe are often interested in reaping the economic benefits that the domestic and inbound tourism industry can bring. We have also seen that, through social tourism initiatives, tourism can bring health benefits to disadvantaged members of the population. How, and whether, tourism is supported by government often depends on the ideological policies of government. Yet even in a free-market economy like the USA, we see governments, often at state level, providing some support for the industry. The government department given responsibility for tourism can often reveal much about the attitude of government towards the industry.

A government becomes involved in tourism through the taxation policy it sets, the financial support it offers and the planning policies it provides, all of which may discourage or encourage tourism to take place. The government may also provide support for tourism development through training schemes and licensing programmes, which can often help to improve the quality of the tourist experience. These activities may take place at the national, regional or local level, although we have seen in the case of the UK that the regional level of governance is being reduced in favour of greater local initiatives between the public and the private sector. Efforts to encourage partnerships with the private sector are likely to continue.

QUESTIONS AND DISCUSSION POINTS

1. In what ways can the involvement of national, regional or local government aid the development and operation of the tourism industry?
2. Social tourism suggests that holidays should be made available to all in society. What is the justification for this?
3. To what extent is technology changing the demand for, and use of, tourist information centres?

TASKS

1. Table 17.2 highlights several European Union programmes for tourism. Focus on one of these programmes and investigate the projects that have been funded in recent years. What are the goals of these projects? Consider the extent to which these actions are helping to develop sustainable tourism within the EU. Summarise your findings on a poster.
2. For a country of your choice, investigate the national tourism policy/strategy. What are the key priorities and actions? To what extent does the government work in partnership to achieve these? Write a brief report that explains your findings.

WEBSITES

Family Holiday Association: www.fhaonline.org.uk

Tourism For All: www.tourismforall.org.uk

Town Twinning: www.twinning.org

VisitBritain: www.visitbritain.com

REFERENCES

Airports Council International (ACI) Europe (2016) *The Ownership of Europe's Airports*. Available online at: www.aci-europe.org/component/downloads/downloads/5095.html [Accessed November 2018].

Arasli, H., Bavik, A. and Ekiz, E. H. (2006) The effects of nepotism on human resource management. *International Journal of Sociology and Social Policy*, 26, 295–308.

Culture and Communities Committee (2018) *Managing our Festival City: Report and scorecard*. Available online at: www.edinburgh.gov.uk/download/meetings/id/55960/item_81_-_managing_our_festival_city_-_report_and_scorecard [Accessed November 2018].

Diebold, C. (2018) Deutsch-französische Städtepartnerschaften bringen Europa zu den Bürgern. Available online at: www.bertelsmann-stiftung.de/de/themen/aktuelle-meldungen/2018/januar/deutsch-franzoesische-staedtepartnerschaften-bringen-europa-zu-den-buergern [Accessed November 2018].

European Commission (EC) (2010) Europe, the world's no. 1 tourist destination: A new political framework for tourism in Europe. *Communication, COM* (2010) 352 final, 30 June.

EC (2016) *Guide on EU Funding for the Tourism Sector 2014–2020*. Available online at: http://ec.europa.eu/growth/content/guide-eu-funding-tourism-sector-updated-version-0_en [Accessed November 2018].

Journal du Cameroun (2018) Nigeria Woos Tourism Investors with Three-year Tax Exemption. Available online at: www.journalducameroun.com/en/nigeria-woos-tourism-investors-with-three-year-tax-exemption [Accessed November 2018].

Loveys, K. (2011) Summer school holidays could be slashed to just four weeks, says Michael Gove. *Daily Mail*, 21 June.

McCabe, S., Minnaert, L. and Diekmann, A. (2012) *Social Tourism in Europe: Theory and practice*. Bristol: Channel View Publications.

Minnaert, L., Maitland, R. and Miller, G. (2006) Social tourism and its ethical foundations. *Tourism, Culture and Communications*, 7 (1), 7–17.

No. 10 (2010) PM's speech on tourism, 12 August. Available online at: www.number10.gov.uk/news/pms-speech-on-tourism [Accessed November 2018].

Northern Ireland Assembly (2015) *Northern Ireland Tourism: Structures*. Paper No. 125/15, 5 November.

Sandford, M. (2011) *The abolition of regional government*. House of Commons Library, 17 March. Standard Note: SN/PC/05842.

Singapore Tourism Board (STB) (2018) Organisational Chart. Available online at: www.stb.gov.sg/about-stb/Pages/Organisation-Chart.aspx [Accessed November 2018].

Smith, H. (2018) Greece relaxes capital controls to prove worst of turmoil is over. *The Guardian*, 3 June.

Stevenson, N. (2002) The role of English local authorities in tourism. *Tourism Insights*, January.

World Travel and Tourism Council (WTTC) (2017) *Governing National Tourism Policy*. London: WTTC.

18

TOUR OPERATING

CONTENTS

LEARNING OUTCOMES

After studying this chapter, you should be able to:

- define the role of a tour operator and distinguish between different types of operator
- explain the functions of each type of operator
- identify how operators interact with other sectors of industry
- summarise how the activities of operators are constrained
- outline the basic principles behind the construction and marketing of a package tour
- explain the appeal of the package tour to its various markets
- evaluate alternative methods of tour distribution and recognise the importance of new forms of electronic reservations and sales systems for operators and their clients.

> People are looking beyond the traditional package holiday, they want a holiday that is handpicked just for them and the next evolution in mass market travel is personalisation and customisation. (Calder, 2018)

INTRODUCTION

The package holiday has made the process of organising holidays much more straightforward than in earlier times. For many holidaymakers, the convenience of booking a package, which provides all the component parts of the holiday, has encouraged travel to locations that otherwise they would not have considered. This has overcome language barriers, as well as concerns regarding the suitability of products like accommodation, airport transfers or tours – and all at a competitive price. However, as the quote above acknowledges, today's traveller demands a holiday experience that is tailored to meet their own expectations. Tour operators have needed to adapt to meet these changes in the market, with varying degrees of success, to the point that now, for the UK, just over a third of main holidays take the form of a package (Mintel, 2018a).

TOUR OPERATORS: WHY A EUROPEAN PERSPECTIVE?

The use of the tour operator as an intermediary in the travel booking process varies across nations. The decision of whether or not to use intermediaries is influenced by a wide variety of factors, including the nature of travel (domestic or international) as well as the experience of the traveller.

It is often generally accepted that the first tour operator was established in the UK, through the activities of Thomas Cook back in the nineteenth century. Many tour operators are an amalgamation of businesses which operate in multiple European countries. For example, Thomas Cook before its failure in September 2019, owned tour operators and charter airlines in the UK, Belgium and Scandinavia. Another giant in tour operations is TUI Group, which is German-owned, while Kuoni, a leading long-haul operator, is Swiss. Furthermore, the largest outbound travel market by far is the European region. The United Nations World Tourism Organization (UNWTO) reported that in 2018 over half of global arrivals were from Europe, the next largest markets being the Asia-Pacific region and the Americas, with 24% and 16%, respectively (UNWTO, 2018) (see Figure 18.1).

As we can see in Figure 18.1, the number of travellers from the European region has seen a slow but steady growth over the past two decades, but the Asia-Pacific region has experienced much more rapid growth, almost trebling (from 110 million in 2000 to 323 million in 2018). This region is dominated by the markets of Japan, South Korea and China, the latter comfortably number one in the world outbound markets (by spend). That said, half of the top ten countries, based on international tourism expenditure, are European (Table 18.1).

For these reasons, this chapter is focused largely on the European tour operator industry, acknowledging the traditional role of the tour operator as well as changing trends that are placing great pressure on tour operators to adapt their activities.

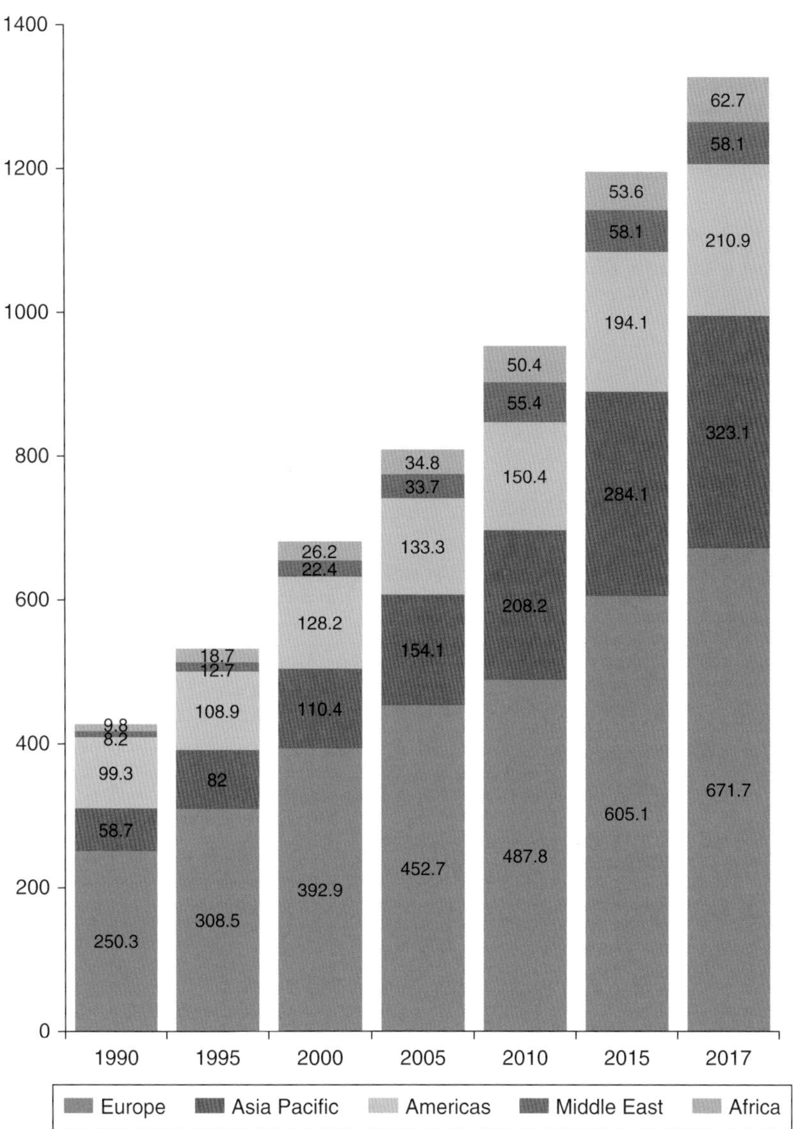

FIGURE 18.1 Region of origin of international travellers (arrivals in millions)

Source: UNWTO, 2018

TABLE 18.1 Tourism spend by top ten outbound markets, 2018

Europe	$US billion	Asia–Pacific	$US billion	Americas	$US billion
Germany	89.1	China	257.7	USA	135.0
Russia	31.1	Australia	34.2	Canada	31.8
UK	71.4	South Korea	30.6		
France	41.4				
Italy	27.7				

Source: UNWTO, 2018

THE ROLE OF THE TOUR OPERATOR

For many years, tour operators have formed the core of what we understand as the travel industry, and, to a large extent, they can be said to have moulded the industry into the form familiar to us today. Traditionally, they provided an essential bridge between travel suppliers and customers, purchasing separately the elements of transport, accommodation and other services and combining them into a package that they then sold direct (or through travel agents) to consumers. Their position in the tourism distribution system is demonstrated by Figure 18.2.

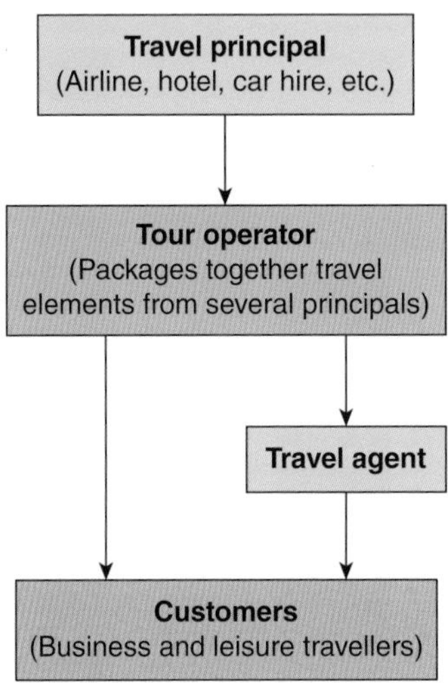

FIGURE 18.2 Tour operators' position in the chain of distribution

Some take the view that tour operators are essentially wholesalers, as they purchase services from the principals in large quantities and break these into individual units to sell to customers. Wholesalers, however, are not normally known to change the product they buy before distributing it, so for this reason some argue that tour operators should be classed as principals in their own right, rather than simply intermediaries. Their argument is based on the premise that by packaging a series of individual tourism elements into a single whole new product – the **inclusive tour** – the operator is actually changing the nature of those products. Like traditional wholesalers, the service the tour operator provides is that of buying in bulk, thus in theory securing considerable discounts from suppliers that could not normally be matched by customers buying direct. The operator is able consequently to assemble and present to the customer a package that is both convenient to purchase and competitively priced.

Recent years have witnessed a change to the ways in which travel products are bought and sold by operators. In the last quarter of the twentieth century, operators had begun to sell unpackaged 'seat only' flights to agents and customers in order to fill seats on their charter flights, and, with the advent of the Internet, which encouraged principals to sell travel arrangements direct to customers, operators have become far more flexible in marketing their products. Many now offer each element of the package separately or give their clients the opportunity to book their flights direct while helping them to organise the remaining elements of their holiday separately. While traditional 7- and 14-day packages remain a popular feature in most operators' brochures, more flexible durations as well as tailor-made arrangements and individual elements of the package are now negotiable.

The packaging of travel elements by tour operators is also valuable to principals in the travel and tourism industry. The travel industry operates in a business environment where supply and demand are seldom in balance; neither can supply expand or contract quickly; both the airline and hotel businesses operate in circumstances that make it difficult to adjust their capacity in the short term.

THE ADVANTAGE OF WORKING WITH A TOUR OPERATOR: THE CASE FOR AIRLINES

Once a flight takes off, the airline has lost the opportunity to sell any empty seats on the plane, and therefore any potential revenue for those seats. Maximising the load factor (the percentage of available seats filled by passengers) is therefore key to maximising revenue. Tour operators can help ensure that more seats are sold.

A charter airline with a single type of aircraft – say, an Airbus A320–200 with a maximum capacity of 174 passengers – can neither expand the number of seats to take advantage of peak opportunities, nor reduce capacity if demand falls slightly. We say that supply is **lumpy**; that is, it cannot be expanded by a *single* seat, but must be expanded in *blocks* of seats – perhaps as many as 150 at a time in the case of aircraft. Carriers, therefore, seek ways to adjust demand to fill the available seats. It is important to do this to keep down costs per passenger and reduce the waste of resources, as flying an aircraft involves fixed costs regardless of the number of passengers on board, and those fixed costs are likely to be the major element in any transport costs. Tour operators have played a very useful role in helping to achieve this for the scheduled airlines, and, in return, the airlines can offer substantial discounts on seats that they know they themselves cannot fill. Example A demonstrates this.

EXAMPLE

A. Costing a scheduled flight

Suppose that the fixed cost of flying a 140-seat plane from Paris to Athens and back is €43,540 (including capital costs, fuel, crew's pay and so on). Suppose also that the additional, or variable, cost per passenger is €30 (to cover administrative expenses such as check-in, the e-ticket and providing in-flight refreshments, extra fuel and so on). If the airline wants to budget for a small profit and estimates that, at a price of €425, it can expect to sell 112 seats, then the cost and pricing look like this:

Fixed cost	€43,540
112 passengers at €30	€3360
Cost of return flight	**€46,900**
Sell 112 tickets at €425 each	€47,600
Profit	**€700**

Of course, in the example, if only 110 passengers are sold seats, then sales drop by €850 (two passengers at €425), costs by only €60 (two passengers at €30), so the airline ends up losing €90:

Fixed cost	€43,540
110 passengers at €30	€3300
Cost of return flight	**€46,840**
Sell 110 tickets at €425 each	€46,750
Profit/loss	**–€90**

The example shows a very simplified picture of pricing on a single route, but the complexity of pricing has substantially increased since the no-frills airlines came into service, with the variations in price becoming far wider (see Chapter 13 for a fuller discussion of this). Airlines also overbook in the expectation that a few passengers will not turn up in time for their flight, or will cancel without refund. Airlines retain the revenue, making a significant contribution to overall profit, especially if the seat can be resold.

Tour operators prove themselves useful to airlines by agreeing to purchase in bulk, say, 25 seats, which can virtually ensure that the airline will fly at a profit. The amount of discount that airlines give to tour operators must be considered, however. For example, if we continue with the example above, as far as the airline is concerned, anything above €30 a head will be profitable, as the fixed costs are already paid for. Tour operators will want the lowest price possible to ensure that they can resell all 25 seats. Obviously, customers are unwilling to pay anything like the original €425 that was being asked or they would have already booked with the airline itself. Let's say that, after negotiating, the airline agrees to sell the seats to a tour operator at a net price of €225 each. The airline's budget for this case is shown in Example B.

EXAMPLE

B. Costing a scheduled flight with a tour operator

Fixed cost	€43,540
137 passengers at €30*	€4110
Cost of return flight	**€47,650**
Sell 112 tickets at €425 each	€47,600
Sell 25 tickets at €225 each	€5625
Revenue	**€53,225**
Profit	**€5575**

Note: *Assumes all 25 seats are sold by the tour operator.

The airline will now achieve a greater profit from this flight than before. What is more, it does not have to take responsibility for marketing the 25 seats, which the tour operator now must sell. This may involve heavy selling costs for the operator, but, as long as it sets a sensible price for each seat that will still deliver a profit for the company after paying overhead costs, the customers are able to buy seats that represent good value. A figure of €299 might be considered reasonable under these circumstances. To ensure that tour operators do not poach existing passengers, airlines usually impose various conditions on the resale of tickets. The main condition is that the tour operator must build the trip into a package and publish a number of brochures to prove it.

As tour operators build their markets, they can eventually decide that they will have enough customers to fill an aircraft and consider either part-chartering a plane with other operators or even chartering a whole plane themselves. Eventually, they may be in a position to buy and operate their own airline to carry their customers, as do the leading tour operators in Europe.

EXAMPLE

TUI Group

TUI Group (formed in 2014 by the merger of TUI AG with TUI Travel plc) owns several airlines, which provide charter flights to service their package holiday operations.

In recent years, rebranding has led to the renaming of some of these operations and now TUI has more than 150 aircraft serving destinations both within and outside Europe. TUI Group airlines include: TUI fly (formerly Hapag-Lloyd Flug and Hapag-Lloyd Express), TUI Airways (formerly Thomson Airways, formed from the merger of Thomsonfly and First Choice Airways, which itself was formerly Britannia UK), TUI fly Nordic (Britannia Nordic), TUI fly Belgium, TUI fly Netherlands and the French airline Corsair. Combined, these airlines would be the seventh largest in Europe in terms of fleet size.

Source: www.tui-group.com

THE ADVANTAGE OF WORKING WITH A TOUR OPERATOR: THE CASE FOR HOTELS

In exactly the same way, hoteliers attempt to use tour operators to fill their unsold bedrooms. They, too, have substantial fixed costs in relation to operating their properties and so are willing to provide substantial discounts to operators and others willing to commit themselves to buying rooms in bulk. This is because, as with airlines, once the fixed costs of the property have been covered by revenue, any price that is greater than the variable cost will represent pure profit for the hotel, which will also then have the opportunity to sell extra services to its clients, such as drinks, leisure activities and meals, those profits compensating for the low room rates that the operators have paid them. Furthermore, if the price is sufficiently attractive, the tour operator may even be able to provide the hotel with guests at times other than peak season. This will allow the hotel to operate all year round rather than have to consider closing during the off-peak period (closure means that no revenue is coming in at all, while the hotel will still attract costs for permanent staff, maintenance and so on).

Some of the larger tour operators started to own and run their own accommodation, but in practice this proved more difficult, and most operators eventually divested themselves of their properties, preferring to sign contracts with proprietors, often for the entire capacity of the hotel and sometimes for several years in advance. The hoteliers' dependence on those contracts and their inability to reach the marketplace in any other way made them overly dependent on tour operators, who, in turn, used their dominant position in the market to force down prices. Consequently, the low profit levels achieved by the hoteliers led some to implement cost-cutting measures in the level of service they provided. The number of customer complaints rose as a result.

EXAMPLE

TUI Hotels and Resorts

TUI Group owns or has management agreements with many hotels across Europe, which operate under brand names such as TUI Blue, Rui, Magic Life, Sensatori, Sensimar, TUI Family Life and Robinson. With more than 320 hotels providing around 235,000 bed spaces, the turnover of TUI Hotels and Resorts exceeded €600 million in 2018.

Source: www.tui-group.com

While elements within the package market appear to be unwilling to pay higher prices for improved levels of service, there is some evidence that higher-quality accommodation is increasingly in demand, with customers prepared to pay slightly higher prices for an opportunity to upgrade. In light of this, some tour operators (such as Club Mediterranée) have elected to upgrade the quality of the accommodation they offer.

The growth of hotel websites is beginning to change this picture. Not only can hoteliers now market their product direct to the public at prices that are competitive with those they offer tour operators, but they can also work with other intermediaries such as website accommodation providers, hotels.com being one such example. These are important opportunities for the hotel sector, which is gradually relinquishing its sales dependence on tour operators.

THE SPECIALISED ROLES OF TOUR OPERATORS

The domestic operator

Tour operators fulfil a number of roles; they do not only carry traffic out of the country, although this is the role with which we most frequently associate them. Operators also exist to organise package holidays domestically; that is, to a destination within the country in which the tourists reside. For many countries, the numbers for domestic travel exceed those for international outbound travel (see Table 18.2).

TABLE 18.2 Domestic tourism

Countries	Domestic trips 2018 (as a % of total domestic and outbound international trips)
India	99.1
China	98.0
USA	91.0
Australia	85.1
Spain	84.1
Russia	82.1
France	78.2
Canada	75.8
Poland	73.9
Germany	68.4
Italy	65.6
Romania	59.5
United Kingdom	56.4
Ireland	47.8
Netherlands	39.7
Switzerland	27.6
Belgium	22.6

Source: calculated from data supplied by Euromonitor

Traditionally, tour operators that served the domestic market have formed just a small part of the travel and tourism industry, because it is relatively simple for tourists to make their own arrangements within their own country. In the past, it was uncommon to find a tour operator that simultaneously organised both domestic and foreign package holidays (although, of course, the originator of the package tour, Thomas Cook, started as a domestic holiday organiser, only later expanding into foreign holidays). As concentration in the industry develops and competition becomes fiercer, however, the larger operators are tending to expand into the domestic market. Despite this, most companies in this sector are relatively small, often dealing directly with the public, and are therefore not involved in retailing through the trade.

The longest established domestic programmes are coach tours operated by companies such as Shearings, based in the UK, OAD Reizen, which operates in the Netherlands, and Orbis Transport in Poland.

The incoming operator

Those countries such as Spain and Greece, which are predominantly destination rather than generating countries, will have an incoming travel sector that is as important as the outgoing sector. Organisations specialising in handling incoming foreign holidaymakers have a rather different role from that of outbound operators. Some are merely **ground-handling** agents, so their role may be limited to organising hotel accommodation on behalf of an overseas tour operator or greeting incoming visitors and transferring them, often by coach, to their hotels. Other companies, however, will offer a comprehensive range of services, which may include negotiating with coach companies and hotels to secure the best quotations for contracts, organising special interest holidays or study tours, or providing dining or theatre arrangements. In some cases, companies specialise according to the markets they serve, catering for the inbound Japanese, Chinese or Israeli markets, for example.

EXAMPLE

Serving the Chinese market to the UK

The number of Chinese visitors to the UK has grown rapidly, rising from 143,000 in 2007 to 337,000 in 2017 (VisitBritain, 2017).

There are many specialist inbound tour operators serving this growing market. For example, Anglo-Chinese Executive Travel (ACE), based in Windsor, with offices in Beijing, Shanghai, Nanjing, Chengdu, Ningxia and Nanchang, provides a range of services for the inbound Chinese market, including arranging accommodation, airport transfers, guided tours and visa application assistance.

To gain business, ACE regularly attends specialist industry events such as the China International Travel Mart held annually in Shanghai and CIBTM in Beijing, the latter focusing on the business tourism sector.

In Britain, there are more than 400 tour companies that derive a major part of their revenue from handling incoming business. As with domestic operators, most of them are small companies and many are members of UKinbound. This organisation provides a forum for the exchange of information and ideas among members, maintains standards of service and acts as a pressure group in dealing with other bodies in the UK who have a role to play in the country's tourism industry.

Incoming tour operators' services are marketed largely through the trade, and organisations work closely with public-sector bodies such as national tourist boards in order to promote their services.

Other specialisations

Many operators recognise that their strengths lie in specialising in a particular niche. For example, some outbound operators choose to specialise according to the mode of transport used by their clients, such as coach tours, rail travel or self-drive holidays. Naturally, such tour operators are in competition with the transport companies seeking to boost their carryings by building inclusive tours around their own forms of transport.

Alternatively, specialisation can be based on the markets they serve or the products they develop. The commonest distinction is between, on the one hand, the **mass-market operators** that have as their products, typically, the sun, sea and sand holiday, designed to appeal to a very broad segment of the market, and, on the other hand, the **specialist operator**, which targets a particular niche market. By trying to distinguish their products from those of their competitors, these operators are not in such intense competition with each other, or with other operators, and their market product is often less price-sensitive as a result.

EXAMPLE

Golf tourism

Golf is the largest segment of the sports tourism market, with an estimated value of more than $2 billion. The International Association of Golf Tour Operators (IAGTO) has more than 700 tour operators as members in 64 countries.

Golf tour operators may choose to specialise in a renowned golf destination, such as Portugal's Algarve or Myrtle Beach in the USA, while others may focus on groups, or particular national or regional markets. Examples include Golfbreaks and Your Golf Travel which provide international golf trips for the UK market. Another example is Classic Golf Tours, located in Colorado and offering domestic and international destinations for the American golf market. The company also serves the corporate market, designing trips which include golf either as an adjunct to a sales meeting or as an incentive or recognition programme for employees or customers.

Specialists have a number of advantages over mass-market companies. Most carry small numbers of tourists and can therefore use smaller accommodation units, such as the many small, family-run hotels in Greece which are popular with tourists but individually too small to interest the larger operators. As the specialist companies generally use scheduled carriers and do not have the level of commitment to a particular destination that their larger colleagues have, they can be more flexible, switching to other destinations if market demand changes. Staff can generally be expected to have a good knowledge of the products and, as the market is often less price-sensitive, the intense price competition found in the mass marketplace is absent, allowing companies to make reasonable profits. If they are successful, however, there is always the danger that one of the larger operators will be attracted to their market and either undercut them or attempt to buy the company.

This has been a feature of the UK tour-operating market for several years, with the largest brands buying out medium-sized niche operators and fitting them into their own specialist products division (sometimes, later dropping the brand altogether or integrating it into their own mainstream brands).

EXAMPLE

Independent tour operators

The Association of Independent Tour Operators (AITO) represents more than 120 tour operators that specialise either by destination or by type of holiday. The specialist nature of the holidays provided can be seen by looking at examples of a few of its members:

- Casa Cantabricas offers tailor-made self-driving holidays to Spain and Portugal, making use of small independent hotels.
- Ffestiniog Travel organises all forms of rail holiday, including escorted rail tours and journeys on historic and scenic railways. The company also offers 'Connoisseur' rail tours for the dedicated rail enthusiast, which include an opportunity to drive the train.
- In The Saddle organises horse-riding holidays around the world. The level of riding experience and the amount of riding desired will influence the choice of trip selected by the equine enthusiasts taking such holidays.
- Scandinavia Only is a specialist operator providing trips to the Nordic countries. The company provides tours that visit places displaying Scandinavia's scenery, culture, history and nature.

More examples of specialist tour operators can be found on the AITO website (www.aito.com).

As with the example of Scandinavia Only, many companies seek to specialise by geographic destination. However, this can be a high-risk decision, as exemplified by the collapse of markets due to factors affecting one country or region. The SARS outbreak in 2003 caused some operators to withdraw their entire China programmes, while the unstable political situation in the Middle East has frequently affected operators specialising in holidays to Israel and neighbouring Arab countries.

Specialisation by market is common. Some companies choose to appeal to a particular age group, as does Saga Holidays, which has for many years been the UK's market leader in holidays for the over-50s. Others target the younger markets, such as Club 18–30 and Scene Hub (formerly 2wentys). The singles market, fast growing as social changes have increased the proportion of divorced people in our society, is served by specialists like Solo Holidays and Page and Moy Group's Just You brand. Other operators specialise by gender. WalkingWomen, for example, as the name implies, offers walking tours for females only. Targets are becoming increasingly tightly focused. One company that has proved itself highly successful in its targeting is Cycling for Softies, which caters for tourists interested in using bicycles as a mode of transport but still seeking comfortable and well-equipped overnight accommodation. This company's main focus is on travel in France and it therefore specialises in both the destination and the market it serves.

Activity and adventure holidays together form one of the fastest-growing areas of specialisation. This market is no longer the preserve of the young, attracting more over-50s.

EXAMPLE

Greycations

One organisation providing adventure holidays for the older age group is ElderTreks. Based in Canada, this tour operator provides small-group trips to over 100 countries. These include African safaris, hiking in the Himalayas, the Andes and the Rockies, and expeditions by icebreaker to the Arctic and Antarctic.

The only concession made to accommodate the mature clientele is that the tours take place at a slightly slower pace, and where possible avoid single-night stops. The company rates the activity levels of each tour, using a five-category scale from Easy (participants are expected to have the fitness to climb two to three flights of stairs or walk one mile) to Challenging (in which participants are expected be fit enough to walk at least five miles).

For further information, see: www.eldertreks.com

THE ROLE OF AIR BROKERS

One other role should be examined here – that of businesses that specialise in providing airline seats in bulk to other tour operators. These specialists are known as **air brokers** or, where their business is principally concerned with consolidating flights on behalf of operators that have not achieved good load factors for their charters, **consolidators**. Their role is discussed in more detail in Chapter 13. Online intermediaries reflect the growth in modern air brokerage, with companies such as ebookers and Opodo becoming major players in the field.

INTEGRATION IN THE INDUSTRY

There have been extensive changes within the competitive environment of the tourism industry. Mergers and takeovers became commonplace, coupled with an increasingly international perspective in the tour-operating business, as operators have come to look abroad for opportunities to expand and dominate the market through purchasing power. The leading European tour operators' attempts to enter the difficult and highly competitive North American markets have tended to prove abortive, although the rationale behind the move was clear: a desire to spread the seasonal flow of traffic, thus obtaining better year-round usage of aircraft. The risk would also be reduced by ensuring a more even spread of revenue between markets in North America, the UK and mainland Europe.

The takeover or merger of businesses is termed **integration**, and it can take place either at the same stage of the supply chain (horizontal integration) or at different stages of the supply chain (vertical integration). This is discussed in more detail in Chapter 7.

Even given the industry integration experienced in the past 30 years, the European Commission (EC) has suggested that the growth of Internet travel providers, as well as the existence of low-cost airlines, has meant that the market remains competitive because smaller tour operators have been able to gain market awareness, travel agents have been able to dynamically package travel (explained in Chapter 19) and consumers have been able to access travel components directly. Thus, it has been accepted that integration is not against the public interest, given that competition still ensures prices are kept down.

TOUR OPERATING WITHIN THE EUROPEAN UNION (EU)

The process of integration has been witnessed extensively across Europe, but some reports have suggested that it may be on the decline in some regions. For instance, established budget airline networks and high levels of Internet use in both the UK and Scandinavia have led business operations in these areas to provide strong challenges to the vertically integrated tour operator model. The integration of travel companies across European borders remains prevalent, however.

Investment companies appear interested in many travel companies. For example, Invesco Asset Management is the largest holder of Thomas Cook Group shares (with 15% holding). Private equity group Carlyle purchased Inca Rail (which provides travel to Machu Picchu) in 2016, while Blackstone purchased Travelport (which includes ebookers, Orbitz and Octopus Travel among its brands). Furthermore, businesses operating in other industry sectors are being attracted to large travel companies. For instance, the large German tour operator DER Touristik is owned by the food retailer REWE, and Hotelplan is a subsidiary of Switzerland's largest supermarket chain, Migros.

The dominance of a few mega-tour operators means that, for many European countries, their largest operators are no longer nationally owned. Some countries, Belgium being one example, have no major nationally owned tour operator. Perhaps the most dominant is TUI, which is the leading tour brand in several European countries, including the UK and Germany.

At the beginning of this century, four tour operators dominated the UK market. However, mergers have reduced this to two operators. At the beginning of 2007, Thomas Cook and My Travel agreed terms to merge the My Travel business, at the time serving more than 5 million customers, into the Thomas Cook Group. Later the same year, TUI and First Choice merged to form TUI Travel (then amalgamating TUI AG to create TUI Group). Now TUI Group earns more than €19 billion in sales annually from 27 million customers.

As we highlighted above, the other major UK operator is the Thomas Cook Group, which now achieves sales of approximately £7 billion annually from its tour operation activities. It is also a major operator in Germany and across Scandinavia. The group serves 20 million customers globally and has some strong brands, including:

- Thomas Cook
- Ving
- Spies
- Airtours
- Neckermann
- Condor
- Hotels4u
- Tourvital.

Despite difficult trading conditions at the beginning of this decade, including £80 million in revenue lost due to the 2010 ash cloud crisis alone, the company implemented cost savings to reduce the debt on its balance sheet. However, Thomas Cook saw share values plunge at the end of 2018 following a troubled year in terms of sales. With £389 million of debts raising concern among investors, the fall in share price meant the business was valued at £348 million. As with TUI, acquisitions were historically important for Thomas Cook. It purchased the German travel operator Oger Tours, specialists in packages to Turkey, Thailand and Cuba, and agreed a merger with the Co-operative Group in the UK which brought economies of scale, and hence efficiencies, in their travel agency operations. However, business transformation plans led to the disposal of the North American, Egyptian and Lebanese sectors of the Thomas Cook business, sale of the ski and activity holiday company Neilson to an investment company and sale of its corporate foreign exchange business.

A third major player in European tour operations is REWE, a leading supermarket chain that controls tour operator DER Touristik and other tour operator brands, including ITS, Jahn Reisen, Dertour, Meier's Weltreisen, Kuoni and ADAC Reisen, together with over 2100 retail travel agencies. Combined, the business serves more than 7 million passengers annually. REWE is active in Germany, Austria and Switzerland, and has expanded (often through company buyouts) to operate in 11 other European countries. Purchase of the Kuoni brand, founded more than 100 years ago, has helped drive this European expansion. Historically, Kuoni focused on the tour-operating sector, which accounted for a significant proportion of the business (upwards of 75% of company revenues), but in recent years this has declined, with destination services growing as a share of company revenue. The destination services sector of the business provides accommodation, tours and other services (for example, booking coaches for transfers and group travel) online and offline to travel agencies and other tour operators.

All these operators have recognised the importance of gaining customer numbers to increase the scale of their operations, thus allowing them to buy at the lowest price and control the markets. Transnational mergers and joint ventures will remain increasingly common, limited only by the anti-monopoly forces of the EC.

THE CHANGING MARKETPLACE IN TOUR OPERATING

Three factors were at work in the second half of the twentieth century that encouraged the growth of the package holiday in Europe:

- There was an expansion of leisure time in the developed countries.
- This was accompanied by greater discretionary income in those countries.
- Package holiday costs were low, both in themselves and in comparison to similar holidays in the home country. This was due to the relatively low costs of accommodation and food in the Mediterranean countries, reductions in air transport costs due to advancing technology, liberalisation of air transport regulations, the introduction of year-round operations, covering both summer and winter seasons, and bulk purchasing by tour operators.

The operators, recognising the strong growth potential in the overseas holiday market, sought to expand their market share and, at the same time, attempted to increase the total size of the market by encouraging those who traditionally took domestic holidays to travel abroad. To achieve this, they slashed prices. Large companies used their purchasing muscle to drive down suppliers' prices (at some cost to quality in a number of cases). They introduced cheap, 'no frills' holidays and, more recently, budget holidays that offered no transfers, no in-flight meals and no resort representatives. Arguably, this new offering can barely be considered a package, in the traditional sense of the word, but budget-conscious consumers have been attracted to it all the same.

Additionally, profit margins were trimmed. Leading tour operators, each determined not to be undersold, engaged in the periodic re-pricing of their holidays throughout the season, using the strategy of brochure reissues with cheaper prices to try to outpace their competitors, but operators always held on to the hope that, given the right conditions, prices could be increased rather than decreased in the later editions.

In the past, overly optimistic forecasts of market growth led to surpluses in supply. Capacity generally exceeded demand each year and operators were then forced into off-loading holidays at bargain basement prices. Not surprisingly, this led to a good deal of dissatisfaction among clients who had booked earlier when the prices were higher. This factor was key to the growth in late bookings.

Traditionally, bookings for package holidays had occurred in the weeks immediately following Christmas, allowing operators time to balance supply and demand and aiding their cash flow; deposits paid by clients in January would be invested and earn interest for the company until its bills had to be paid, which, in some cases, could be as late as September or October. Demanding full balances eight to ten weeks before departure proved similarly lucrative for operators.

Holidaymakers soon came to realise, however, that if they refrained from booking holidays until much nearer to the dates they wanted to travel, they could snap up late-booking bargains. The development of computerised reservation systems allowed operators to update their late availability opportunities quickly, putting cheap offers on the market at very short notice, which made late bookings convenient as well as attractively priced.

The early twenty-first century saw the introduction of online booking, with websites accessible to both retail agents and the general public. This has further promoted the attraction of late booking, reducing the gap between deposits and final payments from months to a matter of weeks, or even removing this gap altogether. The uncertainty caused by this volume of late bookings also made tour operations management more difficult.

The year 2005 appears to have marked the first change of direction, the leading operators reducing their capacity compared with the previous year to reduce the likelihood of overcapacity. In addition, the new technology allowed operators to counteract late-booking trends through the introduction of a policy of fluid pricing. First introduced by Thomson Holidays in 1996 and soon copied by the other leading operators, this entailed offering holidays that were detailed in the brochures for different prices, large discounts being given for early bookings and lower or no discounts for booking nearer the time of the holiday.

EXAMPLE

Holiday pricing by TUI

Historically, brochures included a price table, which detailed the charge for a particular week staying in each category of room. However, this was rarely the price paid; flight and under-occupancy supplements were added, while any discount available at the time of booking reduced the total bill.

Now TUI brochures tend to list only a guide price for adults in low and in high season as well as a guide price for children's places. Customers will establish the exact price at the time of booking. This allows TUI to adjust holiday prices based on the level of demand. This is known as **fluid pricing** and is based on a similar approach to that used by airlines.

Prices will also be influenced by the customer's choice of departure airport, with a premium paid for flights operating during the day (rather than late at night or early in the morning).

(Continued)

Finally, the total cost of the holiday will include any 'extras' selected to improve the service. To take one example, TUI offers passengers the opportunity to pay £18 each to select their seat, ensuring that a family will be able to sit together, something that, generally, frequently happened but could not always be guaranteed on busy flights. Passengers can also choose a host of upgrades; for example, a flight seat upgrade for extra room (£25 each way), extra luggage allowance (£18 for an additional 5kg), or a private taxi transfer to their accommodation on arrival (£55), rather than wait for a coachful of passengers to be delivered to their respective hotels in turn. A sea view room would add, typically, £50 per week per person, or an upgrade to a suite an extra £150.

When all these additional charges and supplements are added, the final price is likely to be nothing close to the basic holiday price. They are, however, relatively transparent, and travel agents or online bookings will display these additional costs separately so passengers can clearly see how the overall cost of the holiday is determined.

Starting in the late 1990s, there was a tendency among operators to launch brochures for the upcoming year at ever earlier dates, resulting, at times, in agents having to find room for brochures covering three different periods: summer and winter of the current year, as well as summer of the following year. More recently, some sense has prevailed and a more rational approach has been apparent. While printed brochures may not be available far in advance, brochures provided digitally online are often available up to 16 months before the holiday period. There is evidence that early launches of brochures did benefit operators, by boosting sales.

EXAMPLE

Online brochures

The major tour operators have now developed apps for smartphones and tablets which provide easy access to, and viewing of, holiday brochures. Digital versions can also be downloaded, and printed if desired. This has thus removed the need for the holidaymaker to visit a travel agent at the start of the holiday search process.

A major advantage of the online publication of brochures is the variety thus available to the holidaymaker, which can stimulate an exploration of destinations and holiday types that may otherwise not have been considered. This shift has, it seems, led to a resurgence of the use of holiday brochures. Research completed for the World Travel Market Industry Report 2016 revealed that a third of holidaymakers made use of a brochure when booking their holiday, up from 6% in 2014 (Greenwood, 2016).

In the past few years, there has been much talk of the demise of the holiday brochure, yet it seems that the holidaymaker likes to have some physical reminder of the details of the holiday booked. Furthermore, the content in brochures is also changing, becoming more a travel magazine than a catalogue of holidays (Baran, 2018). Consequently, we may see the brochure remain in circulation (albeit with smaller print runs) for some time to come.

Tour operators have to estimate their costs for all services up to a year ahead of time. They can anticipate higher costs by raising prices, but this may make them uncompetitive; alternatively, they can take an optimistic approach and price low, in the expectation of stable or declining costs. Originally, the latter was more attractive as moderate cost increases could be passed on to customers (within established limits) in the form of surcharges. Within Europe, however, such surcharges are now no longer acceptable. Legislation implemented by member states in response to the 1992 Directive on Package Travel states that 'a price revision is possible only for variations in transportation costs (including the costs of fuel), dues, taxes or fees chargeable for certain services (such as landing taxes or embarkation or disembarkation fees at ports) and the exchange rates applied to the particular package' (Schulte-Nölke et al., 2008: 288). The update to this legislation in 2015 (implemented by member countries no later than July 2018) maintained this right.

The cost to the tour operator of creating travel packages is affected by changes in the exchange rates for supplies (particularly aviation fuel, which is priced in US dollars). Stability in price can be obtained by 'buying forward' the fuel required for the following year, but this is only practical for the largest operators with sufficient financial reserves.

The introduction of government taxes can also affect the total price paid by tourists. Such taxes might include hotel or bed taxes or departure taxes at ports. In 1996, the UK government introduced an 'exit tax', in the form of air passenger duty (APD), for all flights out of the UK, amounting initially to £5 per person within the EU and £10 outside the EU (a rate that doubled at the end of 1997, and increased again in 2001). An announcement in 2014 removing the requirement for children under 12 to pay APD meant that many tour operators were required to implement systems to refund those families who had already booked travel.

THE LONG-HAUL MARKET

The tendency for all mass-market operators to focus on low price rather than quality or value for money led to this type of tour moving downmarket. As it did so, tourists at the top end of the market, particularly those who had travelled frequently, began to travel independently more often and to more distant destinations. In the UK, independent overseas holiday bookings grew by 33% between 2013 and 2017, while overseas package bookings grew by only 20% (Mintel, 2018a).

The demand for long-haul packages expanded much faster than that for short-haul at the beginning of this century, but the past five years has, particularly in the UK, seen contraction in the market as consumers elect to spread their budget over multiple short trips ahead of a long-haul package (Mintel, 2018b). This sector is expected to see growth though the expansion of offering by low-cost long-haul airlines, allowing for dynamic packaging. The USA, New Zealand and Australia have all witnessed mass-market long-haul growth from the European market, while Thailand and Bali have successfully sold the idea of long-haul sun, sea and sand holidays. South Africa, India and the Middle East (notably Dubai), even Cuba in the Caribbean, have all seen substantial growth in visitors from Western Europe. All of those increases can be directly ascribed to the huge drop in air fares relative to other prices in the past decade.

EXAMPLE

Long-haul at low cost

The long-haul holiday market was predicted to see a decline in 2018 as consumers reconsider the cost of such travel. Furthermore, the European long-haul travel market is changing with the entrance of low-cost carriers such as Norwegian. These airlines now

(Continued)

account for around one-fifth of the long-haul market in the UK (Mintel, 2018b). However, that does mean that consumers are currently more likely to use full-service (e.g. BA) or charter airlines (e.g. TUI Airways).

The collapse of Primera Air (in October 2018), which served transatlantic destinations from Europe, further dissuaded customers from using the emerging low-cost airlines when building their holiday package.

RECENT FACTORS INFLUENCING DEMAND FOR PACKAGE TRAVEL

There is little let-up in the volatility of the tour-operating business. Political conflicts in the Balkans and Turkey at the end of the last century, wars in the Gulf and fears of terrorism that were heightened after the 9/11 tragedy, Bali, Madrid and London bombings, and civil uprisings in northern Africa and the Middle East, all unsettled global travel and tour operations. Natural disasters like the earthquake and subsequent tsunami in the Far East at the end of 2004 and in Japan in 2011 similarly reduced long-haul travel to the affected regions severely. In spite of this catalogue of crises, the sector has shown itself in the past to be resilient and, while in the short term cancelled bookings and hotel reservations would impact severely on these destinations, recovery from even the worst disasters would normally be expected within a year of the event.

European operators have sought new locations to develop where hotel capacity is cheap and readily available, as traditional resorts began to price themselves out of the market. First, the more remote areas of Greece, then Turkey, became boom destinations for Western Europeans seeking sun at rock-bottom prices. The evidence suggests, however, that the inclusive tour market for the traditional sun, sea and sand destinations has probably peaked. For example, in the UK today, despite a recent renaissance, about half of the population choose a package when buying an overseas holiday to Europe.

Second-home ownership has also had a marked effect on patterns of holidaymaking. Many owners disappear from the package holiday market, tending to take most, if not all, of their overseas holidays in their own properties. This, however, has fuelled the growth of the no-frills airlines and the benefits of travel are by no means lost to other sectors of the industry, because second-home owners purchase local products and services at their destinations, invite friends and others to their homes, rent out their properties either privately or through operators and participate in home-exchange opportunities around the world.

In Europe, many in the population have now experienced a foreign holiday at some point in their lives. For example, over 70% of the UK population has travelled overseas. Thus, it is reasonable to assume that the first-time market has been captured and the future growth of the package holiday market is likely to be concentrated on selling a greater frequency of holidays, with a focus on the variety of holidays offered.

The changing nature and demographics of European society are throwing up demand for new kinds of holiday. Growth areas include the following:

- Short breaks and city breaks, especially to more exotic destinations, are increasing. Reykjavik, Barcelona and New York have become popular destinations for short-stay tourism. The entry of the Baltic states into the EU has boosted short breaks to Tallinn and Riga, just as the earlier entry of the Czech Republic boosted Prague as the city break of choice.

- Expansion of the EU has led to increased mobility of the residents of the new accession states. This has the potential to encourage greater VFR (visiting friends and relatives) travel as some choose to work outside their home country, as well as offering wider travel opportunities due to the removal or reduction of visa restrictions, which allows convenient travel to countries across the Continent and further afield.
- In the field of exotic, long-haul activity and adventure holidays, elderly travellers are now far more active than formerly and packages catering to their needs and interests are now common. Early retirement packages at one end of the third age and longer lifespans at the other contribute to this trend.
- Celebration holidays that bring adult groups to a destination are seeing growing demand. The celebration (or commemoration) may focus on the destination (for example, the World War I battlefields), or may be linked to personal celebrations such as significant birthdays or wedding anniversaries.
- Changing attitudes have meant that many tourists are seeking experiences rather than just material products. Living like a local has become an essential part of exploring new destinations for many travellers seeking out authentic experiences. A greater focus on self-development (including learning new skills), culture and health is likely to see customers demanding specialist activities and experiential holidays.

INCLUDING MORE OR LESS?

All-inclusive holidays have grown in popularity. Introduced in the Caribbean, the concept has now been expanded to many European destinations as well, primarily the Mediterranean coastal resorts. These are fully inclusive packages, even down to alcohol and all entertainment at the resort.

EXAMPLE

First Choice goes all-inclusive

Having merged with Thomson Holidays in 2007 (now part of TUI Group), First Choice announced in April 2011 that from the spring of 2012 it would only offer all-inclusive holidays. The holiday price would include all flights, accommodation, meals and drinks in the price of the holiday. Between 2004 and 2009, the all-inclusive market grew by a third. This was viewed as a particularly cost-effective option, especially for a family seeking to control costs once on holiday. However, in recent years there has been a decline in the share of the market taking all-inclusive holidays, down from 18% of the UK market in 2015 to 15% of the market in 2018 (ABTA, 2018).

Of course, the tour operator does charge a higher price for such vacations, and, although the accommodation resort will have negotiated a higher rate with the tour operator to provide an all-inclusive service, the tour operator will gain more of the travellers' holiday spend, which can add to profitability. The sustainability of all-inclusive holidays for destinations is questionable, however, given that customers do not need to go out of their complex to buy anything while they are on holiday; consequently, local shops and services fail to obtain the benefits of the tourists' visit.

At the same time, some operators are electing to **unpackage** elements of the package holiday that would have traditionally been included, such as airport transfers and in-flight catering. The operators are then able to increase their revenue by selling these as 'add-ons', especially common when customers buy no-frills packages. Operators are also making additional charges for early check-in or late check-out of rooms, pre-bookable seats or upgraded seats (as several charter airlines have introduced a premium economy cabin on their planes), the use of prestigious airport lounges and even for guaranteeing a seat next to a friend or relative.

Of course, traditional sales of excursions and car hire at the destination are also lucrative, and resort representatives are actively encouraged to make such sales to the tourists. A further boost to operators' profits can come through the imposition of high cancellation charges as operators retain the revenue while remaining free to sell the same holiday subsequently to other holidaymakers.

THE NATURE OF TOUR OPERATING

An inclusive tour programme, as we have seen, is composed of a series of integrated travel services, each of which is purchased by a tour operator in bulk and resold as part of a package at an all-inclusive price. These integrated services usually consist of an aircraft seat, accommodation at the destination and transfers between the accommodation and the airport on arrival and departure. They may also include other services, such as excursions or car hire.

The inclusive tour is commonly referred to as a package tour and most are single-destination, resort-based holidays. Tours comprising two or more destinations are by no means uncommon, however, and long-haul operators frequently build in optional extensions to another destination in their itineraries. A beach holiday in Kenya might offer an optional extension to one of the game parks, for instance; or a visit to the Chilean fjords, flying to Santiago, might offer tourists the opportunity to extend the itinerary to Chilean-owned Easter Island.

In East Asia, multicentre holidays are very common, as many capital cities in the area are seen as meriting only relatively short stays of three to four nights. Increasingly, itineraries other than the most basic are tailor-made for clients, in terms of length of stay, accommodation, flights and activities at the resort. Dynamic packaging (see Chapter 19) has become a more common booking approach, and it permits either operators or their travel agents to put together tour programmes tailor-made especially to meet the demands of each individual client, using websites to contact suppliers.

Linear tours, such as those offered by coach companies that carry people to different destinations or even through several countries, were at one time the most popular form of trip and still retain a loyal following, but mainly among older clients. Even they lend themselves to tailor-made adaptation, with alternative flights to connect with the tours and short-stay extensions being arranged at the beginning or end of the holiday.

The success of the operator usually depends on an ability to buy a combination of products, put them together and sell them at an inclusive price that is lower than the customers could obtain themselves. The major international operators may book several million hotel beds for a season, thus negotiating very low prices from the hotel owners. Similarly, they bulk-buy seats on aircraft or charter whole aircraft at the best prices they can secure. The end result must be seen by customers as offering value for money, either in terms of the final price paid or time saved shopping around. With package holidays becoming more and more a standardised product, the destination or country has come to play a lesser part in customers' decision-making. Destinations will be readily substituted if customers feel that their first choice is overpriced.

MANAGING AIR TRANSPORT

Tour operators can lower prices by either reducing their profit margins or cutting costs. Cost savings can be achieved initially by chartering whole aircraft instead of merely purchasing a block of seats on a scheduled flight. Further savings can be made by chartering the aircraft over a lengthy period of time, such as a whole season, rather than on an ad hoc basis, this now being the normal pattern of operating for the large companies. Ultimately, the largest operators reduce costs to the minimum by running their own airlines, which allows them to exercise better control over their operations and the standard of their products.

Owning your own aircraft ensures that, when the demand is there, you have the aircraft to meet it at a price you can afford. Emphasis then shifts to ensuring that the highest possible **load factors** (the percentage of seats sold to seats available) are achieved and the aircraft are kept flying for the maximum number of hours each day as they are not earning revenue while stationary on the ground, and parking fees can amount to hundreds of pounds per hour.

This requires careful planning to ensure that **turnarounds** (the time spent between arriving with one load of passengers and taking off with another) are as rapid as possible, commensurate with good standards of safety. Typically, this will result in up to three rotations in a single day, say, between a Northern European point of origin and a Mediterranean destination. These rotations may be made from a single point of origin (an airport) to a number of different destinations abroad or from several points of origin to a single destination abroad or from different points of origin to different foreign destinations. The latter flight plan is commonly known as a 'W' flight pattern (see Figure 18.3), which can be programmed to produce the maximum aircraft usage during a 24-hour period.

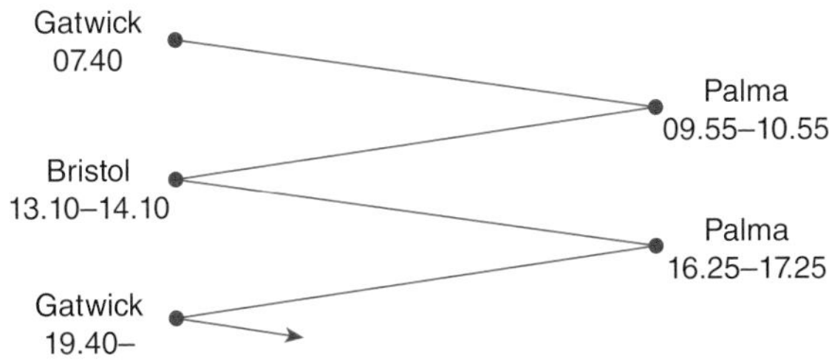

FIGURE 18.3 A typical 'W' flight pattern

W-pattern flights are not necessarily carrying the customers of a single operator (even where the aircraft is owned by a tour operator). Charters can be contracted to carry the passengers of a number of different operators between the same points of origin and destination, either sharing the flights or filling different flights. This can give rise to problems, one of which will occur when different operators contract for morning, afternoon and evening flights. If one operator decides to cancel, the airline concerned has to find alternative users for the aircraft, which may mean a longer flight commitment, causing delays or a change of flights to those passengers already booked on that flight. The knock-on effect of delays can become very apparent if there is a minor maintenance issue with the plane or air traffic controllers go on strike. Tight flight scheduling, particularly into busy airports at the height of the season, can mean that delays on one flight can have repercussions on tour operator movements using the same aircraft over the next two or three days.

EXAMPLE

Aircraft position

The six-day closure of European airspace as a result of the eruption of the Icelandic volcano Eyjafjallajoekull in 2010 caused many problems for tour operators, with passengers unable to fly out to their holiday destinations, or stranded in destinations unable to return home.

But the opening of airspace was not the end of the problems. The cancellation of many flights had left aircraft significantly out of position, at the airports where they were grounded when the ash cloud rolled in. And with aircraft of various sizes, capable of travelling different distances, it was important that they were quickly returned to their schedule as this had an impact not just on the immediate flight but also on those for several weeks ahead.

Not only were aircraft out of position, so too were the crew. Each aircraft requires a set number of cabin staff, based on safety rules linked to capacity. Therefore, crew scheduling also had to be reconfigured to ensure the planes were allowed to take off. Getting both aircraft and crew back on schedule took several weeks.

High load factors are achieved by setting the **breakeven** (the point at which the number of seats sold on each flight covers all the flight's operating, administrative and marketing costs) at a point as close as possible to capacity. This brings down the average seat cost to a level that will encourage the greatest number of people to travel. On many well-marketed charter flights, the breakeven is set as high as 90% or higher, while actual average load factors may be as high as 96–98%. The company makes its profit on the difference between those two figures, and clearly, as every extra person carried is almost pure profit (all fixed costs having been covered), then substantial reductions can be made for last-minute bookings to fill those final seats. Conversely, if very few seats remain, the company may even choose to inflate the price, in the knowledge that there are always a few passengers who are willing to pay for a very specific flight at short notice. Of course, if the breakeven load factors have not been reached, the operator will not cover all costs, but it will still be better to attract as many people as possible for the flight, because they will at least make a contribution to the fixed costs of operating the flight even if all the costs are not recovered. Passengers may also buy duty-free goods on board (if travelling outside the EU countries), and an increasing number of short-haul airlines no longer serve food and drink free of charge, so the sale of these items on board becomes another important source of revenue, making a further contribution to profit for the airline; or, taking a broader view, for the parent company of the jointly owned airline/tour operator. Furthermore, if the operator has contracted for a set number of beds and is committed to pay for that number, it is better to carry passengers to fill those beds than for them to be empty.

Productivity in airline operations can be aided by the procedure of **consolidating flights**. Charter flights with unacceptably low load factors can be cancelled and their passengers transferred to other flights. This helps to reduce the element of risk for the tour operator, otherwise breakevens would have to be set at a lower level of capacity, so fares would be higher. Such consolidations are not available for groups carried on scheduled airline services and are, in any case, subject to considerable restrictions, such as adequate advance notice being given to the clients. Inevitably they are unpopular with clients, so many companies now try to avoid them.

THE PROBLEM OF SEASONALITY

A problem facing all sectors of tourism is the highly seasonal nature of most tourist traffic. Nowhere is this more apparent than in the demand for package holidays in Europe. This market, however, is also highly price-sensitive and longer periods of holiday entitlement over the past 20 years have helped to encourage many people to take their second holiday abroad too, often outside of peak periods. This has meant that operators can spread their fixed costs more evenly over the entire year, rather than concentrating them in the summer period, helping to reduce prices further. Most importantly, it has allowed operators to contract for aircraft and hotels on a year-round basis.

If only a summer season is programmed, any tour operator running a charter airline to service its needs is left with a **dead leg** twice in the year (an aircraft returning empty after the first flight of the season because it has no passengers to pick up, and an empty outbound flight at the end of the season to pick up the last clients returning home). The costs of those empty flights have to be built into the overall pricing structure of the operation, but, if they can be avoided by offering year-round programmes, clearly the savings made can be passed on to customers.

EXAMPLE

Accounting for dead legs

A tour operator is offering a holiday package flying from Edinburgh to Alicante in Spain. It estimates that the cost of the flight is €12,000 for each segment flown. Each flight has the capacity for 160 passengers.

Initially, the cost per passenger for this holiday may appear to be €150 (return flight of €24,000 at 160 passengers). However, the tour operator has chosen to operate only in the summer months (12 separate holiday weeks) and therefore has contracted an airline to serve for 13 weeks – the last week is needed to fly the holidaymakers who travelled in week 12 home. Through successful marketing efforts, all 160 holidays available have been sold so the company is operating at 100% capacity (in reality, tour operators may operate on load factors closer to 95%).

	Week 1	Week 2	Week 3–12	Week 13
Number of passengers flying out to Alicante from Edinburgh	160	160	160	0 (dead leg)
Number of passengers returning from Alicante to Edinburgh	0 (dead leg)	160	160	160

As we can see from the table above, the total number of flight segments is 26 (including the two dead legs) so at €12,000 per flight segment the total cost is €312,000. The total passenger holidays for the 12 weeks is 1920 and therefore the flight cost per passenger is €162.50.

Operators also use marginal costing techniques to attract clients out of season. This means that holidays need to be priced to cover their variable costs and make some contribution to fixed costs. This recognises that many costs, such as those encountered in operating hotels, continue whether the hotel is open or closed, so any guests that the hotel can attract will help to pay the bills. They will also enable the hotel to keep its staff all year round, thus making it easier to retain good staff. Some market segments – the retired, for example – can be attracted to the idea of spending the entire winter abroad if prices are low enough, and hoteliers welcome these budget clients as they can still be expected to spend some additional money in the hotel bars or restaurants.

OPERATING WITH SCHEDULED AIRLINES

Not all destinations allow charter flights to operate into their territory (often, in order to protect bookings on the scheduled flights of the country's airline); neither will there be sufficient demand for flights to many destinations (such as those served by most long-haul programmes) to merit chartering an entire aircraft. For those forms of packaging, the tour operator can arrange the transport element through scheduled airlines, using net inclusive, tour-basing excursion fares (ITX) or group inclusive, tour-basing (GIT) fares, either contracting individual seats based on client demand (around which a tailor-made holiday can be constructed) or contracting a block of seats on flights to satisfy the needs of a brochure programme.

Airlines will allow ITX fares to be applied subject to certain conditions attached to the programme, primarily that it must be packaged with land arrangements. Tour operators may also have access to some seat-only special price fares offered by airlines to tactically stimulate demand on particular routes. Such fares, while often very competitive, tend to have strict ticketing guidelines designed to achieve market objectives. Tour operators in the UK making a forward commitment on seats must also obtain an Air Travel Organizers' Licence (ATOL) through the the Civil Aviation Authority (CAA).

CONTROL OVER TOUR OPERATING

In order to protect both consumers and the wider tourism industry from rogue operators, a variety of regulations have been implemented. In some cases, these have come into force to protect consumers and their money, but in other cases they protect the commercial operations of scheduled airlines or the destinations and regions they serve. Many countries within the EU require some form of licensing or qualification for tour operators (see Table 18.3).

TABLE 18.3 Examples of regulation of tour operators within EU countries

Countries	Type of documentation required
Czech Republic, France, Portugal, Slovakia	Trade licence
Hungary	Statutory public register – managed by the Hungarian Trade Licensing Office
Italy	Licence – procedure managed by regional governments
Malta	Licensed by the National Tourism Authority
Poland	Register for organisers of tourism and tourism intermediaries
Slovenia	Licensed by the Chamber of Commerce
Spain	Qualify as travel agent according to administrative legislation
UK	Air Travel Organizer Licence (ATOL) – managed by the CAA

Source: Schulte-Nölke et al., 2008

European Commissioners, looking at the issue of protecting consumers in member states, introduced the 1992 EC Directive on Package Travel, which was designed to clarify and extend responsibility to all sectors of the industry involved in providing and retailing package travel. Those regulations, which each member state was required to introduce into law, covered non-air-based holidays also. The measures included the following obligations (Schulte-Nölke et al., 2008):

- information duties
- provision of a travel brochure, pre-contractual information and details of elements included in the contract, as well as information before the start of the journey; all information must be accurate as the directive specifically references the prohibition of misleading information
- limitation of price revision
- provision of the regulation of situations where an increase in price (or, for some countries, also a decrease in price) may be possible while identifying the conditions for price revision
- consumer rights
- identification of the right of the purchaser to transfer the booking as well as clarifying consumer rights in case of significant alterations to the package
- additional duties of the organiser
- obligations to make alternative arrangements if the original package cannot be provided as planned, providing consumers with equivalent transport back to their point of origin and compensation when the product cannot be delivered as planned
- a duty on the operator to provide assistance to consumers if they experience emergencies or difficulties while on holiday and, in the case of complaints, to undertake prompt efforts to resolve issues
- liability
- clarification of the organiser's and/or retailer's limits of liability in cases where the package is not delivered according to plan or where the consumer has experienced a loss of enjoyment
- schemes to provide security in case of insolvency of the tour operator are also considered.

Initially, the imposition of these regulations brought considerable problems for many tour operators and travel agents, not least because the interpretation of the regulations was unclear. In particular, it remained unclear what exactly constituted a 'package holiday' – was this to include business trips and tailor-made holidays? Would all organisers of packages, such as clubs or schoolteachers organising educational trips, be included? 'Occasional' organisers were to be excluded, but the interpretation of what constituted 'occasional' posed further problems.

What does appear clear is that the additional burden of responsibility placed on tour operators led to some increases in cost for consumers, as operators attempted to cover themselves against any threat of legislation. The regulations imposed much greater responsibility on operators. For example, they directly penalise an operator if there is any dissemination of misleading information and provide for compensation to be paid for any loss suffered by consumers as a result of being misled. Furthermore, they make the tour operator directly responsible if hotels or other suppliers fail to provide the accommodation or services contracted for.

The growth of dynamic packaging and online travel sales has resulted in the existing regulations no longer protecting many travel purchases. In 2015 the European Commission

(EC) published a revised directive, to be implemented by member states by July 2018. The new regulations aimed to ensure financial protection and clarify liability in the case of problems. The regulations broadened the concept of the package, to include customised holidays developed through dynamic packaging and **linked travel arrangements**. Products are considered to be 'linked' when one company facilitates the booking of a subsequent service (for example, easyJet providing the traveller with the opportunity to book a hotel in the destination to which a flight has just been booked). Regulation changes have also ensured transparency so that customers have greater awareness of the protection they have when purchasing travel products.

One further change to the regulations was designed to benefit travel companies. Specifically, it allowed for the introduction of a system of mutual recognition of insolvency protection schemes so that travel companies could operate in multiple European markets without needing separate protection arrangements in each.

EXAMPLE

The changing regulations for the UK-based tour operator

Regulating air travel packages

Regulations restricting tour operators were very limiting when the mass tour market developed in the 1960s. In particular, the regulation known as Provision 1 made it impossible to price package tours lower than the cheapest regular return air fare to a destination. The sole exception to this rule was in the case of affinity groups, which involved charters arranged for associations that exist for a purpose other than that of obtaining cheap travel. The rule was designed to protect scheduled carriers and ensure adequate profit for tour operators, but it severely hindered the expansion of the package tour business.

When the CAA was established in 1971, restrictions were lifted, initially only during the winter months (leading to a huge increase in out-of-season travel), but by 1973 this was extended to all seasons. At the same time, however, the CAA tightened up control on tour operators themselves, introducing in 1972 the requirement to hold ATOLs for charters and block-booked scheduled seats, while simultaneously introducing a system for vetting operators on their financial viability. By 1995, all tour operators were required to hold ATOLs when selling any flights or air holidays abroad. Licences are not required, however, for domestic air tours or for travel abroad using sea or land transport.

Regulating to ensure financial protection of the industry

Following the collapse of an important tour operator, Fiesta Tours, in 1964, which left some 5000 tourists stranded abroad, the industry and its customers came to recognise the importance of introducing protection against financial failure.

On the whole, in the UK, successive governments have preferred to allow the industry to police itself rather than impose additional controls, so this was initially undertaken relatively effectively by ABTA on behalf of tour operators and travel agents. In 1965, ABTA set up a Common Fund for this purpose, anticipating that there would be legislation for the compulsory registration of tour operators. When this failed to materialise, ABTA introduced its stabiliser regulation, restricting ABTA tour operators to selling their package holidays exclusively through ABTA travel agents. In turn, ABTA agents were restricted to selling tours operated by ABTA tour operators. Many agents, however, resented having to contribute to a fund to insure operators and it also became clear that the provisions against collapse were inadequate.

In 1967, the Tour Operators' Study Group (TOSG – later to become the Federation of Tour Operators, FTO) established its own bonding scheme. A bond is a guarantee given by a third party (usually a bank or an insurance company) to pay a sum of money, up to a specified maximum, in the event that the company becomes insolvent. That money would be used to meet the immediate financial obligations arising from the collapse, such as repatriating tourists stranded at overseas resorts and reimbursing clients booked to travel later with the company.

Later, ABTA itself introduced its own bonding scheme for all tour operating (and retail agency) members. The collapse in 1974, in the height of summer, of the Court Line group brought down Clarksons Holidays – then Britain's leading tour operator – and revealed, once again, that the level of protection was inadequate.

The government introduced an obligatory levy of 2% of operators' turnover between 1975 and 1977, which established the Air Travel Trust Fund (ATTF). These reserves were severely depleted, however, by collapses throughout the 1990s, particularly that of the International Leisure Group at the beginning of that decade, and the ATTF was obliged to call on the government for additional borrowing facilities when reserves ran dry. Since then, a number of alternative schemes have been introduced, in the form of either bonds or trustee accounts, including those schemes operated by the AITO Trust, the Travel Trust Association (TTA) and the Association of Bonded Travel Organizers Trust (ABTOT) for smaller operators. The Confederation of Passenger Transport (CPT), the Passenger Shipping Association (PSA) and the Yacht Charter Association operate their own schemes.

In July 2008, ABTA and the FTO merged, thus providing combined expertise to better serve their tour operator members, while providing comprehensive protection schemes for their customers.

Regulating to manage complaints

ABTA operates its own arbitration scheme to resolve complaints by customers about its members. This is at a low cost to claimants, who are successful in about half of all cases brought. AITO provides a similar scheme. Alternatively, claims can be made through the courts under a new tracking system, which entails only moderate costs for plaintiffs.

PLANNING AND MARKETING OF PACKAGE TOURS

Planning for the introduction of a new tour programme or destination is likely to take place over a lengthy span of time, sometimes as long as two years. A typical timescale for a programme of summer tours is shown in Figure 18.4.

In planning deadlines for the programme, it is necessary to work backwards from the planned launch dates. One critical problem is when to determine prices. These have to be confirmed just before material goes to print, but inevitably this will be several months before the tour programme starts, so it entails a good understanding of the market and the wider economy. Assessments must also be made of what the competition is likely to charge for similar products. The introduction of fluid pricing has now removed the publication of precise brochure prices so there is now greater flexibility.

SELECTING A DESTINATION

In practice, the decision to exploit a destination or region for package tours is as much an act of faith as it is the outcome of carefully considered research. Forecasting future developments in tourism, which, as a product, is affected by changing circumstances to a greater extent than most other consumer products, has proved to be notably inaccurate.

As we have seen, tourism patterns change over time, shifting from one country to another and from one form of accommodation to another. With the emphasis on price, mass tour operators are principally concerned with providing the basic sun, sea and sand package in countries that provide the best value for money. Transport costs will depend on charter rights into the country, distances flown and ground-handling costs.

Accommodation and other costs to be met overseas will be affected by exchange rates against the local currency and operators must consider these in comparison with other competitive countries' currency values when setting the price for the package.

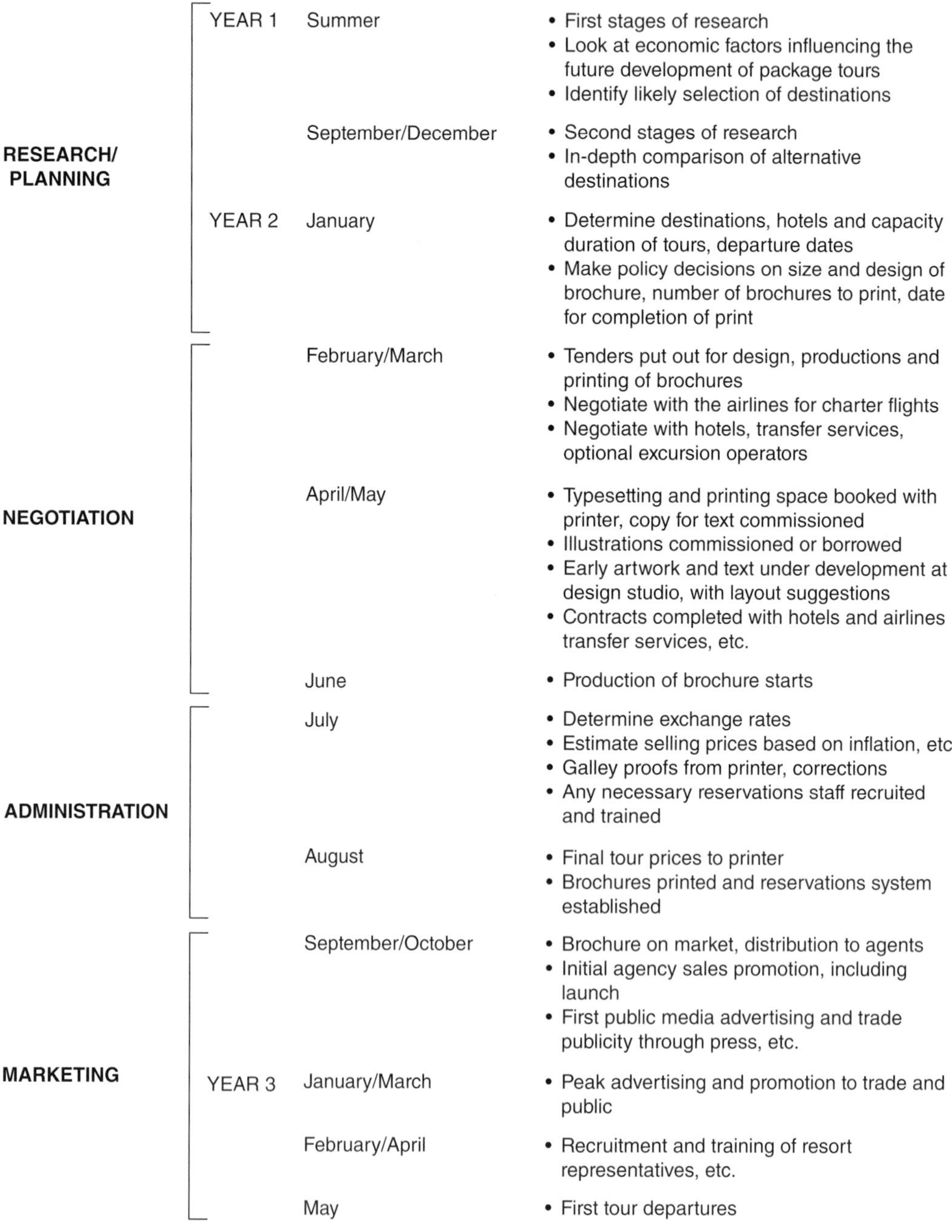

FIGURE 18.4 Typical timescale for planning a summer tour programme

They should also anticipate how changing exchange rates may affect the number of clients likely to select any one destination, as it may appear expensive if the local currency is strong. The introduction of the euro has thus reduced this risk for European tour operators.

Operators also have to take into account such qualitative issues as the political stability of the destination and the support given for developing tourism to the destination by the carriers or tourist office of the country. Increasingly, with an emphasis on sustainability, today's operators are encouraged (if not yet forced by government legislation) to consider the impact on locals and the environment of any new development. Pressure groups and the media are slowly persuading companies to take more seriously the pros and cons of new developments and how these can be effectively managed by the operators, the hotels they work with and the local authorities.

Once the tour operators have made their choice of potential destinations, they must produce a realistic appraisal of the likely demand for those destinations, based on factors such as the number of tourists the destinations presently attract, growth rates over recent years and market share held by any existing travel companies. The mass-market operators are unlikely to look at just a single year's programme – any commitment to a destination is likely to be for a substantial period of time. The specialist operator, however, may be more flexible about switching destinations according to changing demand. In contrast, mass-market operators consider long-term contracts with their hoteliers abroad or even, in some circumstances, establish their own hotels.

The availability of suitable aircraft for the routes must be ascertained. This will, in part, dictate capacities for the programme, as aircraft have different configurations, and, on some routes, where aircraft are operating at the limits of their flight range, some passenger seats may need to be sacrificed in order to take on board sufficient fuel to cover the distance. In some instances, provincial airport runways may be insufficient for larger, fully laden aircraft and, again, fewer passengers may be carried to compensate.

All planning is, of course, also dependent on the company having the necessary finance available to operate and market the programme.

THE PROCESS OF NEGOTIATING

Once the decisions have been made as to destinations to be served, numbers of passengers to be carried during the season and dates of departure, serious negotiations can get under way with airlines, hotels and other principals, leading to formal contracts. Those contracts will spell out payment due dates as well as conditions for the release of unsold accommodation or the cancellation of chartered aircraft flights (or, in the case of block bookings on scheduled services, the aircraft seats), along with details of any penalties that the tour operator will incur for cancellation.

Airline negotiations

Normal terms for aircraft chartering are for a deposit to be paid on signing the contract (generally 10% of the total cost), with the balance becoming due on each flight after it takes place. In negotiating for charter services, the reputation of the tour operator is of paramount importance. If they have worked with that airline or with similar charters in previous years, that will be taken into account when determining the terms and price for the contract. Relationships between the sectors of the industry are still based predominantly on trust, as the threat of legal action, perhaps months after a dispute such as an overbooking problem has arisen, will do little to resolve problems at the time.

Part and parcel of the negotiations is the setting up of the tour-operating flight plan, with decisions being made on the dates and frequency of operations, airports to be used and times of arrival and departure. All of this information will have to be consolidated into a form suitable for publication and easy to understand in the tour brochure.

A well-established operator does not wish to be at the mercy of market forces when dealing with charter airlines. In any given year, the demand for suitable aircraft may exceed the supply, which has encouraged the larger tour operators to form or buy their own airline, just to ensure that the capacity they need is available to them.

EXAMPLE

Tour operator and airline collaboration

Tour operators have long used seats on scheduled airlines to get holidaymakers to their destinations, often through the contracting of blocks of seats. TUI has now expanded its use of the scheduled services offered to include low-cost carriers.

In 2016, TUI Netherlands announced an agreement to block-book flights from Amsterdam Schiphol to Lisbon, Rome Fiumicino and Milan Malpensa. These routes were not served by its own airline subsidiary TUI fly (Netherlands), so this expanded the destinations TUI Netherlands could offer. Such collaboration previously existed in the UK and, as we can see in this example, has now expanded to include other European countries.

TUI recognised that by using flights of airlines such as easyJet and Norwegian, it could offer the customer a greater number of flight options as well as the chance to fly from regional airports. This increased flexibility of the package holiday is demanded by today's customer. Bookings for these airlines are made directly with TUI, thus maintaining customer convenience.

Hotel negotiations

Hotel negotiations – other than in the case of large tour operators, which may negotiate contracts for an entire hotel – are generally far more informal than are airline negotiations. Small and specialist tour operators selling independent inclusive tours may have no more than a **free sale** (or **sell and report**) agreement with hoteliers. These involve the hotel agreeing to guarantee accommodation for a specified maximum number of tourists (usually at least four, although it may be higher in large hotels with plenty of availability for certain days of the week) merely on receipt of the notification of a booking from the tour operator, whether by phone, fax or e-mail. This arrangement may be quite suitable for small tour programmes, but it suffers from the disadvantage that, at times, hoteliers will retain the right to close out certain dates. As these are likely to be the most popular dates in the calendar, the operator stands to lose both potential business and goodwill. The alternative is for the operator to contract for an allocation of rooms in the hotel, with dates agreed for the release of those unsold that are well in advance of the anticipated arrival dates.

Long-term contracts, either for a block of rooms or the entire hotel, have the attraction of providing the operator with the lowest possible prices, but they carry a higher element of risk. Some contracts have been drawn up by operators to cover periods as long as five years and, while at first glance such long, fixed-term price contracts may seem attractive, they are seldom realistic and, in an inflationary period, may well have to be renegotiated to avoid bankrupting the hotelier (such an event would obviously not be in the operator's interest).

EXAMPLE

Balearic hotels sign three-year contracts

At the 2018 World Travel Market, it was announced that an increasing number of hotels in the Balearics agreed to sign a three-year contract with tour operators in an attempt to protect their business from future uncertainty. A decision to sign a contract that would determine room rates for the following three summers provided the hotels with some certainty of operations; but it often comes at a cost of quite low levels of income.

The recovery of other Mediterranean destinations, coupled with activities such as the government-driven strategies of promotion in Turkey and possible changes to demand from the UK market following Brexit, has led to substantial uncertainty regarding demand. Consequently, tying into an agreement with a tour operator can offer the hotel some level of predictability.

In addition to the operator spelling out exact requirements in terms of rooms – required numbers of singles, doubles, twins, with or without private facilities, whether with balconies or sea views and with what catering provision (room only, with breakfast, half or full board, all-inclusive) – it must also clarify a number of other facts, including:

- reservations and registration procedures, including whether or not hotel vouchers are to be issued
- accommodation requirements for any representatives or couriers (usually provided free)
- handling procedures and fees charged for porterage
- special facilities available or needed, such as air-conditioned or non-smoking rooms, facilities for handicapped customers or special catering requirements, such as kosher or vegetarian food
- languages spoken by hotel staff
- systems of payment by guests for drinks or other extras
- reassurance on suitable fire and safety precautions (tour operators based in the EU have responsibility (and liability) for protecting their customers under the Package Travel Directive, no matter where the hotel is situated)
- if appropriate, suitable space for a representative's desk and noticeboard.

In negotiations, consideration may also be given to the availability of alternative hotel accommodation of a comparable standard in the event of overbooking. Of course, a hotel with a reputation for overbooking is to be avoided, but, over the course of time, some errors are bound to occur and so guests will need to be transferred to other hotels. Tour operators must satisfy themselves that the arrangements made by the hotelier for taking care of clients in these circumstances are adequate. Any operator negotiating with a hotelier will be aware that they are likely to be sharing contracted space with other operators, not only within their own country but also from other countries. It is as well to be aware of one's own standing with the hotelier in relation to those other companies. For example, in Spain it was not uncommon in the past to find that the German operators, which tended to pay higher prices for their rooms than did the British, would have their rooms protected in preference to UK operators when overbookings occurred.

Independent companies can find themselves squeezed out of the market for European bed stock in popular resorts and, at times, even the mass-market operators become aware that greater concentration in the industry can lead to more difficulty in tying up contracts with popular hotels. For this reason, as demand rises for key Mediterranean destinations, and also to ensure greater control over the major elements in the package, some operators turn to owning hotels at the destinations or, at the very least, having far more say in their management.

Destination services negotiations

Similar negotiations will take place with locally based incoming operators and coach companies to provide transfers between airports and hotels and any optional excursions. Car hire companies may also be approached to negotiate commission rates on sales to the tour operator's clients and tailor-made transfers between airports and hotels.

The reliability and honesty of local operators is an important issue here. Some smaller tour operators may not be in a position to employ their own resort representatives initially, so their image will depend on the level of service provided by the local operators' staff.

If a local company is also operating optional sightseeing excursions, procedures for booking these and handling the finances involved must be established. It should also be clarified whether qualified guides with a sound knowledge of the clients' language are to be employed on the excursions.

THE ROLE OF THE RESORT REPRESENTATIVE

Tour operators carrying large numbers of package tourists to a destination are in a position to employ their own resort representatives. This has obvious advantages in that the company can count on the loyalty and total commitment of its own staff. A decision must be made as to whether to employ a national of the host country or of the generating country (although it should be acknowledged that, in some cases, the destination may receive customers from several generating countries and the representative will need to be able to serve all customers effectively). The advantage of hiring a representative from the local community is that he or she will be fully acquainted with the local customs and geography, fluent in the language of the country and have good local contacts, which may make it easier to take care of problems effectively (such as dealing with the police, local shopkeepers or hoteliers). The flipside of this is that he or she is likely to be less familiar with the culture, customs or language of the clients, which can act as a negative point for tourists, especially for those on first visits abroad. Exceptional local representatives have been able to overcome this problem and, if they themselves have some common background with their clients, such as having lived for some years in the incoming tourists' country, they can often function as effectively as would representatives from the generating country.

Furthermore, some countries impose restrictions on the employment of foreign nationals at resorts, which is a point that must be clarified before employing any representatives. This used to be a problem at the popular Mediterranean resorts, but, with the development of freedom of labour movement within the EU, tour operators are now free to decide for themselves what should be the background and nationality of their representatives.

Resort representatives are usually given a desk and/or signage space in the hotel lobby from which to work but this may need to be shared with other tour operators (see Figure 18.5). In cases where tour operators have their clients in two or more hotels in the resort, they may have to visit each of these hotels during some part of the day.

FIGURE 18.5 Tour operators share the information stand in a Moroccan hotel

Photo: Claire Humphreys

The representatives' role is far more demanding than is commonly thought. During the high season, they can be expected to work a seven-day week and will need to be on call for 24 hours each day to cope with any emergencies. Their principal functions include:

- handling general enquiries
- advising on currency exchange, shopping and so on
- organising and supervising social activities at the hotels
- publicising, selling and booking optional excursions
- handling special requirements and complaints and acting as an intermediary for clients, interceding with the hotel proprietor, the police or other local authorities as necessary.

These routine functions are supplemented by problems arising from lost baggage, ill health (needing to refer clients to local dentists or doctors) and even, occasionally, death, although serious problems such as these are usually referred to area managers, who may oversee and manage representatives across several resorts in a region or country. The representatives must also relocate clients whose accommodation is for any reason inadequate or when overbookings have occurred, and may also have to rebook flights for those clients whose plans change as a result of an emergency.

The representatives' busiest days are those when groups are arriving or leaving the resort. They will accompany groups returning home on the coach to the airport, ensuring that departure formalities at the hotel have been complied with, arrange to pay any airport or departure taxes due and then wait to greet incoming clients and accompany them, in turn, to their hotels on the transfer coaches. In the not uncommon situation where flights are delayed, this can result in representatives having to spend very long hours at the airport, sometimes missing a night's sleep. On their return to the hotels, they must also ensure that check-in procedures operate smoothly, going over rooming lists with the hotel managers before the latter bill the company.

Most operators also provide a welcome party for their clients on the first or second night of their holiday and it is the representatives' task to organise and host this. It also provides an important opportunity to sell excursions to the newly arrived guests. As profit margins are often tight for tour operators, there has been more emphasis placed on the sale of excursions in recent years. Many representatives have in the past been given sales targets to achieve and may be rewarded financially for good performance in this area.

There has been a substantial reduction in the number of representatives employed and in some cases this has led to their disappearance entirely. The explanation for this move comes partly as a cost-saving measure, but also results from the increasing sophistication of the customers, many of whom are well travelled and no longer feel that they need a rep's help at their destination, as long as a company rep is available at the end of a phone. Technology has allowed the creation of 24-hour helplines, digital communications through the use of SMS, WhatsApp and email, as well as online chat facilities via tour operator-designed apps, all of which have reduced the need for resort reps.

EXAMPLE

Reviewing the need for holiday reps

In 2005 Thomson Holidays reduced the number of reps it employed by 40%. Since then it has aimed to modernise the function of this group of employees. By 2013 TUI, the parent company, had arranged for its 1300 reps, serving customers of the Thomson and First Choice brands, to be empowered to do more, including managing complaints and any corresponding compensation levels.

It employed technology – providing each rep with an iPad – to reduce paperwork levels and improve communication. Early trials of the technology allowed 85% of complaints to be handled in resort, with agreed compensation levels often lower at that stage. Furthermore, improved communication led to an increase in customer satisfaction levels – up by 34%.

Source: Travel Weekly, 2013

Where representatives continue to be favoured, they can expect to spend some time at their resort bases before the start of the season, not just to get to know the site, but also to report back to their companies on the standards of tourist facilities and to pinpoint any discrepancies between descriptions in the brochures and reality. This has become increasingly important since the regulations imposed by the EU Package Travel Directive came into force. Representatives may also be expected to inform their companies if any changes occur during the season about which clients must be notified at the time of booking. In an effort to reduce complaints and handle them at source, some operators give representatives the authority to compensate their clients on the spot for minor claims and complaints which, as we have seen in the example of TUI, is often more cost-effective.

Today, some operators employ full-time staff who spend part of the year as representatives at their resorts, either in the summer or winter, while at other times they are brought back to head office to handle reservations or other administrative work. The job of a representative seldom offers genuine career opportunities, but for some there is the opportunity to progress, starting with a position as a children's representative and moving on to adult representative, senior representative, area supervisor and eventually area manager. Ultimately, the opportunity for progression lies back at head office, where the managers having overall responsibility for resort representatives recruit and train staff, organise holiday rosters, provide uniforms and handle the administration of the representatives' department. Nevertheless, for the large majority, opportunities for employment are limited to the high season.

PRICING THE PACKAGE TOUR

Key to the success of a tour operator's programme is getting the price right. It must be right for the market, right compared with the prices of competitors' package tours and right compared with the prices of other tours offered by the company.

COSTING THE PACKAGE

A tour operator will, as we have noted, normally purchase three main inputs to create inclusive tours: transport, accommodation and services. The latter will include transfers between airports and accommodation abroad and, possibly, the services of the company's resort representative at the site. The operator will also, of course, have to cover costs that arise within the company's headquarters, such as administration, reservations, marketing and advertising. Finally, the operator will have to cover the cost of commission paid to retailers and servicing those retailers.

The cost of producing a package holiday will also be dependent on factors such as the destination (longer journeys may result in higher airline seat costs but popular destinations may bring economies of scale), hotel quality and board basis, and sales channel. However, as a broad estimate, Table 18.4 suggests a typical cost structure.

TABLE 18.4 The typical cost structure of an inclusive tour using charter air services

Costs	Percentage of overall costs
Charter air seat	45
Hotel accommodation	35
Other services at destination	5
Head office overheads	5
Travel agency's commission	10

As the profits achieved by most operators after allowing for agencies' commission are actually quite narrow – perhaps as little as 1–3% of revenue, after covering all costs – operators will seek to top up their revenue in any other way possible. For mass-market operators, the bulk of their revenue – in excess of 50%, normally – is achieved through the sales of summer holidays. Perhaps another 15–20% will be achieved through a winter tour programme and the balance through a mix of sales of excursions at the destination, the interest received on deposits and final payments invested, foreign currency speculation and sale of insurance policies.

One contribution to revenue is achieved by imposing cancellation charges. According to the EU Package Travel Directive 2015, these charges must be 'reasonable', thus operators cannot set extortionate fees. However, the operator may well be able to sell the cancelled holiday again. The Package Travel Directive now allows, in theory, the substitution of names by the clients to replace cancelled bookings, but this is impossible to enforce where many airlines do not accept name changes and countries require arriving passengers to hold visas.

Specialist operators that offer a unique product may have more flexibility and the freedom to determine their prices based on cost plus a mark-up that is sufficient to cover overheads and provide a satisfactory level of profit. The mass operators, however, must take greater account than niche operators of their competitors' prices as demand for package tours is, as we have seen, extremely price-sensitive, especially for programmes offered in the shoulder or low season.

In the following sections, we will examine two alternative, but typical, examples of cost-determined tour pricing. The first will consider pricing for the mass market; the second, pricing for the specialist operator.

Mass-market tour pricing

The first example is based on a German company providing time-series charter travel and a two-week hotel stay at a Mediterranean beach resort destination, such as those found on the island of Majorca, Spain.

EXAMPLE

Mass-market operator pricing

	Flight costs €	Package costs (including flight costs) €
Flight costs, based on 15 holiday departures (back to back) on Boeing 737-800, 189-seat aircraft at €20,725 per flight	621,750	
Plus one empty leg each way at beginning and end of the season:		
out	20,725	
home	20,725	
Total flight costs	**663,200**	
Total cost per flight:		
(€663,200 ÷ 15 holiday departures)	44,213.33	
Cost per seat at 90% occupancy (170 seats), i.e. €44,213.33 ÷ 170		260.08
Plus passenger charges (e.g. airport fees at outbound and inbound airports, government taxes, security fees)		40.00
Net hotel cost per person, 14 nights half-board		245.00
Resort agent's handling fees and transfers, per person		10.00
Gratuities, porterage		5.00

	Flight costs €	Package costs (including flight costs) €
Total cost per person		**560.08**
Add mark-up of approx. 30% on cost price to cover agency commission, marketing costs (including brochure production, advertising, etc.), head office administrative costs and profit		168.02
Selling price (rounded up)		**730.00**

Many companies would add a small fee, say €15, in order to build in a no-surcharge guarantee, especially in times of economic instability. Holidays that are cancelled are presently resold to the public – as mentioned, this is a source of considerable extra income as full refunds do not have to be made to the original customer (who recovers these costs from insurance, if there is a valid claim).

In estimating the cost of a seat on the aircraft, operators must not only calculate the load factor on which this cost is to be based but must also aim to achieve this load factor on average throughout the series of tours they will be operating. This must depend on their estimates of the market demand for each destination and the current supply of aircraft seats available to their competitors. Remember that one flight route may service several destinations; for example, a flight taking skiers to the USA may land in Denver and serve holidaymakers visiting the popular resorts of Vail, Breckenridge or Keystone as well as transferring other passengers onto a short internal flight serving Steamboat Springs. Similarly, flights to Geneva may serve alpine resorts in France, Switzerland and Italy. As the demand at high season will frequently exceed the supply of seats to the destinations, there is scope to increase the price, and hence profits, for those months of the year, even if that results in the company being uncompetitive compared with other leading operators. In the low season, meanwhile, supply is likely to exceed the demand for available packages, so companies may set their prices so low that only the variable costs are covered, with no contribution made to the fixed costs (marketing, administration and so on), in order to fill the seats.

Each tour operator must carefully consider what proportion of its overheads is to be allocated to each tour and destination. As long as the expenses are recovered in full during the term of operation, the allocation of costs can be made on the basis of market forces and need not necessarily be apportioned equally to each programme and destination. There is a case for a marketing-orientated approach to pricing, based on a consideration of market prices and the company's long-term objectives. In entering a new market, for instance, it may be that the principal objective is to penetrate and obtain a targeted share of that market in the first year of operating, which may be achieved by reducing or even forgoing profits during the first year and/or reducing the per capita contribution to corporate costs.

Specialist tour pricing

The second example is of a specialist French long-haul operator that uses the services of scheduled carriers to Hong Kong, with a Group Inclusive Tour (GIT) fare.

In the case of this specialist operator, prices reflect market demand at different periods of the year and there is no equal distribution of office overheads as the profits and most overheads are recoverable in the high-season prices charged to the market. The lead price gives very little profit for bookings made through the trade, but is strictly limited to one or two weeks of the year. Large profits can be obtained, however, over Christmas, Chinese

New Year, during conferences and for other customers committed to specific dates. There is a tendency to be cautious about milking excess profits from periods of increased demand; if charges are set too high, operators may be left with availability during peak times.

The pricing policy shown here is common among the smaller specialist operators, which tend to use less sophisticated pricing techniques when fixing target profits. Many specialists operating in a climate where there is no exact competition for their product could be expected to charge a price that would give them an overall gross profit of 25% or more, while most mass-market operators, and some specialists, will be forced by market conditions to settle for much lower margins.

EXAMPLE

Specialist operator pricing

	Package costs € (including flight costs)
Flight cost, based on net Group Inclusive Tour fares, per person	480
Plus air charges	71
Net hotel cost per person, 7 nights, twin room (HK$680 per room at HK$340 per person per night; HK$10 at €1)	238
Transfers HK$105 each way (equating to €10.50 each way)	21
Subtotal	**810**
Add agent's commission	90
Total cost per person	**900**
Selling prices	
'Lead price' (offered on only one or two low-season flights)	919
Shoulder season price	989
High season price (summer, Christmas and Easter holiday periods)	1229

In developing a pricing strategy for package tours, operators must take into account a number of other variables in addition to those previously mentioned. For example, when setting a price for a departure from a regional airport, the operator will look at how much more the client will be willing to pay to avoid a long trip to a major airport. In the example given above, for flights from France to Hong Kong, a traveller living near Strasbourg may prefer to fly from a regional airport to Hong Kong via Frankfurt with Lufthansa rather than make the journey to Paris. Equally, if a flight is to leave at 2 a.m., the price must be sufficiently attractive compared with others leaving during the day to make people willing to suffer the inconvenience of travelling at that time.

DISCOUNTING STRATEGIES

Discounts on published tour prices have become a widely accepted practice in the industry. Originally applied to late bookings in order to clear seats, the technique has more recently been used by the larger operators to persuade members of the public to book earlier, using a system of **fluid pricing** – the practice of prices for travel products altering as demand levels change, discussed earlier.

Discounting is also influenced by travel retailers. They may elect to sell packages below the prices determined by the operators themselves by passing on to the clients a proportion of their commission. In practice, this has meant that the largest discounts can be allowed by the largest multiple travel agencies, as they can negotiate larger commissions, well above the 10% norm, by achieving higher sales and, in effect, can pass on to their clients almost all the 10% basic commission. As this percentage represents the total commission that most independent agents receive from operators, the independents cannot match their prices and therefore find it impossible to compete on price alone. Instead, many will offer alternative benefits, for example free insurance to secure a sale or an extra service, such as a free taxi transfer to the local airport.

Heavy discounting by the market leaders through their own retail chains has been a major factor in boosting their share of the mass market. Given the problems that have faced the industry over the past few years and the strong competition between operators to survive in a difficult marketplace, there is little likelihood of the industry moving away from deep discounting in the foreseeable future.

CASH FLOW

The normal booking season for summer holidays starts in the autumn of the preceding year, reaching its peak in the three months following Christmas, so a large proportion of deposits will have been paid by the end of March. Although the operators themselves will have had to make deposits for aircraft charters at the beginning of the season and may also have had to make some advances to hoteliers to ensure that the rooms they need are held, the final account for these services will not fall due until after the clients have completed their holiday. Operators will have the use of deposit payments for anything up to a year in advance and will have clients' final payments at least eight weeks before they themselves have to settle their accounts. This money is invested to earn interest and, in some cases, that interest will actually exceed the net profits made by tour operating itself. Clearly, one effect of the tendency of holidaymakers to book their holidays later will be a fall in interest earnings by the operators.

YIELD MANAGEMENT

Yield management (discussed in Chapter 13) has been a key tool for the airline industry, allowing each fare category to be allocated to a set number of seats, with the number of seats in each category being determined by the demand for any flight. Such a technique is now being applied across the industry, including sectors such as hotels, car hire and tour operators.

For tour operators, the smooth running of yield management is frequently defeated by the excess capacity available in the market, forcing companies to 'dump' packages at whatever price they can achieve in order to help make a contribution to their overheads. There is some evidence that companies are improving their skills at yield management by improving their forecasting or a willingness to reduce capacity in order to achieve a better balance between supply and demand. While such actions have been taken largely in the form of implicit agreements between the major operators, there is always the risk that the smaller operators will see this as an opportunity to steal some market share from the brand leaders and increase their own capacity.

If prices are set too low initially and late demand in the season results in a 'sold out' situation, the company will not have maximised its profit opportunities. At the same time, if the company finds itself involved in added expenditure in the course of the summer – for example, providing accommodation and meals for clients delayed by air traffic control strikes (which cannot be foreseen but occur not infrequently in Europe) – what might have been a slim but acceptable profit can soon be turned into an overall loss.

Another aspect to consider is when to launch the new holiday programme. In the past, some operators have even launched programmes more than a year in advance. Companies launching their programmes ahead of their rivals will always hope to steal a larger proportion of the early booking market and, of course, have the consequent revenue that can be invested over a longer period. It is unclear, however, whether the advantages of early sales achieved in this way are sufficient to offset the drawbacks, not least of confusing both agents and customers through the range of choice on offer at any given time. A further issue is that publishing this far in advance gives competitors a full view of your prices, hotels and sales techniques, giving them an opportunity to adjust their marketing when they launch their own programmes.

THE TOUR BROCHURE

For many years, the tour operator's brochure was the critical marketing tool and the main influence on customers' decisions to buy. Tourism is an intangible product that customers are obliged to purchase without having the opportunity to inspect it, and often from a base of very inadequate knowledge. In these circumstances, and given the often limited personal knowledge of products and destinations held by travel agents, the brochure became the principal means of both informing customers about the product and persuading them to purchase it.

For most companies, very large sums are still invested in the brochure itself, as well as advertising designed to persuade customers to access a digital copy of the brochure online or visit travel agents to pick one up. The production of the brochure is likely to represent a very significant proportion of the total marketing budget, with print runs, in the case of the largest operators, running into millions, at a unit cost of well over £2 a copy. Wider use of digital brochures does reduce print costs but these still have to be designed – itself a time-consuming and not inexpensive task. However, for small tour operators, software now exists to allow in-house brochure design that can reduce the total cost of brochure production.

Despite the cost advantages of producing electronic brochures, there is still a demand for printed versions. The opportunity to mark up pages with notes about particular products, to share these brochures with others travelling in the group and to repeatedly review the product as the holiday decision is being made, remains important for many holidaymakers. Personalised brochures sent by e-mail at the request of the traveller may help here, as the brochure can be printed if necessary and shared with others electronically – important if the travellers are geographically spread. One downside of the personalised brochure containing only the sections requested by the holidaymaker is that this may limit the opportunity to cross-sell products; a multi-destination printed brochure provides an opportunity to inspire travellers to consider alternative destinations that may also meet their desires.

EXAMPLE

Digital brochures

Encouraging holidaymakers to access brochures online has the benefit of reducing print and distribution costs for tour operators. It also ensures that every holidaymaker can gain access to the brochure they seek, addressing the common problem of popular brochures being out of stock with travel agents.

However, the cost of producing a brochure is not insignificant. Good graphic design, the time taken in creating the content, and the requirement for proofreading of brochures which can be several hundred pages long, all impact on production costs. Furthermore, customers are now expecting more from the online brochure experience. The now defunct Thomas Cook Brochure Store held more than 60,000 pages across its brochure range. It was designed to be easily viewed from computers, tablets and smartphones, offering functions that allowed holiday ideas to be easily shared. While this site no longer exists others, such as Brochure Bank (discussed late in this chapter), offer customers a similar service.

The brochure is no longer the critical tool it once was, as many operators now sell directly from their websites. Indeed, some small companies no longer print brochures at all, simply printing off relevant pages from their websites for those customers wanting a paper copy of their holiday arrangements. While this trend is likely to continue, for the present the brochure remains an important tool, so must be considered here.

BROCHURE DESIGN AND FORMAT

Larger companies will either have their brochures designed and prepared in their own advertising department or coordinate the production with a design studio, often associated with the advertising agency they use. The agency will help to negotiate with printers to obtain the best quotation for producing the brochure and ensure that print deadlines are met. In other cases, tour operators will tackle the design of the brochure themselves, a process that is being increasingly aided by computer programs that allow desktop publishing. The computer software will organise the layout, selecting the best locations for text and illustrations to minimise use of space, thus helping to reduce the cost.

EXAMPLE

Brochure software

Brochure design can be achieved using widely available software. For example, Microsoft provides templates to create travel brochures using its Office Word software. However, while the result might be suitable for the simplest of tour programmes, it may not project a quality image of the brand.

Specialist software that can be operated on standard desktop computers is widely available. Popular programs include Adobe Illustrator, Canva, Lucidpress and Microsoft Publisher. In most cases, the software is fairly simple to learn and can achieve impressive results, if the user has an eye for good design and an attention to detail.

While this technology allows brochures to be produced in-house, smaller tour operators may achieve better results with the help of an independent design studio, which can provide the professional expertise required in relation to the brochure's layout, artwork and copy that are so important to ensuring that the result is a professional piece of publicity material.

The purposes the brochure serves will dictate its design and format. A single ad hoc programme, for example, for a foreign trade exhibition, may require nothing more than a leaflet, while a limited programme of tours may be laid out in the form of a simple booklet.

Purpose-designed brochures will usually include all of an operator's summer or winter tours within a single brochure. However, many larger operators have diversified into a great many different types of holiday: long-haul and short-haul, coach tours as well as air holidays, lake and mountain resorts as well as seaside resorts. If all these were to be combined in a single brochure, it would run to thousands of pages and be both clumsy to handle and very expensive to produce. There would also be high wastage, as clients who know the type of holiday they want will have to pick up the entire programme just to get details of the particular product they are interested in. Operators therefore produce individual brochures, even in some cases separating brochures by destination. This has the added advantage of filling more of the agents' rack space, leaving less available space for competitors. If the leading half-dozen operators produce as many as 70–80 different brochures, all top sellers for agents, this will require the agency to devote as much as half their rack space to these brands.

While some might contend that there is a disappointing sameness to the leading operators' brochures today, taken individually the quality and professionalism of modern brochure design and printing are outstanding. As brochures must also reinforce an image of quality and reliability, the text and images contained in brochures must not only be attractive but also truthful, accurate and easily understood. Good layout, high-quality photography and suitable paper are all essential if a brochure is to do its job effectively.

OBLIGATIONS AFFECTING TOUR BROCHURES

Tour operators are selling dreams, and their brochures must allow consumers to fantasise a little about their holidays. It is also vitally important, however, that consumers are not misled about any aspect of their holiday. The EU Package Travel Directive 1992 clarified operators' responsibilities regarding misrepresentations of elements of the travel product, which simplified proceedings for tourists, who can sue an operator for offences for which their suppliers abroad are responsible, requiring the operator, in turn, to sue suppliers in the destination country to recover their costs. The 2015 update to this Directive, taking account of changes in the growth of online sales, stated that the provision of information is no longer based exclusively on travel brochures, meaning that tour operators do not have to reprint brochures every time there is a change of information.

The EU Directive recognises that any descriptive material concerning a package should not contain any misleading information and that the holidaymaker should be provided with the following details:

- the price
- the characteristics and categories of transport used
- the type of accommodation, and its location, quality rating and main features
- any excursions or activities included (or excluded) in the package
- the meal plan
- the travel itinerary and dates
- passport and visa requirements
- whether the trip is accessible for people with reduced mobility
- cancellation fees
- the amount of the deposit and timetable for payment of the final balance

- whether a minimum number of persons is required for the package to operate
- the arrangements for financial protection against insolvency of the tour operator
- contact details for the package holiday organiser.

Many tour operators provide guide prices in brochures, with travellers expected to contact travel agents or look at company websites for current rates. Concern that removing prices completely would make it more difficult for the consumer to compare alternative holiday products has meant that brochures still have guide prices included.

THE E-BROCHURE

As mentioned earlier, many tour operators will offer visitors to their website the opportunity to download all or part of their brochure. In most cases, the format used is a PDF file (which can be read using widely available free software). In the past, it was common to allow the brochure to be downloaded through a hyperlink on the website. More and more, however, tour operators are realising that they can make contact with those customers reading their brochures by sending the requested information as an attachment to an e-mail address. This provides the tour operator with the opportunity to follow up the brochure request with relevant e-mails to try to encourage the customer to book with them.

Websites now frequently replace some elements of the traditional brochure, but the preparation of web pages has to be undertaken as carefully as that for brochures. While a website will share many characteristics with a brochure, there are important differences. Customers will read fewer words on a screen than on the printed page, so the visual elements take on greater significance. The particular advantage of a website is that it can be changed frequently and at short notice; in fact, an up-to-date website will be expected. Many companies use their websites to personalise their approach to clients, giving portraits of staff and adding comments from tourists on the resort pages.

NEGOTIATING WITH PRINTERS

Printers do not expect their clients to be experts in printing methods, but those involved with the processing and production of a brochure should be reasonably familiar with current techniques in printing and common terms used. Printers need the following information:

- the number of brochures required
- the number of colours to be used in the printing. Full-colour work normally involves four colours, but some cost savings should be possible if colour photography is not to be included
- the paper to be used – size, format, quality and weight. The choice of paper will be influenced by several factors, including the printing process used. Size may be dictated by industry requirements. For example, a tour operator's brochure needs to fit a standard travel agent's rack. Paper quality varies according to the material from which it is made. It may be glossy or matte, but will be selected for its whiteness and opacity. Inevitably, there is an element of compromise here as very white paper tends to be less opaque and one must avoid print showing through on the other side of the sheet. The weight of paper chosen will, of course, affect the overall weight of the brochure, an important factor if it is to be mailed in quantity. Operators may well cut the size of a brochure if it reduces postage costs to a lower band
- the number and positions of illustrations (photos, artwork, maps and so on) used

- typesetting needs; there are over 6000 typefaces from which to choose, and the style of type chosen should reflect the theme of the brochure, its subject and the image of the company
- completion and delivery dates.

Many operators choose to have their brochures printed abroad at lower cost. Good-quality work can be produced at very competitive prices for long print runs, but obviously the operator will want to see whether or not domestic printers can match the prices quoted by printers abroad as using a local printer will reduce transport costs. Most importantly, operators must avoid cutting corners to save money as an inferior print job can threaten the whole success of the tour programme.

The progress of the printing must be supervised throughout, either by the operator or its advertising agency. Proofs should be submitted at each stage of production to check on accuracy and a final corrected proof should be seen before the actual print run to ensure that there are no outstanding errors. As the brochure is such a crucial legal document, generally several members of staff will read it through before the final proof is passed for printing.

EXAMPLE

Accuracy is everything

Checking the content of a holiday brochure is vital. While ensuring that printers do not make mistakes is important, it is also vital to ensure accuracy in the information provided to the printers. They are unlikely to question the content provided, especially if it is specific to a particular product or destination.

UK holiday company Warner Leisure should have double-checked the content of its 2010 brochures before mailing these to their clients. A case of mistaken identity led to the embarrassing admission that the promotional text encouraging visitors to its Norton Grange venue, in Yarmouth, Isle of Wight, was actually referring to a range of attractions and events taking place in Great Yarmouth – a seaside destination in Norfolk, some 250 miles away!

BROCHURE DISTRIBUTION AND CONTROL

Tour operators must make the decision to either use all of the retail agencies available to them or select those that they feel will be most productive for the company. Whatever decision is made, operators must also establish a policy for distributing their brochures to these agents. If equal numbers of brochures are distributed to every agent, many copies will be wasted.

Wastage can be reduced by establishing standards against which to monitor the performance of travel agents. A key ratio is that of brochures given out to bookings received. 'Average' figures tend to vary considerably for different operators, so, while one will expect to gain a booking for every three to four brochures given out (which may still mean that every booking carries the burden of some £10 in brochure production costs), specialist operators may have to give out as many as 25–30 brochures to obtain a single booking. The overall position is slightly better than this suggests, as each booking will involve typically between two and four people.

If figures consistently poorer than these are achieved by any of its agents, the operator should look to them for an explanation. The problem could be accounted for by an agent's lack of control over their own brochure distribution – do they merely stock their display racks and leave clients to pick up whatever numbers of brochures they wish, or do they make a serious attempt to sell to 'browsers'? Some agents retain all stocks of brochures except a display copy, so that customers have to ask for copies of the brochures they require. This is instrumental in cutting down waste and it increases the number of sales opportunities.

EXAMPLE

Brochure Bank

An online resource for brochures is provided by Brochure Bank. This is a travel marketing company which provides brochures on request for holidaymakers. The marketing company provides access to brochures from a range of companies, to aid their marketing and distribution activities.

Visitors to the Brochure Bank website will find brochures grouped by destination and by holiday style (sun, cruise, skiing, adventure holidays, for example). Holidaymakers can also search for brochures by tour operator – important for those companies with strong customer loyalty.

Brochure Bank promotes more than 35 tour operator brands, many of which are long established in the tourism industry but are insufficient in size to compete with the major operators. Helpfully, as part of the ordering process Brochure Bank records customer contact details, which are then passed to those tour operators whose brochures have been selected. This ensures brochure requests can be followed up by sales calls.

It is now the practice of most operators to categorise their agents in some way, in terms of their productivity. This could typically take the form shown in Table 18.5.

TABLE 18.5 Example categories reflecting sales productivity

Agents	Bookings per year
Category A: top, most productive agents, multiples	100+
Category B: good agents	50–99
Category C: fair agents	20–49
Category D: below average agents	6–19
Category E: poor agents, producing little	0–5

Of course, for a specialist operator, the number of sales per category might be considerably smaller; a good agent may produce as few as ten bookings a year. The principle remains the same, however: the operator will determine, on the strength of these categories, what level of support to give each of the agents. Those agents at the top of the scale can expect to receive as many brochures as they ask for, while at the other end, perhaps the operator will be willing to provide only a file copy or two to three brochures to work with. Many new or independent agents are finding it increasingly difficult to obtain any supplies of brochures from the major operators, which are tending to narrow the focus of their distribution policy.

THE RESERVATIONS SYSTEM

In order to put a package tour programme into operation, a reservations system must exist. The design of the system will depend on whether reservations are to be handled manually or by computer and on whether the operator plans to sell through agents or direct to the public.

Many operators still sell their tours through high street travel agents, although direct sales through the leading operators' websites are increasing rapidly. In the UK, the multiples – retail chains owned by the lead operators – are responsible for over 50% of all package holidays sold by agents.

Manual systems have almost entirely disappeared in favour of **computer reservation systems** (CRSs), which offer a faster, more efficient service at a much cheaper price for the operator. A travel agent needs to contact the operator quickly when serving a client at the counter. If telephone lines are engaged, or not answered for long periods of time, the agent could become frustrated and decide to deal with a competitor who is easier to contact, or the client will go home and then simply search for a holiday on a website.

Initially, the CRS operated only in-house; that is, on the operator's own premises. Agents seeking to make a booking would telephone the operator, who then tapped into the company's computer to check on availability. It was but a short step from this to link the agent directly to the CRS, providing a visual display unit (VDU) in the agent's office. These connections originally depended on the use of telephone lines to link the agent's VDU to the operator's CRS. Subsequently, agents were 'hard-wired' directly into the operators' CRS, reducing the time taken to make bookings.

In the UK, the market leader Thomson Holidays (now part of TUI) was the first operator to decide that all bookings through agents should be handled by a specially developed system called TOPS, forcing agents to invest in the appropriate hardware if they wished to book holidays from this major player. Most other large companies rapidly followed suit.

MAKING A RESERVATION

The computer will allow the agent to see whether or not the particular tour required by the client is available. If it is not, it will automatically display other dates or destinations that match the client's needs as closely as possible. Once the agent has established that a package is acceptable to the client, a booking is made (sometimes an option can be taken for 24 hours, but operators are now tending to accept only firm bookings). Any late changes to the holiday that are not detailed in the brochure can be drawn to the attention of the client and agent on the screen at this time. The agent is provided with a code number to identify the booking and obtains a completed booking form from the client, together with a deposit.

The computer booking alone is sufficient to hold the reservation, so booking forms are now held in the agent's files rather than, as formerly, sent to the operator with the deposit. The operator will issue an interim invoice to confirm the booking, on receipt of the deposit, and a final invoice will be issued, normally about ten weeks before the client is due to leave, requesting that full payment is made eight weeks before departure. Changes to the holiday cannot be made once the final invoice has been issued. After receipt of the final payment, the tour operator will issue all tickets, itineraries and, where necessary, vouchers and despatch them to the agent, who will forward them to the client. The advent of e-tickets and vouchers, however, dramatically reduced the amount of paperwork sent by operators to their clients.

Prior to each departure, a flight manifest is prepared for the airline, with the names of all those booked on it. In the case of flights using US airspace, a considerable amount of personal information has to be supplied for every passenger – a security measure introduced after 9/11. Also, a rooming list is sent to the hotels concerned and resort representatives where appropriate. The latter should go over the rooming list with the hotelier to ensure that all is in order prior to the clients' arrival.

LATE BOOKINGS

Tour operators are anxious to sell every one of their holidays. The ability to react quickly to deal with last-minute demand for bookings plays a key role in fulfilling this objective. In the UK, more than a third of holidays are booked within two months of departure (see Figure 18.6). Many operators have introduced procedures designed to pick up these late bookings, including the rapid updating of availability on computer reservation systems and a booking procedure that allows tickets to be sent to the customer electronically. The new online agents provide an excellent medium for selling off flights and accommodation at short notice.

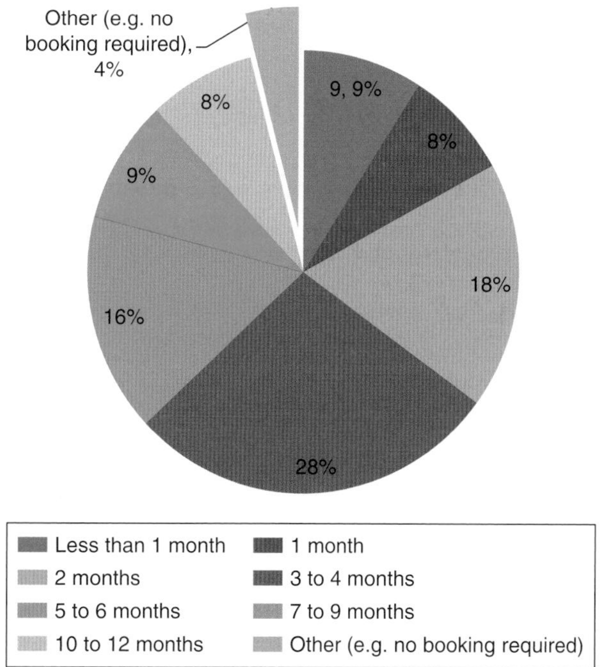

FIGURE 18.6 Lead times for booking holidays – UK domestic and overseas holidays

Source: Adapted from data provided by BDRC Continental, 2017

THE DISTRIBUTION NETWORK

Selecting retailers

Essentially, tour operators have to choose between two alternative methods for selling their holidays: retail travel agents or direct to the public (although websites can have a role in either of these approaches). Larger operators that have products with universal appeal and the market for which is national in scope have tended to sell the bulk of their holidays through the retail trade, but the development of websites has encouraged an increasing number of sales to be made direct, a development welcomed by the operators as they can thus save paying agents' commissions. Websites also aid retailers, in that agents now need to spend less time talking to their clients about the products or ordering brochures and can therefore stress their role as a personal link, which offers clients a sense of security. Companies with a policy of selling direct to the public will be examined in the next main section.

Few operators deal indiscriminately with all retail agents. The cost of servicing the less productive agents is often greater than the revenue they produce as they must not only be provided with expensive brochures, but also receive regular mailings to update their information and be supported by sales material and even, in some cases, visits from the operators' sales representatives. Even in the era of websites, many operators still find that the personal contacts established by a good sales representative lead to more sales than do mail-shots or phone calls. The operators must therefore decide whether to vary the support they offer to different agents, or even dispense with the services of some agents altogether.

We have already seen how brochure supplies are varied according to the productivity of agents. It has also been the practice of operators to support their best agents by offering them an overriding commission of between 1 and 5%, in addition to the basic 10%, for achieving target sales figures. The large multiples, due to the strength of their position in the retail trade, can negotiate the highest overrides, giving them the ability to discount substantially in order to attract yet more business.

Leading operators have reduced both support and commission to their agents in recent years, and their process of directional selling has favoured sales through their own chains. This is proving a challenge for independent agents, who will often work with independent tour operators and other small operators to make up for the shortfall in their sales of mass-market tours.

EXAMPLE

Funjet

This company is an American-based tour operator, with a focus on more luxurious, all-inclusive holidays predominantly in North America, Mexico and the Caribbean. Established in 1974, this longstanding tour operator offers charter flight services to popular destinations from several major US cities including Baltimore, Chicago, Denver, Houston and Minneapolis. The company has a list of preferred travel agents which it encourages customers to use.

To stimulate travel agency sales, instead of increasing commission rates Funjet reduced the amount of commission paid to its lowest-performing preferred agents from 10% to 7%. It has also reduced commission to non-preferred travel agents to 5%. Funjet claimed that this move was an attempt to incentivise agents to sell more Funjet holidays in order to move to a higher commission band on all sales. It remains to be seen whether this will have the desired effect: will travel agents increase their sales of Funjet vacations or will they simply focus on those tour operators which offer higher commission rates regardless of total annual sales?

The smaller operators – those which are strong in certain geographic regions or cater for specific niche markets, often involving quite a small number of customers in total – are obviously not in a position to support a national network of retailers. Most of them will therefore choose to sell direct to their customers, although a handful may try to concentrate sales through a limited number of supportive agents.

Relationships with travel agents

It is customary for tour operators to draw up a formal agreement with the travel agents they appoint to sell their services. Those agreements specify the terms and conditions of trading, including such issues as the normal rates of commission paid and whether or not credit will be extended to the agent or settlement of accounts must be made immediately.

Under the terms of these agreements, the agents agree to support and promote the sale of their principals' services. In return, the operators agree to provide the support and co-operation necessary for the successful merchandising of the companies' products; that is, providing adequate supplies of brochures, sales promotion material and sometimes finance for cooperative regional advertising or promotion campaigns. Operators will also try to ensure that their retailers are knowledgeable about the products they sell. This will be achieved through the circulation of sales letters or mailshots, invitations to workshops or other presentations and inviting selected agents on educational study trips.

The educational study trip

The **educational study trip** (**familiarisation trip**, or 'fam' trip, as it is known in North America) is a trip organised by principals (whether tour operators, carriers or tourist offices of the regions involved) for a variety of purposes. For example, members of the media or travel writers will be taken to tourist destinations in order for the principals to gain free – and, hopefully, positive – media coverage. Travel agents are also offered opportunities to undertake trips in order to improve their knowledge of the destinations or encourage them to sell the region or product. Sometimes, these trips are used by tour operators as incentives to agents; that is, if certain sales targets are reached, trips will be provided as a reward.

Visits to a destination are known to be one of the most effective means of encouraging agents to sell a particular package. These organised trips also have a social function, enabling the operators to get to know their agents better and to obtain feedback from them. The cost of mounting educational trips, however, is high, even if a proportion of the costs is met by the hotels at the destination or the national tourist offices and carriers helping to organise the holidays, so principals will try to do everything they can to ensure that the trips give them value for money. This was not always the case in the past, when such visits abroad were often treated as purely social events, attractive as a travel perk rather than an educational experience.

The effectiveness of the trips has been improved by selecting the candidates more carefully, providing a more balanced mix of visits, working sessions and social activities and imposing a small charge for attendance, so that the managers of travel agencies will take care to ensure that the expense is justified in terms of an increased productivity and expertise of their staff.

The careful selection of candidates will ensure that all those attending share common objectives. Monitoring performance, by soliciting reports from those attending and checking the sales of staff from those agencies invited to participate, will help to ensure that the operators' money has been well spent.

EXAMPLE

Fam trips

Fam trips might sound like a great opportunity for a free holiday for travel agents, but tour operators design them to ensure they are likely to encourage sales of their product. One example is the fam trip to Mauritius organised by Beachcomber Tours in spring 2018. To qualify for the tour, travel agents needed to make at least one sale to Mauritius in the lead-up time. The agent was also required to implement at least one of the following marketing initiatives:

(Continued)

- create a 'Beachcomber'-themed window display for the travel agency
- implement a Facebook campaign that links to the Beachcomber company
- promote the Beachcomber Mauritius promotion page on the company's website.

Agents would also need to pay a £300 fee for the trip, which could be earned back through sales (at a rate of £50 per sale).

It is not uncommon in the USA for travel agents to pay for fam trips, and the industry magazine *Travel Weekly* lists trips being offered for low rates to travel professionals. Each listing outlines an itinerary, the sponsor of the fam trip and, where available, the cost of taking a companion.

For further information, see: www.travelweekly.com/fam-trips

OPERATORS SELLING DIRECT

Apart from those operators that will inevitably sell direct to their clients, for the reasons outlined above, a handful of larger tour operators have chosen deliberately to market their products direct to the public. This movement was spearheaded by the Danish company Tjaereborg, which entered the UK market in the late 1970s with a promotional strategy that asserted that if customers booked holidays direct, by cutting out the agents' commission, they would save money. While isolated bargains were certainly on offer, many holidays were no cheaper and sometimes more expensive than similar packages booked through an agent.

The reasons for this are not hard to understand. While travel agency commissions were indeed saved, huge budgets were required to inform and promote the holidays to the general public. The company had to invest millions in heavy advertising in the media, and similar high costs were incurred by the need to have a large reservations staff and multiple telephone lines to answer queries from the public. Those costs were, of course, fixed, while commissions are only paid to agents when they achieve a sale.

Tjaereborg soon found that, after initial success, which was probably the outcome of curiosity, it was unable to achieve greater market penetration, especially as Thomson Holidays had rapidly joined the competition with a direct sell division, Portland Holidays. Tjaereborg, after turning in an indifferent performance for several years, was sold to First Choice (then called Owners Abroad), which eventually replaced the brand with another direct sell operation, Eclipse.

Whether holidaymakers choose to buy direct or use an intermediary is often dependent on cultural influences related to traditional buying habits for travel products. In the UK, evidence suggests that some British holidaymakers still seek the assurance of face-to-face contact with an agent, even if the product knowledge of that agent is limited. However, the advent of online booking of travel arrangements is now changing this pattern dramatically. In particular, price comparison websites (such as Travel Supermarket) are growing in importance as consumers look for efficient methods to seek out the best deals.

While every country has its own unique purchasing behaviours, many follow similar patterns to those of the UK regarding package travel. In France, high levels of Internet access have led to online sales, although in recent years weak economic conditions have seen sales growth stagnating. Furthermore, it seems that the French are maintaining the use of multiple channels for purchasing their travel products. In Belgium, package holidays make up about one-quarter of the total spent on holiday travel. In the Netherlands, it is reported that online sales are growing in importance, particularly for accommodation, flights and car rental, with two-thirds of summer holidays booked online (CBS, 2018). Domestic travel for the Dutch, however, tends to be booked directly with the principals. This growing popularity for dynamic packaging is likely to lead to the decline of standardised package trips, which may further affect booking patterns.

THE INFORMATION TECHNOLOGY REVOLUTION AND ITS IMPACT ON TOUR OPERATING

No business is being transformed by information technology (IT) faster or more radically than the business of travel; and tour operating, of all the sectors of this business, is arguably the most affected by developments. Of course, the advent of modern technology is no longer a recent phenomenon; after all, computers were widely introduced into the trade as early as the 1960s, hastening the demise of the traditional manual booking system. It is the scale and pace of development, however, that is proving so disruptive for the industry, as new forms of booking and information facility become available both to the trade and to the customer. Even the telephone has become a tool for providing new ways to book holidays, with the development of smartphone applications, which allows customers to access material quickly from various information sources on their mobile phones.

The key question is not whether such new techniques will start to replace traditional methods of booking holidays, but rather how quickly the transition will occur and how completely it will come to dominate distribution. One can only speculate on what kind of future the traditional agency channels will have – or even traditional tour operators, given that suppliers can now reach their customers directly through websites and e-mail, and customers are not slow to recognise that they can put together their own package as well as any operator. The number of holiday sales that are made online through the Internet is growing rapidly each year, with both packages and travel components being purchased.

As holidaymakers from much of Europe and North America become accustomed to booking online, it is the growing markets of China and India that will be of most interest in terms of their move to online travel purchase. Social media and access to smartphones are becoming more mainstream and this is helping to build customer online engagement with travel companies. China has more than 500 million Internet users, a fact that is moving the country up the world rankings in terms of online travel sales. While online sales of transport and accommodation are growing for the outbound market, the popularity of package tours means many travellers will purchase tour operator products through travel agents. In China, forecasts suggest that the online travel booking segment will have increased from $69 billion in 2017 to more than $120 billion by 2022, with around half of this coming from sales of package holidays (Digital Market Outlook, 2018).

Internet penetration in India is only now starting to reach the levels experienced in China. India has 462 million Internet users, not an insignificant number, with the majority being mobile Internet users. A second impediment is that of online payment. Access to and use of credit or debit cards is limiting opportunities for online payment. However, as more residents gain convenient access to the Internet and alternative modes of electronic payment are developed, so travel retail sales are predicted to grow, with forecasts predicting levels reaching $11 billion by 2022.

The leading operators have responded to the growth in Internet booking of travel products, often with the introduction of their own booking sites. This is true not just for package holidays but also for their efforts in trying to capture the growing numbers wishing to use dynamic packaging.

Some observers in the industry are adamant that the growth in online booking will neither lead to the closure of tour operators nor eradicate the travel agent. Some believe that the caution of some consumers, the lack of IT knowledge and skills among the older generation as well as uncertainty about the reliability of the many new dot.com companies will ensure that support for more traditional means of booking will continue. Others, aware of the rise in criminal activity associated with credit cards, are also reluctant to provide their card details over the Internet. Still others believe that independent agents will be more impartial in giving advice about travel products than will the suppliers' websites, as well as providing greater expertise in recommending holidays.

Undoubtedly, all of these views have some validity, discouraging some sales through online channels. Operators and agents fight back by pointing out to the independent travel bookers that they will have no one to turn to when things go wrong, and that accommodation and flights booked separately will not have the level of protection offered by a package in the event of the collapse of suppliers or some other disaster. However, as mentioned earlier in this chapter, changes to the European Directive on Package Travel 2015 have expanded protection, particularly in the case of dynamic packaging.

The development of alternative channels is hindered by two factors. Operators have been slow to realise the potential of the new technology and, in general, marketing costs remain high for suppliers attempting to sell direct to the public. Nonetheless, more and more operators are becoming aware that selling via the Internet allows suppliers to trim, and possibly even eradicate, their two major sources of expenditure – commission and brochures. Already much information on destinations and facilities is available for public viewing on the Internet, and before long all holiday information currently provided by operators through the medium of brochures will become accessible in this way.

The growth of technological development in this field is too rapid to allow a thorough treatment of the subject in a textbook. Students of tour operating must keep abreast of such developments through the trade press or other media. Suffice to say that, in addition to reservation systems, computers are now used widely to provide accounts and management information quickly and accurately to both operators and agents, while larger operators have also introduced accounting systems that allow the direct transfer of agency payments from agents' bank accounts to the operators'.

EXAMPLE

Tour operator software

Companies that establish tour programmes use software to manage customer information, tour details and help with back-office activities such as invoicing and payments. The software also helps operators by allowing quotes to be created based on existing programmes and usually includes an online reservation and payment system for tourists to use.

One example, Tourplan, is designed to provide a software solution for small and medium-sized tour operators. It includes a reservation system as well as functions that assist with the management of package holidays, tailor-made tours and some forms of business travel.

For more information, see: www.tourplan.com

In any examination of the influence of new technology in industry, it would be facile to ignore the counter-argument that impersonal means of communication can only go so far in satisfying consumers' needs. It is helpful to look at parallels in other industries. In the world of print, for example, newspapers remain popular even though their data are available online and, despite the growth of online banking, customers still value direct contact with their bank. Operators would do well to look at developments in other fields and see what lessons can be learned to improve their own means of communication with their clients.

THE FUTURE FOR TOUR OPERATORS

Consolidation within this sector is likely to continue. The merging of companies that has been experienced over the past two decades will also be seen with many online operators, as they seek to establish greater turnover as well as try to control a larger share of loyal customers. The growing popularity of dynamic packaging will give travel agents the opportunity to provide a tailored holiday product to their customers, drawing on travel elements from a range of suppliers. This may require a response from tour operators as the demand for package holidays declines.

As tourists become more experienced and seek out more unusual or exotic experiences, specialist niche products are likely to become more popular. This may provide a distinct opportunity for smaller, independent tour operators, although already it is possible to see that the mega-operators are trying to serve this market, focusing attention on the specialist brands within their operations.

QUESTIONS AND DISCUSSION POINTS

1. What are the benefits to the customer of booking a package holiday ahead of booking each component of a trip separately?
2. With the growth of Internet booking, more hotels can sell their products direct to customers. Given this, why would some hotels decide to work with tour operators?
3. How is IT changing the tour operations business?

TASKS

1. There are numerous tour operator software packages available to the market. Identify at least three different software products, noting what each offers to help the tour operator. Summarise this as a poster.
2. In each brochure, the tour operator is required to provide information about booking conditions. Obtain a brochure and examine these in detail (note that they may run to several pages long). Write a short report that explains the different aspects covered and comment on the extent to which these protect the tourist.

WEBSITES

Association of Independent Tour Operators: www.aito.co.uk

EC Package Travel Directive (90/314/EEC): ec.europa.eu

European Tour Operators Association: www.etoa.org

Thomas Cook (receivership information) – www.thomascook.com

TUI Group: www.tui-group.com

REFERENCES

Association of British Travel Agents (ABTA) (2018) *Holiday Habits Report*. London: ABTA.

Baran, M. (2018) Print lives: The travel brochure is still relevant. *Travel Weekly*, 17 January.

BDRC Continental (2017) *Holiday Trends*. London: BDRC Continental.

Calder, S. (2018) UK's biggest holiday firm rebrands from Thomson to TUI. *The Independent*, 20 September.

CBS (Statistics Netherlands) (2018) *Two-thirds of Summer Holidays Booked Online*. Available online at: www.cbs.nl/en-gb/news/2018/30/two-thirds-of-summer-holidays-booked-online [Accessed January 2018].

Digital Market Outlook (2018) Online travel booking revenue in selected countries worldwide in 2018. *Statista*, April.

Greenwood, A. (2016) *Brochures Making a Comeback among Holidaymakers*. Available online at: www.traveldailymedia.com/brochures-making-a-comeback-among-holidaymakers [Accessed December 2018].

Mintel (2018a) *Package vs Independent Holidays – UK*. London: Mintel, April.

Mintel (2018b) *Long-haul vs Short-haul Holidays – UK*. London: Mintel, October.

Schulte-Nölke, H., Twigg-Flesner, C. and Ebers, M. (2008) *EC Consumer Law Compendium: Comparative analysis*. Bielefeld University, Germany.

Travel Weekly (2013) *How TUI is Updating the Role of Holiday Reps*. Available online at: www.travelweekly.co.uk/articles/45761/special-report-how-tui-is-updating-the-role-of-holiday-reps [Accessed January 2018].

VisitBritain (2017) Quarterly Inbound Update: Full year 2017. Available online at: www.visitbritain.org/sites/default/files/vb-corporate/Documents-Library/documents/2017_uk_and_regional_ips_summary_v3.pdf [Accessed December 2018].

United Nations World Tourism Organization (UNWTO) (2018) *Tourism Highlights*. Madrid: UNWTO.

19

SELLING AND DISTRIBUTING TRAVEL AND TOURISM

CONTENTS

LEARNING OUTCOMES

After studying this chapter, you should be able to:

- explain the role of travel agents as a component of the tourism industry and their relationship with other sectors
- identify the functions performed by an agent
- state the qualities necessary for effective agency management and service
- articulate the considerations and the requirements for establishing and running a travel agency
- assess the constraints and threats to agents' operations and evaluate alternative solutions for their survival.

> The American Society of Travel Agents quietly changed its name to the American Society of Travel Advisors (ASTA) . . . The message was clear: Stop calling us travel agents. Travel agents represent a dying business that no longer serves customers. Travel advisors, which provide a professional service, are the future. (Elliott, 2018)

INTRODUCTION

Half a century ago, as mass-market travel was starting to boom, travellers would actively discuss the use of travel agents vis-à-vis making arrangements independently. Today, as we will discover throughout this chapter, that same debate continues.

The European Commission (1999) has defined **travel agents** as retailers to leisure and business travellers, selling flights (charter or scheduled), accommodation, car hire, foreign currency, travel insurance and other travel services. They are generally paid a commission by the supplier of the service or, in the case of a package holiday, by the operator. In some countries, the term 'travel agent' is used more generally to refer to an organisation operating in the travel industry (this may be as a retailer but also includes those acting as tour operators or tour providers). This chapter, however, specifically focuses on the travel agent as a retailer. The travel agent acts as an intermediary, conveniently linking customers with the providers of travel products. Providers of travel products are often termed **principals**, owning specific travel elements, such as hotels or airlines, as well as tour operators, who put together packages that combine several travel elements (see Figure 19.1).

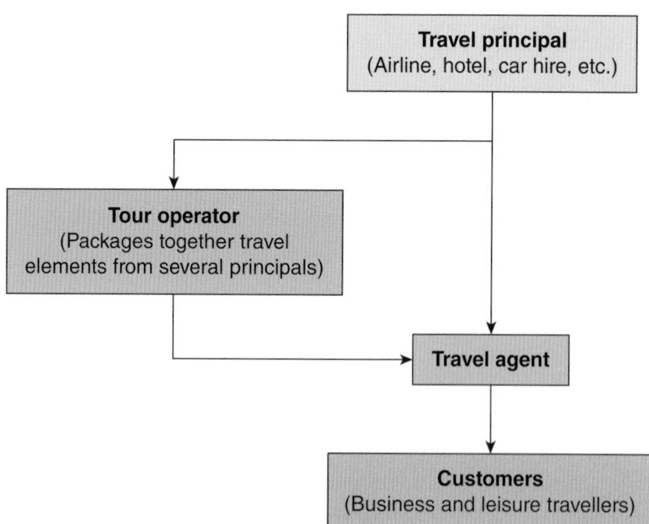

FIGURE 19.1 The position of travel agents in the chain of distribution

Most travel principals continue to rely, to a greater or lesser extent, on travel agents as an important source of distribution, and retailers continue to play a key role in the structure of the industry. Their share of business, however, is declining, even in the key area of **inclusive tours** (package holidays), as customers turn to booking direct. The agent's role is changing – as the quote at the beginning of the chapter highlights – but there are grounds for belief that it is far from collapsing.

HISTORICAL CONTEXT

Agents selling travel arrangements have been in existence in the UK for well over 100 years. Indeed, the oldest – now the tour operator Cox and Kings – traces its origins back to the eighteenth century. The travel agent's principal role in earlier times was to sell shipping and rail services, but, with the coming of air transport and the development of the package tour business after World War II, their product range expanded.

Before World War II, shipping companies had been able to provide a good reservations and ticketing service direct to the public, with sales outlets in their city offices and at leading ports. Railways and coach operators had similarly established city centre terminals from which they could dispense tickets direct to the public. When the airlines arrived on the scene, however, their airport terminals were situated well away from centres of population, and, as a convenient network of travel agents was in place by that time, they did not face the same pressure to establish their own sales offices. Although most leading airlines did establish a main selling office in capital cities and many also opened offices in other leading cities, the new demand for air tickets encouraged travel agents to expand their distribution outlets further. With the deregulation of air travel and a greater willingness on the part of passengers to book direct (first by phone or fax, later via the Internet), many airlines closed their town centre sales offices. Travel agents similarly experienced a fall in air ticket sales.

It was the travel agents themselves who developed the first air package tours. Retail entrepreneurs had the vision to see that, if they could buy seats on flights in bulk at discounted prices, they could reduce the cost of air fares and thus a huge mass market for foreign tours would develop. The packages they developed were, in turn, sold through other agents, eventually to become the retailers' principal source of revenue.

THE SCALE OF THE RETAIL SECTOR

It is difficult to estimate the number of travel agents in existence globally. Many become members of their national association bodies, but, as such organisations often allow those tour operators who also provide retail services to join, their membership statistics can provide only limited detail regarding the number of businesses operating primarily as travel agents (see Table 19.1). While some countries require agents to be licensed, many have no compulsory registration scheme. Licensing schemes can vary in their format. For instance, in Ireland, the licensing of travel agents and tour operators is undertaken by the Commission for Aviation Regulation (almost 200 travel agents were licensed to trade during the last quarter of 2018). Alternatively, licensing may be managed through government bodies or linked to customer financial protection schemes.

TABLE 19.1 Membership of travel agent associations

Association	Membership (percentage of total travel agency sales attributed to members)
Association of Croatian Travel Agencies (UHPA)	221
Association of Danish Travel Agents and Tour Operators	112 (70% of sales)
Association of Finnish Travel Agents	170 (95% of sales)

(Continued)

TABLE 19.1 (Continued)

Association	Membership (percentage of total travel agency sales attributed to members)
Association of South African Travel Agents	461
Association of Turkish Travel Agencies (TURSAB)	7950*
Österreichischer Reisebüroverband (ÖRV) – Austria	468 (80% of sales)
Svenska Resebyråföreningen (SRF) – Sweden	270 (85% of sales)
Travel Agents Federation of India	1400 (70% of sales)
Travel Agents' Association New Zealand	303

Source: Authors' own research, 2019

Note: *figure at 2014

EXAMPLE

Australia changes its approach

Historically, travel agency licensing was obligatory in Australia, each state overseeing the management of this process. Consumer protection was offered through the Travel Compensation Fund, which required travel agents to prove annually their financial stability.

However, through a phased process of reform taking place between 2013 and 2015, both licensing and financial protection have changed. Legislation requiring licensing was repealed in July 2014, to be replaced by voluntary industry accreditation through the Australian Federation of Travel Agents (AFTA). The financial protection scheme has also been terminated, replaced by the expectation that travel agents take out insurance to provide insolvency protection and international passenger protection (IPP).

It should also be noted that customers' use of travel agents varies from country to country. Research (Dumazel and Humphreys, 1999) found that, while 80% of travel purchases in the UK were through travel agents, Belgium, the Netherlands and Switzerland recorded levels closer to 25%. While the market has changed significantly since that time, it highlights the fact that different distribution channels are used in different nations.

The number of travel retail outlets in the UK declined in 2016, by 70 outlets, to 3695 (Mintel, 2017). This continues the pattern of long-term decline; more than 700 travel agencies have closed their doors in the past decade. The number of agents affiliated to the Association of British Travel Agents (ABTA) – the leading trade body representing both tour operators and travel agents in the UK – has seen a decline in members of more than a third since 1991. This was partly attributed to the decision by Thomas Cook to close 195 high street travel agencies. Online travel agencies now dominate the marketplace; globally, the largest agent, Expedia Inc., exceeded $88 billion in sales in 2017. To put this in context, it far surpasses the revenue earned by all UK travel agents (online and high street), which was estimated at $42 billion for the same year.

THE POWER OF THE TRAVEL AGENCY CHAINS

As the demand for travel services grew in the UK, travel agencies expanded their operations, opening new premises (or, in some cases, acquiring smaller existing businesses) in order to service more customers. In addition, several tour operators sought to take control of the retailing element of their business, so they also established large networks of outlets. To take one instance, the purchase in the 1970s of the Lunn Poly travel agency chain by Thomson Holidays (now part of TUI Group) ensured that the tour operator could provide an expanded network of retail outlets. These **multiples** could achieve business advantages through their centralised marketing activities, negotiating higher commission rates based on sales across the group and reduced costs through mass development and purchasing of key resources (such as computer systems).

The concern that the multiples would expand to a point where independents would be squeezed out of the market has receded to some extent in recent years. Indeed, the composition of the travel agency industry has changed dramatically over time. There was a fall in independent agencies (small, privately owned businesses with only a few outlets) as the travel agency chains (with multiple outlets) expanded under the ownership of major tour operators like Thomas Cook and TUI, but, with the growth in call centres and online booking, the multiples are, as previously mentioned, now starting to reduce the number of their own high street outlets.

COMPETING WITH THE MULTIPLES

Although the large number of branches owned by the leading chains appears to give them an insuperable advantage over the independents, this is not always the case. Medium-sized chains (often operating only in a limited geographic region) can provide strong competition. These chains, commonly known as **miniples**, typically control between 40 and 100 shops. They are, however, vulnerable to takeovers, and some of the major players have been absorbed into leading operators' retail organisations.

The independents have recognised that, on their own, they face an almost impossible task in competing with the multiples for the sale of mass-market holidays. Since it became legal to discount the price of travel products at the point of sale, the independent agents have been under particular pressure from discounting undertaken by the multiples. Such large chains, because of their substantial buying power, can negotiate commission overrides (an additional percentage of commission paid when higher sales targets are achieved), making it easier to undercut independent agents on price. The multiples can also invest more in the latest technology, and in national advertising campaigns, than can the independents.

Independent travel agents have realised that, in order to compete on price, they need to collaborate with other travel agencies. This allows them to negotiate for higher commissions based on their joint buying power. As a result, there has been massive growth in alliances, particularly through the establishment of consortia.

EXAMPLE

Consortia

Travelsavers International

Formed in the USA in 1970, this marketing group has some 3000 independently owned travel agencies in 36 countries worldwide. The travel agencies are not marketed under this

(Continued)

brand name – all the agents retain their own identities. In the UK, they must hold ABTA or IATA membership to operate within this group.

Advantage

Established in 1978 and known initially as the National Association of Independent Travel Agents (NAITA), then as Advantage Travel Centres, this consortium supports around 380 branches, which have a combined turnover of £4.5 billion. Agents may use their own trading name, but around half of members have chosen to emphasise the Advantage brand in their name.

The Travel Network Group

Formed in 1976 as WorldChoice, this group operated initially as the Association of Retail Travel Agents' Consortia (ARTAC). Following a merger with the Travel Trust Association (TTA) in 2008, the group, rebranded in 2011 as the Travel Network Group, is one of the largest consortia of independent travel agents in the UK, with 900 members.

Global Travel Group

Formed in 1993, this group has 800 members and operates its own bonding system. The consortium was later purchased by Stella Travel Services, owner of Travelbag and Travel 2. This organisation is particularly keen to see new agencies established and operates its own training academy for those just starting out.

Elite Travel Group

Established in 1977, this small consortium was formerly known as Midconsort Travel Group (reflecting its geographical focus on the Midlands region of England). This group is owned by those travel agencies who are its members.

Freedom Travel Group

Established in 2001, as the trading arm of the Co-operative Travel Group, its members have combined sales of £1.5 billion. A merger between Thomas Cook and the Co-operative Travel Group in 2001 extended its commercial reach. However this company encountered difficulties following the demise of Thomas Cook.

The potential buying power of such groupings of independent agencies provides them with a very real chance of being able to compete with the large chains, as they can share marketing costs as well as work with the smaller tour operators to ensure that they are represented on the high street. In addition, consortium membership can avoid the necessity for each agency to have separate licences when putting different components of a package together.

Franchising has generally been less successful as a strategy for competing with the multiples. The first chain in the UK to attempt to franchise on a wide scale, Exchange Travel, went into liquidation in 1990 and the Canadian-based Uniglobe chain has similarly found it difficult to establish itself in the UK, despite having a chain of offices in 60 countries worldwide. Travel Leaders, based in the USA, has over 1200 franchised locations, suggesting that markets outside of the UK can operate travel franchises more successfully.

THE PROFITABILITY OF TRAVEL AGENTS

Surprisingly few studies of travel agency productivity and profitability exist. One way to measure these is to examine the profit levels and turnover per employee. Earlier studies have generally found multiples to be more profitable than independents. Annual reports allow comparisons to be made between multiples and independent agents (see Table 19.2).

TABLE 19.2 The profitability of UK travel agents, 2017

Company name	Turnover (£000)	Profit before taxation (£000)	Profit as % of turnover	Number of employees	Profit per employee (£000)
Multiple					
Trailfinders Group Limited	728,157	24,259	3.33%	1095	22.15
Miniple					
Dawson and Sanderson	9918	311	3.14%	259	1.20
Independent					
Americana Vacations	2047	3.5	0.17%	7	0.50

Source: Company accounts

There seems to be limited attention given to the issue of cost control for travel agents, yet with profit margins slim this is an important issue. First we consider staffing costs, which can make up a significant portion of operating costs. Employing an

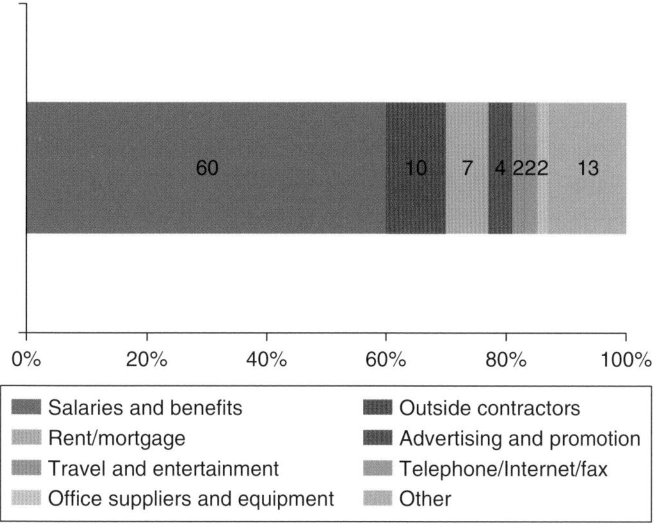

FIGURE 19.2 Average operating expenses (%)

Source: ASTA, 2014

experienced agent may come at a higher cost than, for instance, recruiting a school-leaver on a much lower wage. However, an experienced salesperson is likely to bring in greater levels of revenue, thus there is strategic value in having at least some experienced staff.

Back-office costs, such as those incurred for administering the payroll, HR, accounting and invoicing, for example, may all be managed more profitably with the use of appropriate technology or, in some cases, through outsourcing to specialists who can do it better, faster and cheaper than in-house. The use of technology may be particularly helpful in eliminating time-consuming manual activities.

The cost of operating a travel agency will vary by type of market served (corporate/leisure) and whether operations are online or include a high street presence. Research has looked at the breakdown of costs for travel agencies in the USA, concluding that staff costs make up by far the largest share (Figure 19.2).

THE ROLE OF TRAVEL AGENTS

The travel agent's role is dissimilar to that of most other retailers, in that agents do not purchase products for resale to their customers. Only when a customer has decided on buying a particular holiday do agents approach the principal on their customer's behalf to make a purchase. The travel agent does not, therefore, carry stock. This has three important implications for the business of travel distribution:

1. The cost of setting up in business is relatively small compared to that of other retail businesses.
2. Agents are only able to sell products made available by the tour operators or principals, so in times of peak demand they may be competing with other agencies to access those products that customers wish to purchase.
3. Agents are not seeking to dispose of products that they have already purchased, so may display less brand loyalty towards a particular product or company.

Arguably, the main role of a travel agent has always been to provide a convenient location for the purchase of travel. At those locations, they act as booking agents for holidays and travel, as well as a source of information and advice on travel services. Their customers look to them for expert product knowledge and objectivity in the advice they offer. However, as agents choose to deal with an increasingly limited range of products on which they can maximise their revenue (the competitive nature of retail travel is such that profit margins are small and agents must find whatever means they can of surviving), objectivity in recommendations and travel advice may not be possible. Nor is it realistic to imagine that sales staff have a thorough knowledge of every product available.

The range of products that an agent chooses to offer will vary not only on the basis of the commission each earns, but also by the nature of demand within the catchment area, the degree of specialisation of the agency, and the preferences and marketing policies of the proprietor. An agency that is attempting to provide a full range of services to the public would sell air tickets, cruise and ferry tickets, rail and coach transport, car hire, hotel accommodation and package tours (which might include domestic travel). Additional services, such as travel insurance, traveller's cheques and foreign exchange, may also be offered, and some agents will also undertake to arrange travel documentation (such as visas) for their clients. Some even deal with theatre tickets.

Such all-round agents are rapidly disappearing in the face of commercial pressures, however. Owing to the small amount of revenue achieved on the sale of coach or rail tickets, many agents are now forgoing sales of these types, although some still believe that it is better to offer a full range of services, even if some offer little or no profit, on the grounds that customers may return to buy other travel products later.

An alternative to providing a full range of products is for the agency to specialise in a niche product, such as cruising or golf holidays. Agents may specialise not only in the selection of products they offer, but also in the markets they serve. The clearest distinction is between those which focus on business travel (serving the travel needs of the local, and in some cases national, business community) and those concentrating on leisure travel.

EXAMPLE

Accessible travel

Wheelchair Escapes is based in the USA and is a travel agency serving a market requiring accessible travel. This agency makes travel arrangements that go far beyond the mainstream, including arranging wheelchair-accessible hire cars, wheelchair transportation at airports and mobility scooter hire to help travellers get around their holiday destination.

The owner of the company, Kristy Lacroix, is a member of The Society for Accessible Travel & Hospitality (SATH), an organisation dedicated to expanding travel opportunities in the USA and abroad for people with disabilities.

In 2009, a UK travel trade magazine completed a mystery shopper exercise for a seven-night holiday for two adults, one of whom was in a wheelchair. The response by travel agents was generally poor, with little detailed information sought from the customer about specific needs and a lack of product knowledge on accessibility issues. More recently, a survey of 38 websites of popular travel agents revealed that 20% provided no information on accessibility and a further 70% provided only limited information. With 10 million registered disabled travellers in the UK, this is clearly a substantial niche.

DISTRIBUTION TRENDS

It is becoming clear that the retail sector of the leisure tourism industry is now moving in two distinct directions: towards the fast turnover 'leisure sales shop', a feature of the multiples' approach, which is essentially a booking service offering rock-bottom prices; or towards a more specialised advisory service for complex or expensive tailor-made travel arrangements, which allows the agency to charge fees for their services and avoid the usual pressure to discount.

The move towards charging fees for services has its precedent in the USA, where, for a number of years, travel experts holding the Certified Travel Counsellor (CTC) qualification have dealt with the more lucrative end of the package tour business. It is these operations that seem most likely to benefit if suppliers move to contracts with low or zero commission, as their customers will be more disposed to pay fees for the services that are rendered.

Charging fees is common in the USA, with ASTA reporting that, in 2016, 76% of their members charged transaction fees, having peaked in the mid-2000s. However, the UK has yet to see the extensive introduction of service fees by travel agents.

Meanwhile, the traditional travel agent attempting to provide a wide range of services faces a future that is increasingly uncertain, as there are increasing opportunities for members of the public to book direct with suppliers using the Internet. Nevertheless, while the Internet is still seen as a major threat, the high-profile failure of some tour operators and numerous environmental and political crises have led to many customers using travel agencies, aware of the financial protection and consumer support they provide.

The policy of mass-market tour operators as well as airlines in recent years has been based on selective distribution: that is, favouring a small number of highly productive agents rather than dealing with all retail agencies. This policy has also been favoured by the multiple agents themselves, who choose to stock the products of a few key operators responsible for perhaps 80% of the total revenue in the mass market. Thomas Cook, to take one example, introduced a policy to work with only about 400 companies, of which 30 were identified as 'premium selection'. If this tendency becomes widespread over the next few years, smaller tour operators will have to find other means of reaching their customers.

The tour operator-owned multiples also engage in **directional selling**: that is, they recommend their own companies' products to customers at the expense of those from other suppliers. This ensures that the majority of the sales of the larger tour operators' products are achieved through their own travel agencies. The UK's Foreign Package Holidays (Tour Operators and Travel Agents) Order (2001) requires that the links between operators and their agencies are made clear to customers. While some independents are concerned that tour operators will eventually choose to retail their products exclusively through their own retail chains, currently this is thought unlikely.

EXAMPLE

Agents involved in directional selling

In 2004 Amadeus, a travel technology provider, surveyed British holidaymakers and reported that more than two-thirds of travel agents had tried to encourage their customers to switch from the holiday company they originally requested to other providers.

With over 70% of travel agents admitting that they are likely to push companies paying them higher levels of commission, such directional selling was seen to be a strategic business decision by the management of the agencies. As tour operators drive customers towards direct sell channels and lower commission levels, the fight for customer business has become competitive. Even independent agents are not immune from such behaviour. In many cases, encouraged by their management, they also make their selections from companies offering them the most favourable commission. Technology is aiding this by clearly denoting preferred agents on product search result. There has been criticism of this, suggesting that such activities fly in the face of customer expectation that agents are offering independent advice.

CHANGES TO RETAIL DISTRIBUTION

A number of other notable developments in travel retailing have taken place in the past few years in addition to those already described above.

Home-based sales agents

The field of home selling has expanded rapidly in recent years. Personal travel counsellors and online travel counsellors who work on a freelance basis sell on behalf of an agency and earn commission from that agency. That commission is then shared, with the travel counsellor receiving between 30% and 100% of the total commission earned, depending on the level of support service provided by their host agency.

EXAMPLE

Travel Counsellors

Travel Counsellors is one company that has built up a major retailing base in travel, with more than 1800 home-based employees operating in the UK, the Netherlands, Ireland, Australia, Dubai, South Africa and Canada. Turnover in 2017 was in excess of £216 million, with commissions earned being split 60% to the counsellor and 40% to the company.

In 2006, Travel Counsellors reported that over 40% of its UK-based agents earned more than £300 per week in commission, but acknowledged that more than a third of their counsellors worked between 40 and 60 hours per week to gain such returns. Agents are encouraged to build positive business relationships with their customers, as trust becomes important in developing repeat custom, and developing a loyal customer base can enhance earnings for both the agent and the company.

Direct sales

Perhaps the greatest threat that travel agencies face in the short term is the move to direct selling, which is now accelerating as use of the Internet expands. Can travel principals sell their products directly to the public at a lower cost? That is a vital question for both principals and tour operators.

On the one hand, selling direct to customers cuts out the high cost of servicing intermediaries as well as having to pay commission on each sale. On the other hand, it can involve substantial capital investment to set up sales offices and direct marketing costs can be high, especially if national advertising campaigns have to be mounted. Additional staff must be employed to operate call centres, too, and these must be adequately trained for the job.

Currently, many products available to customers direct on the principals' websites are offered at prices below those quoted to travel agents, leaving customers with little incentive to book through an agent. However, companies that accept bookings from agents, even when selling most of their product direct (small hotels are a good example), usually recognise that to deliberately undermine the retail trade by, for instance, charging a lower price when accepting direct business from their customers may jeopardise their relationship with travel agents, thus impacting on future business.

EXAMPLE

Ryanair

In 2004, the low-cost airline Ryanair moved to direct sell channels only, offering tickets via its own website.

(Continued)

However, in an effort to gain an increasing share of the lucrative business travel market, in 2014 Ryanair returned to using GDS systems, with Travelport the first to host the airline's inventory. This was soon followed by agreements with Amadeus and Sabre, ensuring that business travel agents could offer the airline's product to corporate clients.

Ryanair has a strategy to increase passenger numbers, and a move to selling flights via GDS is, in part, a response to addressing its very narrow distribution strategy.

However, some travel firms have little choice other than to sell their products direct, as their total capacity is too small for it to be considered by the retail distribution network. Consequently, such operators may adopt one of two distributive strategies: find a selection of key agents (likely to be independents rather than chains) that are willing to stock the product; or sell all their holidays direct to the public. The AITO Specialist Travel Agents scheme is an example of the former. The small specialist operators that form the membership of the association have identified some 140 specialist agencies to handle their bookings.

Changes in access to brochures

The proliferation of brochures and the policy of leading tour operators to produce a range of different, branded products, each in their own brochure, have forced travel agents to re-evaluate their policy on stocking brochures for customers. With the typical travel agency only having rack space for around 150 brochures, of which a large proportion may be filled with the products of the leading operators, there is little opportunity for the smaller and specialist operators to get their brochures on those racks. While a few years ago that would have been disastrous for their trade, the introduction of the Internet has led to companies becoming far more dependent instead on their websites to sell their products, and many companies now make brochures available to download.

The product portfolio

The decision about which products to stock is taken not only on the basis of what it is thought will sell quickest or easiest. The introduction of tighter EU legislation over quality and safety has forced many Europe-based agents to reconsider the companies with which they deal and, while override commissions undoubtedly play a role in the decision, equally the service the operator provides to the agent is taken into consideration. Agents who encounter difficulties in getting through to operators on the telephone or who find their e-mail communications or complaints are not answered quickly are less inclined to sell that operator's products.

While the apparently unbiased service provided by independent travel agents appears to be a marketing advantage, it is questionable whether or not clients themselves actually deal through an agent to gain this benefit, as the proportion of sales through travel agents is highest for the standard package holidays, which could, arguably, be booked direct with equal simplicity. This supports the view of many that travel agents represent only a convenient outlet for buying a holiday rather than an advisory service. One should also not dismiss the value of personal contact when making bookings. Some customers are still reluctant to make such a high-price purchase on the Internet; some fear fraud when offering credit card details over the Web, so agents still offer some guarantee of financial security, which customers see as an advantage. Furthermore, concerns that they may make mistakes or misunderstand booking conditions encourage customers to use the expertise of travel agents. Examples of such mistakes include the traveller who mistyped Sydney and, instead of ending up in Australia, flew to the small mining town of Sidney in Montana, USA, and the American customer who mistook the currency used in quotations and found the price quoted for a booked tour was not $789 but, in fact, £789 sterling – at that time meaning that it cost about 40% more than expected.

EXAMPLE

Holiday booking fraud

It is estimated that as many as 4700 unsuspecting UK holidaymakers lost £6.7 million to fraudsters in 2017. Around three-quarters of this was for bookings of flights and hotels. Around half of victims were planning to travel to Africa and a quarter to Asia. The most common fraud tactic was to lure the customer with a cut-price offer that never materialised.

Source: Davies, 2018

The low proportion of bookings achieved by travel agents for domestic holidays owes much to the traditional pattern of booking holidays in the UK. Domestic holidaymakers have tended in the past to contact principals directly, often by writing to resort tourist offices for brochures and details of hotels. Holidays in the UK were neither conveniently packaged nor seen by travel agents as sufficiently remunerative to justify devoting precious rack space to brochures about them, or training staff in domestic product knowledge. Two factors have tended to increase sales through agencies more recently, however.

First, domestic holidays have risen in price in comparison with foreign holidays, so sales of holidays at home can equal or exceed the 'bargain basement' prices now offered overseas. Therefore, holidaymakers wish to be sure that the purchase they make is providing good value and is suitable to their needs. Second, UK holidays are now better packaged by the tour operators, with the larger companies now including domestic holidays in their product portfolios. Combined, these factors provide travel agents with greater opportunity for earning higher returns on conveniently booked packages. Around one-fifth of holidaymakers used a travel agent to book a domestic holiday in 2017 (ABTA, 2018).

Dynamic packaging

The growth of low-cost carriers has encouraged travellers to consider purchasing individual elements of their holiday, allowing greater flexibility in design. Accommodation suppliers and transfer companies have recognised this demand and have ensured their products are now available for independent bookings. Agents have realised this opportunity and are using dynamic packaging to become tailor-made operators for their clients. The Internet, which threatens their livelihoods, also offers the best prospect for their survival, if they adapt.

By accessing the websites of reliable suppliers, putting together a package of components that exactly meets a customer's needs and adding a mark-up, allowing them a reasonable level of profit for the expertise they are delivering, agents are fulfilling a new role. A 2012 survey of Irish travel agents revealed that half made use of a dynamic packaging search engine, with Flexible Trips and Bookabed the most popular. Agents believed that dynamic packaging offered better value to clients and frequently offered better travel agent margins (Steedman, 2012).

Initially, much of the dynamic packaging market focused on short-haul trips, often providing facilities similar to those offered by packages. However, customers are now expecting similar flexibility across all their travel experiences, and this has seen greater demand for dynamic packaging in product areas such as skiing and cruise holidays, where flights, transfers, cruises and shore excursions are packaged to create a tailor-made holiday.

In the UK, ATOL regulations were amended in 2003 so that agents could no longer buy the separate components of an inclusive tour and package them without possession of an ATOL. Agents were faced with the choice of either buying the components from an existing ATOL holder (such as a tour operator's dynamic packaging website) or applying for a mini ATOL to set themselves up as package operators. Consortia often hold an ATOL to cover all members of their group. If flights are not included in the package, an ATOL is not obligatory, but, if bundling other components, the agent must still comply with the conditions of the European Package Travel Regulations. This includes providing clear booking conditions, the service of a representative or 24-hour telephone assistance, and accepting liability for damages, so business insurance is a must.

More recently, changes to the Package Travel Directive 2015 have expanded the definition of a package to include those holidays purchased using dynamic packaging. This has clarified the responsibility of the agent booking the components as well as ensuring liabilities are clear. Flight-Plus arrangers now have obligations to their customers; if a supplier for one element of the trip fails, the travel agent is required to replace that part of the trip (at no extra cost to the customer) or provide a refund for all elements of the trip.

While dynamic packaging has been important in the UK market for some time, the failure of several airlines and travel operators, coupled with events like the Icelandic ash cloud and political unrest in holiday destinations such as Egypt and Greece, led to concerns over financial protection and personal safety. The outcome is that package holidays continue to outsell dynamic packages at a ratio of five to one (Mintel, 2018).

Disintermediation and reintermediation

The growing use of the Internet to purchase travel products direct from the provider has meant that consumers have begun to bypass intermediaries. This removal of travel agents (as well as tour operators in some cases) from the chain of distribution is termed **disintermediation**.

This has caused obvious concern for travel agents, and their response has been to reinforce their role in the chain of distribution by providing customers with an enhanced travel booking experience. Agents have reinforced awareness of their role in providing information, convenient booking and problem-solving in times of crisis.

Many specialist travel organisations (often online) have been established to support customers in purchasing various elements of their travel at their convenience. Such companies allow different elements to be purchased, often providing discounts when more than one element is purchased. The advantage to consumers is that these intermediaries are independent of the suppliers and viewed as unbiased in terms of the range of products they offer. Airlines also value these outlets as a means of unloading surplus stock without degrading the brand. There have been a few great successes in such travel businesses, including Expedia, lastminute.com, travelocity.com and ebookers, which sell, among other things, discounted and late availability travel, mainly airline seats, hotel accommodation and car rental, rather than focusing on package holidays.

The growing inclusion of such businesses within the chain of distribution has been termed **reintermediation**. This century has seen reintermediation grow, as specialist online providers offer customers improved price comparison opportunities as well as greater efficiencies in the time spent booking travel products.

Reforms to the European Package Travel Directive have affected the role of intermediaries in the chain of distribution. A wider definition of packages addressed the specific characteristics of the online retail market, and recognised another growing sales format – termed **linked travel arrangements** – whereby suppliers provide links to multiple products in the sales process (for example, an airline providing a link to accommodation or car hire as part of the flight booking process).

SETTING UP AND RUNNING A TRAVEL AGENCY

THE LEISURE TRAVEL AGENCY

Traditionally, travel agents are located in major city centres, in the suburbs of large towns and, less frequently, in smaller towns. They are often termed **bricks and mortar** or **high street** agents, reflecting the location of their buildings. To be successful, they tend be located close to the centre of main shopping areas. They compete against the other agents, drawing on the market within the local area. In the case of a large city, that area may extend only to the surrounding streets, but, in the case of an important market town, it may draw on residents living within a radius of 30 or 40 miles.

It is also worth noting that agents in city centres attract as their clients not only local residents but also workers employed in the area who may find it more convenient to make their travel arrangements close to their place of work than to do so nearer to their home. It may also be the case, however, that a number of workers in the area will choose to pick up their brochures from the city branch, but make their reservations at an agency near their home, where bookings can be arranged together with their spouse or partner. This may mean a high turnover of brochures with little return for the city agency, a problem particularly common in a major city like London.

As noted earlier, as holiday brochures can be downloaded by customers from the websites of tour operators, there has been a reduction in the printing of brochures as these online browsers will not be calling into a travel agent. In some cases, too, travel agencies themselves may hold only electronic copies of brochures, just printing the required pages for their customers. This has the benefit of reducing the need to stock all brochures, and may mean that customers are not distracted by other products within the brochure, though this shifts the burden of printing costs to the travel agent.

A recent development among specialised agencies is to focus on contacting their clients through websites or recommendation by word of mouth, thus making them less dependent on expensive street-level premises. These agents generally avoid the problem of timewasters – people who pop in to pick up brochures from which they will later book direct online or merely wish to get quotations to compare with those obtained from several other agencies in the area.

Setting up a travel agency requires little capital, although in some countries formal qualifications are a prerequisite. The International Air Transport Association (IATA) also requires that a suitably qualified and experienced staff member is employed if the agency wishes to sell air tickets. As not every staff member has to be suitably qualified when the business is established, however, it is possible to operate with only one or two experienced employees. Consequently, the business appears extremely attractive to outsiders, who see it as a glamorous occupation with wonderful opportunities for cheap travel.

Establish a new business or purchase an existing agency?

Anyone contemplating opening a travel agency will have to consider the merits of buying an existing agency against those of establishing a new one.

There are considerable advantages to taking over an existing agency. To begin with, trading figures for recent years can be examined and the viability of the agency evaluated in relation to the purchase price. An agency that is operating successfully can be expected to retain its loyal clientele, if service remains comparable in the future. Against this, if there is a strong and loyal market already, the price for the agency may be high, to include the goodwill. **Goodwill** embraces the reputation of the business and the expectation that existing customers will continue to buy from there.

Another advantage of buying an existing agency is that licences and **appointments** (agreements with tour operators to sell their products) are generally retained by the new management. Staff, too, can be retained and good, qualified and experienced staff are often not easy to find, especially for those seeking to set up a new agency.

EXAMPLE

Travel agency for sale

There are specialist companies, many of whom advertise online, which sell businesses on behalf of the owner. These companies can offer a wide variety of online and 'bricks-and-mortar' businesses. Here we look at one example to provide an insight into the market for purchasing an established business.

This is the example of 'TA', an independent agency based in the East Midlands. The business consists of one outlet, located in a prime trading position in a busy market town. The premises are leased, with a monthly rent of £950. The business is an ABTA member and operates with a turnover of £2.3 million annually. The sale also includes the client database, which claims to generate 87% repeat custom. The price to purchase this going concern is £395,000.

The attraction of starting from scratch is mainly a financial one: the capital cost will be limited to office furnishings, fixtures, computers, phones and perhaps a new external fascia. Persuading principals to provide you with brochures, offer you appointments and pay commission on sales, however, may prove difficult, especially if the area concerned is already well served by existing agents.

Location, location, location

A popular phrase may be adapted here: 'There are only three things that are important when setting up an agency: location, location, location.' This drives home the fundamental point that, from your customers' point of view, the convenience of the location is the main criterion in their choice of a travel agent, especially if they require little more than a simple holiday booking service offering the best possible price.

Sites need to be researched carefully. Existing pedestrian flows should be noted, as should barriers, whether physical or psychological. For instance, shops close by traffic 'islands' where pedestrians have to use subways to cross the road will find it difficult to attract passing trade. Parking is often difficult in town centres, so if there are too many restrictions and no nearby car parks, this can be a further important disincentive to your customers.

Any agent expecting to attract casual passing trade will need a visible location. If, however, the agent aims to serve clients via the Internet or those seeking a specialist to advise on a complex travel itinerary, then a side street, or even an upper floor office, with low rents or rates, may adequately serve the purpose.

Clients are attracted to roomy shops with plenty of rack space and a bright, cheerful, inviting atmosphere to tempt them in. Increasingly, windows are designed not as settings to display brochures or destination publicity (although, as can be seen in Figure 19.3, some agencies do still take this approach), but as living advertisements for the shop's interior. Good lighting, warm colours, comfortable chairs, desks rather than impersonal counters, all affect clients' perceptions of the agency and their motivation to enter the shop. Once inside, the good agent takes advantage of the opportunity to make a sale, but enticing clients through the door is the first step in selling.

FIGURE 19.3 Window display promoting UK and European holidays suited to a variety of markets

Photo: Claire Humphreys

EXAMPLE

Shop design

Customers may be tempted by the special offers promoted in the storefront, but, unless the atmosphere and the service live up to their expectations, they are unlikely to buy. Current thinking is that a comfortable environment will help to build a relationship with the customer, and it is the trust developed by this relationship which converts the sale.

(Continued)

To improve the shop environment, some agencies have included coffee facilities, provided wireless Internet and included sofas and armchairs to encourage a longer dwell time – especially important if the shop is busy.

Historically, customers sat across a desk from the agent, who faced a terminal screen, hiding the 'secrets' of the travel industry. Now it is more likely that the screens are visible to the customer, making it easier for the agent to explain details; it is possible today to find that the desk has been replaced by a small table surrounded by comfortable chairs. Finally, it is equally important to get the heating, ventilation and lighting right.

Operations

In the past, agents earned their revenue largely in the form of commissions on sales. Levels of commission have varied over time and according to the travel product sold, but typically have been highest for package tour sales (between 10 and 15%), with transportation companies paying slightly lower rates and other services even less. This pattern has changed radically within the past few years, as principals have sought to remain profitable by cutting costs and finding cheaper means of distributing their products.

Many airlines have changed their payment structure to agents, often withdrawing commission entirely, forcing the agents to charge a service fee to their customers for the sale of tickets. This has been a noted practice of the low-cost carriers, led by Ryanair, whose bookings are made almost entirely via the Internet, but this soon became the practice of many more traditional international carriers, too. In September 2007, Qatar Airlines announced that it would eliminate commission payments (this was 9% in 2004). This followed an announcement by its rival, Emirates, which chose to reduce its commission payments to 5%. Some airlines pay a fixed-level fee according to the class of ticket purchased (paying higher fees for business or first-class tickets). KLM moved from paying 7% commission to a fixed fee in January 2001, while Lufthansa moved to a service fee in January 2002. BA (now taking over half its bookings via the Internet) has moved in a similar direction, not only reducing commission, but also withdrawing ticketing and GDS privileges for agents achieving less than £50,000 worth of sales. To put this in context, in 2015 American travel agencies earned, on average, 1.36% in commission on airline sales.

The nature of the local market significantly affects commission structures, however. For example, in India, the use of travel agents is high, so the decision to reduce commission in India was only announced in the summer of 2008, although neither SpiceJet nor GoAir, both low-cost airlines, had paid commission in recent years. In 2006, Kingfisher bucked the trend and announced that it would double the commission it paid (to 10%), recognising that it sold 60% of its tickets through travel agents in India. In the summer of 2008, however, it too announced a plan to bring in zero commission, after its competitor Air India implemented such a policy. By 2010, most travel agents were earning little or no commission and, as a response, they now charge transaction fees, varied according to the type of airline ticket purchased.

Among tour operators, Thomson led the way in reducing the basic rates of commission paid to its agents and introducing a complex reward system for greater sales effort, including directional selling. However, there appears to be a general move towards increasing commission levels again to encourage loyalty from agents. Those principals that do pay commission will generally offer higher levels to agents that are members of consortia: that is, they have banded together to achieve agreed sales targets in order to compete with the multiples. This can add 2.5% or more to the earnings of the agent, particularly for the sale of package tours. It is still rare, though, to find an agent averaging earnings of more than 10–11% on the total revenue achieved during the year.

EXAMPLE

It's not just commission that is important

The reality is that many travel agents earn their money through commission and therefore their turnover will be affected by total sales and which companies' holidays they sell.

However, where commission is not available some travel agencies will charge a service fee to the client. This is particularly common in the USA and may take the form of a one-time payment, for example £25, to book an economy-class airline ticket. Alternatively, an advisor fee – much like a lawyer would charge for their professional advice – may be charged, with a fee of $100–$250 per booking not uncommon. This move from transaction fees to consultancy fees has become more widespread among American agents. Still, in the USA travel agents make almost four-fifths of their revenue from commission, with one-fifth coming from service fees (*Travel Weekly*, 2017).

Agents at first resisted changes to the commission structure, arguing that their customers would be angered by attempts to charge a transaction fee and would therefore be more likely to book direct with the airlines.

Evidence from the USA tends to support the agents in their view that service charges have been difficult to impose. Commissions were capped by the airlines there in the mid-1990s, but the public initially resisted attempts to impose fees, turning instead to booking on the Internet. In 1995, 70% of all airline tickets issued in the USA were sold through agents, but this had dropped to just 30% a decade later. About four-fifths of US agents now charge transaction fees, payable even if no booking is made, but almost half will discount the charge when a booking is made.

EXAMPLE

Commission on cruises

Cruise companies often pay additional levels of commission when supplementary services or product upgrades are sold by agents.

For example, MSC Cruises announced it would pay 5% commissions on pre-paid cruise activities such as on-board spa treatments or the use of climbing walls or surf machines. This is in addition to the commission it pays on shore excursions. It also offered a massive 25% commission on the sale of higher-grade balcony cabins. Similarly, Royal Caribbean offered a $250 bonus commission for bookings for the higher-grade suites on its two largest ships, *Oasis* and *Allure of the Seas*.

In some cases, commissions are used to develop specific products or markets. For example, Cruise Norway has offered an additional 3% commission on Hurtigruten cruises to its Indian travel agency partners, through a dedicated booking portal. The bonus commission is designed to expand Cruise Norway operations in the major cities of India.

Sources: Steighorst, 2014a, b; Travel Talk, 2014

In the UK, package tours represent by far the largest proportion of all agents' sales, although an increasing proportion of these involve some tailor-made elements. Typically, overseas holidays account for the majority of those sales, with air transport a declining element. Domestic holidays, a growing area of potential sales, have been estimated to take up to 4%, while the remainder is divided between cruises, rail and coach bookings and miscellaneous services. Tailor-made packages, or dynamic packaging, are steadily eroding the traditional tour operator-based package tour product for many agencies.

THE BUSINESS TRAVEL AGENCY

Those agents located close to city centres or other centres of business and industry, such as an industrial estate, may also try to capture the business travellers within their territory. This is a highly specialised market, however, for which staff must have greater skills and will be competing against the large business travel corporations that have contacts with suppliers, allowing them greater flexibility in negotiating prices.

Any commission earned from suppliers may have to be split with business clients, as part of the contract to act as the travel agency for the company. It is increasingly common for business travel agents to negotiate discounted travel with the principal (receiving no commission), then pass on those improved rates to the company they serve, but charge a management fee for the service.

There are a number of approaches that these travel management companies (TMCs) use in fee-based contracts, the most common being:

- a flat fee, usually payable per month, based on predicted levels of business
- rebate of any commission paid to the agency, the agency charging a fixed amount per transaction
- a simple fee per ticket set-up
- variable fees charged according to the complexity of the transaction
- a minimum fee charged per transaction with the guarantee of there being a minimum number of transactions per month.

It is also common to find contracts drawn up based on fees that depend on the agency achieving a certain level of cost savings for the company. Agreements will also generally include extended credit terms, whereby accounts do not have to be settled until 10–12 weeks after the receipt of tickets. One drawback of a system in which commission is fully rebated to the client is that the supplier, such as a hotel, gains no sales benefit from increasing its commission rates to its distributors, so must look for other strategies to gain the agency's support.

Management issues

Businesses are extremely demanding customers. The level of service that agencies must offer to retain their patronage is considerable. Focusing on the business community requires not only additional skills and knowledge, but also a willingness to provide extended hours of service (for the convenience of the businesses) and a level of service far beyond what would be expected of counter staff in a leisure agency. Documentation such as visas may have to be arranged for clients, often at short notice, then delivered to the customer, possibly out of normal business hours. Senior staff must be accessible at any time to arrange last-minute travel. Professional business travel staff will expect to be paid well above the rates paid to counter staff in leisure agencies, yet the margins may be slimmer. The additional costs of handling these arrangements must be considered by the agent, particularly where credit is offered to businesses. It is not unusual for companies to delay payments until well beyond the dates they were due, while the agent is still obliged to make payments to principals on time. Thus, the agency is helping to fund those companies' cash flow at its own expense.

All of this makes business travel a difficult field for an independent operator to enter, regardless of the level of personal service it is willing to offer. The financial attraction of the larger business accounts, which often exceed a million pounds a year, nevertheless results in many agents competing for the business by offering extra levels of service, fares expertise to guarantee lowest prices, and implant offices.

Implant offices are those based in the business client's own premises but staffed by the agency, specifically to handle the company's travel needs exclusively. To justify this, the company must be certain that the revenue generated will be sufficient to cover the high costs of setting up and operating such an additional branch.

As the highest discounts can be offered by agents negotiating the best deals with their principals, this has once again led to the multiple branch agencies dominating the business travel agency market: American Express, Carlson Wagonlit, BCD, Hogg Robinson, FCm and Omega World Travel. Furthermore, some business travel agents are also members of international consortia (for example, Advantage Business Travel), which offer them even greater influence and purchasing power with the principals. With the global buying power of such groups, airline and other tickets can be purchased at the lowest possible price for business house clients.

EXAMPLE

HRG

The Hogg Robinson Group (HRG) has 70 years of corporate travel expertise. The company provides a comprehensive range of corporate travel services, including:

- corporate travel management – travel planning and booking, including ground transport, air, hotel and car hire
- expense management – assisting corporate clients with managing their travel budgets
- travel management services for sports events and sports teams
- meetings and events management, including sourcing venues, and delegate and programme management
- crisis management services that include people-tracking.

Its global network employs 14,000 people and operates in 120 counties across Europe, North America and Asia. It has regional service centres and also provides support through implant offices at client premises.

HRG may charge transaction fees, service fees based on the services required (usually through the regional service centres) or management fees, which are common in cases where implant offices exist.

In 2018, an agreed takeover of HRG resulted in the company becoming a wholly owned subsidiary of American Express Global Business Travel.

The Guild of Travel Management Companies, established in 1967, is the professional body representing the leading business travel agents in the UK and accounts for some 80% of all managed business travel sold in the UK. The Guild's role is to represent the interests of business agents and their clients and improve the standards and quality of travel for its members through negotiation with suppliers such as airlines, airports and hotel chains. With its encouragement, associations have been established in Germany, Ireland, Italy, the Netherlands, Portugal and Spain, and these groups work together as the Guild of European Business Travel Agents.

Large companies often employ specialist travel managers, who act as buyers of travel products for their employees and liaise between the employees and the travel agency. Purchases arranged centrally allow the company to manage travel arrangements (perhaps to adhere to company travel policies) and use the specialist knowledge of the travel manager to gain better prices. These managers have their own professional body in the UK, the Institute of Travel and Meetings (formerly the Institute of Travel Management (ITM)). This organisation seeks to use its influence to obtain better deals for its members, while acting as a mouthpiece and watchdog for this section of the industry.

The Global Business Travel Association (GBTA) is an international trade association for this sector, based in the USA and operating regional chapters in Africa, Asia, Europe, Latin America and North America. Its 9000 members control more than $345 billion of business travel and meetings expenditure. The organisation provides industry training, advocacy, and lobbying, research and networking opportunities.

Some large corporations have gone a stage further. Recognising that they have the buying power to organise their own travel arrangements without the intercession of a travel agent, they will negotiate direct with airlines for their tickets and discount agreements, cutting out intermediaries entirely. Once again, online suppliers and agencies are making it easier for the customer to benefit by going direct.

TRAVEL AGENCY SKILLS AND COMPETENCES

Due to the extremely competitive nature of the retail travel business, two factors become important if the agency is to succeed: good management and good service. Good management will ensure that costs are kept under control, members of staff are motivated and the agency goes out actively to seek customers rather than wait for them to come through the door. Good service will ensure satisfied clients, help to build a loyal clientele and encourage word-of-mouth recommendation, which will increase the local share of the market for the agency.

Despite the expansion of the large multiples, most independent travel agents are still small businesses, in which the owner acts as manager and employs two or three members of staff. In such an agency, there is little specialisation in terms of the usual division of labour, and staff will be expected to cope with all the activities normally associated with the booking of travel, which will include:

- advising potential travellers about resorts, carriers, travel companies and travel facilities worldwide
- making reservations for all travel requirements
- planning itineraries of all kinds, including complex, multi-stopover independent tours
- accessing relevant supplier and destination websites
- issuing documentation, including travel tickets and vouchers

- communicating by telephone, e-mail and letter with travel principals, tour operators and customers
- maintaining accurate files on reservations
- maintaining and displaying stocks of travel brochures
- mediating and negotiating with suppliers in the event of customer complaints.

It is ironic that the travel product requires perhaps greater knowledge on the part of retail staff than does virtually any other product, yet in many countries travel agents' salaries still lag behind those of others in the retail industry. This makes it particularly hard for agency managers to attract and retain skilled staff. Agents argue that competition and discounted prices make it impossible to pay higher salaries, although the opportunity for free or discounted travel does provide an additional employee benefit. Principals have come to accept that their retailers cannot be expected to have detailed knowledge of every product, and concentrate instead on providing agents with easier access to information through websites, reservation systems and brochures.

In addition to product knowledge, therefore, the main skills that counter staff require are the ability to read timetables and other data sources, source 'best buy' airline fares, complete tickets and have sufficient knowledge of their customers to be able to match their needs with the products available. All staff today are also required to be familiar with the latest technology, including accessing online travel portals and CRSs of all types.

The ticketing function is largely undertaken via computer and, arguably, fare quotations and ticketing skills are becoming less important for most agency staff, apart from those dealing with business travel. An understanding of the principles underlying the construction of fares, however, can be helpful. For example, it allows staff to explain complex fares to customers; and, of course, there will be a continuing need for fare experts in the industry.

EXAMPLE

Fares expertise

Constructing fares is a complex subject and entails a lengthy period of training, coupled with continuous exercise of these skills. A number of internationally recognised courses are available to provide these skills, to meet IATA requirements, and can be taken up to the Fares and Ticketing Part II level, indicating full competence in meeting any requirement for fare construction and ticketing.

In some cases, large travel agency chains have centralised the fare calculation role so that a handful of experts can quickly determine the lowest prices for a particular journey by air when requested by a member of their counter staff. For most air fares, however, agents are now dependent on quotations given by carriers or intermediaries via the CRS and websites.

In addition to the counter staff functions, agency managers (who frequently spend time at the counter themselves) are required to fulfil a number of administrative functions. On the financial side, these will include:

- maintenance and control of the agency's accounts
- invoicing clients
- effecting bank reconciliations (matching payments made and received on the bank statement with those in the customer and supplier accounts records)
- preparing and controlling budgets
- providing an estimate of the cash flow in the company on a month-by-month basis
- controlling expenditure.

Sales records must be kept and sales returns completed regularly for travel principals. All these back-office jobs are often computerised, even in the case of small, independent agencies.

Managers are also responsible for safeguarding access to their booking systems, promoting their business and recruiting, training and supervising office staff. Managers will try to ensure that staff are motivated: in general, to provide good customer service and, specifically, to achieve particular sales targets or goals. Managers will often use educational study or familiarisation (fam) trips and training programmes as well as commission bonuses to enhance staff knowledge and motivation. Trips are usually provided by tour operators or destination marketing organisations (DMOs) in order to enhance the product awareness of travel agents, and thus increase sales. There is now much greater emphasis on the educational element of such trips, rather than these being free holidays with little opportunity to develop product knowledge.

Finally, managers need to control and regularly update their websites and oversee the preparation and distribution of e-newsletters to clients. Regular contact with clients via the Internet or by post is now essential if business is to be retained and clients discouraged from booking direct on the Web.

Customer contact skills

The way in which staff communicate with clients is, together with the essential product knowledge they display, a key ingredient in an agency's success. These communication skills can be divided into three distinct categories:

- language skills
- personal and social skills
- sales skills.

Written communications with clients that demonstrate poor sentence construction, grammar or spelling reflect not just on the employee but also on the company itself. When such correspondence goes out under the signature of a senior member of staff, the image of the company suffers a still more serious blow.

Personal and social skills are also very important. Serving the public should not be confused with servility (being a servant). The key is ensuring that customers are served effectively and with respect. Customers expect to be received warmly, with a genuine smile or greeting. Staff are expected to be unfailingly calm and cheerful, whatever stress they may be experiencing during their working day. These qualities need to become second nature to counter staff.

EXAMPLE

First impressions

First impressions weigh heavily and staff are judged by their dress and appearance. Employers often insist on neat hairstyles, suitably discreet makeup for female staff and high overall standards of grooming and appearance, often to the extent that counter staff in the agency chains will be required to wear a uniform. Personal hygiene is, of course, essential.

The way employees sit, stand or walk says a great deal about them and their attitude towards their customers. Staff who meet face-to-face with customers will be expected to look alert and interested, avoid slouching when they walk and sit upright rather than slump in their chairs. These non-verbal signals all say a lot about the attitude of the company to its customers.

Studies reveal that first impressions are created in under 30 seconds and, while not irreversible, can assist the sales process, if positive. Tips to making a great first impression include: be yourself, look sharp, smell great and smile.

Attentiveness to the customer is not only polite, it ensures that vital client needs are recognised, enabling the employee to match needs with products. When talking to customers and greeting them, the employee should maintain eye contact and a manner that will breed confidence in the agency and its staff's product knowledge. Even handshakes are important cues to confidence – they should be firm and offered willingly. Use of the client's name enhances the relationship.

How staff answer the telephone can help to generate the right image of the company. The telephone should be answered quickly and competently. As there are no dress and appearance cues that enable the client to make a judgement, the voice becomes the sole factor. Trainers emphasise the need to smile, even when on the telephone, as an impression of friendliness can still be conveyed in the voice. If clients are asked to hold, they should be given the reason and regularly checked to ensure that they are still holding. If employees cannot give an answer immediately to a problem, they should offer to call the client back with the answer in a short while and then ensure that they do so. Failure to call back is one of the commonest sources of frustration for clients and can easily lead to the loss of their business to a competitor.

E-mail has become a significant mode of communication with customers. Research suggests that, as a booking tool, an e-mail takes 30% less staff time than the telephone, but it is vital that e-mails are dealt with promptly and accurately to ensure that customers feel they are receiving a high quality of service.

EXAMPLE

It's a mystery

For many years, the UK travel trade magazines have operated a mystery shopper programme, reporting the results in their publications.

(Continued)

Historically, *Travel Trade Gazette* (TTG) would compare different high street agents in the same locality. Now, however, it tests online agents alongside high street ones. TTG assesses the staff on four criteria: first impressions, sales process, product and budget match, and incentive and extras offered to encourage booking.

Travel Weekly uses a similar approach, scoring agency appearance (15%), brochure racking (10%), product knowledge (25%), sales technique (25%) and staff attitude (25%). It currently focuses on visiting high street agents and ensures both independent and tour operator-owned agencies are examined.

Both magazines assert that these mystery shopper exercises are not designed to cause detriment to businesses receiving a low score; rather, they are designed to encourage improvements in service quality and to give recognition to high performers.

Good customer contact is deemed so important that many of the multiples use mystery shoppers to monitor the experience provided to customers. In such cases, mystery shoppers will telephone or visit the shop to make travel arrangements. After the visit, they will report back to management regarding the quality of the service they received. This technique can be used to identify weak points in service delivery and encourage staff to maintain or improve service levels by linking assessment to bonuses. It can also be used to evaluate the services of competitors, too, and establish comparison benchmarks.

The sales sequence

Good social skills and high-quality customer service can build an atmosphere that encourages buying, but closing a sale requires an understanding of the techniques involved. Effective selling is the outcome of four stages in the selling process, which together make up the sales sequence:

- establishing **rapport** with clients
- **investigating** clients' needs
- **presenting** the product to clients
- getting clients to take action by **committing** themselves to the purchase
- follow-up with **after-sales service**.

Below, each of these stages is examined in more detail.

Rapport

To sell products successfully, one must first match them to customers' needs. If a client buys a product that does not provide the satisfaction they were looking for, they simply will not come back again. As no travel agency can survive without a high level of repeat business, achieving one-time sales is clearly not enough; customers must be satisfied in the longer term.

To achieve this, the first step is to build **rapport** (a trusting relationship), by engaging clients in conversation, gaining their trust and learning about their needs. This process also allows the salesperson to judge how receptive clients are to new ideas and how willing they are to have products sold to them. Some customers prefer to self-select, so should not be badgered into a sale, while others need and seek advice more openly.

To generate a two-way conversation, the opening phrase 'Can I help you?' has to be avoided – it simply invites the reply, 'No thanks, I'm just looking'. A more useful way of opening a conversation would be to use a phrase such as 'Do you have a particular type of holiday in mind?' or, to a customer who has just picked up a brochure, 'Were you just looking for sun, sea and sand holidays or had you something more adventurous in mind?'. This forces a reply, and encourages the client to open a conversation.

Investigation

Once you have gained clients' trust, the next step is to **investigate** their needs more thoroughly. Once again, it is necessary to ask open questions that elicit full answers rather than a simple 'yes' or 'no'. The sort of information needed to draw out the client will include:

- who is travelling and the number in the group
- when they wish to travel and how long they want to stay at a destination
- their preferred mode of travel
- their choice of destination
- what they expect to pay.

The last is one of the hardest for junior staff. It requires good judgement to know whether the cost of the holiday is critical and, if so, what the limits might be. If customers mention a figure, one should not take it for granted that this is the maximum they are willing to pay. The industry has encouraged holidaymakers to believe that holidays are invariably cheap, but one is doing clients a disservice not to point out that cheapness is not necessarily value for money and, by paying a little more, one might have a better guarantee of satisfaction. The good salesperson is one who can encourage clients to consider products at a higher price while reassuring them that their best interests are being considered. It is generally better to wait for clients to give an indication of their budget than to question them directly on this point.

Clients may have only the vaguest idea about where they want to go, what they want to do, even what they expect to pay. Needs must never be assumed, even when there is a clear statement of intent. For example, clients who say that they do not want to go on a package holiday may merely be revealing a deep-seated prejudice that such holidays are downmarket. Alternatively, they may have had a bad experience of earlier such holidays. The salesperson's task is to tease out the real reason so that the appropriate product can be offered. For example, a tailor-made, independent inclusive tour may offer the best solution, as the client would not be part of a crowd.

Sometimes it will be clear to the salesperson that the client has superior knowledge about the destination or is seeking information about a little-known destination. In these conditions, it is preferable to admit ignorance and either offer an introduction to another member of staff with better knowledge of the destination or offer to obtain more information for them.

Presentation

Once the salesperson is satisfied that they know exactly what the client needs, they may go on to the next stage – **presenting** the products that they feel will suit the client. The aim will be to present not only the features of the holiday being offered, but also the benefits.

It has more recently been suggested that the presentation is about telling the customer the story about the product and how it is suited to them. It is not about a 'hard-sell' but about buying into the life of the customer and placing them at the centre of the holiday search. Thus, the customer can feel that purchasing a holiday is a positive experience, rather than merely a transaction.

Product knowledge is, of course, critical for success in gaining clients' confidence to the point where they will be willing to accept the salesperson's recommendations. Even if they feel that what they are offering is exactly suitable for their client, it is always a good idea to offer an alternative, so that the client has the opportunity to choose. If the salesperson then demonstrates just how one holiday is a better buy than the other, this will make it easier for the client to understand the options being recommended.

At this stage in the sales sequence, the salesperson will often have to handle objections. Sometimes, objections are voiced only because the client needs reassurance or they have not yet fully understood the benefits being offered to them. At other times, objections occur because not all the client's needs have yet been met and then a process of patient questioning may be needed once again to draw out the possibly hidden motives for these objections.

Commitment

This final stage closes the sale. This means getting clients to take action – ideally, to buy, but some clients will need more time to consider the offer. The aim of the salesperson is to get the best possible outcome from the sales sequence: taking an option (placing the required product on hold for the customer), getting the client to call back later or getting them to agree that the salesperson may call them later to follow up the sale.

The good salesperson is always looking for the buying signals that reveal clients are ready to buy: 'Would you like me to see if I can get you a reservation for that date?' can prompt clients who are dithering about taking action. Care must be taken, however. Never push clients into a sale before they are ready to buy or they may be lost forever.

In some cases, offering extras, such as access to an airport lounge, may be enough to encourage purchase. Here again, knowing the customer, and the things they prize, can help to ensure the right extras are offered. For example, there is little benefit in offering an upgrade to a larger hire car if the customer plans to spend little time driving.

After-sales service

Finally, having received the deposit for a firm booking, the salesperson must remember that the sales job is not yet finished. Different countries place various legal obligations on travel agents, so it may be necessary to provide customers with detailed information on visas or other terms and conditions of the booking (such as rights with regard to cancellation). Even after the booking has been confirmed, the tour operator or principal may make changes (such as altering flight times) and customers will need to be notified of these by the agent. In some cases, flights may be cancelled and alternative arrangements will need to be discussed and agreed with the travellers. Clients may also want to make changes to bookings and will expect the salesperson to provide advice and make the arrangements accordingly.

It is beneficial for agencies to try to gain the loyalty of customers, so the salesperson must continue to show interest and concern for clients, helping to reinforce the sale and their commitment to return to make future travel arrangements. The medium of e-mail is invaluable for keeping in touch with clients to assist this.

Training and qualifications

Formal training qualifications for the industry are both diverse and confusing. Not all courses that have been introduced are universally welcomed or understood by the industry. Some national associations provide professional development training, which can help to maintain quality within the industry as well as enhancing the career opportunities of their members.

In the USA, ASTA operates sales courses, consultancy fees education and the popular Travel Agent's Management Toolkit (the successor to its Model Agency Program training), which encourages agency managers to evaluate their business operations and improve their services. ASTA also offers specialist training, to enhance destination or niche market knowledge.

The Australian Federation of Travel Agents (AFTA) offers certificated courses to develop the knowledge and skills of those entering the industry, as well as continuous professional development through a skills accreditation initiative – the Australian Travel Professionals Program.

In the UK, ABTA has supported professional qualifications and lifelong learning in the travel industry and established the Accredited Travel Professional (ATP) scheme. This scheme was developed to allow agents to gain recognition for the qualifications and training programmes they attend throughout their years of employment. ABTA encourages continuous professional development and provides online training resources to support knowledge and skills development within the industry.

EXAMPLE

ABTA training and education

ABTA members have access to specialist training materials that improve skills, such as sales techniques and destination knowledge. ABTA also provides access to educational materials that are designed to expand knowledge of all travel industry professionals. This has included:

- a Webinar on the future of the ATOL scheme
- a video explaining reform proposals of the Package Travel Directive
- online training on Accessible Travel
- online training on Making Travel Greener
- a training DVD on travel safety (including fire, food hygiene and the protection of children).

Some of these resources are produced in collaboration with industry partners, such as training companies and national tourist boards.

TRAVEL AGENCY APPOINTMENTS

Most principals license the sale of their services through a process of contractual agreements with travel agencies, which, as noted earlier, are called **appointments**. In effect, these are a licence to trade and receive commission for sales achieved. Some principals dispense with this formality. Hotels, for example, will normally pay commission on any sales made through a reputable travel agency without any formal agreement. In addition, agents may join trade associations to gain formal national recognition as travel agents.

DEALING WITH PRINCIPALS

Most contracts with principals are non-exclusive: that is, they do not prevent an agent from dealing with the principal's competitors. Occasionally, however, a contract may offer an agency the exclusive right to sell a product, and may furthermore restrict an agent's ability to deal with other, directly competing companies.

Unless expressly stated in a contract, agents do not have the automatic right to deduct their commission from the monies due to principals. If bonus commissions are paid for targets achieved, it is generally the case that these sums of money are paid to agents at the end of the season, rather than immediately following the achievement of a target. These facts must be kept in mind by agents when estimating their business cash flow.

A licence is required if commission is to be paid on the sale of services of members of IATA (apart from sales of purely domestic tickets). Thus, it is important for travel agents who wish to offer a full range of services either to hold the necessary IATA appointment or to have an arrangement with another agency that does so, that agent issuing tickets on their behalf.

There are around 60,000 IATA-accredited agencies worldwide. IATA's Agency Distribution Office deals with applications for licences, a process that can take up to 45 days. The cost of application is in the region of £1000 for a new travel agency (slightly less if the application is to add a new branch to an existing agency). An explanation of the application process for each country is available on the IATA website (www.iata.org/services/accreditation/accreditation-travel/Pages/application.aspx). If approved, a bond is taken out to cover the agency's anticipated monthly IATA turnover.

Approval is also required for making commissionable sales on the services of railways, coach tickets, domestic airline services and other principals, such as shipping and car hire firms. Obtaining approval for most of these has been largely a formality for agents holding ABTA and IATA appointments. Appointments to sell travel insurance, however, involve closer scrutiny as the agent will be acting as a broker for the insurance service concerned. Insurance companies have generally tightened up on standards for their brokers, including those retailers operating in the travel industry.

MEMBERSHIP OF TRADE BODIES

In the UK, there are no legal requirements to meet when setting up as a travel agent, but in some countries, including many of those within the EU, governments do exercise licensing control over agencies (see Table 19.3). Occasionally, licensing is carried out by the government but more commonly any licensing is managed by national associations, set up to promote the interests of their members, which establish standards of practice to protect customers and the industry, as well as lobbying government on policy affecting travel agents and their customers.

TABLE 19.3 Travel agency licensing requirements

Country	Regulation
Association of Croatian Travel Agencies (UHPA)	Must register and obtain an identification code
Association of Danish Travel Agents and Tour Operators	Must register with Travel Guarantee Fund if selling packages
Association of Finnish Travel Agents	Required to register with Consumer Agency and protect against financial insolvency
Association of Turkish Travel Agencies (TURSAB)	Must register with TURSAB
Federation of Associations of Travel & Tourism Agents, Malta	Required to hold a licence issued by the Malta Tourism Authority
Swiss Federation of Travel Agencies	No licence is required but customer payments must be protected
Travel Agents' Association New Zealand	No licence, but must have a financial bond

Source: C. Humphreys, correspondence with membership managers of travel agents' associations, 2011

EXAMPLE

The role of trade associations: the case of the Association of British Travel Agents (ABTA)

Until 1993, any travel agent wishing to sell the products of an ABTA tour operator had to be a member of ABTA. In turn, ABTA tour operators could only sell their services through ABTA retailers. This reciprocal agreement, known as Stabiliser, was technically a constraint on trade and, as such, was challenged by the Office of Fair Trading. The Restrictive Practices Court upheld the agreement in 1982, however, after an appeal by ABTA, on the grounds that it was in the public interest, as ABTA's in-house scheme of protection for consumers against the collapse of a member company was recognised as one of the best in the world. A Common Fund, provided out of membership subscriptions, allowed clients of a travel agency to continue with their holiday even if the travel agency they had booked with went into liquidation before the tour operator received payment for the tour. This complemented the protection offered by ABTA against the collapse of a tour operator. Many earlier conditions imposed on members by ABTA, however, such as a prohibition on discounting and the sale of non-travel products ('mixed selling'), were overturned by the Restrictive Practices Court.

In 2000, ABTA also removed the distinction between tour operator and retail agent membership, absorbing members into a single class. In July 2008, ABTA merged with the Federation of Tour Operators (FTO) to enhance its ability to support its members across the industry.

Members must satisfy ABTA on their financial standing and qualifications. ABTA also requires its members to have at least one member of its customer-facing staff with a minimum of two years' experience (reduced by six months for staff holding formal qualifications).

(Continued)

The abolition of the Stabiliser agreement and the introduction of the EU's Package Travel Directive led to much greater freedom for agents to operate outside of ABTA membership, however, and so it lost many of its controlling functions. Agents became free to trade with ABTA and non-ABTA tour operators and are now subject only to legal requirements to carry satisfactory bonds against financial collapse. These changes did not lead to the wholesale withdrawal of members from ABTA.

ABTA represents the interests of both tour operators and travel agents. Given the potential conflicts of interest between these two groups, and other conflicts that can arise between the multiples and the independent agencies, the continuing support for ABTA within the trade may seem surprising, but the importance of having a strong body to represent trade interests in consultations with government and other industry bodies and the organisation's role as a mouthpiece for the industry have ensured its survival.

Customer recognition of the financial protection afforded to ABTA members is extensive and retailers benefit from this brand recognition. Retailers also benefit from the clearing house that processes payments to tour operators.

Bonding

The introduction of the European Package Travel Directive meant that member states were required to incorporate financial protection within their legislation on travel operations. It should be noted that bonding is also often a requirement of operating as a travel agent in many non-European countries. It may be undertaken in one of three ways:

1. A sum of money equal to the value of the bond can be placed in a trust account. The agent can benefit from the interest accruing on the account, but cannot touch the capital itself. As this could involve putting up a substantial amount of money, it is rarely chosen except by the largest corporations.
2. The agent can obtain an insurance policy for the amount required, paying an annual premium.
3. The agent has the bank put up the bond, against either company assets or, more commonly, the personal guarantees of the directors. A fee is charged that is substantially less than the premium paid for an insurance policy, but the directors become personally liable for the amount of the bond in the event of the company's failure.

THE IMPACT OF COMPUTER TECHNOLOGY

As we saw earlier, the industry has been profoundly affected by developments in technology over the past decade, particularly computers. As innovations in this field are constantly being launched or improved, information about this sphere of travel activity tends to date very quickly, so there will be little benefit to be gained from examining the detailed merits of any existing system here, but this section of the chapter will provide an overview of the topic.

Computer systems in travel agencies are designed to offer three distinct facilities:

- front-office 'client relations' systems, enabling staff to access principals' CRSs/GDSs and websites, check availability and make reservations

- back-office systems, enabling documents such as invoices, vouchers, tickets and itineraries to be issued and accounts to be processed with principals
- management systems, producing updated figures on the company's performance to assist managers in guiding and controlling operations.

Systems have now been developed that will provide all three facilities for even the smallest independent agent, at prices that continue to fall. Alternatively, equipment can be leased to reduce capital investment and spread costs.

With regard to front-office sales and reservation activities, it is now mandatory to use computers rather than the telephone to make bookings with the leading tour operators and many principals. The retail travel sector is ideally suited to benefit from the use of computer technology. The products sold cannot be inspected directly before purchase, but may be viewed with the use of brochures or digitally; sales outlets require systems for determining the availability of transport and accommodation, and the ability to make immediate reservations, amendments or cancellations; complex fares and conditions of travel must be accessed in order to provide customers with accurate and current quotes.

Back-office functions can be greatly assisted by computer technology. It can produce travel documents such as tickets, invoices, vouchers and itineraries, all which can now be processed efficiently and, when needed, quite rapidly (many providers are moving towards automated systems to provide computer-generated e-tickets, which can further enhance this process).

The travel agent also needs to process an ever-increasing amount of accounting and management information quickly and computers are invaluable for this. Computers can also assist with processing customer payments, chasing customers for the balance on their travel account, as well as managing supplier accounts. Storing customer details using database technology means they can easily be used to support marketing activities such as mailshots. It is common now to e-mail newsletters and special offers to customer e-mail addresses, to maintain contact and stimulate a purchase. More general office administration, such as personnel and payroll functions, can also be performed easily using dedicated software. In addition, business performance data can be retrieved to quickly assess areas such as sales levels and profit margins.

EXAMPLE

Data protection (GPDR)

In the spring of 2018, a European Union regulation designed to protect the privacy of its citizens came into law. The General Data Protection Regulation (GPDR) requires holders of data to ensure protection of the information collected. Consent from the individual for the data to be held and used is now explicitly required.

The law also made it easier for the individual citizen to request access to the data held about them, as well as require its erasure (termed the 'Right to be Forgotten').

GLOBAL DISTRIBUTION SYSTEMS (GDS)

In considering systems that are designed to access travel principals' reservations systems, one can distinguish between those developed by airlines and those developed by tour operators.

The airlines' travel reservation systems must be capable of booking seats on a large number of different airlines to allow maximum flexibility regarding route options (to allow a variety of origin and destination options to be available to customers). Agents currently achieve this principally by using one of the four major global distribution systems: Galileo, Amadeus, Sabre or Worldspan. In 2007, Galileo merged with Worldspan, moving Galileo data operations to the Worldspan site in Atlanta but continuing to operate both systems. In recent years, there has been an effort to increase the range of products available through such systems, including, as we mentioned earlier in this chapter, low-cost airlines such as Ryanair, and this may further increase the use of GDS by travel agents.

American Airlines has rocked this approach, placing pressure on agents to connect directly to the American Airlines system rather than via GDS. The airline sees this as a key way of reducing distribution costs, but this was not without industry recriminations (and lawsuits in US courts), with American Airlines battling with Travelport (owner of Galileo and Worldspan), Orbitz and Expedia, supported by GDS provider Sabre. Advances in technological capabilities which make a direct connection to the airline feasible and concentration of sales through a few large online travel agency websites have combined to reduce the benefit of a wider distribution network.

TOUR OPERATORS' RESERVATION SYSTEMS

Systems to reserve products from the major tour operators are likewise accessed live on the computer. In the past, this was done through a direct connection to the system using a specially designed terminal system known as Viewdata. More recently, however, many tour operators (as well as principals) have moved their operations to Internet-based systems, often incorporating specially designed reservations systems, such as the 'Genie' system developed for TUI to replace Viewdata.

TECHNOLOGY PROVIDING NEW RETAILING SYSTEMS

Although connections between suppliers and agents are being made simpler, there is still the need to provide travel agents with computer training to operate the many different systems used by suppliers (such training may be provided by the supplier). Many of those agents who have embraced technology wholeheartedly have also recognised the advantage of becoming online retailers. Such agencies are adapting new technology to reach their clients online through the Web. The largest **online travel agencies** (OTAs) are Expedia and Priceline, both of which achieve in excess of $55 billion in sales annually. Leading Asia Pacific companies are the Chinese-based Ctrip and Indian-based MakeMyTrip, both much smaller with sales under $1 billion, but markets in these countries are experiencing annual growth rates of up to 13% (Euromonitor, 2018a, b) and the value of sales through travel intermediaries in the Asia-Pacific region is expected to double in size by 2023.

Web-based travel retailers are also providing other Internet companies with the capability to sell travel products, by embedding their search and booking facilities within the host's website. In such cases, the design of the site is dictated by the host company, while the travel content is externally provided by the travel retailer. This allows the host the opportunity to offer its customers a range of travel products, while the Web retailer expands its sales opportunities. The host provider may also earn a small fee for each booking made through its portal.

TECHNOLOGY HELPS SUPPLIERS TO SERVE CUSTOMERS DIRECTLY

Suppliers, notably the airlines, are creating their own websites, and it is against these that the online intermediaries will have to compete. More widely, there is a rapid growth in business-to-consumer (B2C) sites, which are designed to cut out the intermediaries and sell direct to the public. The airlines have formed their own intermediaries, as with Opodo and Orbitz, while their own websites attract consumers with competitive prices, both of which challenge sales through agents using the traditional GDSs.

The critical question is whether or not the high street agent can survive in the face of these new methods of distribution. There are claims that, while the Internet offers more options to customers, it does not necessarily replace existing forms of distribution, as answers to specific questions will still need to be raised with agents. The question remains as to how agents can avoid clients coming to them to pick their brains and then going home to book their holidays online. In addition, the growth of sites such as tripadvisor.com, which allows travellers to post reports on travel products such as hotels, provides customers with extensive information to aid their decisions. However, the Advertising Standards Authority (ASA) has expressed concern about fake or misleading reviews on TripAdvisor, which include favourable reviews paid for by principals and cases where customers have threatened to write bad reviews unless compensated.

TECHNOLOGY AND GENERATING MARKETS FOR TRAVEL PRODUCTS

Not all markets are currently threatened by the changes in distribution network that have occurred though the development of technology and use of the Internet. While access to computers as well as connection to the Internet have occurred in many key markets, it has not penetrated all areas; in the Asia region, around 45% of the population currently has access to the Internet, although this area is seeking a rapid growth in access. For example, it has been reported that in India, although online travel companies exist, low Internet usage, limited access to credit cards (with sufficiently high credit limits) and concern over payment security have restricted online sales.

Opinion is divided on whether the majority of agents or only a handful of the most adaptable can survive the Internet explosion that has occurred in major travel-generating markets. Mandelbaum (2004) proposed that demand for good travel agents will continue, as these can assist clients when travel problems occur; they are aware of the track records of products and can locate the latest special deals, often more quickly than a customer can find products though Internet searches. Certainly in the period since this report was published, many high street travel agents successfully continue to operate. Those who are the most adaptable, offering a personal service, including expert advice, are the ones which survive. The fact remains, however, that many agents have neither the knowledge nor the resources to undertake major change. The move to cutting commission and, in the case of the airlines, withdrawing commission entirely, may encourage many agents to charge fees. If agents are to become professionals, like lawyers, as many are arguing, how do they ensure their staff can deliver this level of expertise?

THE FUTURE OF TRAVEL RETAILING

Not only travel agents, but the entire travel industry faces greater uncertainty than ever before. The introduction of B2C in travel – suppliers providing a direct interface with their clients – threatens both agents and tour operators. This is because, if customers are encouraged to book flights and hotels direct for less than is possible through intermediaries, how long will it be before it becomes customary for those same customers to put together their own packages? To compete against this, travel agents need to add value for the customer, rather than assuming quotes for travel are always about the cheapest price. Consequently, travel agents need to identify and build relationships with those customers who buy on total value rather than just price.

To meet the demands of more experienced travellers who seek tailor-made trips, dynamic packaging has grown rapidly, the technology now allowing travel agents to conveniently create packages at cheaper overall prices than by purchasing products separately. Legislation is starting to catch up, providing greater protection to customers taking this approach to travel booking and, once in place and publicised, it is likely that dynamic packaging will expand further.

Building close ties with a travel agent may address the concerns of holidaymakers worried about the failure of tour operators that then leave passengers stranded overseas. Events like the Icelandic ash cloud have also highlighted the need for support in troubled times. As customers seek greater value for their money, financial protection and support in emergencies, so the traditional travel agent may benefit from the return of customers to their doors.

QUESTIONS AND DISCUSSION POINTS

1. When considering travel retail, what is meant by the terms disintermediation and reintermediation?
2. What factors have influenced the growth of dynamic packaging?
3. What are the benefits of joining a consortium when establishing a new travel agency business?

TASKS

1. In small groups, complete a piece of research that examines the behaviour of recent purchasers of travel products, specifically focusing on whether travel agents (either online or on the high street) were used to assist the process. Evaluate your results to offer some conclusions as to the use of travel agents by different types of travellers, and for different travel products.
2. Visit a high street travel agent in your area and interview the manager. Ask about the day-to-day activities undertaken in their job role. Also ask about the benefits of working as a travel agent. Give a presentation that sets out your findings.

WEBSITES

ABTA: www.abta.com

Americana Vacations: www.americanavacations.com

Dawson and Sanderson: www.holidayco.co.uk

European Travel Agents' and Tour Operators' Associations: www.ectaa.org

IATA: www.iata.org

CONSORTIA

Advantage: www.advantagemember.co.uk

Elite Travel Group: www.elitetravelgroup.co.uk

Freedom Travel Group: www.freedomtravelgroup.co.uk

Global Travel Group: www.globaltravelgroup.com

The Travel Network Group: www.thetravelnetworkgroup.co.uk

Travelsavers International: www.travelsavers.com

REFERENCES

American Society of Travel Advisors (ASTA) (2014) *Benchmarking Research Highlights*. Washington, DC: ASTA.

Association of British Travel Agents (ABTA) (2018) *Holiday Habits Report*. London: ABTA.

Davies, P. (2018) Holiday booking fraud costs holidaymakers £6.7m. *Travel Weekly*, 7 April.

Dumazel, R. and Humphreys, I. (1999) Travel agent monitoring and management. *Journal of Air Transport Management*, 5 (2), 63–72.

Elliott, C. (2018) This is why travel agents want to be called travel advisors. *Forbes*, 11 November. Available online at: www.forbes.com/sites/christopherelliott/2018/11/11/this-is-why-travel-agents-want-to-be-called-travel-advisors/#3d3548561ca3 [Accessed January 2019].

Euromonitor (2018a) Online travel sales and intermediaries in India. *Euromonitor*, 14 September.

Euromonitor (2018b) Online travel sales and intermediaries in China. *Euromonitor*, 14 September.

European Commission (1999) Commission decision – declaring a concentration to be incompatible with the common market and the EEA Agreement. Case No. IV/M.1524 – Airtours/First Choice, EC, C (1999) 3022 final – EN, 22 September.

Mandelbaum, R. (2004) Travel agents – it still pays to hire one, even in the Internet age. *Money*, April.

Mintel (2017) *Travel Agents – UK*. London: Mintel, December.

Mintel (2018) *Package vs Independent Holidays – UK*. London: Mintel, April.

Steedman, N. (2012) Dynamic packaging survey reveals 50 per cent of travel agents use a booking engine. *Irish Travel Trade News*, 2 April.

Steighorst, T. (2014a) MSC pays 5% commission on prepaid cruise activities. *Travel Weekly*, 27 May.

Steighorst, T. (2014b) Royal Caribbean pays bonus on high-end Oasis-class bookings. *Travel Weekly*, 10 June.

Travel Talk (2014) Cruises: Bonus commission from Cruise Norway. *TT Bureau*, 16 November.

Travel Weekly (2017) Travel Industry Survey. *Travel Weekly*, 23 October.

20

ANCILLARY TOURISM SERVICES

CONTENTS

LEARNING OUTCOMES

After studying this chapter, you should be able to:

- explain the roles of guides, couriers and animateurs in meeting tourists' needs
- describe the use of insurance and financial services to assist the tourist
- identify the principal sources of information in use by travel agents
- summarise the marketing and consultancy services available to the tourism industry.

> Two factors interact in the tourism process. There is the tourist, in search of experiences and needing support services and facilities which are also experiential . . . Secondly, there is a diverse spectrum of resources which provides the experiences, services and facilities. (Leiper, 1979: 390)

INTRODUCTION

As we can see from the quote above, the search for travel experiences employs the use of numerous support services and facilities. While many of these would be considered to be a part of the tourism industry, there are some services that support the needs of the tourist but which are seldom considered to be a part of the tourism industry: customs and border control operations, visa issuing services and currency transfer systems, for example.

Consequently, there is a further category of miscellaneous tourism services that deserves to be examined more closely here. We will call these **ancillary services** – these are provided either to the tourist or to the suppliers of tourist services. Each of these will be dealt with in turn.

SERVICES TO THE TOURIST

Guides and courier services

Unfortunately, there is as yet no term that conveniently embraces all the mediators whose function it is to shepherd, guide, inform and interpret for groups of tourists; nor can one conveniently link their functions to one particular sector of the industry. Some are employed by transport providers and tour operators; others work independently or provide their services freelance to companies in the industry.

In an industry that is becoming increasingly impersonal, as companies grow in size and tourism products themselves become more homogeneous, the role of those who interface with tourists becomes more and more important. Indeed, it may be the only feature of a package tour that distinguishes one product from another, yet curiously it is a role that has been progressively downgraded by the larger companies, often as a means of cutting costs. As experienced travellers see the provision of such support as less important, many tour operators have reduced the number of representatives in resort, often providing any emergency assistance via telephone contacts instead. There are some areas where the use of support personnel is still popular, however, so we will examine these two similar roles – the courier and the guide. Couriers differ from guides in the sense that the latter considers imparting information as the most important function of their job, while couriers may attach more importance to their social and people-management functions.

Couriers

Couriers are employed by coach companies or tour operators to supervise and shepherd groups of tourists participating in tours (either on extended tours or day excursions). As well as being called couriers, they may be known as tour escorts, tour leaders, tour managers or tour directors (the latter terms imply greater levels of responsibility and status). One of their functions is to offer a sightseeing commentary on the country or region through which tourists are travelling and to act as a source of information.

Some companies dispense with the separate services of a courier in favour of a driver who is also a courier, taking on the responsibility of both driving the coach and looking after the passengers. Many drivers, however, have neither adequate general knowledge nor the necessary training to offer a truly professional guiding service and they should not, in any case, be diverted from their prime responsibility – that of driving the coach safely and expertly. Some countries frown on coach drivers who give commentaries while their coach is in motion, sometimes going as far as to forbid the practice.

Courier work is often freelance and offers little opportunity to develop a career. Apart from a handful of destinations that have truly year-round appeal (such as capital cities), most guiding work is temporary and seasonal, even though many professional guides choose to return to the job year after year. Some are able to find a combination of posts in summer and winter resorts, enabling them to take up paid employment for most of the year.

Prior experience is the principal criterion in gaining employment. While qualifications exist in many countries, they are not always essential to the role, and in the UK professional training is available but by no means obligatory. The role attracts graduates with relevant qualifications such as languages or history, but many companies prefer to recruit couriers largely on the strength of their personality, their ability to handle clients with sensitivity and tact, and their stamina – both physical and mental. In some posts, employers will lay emphasis on sales ability, as couriers may be required to sell supplementary services such as optional excursions. Arguably, this is changing the nature of the role, with commercial acumen replacing sociability.

Guides

Guides, or guide lecturers as they are frequently known, are retained by principals for their expertise in general or specialist subjects. Employment tends to be freelance and intermittent, with low-season jobs rare outside the large cities. Guides take pride in their professionalism and will often have well-established regional and national bodies to represent their interests.

In the UK, the Blue Badge is seen as the mark of attainment of professional status. It is awarded following formal periods of training and examinations, the wearer thus qualified to guide walking tours, at sites and on a moving vehicle. The Green Badge is awarded for Associate status, with holders trained to deliver guided walks and at sites in their specified area. White Badge holders are qualified for one mode of guiding only, either at a specific site such as a cathedral or museum or to guide a walk along one fixed route.

In some countries, professional qualifications are essential to secure a licence to operate. In France, for example, a local guide must be employed to guide in Paris, having demonstrated local knowledge in formally approved qualifications (although such qualifications can also be obtained by workers from other countries, of course). In the USA, the right to act as a tour guide without being licensed has become a hot topic, with court cases challenging such schemes, as the example below highlights.

EXAMPLE

Paid guide or free speech?

In 2014, the courts ruled that the New Orleans licensing scheme was constitutional. However, later the same year, a Washington district court of appeal ruled that a scheme operating in the capital city was unconstitutional under rights of free speech. The

(Continued)

Washington scheme required guides to take a 100-question exam and pay a $200 fee to gain a licence.

In 2018, a US district court in Charleston (South Carolina) also ruled against the city's licensing requirements, stating that it placed 'real burdens on those hoping to be tour guides in Charleston ... a lucrative profession in a city where tourism is the most profitable industry' (*Charleston Regional Business Journal*, 2018). The city had introduced the regulations more than 30 years earlier, as part of its first tourism management plan. The outcome of this legal decision was for the city to change its mandatory scheme into a voluntary certification programme, with the view that such controls can ensure quality and accuracy of tours.

While qualified guides offer high levels of quality, many companies running coach sightseeing tours prefer to recruit amateur guides without qualifications to keep down costs. The 'added value' of a qualified guide is still seen by many employers as a luxury they cannot afford in a climate where cutting costs to achieve sales is imperative.

A separate category of guide is the *driver* who is also a *guide*. These are professional guides who operate on a freelance basis, taking up to four individuals on tour in their own vehicles. The close personal relationship that is built up on these tours between guide and clients is valued on both sides. This form of tailor-made package is popular with wealthier visitors.

EXAMPLE

International Tour Guide Day

The importance of tour guides to the image and reputation of a destination has not always been overtly recognised; yet they are 'of critical importance in the smooth and successful running of the tourism industry because their contact with tourists often has direct influence on the tourist's experience in the country' (*Business Day*, 2009). Efforts to increase awareness of their activities have come with greater media reporting of the official 'International Tour Guide Day'.

Developed at the 1987 summit of the World Federation of Tourist Guide Associations, in order to raise the profile of their profession (and first launched in 1990), the International Tour Guide Day – on 21 February – often sees tour guides providing events for their local communities and tourism industry representatives, or participating in training events for themselves.

The role of the guide

Not only should the guide have extensive knowledge of the attraction or destination linked to their work, they take on a number of other roles. First, they will act not just as an educator, but also may need to provide translations of information and directional signage as well as menus and other documents. This is important in enhancing visitor experience as well as ensuring safety. Maintaining control over visiting groups, selecting the direction of walking routes, timings of visits and the speed of movement around attractions can ensure safety as well as ensuring visitor flow, which can be beneficial to the attraction, to other visitors and possibly to the local population. Control can also ensure that tourists are kept away from high-crime areas, reducing overall risk of danger. Finally, the tour guide may take on a social role, perhaps as entertainer or as mediator between visitors within the group. Taking the opportunity to dine with the tour party may enhance the experience of the tourist as they feel they have had opportunities to interact with a member of the local community.

THE ROLE OF THE ANIMATEUR

The term **animateur** is now becoming more widely known within the tourism industry. It applies to those members of the industry who entertain tourists, either by acting out a role or providing entertainment or instruction. The English term 'entertainer' is not strictly comparable as this tends to be associated with either a stage role or street entertainers, who are typically jugglers, acrobats, fire-eaters or, increasingly popular in leading resorts, 'living sculptures' (see Figure 20.1).

FIGURE 20.1 Street entertainers in Brussels

Photo: Claire Humphreys

The French term, however, relates to those whose task it is to interact with tourists in a broad range of roles that will enhance the destination or attraction where they work. It applies to the British role of the Butlin's holiday camp redcoat and to the US camp counsellor, as well as the compère on stage on a cruise ship. Other tasks include instructing tourists in sports or hobbies (ski instructors, surfing instructors), lecturing to cruise passengers or teaching them how to play bridge or other card games. Resort representatives are often expected to take on the role of animateurs when they form part of the evening's entertainment on stage at European campsites. In Disney's theme parks there are a variety of animateur roles, the best-known of which is Mickey Mouse, but a host of other Disney characters are to be found on site, such as Alice in Wonderland, Snow White and even the Chipmunks. These workers normally have no speaking role and are there to make friends with younger visitors, posing for photographs and so on. Elsewhere, you might find animateurs dressed as historical figures at a heritage site. For example, at historic Williamsburg in Virginia, a number of staff are dressed in eighteenth-century costume and will maintain their roles if questioned by visitors.

The job might be thought of as fairly basic, in terms of skills, but continental Europeans take a different view; animation appears on the syllabus of French tourism and leisure qualifications, to cite just one example. This reflects the seriousness with which continental tourism employees and employers view the role – it is one way to provide a professional service for the industry.

EXAMPLE

Animateurs add to the theme park experience

Warner Bros Movie World, located on Queensland's Gold Coast, is Australia's only movie-related theme park. It opened in 1991 and, throughout this time, it has included shows related to the long-time favourite *Looney Tunes* cartoon characters as well as hit movies. Attractions have included the Police Academy stunt show, the Batman Adventure and the Harry Potter magical experience.

Like its well-known rival, Disney, the park employs staff to dress in costume and entertain the visitors. This can help add to the excitement, providing picture opportunities for children and adults alike. However, it can be hard work for the actors inside the costumes – being mobbed by eager parents keen to get photo opportunities of their offspring; remaining in character despite being prodded, mauled and kicked; and dealing with the heat inside large and unwieldy costumes.

The actors may form part of a stage show (see Figure 20.2) or wander around the park, interacting with the visitors. In some cases, their work may take them further afield. To take one example, the airline Etihad, in a promotional campaign for its Queensland route, provided customers to its holiday shop in Abu Dhabi with the opportunity to have their photo taken with Tweety Bird and Bugs Bunny.

FIGURE 20.2 Looney Tunes stage show – Movie World

Photo: Claire Humphreys

FINANCIAL SERVICES

This section will deal with the financial services offered to tourists – insurance, foreign exchange and credit.

Insurance

Insurance is an important, very often obligatory, aspect of a tourist's travel arrangements, embracing coverage for one or more of the following contingencies:

- medical care and hospitalisation (and, where necessary, repatriation – important where local hospital services are of a low standard)
- personal accident
- cancellation or curtailment of holiday
- delayed departure
- baggage loss or delay
- money loss
- personal liability.

Some policies now also include coverage for the collapse of the travel agent or tour operator through which the tour was purchased, an increasingly important option in view of the growing instability in the industry – although bonded tours should be refundable in the event of a cancellation. The growth of budget airlines and their not infrequent demise point to the importance of adequate insurance, as scheduled air travel, apart from that in a package tour, is not currently protected by bonding. The inclusion of airline failure insurance (AFI) is commonly offered to travellers when booking flights online.

Tourists may purchase insurance either in the form of a selective policy, covering one or more of the above items, or, more commonly, in the form of a standard 'package', which will include all or most of the above. The latter policy, although inflexible in its coverage, invariably offers the best value if comprehensive coverage is sought. Although most tour operators encourage clients to buy their company's comprehensive policies, they are often more expensive than a comprehensive policy arranged by an independent insurance company. Travel agents may offer better-value insurance policies than those of an operator, but they, too, may be biased in favour of schemes paying them higher levels of commission. It is no longer legal to force clients to purchase a particular policy, although in the UK operators can demand evidence that customers are insured. Free insurance has become an attractive incentive in marketing package tours.

Other retailers are now competing with travel agents to sell travel insurance, including supermarkets, banks and high street shops, while cut-price annual policies are marketed direct by insurance agents, so travel agents are faced with a very competitive environment in which to sell their insurance products notwithstanding the attractive commissions paid.

Key issues in choosing a policy are to ensure that medical coverage is sufficient to meet need (in the USA, bills in excess of $1 million are not uncommon for serious illnesses) and that valuable individual items are also sufficiently covered. The normal comprehensive coverage will limit compensation for total valuables and may restrict the total value of any individual item, which may mean claims do not fully reimburse the traveller in situations where luggage items are lost or stolen.

Insurance at reasonable cost for older travellers is becoming harder to find; older people are travelling more frequently, but are more likely to suffer medical difficulties than younger travellers. Doubling, or even tripling, the price of a policy is common for travellers above the age of 65. Of equal concern are the high numbers of travellers who fail to insure themselves when travelling abroad. The availability of cheap flights through budget airlines and ownership of second homes abroad have encouraged people to take more short breaks, but a UK government study has revealed that in 2012 almost a quarter of travellers holidaying abroad were uninsured. For younger travellers (aged 15–24) this figure climbed to 48%, yet this group are more likely to take part in adventurous activities while on holiday (FCO, 2014). Australians are similarly also likely to travel overseas without insurance; a 2016 survey revealed that one-third of travellers thought it was acceptable to travel to a developed country without insurance (Quantum Market Research, 2016).

EXAMPLE

The cost of not having travel insurance

The volcano ash cloud, which affected European travel in 2010, and briefly again in 2011, helped to highlight the importance of travel insurance, as vacationers were stranded overseas with little help and unexpected costs. Efforts by governments in the UK, the USA, Australia,

Ireland and Germany, among others, have sought to encourage travellers to take out insurance in case the worst happens.

The UK Foreign and Commonwealth Office reported that although many of its nationals consider insurance for package trips, nearly half did not take out cover when travelling abroad to visit friends and family; yet the cost of treatment for illness, such as a heart attack, could be as much as £25,000 (Smithers, 2011). The Department of Foreign Affairs in Australia reported that hospital stays in South-East Asia can amount to more than $800 a day, with the cost of medical evacuation from Bali to Australia running into thousands. As an example, in July 2012 a New Zealander on holiday in Bali incurred over $80,000 in medical and evacuation bills to address injuries suffered while riding a scooter (Southern Cross Healthcare, 2013).

As a humorous aside, it should be highlighted that travel insurance pays out on the most unexpected of events, many of which could perhaps not be predicted but have the potential to ruin a holiday. Here are some examples:

- Two children in Cornwall buried their parents' video camera in the sand to prevent it from being stolen while they went swimming, but could not remember where. Travel insurance covered the cost of the camera.
- A couple on holiday in Malaysia returned to their lodge to find that monkeys had stolen their clothes and scattered them all across the neighbouring rainforest. Their claim was paid.
- A holidaymaker in Sri Lanka needed hospital treatment after a coconut fell on her head while she was reading in the shade below. Her insurer covered her medical expenses.

Source: Telegraph Travel, 2014

Insurance remains a lucrative business for both operators and agents, although claims have been rising in recent years. Some reports estimate that 10% of holidaymakers make claims, often fraudulently, against their policies and this has led insurers to increase premiums to offset those losses.

Foreign transactions

Travellers today have an ever-widening choice of ways in which they can pay for services and goods while abroad. These include:

- taking sterling, euros, US dollars or foreign banknotes with them (however, this can lead to loss or theft, and certain foreign countries have restrictions on the import or export of their currency)
- arranging for the advance transfer of funds to a specified foreign bank or an open credit to be made available, through their own bank, at a foreign bank
- using credit cards or charge cards
- taking traveller's cheques, in sterling, US dollars or euros
- taking travel money cards.

The introduction of the euro as common currency in many EU countries has made life easier for visitors touring a number of countries on the Continent. Purchasing foreign currency is relatively convenient, with many outlets offering exchange facilities. Leading travel agency chains operate their own foreign exchange desks, as do the high street banks, and the UK Post Office has also introduced a foreign exchange desk offering highly competitive rates. Some large department stores also provide currency exchange facilities in their major branches. Companies such as Travelex and TTT Moneycorp provide such facilities at airports and other transport hubs. The large number of foreign exchange facilities available provide people with a very wide choice, but charges fluctuate considerably and both rates of conversion and fixed charges need to be compared to judge what represents best value for money.

Sending money abroad in advance of travel is useful when planning to spend some time in the same place, but anti-money-laundering regulations have made such activities more complex and often time-consuming to arrange. However, companies such as Western Union and MoneyGram have tried to ease this process and have now made it possible to send money electronically from a bank account to be collected in cash at a local office. This might be particularly useful if a traveller has had their wallet stolen and needs cash to continue their holiday.

Credit cards such as those of Visa and Mastercard (Eurocard on the Continent) are widely accepted throughout the world. Some retailers will quote their prices either in local currency or in the national currency of the card and will debit accounts accordingly, so that purchasers abroad will be aware of the actual cost for the item in their own currency. Bank charges for drawing cash abroad against both credit and debit cards can also be high. Charge cards such as American Express or Diners Club provide similar advantages and drawbacks (charge cards differ from credit cards in that accounts are due for settlement in full after receipt of an invoice from the company – credit is not extended – but the limit on charge card transactions is generally much higher than on credit cards; indeed, the company may impose no ceiling on the amount the holder may charge to their account).

As travel companies are required to pay a fee to the card companies when accepting credit cards in payment for travel services, until recently it was common practice to pass these costs on to their clients in the form of card payment fees. However, a change in EU legislation in January 2018 banned such practices.

In the UK, payment by credit card offers the additional advantage to the traveller of the funds being protected under the Consumer Credit Act 1974 on amounts in excess of £100 in the event of the collapse of the agent, operator or airline with which they are dealing. Travellers would then be able to reclaim payments from their credit card company in the event of a business failure.

Although declining in use, traveller's cheques are still available, being accepted throughout the world by banks and some commercial institutions. They offer the holder guaranteed security, with rapid compensation for theft or loss, an advantage that outweighs the standard premium charged of 1–3% of face value. The value of the system for suppliers is that there is generally a considerable lapse of time between the tourist purchasing traveller's cheques and encashing them. The money invested in the interim at market rates of interest provides the supplier with substantial profits. Market leaders in traveller's cheque sales are American Express, which first introduced the concept in 1891; those issued in US$ are the most widely accepted. In recent years, the use of traveller's cheques has declined in favour of payment cards, and Travelex and Visa now provide travel card equivalents to the paper cheque. Mintel research (2014) reported that only 8% of travellers abroad used cheques for their holiday money.

An alternative to traveller's cheques is the travel money card, provided by companies like Western Union, American Express, Mastercard and many others. These are prepaid cards loaded with a fixed sum of euros, dollars or sterling in the form of 'e-money' and a PIN code. Additional amounts may be loaded on to the card at any point, subject to an authorised maximum. The card can then be tendered for purchases or used to withdraw cash from ATMs abroad. Their clear value is their relative protection against theft and fraudulent misuse as they cannot be used to clear a bank account and they also make it impossible for the holidaymaker to overspend. They are, however, rather expensive to use for withdrawing cash abroad and charges are made for encashing any unused balance after completing a journey.

Many countries now use chip and PIN cards, although, when used abroad, a signature is often required instead, which is felt to be less secure. Theft and the fraudulent use of cards are discouraging total reliance on plastic to make purchases and draw money when abroad. Tourists are now recommended to carry an assortment of small denomination notes and a variety of plastic cards when travelling.

EXAMPLE

New ways to pay

The introduction of Apple Pay in 2014 led to the use of mobile phones as a means of payment. After registering a credit or debit card to the Apple digital wallet, small payments (up to £30 or €30) could be made at contactless point-of-sale terminals. Its success has led to competitors entering the market, predominantly Google Pay. Payments are made using near-field communication (NFC) technology, which is found in phones and other connected devices such as smart watches. Payments are recorded instantly with apps used to keep track of payments.

This increasing use of apps to monitor spending has led to the introduction of a new wave of digital banks, with Revolut and Monza among the biggest. Popular with the younger generation, these financial tech companies provide apps that help keep track of spending, make it easier to make transfers and payments to other people and businesses, and, like traditional banks, provide a debit card to allow payment via point-of-sale terminals. In terms of travel money, these companies offer free or low-cost foreign currency transactions, using inter-bank rates to improve the exchange rate received.

Travel vouchers

Incentive travel (discussed in more detail in Chapter 11) has grown over the past few years, with companies providing their employees or dealers with attractive travel packages as a reward for achievement. One option taken up by some companies is travel vouchers, issued in various denominations, which allow the recipient to choose their own travel arrangements. This is simply monetary reward for achievement in another form, but the appeal of travel has proved to be a stronger motivator than either cash or consumer durables. The vouchers offer some flexibility and can be given in small denominations – to reward, for example, low absenteeism or the achievement of weekly targets. Some of these vouchers can only be exchanged against specific travel products or through certain travel agents, while others can be used to pay for any holiday arrangements purchased through any agent.

EXAMPLE

ANCV Chèque-Vacances

In France, providing incentive vouchers for holidays has long been established though the Chèque-Vacances system operated by ANCV. Companies boost the loyalty of employees by offering travel vouchers, with the employer contributing up to 80% of the cost.

The travel vouchers can then be redeemed at tourism businesses operating in the accommodation, transport, cultural, leisure and hospitality sectors (including travel agents, theme parks, ski schools and festivals).

Source: www.groupe-cheque-dejeuner.com

Duty-free shopping

Under the category of services to tourists, mention should also be made of duty-free shopping facilities, a subject that has been discussed in more detail elsewhere in this text. The purchase of duty-free goods at airports, on board ships and aircraft or at specially designated duty-free ports has been a strong attraction for tourists for a very long time.

Introduced during the first half of the twentieth century, mainly to satisfy the demands of travellers on the great ocean liners, it was extended to aircraft in 1944. The first airport duty-free shop arrived in 1947, when the Irish Parliament passed the Custom-free Airport Act, giving Shannon this honour. Since those days, duty-free purchases of spirits and tobacco in particular have been effectively marketed by airports and carriers alike and the profits and sales of such items have always been substantial, accounting for large shares in the profits of many companies. Airports have achieved up to half their total operating profits through such sales, while some Scandinavian ferry companies obtain up to 70% of their income in this manner.

This has led in some quarters to criticisms of profiteering, but airports reply to this by claiming that, without these profits, they would be forced to increase their landing charges, which would have a knock-on effect on carriers, forcing these in turn to raise their fares. Without the benefit of duty-free shopping, transport fares do tend to rise appreciably; estimates typically point to increases ranging from 10% to as high as 30%. Rising congestion at airports, the requirement for earlier check-in times and flight delays all tend to enhance sales in airport shops.

EXAMPLE

Airport shopping

Recent research suggests that travellers are less confident that duty-free shopping offers good value, believing that goods can be purchased online or on the high street at lower prices. This supports earlier research that concluded that only 8% of Germans, 12% of British travellers and 13% of Spanish and Italian travellers appear to believe that duty-free products are cheaper than can be found elsewhere. Nevertheless, global duty free sales exceeded $68 billion in 2017.

Sources: Mintel, 2013, 2018; Morris, 2018

Tax harmonisation in the EU led to the withdrawal of duty-free privileges for travel between member states in July 1999, and many companies were badly hit by the move. To take one example, Eurotunnel alone saw a 72% fall in its retail revenue in the months following the ending of duty-free sales across the Channel. Fares on cross-Channel services were raised sharply, although heightened competition succeeded in pushing them down again. In response to the decline in sales at UK ports, marketing efforts highlighted the opportunity to purchase duty-paid goods, often at French prices, which substantially undercut those in the UK. Countries such as Tunisia, Morocco and Turkey are close enough to provide alternatives for tourists, for whom duty-free sales are an important component of the holiday.

SERVICES TO THE SUPPLIER

EDUCATION AND TRAINING

Historically, the approach to training in the tourism industry has been a sectoral one, each primarily concerned with training staff to become competent within its own sector, often focusing on narrow job-specific abilities. In an industry comprising mainly small units with entrepreneurial styles of management, the benefits of formal education and training were seldom acknowledged. Most employees of travel agencies, tour operators and hotels were trained on the job, often by observing supervisors at work. However, a handful of companies, including Thomas Cook, were notable for their early recognition of the need for more formal, although still in-house, training.

With the growing professionalisation of sectors, greater emphasis is placed on more formal modes of training supported by the introduction of national standards. The difficulty of organising day release for employees of small travel companies encouraged the development of distance-learning packages. Airline fares and ticketing courses, for example, offered by the International Air Transport Association (IATA), deliver internationally recognised distance-learning opportunities for students of tourism throughout the world. The United Nations World Tourism Organization (UNWTO) also has a training academy providing education through its Themis foundation.

EXAMPLE

UNWTO Academy

Founded in June 1998, the goal of the Themis foundation is to provide support to member states in their provision of policies and programmes to deliver education and training that will improve the quality, competitiveness and sustainability of the tourism sector. This is delivered through the UNWTO Academy.

The expected expansion of tourism over the coming decade will lead to a demand for labour that is well qualified, motivated and highly skilled. This should ensure that the benefits of tourism are reaped by the local communities that deliver tourism services. The UNWTO Academy points to the need for an abundant supply of suitably skilled individuals in all sectors of the industry. Consequently, the training sessions offered cover many different needs of the industry. In 2018, these included the following:

- UNWTO training programme in the Kingdom of Bahrain on 'Tour Guiding'

(Continued)

- UNWTO-UOC course on 'Strategy and Sustainable Management of Tourism Destinations'
- UNWTO/GWU online course on 'Tourism as a Path to International Cooperation & Sustainable Development'
- UNWTO-UAE executive training workshop on 'Innovative Approaches to Destination Branding'.

Source: UNWTO Academy, http://academy.unwto.org

With vocational courses, the question of balance between job-specific skills and broader conceptual knowledge has long taxed employers and educationalists alike. Unlike most countries in Europe, many tourism employers in the UK still do not hold formal qualifications in high regard, preferring to provide the job skills that are seen as essential to fulfil basic, sector-specific roles in the industry. Across the globe, however, universities and colleges now offer courses designed to provide not just essential skills but also a broader knowledge of the industry and the world of business. This includes undergraduate studies as well as postgraduate diplomas and Master's qualifications in tourism-related studies (including specialist areas, such as e-tourism, destination marketing and events management).

THE TRADE PRESS

In addition to specialist academic journals, there is a large selection of weekly and monthly journals devoted to the travel and tourism industry. The weekly trade papers *Travel Trade Gazette* and *Travel Weekly* provide an invaluable service to the industry, covering news of both social and commercial activities, as well as providing the heaviest concentration of advertisements for jobs in the industry. Updates on the industry are also available to readers online.

In an industry as fast-moving as tourism, employees can only update their knowledge of travel products by regularly reading the trade press, whether in hard copy or online. The newspapers complement the work of the training bodies, while, for untrained staff, they may well act as the principal source of new information.

The trade press depends largely on advertising for its revenue, as the two weeklies are distributed free to members of the industry. In return, they support the industry by sponsoring trade fairs, seminars and other events. Today, these trade journals also provide a significant amount of their news content online (www.ttgmedia.com and www.travelweekly.co.uk).

Within the general category of the press, one must also include those who are responsible for the publication of travel guides and timetables. The task of updating this information is obviously immense, especially in view of the worldwide scope of many of these publications. As their production becomes more complex each year, this is also a field that lends itself to computerisation. Most guides now provide access for agents – and the public – electronically, and it is questionable whether there will still be a demand for hard-copy guides of this nature for very much longer.

Many travel guides are bought by both the trade and the travelling public (see Table 20.1). Corporate travel managers and frequent travellers on business are likely to want their own copies of guides, and agents may want hard copies to show to their customers when discussing alternatives.

TABLE 20.1 Examples of travel publications

Publication	Details
	Industry guides
OAG flight guide	Printed guide providing information on airline schedules. This guide supports the online database of flight details
World Travel Guide	Detailed country information, including details of passports and visas, health and climate, as well as resorts and excursions
	Travel magazines
Business Traveller	A magazine aimed at the frequent business traveller, published worldwide
Condé Nast Traveller	Aimed at the upmarket leisure sector, this magazine provides information on upcoming destinations and resorts as well as current issues for travellers
National Geographic Traveler	An international magazine focusing on travel environments, landscapes and cultures
	In-flight magazines
American Way	American Airlines
Discovery	Cathay Pacific
Open Skies	Emirates
High Life	British Airways
The Australian Way	Qantas Airlines
	Destination travel guides
Lonely Planet	Country and destination travel guides, often used by budget and gap year travellers
Fodor's	Country and city guides, aimed at discerning travellers
Michelin Red and Green guides	Guides to restaurants, travel and tourism businesses and sites of interest

Note: Many travel agents now use the Internet to access directories for which they have paid subscriptions

HOTEL GUIDEBOOKS

Hotel guides, of course, have always served the needs of both the trade and the public, although many are produced commercially for purchase by the travelling public. They fall into three distinct categories:

- independent guides that do not charge for entries and inspections are made anonymously – examples include the *Michelin Red Guide* and the *Good Hotel Guide*
- paid-entry guides that make a charge for listing – examples include Alastair Sawday's *Special Places to Stay* and Condé Nast Johansen's *Recommended Hotels*
- registration guides that are funded by membership fees – examples include the AA and RAC handbooks.

The Internet has had an impact on the information available for this sector particularly, with many websites – Trip Advisor being one such example – encouraging guests who have stayed at hotels to post their own reviews, rating the performance and overall quality of the accommodation. As these data become conveniently available, both online and through mobile phone apps, hotels will need to be ever more responsive in their monitoring of information published about their properties.

TRAVEL GUIDEBOOKS

Travel guidebooks are enjoying huge popularity as more and more holidaymakers travel further afield each year and specialist bookshops, such as Stanfords, cater to this growing demand. Such guidebooks must be updated frequently if they are to remain of any value, so many are produced on an annual basis. This, again, is an area that lends itself to computerisation, and much of the information held in guidebooks can be readily accessed using a computer. Travel guides for longer trips, such as Lonely Planet or Rough Guides, or for cities, such as Dorling Kindersley's Eyewitness series, include accommodation and transport details alongside historical details of destinations, places to visit and restaurant recommendations for a variety of budgets.

MARKETING SERVICES

A number of services exist to provide marketing support, either wholly or in part, to members of the travel industry. These include marketing consultants, representative agencies, advertising agencies, brochure design, printing and distribution services, suppliers of travel point-of-sale material, and research and public relations organisations. To this list must be added the organisations that provide the hardware and software for the travel industry's computer systems.

This book does not propose to discuss in depth the marketing of tourism as the subject is comprehensively covered in a companion book (Holloway, 2004). The point to be made here is that both large and small companies in the industry can benefit from employing these specialist agencies and, in some instances, their services are, in fact, indispensable.

TOURISM CONSULTANTS

Management and marketing consultants offer advice to companies on the organisation and operation of their business. They bring to the task two valuable attributes: expertise and objectivity.

Most tourism consultants will have had years of experience in the industry on which to draw, having been successful in their own field before turning to consultancy, but, with the economic and political crises that have occurred over the past two decades and the resultant mergers and takeovers that have led to downsizing in the industry, it is inevitable that the pool of former executives in the industry have turned to consultancy work. The consultants' group affiliated to the Tourism Society alone lists over 100 individuals.

Consultants, not being directly involved in the day-to-day running of the companies they are employed to help, can approach their task without any preconceived ideas. They can therefore advise companies on either the general reorganisation of the business or on some ad hoc issues, such as undertaking a feasibility study or the introduction of a new computer system.

EXAMPLE

Tourism consultancy

An insight into the kind of activities undertaken by tourism consultants is possible through an examination of the work being advertised, often in the form of a call for *tenders*. Tendering requires consultancy companies to bid for the work available, setting their price and providing an explanation of how their approach will meet the tender objectives. Four examples of publically advertised tenders are listed in Table 20.2.

TABLE 20.2 Tender activities

Organisation	Tender activity
Government of South Australia	Consultancy completing a comprehensive review of the current business model and legislative framework for the Adelaide Festival Centre
Ministry of Tourism, India	Consultancy for the development of Dholavira as an iconic tourism site
Ministry of Tourism, Trinidad and Tobago	Consultancy for the revision of the National Tourism Policy and Tourism Master Plan
UNESCO	Consultancy services for the development of a comprehensive tourism strategy for Iraq

REPRESENTATIVE AGENCIES

For a retainer or payment of royalties on sales, these organisations act as general sales agents for a company within a defined territory. This is a valuable service for smaller companies seeking representation abroad, for example. In the travel industry, it is most commonly found in the hotel sector, but carriers, excursion operators and public-sector tourist offices all make use of the facility in marketing their services in other countries. As with consultants, many of the employees of these agencies will have had prior work experience in the sector that they represent.

ADVERTISING AND PROMOTIONAL AGENCIES

Many large travel companies, and an increasing number of smaller ones, retain an advertising agency. A number of these specialise in handling travel accounts.

Advertising agents do much more than design advertisements and place them in the media. They should be closely involved in the entire marketing strategy of the company and will be involved with the design and production of travel brochures. Many are equipped to carry out market research, the production of publicity material and merchandising or public relations activities. Some larger agencies also produce their own hotel/resort guides, using their own staff's extensive knowledge.

Travel companies may have their brochures created by the design studio of their advertising agent, arrange for them to be produced by an independent design studio or, in some cases, their printer's studio may undertake the work. A growing number of brochures are now put together in-house instead, however, with the aid of sophisticated computer software available to allow desktop publishing. Advertising agents can also help and advise on the selection of a printer for the production of brochures or other publicity material.

Innovation in publicity material for the trade saw the use of technology to replace the printed travel brochure. Initially, this took the form of video cassettes, but these gave way to CD-ROMs, then DVDs; but such resources are now more likely to be provided online. These are designed to help customers reach a decision on holiday destination, facilities and services. They are sometimes produced by tour operators, but frequently the production costs are borne by the principals – operators, hotels, airlines – whose services are promoted. A number of companies now specialise in the production of these travel aids.

There was some initial concern that online resources might come to replace the brochure entirely, but, to date, there is little evidence to suggest that this is occurring; holidaymakers still like something tangible to flick through and refer to. With the development of direct communication between principals and consumers via the Internet and digital TV channels, if brochures are ever to be replaced, it is more likely that it will be by webpages using text, video, maps and images, which can be quickly updated and re-priced. Changes affecting the tour brochure are discussed in more detail in Chapter 18.

Finally, mention should be made of direct mail and distribution services, some of which specialise in handling travel accounts. Some of these companies design and organise direct mail promotional literature aimed at specific target markets or travel retailers. They will also undertake distribution of a principal's brochures to travel agents.

TECHNICAL SERVICES

The rapid spread of the computer within all sectors of the travel industry has led to the establishment of specialist computer experts, who concentrate on designing and implementing purpose-made systems for their travel industry clients. Such systems include not only travel information and reservations functions, but also accounting and management information.

EXAMPLE

Corporate travel management software

Managing corporate travel, both in terms of travel costs and employee safety, has led to the introduction of travel management software. Several companies provide systems that can be linked to accounting software to manage travel bookings and expense payments.

One such example is that provided by KDS. Its system links together software for tourism companies (GDS systems, low-cost airline, hotel, car rental reservations), credit card payment systems (to manage expense payments) and corporate accounting and payroll systems.

The benefit of using travel management software is that it can control spend and ensure that travel bookings are in line with corporate travel policies. It can also reduce costs because of lower booking fees or negotiated discount rates with travel suppliers.

Companies also have a duty of care when employees travel, and such systems can use booking information to keep track of employees in case of emergencies.

Source: www.kds.com

Other computer organisations have been set up to provide networks that allow agents to access principals' computer reservations systems. With the pace of change that one has come to expect of this field, updating equipment and software is a regular function of the modern business, and these organisations fulfil a vital role in ensuring that businesses are up to date and efficient in improving their service, while keeping costs under control.

THE FUTURE OF ANCILLARY SERVICES

For more than a decade, academics have been reporting that tourists are changing, seeking out travel opportunities that allow them to experience the unusual or rare, or even provide for self-development and education. While the concept of a tourist guide may have often been seen as old-fashioned or outdated, as these tourists seek out such personal experiences, the role of the animateur or guide will remain important. The provision of human interaction to inform and entertain will provide opportunities for attractions, destinations and tourist resorts to enhance their offering.

Furthermore, as tourists gain greater access to information (with access to the Internet expanding to all corners of the globe and via mobile technology), the need to provide knowledge in a format that conveniently adds to the experience of visiting a place will become ever more important. Walking tours that can be downloaded on to mobile phones or MP3 players and virtual tours online will provide many visitors with a perception of the destination, but it will be the guides or animateurs who can bring the visit to life and make the experience memorable.

While modern film technology, including virtual reality animation, can provide stunts and scenes that are nearly impossible to achieve in real life (certainly not on a budget that most tourist attractions or destinations can afford), it is noticeable that many tourists still seek out 'low-tech' experiences where their interaction with humans (often perceived as 'locals') is a main attraction.

Mobile technology and social media systems have provided convenient opportunities for customers to feed back their opinions on the products they experience, whether it is choosing to 'like' a company on Facebook or tweeting about the poor experience received at the reception desk of a hotel. The consequence is that companies will need to monitor, and respond to, the feedback they are receiving from their customers in a timely and professional manner. This requires familiarity with the ever-advancing technology.

QUESTIONS AND DISCUSSION POINTS

1. Summarise the benefits of taking out travel insurance.
2. Why are human guides an important part of the offer at many tourist attractions?
3. In this chapter we discussed the existence of hotel guidebooks. Why might a hotel decide to pay for entry in such a guide?

TASKS

1. Complete a small piece of research, asking travellers about their use of cash, credit and debit cards, travellers cheques and pre-paid travel cards. Examine the reasons for their decisions regarding each type of payment method. Produce a short report that summarises your findings.
2. The *Travel Trade Gazette* website lists current job vacancies (www.ttgmedia.com/all-jobs). Select a vacancy that interests you and review the skills and education needed to apply for this role. Create your own CV that is tailored to this job.

WEBSITES

Foreign and Commonwealth Office (travel insurance advice): www.gov.uk/guidance/foreign-travel-insurance

Travel Trade Gazette: www.ttgmedia.com

Travel Weekly: www.travelweekly.com

UNWTO Themis Academy: http://academy.unwto.or

REFERENCES

Business Day (2009) Guiding lights gather, South Africa. *Business Day*, 6 March.

Charleston Regional Business Journal (2018) Court strikes down tour guide license requirement. *Charleston Regional Business Journal*, 6 August. Available online at: http://link.galegroup.com/apps/doc/A549547143/STND?u=lmu_web&sid=STND&xid=458f2998. [Accessed 31 October 2018].

Foreign & Commonwealth Office (FCO) (2014) Travel Insurance Facts. Available online at: https://assets.publishing.service.gov.uk/government/uploads/system/uploads/attachment_data/file/206692/Insurance_Infographic_v5.pdf (Accessed November 2018).

Holloway, J. C. (2004) *Marketing for Tourism*, 4th edn. Harlow: Prentice Hall.

Leiper, N. (1979) The framework of tourism: Towards a definition of tourism, tourist, and the tourist industry. *Annals of Tourism Research*, 6 (4), 390–407.

Mintel (2013) *Airport Retailing – Europe*. London: Mintel, March.

Mintel (2014) *Travel Money – UK*. London: Mintel, May.

Mintel (2018) *Shopping in Duty Free Stores – China*. London: Mintel, September.

Morris, H. (2018) The truth about airport duty free – and why the bargains aren't what they seem. *The Telegraph*, 29 August.

Quantum Market Research (2016) Survey of Australians' Travel Insurance Behaviour. Available online at: https://smartraveller.gov.au/guide/all-travellers/insurance/Documents/survey-travel-insurance-behaviour-web.pdf [Accessed October 2018].

Smithers, R. (2011) Britons urged to take out travel insurance if visiting family abroad. *The Guardian*, 2 June.

Southern Cross Healthcare (2013) The highest travel insurance claims of 2012. *Fuseworks Media*, 20 January.

Telegraph Travel (2014) *Ten Ridiculous Travel Insurance Claims*. Available online at: www.telegraph.co.uk/travel/weird-wide-world/5119218/Ten-ridiculous-travel-insurance-claims.html [Accessed November 2014].

INDEX

684040742617

Deborah Har ing author of *A Discover* e. A history professor at the University of Southern California, Harkness has received Fulbright, Guggenheim, and National Humanities Center fellowships.

Follow Deborah on Twitter @DebHarkness and visit www.deborahharkness.com and www.facebook.com/AuthorDeborahHarkness.

Praise for Deborah Harkness:

'We literally fell head over stilettos in love with volume one in the trilogy . . . If you loved *Twilight* but need to sink your teeth into a much more meaty, intelligent and feisty story – with an addictive love thread to boot – then read *A Discovery of Witches* quick' *Glamour*

'Gripping and impossible to put down, this is *Twilight* for grown ups – a wonderful read!' Katie Fforde

'Romantic, erudite, and suspenseful' *O, The Oprah Magazine*

'One of the most exciting novels I've read in years . . . I fell in love with it from the very first page' Danielle Trussoni, author of *Angelology*

'This might just be a *Twilight* for the tweedy set' *Entertainment Weekly*

'A spellbinding saga . . . unputdownable' *Woman & Home*

'A vast, sexy, historical romp of a novel. There's no doubting Harkness's vivid imagination' *Daily Mirror*

'The perfect summer read' *Prima*

'A romp through magical academia' *Guardian*

By Deborah Harkness

A Discovery of Witches
Shadow of Night
The Book of Life
The World of All Souls
Time's Convert